Illustrated Sterling Edition

The Member for Arcis

The Seamy Side of History

AND OTHER STORIES

BY

HONORÉ de BALZAC

With Introductions by

GEORGE SAINTSBURY

BOSTON

DANA ESTES & COMPANY

PUBLISHERS

CONTENTS

PART I

PART II

CONTENTS

(Translated by CLARA BELL and others)

THE MEMBER FOR ARCIS

INTRODUCTION

Le Député d'Arcis, like the still less generally known *Les Petits Bourgeois,* stands on a rather different footing from the rest of Balzac's work. Both were posthumous, and both, having been left unfinished, were completed by the author's friend, Charles Rabou. Rabou is not much known nowadays as a man of letters; he must not be confused with the writer Hippolyte Babou, the friend of Baudelaire, the reputed inventor of the title *Fleurs du Mal,* and the author of some very acute articles in the great collection of Crepet's *Poètes Français.* But he figures pretty frequently in association of one kind or another with Balzac, and would appear to have been thoroughly imbued with the scheme and spirit of the *Comédie.* At the same time, it does not appear that even the indefatigable and most competent M. de Lovenjoul is perfectly certain where Balzac's labors end and those of Rabou begin.

It would seem, however (and certainly internal evidence has nothing to say on the other side), that the severance, or rather the junction, must have taken place somewhere about the point where, after the introduction of Maxime de Trailles, the interest suddenly shifts altogether from the folk of Arcis and the conduct of their election to the hitherto unknown Comte de Sallenauve. It would, no doubt, be possible, and even easy, to discover in Balzac's undoubted work—for instance, in *Le Curé de Village* and *Illusions Perdues*—instances of shiftings of interest nearly as abrupt and of

(ix)

changes in the main centre of the story nearly as decided. Nor is it possible, considering the weakness of constructive finish which always marked Balzac, to rule out offhand the substitution, after an unusually lively and business-like beginning, of the nearly always frigid scheme of letters, topped up with a conclusion in which, with very doubtful art, as many personages of the *Comédie,* and even direct references to as many of its books as possible, are dragged in. But it is nearly as possible certain that he would never have left things in such a condition, and I do not even think that he would ever have arranged them in quite the same state, even as an experiment.

The book belongs to the Champenois or Arcis-sur-Aube series, which is so brilliantly opened by *Une Ténébreuse Affaire.* It is curious and worth notice, as showing the conscientious fashion in which Balzac always set about his mature work, that though his provincial stories are taken from parts of France widely distant from one another, the selection is by no means haphazard, and arranges itself with ease into groups corresponding to certain haunts or sojourns of the author. There is the Loire group, furnished by his youthful remembrances of Tours and Saumur, and by later ones down to the Breton coast. There is the group of which Alençon and the Breton-Norman frontiers are the field, and the scenery of which was furnished by early visits of which we know little, but the fact of the existence of which is of the first importance, as having given birth to the *Chouans,* and so to the whole *Comédie* in a way. There is the Angoumois-Limousin group, for which he informed himself during his frequent visits to the Carraud family. And lastly, there is one of rather wider extent, and not connected with so definite a centre, but including the Morvan, Upper Burgundy, and part of Champagne, which seems to have been commended to him by his stay at Saché and other places. This was his latest set of studies, and to this *Le Député d'Arcis* of course belongs. To round off the subject, it is noteworthy that no part of the coast except a little in the north, with the remarkable exceptions of the scenes of *La Recherche de l'Absolu* and one or two others; nothing in the greater part of Brittany and Normandy; nothing in Guienne, Gascony, Languedoc, Provence, or Dauphiné, seems to have attracted him. Yet some of these scenes—and with some of them he had meddled in the Days of Ignorance—are the most tempting of any in France to the romancer, and his abstention from them is one of the clearest proofs of his resolve to speak only of that he did know.

The certainly genuine part of the present book is, as certainly, not below anything save his very best work. It belongs, indeed, to the most minute and "meticulous" part of that work, not to the bolder and more ambitious side. There is no Goriot, no Eugénie Grandet, not even any Corentin or Vautrin, hardly so much as a Rastignac about it. But the good little people of Arcis-sur-Aube are represented "in their natural," as Balzac's great compatriot would have said, with extraordinary felicity and force. The electoral meeting in Madame Marion's house is certainly one of the best things in the whole *Comédie* for completeness within its own limits, and none of the personages, official or other, can be said to suffer from that touch of exaggeration which, to some tastes, interferes with the more celebrated and perhaps more generally attractive delineations of Parisian journalism in *Illusions Perdues* and similar books. In fact, in what he wrote of *Le Député d'Arcis,* Balzac seems to have had personal knowledge to go upon, without any personal grievances to revenge or any personal crazes to enforce. The latter, it is true, often prompted his sublimest work; but the former frequently helped to produce his least successful. In *Le Député d'Arcis* he is at the happy mean. It is not necessary to give an elaborate bibliography of it, for, as has been said, only the "Election" part is certainly Balzac's. This appeared in a newspaper, *L'Union Monarchique,* for April and May 1847.

G. S.

THE MEMBER FOR ARCIS

PART I.

THE ELECTION.

BEFORE entering on a study of a country election, I need hardly say that the town of Arcis-sur-Aube was not the scene of the events to be related. The district of Arcis votes at Bar-sur-Aube, which is fifteen leagues away from Arcis; so there is no member for Arcis in the Chamber of Deputies. The amenities demanded by the history of contemporary manners require this precaution. It is perhaps an ingenious notion to describe one town as the setting for a drama played out in another; indeed, the plan has been already adopted in the course of this Human Comedy, in spite of the drawback that it often makes the frame as elaborate as the picture.

Towards the end of April 1839, at about ten in the morning, a strange appearance was presented by Madame Marion's drawing-room—the lady was the widow of a revenue collector in the department of the Aube. Nothing remained in it of all the furniture but the window curtains, the chimney hangings and ornaments, the chandelier, and the tea-table. The Aubusson carpet, taken up a fortnight sooner than was necessary, encumbered the balcony steps, and the parquet had been energetically rubbed without looking any the brighter.

This was a sort of domestic forecast of the coming elections, for which preparations were being made over the whole face of the country. Things are sometimes as humorous as men. This is an argument in favor of the occult sciences.

An old man-servant, attached to Colonel Giguet, Madame Marion's brother, had just finished sweeping away the dust that had lodged between the boards in the course of the winter. The housemaid and cook, with a nimble zeal that showed as much enthusiasm as devotion, were bringing down all the chairs in the house and piling them in the garden. It must be explained that the trees already displayed large leaves, between which the sky smiled cloudless. Spring breezes and May sunshine allowed of the glass doors and windows being thrown open from the drawing-room, a room longer than it was wide.

The old lady, giving her orders to the two women, desired them to place the chairs in four rows with a space of about three feet between. In a few minutes there were ten chairs across the rows, a medley of various patterns; a line of chairs was placed along the wall in front of the windows. At the end of the room opposite the forty chairs Madame Marion placed three armchairs behind the tea-table, which she covered with a green cloth, and on it placed a bell.

Old Colonel Giguet appeared on the scene of the fray just as it had occurred to his sister that she might fill up the recess on each side of the chimney-place by bringing in two benches from the ante-room, in spite of the baldness of the velvet, which had seen four-and-twenty years' service.

"We can seat seventy persons," said she, with exultation.

"God send us seventy friends!" replied the Colonel.

"If, after receiving all the society of Arcis-sur-Aube every evening for twenty-four years, even one of our usual visitors should fail us—well!" said the old lady in a threatening tone.

"Come," said the Colonel with a shrug, as he interrupted his sister, "I can name ten who cannot—who ought not to come. To begin with," said he, counting on his fingers: "Antonin Goulard, the sous-préfet, for one; the public prosecutor, Frédéric Marest, for another; Monsieur Olivier Vinet, his deputy, three; Monsieur Martener, the examining judge, four; the justice of the peace——"

"But I am not so silly," the old lady interrupted in her turn, "as to expect that men who hold appointments should attend a meeting of which the purpose is to return one more deputy to the Opposition.—At the same time, Antonin Goulard, Simon's playfellow and school-mate, would be very glad to see him in the Chamber, for——"

"Now, my good sister, leave us men to manage our own business.—Where is Simon?"

"He is dressing. He was very wise not to come to breakfast for he is very nervous; and though our young lawyer is in the habit of speaking in Court, he dreads this meeting as much as if he had to face his enemies."

"My word! Yes. I have often stood the fire of a battery and my soul never quaked—my body I say nothing about; but if I had to stand up here," said the old soldier, placing himself behind the table, "opposite the forty good people who will sit there, open-mouthed, their eyes fixed on mine, and expecting a set speech in sounding periods—my shirt would be soaking before I could find a word."

"And yet, my dear father, you must make that effort on my behalf," said Simon Giguet, coming in from the little drawing-room; "for if there is a man in the department whose word is powerful, it is certainly you. In 1815——"

"In 1815," said the particularly well-preserved little man, "I had not to speak; I merely drew up a little proclamation which raised two thousand men in twenty-four hours. And there is a great difference between putting one's name at the bottom of a broadsheet and addressing a meeting. Napoleon himself would have lost at that game. On the 18th Brumaire he talked sheer nonsense to the Five Hundred."

"But, my dear father, my whole life is at stake, my prospects, my happiness—— Just look at one person only, and fancy you are speaking to him alone—you will get through it all right."

"Mercy on us! I am only an old woman," said Madame

Marion; "but in such a case, and if I knew what it was all about—why, I could be eloquent!"

"Too eloquent, perhaps," said the Colonel. "And to shoot beyond the mark is not to hit it.—But what is in the wind?" he added, addressing his son. "For the last two days you have connected this nomination with some notion—— If my son is not elected, so much the worse for Arcis, that's all."

These words, worthy of a father, were quite in harmony with the whole life of the speaker.

Colonel Giguet, one of the most respected officers in the GRANDE ARMÉE, was one of those admirable characters which to a foundation of perfect rectitude add great delicacy of feeling. He never thrust himself forward; honors came to seek him out; hence for eleven years he had remained a captain in the artillery of the guards, rising to command a battalion in 1813, and promoted Major in 1814. His almost fanatical attachment to Napoleon prohibited his serving the Bourbons after the Emperor's first abdication. And in 1815 his devotion was so conspicuous that he would have been banished but for the Comte de Gondreville, who had his name erased from the list, and succeeded in getting him a retiring pension and the rank of Colonel.

Madame Marion, *née* Giguet, had had another brother who was Colonel of the Gendarmerie at Troyes, and with whom she had formerly lived. There she had married Monsieur Marion, receiver-general of the revenues of the department.

A brother of the late lamented Marion was presiding judge of one of the Imperial Courts. While still a pleader at Arcis this lawyer had, during the "Terror," lent his name to the famous Malin (deputy for the Aube), a representative of the people, to enable him to purchase the estate of Gondreville. Consequently, when Malin had become a senator and a count, his influence was entirely at the service of the Marions. The lawyer's brother thus got his appointment as receiver-general at a time when the Government, far from having to choose from among thirty applicants, was only too glad to find men to sit in such slippery seats.

Marion, the receiver-general, had inherited the property of his brother the judge; Madame Marion came in for that of her brother Colonel Giguet of the Gendarmerie. In 1814 Monsieur Marion suffered some reverses; he died at about the same time as the Empire, and his widow was able to make up fifteen thousand francs a year from the wreck of these fag-ends of fortune. Giguet of the Gendarmerie had left all his little wealth to his sister on hearing of his brother's marriage in 1806 to one of the daughters of a rich Hamburg banker. The admiration of all Europe for Napoleon's magnificent troopers is well known.

In 1814 Madame Marion in very narrow circumstances came to live at Arcis, her native town, where she bought a house in the Grande Place, one of the handsomest residences in the town, on a site suggesting that it had formerly been dependent on the château. Being used to entertain a great deal at Troyes, where the revenue-collector was a person of importance, her drawing-room was open to the prominent members of the Liberal circle at Arcis. A woman who is used to the position of queen of a country salon does not readily forego it. Of all habits, those of vanity are the most enduring.

Colonel Giguet, a Liberal, after being a Bonapartist—for by a singular metamorphosis, Napoleon's soldiers almost all fell in love with the constitutional system—naturally became, under the Restoration, the President of the Town Council of Arcis, which included Grévin, the notary, and Beauvisage, his son-in-law; Varlet *fils,* the leading physician in the town and Grévin's brother-in-law, with sundry other Liberals of importance.

"If our dear boy is not elected," said Madame Marion, after looking into the ante-room and the garden to make sure that nobody was listening; "he will not win Mademoiselle Beau-visage; for what he looks for in the event of his success is marrying Cécile."

"Cécile?" said the old man, opening his eyes wide to gaze at his sister in amazement.

"No one but you in all the department, brother, is likely to forget the fortune and the expectations of Mademoiselle Beauvisage."

"She is the wealthiest heiress in the department of the Aube," said Simon Giguet.

"But it seems to me that my son is not to be sneezed at!" said the old Colonel. "He is your heir; he has his mother's money; and I hope to leave him something better than my bare name."

"All that put together will not give him more than thirty thousand francs a year, and men have already come forward with as much as that—to say nothing of position——"

"And?——" asked the Colonel.

"And have been refused."

"What on earth do the Beauvisages want, then?" said Giguet, looking from his sister to his son.

It may seem strange that Colonel Giguet, Madame Marion's brother—in whose house the society of Arcis had been meeting every evening for the last four-and-twenty years, whose salon rang with the echo of every rumor, every slander, every piece of gossip of the countryside—where perhaps they were even manufactured—should be ignorant of such facts and events. But his ignorance is accounted for when it is pointed out that this noble survivor of the Imperial phalanx went to bed and rose with the fowls, as old men do who want to live all the days of their life. Hence he was never present at confidential "talks."

There are, in provincial life, two kinds of confidential talk: that held in public when everybody is assembled to play cards and gossip, and that which simmers like a carefully watched pot when only two or three trustworthy friends remain, who will certainly not repeat anything that is said, excepting in their own drawing-room to two or three other friends equally to be relied on.

For the past nine years, since his political party had come to the top, the Colonel lived almost out of the world. He always rose with the sun, and devoted himself to horticulture :

he was devoted to flowers; but of all flowers, he only cherished his roses. He had the stained hands of a true gardener. He himself tended his beds—his squares he called them. His squares! The word reminded him of the gaudy array of men drawn up on the field of battle. He was always holding council with his man, and, especially for the last two years, seldom mingled with the company, rarely seeing any visitors. He took one meal only with the family—his dinner; for he was up too early to breakfast with his sister and his son. It is to the Colonel's skill that the world owes the Giguet rose, famous among amateurs.

This old man, a sort of domestic fetich, was brought out, of course, on great occasions; some families have a demi-god of this kind, and make a display of him as they would of a title.

"I have a suspicion that since the Revolution of July Madame Beauvisage has a hankering after living in Paris," said Madame Marion. "Being compelled to remain here till her father dies, she has transferred her ambition and placed her hopes in her future son-in-law; the fair matron dreams of the splendors of a political position."

"And could you love Cécile?" asked the Colonel of his son.

"Yes, father."

"Does she take to you?"

"I think so. But the important point is that her mother and her grandfather should fancy me. Although old Grévin is pleased to oppose my election, success would bring Madame Beauvisage to accept me, for she will hope to govern me to her mind, and be minister under my name."

"A good joke!" cried Madame Marion. "And what does she take us for?"

"Whom has she refused then?" asked the Colonel of his sister.

"Well, within the last three months they say that Antonin Goulard and Monsieur Frédéric Marest, the public prosecutor, got very equivocal replies, meaning anything excepting Yes."

"Good Heavens!" exclaimed the old man, throwing up
his arms, "what times we live in! Why, Cécile is a hosier's
daughter, a farmer's grandchild.—Does Madame Beauvisage
look for a Comte de Cinq-Cygne for a son-in-law?"

"Nay, brother, do not make fun of the Beauvisages. Cécile
is rich enough to choose a husband wherever she pleases—
even of the rank of the Cygnes.—But I hear the bell announcing the arrival of some elector; I must go, and am
sorry that I cannot listen to what is said."

Though, politically speaking, 1839 is far enough from
1847, we can still remember the elections which produced
the Coalition, a brief attempt made by the Chamber of
Deputies to carry into effect the threatened parliamentary
government; a Cromwellian threat which, for lack of a Crom-
well, and under a King averse to fraud, could only result
in the system we now live under, of a Ministry and Chamber
for all the world like the puppets that are worked by the
owner of a show, to the great delight of the always gaping
passer-by.

The district of Arcis-sur-Aube was at that time in a strange
position, believing itself free to elect a deputy. From 1816
till 1836 it had always returned one of the most ponderous
orators of the Left, one of those seventeen whom the Liberal
party loved to designate as *great citizens*—no less a man, in
short, than François Keller, of the firm of Keller Brothers,
son-in-law to the Comte de Gondreville.

Gondreville, one of the finest estates in France, is not
more than a quarter of a league from Arcis. The banker,
lately created count and peer of France, proposed, no doubt,
to hand on to his son, now thirty years of age, his position as deputy, so as to fit him in due time to sit among
the peers.

Charles Keller, already a major holding a staff appointment, and now a viscount, as one of the Prince Royal's
favorites, was attached to the party of the Citizen King. A
splendid future seemed to lie before a young man of immense
wealth, high courage, and noteworthy devotion to the new

dynasty—grandson to the Comte de Gondreville, and nephew of the Maréchale de Carigliano. But this election, indispensable to his future plans, presented very great difficulties.

Ever since the advancement to power of the citizen class, Arcis had felt a vague yearning for independence. The last few elections, at which François Keller had been returned, had been disturbed by certain Republicans whose red caps and wagging beards had not proved alarming to the good folk of Arcis. By working up the feeling of the country, the radical candidate had secured thirty or forty votes. Some of the residents, humiliated by seeing their town a rotten borough of the Opposition, then joined these democrats, but not to support democracy. In France, when the votes are polled, strange politico-chemical products are evolved in which the laws of affinity are quite upset. Now to nominate young Major Keller, in 1839, after returning his father for twenty years, would be positively slavish, a servitude against which the pride of many rich townsmen rose in arms—men who thought themselves quite the equals of Monsieur Malin Comte de Gondreville or of Keller Brothers, bankers, or the Cinq-Cygnes or the King himself, if it came to that! Hence the numerous partisans of old Gondreville, the king of the department, hoped for some fresh stroke of the astuteness he had so often shown. To keep up the influence of his family in the district of Arcis, the old statesman would, no doubt, put forward some man of straw belonging to the place, who would then accept public office and make way for Charles Keller, a state of things which requires the elect of the people to stand another election.

When Simon Giguet sounded Grévin the notary, the Count's faithful ally, on the subject of the candidature, the old man replied that, without knowing anything of the Comte de Gondreville's intentions, Charles Keller was the man for him, and that he should do his utmost to secure his return.

As soon as Grévin's announcement was made known in Arcis there was a strong feeling against him. Although this Aristides of Champagne had, during thirty years of practice,

commanded the fullest confidence of the citizens; although
he had been mayor of the town from 1804 till 1814, and again
during the Hundred Days; although the Opposition had
recognized him as their leader till the days of triumph in
1830, when he had refused the honor of the mayoralty in
consideration of his advanced age; finally, although the
town, in proof of its attachment, had then elected his son-
in-law, Monsieur Beauvisage, they now all turned against
him, and some of the younger spirits accused him of being
in his dotage.   Simon Giguet's supporters attached themselves
to Philéas Beauvisage the mayor, who was all the more ready
to side with them because, without being on bad terms with
his father-in-law, he affected an independence which resulted
in a coolness, but which the cunning old father-in-law overlooked, finding in it a convenient lever for acting on the
townspeople of Arcis.

Monsieur le Maire, questioned only the day before on the
market-place, had declared that he would sooner vote for
the first name on the list of eligible citizens of Arcis than
for Charles Keller, for whom he had, however, the highest
esteem.

"Arcis shall no longer be a rotten borough!" cried he.   "Or
I go to live in Paris."

Flatter the passions of the day, and you become a hero at
once, even at Arcis-sur-Aube.

"Monsieur le Maire has given crowning proof of his firmness of temper," they said.

Nothing gathers faster than a legalized rebellion.   In the
course of the evening Madame Marion and her friends had
organized for the morrow a meeting of "Independent Electors" in favor of Simon Giguet, the Colonel's son.   And now
that morrow was to-day, and she had turned the whole house
topsy-turvy for the reception of the friends on whose independence they relied.

Simon Giguet, the home-made candidate of a little town
that was jealously eager to return one of its sons, had, as
has been seen, at once taken advantage of this little stir to

make himself the representative of the wants and interests of Southwestern Champagne. At the same time, the position and fortune of the Giguet family were wholly due to the Comte de Gondreville. But when an election is in the case, can feelings be considered?

This drama is written for the enlightenment of lands so unhappy as to be ignorant of the benefits of national representation, and unaware, therefore, of the intestinal struggles and the Brutus-like sacrifices a little town has to suffer in giving birth to a deputy—a natural and majestic spectacle which can only be compared to child-birth—there are the same efforts, the same defilement, the same travail, the same triumph.

It may be wondered how an only son with a very sufficient fortune happened to be, like Simon Giguet, an unpretending advocate in the little town of Arcis, where advocates have hardly any employment. So a few words are here necessary describing the candidate.

During his wife's lifetime, from 1806 to 1813, the Colonel had had three children, of whom Simon, the eldest, survived the other two. The mother died in 1814, one of the children in 1818, the other in 1825. Until he remained the sole survivor, Simon had, of course, been brought up with a view to making his own living by some lucrative profession. Then, when he was an only son, Simon's prospects underwent a reverse. Madame Marion's hopes for her nephew had been largely founded on his inheriting considerable wealth from his grandfather, the Hamburg banker; but the German, dying in 1826, left his grandson Giguet no more than two thousand francs a year. The financier, endowed with great powers of procreation, had counteracted the monotony of commercial life by indulging in the joys of fatherhood; hence he favored the families of the eleven other children who clung to him, as it were, and made him believe—what, indeed, seemed not unlikely—that Simon would be a rich man.

The Colonel was bent on putting his son into an independent profession; and this was why: the Giguets could not hope for any favor from Government under the Restoration. Even if Simon had not had an ardent Bonapartist for his father, he belonged to a family all of whom had justly incurred the disapprobation of the Cinq-Cygne family, in consequence of the part taken by Giguet, the Colonel of Gendarmes, and all the Marions—Madame Marion included—as witnesses for the prosecution in the famous trial of the Simeuses. These brothers were unjustly sentenced, in 1805, as guilty of carrying off and detaining the Comte de Gondreville (at that time a senator, after having been the people's representative), who had despoiled their family of its fortune.

Grévin had been not only one of the most important witnesses, but also an ardent promoter of the proceedings. At this time this trial still divided the district of Arcis into two factions—one believing in the innocence of the condemned parties and upholding the family of Cinq-Cygne, the other supporting the Comte de Gondreville and his adherents. Though, after the Restoration, the Comtesse de Cinq-Cygne made use of the influence she acquired by the return of the Bourbons to settle everything to her mind in the department, the Comte de Gondreville found means to counterbalance the supremacy of the Cinq-Cygnes by the secret authority he held over the Liberals by means of Grévin and Colonel Giguet. He also had the support of his son-in-law Keller, who was unfailingly elected deputy in spite of the Cinq-Cygnes, and considerable influence in the State Council so long as Louis XVIII. lived.

It was not till after the death of that king that the Comtesse de Cinq-Cygne was successful in getting Michu appointed presiding judge of the Lower Court at Arcis. She was bent on getting this place for the grandson of the land steward who had perished on the scaffold at Troyes, the victim of his attachment to the Simeuses, and whose full-length portrait was to' be seen in her drawing-room both in Paris and at Cinq-Cygne. Until 1823 the Comte constantly hindered the appointment of Michu.

It was by the Comte de Gondreville's advice that Colonel Giguet had made a lawyer of his son. Simon had all the better chance of shining in the Arcis district, because he was the only pleader there; as a rule, in these small towns, the attorneys plead in their own cases. Simon had had some little success at the assizes of the department; but he was not the less the butt of many pleasantries from Frédéric Marest, the public prosecutor; Olivier Vinet, his deputy; and Michu, the presiding judge—the three wits of the court. Simon Giguet, it must be owned, like all men who are laughed at, laid himself open to the cruel power of ridicule. He listened to his own voice, he was ready to talk on any pretence, he spun out endless reels of cut-and-dried phrases, which were accepted as eloquence among the superior citizens of Arcis. The poor fellow was one of the class of bores who have an explanation for everything, even for the simplest matters. He would explain the rain; the causes of the Revolution of July; he would also explain things that were inexplicable—he would explain Louis-Philippe, Monsieur Odilon Barrot, Monsieur Thiers; he explained the Eastern Question; the state of the province of Champagne; he explained 1789, the custom-house tariff, the views of humanitarians, magnetism, and the distribution of the civil list.

This young man, who was lean and bilious-looking, and tall enough to account for his sonorous emptiness—for a tall man is rarely remarkable for distinguished gifts—caricatured the puritanism of the Extreme Left, whose members are all so precise, after the fashion of a prude who has some intrigue to conceal. Always dressed in black, he wore a white tie that hung loose round his neck, while his face seemed to be set in stiff white paper, for he still affected the upright starched collars which fashion has happily discarded. His coat and trousers were always too big for him. He had what, in the country, is termed dignity, that is to say, he stood stiffly upright while he was boring you—Antonin Goulard, his friend, accusing him of aping Monsieur Dupin. And, in fact, he was rather too much given to low shoes, and coarse black spun-silk stockings.

Under the protection of the respect constantly shown to his old father, and the influence exerted by his aunt in a small town whose principal inhabitants had haunted her receptions for four-and-twenty years, Simon Giguet, already possessed of about ten thousand francs a year, irrespective of the fees he earned, and his aunt's fortune, which would some day certainly be his, never doubted of his election. At the same time, the first sound of the door-bell, announcing the advent of the more important electors, made the ambitious youth's heart beat with vague alarms. Simon did not deceive himself as to the cleverness or the vast resources at the command of old Grévin, nor as to the effect of the heroic measures that would be taken by the Ministry to support the interests of the brave young officer—at that time in Africa on the staff of the Prince—who was the son of one of the great citizen-lords of France, and the nephew of a Maréchale.

"I really think I have the colic," said he to his father. "I have a sickly burning just over the pit of my stomach, which I do not at all like——"

"The oldest soldiers," replied the Colonel, "felt just the same when the guns opened fire at the beginning of a battle."

"What will it be, then, in the Chamber!" exclaimed the lawyer.

"The Comte de Gondreville has told us," the old soldier went on, "that more than one speaker is liable to the little discomforts which we old leather-breeches were used to feel at the beginning of a fight. And all for a few empty words! —But, dear me, you want to be a deputy," added the old man, with a shrug. "Be a deputy!"

"The triumph, father, will be Cécile! Cécile is enormously rich, and in these days money is power."

"Well, well, times have changed! In the Emperor's time it was bravery that was needed."

"Every age may be summed up in a word!" said Simon, repeating a remark of the old Comte de Gondreville's, which was thoroughly characteristic of the man. "Under the

Empire to ruin a man you said, 'He is a coward!' Nowadays we say, 'He is a swindler.' "

"Unhappy France, what have you come to!" cried the Colonel. "I will go back to my roses."

"No, no, stay here, father. You are the keystone of the arch!"

The first to appear was the Mayor, Monsieur Philéas Beauvisage, and with him came his father-in-law's successor, the busiest notary in the town, Achille Pigoult, the grandson of an old man who had been justice of the peace at Arcis all through the Revolution, the Empire, and the early days of the Restoration. Achille Pigoult, a man of about two-and-thirty, had been old Grévin's clerk for eighteen years, without a hope of getting an office as notary. His father, the old justice's son, had failed badly in business, and died of an apoplexy so called. Then the Comte de Gondreville, on whom old Pigoult had some claims outstanding from 1793, had lent the necessary security, and so enabled the grandson to purchase Grévin's office; the old justice of the peace had, in fact, conducted the preliminary inquiry in the Simeuse case. So Achille had established himself in a house in the Church Square belonging to the Count, and let at so low a rent that it was easy to perceive how anxious the wily politician was to keep a hold over the chief notary of the town.

This young Pigoult, a lean little man, with eyes that seemed to pierce the green spectacles which did not mitigate their cunning expression, and fully informed of everybody's concerns in the district, had acquired a certain readiness of speech from the habit of talking on business, and was supposed to be a great wag, simply because he spoke out with rather more wit than the natives had at their command. He was still a bachelor, looking forward to making some good match by the intervention of his two patrons—Grévin and the Comte de Gondreville. And lawyer Giguet could not repress a start of surprise when he saw Achille as a satellite to Monsieur Philéas Beauvisage.

The little notary, his face so seamed with the small-pox that

it looked as if it were covered with a white honeycomb, was
a perfect contrast to the burly mayor, whose face was like a
full moon, and a florid moon too.   This pink-and-white complexion was set off by a beaming smile, the result less of a
happy frame of mind than of the shape of his mouth; but
Philéas Beauvisage was blessed with such perfect self-satisfaction, that he smiled incessantly on everybody and under
all circumstances.   Those doll-like lips would have grinned
at a funeral.   The bright sparkle in his round blue eyes did
not belie that insufferable and perpetual smile.

The man's entire self-satisfaction passed, however, for
benevolence and friendliness, all the more readily because he
had a style of speech of his own, marked by the most extravagant use of polite phraseology.   He always "had the
honor" to inquire after the health of a friend, he invariably
added the adjectives *dear, good, excellent;* and he was prodigal
of complimentary phrases on every occasion of the minor
grievances or pleasures of life.   Thus, under a deluge of
commonplace, he concealed his utter incapacity, his lack of
education, and a vacillating nature which can only find
adequate description in the old-fashioned word weathercock.
But then this weathercock had for its pinion handsome Madame Beauvisage, Séverine Grévin, the notable lady of the
district.

When Séverine had heard of what she was pleased to call
her husband's freak *à propos* to the election, she had said
to him that very morning:

"You did not do badly by asserting your independence;
but you must not go to the meeting at the Giguets' without
taking Achille Pigoult; I have sent to tell him to call for
you."

Now sending Achille Pigoult to keep an eye on Beauvisage
was tantamount to sending a spy from the Gondreville faction to attend the Giguets' meeting.   So it is easy to imagine
what a grimace twisted Simon's puritanical features when
he found himself extending a civil welcome to a regular
visitor in his aunt's drawing-room, and an influential elector,
in whom he scented an enemy.

"Ah!" thought he to himself, "I was a fool when I refused the security money he asked me to lend him! Old Gondreville was sharper than I.—Good-day, Achille," he said aloud, with an air of ease. "You will give me a tough job or two."

"Your meeting is not a conspiracy against the independence of our votes, I suppose," replied the notary with a smile. "We are playing above board?"

"Above board!" repeated Beauvisage.

And the Mayor laughed that meaningless laugh with which some men end every sentence, and which might be called the burden of their song. Then Monsieur le Maire assumed what we may call his third position, full-face, and very upright, with his hands behind his back. He was in a whole suit of black, with a highly decorative white waistcoat, open so as to show a glimpse of two diamond studs worth several thousand francs.

"We will fight it out, and be none the worse friends," Philéas went on. "That is the essential feature of constitutional institutions.—Hah, ha, ha! That is my notion of the alliance between monarchy and liberty.—He, he, he!"

Thereupon the Mayor took Simon by the hand, saying:

"And how are you, my dear friend? Your dear aunt and the worthy Colonel are, no doubt, as well to-day as they were yesterday—at least we may presume that they are.—Heh, heh! A little put out, perhaps, by the ceremony we are preparing for, perhaps.—So, so! Young man" (*yong maan,* he said), "we are starting in our political career?—Ah, ha, ha! This is our first step!—We must never draw back—it is a strong measure! Ay, and I would rather you than I should rush into the tempests of the Chamber.—He, he! pleasing as it may be to find the sovereign power of France embodied in one's own person—he, he!—one four-hundred-and-fifty-third part of it—he, he!"

There was a pleasant fulness in Philéas Beauvisage's voice that corresponded admirably with the gourd-like rotundity of his face and its hue as of a pale buff pumpkin, his round

back, and broad protuberant person. His voice, as deep
and mellow as a bass, had the velvety quality of a baritone,
and the laugh with which he ended every sentence had a
silvery ring.   If God, in stocking the earthly paradise, had
wanted to complete the set of species by adding a country
citizen, He could not have moulded a more magnificent and
developed specimen than Philéas Beauvisage.

"I admire the devotion of men who can throw themselves
into the storms of political life," he went on.   "He, he, he!
You need a nerve that I cannot boast of.   Who would have
said in 1812—in 1813 even—that this was what we were
coming to?—For my part, I am prepared for anything, now
that asphalt and india-rubber, railways and steam, are
metamorphosing the ground under our feet, our greatcoats,
and the length of distances.—Ha, ha!"

This speech was freely seasoned with the eternal laugh
by which Philéas pointed the commonplace facetiousness that
passes muster with his class, and he emphasized it by a gesture he had made his own: he clenched his right fist and
rubbed it into the hollow palm of the left hand with a
peculiarly jovial air.   This action was an accompaniment to
his giggle on the many occasions when he flattered himself
that he had been witty.

It is, no doubt, superfluous to add that Philéas was regarded at Arcis as an agreeable and charming man.

"I will endeavor," said Simon Giguet, "to be a worthy
representative——"

"Of the sheep of Champagne," said Achille Pigoult quickly,
interrupting his friend.

The aspirant took the irony without replying, for he had
to go forward and receive two more electors.   One was the
owner of the *Mulet,* the best inn of the town, situated in the
market square, at the corner of the Rue de Brienne.   This
worthy innkeeper, whose name was Poupart, had married the
sister of a man in the Comtesse de Cinq-Cygne's service, the
notorious Gothard, who had figured at the great trial.   Gothard had been acquitted.   Poupart, though he was of all

the townsfolk one of the most devoted to the Cinq-Cygnes, had, two days since, been so diligently and so cleverly wheedled by Colonel Giguet's servant, that he fancied he would be doing their enemy an ill turn by bringing all his influence to bear on the election of Simon Giguet; and he had just been talking to this effect to a chemist named Fromaget, who, as he was not employed by the Gondreville family, was very ready to plot against the Kellers. These two men, important among the lower middle class, could control a certain number of doubtful votes, for they were the advisers of several electors to whom the political opinions of the candidates were a matter of indifference.

Simon, therefore, took Poupart in hand, leaving Fromaget to his father, who had just come in, and was greeting those who had arrived.

The deputy inspector of public works of the district, the secretary to the Mairie, four bailiffs, three attorneys, the clerk of assize, and the justice's clerk, the revenue collector, and the registrar, two doctors—old Varlet's rivals, Grévin's brother-in-law—a miller named Laurent Coussard, leader of the Republican party at Arcis—the mayor's two deputies, the bookseller and printer of the place, and a dozen or so of townsfolk came in by degrees, and then walked about the garden in groups while waiting till the company should be numerous enough to hold a meeting.

Finally, by twelve o'clock, about fifty men in their Sunday attire, most of them having come out of curiosity to see the fine rooms of which so much had been said in the district, were seated in the chairs arranged for them by Madame Marion. The windows were left open, and the silence was presently so complete that the rustle of a silk dress could be heard; for Madame Marion could not resist the temptation to go out into the garden and sit where she could hear what was going on. The cook, the housemaid, and the man-servant remained in the dining-room, fully sharing their master's feelings.

"Gentlemen," said Simon Giguet, "some of you wish to

do my father the honor of placing him in the chair as presi‑
dent of this meeting, but Colonel Giguet desires me to express
his acknowledgments and decline it, while deeply grateful to
you for the proposal, which he takes as a recompense for his
services to his country.—We are under my father's roof, and
he feels that he must beg to be excused; he proposes a
merchant of the highest respectability—a gentleman on whom
your suffrages conferred the mayoralty of this town—Mon‑
sieur Philéas Beauvisage."

"Hear, hear !"

"We are, I believe, agreed that in this meeting—purely
friendly, and perfectly free, without prejudice in any way
to the great preliminary meeting, when it will be your busi‑
ness to question your candidates and weigh their merits—we
are agreed, I say, to follow the forms—the constitutional
forms—of the elective Chamber?"

"Yes, yes !" unanimously.

"Therefore," said Simon, "I have the honor, speaking in
the name of all present, to request Monsieur the Mayor to
take the president's chair."

Philéas rose and crossed the room, feeling himself turn
as red as a cherry. When he found himself behind the tea‑
table, he saw not a hundred eyes, but a hundred thousand
lights. The sunshine seemed to put the room in a blaze, and,
to use his own words, his throat was full of salt.

"Return thanks !" murmured Simon in his ear.

"Gentlemen——"

The silence was so alarming that Philéas felt his heart in
his mouth.

"What am I to say, Simon?" he whispered.

"Well ?" said Achille Pigoult.

"Gentlemen," said Simon, prompted by the little notary's
spiteful interjection, "the honor you have done the mayor
may have startled without surprising him."

"It is so," said Beauvisage. "I am too much overpowered
by this compliment from my fellow-citizens not to be ex‑
cessively flattered."

"Hear, hear!" cried the notary only.

"The devil may take me," said Beauvisage to himself, "if I am ever caught again to make speeches!"

"Will Monsieur Fromaget and Monsieur Marcelin accept the functions of tellers?" asked Simon.

"It would be more in order," said Achille Pigoult, rising, "if the meeting were to elect the two members who support the chair—in imitation of the Chamber."

"It would be far better," observed Monsieur Mollot, an enormous man, clerk of the assizes, "otherwise the whole business will be a farce, and we shall not be really free. There would be no just cause why the whole of the proceedings should not be regulated as Monsieur Simon might dictate."

Simon muttered a few words to Beauvisage, who rose, and was presently delivered of the word, "Gentlemen!" which might be described as of thrilling interest.

"Allow me, Mr. President," said Achille Pigoult; "it is your part to preside, not to discuss."

"Gentlemen," said Beauvisage again, prompted by Simon, "if we are to—to conform to—to parliamentary usage—I would beg the Honorable Monsieur Pigoult to—to come and speak from the table—this table."

Pigoult started forward and stood by the tea-table, his fingers lightly resting on the edge, and showed his courage by speaking fluently—almost like the great Monsieur Thiers.

"Gentlemen, it was not I who proposed that we should imitate the Chamber; till now it has always appeared to me that the Chambers are truly inimitable. At the same time, it was self-evident that a meeting of sixty-odd notables of Champagne must select a president, for no sheep can move without a shepherd. If we had voted by ballot, I am quite sure our esteemed mayor would have been unanimously elected. His antagonism to the candidate put forward by his relations shows that he possesses civic courage in no ordinary degree, since he can shake off the strongest ties—those of family connection.

"To set public interest above family feeling is so great an effort, that, to achieve it, we are always obliged to remind ourselves that Brutus, from his tribune, has looked down on us for two thousand five hundred odd years. It seemed quite natural to Maître Giguet—who was so clever as to divine our wishes with regard to the choice of a chairman—to guide us in our selection of the tellers; but, in response to my remark, you thought that once was enough, and you were right. Our common friend, Simon Giguet, who is, in fact, to appear as a candidate, would appear too much as the master of the situation, and would then lose that high place in our opinion which his venerable father has secured by his diffidence.

"Now, what is our worthy chairman doing by accepting the presidency on the lines suggested to him by the candidate? Why, he is robbing us of our liberty. And, I ask you, is it seemly that the chairman of our choice should call upon us to vote, by rising and sitting, for the two tellers? Gentlemen, that would be a choice already made. Should we be free to choose? Can a man sit still when his neighbor stands? If I were proposed, every one would rise, I believe, out of politeness; and so, as all would rise for each one in turn, there would be simply no choice when every one had voted for every one else."

"Very true!" said the sixty listeners.

"Well, then, let each of us write two names on a voting-paper, and then those who take their seats on each side of the chairman may regard themselves as ornaments to the meeting. They will be qualified, conjointly with the chairman, to decide on the majority when we vote by rising and sitting on any resolution to be passed.

"We have met, I believe, to promise the candidate such support as we can command at the preliminary meeting, at which every elector in the district will be present. This I pronounce to be a solemn occasion. Are we not voting for the four-hundredth part of the governing power, as Monsieur le Maire told us just now with the appropriate and characteristic wit that we so highly appreciate?"

During this address Colonel Giguet had been cutting a sheet of paper into strips, and Simon sent for an inkstand and pens. There was a pause.

This introductory discussion had greatly disturbed Simon and aroused the attention of the sixty worthies in convocation. In a few minutes they were all busy writing the names, and the cunning Pigoult gave it out that the votes were in favor of Monsieur Mollot, clerk of assize, and Monsieur Godivet, the registrar. These two nominations naturally displeased Fromaget the druggist and Marcelin the attorney.

"You have been of service," said Achille Pigoult, "by enabling us to assert our independence; you may be prouder of being rejected than you could have been of being chosen."

Everybody laughed. Simon Giguet restored silence by asking leave of the chairman to speak. Beauvisage was already damp with perspiration, but he summoned all his courage to say:

"Monsieur Simon Giguet will address the meeting."

"Gentlemen," said the candidate, "allow me first to thank Monsieur Achille Pigoult, who, although our meeting is a strictly friendly one——"

"Is preparatory to the great preliminary meeting," Marcelin put in.

"I was about to say so," Simon went on. "In the first place, I beg to thank Monsieur Achille Pigoult for having proceeded on strictly parliamentary lines. To-day, for the first time, the district of Arcis will make free use——"

"Free use!" said Pigoult, interrupting the orator.

"Free use!" cried the assembly.

"Free use," repeated Simon, "of the right of voting in the great contest of the general election of a member to be returned to Parliament; and as, in a few days, we shall have a meeting, to which every elector is invited, to form an opinion of the candidates, we may think ourselves fortunate to acquire here, on a small scale, some practice in the customs of such meetings. We shall be all the forwarder as to a decision on the political prospects of the town of Arcis; for what we have to do to-day is to consider the town instead of a family, the country instead of a man."

He went on to sketch the history of the elections for the past twenty years. While approving of the repeated election of François Keller, he said that now the time had come for shaking off the yoke of the Gondrevilles. Arcis could not be a fief of the Liberals any more than it could be a fief of the Cinq-Cygnes. Advanced opinions were making their way in France, and Charles Keller did not represent them. Charles Keller, now a viscount, was a courtier; he could never be truly independent, since, in proposing him as a candidate for election, it was done more with a view to fitting him to succeed his father as a peer than as a deputy to the Lower Chamber—and so forth, and so forth. Finally, Simon begged to offer himself as a candidate for their suffrages, pledging himself to sit under the wing of the illustrious Odilon Barrot, and never to desert the glorious standard of Progress. Progress!—a word behind which, at that time, more insincere ambitions took shelter than definite ideas; for, after 1830, it could only stand for the pretensions of certain hungry democrats.

Still, the word had much effect in Arcis, and lent importance to any man who wrote it on his flag. A man who announced himself as a partisan of Progress was a philosopher in all questions, and politically a Puritan. He was in favor of railways, mackintoshes, penitentiaries, negro emancipation, savings-banks, seamless shoes, gas-lighting, asphalt pavements, universal suffrage, and the reduction of the civil list It was also a pronouncement of opposition to the treaties of 1815, to the Elder Branch (the Bourbons), to the Giant of the North, "perfidious Albion," and to every undertaking, good or bad, inaugurated by the Government. As may be seen, the word Progress can stand equally well for black or white. It was a furbishing up of the word Liberalism, a new rallying cry for new ambitions.

"If I rightly understand what we are here for," said Jean Violette, a stocking-weaver, who had, two years since, bought the Beauvisage business, "we are to bind ourselves to secure, by every means in our power, the return of Monsieur Simon Giguet at the election as member for Arcis in the place of the Count François Keller. And if we are all agreed to combine to that end, we have only to say *Yes* or *No* to that question."

"That is going much too fast. Political matters are not managed in that way, or they would cease to be politics!" cried Pigoult, as his grandfather, a man of eighty-six, came into the room. "The last speaker pronounces a decision on what is, in my humble opinion, the very subject under discussion. I beg to speak."

"Monsieur Achille Pigoult will address the meeting," said Beauvisage, who could now get through this sentence with due municipal and constitutional dignity.

"Gentlemen," said the little notary, "if there be in all Arcis a house where no opposition ought to be made to the influence of the Comte de Gondreville and the Keller family, is it not this? The worthy Colonel—Colonel Giguet—is the only member of this household who has not experienced the benefits of senatorial influence, since he never asked anything of the Comte de Gondreville, who, however, had his name erased from the list of exiles in 1815, and secured him the pension he enjoys, without any steps on the part of the Colonel, who is the pride of our town——"

A murmur, flattering to the old man, ran through the crowd.

"But," the orator went on, "the Marion family are loaded with the Count's favors. But for his patronage the late Colonel Giguet never would have had the command of the Gendarmerie of this department. The late Monsieur Marion would not have been presiding judge of the Imperial Court here but for the Count—to whom I, for my part, am eternally indebted. You will therefore understand how natural it is that I should take his part in this room.—And, in fact, there are few persons in this district who have not received some kindness from that family."

There was a stir among the audience.

"A candidate comes forward," Achille went on with some vehemence, "and I have a right to inquire into his past before I intrust him with power to act for me. Now I will not accept ingratitude in my delegate, for ingratitude is like misfortune—it leads from bad to worse. We have been a stepping-stone for the Kellers, you will say; well, what I have just listened to makes me fear that we may become a stepping-stone for the Giguets. We live in an age of facts, do we not? Well, then, let us inquire what will be the results for the electors of Arcis if we return Simon Giguet?

"Independence is your cry?—Well, Simon, whom I am scouting as a candidate, is my friend—as he is the friend of all who hear me—and personally I should be delighted to see him as an orator of the Left, between Garnier-Pagès and Laffitte; but what will be the result for the district represented?—It will have lost the countenance of the Comte de Gondreville and the Kellers, and in the course of five years we shall all feel the want of one or the other. If we want to get leave for a poor fellow who is drawn for the conscription, we apply to the Maréchale de Carigliano. We rely on the Kellers' interest in many matters of business which their good word settles at once. We have always found the old Comte de Gondreville kind and helpful; if you belong to Arcis, you are shown in without being kept waiting. Those three families know every family in the place.—But where is the Maison Giguet's bank, and what influence has it on the Ministry? What credit does it command in the Paris markets? If we want to have a good stone bridge in the place of our wretched timber one, will the Giguets extract the necessary funds from the Department and the State?

"If we return Charles Keller, we shall perpetuate a bond of alliance and friendship which till now has been entirely to our advantage. By electing my good, my excellent friend and schoolfellow Simon Giguet, we shall be constantly the worse till he is in office! And I know his modesty too well to think that he will contradict me when I express a doubt as to his rapid advancement to the Ministry! (*Laughter.*)

"I came to this meeting to oppose a resolution which, I think, would be fatal to our district. 'Charles Keller is a courtier,' I am told.—So much the better. We shall not have to pay for his political apprenticeship; he knows all the business of the place, and the requirements of parliamentary etiquette; he is more nearly a statesman than my friend Simon, who does not pretend that he has trained himself to be a Pitt or a Talleyrand in our little town of Arcis——"

"Danton was a native of Arcis!" cried Colonel Giguet, furious at this harangue, which was only too truthful.

"*Hear, hear!*" The word was shouted, and sixty listeners clapped the speaker.

"My father is very ready," said Simon in an undertone to Beauvisage.

"I cannot understand why, in discussing an election matter, there should be so much exaggeration of any ties between us and the Comte de Gondreville," the old Colonel went on, starting to his feet, while the blood mounted to his face. "My son inherits his fortune from his mother; he never asked the Comte de Gondreville for anything. If the Count had never existed, my son would have been just what he is— the son of an artillery Colonel who owes his promotion to his services—a lawyer who has always held the same opinions.— I would say to the Comte de Gondreville himself, 'We have elected your son-in-law for twenty years. Now we wish to prove that when we did so it was of our own free-will, and we are returning an Arcis man to show that the old spirit of 1793—to which you owed your fortune—still lives on the native soil of Danton, Malin, Grévin, Pigoult, Marion——' And so——"

The old man sat down.

There was a great commotion. Achille opened his mouth to speak. Beauvisage, who would not have felt himself presiding if he had not rung his bell, added to the racket by ringing for silence. It was by this time two o'clock.

"I must be permitted to point out to the honored Colonel, whose feelings we can all understand, that he spoke without authority from the chair, which is contrary to parliamentary usage," said Achille Pigoult.

"I see no necessity for calling the Colonel to order," said Beauvisage. "As a father——"

Silence was restored.

"We did not come here," said Fromaget, "to say *Amen* to everything put forward by the Giguets father and son——"

"No, no!" cried the audience.

"This looks badly!" said Madame Marion to the cook.

"Gentlemen," said Achille, "I will confine myself to asking my friend Simon Giguet to set forth categorically what he proposes to do to further our interests."

"Yes, yes!"

"And when, may I ask," said Simon Giguet, "did good citizens like the men of Arcis first begin to make the sacred mission of a deputy a matter of bargaining and business?"

It is impossible to overestimate the effect of fine sentiment on a crowd. Noble maxims are always applauded, and the humiliation of the country voted for all the same; just as a jail-bird who yearns for the punishment of Robert Macaire when he sees the play, will nevertheless murder the first Monsieur Germeuil who comes in his way.

"Hear, hear!" cried some thorough-going partisans.

"If you send me to the Chamber, it will be to represent your principles—the principles of 1789—to be a cipher, if you will, of the Opposition; but to vote with it, to enlighten the Government, to make war against abuses, and insist on progress in all particulars——"

"But what do you call progress? Our notion of progress would be to bring all this part of the country under cultivation," said Fromaget.

"Progress? I will explain to you what I mean by progress," cried Giguet, provoked by the interruption.

"It is the Rhine-frontier for France," said Colonel Giguet, "and the treaties of 1815 torn across."

"It is keeping up the price of wheat and keeping down the price of bread!" said Pigoult mockingly, and uttering in jest one of the nonsensical cries which France believes in.

"It is the happiness of the multitude achieved by the triumph of humanitarian doctrines."

"What did I tell you?" the wily notary muttered to his neighbors.

"Hush, silence—we want to hear!" said some.

"Gentlemen," said Mollot, with a fat smile, "the debate is noisy; give your attention to the speaker; allow him to explain——"

"Ba-a-a, ba-a-aa," bleated a friend of Achille's, who was gifted with a power of ventriloquism that was invaluable at elections.

A roar of laughter burst from the audience, who were essentially men of their province. Simon Giguet folded his arms and waited till the storm of merriment should be over.

"If that was intended as a reproof," he said, "a hint that I was marching with the flock of those noble defenders of the rights of man, who cry out, who write book after book—of the immortal priest who pleads for murdered Poland—of the bold pamphleteers—of those who keep an eye on the civil list—of the philosophers who cry out for honesty in the action of our institutions—if so, I thank my unknown friend.—To me progress means the realization of all that was promised us at the Revolution of July; electoral reform—and——"

"Then you are a democrat," interrupted Achille Pigoult.

"No," replied the candidate. "Am I a democrat because I aim at a regular and legal development of our institutions? To me progress is fraternity among all the members of the great French family, and we cannot deny that much suffering——"

At three o'clock Simon Giguet was still explaining the meaning of progress, and some of the audience were emitting steady snores expressive of deep slumbers.

Achille Pigoult had artfully persuaded them to listen in religious silence to the speaker, who was sinking, drowning, in his endless phrases and parentheses.

At that hour several groups of citizens, electors, and non-electors were standing about in front of the Château d'Arcis. The gate opens on to the Place at a right angle to that of Madame Marion's house. Several streets turn out of this square, and in the middle of it stands a covered market. Opposite the château, on the further side of the square, which is neither paved nor macadamized, so that the rain runs off in little gullies, there is a fine avenue known as the Avenue des Soupirs (of Sighs). Is this to the honor or the discredit of the women of the town? The ambiguity is, no doubt, a local witticism. Two broad walks, shaded by handsome old lime-trees, lead from the market-square to a boulevard forming another promenade, deserted, as such walks always are in a country town, and where stagnant filth takes the place of the bustling crowd of the capital.

While the discussion was at its height, to which Achille Pigoult had given a dramatic turn, with a coolness and dexterity worthy of a member of the real Parliament, four men were pacing one of the lime-walks of the Avenue des Soupirs. When they came to the square they stopped with one accord to watch the townsfolk, who were buzzing round the château like bees going into a hive at dusk. These four were the whole Ministerial party of Arcis: the sous-préfet, the public prosecutor, his deputy, and Monsieur Martener, the examining judge. The presiding judge was, as has already been explained, a partisan of the Elder Branch, and devoted to the family of Cinq-Cygne.

"Well, I cannot understand what the Government is about," the sous-préfet declared, pointing to the growing crowd. "The position is serious, and I am left without any instructions."

"In that you are like many other people," said Olivier Vinet, smiling.

"What complaint have you against the Government?" asked the public prosecutor.

"The Ministry is in a difficulty," said young Martener. "It is well known that this borough belongs, so to speak, to the Kellers, and it has no wish to annoy them. Some consideration must be shown to the only man who can at all compare with Monsieur de Talleyrand. It is to the Comte de Gondreville that the police should go for instructions, not to the préfet."

"And meanwhile," said Frédéric Marest, "the Opposition is making a stir, and you see that Colonel Giguet's influence is strong. The mayor, Monsieur Beauvisage, is in the chair at this preliminary meeting."

"After all," said Olivier Vinet slily to the sous-préfet, "Simon Giguet is a friend of yours, a school-fellow. Even if he were a supporter of Monsieur Thiers, you would lose nothing by his being elected."

"The present Ministry might turn me out before its fall. We may know when we are likely to be kicked out, but we can never tell when we may get in again," said Antonin Goulard.

"There goes Collinet the grocer. He is the sixty-seventh qualified elector who has gone into Colonel Giguet's house," said Monsieur Martener, fulfilling his functions as examining judge by counting the electors.

"If Charles Keller is the Ministerial candidate, I ought to have been informed," said Goulard. "Time ought not to have been given for Simon Giguet to get hold of the voters."

The four gentlemen walked on slowly to where the avenues end at the market-place.

"There comes Monsieur Groslier!" said the judge, seeing a man on horseback.

The horseman was the superintendent of the police. He saw the governing body of Arcis assembled on the highway, and rode up to the four functionaries.

"Well, Monsieur Groslier?" questioned the sous-préfet, meeting him at a few paces from the other three.

"Monsieur," said the police-officer in a low voice, "Monsieur le Préfet sent me to tell you some very sad news—the Vicomte Charles Keller is dead. The news reached Paris by telegraph the day before yesterday; and the two Messieurs

Keller, the Comte de Gondreville, the Maréchale de Carigliano, in fact, all the family, came yesterday to Gondreville. Abdel-Kader has reopened the fighting in Africa, and there has been some very hot work. The poor young man was one of the first victims to the war. You will receive confidential instructions, I was told to say, with regard to the election."

"Through whom?" asked Goulard.

"If I knew, it would cease to be confidential," replied the other. "Monsieur le Préfet himself did not know. 'It would be,' he said, 'a private communication to you from the Minister.' "

And he went on his way, while the proud and happy official laid a finger to his lips to impress on him to be secret.

"What news from the préfecture?" asked the public prosecutor when Goulard returned to join the other three functionaries.

"Nothing more satisfactory," replied Antonin, hurrying on as if to be rid of his companions.

As they made their way towards the middle of the square, saying little, for the three officials were somewhat nettled by the hasty pace assumed by the sous-préfet, Monsieur Martener saw old Madame Beauvisage, Philéas' mother, surrounded by almost all the people who had gathered there, and apparently telling them some long story. An attorney named Sinot, whose clients were the royalists of the town and district, and who had not gone to the Giguet meeting, stepped out of the crowd, and hurrying up to Madame Marion's house, rang the bell violently.

"What is the matter?" asked Frédéric Marest, dropping his eyeglass, and informing the other two of this proceeding.

"The matter, gentlemen," replied Antonin Goulard, seeing no occasion for keeping a secret which would at once be told by others, "is that Charles Keller has been killed in Africa, an event which gives Simon Giguet every chance!—You know Arcis; there could be no ministerial candidate other than Charles Keller. Parochial patriotism would rise in arms against any other——"

"And will such a simpleton be elected?" asked Olivier Vinet, laughing.

The judge's deputy, a young fellow of three-and-twenty, the eldest son of a very famous public prosecutor, whose promotion dated from the Revolution of July, had, of course, been helped by his father's interest to get into the upper ranks of his profession. That father, still a public prosecutor, and returned as deputy by the town of Provins, is one of the buttresses of the Centre. Thus the son, whose mother had been a Mademoiselle Chargebœuf, had an assurance, alike in his official work and his demeanor, which proclaimed his father's influence. He expressed his opinions unhesitatingly on men and things, for he counted on not remaining long at Arcis, but on getting a place as public prosecutor at Versailles, the infallible stepping-stone to an appointment in Paris.

The free-and-easy air, and the sort of judicial conceit assumed by this personage on the strength of his certainty of "getting on," annoyed Frédéric Marest, and all the more because a very biting wit effectually supported his young subaltern's undisciplined freedom. The public prosecutor himself, a man of forty, who had waited six years under the Restoration to rise to the post of first deputy judge, and whom the Revolution of July had left stranded at Arcis, though he had eighteen thousand francs a year of his own, was always torn between his anxiety to win the good graces of the elder Vinet, who had every chance of becoming Keeper of the Seals —an office commonly conferred on a lawyer who sits in Parliament—and the necessity for preserving his own dignity. Olivier Vinet, a thin stripling, with fair hair and a colorless face, accentuated by a pair of mischievous greenish eyes, was one of those mocking spirits, fond of pleasure, who can at any moment assume the precise, pedantic, and rather abrupt manner which a magistrate puts on when in Court.

The burly public prosecutor, very stout and solemn, had, for a short time past, adopted a method by which, as he hoped, to get the upper hand of this distracting youth: he treated him as a father treats a spoilt child.

"Olivier," said he to his deputy, patting him on the shoulder, "a man as clear-sighted as you are must see that Maître Giguet is likely enough to be elected. You might have blurted out that speech before the townsfolk instead of among friends."

"But there is one thing against Giguet," remarked Monsieur Martener.

This worthy young fellow, dull, but with very capable brains, the son of a doctor at Provins, owed his position to Vinet's father, who during the long years when he had been a pleader at Provins, had patronized the townsfolk there as the Comte de Gondreville did those of Arcis.

"What?" asked Antonin.

"Parochial feeling is tremendously strong against a man who is forced on the electors," replied the judge; "but when, in a place like Arcis, the alternative is the elevation of one of their equals, jealousy and envy get the upper hand even of local feeling."

"That seems simple enough," said the public prosecutor, "but it is perfectly true. If you could secure only fifty Ministerial votes, you would not unlikely find the first favorite here," and he glanced at Antonin Goulard.

"It will be enough to set up a candidate of the same calibre to oppose Simon Giguet," said Olivier Vinet.

The sous-préfet's face betrayed such satisfaction as could not escape the eye of either of his companions, with whom, indeed, he was on excellent terms. Bachelors all, and all well to do, they had without premeditation formed a defensive alliance to defy the dulness of a country town. The other three were already aware of Goulard's jealousy of Giguet, which a few words here will suffice to account for.

Antonin Goulard, whose father had been a huntsman in the service of the Simeuse family, enriched by investments in nationalized land, was, like Simon Giguet, a native of Arcis. Old Goulard left the Abbey of Valpreux—a corruption of Val-des-Preux—to live in the town after his wife's death, and sent his son Antonin to school at the Lycée Impérial, where Colonel Giguet had placed his boy. The two lads, after being school-fellows, went together to Paris to study law, and, their friendship persisting, they took their amusements together. They promised to help each other in life, since they adopted different branches of their profession; but fate decided that they were to become rivals.

In spite of his sufficiently evident personal advantages, and the cross of the Legion of Honor, which the Count had obtained for Goulard to compensate him for lack of promotion, and which he displayed at his button-hole, the offer of his heart and prospects had been civilly declined when, six months before the day when this narrative opens, Antonin had secretly called on Madame Beauvisage as her daughter's suitor. But no step of this kind is a secret in the country. Frédéric Marest, whose fortune, whose order, and whose position were the same three years before, had then been also dismissed on the score of disparity of years. Hence both Goulard and the public prosecutor were never more than strictly polite to the Beauvisages, and made fun of them between themselves.

As they walked just now, they both had guessed, and had told each other, the secret of Simon Giguet's candidature, for they had got wind, the night before, of Madame Marion's ambitions. Animated alike by the spirit of the dog in the manger, they were tacitly but heartily agreed in a determination to hinder the young lawyer from winning the wealthy heiress who had been refused to them.

"Heaven grant that I may be able to control the election!" said the sous-préfet, "and the Comte de Gondreville may get me appointed préfet, for I have no more wish to remain here than you have, though I am a native born."

"You have a very good opportunity of being elected deputy, sir," said Olivier Vinet to Marest. "Come and see my father, who will, no doubt, arrive at Provins within a few hours, and we will get him to have you nominated as the Ministerial candidate."

"Stay where you are," said Goulard. "The Ministry has ideas of its own as to its candidate——"

"Pooh! Why, there are two Ministries—one that hopes to control the election, and one that means to profit by it," said Vinet.

"Do not complicate Antonin's difficulties," replied Frédéric Marest, with a knowing wink to his deputy.

The four officials, now far away from the Avenue des Soupirs, crossed the market-place to the *Mulet* inn on seeing Poupart come out of Madame Marion's house. At that moment, in fact, the sixty-seven conspirators were pouring out of the carriage gate.

"And you have been into that house?" asked Antonin Goulard, pointing to the wall of the Marion's garden, backing on the Brienne road opposite the stables of the *Mulet*.

"And I go there no more, Monsieur le Sous-préfet," returned the innkeeper. "Monsieur Keller's son is dead; I have nothing more to do with it. God has made it his business to clear the way——"

"Well, Pigoult?" said Olivier Vinet, seeing the whole of the Opposition coming from the meeting.

"Well," echoed the notary on whose brow the moisture still testified to the energy his efforts, "Sinot has just brought us news which result in unanimity. With the exception of five dissidents—Poupart, my grandfather, Mollot, Sinot and myself—they have all sworn, as at a game of tennis, to use every means in their power to secure the return of Simon Giguet—of whom have made a mortal enemy.—We all got very heated! At any rate, I got the Giguets to fulminate against the Cindrevilles, so the old Count will side with me. Not later than to-morrow he shall know what the self-styled patriots of Arcis said about him, and his corruption, and his famous conduct, so as to shake off his protection, or, as they say, his yoke."

"And they are unanimous?" said Vinet, with a smile.

"To-day," replied Monsieur Marest.

"Oh!" cried Pigoult, "the general feeling is in favor of

electing a man of the place. Whom can you find to set up in opposition to Simon Giguet, who has spent two mortal hours in preaching on the word Progress!"

"We can find old Grévin!" cried the sous-préfet.

"He has no ambition," said Pigoult. "But first and foremost we must consult the Count.—Just look," he went on, "how attentively Simon is taking care of that old noodle Beauvisage!"

And he pointed to the lawyer, who had the mayor by the arm, and was talking in his ear.

Beauvisage bowed right and left to all the inhabitants, who gazed at him with the deference of country townspeople for the richest man in the place.

"He treats him as a father—and mother!" remarked Vinet.

"Oh! he will do no good by buttering him up," replied Pigoult, who caught the hint conveyed in Vinet's retort. "Cécile's fate does not rest with either father or mother."

"With whom, then?"

"My old master. If Simon were the member for Arcis, he would be no forwarder in that matter."

Though the sous-préfet and Marest pressed Pigoult hard, they could get no explanation of this remark, which, as they shrewdly surmised, was big with meaning, and revealed some acquaintance with the intentions of the Beauvisage family.

All Arcis was in a pother, not only in consequence of the distressing news that had stricken the Gondrevilles, but also because of the great resolution voted at the Giguets'—where, at this moment, Madame Marion and the servants were hard at work restoring order, that everything might be in readiness for the company who would undoubtedly drop in as usual in the evening in full force, attracted by curiosity.

Champagne looks, and is, but a poor country. Its aspect is for the most part dreary, a dull plain. As you pass through the villages, or even the towns, you see none but shabby buildings of timber or concrete; the handsomest are of brick. Stone is scarcely used even for public buildings. At Arcis the château, the Palais de Justice, and the church are the only edifices constructed of stone. Nevertheless, the province—or, at any rate, the departments of the Aube, the Marne, and the Haute-Marne, rich in the vineyards which are famous throughout the world—also support many flourishing industries. To say nothing of the manufacturing centre at Reims, almost all the hosiery of every kind produced in France, a very considerable trade, is woven in and near Troyes. For ten leagues round, the country is inhabited by stocking-weavers, whose frames may be seen through the open doors as you pass through the hamlets. These workers deal through factors with the master speculator, who calls himself a manufacturer. The manufacturer sells to Paris houses, or more often, to retail hosiers, who stick up a sign proclaiming themselves manufacturing hosiers.

None of these middlemen ever made a stocking, or a nightcap, or a sock. A large proportion of such gear comes from Champagne—not all, for there are weavers in Paris who compete with the country workers.

These middlemen, coming between the producer and the consumer, are a curse not peculiar to this trade. It exists in most branches of commerce, and adds to the price of the goods all the profit taken by the intermediary. To do away with these expensive go-betweens, who hinder the direct sale of manufactured goods, would be a benevolent achievement, and the magnitude of the results would raise it to the level of a great political reform. Industry at large would be benefited, for it would bring about such a reduction of prices to the home-consumer as is needed to maintain the struggle against foreign competition, a battle as murderous as that of hostile armies.

But the overthrow of such an abuse as this would not secure to our modern philanthropists such glory or such profit as are to be obtained by fighting for the Dead Sea apples of negro emancipation, or the penitentiary system; hence this illicit commerce of the middleman, the producer's banker, will weigh for a long time yet on the workers and consumers alike. In France—so clever as a nation—it is always supposed that simplification means destruction. We are still frightened by the Revolution of 1789.

The industrial energy that always thrives in a land where Nature is a grudging step-dame, sufficiently shows what progress agriculture would make there if only wealth would join its partnership with the land, which is not more barren in Champagne than in Scotland, where the outlay of capital has worked miracles. And when agriculture shall have conquered the unfertile tracts of that province, when industry shall have scattered a little capital on the chalk fields of Champagne, prosperity will multiply threefold. The land is, in fact, devoid of luxury, and the dwelling-houses are bare; but English comfort will find its way thither, money will acquire that rapid circulation which is half of what makes wealth, and which is now beginning in many of the torpid districts of France.

Writers, officials, the Church from its pulpits, the Press in its columns—all to whom chance has given any kind of influence over the masses—ought to proclaim it again and again: "Hoarding is a social crime." The miserliness of the provinces stagnates the vitality of the industrial mass, and impairs the health of the nation. The little town of Arcis, for instance, on the way to nowhere, and apparently sunk in complete quiescence, is comparatively rich in the possession of capital slowly amassed in the hosiery trade.

Monsieur Philéas Beauvisage was the Alexander—or, if you will, the Attila—of his native town. This is how that respectable and hardworking man had conquered the dominion of cotton. He was the only surviving child of the Beauvisages, long settled on the fine farm of Bellache, part of the Gondreville estate; and in 1811 his parents made a considerable sacrifice to save him from the conscription by purchasing a substitute. Then his mother, as a widow, had again, in 1813, rescued her only son from being enlisted in the Guards by the good offices of the Comte de Gondreville.

In 1813 Philéas, then twenty-one, had for three years past been engaged in the pacific business of a hosier. The lease of the farm of Bellache having run out, the farmer's widow decided that she would not renew it. In fact, she foresaw ample occupation for her old age in watching the investment of her money.

That her later days might not be disturbed by anxiety, she had a complete valuation made by Monsieur Grévin, the notary, of all her husband's estate, though her son had made no claims on her ; and his share was found to amount to about a hundred and fifty thousand francs. The good woman had not to sell her land, most of it purchased from Michu, the luckless steward of the Simeuse family. She paid her son in cash, advising him to buy up his master's business. This old Monsieur Pigoult was the son of the old justice of the peace, and his affairs were already in such disorder that his death, as has been hinted, was supposed to have been due to his own act.

Philéas Beauvisage, a prudent youth, with a proper respect for his mother, had soon concluded the bargain ; and as he inherited from his parents the bump of acquisitiveness, as phrenologists term it, his youthful zeal was thrown into the business, which seemed to him immense, and which he pro- posed to extend by speculation.

The Christian name Philéas, which may, perhaps, seem extraordinary, was one of the many whimsical results of the Revolution. The Beauvisages, as connected with the Simeuses, and consequently good Catholics, had their infant baptized. The curé of Cinq-Cygne, the Abbé Goujet, being consulted by the farmers, advised them to take Philéas as his patron saint, his Greek name being likely to find favor in the eyes of the municipality, for the boy was born at a time when chil- dren were registered by the strange names in the Republican calendar.

In 1814, hosiery—as a rule, a fairly regular trade—was liable to all the ups and downs of the cotton market. The price of cotton depended on the Emperor's successes or defeats; his adversaries, the English generals in Spain, would say, "The town is ours; send up the bales." Pigoult, Philéas' retiring master, supplied his weavers in the country with yarns. At the time when he sold his business to young Beauvisage, he had in stock a large supply of cotton yarns, purchased when they were at the dearest, while cotton was now being brought in through Lisbon in vast quantities at six sous the kilogramme, in virtue of the Emperor's famous decree. The reaction in France, caused by the importation of this cheap cotton, brought about Pigoult's death, and laid the foundation of Beauvisage's fortune; for he, instead of losing his head like his old master, bought up twice as much cotton as his predecessor had in stock, and so struck a medium average price. This simple transaction enabled Philéas to triple his output of manufactured goods, while apparently a benefactor to the workers; and he could sell his produce in Paris and the provinces at a profit when others were merely recovering the cost price. By the beginning of 1814 his manufactured stock was exhausted.

The prospect of war on French soil, which would be especially disastrous to Champagne, made him cautious. He manufactured no more goods, and by realizing his capital in solid gold, stood prepared for the event. At that time the custom-houses were a dead letter. Napoleon had been obliged to enlist his thirty thousand customs officials to defend the country. Cotton, smuggled in through a thousand gaps in the hedge, was flung into every market. It is impossible to give an idea of the liveliness and cunning of cotton at that date, or of the avidity with which the English clutched at a country where cotton stockings were worth six francs a pair, and cambric shirts were an article of luxury.

Manufacturers on a smaller scale and the master workmen, counting on Napoleon's genius and luck, had invested in cotton coming through Spain. This they were working up, in the hope of presently dictating terms to the Paris retail shops. All this Philéas noted. Then, when the province was devastated by war, he stood between the army and Paris.

As each battle was lost he went to the weavers who had hidden their goods in casks—silos of hosiery—and, cash in hand, this Cossack of the trade, going from village to village, bought up, below cost price, these barrels of stockings, which might fall any day into the hands of foes whose feet wanted covering as badly as their throats wanted liquor.

At this period of disaster, Philéas displayed a degree of energy that was almost a match for the Emperor's. This captain of the hosiery trade fought the commercial campaign of 1814 with a courage that remains unrecognized. One league behind, wherever the General was one league in advance, he bought up cotton nightcaps and stockings as his trophies, while the Emperor in his reverses plucked immortal palms. The genius was equal in both, though exercised in widely different spheres, since one was eager to cover as many heads as the other hoped to fell. Compelled to create means of transport to save his casks full of stockings, which he stored in a Paris suburb, Philéas often requisitioned horses and wagons, as though the safety of the Empire depended on him. And was not the majesty of Trade as good as that of Napoleon? Had not the English merchants, after subsidizing Europe, got the upper hand of the giant who threatened their ships?

While the Emperor was abdicating at Fontainebleau, Philéas was the triumphant master of the "article." As a result of his clever manœuvres, the price of cotton was kept down, and he had doubled his fortune when many manufacturers thought themselves lucky to get rid of their goods at a loss of fifty per cent. He returned to Arcis with three hundred thousand francs, half of which, invested in the Funds, brought him fifteen thousand francs a year. One hundred thousand he used to double the capital needed for his business; and he spent the remainder in building, decorating, and furnishing a fine house in the Place du Pont, at Arcis.

On his return in triumph, the hosier naturally confided his story to Monsieur Grévin. The notary had a daughter to marry, just twenty years of age. Grévin's father-in-law, who for forty years had practised as a doctor at Arcis, was at that time still alive. Grévin was a widower; he knew that old Madame Beauvisage was rich; he believed in the energy and capacity of a young man who had thus boldly utilized the campaign of 1814. Séverine Grévin's fortune from her mother was sixty thousand francs. What was old Dr. Varlet to leave her? As much again, at most! Grévin was already fifty; he was very much afraid of dying; he saw no chance, after the Restoration, of marrying his daughter as he would wish—for her he was ambitious.

Under these circumstances, he contrived to have it suggested to Philéas that he should propose for Séverine. Mademoiselle Grévin, well brought up and handsome, was regarded as one of the good matches of the town. Also, the connection with the most intimate friend of the Comte de Gondreville, who retained his dignity as a peer of France, was, of course, an honor for the son of one of the Gondreville farmers. The widow would, indeed, have made a sacrifice to achieve it. But when she heard that her son's suit was successful, she held her hand, and gave him nothing, an act of prudence in which the notary followed suit. And thus the marriage was brought about between the son of the farmer who had been so faithful to the Simeuses, and the daughter of one of their most determined enemies. This, perhaps, was the only instance in which Louis XVIII.'s motto found application—"*Union et oubli*" (union and oblivion).

When the Bourbons returned for the second time, old Dr. Varlet died, at the age of seventy-six, leaving in his cellar two hundred thousand francs in gold, besides other property valued at an equal sum. Thus, in 1816, Philéas and his wife found themselves possessed of thirty thousand francs a year, apart from the profits of the business; for Grévin wished to invest his daughter's money in land, and Beauvisage made no objection. The interest on Séverine Grévin's share of her grandfather's money amounted to scarcely fifteen thousand francs a year, in spite of the good opportunities for investment which Grévin kept a lookout for.

The first two years of married life were enough to show Grévin and his daughter how incapable Philéas really was. The hawk's eye of commercial greed had seemed to be the effect of superior capacity, and the old notary had mistaken youthfulness for power, and luck for a talent for business. But though Philéas could read and write, and do sums to admiration, he had never read a book. Miserably ignorant, conversation with him was out of the question; he could respond by a deluge of commonplace, expressed pleasantly enough. But, as the son of a farmer, he was not wanting in commercial acumen.

Other men must be plain with him, clear and explicit; but he never was the same to his adversary.

Tender and kind-hearted, Philéas wept at the least touch of pathos. This made him reverent to his wife, whose superiority filled him with unbounded admiration. Séverine, a woman of brains, knew everything—according to Philéas. And she was all the more accurate in her judgments because she consulted her father on every point. Also, she had a very firm temper, and this made her absolute mistress in her own house. As soon as this point was gained, the old notary felt less regret at seeing his daughter happy through a mastery which is always gratifying to a wife of determined character. —Still, there was the woman!

This, it was said, was what befell the woman.

At the time of the reaction of 1815, a certain Vicomte de Chargebœuf, of the poorer branch, was appointed sous-préfet at Arcis by the influence of the Marquise de Cinq-Cygne, to whom he was related. This young gentleman remained there as sous-préfet for five years. Handsome Madame Beauvisage, it was said, had something to do with the long stay—much too long for his advantage—made by the Vicomte in this small post. At the same time, it must at once be said that these hints were never justified by the scandals which·betray such love-affairs, so difficult to conceal from the

Argus eyes of a small country town. "If Séverine loved the Vicomte de Chargebœuf, if he loved her, it was a blameless and honorable attachment," said all the friends of the Grévins and the Marions. And these two sets imposed their opinion on the immediate neighborhood. But the Grévins and the Marions had no influence over the Royalists, and the Royalists declared that the sous-préfet was a happy man.

As soon as the Marquise de Cinq-Cygne heard what was rumored as to her young relation, she sent for him to Cinq-Cygne; and so great was her horror of all who were ever so remotely connected with the actors in the judicial tragedy that had been so fatal to her family, that she desired the Viscount to live elsewhere. She got him appointed to Sancerre as sous-préfet, promising to secure his promotion. Some acute observers asserted that the Viscount had pretended to be in love, so as to be made préfet, knowing how deeply the Marquise hated the name of Grévin. Others, on the other hand, remarked on the coincidence of the Vicomte de Chargebœuf's visits to Paris with those made by Madame Beauvisage under the most trivial pretexts. An impartial historian would find it very difficult to form an opinion as to facts thus enwrapped in the mystery of private life.

A single circumstance seemed to turn the scale in favor of scandal. Cécile Renée Beauvisage was born in 1820, when Monsieur de Chargebœuf was leaving Arcis, and one of the sous-préfet's names was René. The name was given her by the Comte de Gondreville, her godfather. If the mother had raised any objection to her child's having that name, she might possibly have confirmed these suspicions; and as the world must always be in the right, this was supposed to be a little bit of mischief on the part of the old peer. Madame Keller, the Count's daughter, was the godmother, and her name was Cécile.

As to Cécile Renée Beauvisage's face, the likeness is striking!—not to her father or her mother; as time goes on, she has become the living image of the Viscount, even to his aristocratic manner. This likeness, moral and physical, has

however escaped the ken of the good folks of Arcis, for the
Vicomte never returned there.

At any rate, Séverine made Philéas happy in his own way.
He was fond of good living and the comforts of life; she
gave him the choicest wines, a table fit for a bishop, catered
for by the best cook in the department; but she made no
display of luxury, keeping house in the style required by
the plain citizens of Arcis. It was a saying at Arcis that
you should dine with Madame Beauvisage, and spend the
evening with Madame Marion.

The importance to which the House of Cinq-Cygne was at
once raised by the Restoration had naturally tightened the
bonds that held together all the families in the district who
had been in any way concerned in the trial as to the temporary
disappearance of Gondreville. The Marions, the Grévins,
and the Giguets held together all the more closely because,
to secure the triumph of their so-called constitutional party
at the coming elections, harmonious co-operation would be
necessary.

Séverine, of aforethought, kept Beauvisage busy with his
hosiery trade, from which any other man might have retired,
sending him to Paris or about the country on business. Indeed, till 1830, Philéas, who thus found work for his bump
of acquisitiveness, earned every year as much as he spent, besides the interest on his capital, while taking things easy
and doing his work *in slippers,* as they say. Hence, the interest and fortune of Monsieur and Madame Beauvisage, invested for fifteen years past by the constant care of old
Grévin, would amount, in 1830, to five hundred thousand
francs. This, in fact, was at that time Cécile's marriage-
portion; and the old notary invested it in three and a half per
cents bought at fifty, and so yielding thirty thousand francs
a year. So no one was mistaken when estimating the fortune
of the Beauvisages at a guess at eighty thousand francs a
year.

In 1830 they sold the business to Jean Violette, one of
their agents, the grandson of one of the most important

witnesses for the prosecution in the Simeuse trial, and had invested the purchase-money, estimated at three hundred thousand francs. And Monsieur and Madame Beauvisage had still in prospect the money that would come to them from old Grévin and from the old farmer's widow, each supposed to be worth fifteen to twenty thousand francs a year.

These great provincial fortunes are the product of time multiplied by economy. Thirty years of old age are in themselves a capital. Even if they gave Cécile a portion of fifty thousand francs a year, Monsieur and Madame Beauvisage would still inherit two fortunes, besides keeping thirty thousand francs a year and their house at Arcis.

As soon as the old Marquise de Cinq-Cygne should die, Cécile would be an acceptable match for the young Marquis; but that lady's health—strong, and almost handsome still at the age of sixty—negatived any such hope, if, indeed, it had ever entered into the mind of Grévin and his daughter, as some persons asserted who were surprised at the rejection of suitors so eligible as the sous-préfet and the public prosecutor.

The house built by Beauvisage, one of the handsomest in Arcis, stands in the Place du Pont, in a line with the Rue Vide-Bourse, and at the corner of the Rue du Pont, which slopes up to the Church Square. Though, like many provincial town-houses, it has neither forecourt nor garden, it has a rather good effect in spite of some bad taste in the decorations. The house door—a double door—opens from the street. The windows on the ground floor overlook the *Poste* inn, on the street side, and on the side towards the Square have a view of the picturesque reaches of the Aube, which is navigable below this bridge. On the other side of the bridge is a corresponding place or square. Here stood Monsieur Grévin's house, and here begins the road to Sézanne.

The Maison Beauvisage, carefully painted white, might pass for being built of stone. The height of the windows, and the enriched outside mouldings, contribute to give the building a certain style, enhanced, no doubt, by the poverty-stricken appearance of most of the houses in the town, constructed as they are of timber, and coated with stucco made to imitate stone. Still, even these dwellings have a stamp of originality, since each architect, or each owner, has exerted his ingenuity to solve the problems of this mode of construction.

On each of the open spaces at either end of the bridge, an example may be seen of this peculiar architecture. In the middle of the row of houses in the square, to the left of the Maison Beauvisage, may be seen the frail shop—the walls painted plum-color, and the woodwork green—occupied by Jean Violette, grandson of the famous farmer of Grouage, one of the chief witnesses in the case of the senator's disappearance; to him, in 1830, Beauvisage had made over his connection and his stock-in-trade, and, it was said, had lent him capital.

The bridge of Arcis is of timber. At about a hundred yards above this bridge the current is checked by another bridge supporting the tall wooden buildings of a mill with several wheels. The space between the road bridge and this private dam forms a pool, on each side of which stand some good houses. Through a gap, and over the roofs, the hill is seen where stands the Château d'Arcis, with its gardens, its paddock, its surrounding walls and trees, commanding the upper river of the Aube and the poor meadows of the left bank.

The noise of the water tumbling over the dam behind the foot-bridge to the mills, and the hum of the wheels as they thrash the water ere it falls into the pool in cascades, make the street above the bridge quite lively, in contrast with the silence of the stream where it flows below between Monsieur Grévin's garden, his house being next to the bridge on the left bank, and the quay on the right bank, where boats unload, in front of a row of poor but picturesque houses. The Aube meanders in the distance between trees, singly or in groups, tall or stumpy, and of various kinds, according to the caprice of the residents.

The character of the buildings is so various that the tourist might find a specimen representative of every country. On the north side of the pool, where ducks sport and gobble in the water, there is, for instance, an almost southern-looking house with an incurved roof covered with pan-tiles, such as are used in Italy; on one side of it is a small garden plot on the quay in which vines grow over a trellis, and two or three trees. It recalls some corner of Rome, where, on the banks of the Tiber, houses of this type may be seen. Opposite, on the other shore, is a large dwelling with a pent-house roof and balconies like those of a Swiss châlet; to complete the illusion, between it and the weir lies a wide meadow, planted with poplars on each side of a narrow graveled path. And, crowning the town, the buildings of the château, looking all the more imposing as it stands up amid such frail structures, seem to represent the grandeur of the old French aristocracy.

Though the two squares at the ends of the bridge are intersected by the Sézanne road, an abominable road too, and very ill kept, and though they are the liveliest spots in the town—for the offices of the Justice of the Peace and of the Mayor of Arcis are both in the Rue Vide-Bourse—a Parisian would think the place strangely rustic and deserted. The landscape is altogether artless; standing on the square by the bridge, opposite the *Poste* inn, a farmyard pump is to be seen; to be sure, for nearly half a century a similar one commanded our admiration in the grand courtyard of the Louvre.

Nothing can more aptly illustrate provincial life than the utter silence that reigns in this little town, even in its busiest quarter. It may easily be supposed how agitating is the presence of a stranger, even if he stays but half a day, and what eager faces lean from every window to watch him; and, then, picture the chronic espionage exercised by the residents over each other. Life becomes so nearly monastic that excepting on Sundays and fête-days, a visitor will not meet a creature on the Boulevards or in the Avenue des Soupirs—nowhere, in short, not even in the streets.

It will now be obvious why the front of Monsieur Beauvisage's house was in a line with the street and the square: the square served as a forecourt. As he sat at the window, the retired hosier could get a raking view of the Church Square, of those at the two ends of the bridge, and of the Sézanne road. He could see the coaches and travelers arrive at the *Hôtel de la Poste*. And on days when the Court was sitting, he could see the stir in front of the Justice-house and the Mairie. And, indeed, Beauvisage would not have exchanged his house for the château in spite of its lordly appearance, its stone masonry, and its commanding position.

On entering the house, you found yourself in a hall, and facing a staircase beyond. On the right was a large drawing-room, with two windows to the square, on the left a handsome dining-room looking on to the street. The bedrooms were on the first floor.

In spite of their wealth, the Beauvisage household consisted of the cook and a housemaid, a peasant woman who washed, ironed, and cleaned, not often being required to wait on madame and mademoiselle, who waited on each other to fill up their time. Since the hosiery business had been sold, the horse and trap, formerly used by Philéas, and kept at the inn, had also been disposed of.

Just as Philéas went in, his wife, who had been informed of the resolution passed at the meeting, had put on her boots and her shawl to call on her father; for she rightly guessed that in the course of the evening Madame Marion would throw out some hints preliminary to proposing Simon for Cécile.

After telling her about Charles Keller's death, Philéas asked her opinion with a simplicity that proved a habit of respecting Séverine's views on all subjects.

"What do you say to that, wife?" said he, and then sat down to await her reply.

In 1839 Madame Beauvisage, though forty-four years of

age, still looked so young, that she might have been the
"double" of Mademoiselle Mars.   If the reader can remember
the most charming Célimène ever seen on the stage of the
Français, he may form an exact idea of Séverine Beauvisage.
There were in both the same roundness of form, the same
beautiful features, the same finished outline; but the hosier's
wife was too short, and thus missed the dignified grace, the
coquettish air *à la Sévigné,* which dwell in the memory of
those who have lived through the Empire and the Restoration.   And then provincial habits, and the careless way of
dressing which Séverine had allowed herself to drift into for
ten years past, gave a common look to that handsome profile
and fine features, and she had grown stout, which disfigured
what for the first twelve years of her married life had been
really a magnificent person.   Séverine's imperfections were
redeemed by a queenly glance, full of pride and command,
and by a turn of the head that asserted her dignity.   Her
hair, still black, long, and thick, crowning her head with a
broad plait, gave her a youthful look.   Her shoulders and
bosom were as white as snow, but all too full and puffy, spoiling the lines of the throat, and making it too short.   Her
arms, too stout and dimpled, ended in hands which, though
pretty and small, were too plump.   She was so overfull of
life and health, that the flesh, in spite of all her care, made
a little roll above her shoe.   A pair of earrings without
pendants, each worth a thousand crowns, adorned her ears.

She had on a lace cap with pink ribbons, a morning gown
of *mousseline de laine,* striped in pink and gray, and trimmed
with green, opening over a petticoat with a narrow frill of
Valenciennes edging, and a green Indian shawl, of which the
point hung to the ground.   Her feet did not seem comfortable
in their bronze kid boots.

"You cannot be so hungry," said she, looking at her husband, "but that you can wait half an hour.   My father will
have finished dinner, but I cannot eat mine in comfort till
I know what he thinks, and whether we ought to go out to
Gondreville——"

"Yes, yes, go, my dear; I can wait," said the hosier.

"Bless me! shall I never cure you of addressing me as *tu?*"* she exclaimed, with a meaning shrug.

"I have never done so in company by any chance—since 1817," replied Philéas.

"But you constantly do so before your daughter and the servants——"

"As you please, Séverine," said Beauvisage dejectedly.

"Above all things, do not say a word to Cécile about the resolution of the electors," added Madame Beauvisage, who was looking at herself in the glass while arranging her shawl.

"Shall I go with you to see your father?" asked Philéas.

"No; stay with Cécile.—Besides, Jean Violette is to call to-day to pay the rest of the money he owes you. He will bring you his twenty thousand francs. This is the third time he has asked for three months' grace; grant him no more time, and if he cannot pay up, take his note of hand to Courtet the bailiff; we must do things regularly, and apply to the Court. Achille Pigoult will tell you how to get the money. That Violette is the worthy descendant of his grandfather! I believe him quite capable of making money out of a bankruptcy. He has no sense of honor or justice."

"He is a very clever fellow," said Beauvisage.

"You handed over to him a connection and stock-in-trade that were well worth fifty thousand francs for thirty thousand, and in eight years he has only paid you ten thousand——"

"I never had the law of any man," replied Beauvisage, "and would rather lose my money than torment the poor fellow——"

"A poor fellow who is making a fool of you."

Beauvisage was silent. Finding nothing to say in reply to this brutal remark, he stared at the drawing-room floor.

---

* *Tu* (thou) instead of *vous* (you) is used in domestic and familiar intercourse.— *Translator.*

The gradual extinction of Beauvisage's intellect was perhaps due to too much sleep. He was in bed every night by eight o'clock, and remained there till eight next morning, and for twenty years had slept for twelve hours on end without ever waking; or, if such a serious event should supervene, it was to him the most extraordinary fact—he would talk about it all day. He then spent about an hour dressing, for his wife had drilled him into never appearing in her presence at breakfast till he was shaved, washed, and properly dressed.

When he was in business he went off after breakfast to attend to it, and did not come in till dinner-time. Since 1832 he would call on his father-in-law instead, and take a walk, or pay visits in the town. He always was seen in boots, blue cloth trousers, a white waistcoat, and a blue coat, the dress insisted on by his wife. His linen was exquisitely fine and white, Séverine requiring him to have a clean shirt every day. This care of his person, so unusual in the country, contributed to the respect in which he was held, as in Paris we remark a man of fashion.

Thus the outer man of this worthy and solemn night-cap seller denoted a person of worship; and his wife was too shrewd ever to have said a word that could let the public of Arcis into the secret of her disappointment and of her husband's ineptitude; while he, by dint of smiles, obsequious speeches, and airs of wealth, passed muster as a man of great importance. It was reported that Séverine was so jealous that she would not allow him to go out in the evening, while Philéas was expressing roses and lilies for his complexion under the weight of blissful slumbers.

Beauvisage, whose life was quite to his mind, cared for by his wife, well served by the two maids, and petted by his daughter, declared himself—and was—the happiest man in Arcis. Séverine's feeling for her commonplace husband was not without the hue of protective pity that a mother feels for her children. She disguised the stern remarks she felt called upon to make to him under a jesting tone. There was not a more peaceful household; and Philéas' dislike to company, which sent him to·sleep, as he could not play any games of cards, had left Séverine free to dispose of her evenings.

Cécile's entrance put an end to her father's embarrassment. He looked up.

"How fine you are!" he exclaimed.

Madame Beauvisage turned round sharply with a piercing look at her daughter, who blushed under it.

"Why, Cécile! who told you to dress up in that style?" asked the mother.

"Are we not going to Madame Marion's this evening? I dressed to see how my gown fits."

"Cécile, Cécile!" said Séverine, "why try to deceive your mother? It is not right; I am not pleased with you. You are trying to hide something——"

"Why, what has she done?" asked Beauvisage, enchanted to see his daughter so fresh and smart.

"What has she done? I will tell her," said the mother, threatening her only child with an ominous finger.

Cécile threw her arms round her mother's neck, hugged and petted her, which, in an only child, is a sure way of winning the day.

Cécile Beauvisage, a young lady of nineteen, had dressed herself in a pale gray silk frock, trimmed with *brandenburgs* of a darker shade to look in front like a coat. The body, with its buttons and jockey tails, formed a point in front, and laced up the back, like stays. This sort of *corset* fitted exactly to the line of the back, hips and bust. The skirt, with three rows of narrow fringe, hung in pretty folds, and the cut and style proclaimed the hand of a Paris dressmaker. A light handkerchief trimmed with lace was worn over the body. The heiress had knotted a pink kerchief round her throat, and wore a straw hat with a moss rose in it. She had fine black netted mittens and bronze kid boots; in short, but for a certain "Sunday-best" effect, this turnout, as of a figure in a fashion-plate, could not fail to charm her father and mother. And Cécile was a pretty girl, of medium height.

and well proportioned. Her chestnut hair was dressed in the fashion of the day, in two thick plaits, forming loops on each side of her face, and fastened up at the back of her head. Her face, bright with health, had the aristocratic stamp which she had not inherited from her father or her mother. Thus her clear brown eyes had not a trace of the soft, calm, almost melancholy look so common in young girls. Sprightly, quick, and healthy, Cécile destroyed the romantic cast of her features by a sort of practical homeliness and the freedom of manner often seen in spoilt children. At the same time, a husband who should be capable of recommencing her education and effacing the traces of a provincial life, might extract a charming woman from this rough-hewn marble.

In point of fact, Séverine's pride of her daughter had counteracted the effects of her love for her. Madame Beauvisage had had firmness enough to bring her daughter up well; she had assumed a certain severity which exacted obedience and eradicated the little evil that was indigenous in the child's soul. The mother and daughter had never been separated; and Cécile was blessed with what is rarer among girls than is commonly supposed—perfect and unblemished purity of mind, innocence of heart, and genuine guilelessness.

"Your dress is highly suggestive," said Madame Beauvisage. "Did Simon Giguet say anything to you yesterday which you did not confide to me?"

"Well, well!" said Philéas, "a man who is to be the representative to his fellow-citizens——"

"My dear mamma," said Cécile in her mother's ear, "he bores me to death—but there is not another man in Arcis!"

"Your opinion of him is quite correct. But wait till we know what your grandfather thinks," said Madame Beauvisage, embracing her daughter, whose reply betrayed great good sense, though it showed that her innocence had been tarnished by a thought of marriage.

Monsieur Grévin's house, situated on the opposite bank of the river. at the corner of the little Place beyond the

bridge, was one of the oldest in the town. It was built of
wood, the interstices between the timbers being filled up with
pebbles, and it was covered with a smooth coating of cement
painted stone-color. In spite of this coquettish artifice, it
looked, all the same, like a house built of cards.

The garden, lying along the river bank, had a terrace wall
with vases for flower-pots.

This modest dwelling, with its stout wooden shutters
painted stone-color like the walls, was furnished with a
simplicity to correspond with the exterior. On entering you
found yourself in a small pebbled courtyard, divided from the
garden by a green trellis. On the ground floor the old
notary's office had been turned into a drawing-room, with
windows looking out on the river and the square, furnished
with very old and very faded green Utrecht velvet. The lawyer's study was now his dining-room. Everything bore the
stamp of the owner, the philosophical old man who led one
of those lives that flow like the waters of a country stream,
the envy of political harlequins when at last their eyes are
opened to the vanity of social distinctions, and when they
are tired of a mad struggle with the tide of human affairs.

While Séverine is making her way across the bridge to
see if her father has finished his dinner, it may be well to
give a few minutes' study to the person, the life, and the
opinions of the old man whose friendship with the Comte
Malin de Gondreville secured him the respect of the whole
neighborhood. This is the plain unvarnished tale of the
notary who for a long time had been, to all intents and purposes, the only notary in Arcis.

In 1787 two youths set out from Arcis with letters of
recommendation to a member of the Council named Danton. This famous revolutionary was a native of Arcis. His
house is still shown, and his family still lives there. This
may perhaps account for the influence of the Revolution being so strongly felt in that part of the province.

Danton articled his young fellow-countrymen to a lawyer
of the Châtelet, who became famous for an action against

the Comte Morton de Chabrillant concerning his box at the theatre on the occasion of the first performance of the *Mariage de Figaro,* when the *Parlement* took the lawyer's side as considering itself insulted in the person of its legal representative.

One of the young men was named Malin, and the other Grévin; each was an only son. Malin's father was at that time the owner of the house in which Grévin was now living. They were mutually and faithfully attached. Malin, a shrewd fellow, with good brains and high ambitions, had the gift of eloquence. Grévin, honest and hardworking, made it his business to admire Malin.

They returned to the country when the Revolution began; Malin as a pleader at Troyes, Grévin to be a notary at Arcis. Grévin, always Malin's humble servant, got him returned as deputy to the Convention; Malin had Grévin appointed prosecuting magistrate at Arcis. Until the 9th Thermidor, Malin remained unknown; he always voted with the strong to crush the weak; but Tallien showed him the necessity for crushing Robespierre. Then in that terrific parliamentary battle, Malin distinguished himself; he showed courage at the right moment.

From that day he began to play a part as a politician; he was one of the heroes of the rank and file; he deserted from the party of the "Thermidoriens" to join that of the "Clichyens," and was one of the Council of Elders. After allying himself with Talleyrand and Fouché to conspire against Bonaparte, he—with them—became one of Bonaparte's most ardent partisans after the victory of Marengo. Appointed tribune, he was one of the first to be elected to the Council of State, worked at the revision of the Code, and was soon promoted to senatorial dignity with the title of Comte de Gondreville.

This was the political side of their career. Now for the financial side.

Grévin was the most active and most crafty instrument of the Comte de Gondreville's fortune in the district of

Arcis. The estate of Gondreville had belonged to the
Simeuse family, a good old house of provincial nobility,
decimated by the guillotine, of which the two surviving heirs,
both young soldiers, were serving in Condé's army. The
estate, sold as nationalized land, was purchased by Grévin for
Malin, under Marion's name. Grévin, in fact, acquired for
his friend the larger part of the Church lands sold by the
Republic in the department of the Aube. Malin sent the
sums necessary for these purchases, not forgetting a bonus to
the agent. When, presently, the Directory was supreme—
by which time Malin was a power in the Republic—the sales
were taken up in his name.

Then Grévin was a notary, and Malin in the Council of
State; Grévin became Mayor of Arcis, Malin was Senator
and Comte de Gondreville. Malin married the daughter of
a millionaire army-contractor; Grévin married the only
daughter of Monsieur Varlet, the leading doctor in Arcis.
The Comte de Gondreville had three hundred thousand francs
a year, a fine house in Paris, and the splendid château of
Gondreville. One of his daughters married a Paris banker,
one of the Kellers; the other became the wife of Marshal the
Duc de Carigliano.

Grévin, a rich man too, with fifteen thousand francs a
year, owned the house where he was now peacefully ending
his days in strict economy, having managed his friend's business for him, and bought this house from him for six thousand francs. The Comte de Gondreville was eighty years of
age, and Grévin seventy-six. The peer, taking his walk in
his park, the old notary in what had been that peer's father's
garden, each in his warm morning wrapper, hoarded crown
upon crown. Not a cloud had chequered this friendship of
sixty years. The notary had always been subservient to the
Member of the Convention, the Councillor of State, the Senator, the Peer of France.

After the Revolution of July, Malin, being in Arcis, had
said to Grévin:

"Would you care to have the Cross?" (of the Legion of
Honor).

"And what would I do with it?" replied Grévin.

Neither had ever failed the other. They had always advised and informed each other without envy on one side or arrogance or offensive airs on the other. Malin had always been obliged to do his best for Grévin, for all Grévin's pride was in the Comte de Gondreville. Grévin was as much the Comte de Gondreville as Malin himself. At the same time, since the Revolution of July, when Grévin, already an old man, had given up the management of the Count's affairs, and when the Count, failing from age and from the part he had played in so many political storms, was settling down to a quiet life, the old men—sure of each other's regard, but no longer needing each other's help—had met but rarely. On his way to his country place or on his return journey to Paris, the Count would call on Grévin, who paid the Count a visit or two while he was at Gondreville.

Their children were scarcely acquainted. Neither Madame Keller, nor the Duchesse de Carigliano, had ever formed any intimacy with Mademoiselle Grévin either before or since her marriage to Beauvisage the hosier. This scorn, whether apparent or real, greatly puzzled Séverine. Grévin, as Mayor of Arcis under the Empire, a man kind and helpful to all, had, in the exercise of his power, conciliated and overcome many difficulties. His good humor, bluntness, and honesty had won the regard and affection of his district; and besides, everybody respected him as a man who could command the favor, the power, and the influence of the Comte de Gondreville.

By this time, however, when the notary's active participation in public business was a thing of the past, when for eight years he had been almost forgotten in the town of Arcis, and his death might be expected any day, Grévin, like his old friend Malin, vegetated rather than lived. He never went beyond his garden; he grew his flowers, pruned his trees, inspected his vegetables and his grafts—like all old men, he seemed to practise being a corpse. His life was as regular as clockwork. Like his friend Colonel Giguet, he was up with the sun and in bed before nine; he was as frugal as a miser, and drank very little wine—but it was the best. He allowed himself coffee, but never touched liqueurs, and took no exercise but that involved in gardening.

In all weathers he wore the same clothes: heavy shoes, oiled to keep out the wet, loose worsted stockings, thick gray flannel trousers strapped round the waist, without braces; a wide waistcoat of thin sky-blue cloth with horn buttons, and a coat of gray flannel to match the trousers. On his head he wore a little round beaver-skin cap, which he never took off in the house. In the summer a black velvet cap took the place of the fur cap, and he wore an iron-gray cloth coat instead of the thick flannel one.

He was of medium height, and stout, as a healthy old man should be, which made him move a little heavily; his pace was slow, as is natural to men of sedentary habits. Up by daybreak, he made the most careful and elaborate toilet; he shaved himself, he walked round his garden, he looked at the weather and consulted the barometer, opening the drawing-room shutters himself. He hoed, he raked, he hunted out the caterpillars—he would always find occupation till breakfast time. After breakfast he devoted two hours to digestion, thinking—of heaven knows what. Almost every day, between two and five, his granddaughter came to see him, sometimes brought by the maid, and sometimes by her mother.

There were days when this mechanical routine was upset. He had to receive the farmers' rents, and payments in kind, to be at once resold; but this little business was but once a month on a market-day. What became of the money? No one knew, not even Séverine or Cécile; on that point Grévin was as mute as the confessional. Still, all the old man's feelings had in the end centered in his daughter and his grandchild; he really loved them more than his money.

This septuagenarian, so neat in his person, with his round face, his bald forehead, his blue eyes and thin white hair, had a tinge of despotism in his temper, as men have when they have met with no resistance from men and things. His

only great fault, and that deeply hidden, for nothing had
ever called it into play, was a persistent and terrible vindic-
tiveness, a rancor which Malin had never roused. Grévin
had always been at Malin's service, but he had always found
him grateful; the Count had never humiliated or offended
his friend, whose nature he knew thoroughly. The two men
still called each other *tu*, as in their boyhood, and still affectionately shook hands. The Senator had never allowed Grévin
to feel the difference in their positions; he always anticipated
the wishes of his old comrade, and offered him all, knowing
that he would be content with little. Grévin, who was devoted to classical literature, a purist in taste, and a good lawyer, was deeply and widely learned in legal studies; he had
done work for Malin which won the editor of the *Code* much
honor in the Council of State.

Séverine was affectionately attached to her father; she and
her daughter never left the making of his linen to any one
else. They knitted his winter stockings, and watched his
health with minute care. And Grévin knew that no thought
of self-interest mingled with their love for him; a possible
inheritance of a million francs would not dry their tears, and
old men are keenly alive to disinterested affection. Before
leaving the good man's house, every day Séverine or Cécile inquired as to what his dinner was to be next day, and sent him
early vegetables from market.

Madame Beauvisage had-always wished that her father
should introduce her at the Château de Gondreville to make
acquaintance with the Count's daughters; but the prudent
old man had frequently explained to her how difficult it would
be to keep up any connection with the Duchesse de Carigliano,
who lived in Paris, and seldom came to Gondreville, or with
a woman of fashion, like Madame Keller, when she herself
had a hosier's shop at Arcis.

"Your life is settled," said Grévin to his daughter. "Place
all your hopes of enjoyment in Cécile, who, when you give
up business, will certainly be rich enough to give you the free
and handsome style of living that you deserve Choose a

son-in-law who has ambitions and brains, and then you can some day go to Paris and leave that simpleton Beauvisage here. If I should live long enough to have a grandson-in-law, I will steer you over the sea of politics as I steered Malin, and you shall rise as high as the Kellers."

These words, spoken before the Revolution of 1830, and one year after the old notary had established himself in his little house, account for his calm existence. Grévin wished to live; he wished to start his daughter, his granddaughter, and his great-grandchildren on the highroad to greatness. Grévin was ambitious for the third generation.

When he made that speech the old man was thinking of seeing Cécile married to Charles Keller, and at this moment he was mourning over his disappointed hopes: he did not know what determination to come to.

He had no connections in Paris society; and seeing nobody else whom Cécile could advantageously marry but the young Marquis de Cinq-Cygne, he was wondering whether by sheer force of gold he might not smooth away the difficulties raised by the Revolution of July between the Royalists who were faithful to their principles and their conquerors. In fact, it seemed to him that there would be so little chance of happiness for Cécile if she fell into the hands of the Marquise de Cinq-Cynge, that he made up his mind to leave it to time to settle matters—that trusted friend of the aged. He hoped that his arch-enemy the Marquise might die, and then he thought he could capture the son through the grandfather, old Hauteserre, who was living with them at Cinq-Cygne, and whom he knew to be open to the bribery of his avarice. If this scheme should fail, when Cécile Beauvisage should be two-and-twenty with no hope of success, Grévin would consult his friend Gondreville, and leave him to find her a husband in Paris, in accordance with her taste or ambition, among the dukes of the Empire.

Séverine found her father sitting on a wooden bench at the end of his terrace, under the blossoming lilacs, and taking his coffee, for it was half-past five. She saw at once by the sorrowful gravity of her father's expression that he had heard the news. In fact, the old Count had sent a man-servant to beg his friend to go to him. Hitherto, Grévin had been unwilling to encourage his daughter's hopes; but now, in the conflict of mingled considerations that struggled in his sorrowful mind, his secret slipped out.

"My dear child," said he, "I had dreamed of such splendid and noble prospects for your future life, and death has upset them all. Cécile might have been the Vicomtesse Keller; for Charles, by my management, would have been elected member for Arcis, and he would certainly some day have suc-ceeded his father as peer. Neither Gondreville nor Madame Keller, his daughter, would have sneezed at Cécile's sixty thousand francs a year, especially with the added prospect of a hundred thousand more which will come to you some day. You could have lived in Paris with your daughter, and have played your part as mother-in-law in the higher spheres of power."

Madame Beauvisage nodded approval.

"But we are struck down by the blow that has killed this charming young man, who had already made a friend of the Prince.—And this Simon Giguet, who is pushing forward on the political stage, is a fool, a fool of the worst kind, for he believes himself an eagle.—You are too intimate with the Giguets and the Marion family to refuse the alliance without a great show of reason, but you must refuse——"

"We are, as usual, quite agreed, my dear father."

"All this necessitates my going to see my old friend Malin; in the first place, to comfort him; and in the second place, to consult him.—You and Cécile would be miserable with an old family of the Faubourg Saint-Germain; they would make you feel your humble birth in a thousand little ways. What we must look out for is one of Napoleon's dukes who is in want of money; then we can get a fine title for Cécile, and we will tie up her fortune.

"You can say that I have arranged for the disposal of Cécile's hand, and that will put an end to all such impertinent

proposals as Antonin Goulard's.   Little Vinet is sure to come
forward; and of all the suitors who will nibble at her fortune, he is the preferable.   He is clever, pushing, and connected through his mother with the Chargebœufs.   But he is
too determined not to be master, and he is young enough to
make her love him; between the two you would be done for.
—I know what you are, my child!"

"I shall feel very much embarrassed this evening at the
Marions," said Séverine.

"Well, my dear, send Madame Marion to me.   I will talk
to her!"

"I knew that you were planning for our future, dear father,
but I had no idea that it would be anything so brilliant,"
said Madame Beauvisage, taking her father's hands and kissing them.

"I have planned so deeply," replied Grévin, "that in 1831 I
bought a house you know very well—the Hôtel Beauséant——"

Madame Beauvisage started with surprise at hearing this
well-kept secret, but she did not interrupt her father.

"It will be my wedding gift," he added.   "I let it in 1832
to some English, for seven years, at twenty-four thousand
francs a year—a good stroke of business, for it only cost
me three hundred and twenty-five thousand, and I have got
back nearly two hundred thousand.   The lease is out on the
15th of July next."

Séverine kissed her father on the forehead and on both
cheeks.   This last discovery promised such splendor in the
future that she was dazzled.

"If my father takes my advice," said she to herself, as she
recrossed the bridge, "he will leave the property only in reversion to his grandchildren, and I shall have the life-in-
terest; I do not wish that my daughter and her husband
should turn me out of their house; they shall live in mine."

At dessert, when the maids were dining in the kitchen,
and Madame Beauvisage was sure of not being overheard,
she thought it well to give Cécile a little lecture.

"My dear child," said she, "behave this evening as a well-brought-up girl should; and henceforth try to have a quiet reserved manner; do not chatter too freely, nor walk about alone with Monsieur Giguet, or Monsieur Olivier Vinet, or the Sous-préfet, or Monsieur Martener—or anybody, in short, not even Achille Pigoult. You will never marry any young man of Arcis or of the department. Your fate will be to shine in Paris. You shall have some pretty dresses for every-day wear, to accustom you to being elegant; and I will try to bribe some waiting-woman of the Duchesse de Maufrigneuse's to find out where the Princesse de Cadignan and the Marquise de Cinq-Cygne buy their things. Oh, we will not look in the least provincial! You must practise the piano three hours a day, and I will have Moïse over from Troyes every day till I can find out about a master who will come from Paris. You must cultivate all your talents, for you have not more than a year before you at most before getting married.—So, now, I have warned you, and I shall see how you conduct yourself this evening. You must keep Simon at arm's length without making him ridiculous."

"Be quite easy, ma'am, I will begin at once to adore the Unknown."

This speech, which made Madame Beauvisage smile, needs a word of explanation.

"Ah, I have not seen him yet," said Philéas, "but everybody is talking of him. When I want to know who he is, I will send the sergeant or Monsieur Groslier to inspect his passport."

There is not a country town in France where sooner or later the Comedy of the Stranger is not played. The Stranger is not unfrequently an adventurer who takes the natives in, and goes off, carrying with him a woman's reputation or a family cash-box. More often he is really a stranger, whose life is a mystery for long enough to set the town talking of his acts and deeds.

Now, the possible accession of Simon Giguet to representative power was not the only great event of the day. The attention of the citizens of Arcis had been much engaged by the proceedings of an individual who had arrived three days previously, and who was, as it happened, the first Stranger to the rising generation. Hence, the *Unknown* was the chief subject of conversation in every family circle. He was the log that had dropped from the clouds into a community of frogs.

The position of Arcis-sur-Aube sufficiently accounts for the effect that the advent of a visitor was likely to produce. Within six leagues from Troyes, by a farm called La Belle-Étoile, on the highway from Paris, a country road turns off, leading to the town of Arcis, across the wide flats where the Seine traces a narrow green valley, shaded with poplars, in sharp contrast to the white chalky marl of the soil. The road from Arcis to Troyes is also about six leagues long, and forms the chord of an arc with Arcis and Troyes at either end, so that the shortest way from Paris is by the cross-road turning off by La Belle-Étoile. The river Aube, as has been said, is not navigable above Arcis; and so this town, at six leagues from the main road, divided from Troyes by a monotonous level, lies lost in a desert, as it were, with no traffic or trade by land or water. Sézanne, at some leagues from Arcis on the other side of the river, stands on a highroad which shortens, by eight stages, the old post road to Germany, *via* Troyes. Thus, Arcis is isolated; no mails pass through the town; there is only a service of coaches to La Belle-Étoile on one hand, and to Troyes on the other.

All the residents know each other, and they know every commercial traveler who comes on business from the Paris houses; thus, as in every small town in a similar position, the arrival of a stranger in Arcis sets every tongue wagging, and excites every imagination, if he should stay more than two days without announcing his name and his business.

Now, while Arcis was still stagnantly peaceful, three days before that on which—by the fiat of the creator of so many fictions—this story begins, everybody had witnessed the arrival, by the road from La Belle-Étoile, of a Stranger, in a neat tilbury, driving a well-bred horse, and followed by a tiger no bigger than your thumb, mounted on a saddle-horse. The coach in connection with the mails for Troyes had brought from La Belle-Étoile three trunks from Paris, with no name on them, but belonging to the newcomer, who took rooms at the *Mulet*. Everybody in Arcis that evening supposed that this individual wanted to purchase land at Arcis, and he was spoken of in many family councils as the future owner of the château.

The tilbury, the traveler, the tiger, and the steeds all seemed to have dropped from some very superior social sphere. The stranger, who was tired no doubt, remained invisible; perhaps he spent part of his time in settling in the rooms he selected, announcing his intention of remaining some little time. He insisted on seeing where his horses were housed in the stable, and was exceedingly particular; they were to be kept apart from those belonging to the inn, and from any that might arrive. So much eccentric care led the host of the *Mulet* to the conclusion that the visitor must be an Englishman.

On the very first evening some attempts were made on the *Mulet* by curious inquirers; but no information was to be got out of the little groom, who refused to give any account of his master, not by misleading answers or silence, but by such banter as seemed to indicate deep depravity far beyond his years.

After a careful toilet, the visitor ate his dinner at about six o'clock, and then rode out, his groom in attendance, on the Brienne road, and returned very late. The innkeeper, his wife, and the chambermaids vainly examined the stranger's luggage and possessions; they discovered nothing that could throw any light on the mysterious visitor's rank, name, profession, or purpose.

The effect was incalculable; endless surmises were put forward, such as might have justified the intervention of the public prosecutor.

When he returned, the stranger admitted the mistress of

the house, who laid before him the volume in which, by the regulations of the police, he was required to write his name and dignity, the object of his visit, and the place whence he came.

"I shall write nothing whatever, madame," said he to the innkeeper's wife. "If anybody troubles you on the subject, you can say that I refused, and send the Sous-préfet to me if you like, for I have no passport.—People will ask you a great many questions about me, madame," he added. "And you can answer what you please; I do not intend that you should know anything about me, even if you should obtain information in spite of me. If you annoy me, I shall go the *Hôtel de la Poste,* on the square by the bridge; and, observe, that I propose to remain a fortnight at least. I should be very sorry to go, for I know you to be a sister of Gothard, one of the heroes of the Simeuse case."

"Certainly, sir!" replied the sister of Gothard—the Cinq-Cygnes' steward.

After this, the stranger had no difficulty in detaining the good woman for nearly two hours, and extracting from her all she could tell him concerning Arcis—everybody's fortune, everybody's business, and who all the officials were.

Next morning he again rode out attended by the tiger, and did not come in till midnight.

The reader can now understand Cécile's little jest, which Madame Beauvisage thought had nothing in it.

Beauvisage and Cécile, equally surprised by the order of the day set forth by Séverine, were no less delighted. While his wife was changing her dress to go to Madame Marion's, the father listened to the girl's hypotheses—guesses such as a young lady naturally indulges in under such circumstances. Then, tired by the day's work, as soon as his wife and daughter were gone, he went to bed.

As all may suppose who know France, or the province of Champagne—which is not quite the same thing—or yet more, the ways of country towns, there was a perfect mob in Madame Marion's rooms that evening. Simon Giguet's success was regarded as a victory over the Comte de Gondreville, and the independence of Arcis in electioneering matters as established for ever. The news of poor Charles Keller's death was felt to be a special dispensation from Heaven, and silenced rivalry.

Antonin Goulard, Frédéric Marest, Olivier Vinet, Monsieur Martener, in short, all the authorities who had ever frequented the house, whose opinions could hardly be adverse to the Government as established by popular suffrage in July 1830, were there as usual, but all brought thither by curiosity as to the attitude assumed by the Beauvisages, mother and daughter.

The drawing-room, restored to order, bore no traces of the meeting which had presumably decided Maître Simon's fate.

By eight o'clock, four card-players, at each of the four tables, were busily occupied. The small drawing-room and the dining-room were full of company. Never, excepting on great occasions when there was dancing, or on some public holiday, had Madame Marion seen people crowded at the door of her room, and streaming in like the tail of a comet.

"It is the dawn of advancement," said Olivier, remarking to her on a sight so delightful to a woman who is fond of entertaining.

"It is impossible to foresee what Simon may rise to," replied Madame Marion. "We live in an age when a man who has perseverance and the art of getting on may aspire to the best."

This speech was made less to Vinet than for the benefit of Madame Beauvisage, who had just come in with her daughter and congratulated her friend.

To avoid any direct questioning, and to forefend any misinterpretation of chance remarks, Cécile's mother took a seat at a whist-table, and threw all her concentrated energies into the task of winning a hundred points. A hundred points means fifty sous! If a player loses so large a sum, it is a two days' wonder at Arcis.

Cécile went to gossip with Mademoiselle Mollot, one of her bosom friends, and seemed more affectionate to her than ever. Mademoiselle Mollot was the beauty of Arcis, as Cécile was the heiress. M. Mollot, clerk of assize at Arcis, lived in the Grande Place, in a house situated very much as that of the Beauvisages' was at the bridge end. Madame Mollot, who never sat anywhere but at the drawing-room window on the ground floor, suffered in consequence from acute and chronic curiosity, a permanent and inveterate malady. Madame Mollot devoted herself to watching her neighbors, as a nervous woman talks of her ailments, with airs, and graces, and thorough enjoyment. If a countryman came on the Square from the road to Brienne, she watched and wondered what his business could be at Arcis, and her mind knew no rest till she could account for that peasant's proceedings. She spent her whole life in criticising events, men and things, and the household affairs of Arcis.

She was a tall, meagre woman, the daughter of a judge at Troyes, and she had brought Monsieur Mollot, formerly Grévin's managing clerk, fortune enough to enable him to pay for his place as clerk of assize. The clerk of assize ranks with a judge, just as in the Supreme Court the chief clerk ranks with a councillor. Monsieur Mollot owed his nomination to the Comte de Gondreville, who had settled the matter by a word in season at the Chancellor's office in favor of Grévin's clerk. The whole ambition of these three persons—Mollot, his wife, and his daughter—was to see Ernestine Mollot, who was an only child, married to Antonin Goulard. Thus the rejection by the Beauvisages of every advance on the part of the Sous-préfet had tightened the bonds of friendship between the two families.

"There is a much-provoked man!" said Ernestine to Cécile, pointing to Simon Giguet. "He is pining to come and talk to us; but everybody who comes in feels bound to congratulate and detain him. Fifty times at least I have heard him say— 'The goodwill of my fellow-citizens is towards my father, I believe, rather than myself; be that as it may, rely upon it,

I shall devote myself not merely to our common interests, but more especially to yours'—I can hear the words from the movement of his lips, and every time he looks round at you with the eyes of a martyr."

"Ernestine," said Cécile, "stay by me all the evening, for I do not want to hear his hints hidden under speeches full of *Alas!* and punctuated with sighs."

"Then you do not want to be the wife of a Keeper of the Seals!"

"Have they got no higher than that?" said Cécile, laughing.

"I assure you," said Ernestine, "that just now, before you came in, Monsieur Godivet the registrar declared in his enthusiasm that Simon would be Keeper of the Seals before three years were out."

"And do they rely on the patronage of the Comte de Gondreville?" asked Goulard, seating himself by the two girls, with a shrewd suspicion that they were laughing at his friend Giguet.

"Ah, Monsieur Antonin," said pretty Ernestine, "you promised my mother to find out who the handsome stranger is! What is your latest information?"

"The events of to-day, mademoiselle, have been of far greater importance," said Antonin, seating himself by Cécile like a diplomate enchanted to escape from general observation by taking refuge with a party of girls. "My whole career as Sous-préfet or full Préfet hangs in the balance."

"Why! Will you not allow your friend Simon to be returned as unanimously elected?"

"Simon is my friend, but the Government is my master, and I mean to do all I can to hinder Simon's return.—And Madame Mollot ought to lend me her assistance as the wife of a man whose duties attach him to the Government."

"We are quite prepared to side with you," said Madame Mollot. "My husband told me," she went on in an undertone, "of all the proceedings here this morning. It was lamentable.' Only one man showed any talent—Achille Pigoult.

Every one agrees in saying that he is an orator, and would shine in Parliament. And though he has nothing, and my daughter is an only child with a marriage portion of sixty thousand francs—to say nothing of what we may leave her—and money from her father's uncle the miller, and from my aunt Lambert at Troyes—well, I declare to you that if Monsieur Achille Pigoult should do us the honor of proposing for her, for my part, I would say yes—that is, if my daughter liked him well enough. But the little simpleton will not marry any one she does not fancy.—It is Mademoiselle Beauvisage who has put that into her head."

The Sous-préfet took this broadside as a man who knows that he has thirty thousand francs a year of his own, and expects to be made Préfet.

"Mademoiselle Beauvisage is in the right," said he, looking at Cécile; "she is rich enough to marry for love."

"We will not discuss marriage," said Ernestine. "It only distresses my poor little Cécile, who was confessing to me just now that if she could only be married for love, and not for her money, she would like to be courted by some stranger who knew nothing of Arcis or the fortunes which are to make her a female Crœsus; and she only wishes she could go through some romantic adventure that would end in her being loved and married for her own sake——"

"That is a very pretty idea. I always knew that mademoiselle had as much wit as money!" exclaimed Olivier Vinet, joining the group, in detestation of the flatterers surrounding Simon Giguet, the idol of the day.

"And that was how, from one thing to another, we were led to talk of the Unknown——"

"And then," added Ernestine, "she thought of him as the possible hero of the romance I have sketched——"

"Oh!" cried Madame Mollot, "a man of fifty! Never!"

"How do you know that he is a man of fifty?" asked Vinet, with a smile.

"To tell the truth," said Madame Mollot, "I was so mystified, that this morning I took my opera-glass——"

"Well done!" exclaimed the inspector of works, who was courting the mother to win the daughter.

"And so," Madame Mollot went on, "I could see the stranger shaving himself—with such elegant razors! Gold handles—or silver-gilt."

"Gold! gold!" cried Vinet. "When there is any doubt, let everything be of the best!—And I, who have never seen the gentleman, feel quite sure that he is at least a Count." This, which was thought very funny, made everybody laugh.*

The little group who could be so merry excited the envy of the dowagers and attracted the attention of the black-coated men who stood round Simon Giguet. As to Giguet himself, he was in despair at not being able forthwith to lay his fortune and his prospects at the heiress' feet.

"Oh, my dear father," thought the deputy clerk, finding himself complimented for the involuntary witticism, "what a place you have sent me to as a beginning of my experience!—A count—*Comte* with an *m,* ladies," he explained. "A man as illustrious by birth as he is distinguished in manners; noteworthy for his fortune and his carriages—a dandy, a man of fashion—a lemon-kid glove man——"

"He has the smartest tilbury you ever saw, Monsieur Olivier," said Ernestine.

"And you never told me of his tilbury, Antonin, this morning when we were discussing this dark conspirator; the tilbury is really an attenuating circumstance. A man with a tilbury cannot be a Republican."

"Young ladies," said Antonin Goulard, "there is nothing I would not do to promote your pleasure.—We will know, and that soon, if he is a *Comte,* with an *m,* so that you may be able to construct your *conte* with an *n.*"

"And it may then become history," said the engineer.

"As written for the edification of Sous-préfets," said Olivier Vinet.

"And how will you set about it?" asked Madame Mollot.

* There is a pun in the French on the words *Comte,* a Count, and *Conte,* a romance, a fib.

"Ah!" replied the Sous-préfet. "If you were to ask Mademoiselle Beauvisage whom she would marry, if she were condemned to choose from the men who are here now, she would not tell you! You must grant some reticence to power.—Be quite easy, young ladies, in ten minutes you shall know whether the stranger is a count or a bagman."

Antonin left the little coterie of girls—for there were besides Cécile and Ernestine, Mademoiselle Berton, the daughter of the collector of revenue, an insignificant damsel who was a sort of satellite to the heiress and the beauty, and Mademoiselle Herbelot, sister of the second notary of Arcis, an old maid of thirty, sour, pinched, and dressed after the manner of old maids—she wore a green tabinet gown, and a kerchief with embroidered corners, crossed and knotted in front after the manner in fashion during the Reign of Terror.

"Julien," said the Sous-préfet to his servant in the vestibule, "you were in service for six months with the Gondrevilles; do you know a count's coronet when you see it?"

"It has nine points, sir, with balls."

"Very good. Then go over to the *Mulet* and try to get a look at the tilbury belonging to the strange gentleman who is staying there; and come back and tell me what is painted on it. Do the job cleverly, pick up anything you can hear.—If you see the little groom, ask him at what hour to-morrow his master can receive the Sous-préfet—say Monsieur le Comte, if by chance you see such a coronet. Don't drink, say nothing, come back quickly, and when you return let me know by just showing yourself at the drawing-room door."

"Yes, Monsieur le Sous-préfet."

The *Mulet* inn, as has been said, stands on the Place at the opposite corner to the garden wall of Madame Marion's house on the other side of the Brienne road. So the problem would be quickly solved.

Antonin Goulard returned to his seat by Mademoiselle Beauvisage.

"We talked of him so much here last evening," Madame Mollot was saying, "that I dreamed of him all night——"

"Dear, dear!" said Vinet; "do you still dream of the Unknown, fair lady?"

"You are very impertinent. I could make you dream of me
if I chose!" she retorted. "So this morning when I got
up——"

It may here be noted that Madame Mollet was regarded at
Arcis as having a smart wit—that is to say, she talked
fluently, and took an unfair advantage of the gift. A Parisian wandering in those parts, like the Stranger in question,
would have probably thought her an intolerable chatterbox.

—"And was dressing, in the natural course of things, as I
looked straight before me——"

"Out of window?" said Goulard.

"Certainly.—My dressing-room looks out on the market-
place.—You must know that Poupart has given the Stranger
one of the rooms that face mine——"

"One room, mamma!" exclaimed Ernestine. "The Count
has three rooms! The groom, who is all in black, is in the
first room; the second has been turned into a sort of drawing-
room; and the gentleman sleeps in the third."

"Then he has half the inn," remarked Mademoiselle
Herbelot.

"Well, what has that to do with the man himself?" said
Madame Mollot, vexed at being interrupted by girls; "I am
speaking of his person."

"Do not interrupt the orator," said Olivier Vinet.

"As I was stooping——"

"Sitting," said Antonin Goulard.

"Madame was as she ought to be—dressing, and looking
at the *Mulet*," said Vinet.

These pleasantries are highly esteemed in the country; for
everybody has said everything there for too long not to be
content with the same nonsense as amused our fathers before
the importation of English prudery, one of the forms of
merchandise which custom-houses cannot prohibit.

"Do not interrupt the orator," said Mademoiselle Beauvisage to Vinet, with a responsive smile.

—"My eyes involuntarily fell on the window of the room in which last night the Stranger had gone to bed—at what hour I cannot imagine, for I lay awake till after midnight!—It is my misfortune to have a husband who snores till the walls and ceiling tremble. If I get to sleep first, I sleep so heavily that I hear nothing; but if Mollot gets the start, my night's rest is done for."

"There is a third alternative—you might go off together," said Achille Pigoult, coming to join this cheerful party. "It is your slumbers that are in question, I perceive——"

"Hold your tongue, and get along with you," said Madame Mollot, very graciously.

"You see what that means?" said Cécile in Ernestine's ear.

"Well, he had not come in by one o'clock," Madame Mollot went on.

"He is a fraud! Sneaking in when you could not see him," said Achille Pigoult. "Oh, he is a knowing one, you may depend! He will get us all into a bag and sell us on the market-place!"

"To whom?" asked Vinet.

"To a business, to an idea, to a system!" replied the notary, and the other lawyer answered with a cunning smile.

"Imagine my surprise," Madame Mollot returned, "when I caught sight of a piece of stuff, so magnificent, so elegant, so gaudy!—Said I to myself, 'He must have a dressing-gown of that stuff woven with spun glass which we saw at the Industrial Exhibition.'—And I went for my opera-glass and looked.—But, good Heavens! what did I see? Above the dressing-gown, where his head should have been, I saw a huge mass, like a big knee.—No, I cannot tell you how curious I was!"

"I can quite imagine it," said Antonin.

"No, you cannot imagine it," said Madame Mollot, "for that knee——"

"Oh, I see it all," said Olivier Vinet, shouting with

laughter. "The Stranger was dressing too, and you saw his two knees——"

"Not at all," said Madame Mollot; "you are putting things into my mouth.—The Stranger was standing up; he held a sponge over a huge basin, and your rude joke be on your own head, Monsieur Olivier. I should have known if I had seen what you suppose——"

"Oh! have known—— Madame, you are committing yourself!" said Antonin Goulard.

"Do let me speak!" said Madame Mollot. "It was his head! He was washing his head! he has not a hair."

"Rash man!" said Antonin Goulard. "He certainly cannot have come to look for a wife. To get married here a man must have some hair. Hair is in great request."

"So I have my reasons for saying that he must be fifty. A man does not take to a wig before that age. For, in fact, the Unknown, when he had finished his toilet, opened his window, and I beheld him from afar, the owner of a splendid head of black hair. He stuck up his eyeglass when I went to the balcony.—So, my dear Cécile, that gentleman will hardly be the hero of your romance."

"Why not? Men of fifty are not to be disdained when they are Counts," said Ernestine.

"Perhaps he had fair hair after all," said Olivier Vinet mischievously, "and then he would be very eligible. The real question is whether it was his bald head that Madame Mollot saw, or——"

"Be quiet!" said Madame Mollot.

Antonin Goulard went out to send Madame Marion's servant across to the *Mulet* with instructions for Julien.

"Bless me, what does a husband's age matter?" said Mademoiselle Herbelot.

"So long as you get one," Vinet put in. He was much feared for his cold and malignant sarcasm.

"Yes," replied the old maid, piqued by the remark, "I would rather have a husband of fifty, kind and indulgent to his wife, than a young man of between twenty and thirty who had no heart, and whose wit stung everybody—even his wife."

"That," said Olivier Vinet, "is mere talk, since to prefer a man of fifty to a young man one must have the choice!"

"Oh!" said Madame Mollot, to stop this squabble between Mademoiselle Herbelot and young Vinet, who always went too far, "when a woman has seen something of life, she knows that whether a husband is fifty or five-and-twenty, it comes to exactly the same thing if he is merely esteemed.— The really important thing in marriage is the suitability of circumstances to be considered.—If Mademoiselle Beauvisage wishes to live in Paris—and that would be my notion in her place—I would certainly not marry anybody in Arcis. If I had had such a fortune as she will have, I might very well have given my hand to a Count, a man who could have placed me in a good social position, and I should not have asked to see his pedigree."

"It would have been enough for you to have seen him at his toilet," said Vinet in a murmur to Madame Mollot.

"But the King can make a Count, madame," observed Madame Marion, who had been standing for a minute or two looking at the circle of young people.

"But some young ladies like their Counts ready-made," said Vinet.

"Now, Monsieur Antonin," said Cécile, laughing at Olivier Vinet's speech, "the ten minutes are over, and we do not yet know whether the Stranger is a Count."

"The Government must prove itself infallible," said Vinet, turning to Antonin.

"I will keep my word," replied the Sous-préfet, seeing his servant's face in the doorway. And he again left his seat.

"You are talking of the Stranger!" said Madame Marion. "Does any one know anything about him?"

"No, madame," said Achille Pigoult. "But he, without knowing it, is like an athlete in a circus—the object of interest to two thousand pairs of eyes.—I do know something," added the little notary.

"Oh, tell us, Monsieur Achille!" Ernestine eagerly exclaimed.

"His servant's name is Paradis."

"Paradis!" echoed everybody.

"Can any one be called Paradis?" asked Madame Herbelot, taking a seat by her sister-in-law.

"It goes far to prove that his master is an angel," the notary went on, "for when his servant follows him you see——"

" 'C'est le chemin du Paradis.' That is really very neat," said Madame Marion, who was anxious to secure Achille Pigoult in her nephew's interest.

"Monsieur," Julien was saying to his master in the dining-room, "there is a coat-of-arms on the tilbury."

"A coat-of-arms?"

"And very queer they are. There is a coronet over them—nine points with balls——"

"Then he is a Count——"

"And a winged monster running like mad, just like a postilion that has lost something.—And this is what is written on the ribbon," said he, taking a scrap of paper out of his waistcoat pocket. "Mademoiselle Anicette, the Princesse de Cadignan's maid who had just come—in a carriage, of course—to bring a letter to the gentleman (and the carriage from Cinq-Cygne is waiting at the door) copied the words down for me."

"Give it me."

The Sous-préfet read:

"Quo me trahit fortuna."

Though he was not a sufficiently accomplished herald to know what family bore this motto, Antonin supposed that the Cinq-Cygnes would hardly lend their chaise for the Princesse de Cadignan to send an express messenger to any one not of the highest nobility.

"Oho! so you know the Princess' maid? You are a lucky beggar," said Antonin to the man.

Julien, a native of the place, after being in service at Gondreville for six months, had been engaged by Monsieur le Sous-préfet, who wished to have a stylish servant.

"Well, monsieur, Anicette was my father's god-daughter.

And father, who felt kindly to the poor child, as her father was dead, sent her to Paris to learn dressmaking; my mother could not bear the sight of her."

"Is she pretty?"

"Not amiss, Monsieur le Sous-préfet. More by token she had her little troubles in Paris. However, as she is clever, and can make dresses and understands hairdressing, the Princess took her on the recommendation of Monsieur Marin, head-valet to Monsieur le Duc de Maufrigneuse."

"And what did she say about Cinq-Cygne? Is there a great deal of company?"

"Yes, sir, a great deal. The Princess is there, and Monsieur d'Arthez, the Duc de Maufrigneuse and the Duchess, and the young Marquis. In short, the house is full. Monseigneur the Bishop of Troyes is expected this evening."

"Monseigneur Troubert. Oh, I should like to know whether he makes any stay there."

"Anicette thought he would. She fancies he has come on account of the gentleman who is lodging at the *Mulet*. And more people are expected. The coachman said there was a great talk about the elections. Monsieur le Président Michu is to spend a few days there."

"Just try to get that maid into the town on some pretext. Have you any fancy for her?"

"If she had anything of her own, there is no knowing. She is a smart girl."

"Well, tell her to come to see you at the Sous-préfecture."

"Very well, sir; I will go at once."

"But do not mention me, or she will not come. Tell her you have heard of a good place——"

"Oh, sir! I was in service at Gondreville——"

"And you do not know the history of that message sent from Cinq-Cygne at such an hour. For it is half-past nine."

"It was something pressing, it would seem; for the Count, who had just come in from Gondreville——"

"The Stranger had been to Gondreville!"

"He dined there, Monsieur le Sous-préfet. And, you shall

see, it is the greatest joke. The little groom is as drunk as an owl, saving your presence. They gave him so much champagne wine in the servants' hall that he cannot keep on his legs. They did it for a joke, no doubt."

"Well—but the Count?"

"The Count had gone to bed, but as soon as he read the note he got up. He is now dressing. They were putting the horse in, and he is going out in the tilbury to spend the rest of the evening at Cinq-Cygne."

"Then he is a person of importance?"

"Oh yes, sir, no doubt; for Gothard, the steward at Cinq-Cygne, came this morning to see Poupart, who is his brother-in-law, and told him to be sure to hold his tongue about the gentleman and his doings, and to serve him as if he were the King."

"Then can Vinet be right?" thought Goulard to himself. "Is there some plot brewing?"

"It was the Duc Georges de Maufrigneuse who sent Monsieur Gothard to the *Mulet;* and when Poupart came here to the meeting this morning, it was because this Count made him come. If he were to tell Monsieur Poupart to set out for Paris to-night, he would go. Gothard told his brother-in-law to throw everything over for the gentleman and hoodwink all inquirers."

"If you can get hold of Anicette, be sure to let me know," said Antonin.

"Well, I could go to see her at Cinq-Cygne, sir, if you were to send me out to your house at le Val-Preux."

"That is a good idea. You might get a lift on the chaise. But what about the little groom?"

"He is a smart little chap, Monsieur le Sous-préfet! Just fancy, sir, screwed as he is, he has just ridden off on his master's fine English horse, a thoroughbred that can cover seven leagues an hour, to carry a letter to Troyes, that it may reach Paris to-morrow! And the brat is no more than nine and a half years old! What will he be by the time he is twenty?"

The Sous-préfet listened mechanically to this last piece of

domestic gossip. Julien chattered on for a few minutes, and Goulard heard him vaguely, thinking all the time of the great Unknown.

"Wait a little," he said to the servant.

"What a puzzle!" thought he, as he slowly returned to the drawing-room. "A man who dines with the Comte de Gondreville, and who spends the night at Cinq-Cygne! Mysterie**s** with a vengeance!"

"Well!" cried Mademoiselle Beauvisage's little circle as h**e** joined them.

"Well, he is a count, and of the right sort, I will answer for it!"

"Oh, how I should like to see him!" exclaimed Cécile.

"Mademoiselle," said Antonin, with a mischievous smile at Madame Mollot, "he is tall and well made, and does not wear a wig! His little tiger was as tipsy as a lord; they had filled him up with wine in the servants' hall at Gondreville; and the child, who is but nine, replied to Julien with all the dignity of an old valet when my man said something about his master's wig. 'A wig! My master! I would not stay with him. He dyes his hair, and that is bad enough.' "

"Your opera-glasses magnify a good deal," said Achille Pigoult to Madame Mollot, who laughed.

"Well, and this boy of our handsome Count's, tipsy as he is, has flown off to Troyes to carry a letter, and will be there in an hour and a quarter, in spite of the darkness."

"I should like to see the tiger!" said Vinet.

"If he dined at Gondreville, we shall soon know all about this Count," said Cécile, "for grandpapa is going there to-morrow morning."

"What will seem even more strange," said Antonin Goulard, "is that a special messenger, in the person of Mademoiselle Anicette, the Princesse de Cadignan's maid, has come from Cinq-Cygne to the stranger, and he is going to spend the night there."

"Bless me!" said Olivier Vinet; "but he is not a man—he is a demon, a phœnix! He is the friend of both parties! He can ingurgitate——"

"For shame, monsieur!" said Madame Mollot, "you use words——"

"Ingurgitate is good Latin, madame," replied Vinet very gravely. "He ingurgitates, I say, with King Louis-Philippe in the morning, and banquets at Holyrood in the evening with Charles X. There is but one reason that can allow a respectable Christian to frequent both camps and go alike to the Capulets' and the Montagues'. Ah! I know what the man is! He is the manager of the railway line between Paris and Lyons, or Paris and Dijon, or Montereau and Troyes——"

"Of course!" cried Antonin. "You have hit it. Only finance, interest, or speculation are equally welcome wherever they go."

"Yes, and just now the greatest names, the greatest families, the old and the new nobility are rushing full tilt into joint-stock concerns," said Achille Pigoult.

"Francs to the Frank!" said Olivier, without a smile.

"You can hardly be said to be the olive branch of peace," said Madame Mollot.

"But is it not disgusting to see such names as Verneuil, Maufrigneuse, and d'Hérouville cheek by jowl with Tillet and Nucingen in the quotations on 'Change?"

"Our stranger is, you may depend, an infant railway line," said Vinet.

"Well, all Arcis will be topsy-turvy by to-morrow," said Achille Pigoult. "I will call on the gentleman to get the notary's work in the concern. There will be two thousand deeds to draw up!"

"And so our romance is a locomotive!" said Ernestine sadly to Cécile.

"Nay, a count and a railway company in one is doubly conjugal," said Achille. "But—is he a bachelor?"

"I will find out to-morrow from grandpapa!" cried Cécile with affected enthusiasm.

"A pretty joke!" exclaimed Madame Marion with a forced laugh. "Why, Cécile, child, is your brain running on the Unknown?"

"A husband is always the Unknown," remarked Olivier Vinet hastily, with a glance at Mademoiselle Beauvisage, which she perfectly understood.

"And why not?" said she. "There is nothing compromising in that. Besides, if these gentlemen are right, he is either a great lord or a great speculator. My word! I can do with either. I like Paris! I want a carriage, and a fine house, and a box at the Opera, et cetera."

"To be sure," said Vinet. "Why refuse yourself anything in a day-dream? Now, if I had the honor to be your brother, you should marry the young Marquis de Cinq-Cygne, who is, it strikes me, the young fellow to make the money fly, and to laugh at his mother's objections to the actors in the judicial drama in which our presiding judge's father came to such a sad end."

"You would find it easier to become Prime Minister!" said Madame Marion. "There can never be an alliance between Grévin's granddaughter and the Cinq-Cygnes."

"Romeo was within an ace of marrying Juliet," said Achille Pigoult; "and Mademoiselle Cécile is handsomer——"

"Oh, if you quote opera!" said Herbelot feebly, as he rose from the whist-table.

"My colleague," said Achille Pigoult, "is evidently not strong in mediæval history."

"Come along, Malvina," said the sturdy notary, without answering his young brother of the law.

"Tell me, Monsieur Antonin," said Cécile, "you spoke of Anicette, the Princesse de Cadignan's maid—do you know her?"

"No; but Julien does. She is his father's godchild, and they are old friends."

"Oh, do try, through Julien, to get her for us; mamma will give any wages——"

"Mademoiselle, to hear is to obey, as they say to the despots in Asia," replied the Sous-préfet. "To serve you, see how prompt I will be."

He went off to desire Julien to get a lift in the chaise

returning to Cinq-Cygne, and to win over Anicette at any cost.

At this moment Simon Giguet, who had been put through his paces by all the influential men of Arcis, and who believed himself secure of his election, joined the circle round Cécile and Mademoiselle Mollot.

It was getting late; ten had struck.

Having consumed an enormous quantity of cakes, of orgeat, punch, lemonade, and various fruit syrups, all who had come that evening to Madame Marion's on purely political grounds, and who were unaccustomed to tread these boards—to them quite aristocratic—disappeared promptly, all the more so because they never sat up so late. The party would now be more intimate in its tone; Simon Giguet hoped to be able to exchange a few words with Cécile, and looked at her with a conquering air. This greatly offended Cécile.

"My dear fellow," said Antonin to Simon, as he saw the aureole of triumph on his friend's brow, "you have joined us at a moment when all the men of Arcis are in the wrong box——"

"Quite wrong," said Ernestine, nudged by Cécile. "We are quite crazy about the Unknown. Cécile and I are quarreling for him."

"To begin with, he is no longer unknown," said Cécile. "He is a Count."

"Some adventurer!" said Simon Giguet scornfully.

"Would you say that to his face," retorted Cécile, much nettled. "A man who has just had a message by one of the Princesse de Cadignan's servants, who dined to-day at Gondreville, and is gone to spend this very evening with the Marquise de Cinq-Cygne?"

She spoke so eagerly and sharply that Simon was put out of countenance.

"Indeed, mademoiselle," said Olivier Vinet, "if we all said to people's faces what we say behind each other's backs, society would be impossible. The pleasure of society, especially in the country, consists in speaking ill of others."

"Monsieur Simon is jealous of your enthusiasm about the strange Count," remarked Ernestine.

"It seems to me," said Cécile, "that Monsieur Simon has no right to be jealous of any fancy of mine!"

And saying this in a tone to annihilate Simon, Cécile rose. Everybody made way for her, and she joined her mother, who was settling her gambling account.

"My dear girl," said Madame Marion, close at her heels, "it seems to me that you are very hard on my poor Simon."

"Why, what has the dear little puss been doing?" asked her mother.

"Mamma, Monsieur Simon gave my Unknown a slap in the face by calling him an adventurer."

Simon had followed his aunt, and was now on the battle-field by the whist-table. Thus the four persons, whose interests were so serious, were collected in the middle of the room; Cécile and her mother on one side of the table, Madame Marion and her nephew on the other.

"Really, madame," said Simon Giguet, "you must confess that a young lady must be very anxious to find me in the wrong, to be vexed by my saying that a man of whom all Arcis is talking, and who is living at the *Mulet*——"

"Do you suppose he is competing with you?" said Madame Beauvisage jestingly.

"I should certainly feel it a deep grievance if he should be the cause of any misunderstanding between Mademoiselle Cécile and me," said the candidate, with a beseeching look at the girl.

"But you pronounced sentence, monsieur, in a cutting tone, which proved you to be despotic—and you are right; if you hope ever to be Minister, you must cut a good deal!"

Madame Beauvisage took Madame Marion by the arm and led her to a sofa. Cécile, left alone, went to join the circle, that she might not hear any reply that Simon might make; and he remained by the table, looking foolish enough, mechanically playing tricks with the bone fish.

"There are as good fish in the sea!" said Olivier Vinet,

who had observed the little scene; and Cécile, overhearing the remark, though it was spoken in a low tone, could not help laughing.

"My dear friend," said Madame Marion to Madame Beauvisage, "nothing now, you see, can hinder my nephew's election."

"I congratulate you—and the Chamber," said Séverine.

"And my nephew will make his mark, my dear.—I will tell you why: his own fortune, and what his father will leave him with mine, will bring him in about thirty thousand francs a year. When a man is a member of parliament and has such a fortune, there is nothing he may not aspire to."

"Madame, he will command our admiration, and our best wishes will be with him throughout his political career, but——"

"I ask for no reply," exclaimed Madame Marion, eagerly interrupting her friend "I only ask you to think it over. Do our young people like each other? Can we arrange the match? We shall live in Paris whenever the Chambers are sitting, and who knows but the Member for Arcis may be settled there by getting some good place in office?—See how Monsieur Vinet of Provins has got on! Mademoiselle de Chargebœuf was thought very foolish to marry him; and before long she will be the wife of the Keeper of the Seals, and Monsieur Vinet may have a peerage if he likes."

"Madame, it does not rest with me to settle my daughter's marriage. In the first place, her father and I leave her absolutely free to choose for herself. If she wanted to marry the *Unknown,* if he were a suitable match, we should give our consent. Then Cécile depends entirely on her grandfather, who, as a wedding gift, will settle on her a house in Paris, the Hôtel Beauséant, which he bought for us ten years ago, and which at the present day is worth eight hundred thousand francs. It is one of the finest mansions in the Faubourg Saint-Germain. He has also a sum of two hundred thousand francs put by for furnishing it. Now a grandfather who behaves in that way, and who will persuade my mother-in-law on her part to do something for her grandchild, has some right to an opinion on the question of a suitable match——"

"Certainly!" said Madame Marion, amazed at this revelation, which would add to the difficulties of her nephew's marriage with Cécile.

"And even if Cécile had no expectations from her grandfather," Madame Beauvisage went on, "she would not marry without consulting him. The young man my father had chosen is just dead; I do not know what his present intentions may be. If you have any proposals to make, go and see my father."

"Very well, I will," said Madame Marion.

Madame Beauvisage signaled to Cécile, and they left.

On the following afternoon Antonin and Frédéric Marest were walking, as was their after-dinner custom, with Monsieur Martener and Olivier under the limes of the Avenue des Soupirs, smoking their cigars. These walks are one of the little pleasures of provincial bigwigs, when they live on good terms with each other.

They had taken but a few turns when they were joined by Simon Giguet, who said to the Sous-préfet with an air of mystery:

"You will surely stick by an old comrade, who will make it his business to get you the Legion of Honor and a *préfecture!*"

"Are you beginning your political career already?" said Antonin, laughing. "So you are trying to bribe me—you who are such a puritan?"

"Will you support me?"

"My dear fellow, you know that Bar-sur-Aube registers its votes here. Who can guarantee a majority under such circumstances? My colleague at Bar-sur-Aube would show me up if I did not do as much as he to support the Government; and your promises are conditional, while my overthrow would be a certainty."

"But I have no opponent."

Antonin Goulard, meanwhile, shown up by the innkeeper, found the Unknown in the room he used for a drawing-room, and himself under inspection through a most impertinent eyeglass.

"Monsieur," said Antonin Goulard in a rather lofty tone, "I have just heard from the innkeeper's wife that you refuse to conform to the police regulations; and as I have no doubt that you are a man of some consequence, I have come myself——"

"Your name is Goulard?" said the Stranger in a head-voice.

"I am Sous-préfet, monsieur," said Antonin Goulard.

"Your father, I think, was attached to the Simeuses?"

"And I am attached to the Government. Times have changed."

"You have a servant named Julien who wants to bribe away the Princesse de Cadignan's waiting-maid?"

"Monsieur, I allow no one to speak to me in such a way; you misunderstand my character——"

"But you wish to understand mine," interrupted the other. "You may write it in the inn-register: 'An impertinent person, from Paris, age doubtful, traveling for his pleasure.'—It would be an innovation highly appreciated in France to imitate the English method of allowing people to come and go as they please without annoying them and asking them for their papers at every turn.—I have no passport: what will you do to me?"

"The public prosecutor is out there under the limes——" said the Sous-préfet.

"Monsieur Marest?—Wish him from me a very good morning."

"But who are you?"

"Whatever you wish me to be, my dear Monsieur Goulard," said the Stranger, "since it is you who must decide how I should appear before the good folks of this district. Give me some advice as to my demeanor. Here—read this."

And the visitor held out a note as follows:—

(*Private.*)   PRÉFECTURE OF THE AUBE.

"MONSIEUR LE SOUS-PRÉFET,—Be good enough to take steps with the bearer as to the election in Arcis, and conform to his requirements in every particular. I request you to be absolutely secret, and to treat him with the respect due to his rank."

The note was written and signed by the Préfet of the department.

"You have been talking prose without knowing it," said the Stranger, as he took the letter back.

Antonin Goulard, already impressed by the man's gentlemanly appearance and manner, spoke respectfully.

"How is that, monsieur?" said he.

"By trying to bribe Anicette. She came to tell me of Julien's offers—you may call him Julien the Apostate, for little Paradis, my tiger, routed him completely, and he ended by confessing that you were anxious to place Anicette in the service of the richest family in Arcis. Now, as the richest family in Arcis are the Beauvisages, I presume that it is Mademoiselle Cécile who is anxious to secure such a treasure."

"Yes, monsieur."

"Very well, Anicette can go to the Beauvisages at once."

He whistled. Paradis appeared so promptly that his master said:

"You were listening."

"I cannot help myself, Monsieur le Comte, the walls are made of paper.—If you like, Monsieur le Comte, I can go to an upstairs room."

"No, you may listen; it is your privilege. It is my business to speak low when I do not want you to hear. Now, go back to Cinq-Cygne, and give this twenty-franc piece to Anicette from me.—Julien will be supposed to have bribed her on your account," he added, turning to Goulard. "This gold piece means that she is to do as Julien tells her. Anicette may possibly be of use to our candidate."

"Anicette!"

"You see, Monsieur le Sous-préfet, I have made use of waiting-maids for two-and-thirty years. I had my first adventure at the age of thirteen, exactly like the Regent, the present King's great-great-grandfather.—Now, do you know the amount of this demoiselle Beauvisage's fortune?"

"No one can help knowing it, monsieur; for last evening at Madame Marion's, Madame Séverine said that Monsieur Grévin, Cécile's grandfather, would give her the Hôtel Beauséant and two hundred thousand francs on her wedding day."

The Stranger's eyes betrayed no surprise; he seemed to think it a very moderate fortune.

"Do you know Arcis well?" he asked Goulard.

"I am Sous-préfet of the town, and I was born here."

"Well, then, how can I balk curiosity?"

"By satisfying it, Monsieur le Comte. Use your Christian name; enter that and your title on the register."

"Very good: Comte Maxime."

"And if you would call yourself the manager of a railway company, Arcis would be content; you could keep it quiet for a fortnight by flying that flag."

"No, I prefer water-works; it is less common. I have come to improve the waste-lands of the province. That, my dear Monsieur Goulard, will be an excuse for inviting myself to dine at your house to meet the Beauvisages—to-morrow. I particularly wish to see them and study them."

"I shall be only too happy," said the official. "But I must ask your indulgence for the poverty of my establishment——"

"If I succeed in directing the election at Arcis in accordance with the wishes of those who have sent me here, you, my good friend, will be made a Préfet.—Read these——" and he held out two other letters.

"Very good, Monsieur le Comte," said Goulard, as he returned them.

"Make out a list of all the votes at the disposal of the Government. Above all, we must not appear to have any mutual understanding. I am merely a speculator, and do not care a fig about the election."

"I will send the police superintendent to compel you to write your name on Poupart's register."

"Yes, that is very good. Good-morning, monsieur.—What a land we live in!" he went on in a loud tone. "It is impossible to stir a step without having the whole posse at your heels—even the Sous-préfet!"

"You will have to settle that with the head of the police," replied Antonin emphatically.

And twenty minutes later there was a great talk at Madame Mollot's of high words between the Sous-préfet and the Stranger.

"Well, and what wood is the log made of that has dropped into our pool?" asked Olivier Vinet of Goulard, as he came away from the inn.

"A certain Comte Maxime, come to study the geology of the district in the hope of finding mineral sources," said Goulard indifferently.

"*Re*-sources you should say," replied Olivier.

"Does he fancy he can raise any capital in these parts?" asked Monsieur Martener.

"I doubt our royalist people seeing anything in that form of mining," said Vinet, smiling.

"What do you expect, judging from Madame Marion's looks and movements?" said Antonin, changing the conversation by pointing out Simon and his aunt in eager conference.

Simon had gone forward to meet Madame Marion, and stood talking in the square.

"Well, if he were accepted, a word would be enough to tell him so, I should think," observed Vinet.

"Well?" asked the two men at once as Simon came up the lime walk.

"My aunt has hopes. Madame Beauvisage and old Grévin, who was starting for Gondreville, were not surprised at our proposal; our respective fortunes were discussed. Cécile is absolutely free to make her own choice. Finally, Madame Beauvisage said that for her part she saw no objection to a connection which did her honor, though, at the same time, she must make her consent depend on my election, and possibly on my appearing in the Chamber; and old Grévin said he must consult the Comte de Gondreville, as he never came to any important decision without taking his advice."

"So you will not marry Cécile, old boy," said Goulard bluntly.

"And why not?" said Giguet ironically.

"My dear fellow, Madame Beauvisage and her daughter spend four evenings a week in your aunt's drawing-room; Madame Marion is the most thoroughly fine lady in Arcis. Though she is twenty years the elder, she is the object of Madame Beauvisage's envy; and do you suppose they could refuse you point-blank without some little civility?"

"Neither Yes nor No is No," Vinet went on, "in view of the extreme intimacy of your two families. If Madame Beauvisage is the woman of fortune, Madame Marion is the most looked up to; for, with the exception of the presiding judge's wife—who sees no one—she is the only woman who can entertain at all; she is the queen of Arcis. Madame Beauvisage wishes to refuse politely—that is all."

"It seems to me that old Grévin was making a fool of your aunt, my dear boy," said Frédéric Marest. "Yesterday you attacked the Comte de Gondreville; you hurt him, you offended him deeply—for Achille Pigoult defended him bravely—and now he is to be consulted as to your marrying Cécile!"

"No one can be craftier than old Grévin," said Vinet.

"Madame Beauvisage is ambitious," Goulard went on, "and knows that her daughter will have two millions of francs. She means to be the mother-in-law of a minister or of an ambassador, so as to lord it in Paris."

"Well, and why not that?" said Simon Giguet.

"I wish you may get it!" replied Goulard, looking at Vinet, and they laughed as they went on their way. "He will not even be elected!" he went on to Olivier. "The Government has schemes of its own. You will find a letter at home from your father, desiring you to secure every one in your connection who ought to vote for their masters. Your promotion depends upon it, and you are to keep your own counsel."

"And who is the man for whom they are to vote—ushers, attorneys, justice of the peace, and notaries?" asked Vinet.

"The man I will tell you to vote for."

"But how do you know that my father has written to me, and what he has written?"

"From the Unknown."

"The man of mines?"

"My dear Vinet, we are not to know him; we must treat him as a stranger.—He saw your father as he came through Provins. Just now this individual showed me a letter from the Préfet instructing me to act in the matter of the elections as I shall be directed by this Comte Maxime. I should not get off without having to fight a battle, that I knew! Let us dine together and plan our batteries: You want to be Public Prosecutor at Mantes, and I to be Préfet, and we must not appear to meddle in the elections, for we are between the hammer and anvil. Simon is the candidate put forward by the party who want to upset the present Ministry, and who may succeed. But for clear-sighted men like us there is but one thing to do."

"And that is?"

"To obey those who make and unmake ministries. The letter that was shown to me was from a man in the secrets of the immutable idea."

Before going any further, it will be necessary to explain who this "miner" was, and what he hoped to extract out of the province of Champagne.

About two months before Simon Giguet's day of triumph

as a candidate, at eleven o'clock one evening, just as tea was being served in the Marquise d'Espard's drawing-room in the Rue du Faubourg Saint-Honoré, the Chevalier d'Espard, her brother-in-law, as he set his cup down on the chimney-shelf and looked at the circle round the fire, observed:

"Maxime was very much out of spirits this evening—did not you think so?"

"Well," replied Rastignac, "his depression is very natural. He is eight-and-forty; at that age a man does not make friends; and when we buried de Marsay, Maxime lost the only one who could thoroughly understand him, who could be of use to him, or make use of him."

"And he probably has some pressing debts. Could not you put him in the way of paying them off?" said the Marquise to Rastignac.

Rastignac at this juncture was in office for the second time; he had just been created Count, almost in spite of himself; his father-in-law, the Baron de Nucingen, had been made a peer of France; his brother was a bishop; the Comte de la Roche-Hugon, his brother-in-law, was ambassador; and he was supposed to be an indispensable element in the composition of any future ministry.

"You always forget, my dear Marquise," replied Rastignac, "that our Government changes its silver for nothing but gold; it takes no account of men."

"Is Maxime a man to blow his brains out?" asked du Tillet the banker.

"You only wish he were! Then we should be quits," replied Maxime de Trailles, who was supposed by all to have left the house.

And the Count rose like an apparition from the depths of a low chair behind that of the Chevalier d'Espard.

Everybody laughed.

"Will you have a cup of tea?" asked young Madame de Rastignac, whom the Marquise had begged to do the honors of the tea-table.

"With pleasure," said the Count, coming to stand in front of the fire.

This man, the prince of the rakes of Paris, had, till now, maintained the position of superiority assumed by dandies— in those days known in Paris as *gants jaunes* (*lemon-kids*), and since then as *lions*. It is needless to tell the story of his youth, full of disreputable adventures and terrible dramas, in which he had always managed to observe the proprieties. To this man women were but means to an end; he had no belief in their sufferings or their enjoyment; like the deceased de Marsay, he regarded them as naughty children.

After running through his own fortune, he had devoured that of a famous courtesan known as *La belle Hollandaise,* the mother of the no less famous Esther Gobseck. Then he brought trouble on Madame de Restaud, Madame Delphine de Nucingen's sister; the young Comtesse de Rastignac was Madame de Nucingen's daughter.

Paris society is full of inconceivable anomalies. The Baronne de Nucingen was at this moment in Madame d'Espard's drawing-room, face to face with the author of all her sister's misery—an assassin who had only murdered a woman's happiness. That, no doubt, was why he was there.

Madame de Nucingen had dined with the Marquise, and her daughter with her. Augusta de Nucingen had been married for about a year to the Comte de Rastignac, who had started on his political career by holding the post of Under-secretary of State in the Ministry formed by the famous de Marsay, the only great statesman brought to the front by the Revolution of July. Count Maxime de Trailles alone knew how much disaster he had occasioned; but he had always sheltered himself from blame by obeying the code of manly honor. Though he had squandered more money in his life than the felons in the four penal establishments of France had stolen in the same time, justice treated him with respect. He had never failed in any question of technical honor; he paid his gambling debts with scrupulous punctuality. He was a

capital player, and the partner of the greatest personages
and ambassadors. He dined with all the members of the
Corps diplomatique. He would fight; he had killed two or
three men in his time—nay, he had murdered them, for his
skill and coolness were matchless.

There was not a young man in Paris to compare with him
in dress, in grace of manner, in pleasant wit, in ease and
readiness, in what used to be called the *grand air.* As page
to the Emperor, trained from the age of twelve in horse
exercise of every kind, he was a noted rider. He had always
five horses in his stables, he kept racers, he set the fashion.
Finally, no man was more successful than he in giving a
supper to younger men; he would drink with the stoutest,
and come out fresh and cool, ready to begin again, as if orgies
were his element.

Maxime, one of the men whom everybody despises, but
who control that contempt by the insolence of audacity and
the fear they inspire, never deceived himself as to his position.
This was where his strength lay. Strong men can always
criticise themselves.

At the time of the Restoration he had turned his employment as page to the Emperor to good account. He attributed his supposed Bonapartist proclivities to the repulses
he had met with from a succession of ministers when he had
wanted to serve under the Bourbons; for, in fact, notwithstanding his connections, his good birth, and his dangerous
cleverness, he had never succeeded in getting an appointment.
Then he had joined the underground conspiracy, which ended
in the fall of the elder branch of the Bourbons. When the
younger branch, at the heels of the Paris populace, had
trampled down the senior branch, and established itself on the
throne, Maxime made the most of his attachment to Napoleon,
for whom he cared no more than for the object of his first
flirtation. He then did good service, for which it was difficult
to make a return, as he wanted to be repaid too often by
people who knew how to keep accounts. At the first refusal
Maxime assumed a hostile attitude, threatening to reveal

certain not very creditable details; for a dynasty first set up has, like infants, dirty linen to hide.

De Marsay, in the course of his career, made up for the blunders of those who had undervalued the usefulness of this person; he employed him on such secret errands as need a conscience hardened by the hammer of necessity, an address which is equal to any mode of action, impudence, and, above all, the coolness, presence of mind, and swift apprehension of affairs, which are combined to make a *bravo* of scheming and superior policy. Such an instrument is at once rare and indispensable. De Marsay intentionally secured to Maxime de Trailles a firm footing in the highest social circles; he represented him as being a man matured by passion, taught by experience, knowing men and things, to whom traveling and a faculty of observation had given great knowledge of European interests, of foreign Cabinets, and of the connections of all the great continental families. De Marsay impressed on Maxime the necessity for doing himself credit; he explained to him that discretion was not so much a virtue as a good speculation; he proved to him that power never evades the touch of a strong and trustworthy tool, at the same time elegant and polished.

"In political life you can only squeeze a man once," said he, blaming him for having uttered a threat.

And Maxime was the man to understand all the significance of the axiom.

At de Marsay's death, Comte Maxime de Trailles fell back into his old life. He went every year to gamble at watering-places, and returned to spend the winter in Paris; but, although he received from time to time some considerable sums dug out of the depths of very tight-locked chests, this sort of half-pay due to a man of spirit, who might at any moment be made use of, and who was in the confidence of many mysteries of antagonistic diplomates, was insufficient for the extravagant splendor of a life like that of this king of the dandies, the tyrant of four or five Paris clubs. Hence the Count had many hours of uneasiness over the financial question.

Having no estates or investments, he had never been able to strengthen his position by being elected député; and having no ostensible duties, it was out of his power to hold the knife to a great man's throat, and get himself made a peer of France. And time was gaining on him; dissipation of all kinds had damaged his health and person. In spite of a handsome appearance, he knew it; he did not deceive himself. He determined to settle, to marry. He was too clever a man to overestimate the true value of his position; it was, he knew, an illusion. So he could not find a wife in the highest Paris society, nor in the middle class. He required a vast amount of spite, with apparent sincerity and real service done, to make himself acceptable; for every one hoped for his fall, and a vein of ill-luck might be his ruin.

If once he should find himself in prison, at Clichy or abroad, as a result of some bill of exchange that he failed to negotiate, he would drop into the gulf where so many political dead men are to be seen who do not comfort each other. At this very hour he was dreading the falling stones from some portions of the awful vault which debts build up over many a Parisian head. He had allowed his anxiety to be seen in his face; he had refused to play here at Madame d'Espard's; he had been absent-minded while talking to ladies; and he had ended by sitting mute and absorbed in the armchair from which he now rose like Banquo's ghost.

Comte Maxime de Trailles, standing in the middle of the fire-front, under the cross-lights of two large candelabra, found himself the centre of direct or indirect observation. The few words that had been said required him to assume an attitude of defiance; and he stood there like a man of spirit, but without arrogance, determined to show himself superior to suspicion. A painter could not have had a more favorable moment for sketching this really remarkable man.

For must not a man have extraordinary gifts to play such a part as his, to have fascinated women for thirty years, to have commanded himself to use his talents only in a secret sphere—exciting a people to rebel, discovering the mysteries of the astutest politicians, and triumphing only in ladies' boudoirs or men's private rooms? Is there not something grand in being able to rise to the highest schemes of political life, and then calmly drop back into the insignificance of a frivolous existence? A man must be of iron who can live through the alternations of the gaming table and the sudden journeys of a political agent, who can keep up the war footing of elegance and fashion and the expenses of necessary civilities to the fair sex, whose memory is a perfect library of craft and falsehood, who can hide so many and such different ideas, and so many tricks of craft, under such impenetrable suavity of manner. If the breeze of favor had blown steadily on those ever-spread sails, if the course of events had served Maxime better, he might have been a Mazarin, a Maréchal de Richelieu, a Potemkin—or perhaps, more exactly, a Lauzun, *minus* Pignerol.

The Count, a fairly tall man, and not inclining to be fat, had a certain amount of stomach; but he suppressed it majestically—to use Brillat-Savarin's words. His clothes, too, were so well made that his figure preserved a youthful aspect, and there was something light and easy in his movements, which was due, no doubt, to constant exercise, to the habit of fencing, riding, and shooting. Maxime had, in fact, all the physical grace and distinction of an aristocrat, enhanced by his admirable "get-up." His face was long, of the Bourbon type, framed in whiskers and a beard under his chin, carefully cut and curled, and as black as jet. This hue, matching that of his thick hair, was preserved by the use of an Indian cosmetic, very expensive, and known only in Persia, of which Maxime kept the secret. He thus cheated the keenest eye as to the white hairs which had long since streaked the natural black. The peculiarity of this dye, used by the Persians for thin beards, is that it does not make the features look hard; it can be softened by an admixture of indigo, and harmonizes with the color of the skin. This, no doubt, was the operation seen by Madame Mollot; but it remains to this day a standing joke at Arcis to wonder now and again, at the evening meetings, "what Madame Mollot did see."

Maxime had a fine forehead, blue eyes, a Grecian nose, a pleasant mouth, and well-shaped chin; but all round his eyes were a myriad wrinkles, as fine as if they had been marked with a razor—invisible, in fact, at a little distance. There were similar lines on his temples, and all his face was a good deal wrinkled. His eyes, like those of gamblers who have sat up night after night, were covered with a sort of glaze; but their look, if dimmed, was only the more terrible—nay, terrifying. It so evidently covered a brooding fire, the lavas of half-extinguished passions. The mouth too, once fresh and scarlet, had a cold shade, and it was not quite straight; the right-hand corner drooped a little. This sinuous line seemed to hint at falsehood. Vice had disfigured the smile, but his teeth were still sound and white.

These blemishes, too, were overlooked in the general effect of his face and figure. His grace was still so attractive that no younger man could compare with Maxime on horseback in the Bois de Boulogne, where he appeared more youthful and graceful than the youngest and most graceful of them all. This privilege of eternal youth has been seen in some men of our day.

De Trailles was all the more dangerous because he seemed yielding and indolent, and never betrayed his obstinate foregone conclusions on every subject. This charming indifference, which enabled him to back up a seditious mob with as much skill as he could have brought to bear on a Court intrigue to strengthen the position of a King, had a certain charm. No one, especially in France, ever distrusts what seems calm and homogeneous; we are accustomed to so much stir about trifles.

The Count, dressed in the fashion of 1839, had on a black coat, a dark blue cashmere waistcoat embroidered with light blue sprigs, black trousers, gray silk socks, and patent leather shoes. His watch, in his waistcoat pocket, was secured through a button-hole by a neat gold chain.

"Rastignac," said he, as he accepted the cup of tea held out to him by the pretty Countess, "will you come with me to the Austrian embassy?"

"My dear fellow, I am too recently married not to go home with my wife."

"Which means that by and by——?" said the young Countess, looking round at her husband.

"By and by is the end of the world," replied Maxime. "But if you make madame the judge, that will win the case for me, I think?"

Count Maxime, with a graceful gesture, drew the pretty Countess to his side; she listened to a few words he said, and then remarked, "If you like to go to the embassy with Monsieur de Trailles, my mother will take me home."

A few minutes later the Baronne de Nucingen and the Comtesse de Rastignac went away together. Maxime and Rastignac soon followed; and when they were sitting together in the carriage:

"What do you want of me, Maxime?" asked the husband. "What is the hurry, that you take me by the throat? And what did you say to my wife?"

"That I wanted to speak to you," replied Monsieur de Trailles. "You are a lucky dog, you are! You have ended by marrying the sole heiress of the Nucingen millions—but you have worked for it. Twenty years of penal servitude——"

"Maxime!"

"While I find myself looked at askance by everybody," he went on, without heeding the interruption. "A wretched creature—a du Tillet—asks if I have courage enough to kill myself! It is time to see where we stand.—Do they want me out of the way, or do they not? You can find out—you *must* find out," said Maxime, silencing Rastignac by a gesture. "This is my plan; listen to it. You ought to do me a service —I have served you, and can serve you again. The life I am leading bores me, and I want a pension. Help me to conclude a marriage which will secure me half a million; once married, get me sent as Minister to some wretched American republic. I will stay there long enough to justify my appointment to a similar post in Germany. If I am good for anything, I shall be promoted; if I am good for nothing, I shall be cashiered.—I may have a son; I will bring him up strictly; his mother will be rich; I will train him to diplomacy; he may become an ambassador!"

"And this is my answer," said Rastignac. "There is a harder struggle to be fought out than the outside world imagines between a power in swaddling clothes and a child in power. The power in swaddling clothes is the Chamber of Deputies, which, not being restrained by a hereditary Chamber——"

"Aha!" said Maxime, "you are a peer of France!"

"And shall I not remain so under any government?" said the newly-made peer. "But do not interrupt, you are interested in all this muddle. The Chamber of Deputies will inevitably be the whole of the Government, as Marsay used to tell us—the only man who might have rescued France; for a nation does not die; it is slave or free, that is all. The child in power is the dynasty crowned in the month of August 1830.

"The present Ministry is beaten; it has dissolved the Chamber, and will call a general election to prevent the next Ministry from having the chance; but it has no hope of a victory. If it should be victorious in the elections, the dynasty would be in danger; whereas, if the Ministry is turned out, the dynastic party may struggle on and hold its own for some time yet. The blunders of the Chamber will turn to the advantage of a Will, which, unfortunately, is the mainspring of politics. When one man is all in all, as Napoleon was, the moment comes when he must have representatives; and as superior men are rejected, the great Head is not represented. The representative is called the Cabinet, and in France there is no Cabinet—only a Will for life. In France only those who govern can blunder, the Opposition can never blunder; it may lose every battle and be none the worse; it is enough if, like the Allies in 1814, it wins but one victory. With 'three glorious days' is could destroy everything. Hence not to govern, but to sit and wait, is to be the next heir to power. Now, my personal feelings are on the side of the aristocracy, my public opinions on that of the dynasty of July. The House of Orleans has helped me to reinstate the fortunes of my family, and I am attached to it for ever."

"The for ever of Monsieur de Talleyrand, of course," de Trailles put in.

"So at the present moment I can do nothing for you," Rastignac went on. "We shall not be in power these six months. —Yes, for those six months we shall be dying by inches; I have always known it. We knew our fate from the first; we were but a stop-gap ministry.—But if you distinguish yourself in the thick of the electoral fray that is beginning, if you become a vote—a member—faithful to the reigning dynasty, your wishes shall be attended to. I can say a great deal about your zeal, I can poke my nose into every secret document, every private and confidential letter, and find you some tough place to work up. If you succeed, I can urge your claims—your skill and devotion—and demand the reward.

"As to your marriage, my dear fellow, that can only be arranged in the country with some family of ambitious manufacturers. In Paris you are too well known. The thing to find is a millionaire, a parvenu, with a daughter, and possessed with the ambition to swagger at the Tuileries."

"Well; but get your father-in-law to lend me twenty-five thousand francs to carry me over meanwhile; then he will be interested in my not being dismissed with empty promises, and will promote my marriage."

"You are wide-awake, Maxime, and you do not trust me. but I like a clever fellow; I will arrange that little business for you."

The carriage stopped.

The Comte de Rastignac saw the Minister of the Interior in the Embassy drawing-room, and drew him into a corner. The Comte de Trailles was apparently devoting himself to the old Comtesse de Listomère, but in reality he was watching the two men; he marked their gestures, interpreted their glances, and at last caught a friendly look towards himself from the Minister's eye.

Maxime and Rastignac went away together at one in the morning, and before they each got into his own carriage, Rastignac said on the stairs:

"Come to see me when the elections are coming on. Between this and then I shall find out where the Opposition is likely to be strongest, and what remedy may be devised by two such minds as ours."

"I am in a hurry for those twenty-five thousand francs!" replied de Trailles.

"Well, keep out of sight."

About seven weeks later, one morning before it was light, the Comte de Trailles drove mysteriously in a hackney cab to the Rue de Varenne. He dismissed the cab on arriving at the door of the Minister of Public Works, looked to see that he was not watched, and then waited in a small room on the first floor till Rastignac should be up. In a few minutes the man-servant, who had carried in Maxime's card, showed him into his master's room, where the great man was finishing his toilet.

"My dear fellow," said the Minister, "I can tell you a secret which will be published in the newspapers within two days, and which you can turn to good account. That poor Charles Keller, who danced the mazurka so well, has been killed in Africa, and he was our candidate for the borough and district of Arcis. His death leaves a gap. Here are copies of the two reports—one from the Sous-préfet, the other from the Police Commissioner—informing the Ministry that there were difficulties in the way of our poor friend's election. In the Police Commissioner's letter you will find some information as to the state of the town which will be sufficient to guide a man of your ability, for the ambition of poor Charles Keller's opponent is founded on his wish to marry an heiress. To a man like you this is hint enough.—The Cinq-Cygnes, the

Princesse de Cadignan, and Georges de Maufrigneuse are within a stone's throw of Arcis; you could at need secure the legitimist votes.—So——"

"Do not wear your tongue out," said Maxime. "Is the Police Commissioner still at Arcis?"

"Yes."

"Give me a line to him."

"My dear fellow," said Rastignac, giving Maxime a packet of papers, "you will find there two letters written to Gondreville to introduce you. You have been a page, he was a senator—you will understand each other.—Madame François Keller is addicted to piety; here is a letter to her from the Maréchale de Carigliano. The Maréchale is now Orleanist; she recommends you warmly, and will, in fact, be going to Arcis.— I have only one word to add: Be on your guard against the Sous-préfet; I believe him to be very capable of taking up this Simon Giguet as an advocate with the ex-President of the Council. If you need more letters, powers, introductions— write to me."

"And the twenty-five thousand francs?" asked Maxime.

"Sign this bill on du Tillet; here is the money."

"I shall succeed," said the Count, "and you can promise the authorities that the Member for Arcis will be theirs, body and soul. If I fail, pitch me overboard!"

And within an hour Maxime de Trailles, driving his tilbury, was on the road to Arcis.

As soon as he was furnished with the information supplied by the landlady of the *Mulet* and Antonin Goulard, Monsieur de Trailles lost no time in arranging the plan of his electoral campaign—a plan so obvious that the reader will have divined it at once. This shrewd agent for his own private politics at once set up Philéas as the candidate in opposition to Simon Giguet; and, notwithstanding that the man was an unlikely cipher, the idea, it must be admitted, had strong chances in its favor. · Beauvisage, as wearing the halo of municipal authority, had, with the great mass of indifferent voters, the advantage of being known by reputation.

Logic rules the development of affairs here below more than might be supposed—it is like a wife to whom, after every infidelity, a man is sure to return.

Plain sense demands that the electors called upon to choose a representative of their common interests should always be amply informed as to his fitness, his honesty, and his character. In practice, no doubt, this theory is often considerably strained; but whenever the electoral flock is left to follow its instincts, and can believe that it is voting in obedience to its own lights and intelligence, it may be trusted to throw zeal and conscious pride into its decisions; hence, while knowing their man is half the battle in the electoral sense, to know his name is, at any rate, a good beginning.

Among lukewarm voters, beginning with the most fervent, Philéas was certain, in the first instance, to secure the Gondreville party. Any candidate would be certain of the support of the *Viceroy* of Arcis, if it were only to punish the audacity of Simon Giguet. The election of an upstart, in the very act of flagrant ingratitude and hostility, would cast a slur on the Comte de Gondreville's provincial supremacy, and must be averted at any cost. Still, Beauvisage must expect, at the first announcement of his parliamentary ambition, a far from flattering or encouraging expression of surprise on the part of his father-in-law Grévin. The old man had, once for all, taken his son-in-law's measure; and to a mind as well balanced and clear as his, the notion of Philéas as a statesman would have the same unpleasant effect as a startling discord has on the ear. Also, if it is true that no man is a prophet in his own country, he is still less so in his own family, where any recognition of even the most indisputable success is grudged or questioned long after it has ceased to be doubted by the outer world. But, the first shock over, Grévin would probably become accustomed to an alternative, which, after all, was not antagonistic to his own notions for the future existence of Séverine. And then what sacrifice would he not be ready to make to save the high influence of the Gondrevilles, so evidently endangered?

To the legitimist and republican parties, neither of which could have any weight in the elections excepting to turn the scale, Monsieur de Trailles' nominee had one strange recommendation—namely, his acknowledged ineptitude. These two fractional elements of the anti-dynastic opposition knew that neither was strong enough to return a member; hence they would probably be eager to embrace an opportunity of playing a trick on what they disdainfully called the established order of things; and it might confidently be expected that, in cheerful desperation, they would heartily contribute to the success of a candidate so grossly ridiculous as to reflect a broad beam of ridicule on the Government that could support his election. Finally, in the suffrages of the Left Centre, which had provisionally accepted Simon Giguet as its candidate, Beauvisage would give rise to a strong secession, since he too gave himself out as opposed to the reigning dynasty; and Monsieur de Trailles, pending further orders, while assuring the Mayor of the support of the Ministry, meant to encourage that political bias, which was undoubtedly the most popular on the scene of operations.

Whatever budget of convictions the incorruptible representative might carry with him to Paris, his horoscope was drawn; it was quite certain that on his very first appearance at the Tuileries, august fascination would win him over to fanaticism, if the mere snares of ministerial enticement were not enough to produce that result.

Public interest being so satisfactorily arranged for, the electoral agent had now to consider the personal question: Whether, while manufacturing a deputy, he could find the stuff that would also make a father-in-law. The first point —the fortune, and the second point—the young lady, met his views; the first without dazzling him, the second without his being blind to the defects of a provincial education which must be corrected from the beginning, but which would probably not offer any serious resistance to his skilful marital guidance. Madame Beauvisage carried her husband away by storm; she was an ambitious woman, who, in spite of her four-and-forty years, still seemed conscious of a heart. Consequently, the best game to play would perhaps be a feint attack on her, to be subsequently turned on the daughter.

How far must the advanced works be carried? A question to be answered as circumstances might direct. In any case, so far as the two women were concerned, Maxime felt that he had the strong recommendation of his title, his reputation as a man of fashion, and his peculiar fitness to initiate them into the elegant and difficult arcana of Paris life; and, finally, as the founder of Beauvisage's political fortunes, which promised such a happy revolution in the life of these two exiled ladies, might not Monsieur de Trailles expect to find them enthusiastically grateful?

At the same time, there remained one serious difficulty in the way of a successful matrimonial campaign. He must obtain the consent of old Grévin, who was not the man to allow Cécile's marriage without making the strictest inquiries into the past career of her suitor. Now, in the event of such an inquiry, was there not some fear that a punctilious old man might fail to find a record of such complete security and conventional virtues as his prudence might insist on?

The semi-governmental mission which had brought Monsieur de Trailles to Arcis would indeed give a semblance of such importance and amendment as might be calculated to neutralize the effect of certain items of information. And if, before this mission were made public, it were confided as a great secret to Grévin by Gondreville, the old man's vanity would be flattered, and that would score in Maxime's favor.

He then resolved, in this difficult predicament, to adopt the very old trick attributed to Gribouille, consisting in throwing himself into the water to avoid getting wet. He would anticipate the old notary's suspicions; he himself would seem to doubt his own prudence; and, by way of a precaution against the temptations that had so long beset him, he determined to make it a preliminary condition that Cécile's fortune should be expressly settled on herself. By this means they would feel safe against any relapse on his part into habits of extravagance.

It would be his business to acquire such influence over his young wife as would enable him, by acting on her feelings, to recover the conjugal authority of which such a marriage-contract would deprive him.

At first nothing occurred to make him doubt the wisdom and perspicacity of all these projects. As soon as it was mooted, the nomination of Beauvisage caught fire like a train of gunpowder; and Monsieur de Trailles thought the success of all his schemes so probable, that he felt justified in writing to Rastignac, pledging himself to carry out his mission with the happiest and completest results.

But, suddenly, in opposition to Beauvisage the triumphant, another candidate appeared on the scene; and, it may be incidentally noted, that, for the good fortune of this piece of history, the competitor presented himself under conditions so exceptional and so unforeseen that, instead of a picture of petty conflicts attending a country election, it may very probably afford the interest of a far more exciting drama.

The man who intervenes in this narrative to fill so high a calling will be called upon to play so important a part that it is necessary to introduce him by a somewhat lengthy retrospective explanation. But at the stage we have reached, to interrupt the story by a sort of argument in the middle would be a breach of all the laws of art, and expose me to the wrath of the Critic, that sanctimonious guardian of literary orthodoxy.

In the presence of such a dilemma, the author would find himself in serious difficulties, but that his lucky star threw in his way a correspondence in which he found every detail he could wish to place before the reader set forth in order, with a brilliancy and vividness he could not have hoped to achieve.

These letters are worthy of being read with attention. While they bring on to the scene many actors in the Human Comedy who have appeared before, they explain a number of facts indispensable to the understanding and progress of this particular drama. When they have been presented, and the narrative thus brought up to the point where it now apparently breaks off, it will resume its course without any hiatus; and the author flatters himself that the introduction for a time of the epistolary form, instead of destroying its un ty, may, in fact, enhance it.

PART II.

*The Comte de l'Estorade to Marie-Gaston.**

MY DEAR SIR,—In obedience to your request, I have seen
M. the Préfet of Police, to ascertain whether the pious purpose of which you speak in your letter dated from Carrara
will meet with any opposition on the part of the authorities.
He informs me that the Imperial decree of the 23rd Prairial
of the year XII., which is still paramount on all points connected with interments, establishes beyond a doubt the right
of every landowner to be buried in his own ground. You
have only to apply for permission from the Préfet of the Department—Seine-et-Oise—and without any further formality,
you can transfer the mortal remains of Madame Marie-
Gaston to the monument you propose to erect to her in your
park at Ville-d'Avray.

But I may now be so bold as to suggest to you some objections. Are you quite sure that difficulties may not be
raised by the Chaulieu family, with whom you are not on the
best terms? In fact, might they not, up to a certain point, be
justified in complaining that, by removing a tomb—dear to
them as well as to you—from a public cemetery to private and
enclosed ground, you are regulating the visits they may wish
to pay to that grave by your own arbitrary will and pleasure?
Since, evidently, it will be in your power to prohibit their
coming on to your property.

I am well aware that, strictly speaking, a wife, living or
dead, belongs to her husband, to the exclusion of all other
relationship however near. But if, under the promptings of

* See *Mémoires de deux jeunes Mariées.*

(114)

the ill-feeling they have already manifested towards you on more than one occasion, Madame Marie-Gaston's parents should choose to dispute your decision by an action at law, what a painful business it must be! You would gain the day, I make no doubt, the Duc de Chaulieu's influence being no longer what it was at the time of the Restoration; but have you considered what venom an advocate's tongue can infuse into such a question, especially when arguing a very natural claim: that of a father, mother, and two brothers, pleading to be left in possession of the melancholy gratification of praying over a grave?

And if I must indeed tell you my whole mind, it is with deep regret that I find you inventing new forms of cherishing your grief, too long inconsolable. We had hoped that, after spending two years in Italy, you would return more resigned, and would make up your mind to seek some diversion from your sorrow in active life. But this sort of temple to ardent memories which you are proposing to erect in a place where they already crush you too closely, can only prolong their bitterness, and I cannot approve the perennial renewal you will thus confer on them.

However, as we are bound to serve our friends in their own way, I have conveyed your message to Monsieur Dorlange; still, I cannot but tell you that he was far from eager to enter into your views. His first words, when I announced myself as representing you, were that he had not the honor of knowing you; and, strange as the reply may seem to you, it was spoken with such perfect simplicity, that at first I imagined I had made some mistake, some confusion of names. However, as your oblivious friend presently admitted that he had been at school at the college of Tours, and also that he was the same M. Dorlange who, in 1831, had taken the first prize for sculpture under quite exceptional circumstances, I could entertain no doubt as to his identity. I then accounted to myself for his defective memory by the long break in your intercourse, of which you wrote. That neglect must have wounded him more than you imagined;

and when he affected not even to recollect your name, it was
a revenge he was not sorry to take.

This, however, is not the real obstacle.

Remembering on what brotherly terms you had formerly
been, I could not believe that M. Dorlange's wrath would be
inexorable. And so, after explaining to him the work he
was invited to undertake, I was about to enter on some explanations as to his grievance against you, when I was met by
the most unlooked-for obstacle.

"Indeed," said he, "the importance of the commission you
are good enough to propose to me, the assurance that no out-
lay will be thought too great for the dignity and perfection
of the work, the invitation to set out myself for Carrara to
superintend the choice and extraction of the marbles,—the
whole thing is a piece of such great good fortune for an
artist, that at any other time I should have accepted it
eagerly. But at this moment, when you honor me with a
call, though I have no fixed intention of abandoning my
career as an artist, I am possibly about to be launched in
political life. My friends are urging me to come forward
as a candidate at the coming elections; and, as you will understand, monsieur, if I should be returned, the complication
of parliamentary duties, and my initiation into a new experience, would, for some time at any rate, stand in the way of
undertaking such a work as you propose, with the necessary
leisure and thought. Also," added M. Dorlange, "I should
be working in the service of a great sorrow anxious to find
consolation at any cost in the projected monument. That
sorrow would naturally be impatient; I should inevitably be
slow, disturbed, hindered; it will be better, therefore, to apply
to some one else—which does not make me less grateful for
the honor and confidence you have shown me."

After listening to this little speech, very neatly turned, as
you perceive, it struck me that your friend was anticipating
parliamentary triumphs, perhaps a little too confidently,
and, for a moment, I thought of hinting at the possibility
of his failing at the election, and asking whether, in that

case, I might call on him again. But it is never polite to cast doubts on popular success; and as I was talking to a man already much offended, I would not throw oil on the fire by a question that might have been taken amiss. I merely expressed my regrets, and said I would let you now the result of my visit.

I need hardly say that within a few days I shall have found out what are the prospects of this parliamentary ambition which has arisen so inopportunely in our way. For my part, there seem to me to be a thousand reasons for expecting it to miss fire. Assuming this, you would perhaps do well to write to M. Dorlange; for his manner, though perfectly polite and correct, appeared to confess a still lively memory of some wrong for which you will have to obtain forgiveness. I know that it must be painful to you to explain the very singular circumstances of your marriage, for it will compel you to retrace the days of your happiness, now so cruel a memory. But, judging from what I saw of your old friend, if you are really bent on his giving you the benefit of his talents, if you do not apply to him yourself, but continue to employ a go-between, you will be persisting in a course which he finds disobliging, and expose yourself to a final refusal.

At the same time, if the step I urge on you is really too much for you, there is perhaps another alternative. Madame de l'Estorade has always seemed to me a very tactful negotiator in any business she undertakes, and in this particular instance I should feel entire confidence in her skill. She endured, from Madame Marie-Gaston's gusts of selfish passion, treatment much like that of which Monsieur Dorlange complains. She, better than anybody, will be in a position to explain to him the absorbing cares of married life which you shut in its own narrow folds; and it seems to me that the example of long-suffering and patience which she always showed to her whom she would call her "dear crazy thing," cannot fail to infect your friend.

You have ample time to think over the use you may wish to make of the opening that thus offers. Madame de l'Estorade is just now suffering from a nervous shock, the result of a terrible fright. A week ago our dear little Naïs was within an ace of being crushed before her eyes; and but for the courage of a stranger who rushed at the horses' heads and brought them up short, God knows what dreadful misfortune would have befallen us. This fearful moment produced in Madame de l'Estorade an attack of nervous excitement which made us for a time excessively anxious. Though she is much better to-day, it will be some days yet before she can see Monsieur Dorlange, supposing you should think her feminine intervention desirable and useful.

Still, once again, my dear sir, would it not be wiser to give up your idea? All I can foresee as the outcome for you is enormous expense, unpleasant squabbles with the Chaulieus, and a renewal of your sorrows. Notwithstanding, I am none the less at your service in and for anything, as I cannot fail to be, from every sentiment of esteem and friendship.

The Comtesse de l'Estorade to Madame Octave de Camps.

PARIS, *February* 1839.

DEAR FRIEND,—Of all the expressions of sympathy that have reached me since the dreadful accident to my poor child, none has touched me more deeply than your kind letter. To answer your affectionate inquiry, I must say that in that terrible moment Naïs was marvelously composed and calm. It would be impossible, I think, to see death more imminent, but neither at the time nor afterwards did the brave child flinch; everything shows her to have a firm nature, and her health, thank God, has not suffered in the faintest degree.

I, for my part, as a consequence of my intense fright, have had an attack of spasmodic convulsions, and for some days, it would seem, alarmed my doctor, who feared I might go out of my mind. Thanks, however, to a strong constitution, I am now almost myself again, and no traces would remain of that painful shock if it had not, by a singular fatality, been connected with another unpleasant circumstance which had for some time thought fit to fill a place in my life.

Even before this latest kind assurance of your goodwill towards me, I had thought of turning to the help of your friendship and advice; and now, when you are so good as to write that you would be happy and proud if in any degree you might take the place of poor Louise de Chaulieu, the dear, incomparable friend snatched from me by death, how can I hesitate? I take you at your word, my dear madame, and boldly request you to exert in my favor the delicate skill which enabled you to defy impertinent comment when the impossibility of announcing your marriage to Monsieur de Camps exposed you to insolent and perfidious curiosity—the peculiar tact by which you extricated yourself from a position of difficulty and danger—in short, the wonderful art which allowed you at once to keep your secret and maintain your dignity. I need their help in the disagreeable matter to which I have alluded. Unfortunately, to benefit by the doctor's advice, the patient must explain the case; and here M. de Camps, with his genius for business, seems to me an atrocious person. Owing to those odious forges he has chosen to buy, you are as good as dead to Paris and the world. Of old, when you were at hand, in a quarter of an hour's chat I could have told the whole story without hesitancy or preparation; as it is, I have to think it all out and go through the solemn formality of a confession in black and white.

After all, effrontery will perhaps best serve my turn; and since, in spite of circumlocutions and preambles, I must at last come to the point, why not confess at once that at the kernel of the matter is that very stranger who rescued my poor little girl. A stranger—be it clearly understood—to M. de l'Estorade, and to all who may have reported the accident; a stranger to the whole world, if you please—but not to your humble servant, whom this man has for three months past condescended to honor with the most persistent attention. It cannot seem any less preposterous to you than it does to me, my dear friend, that I, at two-and-thirty, with three children, one a tall son of fifteen, should have become the object of unremitting devotion, and yet that is the absurd misfortune against which I have to protect myself.

And when I say that I know the unknown, this is but partly true: I know neither his name nor his place of residence, nor anything about him; I never met him in society; and I may add that though he has the ribbon of the Legion of Honor, nothing in his appearance, which has no trace of elegance, leads me to suppose that I ever shall meet him in society.

It was at the Church of Saint-Thomas d'Aquin, where, as you know, I was in the daily habit of attending Mass, that this annoying "shadowing" first began. I also took the children out walking in the Tuileries almost every day, M. de l'Estorade having taken a house without a garden. This custom was soon noted by my persecutor, and gave him boldness; for wherever I was to be found out of doors I had to put up with his presence. But this singular adorer was as prudent as he was daring; he always avoided following me to my door; and he steered his way at such a distance and so undemonstratively, that I had at any rate the comforting certainty that his foolish assiduity could not attract the notice of anybody who was with me. And yet, Heaven alone knows to what inconveniences and privations I have submitted to put him off my track. I never entered the church but on Sunday; and to the risk of the dear children's health I have often kept them at home, or invented excuses for not going out with them, leaving them to the servants—against all my principles of education and prudence.

Visits, shopping—I can do nothing but in a carriage; and all this could not hinder that, just when I fancied I had routed this tiresome person and exhausted his patience, he was on the spot to play so brave and providential a part in that dreadful accident to Naïs. But it is this very obligation which I now owe him that introduces a vexatious complication into a position already so awkward. If I had at last been too much annoyed by his persistency I might by some means, even by some decisive action, have put an end to his persecution; but now, if he comes across my path, what can I do? How am I to proceed? Merely to thank him would be to encourage him; and even if he should not try to take advantage of my civilities to alter our relative position, I should have him at my heels closer than ever.—Am I then not to notice him, to affect not to recognize him? But, my dear madame, think! A mother who owes her child's life to his efforts and pretends not to perceive it—who has not a word of gratitude——!

This, then, is the intolerable dilemma in which I find myself, and you can see how sorely I need your advice and judgment. What can I do to break the odious habit this gentleman has formed of following me like my shadow? How am I to thank him without exciting his imagination, or to avoid thanking him without suffering the reproaches of my conscience? This is the problem I submit to your wisdom.

If you will do me the service of solving it—and I know no one else so capable—I shall add my gratitude to the affection which, as you know, dear madame, I already feel for you.

The Comte de l'Estorade to Marie-Gaston.

PARIS, *February* 1839.

The public prints, my dear sir, may have been beforehand in giving you an account of a meeting between your friend M. Dorlange and the Duc de Rhétoré. But the newspapers, by announcing the bare facts—since custom and propriety do not allow them to expatiate on the motives of the quarrel —will only have excited your curiosity without satisfying it. I happen to know on good authority all the details of the affair, and I hasten to communicate them to you, as they must to you be of the greatest interest.

Three days ago, that is to say, on the evening of the day when I had called on M. Dorlange, the Duc de Rhétoré was in a stall at the opera. M. de Ronquerolles, who has lately returned from a diplomatic mission that had detained him far from Paris for some years, presently took the seat next to him. Between the acts these gentlemen did not leave their place to walk in the gallery; but, as is commonly done in the theatre, they stood up with their back to the stage, consequently facing M. Dorlange, who sat behind them and seemed absorbed in the evening's news. There had been a very uproarious scene in the Chamber—what is termed a very interesting debate.—The conversation turned very naturally on the events in Paris society during M. de Ronquerolles' absence, and he happened to make this remark, which, of course, attracted M. Dorlange's attention:

"And that poor Madame de Macumer—what a sad end, and what a strange marriage!"

"Oh, you know," said M. de Rhétoré in the high-pitched tone he affects, "my sister had too much imagination not to be a little chimerical and romantic. She was passionately in love with M. de Macumer, her first husband; still, one may tire of all things, even of widowhood. This M. Marie-Gaston came in her way. He is attractive in person; my sister was rich, he very much in debt; he was proportionately amiable and attentive; and, on my honor, the rogue managed so cleverly, that, after stepping into M. de Macumer's shoes, and making his wife die of jealousy, he got out of her everything that the law allowed the poor silly woman to dispose of.—Louise left a fortune of at least twelve hundred thousand francs, to say nothing of magnificent furniture and a delightful villa she had built at Ville-d'Avray. Half of this came to our gentleman, the other half to my father and mother, the Duc and Duchesse de Chaulieu, who, as parents, had a right to that share. As to my brother Lenoncourt and me—we were simply disinherited for our portion."

As soon as your name was pronounced, my dear sir, M. Dorlange laid down his paper; then, as M. de Rhétoré ceased speaking, he rose.

"I beg your pardon, M. le Duc, for taking the liberty of correcting your statements; but, as a matter of conscience,

I must assure you that you are to the last degree misinformed."

"You say?——" replied the Duke, half closing his eyes, and in a tone of contempt which you can easily imagine.

"I say, Monsieur le Duc, that Marie-Gaston has been my friend from childhood, and that he has never been called a *rogue*. On the contrary, he is a man of honor and talent; and far from making his wife die of jealousy, he made her perfectly happy during three years of married life. As to her fortune——"

"You have considered the consequences of this step?" said the Duke, interrupting him.

"Certainly, monsieur. And I repeat that, with regard to the fortune left to Marie-Gaston by a special provision in his wife's will, he coveted it so little that, to my knowledge, he is about to devote a sum of two or three hundred thousand francs to the erection of a monument to the wife he has never ceased to mourn."

"And, after all, monsieur, who are you?" the Duc de Rhétoré broke in again, with growing irritation.

"In a moment I shall have the honor to inform you," replied M. Dorlange. "But, first, you will allow me to add that Madame Marie-Gaston could have no pangs of conscience in disposing as she did of the fortune of which you have been deprived. All her wealth, as a matter of fact, came to her from M. le Baron de Macumer, her first husband, and she had previously renounced her patrimony to secure an adequate position to your brother, M. le Duc de Lenoncourt-Givry, who, as a younger son, had not, like yourself, M. le Duc, the benefit of the entail."

M. Dorlange felt in his pocket for his card-case, but it was not there.

"I have no cards about me," he said; "but my name is Dorlange—a sort of stage-name, and easy to remember—42 Rue de l'Ouest."

"Not a very central position," M. de Rhétoré remarked ironically.

At the same time he turned to M. de Ronquerolles, and taking him as a witness and as his second:

"I must apologize to you, my dear fellow," said he, "for sending you on a voyage of discovery to-morrow morning." Then he added, "Come to the smoking-room; we can talk there in peace, and at any rate in *security.*"

By the emphasis he laid on the last word, it was impossible to misunderstand the innuendo it was meant to convey. The two gentlemen went out, without the scene having given rise to any commotion or fuss, since the stalls all round them were empty, and M. Dorlange then caught sight of M. Stidmann, the famous sculptor, at the other end of the stalls. He went up to him.

"Do you happen to have," said he, "such a thing as a memorandum or sketch book in your pocket?"

"Yes—always."

"Then would you lend it me and allow me to tear a leaf out? I have just had an idea that I do not want to lose. If I should not see you as you go out, to return the book, you shall have it without fail to-morrow morning."

On returning to his seat, M. Dorlange made a hasty pencil sketch; and when the curtain rose, and MM. de Rhétoré and de Ronquerolles came back to their places, he lightly touched the Duke on the shoulder, and handing him the drawing, he said, "My card, which I have the honor of giving to your grace."

The card was a pretty sketch of sculpturesque architecture set in a landscape. Underneath it was written: "Sketch for a monument to be erected to the memory of Madame Marie-Gaston, *née* Chaulieu, by her husband, from the designs of Charles Dorlange, sculptor, Rue de l'Ouest, 42."

He could have found no more ingenious way of intimating to M. de Rhétoré that he had no mean adversary; and you may observe, my dear sir, that M. Dorlange thus gave weight to his denial by giving substance, so to speak, to his statement as to your disinterestedness and conjugal devotion and grief.

The performance ended without any further incident. M. de Rhétoré parted from M. de Ronquerolles.

M. de Ronquerolles then addressed M. Dorlange, very courteously endeavoring to effect a reconciliation, observing that though he might be in the right, his conduct was unconventional and offensive, that M. de Rhétoré had behaved with great moderation, and would certainly accept the very slightest expression of regret—in fact, said everything that could be said on such an occasion. M. Dorlange would not hear of anything approaching an apology, and on the following day he received a visit from M. de Ronquerolles and General de Montriveau as representing M. de Rhétoré. Again they were urgent that M. Dorlange should consent to express himself in different language. But your friend would not be moved from this ultimatum.

"Will M. de Rhétoré withdraw the expressions I felt myself bound to take exception to? If so, I will retract mine."

"That is impossible," said they. "The offence was personal to M. de Rhétoré, to you it was not. Rightly or wrongly, he firmly believes that M. Marie-Gaston did him an injury. Allowance must always be made for damaged interests; perfect justice is never to be got from them."

"So that M. le Duc may continue to slander my friend at his pleasure!" said M. Dorlange, "since, in the first place, my friend is in Italy; and in the second, he would always, if possible, avoid coming to extreme measures with his wife's brother. And," he added, "it is precisely this impossibility of his defending himself which gives me a right—nay more, makes it my duty to intervene. It was by a special grace of Providence that I was enabled to catch some of the malignant reports that are flying about on the wing; and since M. le Duc de Rhétoré sees no reason to mitigate his language, we will, if you please, carry the affair through to the end."

The dispute being reduced to these terms, the duel was inevitable, and in the course of the day the seconds on both sides arranged the conditions. The meeting was fixed for the next morning; the weapons, pistols. On the ground, M.

Dorlange was perfectly cool. After exchanging shots without effect, as the seconds seemed anxious to stop the proceedings—

"Come," said he cheerfully, "one shot more!" as if he were firing at a dummy in a shooting gallery.

This time he was wounded in the fleshy part of the thigh, not a dangerous wound, but one which bled very freely. While he was being carried to the carriage in which he had come, M. de Rhétoré was anxiously giving every assistance, and when he was close to him—"All the same," said Dorlange, "Marie-Gaston is an honest gentleman, a heart of gold——" and he fainted away almost as he spoke.

This duel, as you may suppose, my dear sir, has been the talk of the town; I have only had to keep my ears open to collect any amount of information concerning M. Dorlange, for he is the lion of the day, and all yesterday it was impossible to go into a house where he was not the subject of conversation. My harvest was chiefly gathered at Mme. de Montcornet's. She, as you know, has a large acquaintance among artists and men of letters; and to give you a notion of the position your friend holds in their regard, I need only report a conversation in which I took part last evening in the Countess' drawing-room. The speakers were M. Émile Blondet, of the *Débats;* M. Bixiou the caricaturist, one of the best informed eavesdroppers in Paris—I believe you know them both, but at any rate I am sure that you are intimate with Joseph Bridau, our great painter, who was the third speaker, for I remember that he and Daniel d'Arthez signed for you when you were married.

Bridau was speaking when I joined them.

"Dorlange began splendidly," said he. "There was the touch of a great master even in the work he sent in for competition, to which, under the pressure of opinion, the Academy awarded the prize, though he had laughed very audaciously at their programme."

"Quite true," said M. Bixiou. "And the Pandora he exhibited in 1837, on his return from Rome, was also a very strik-

This time he was wounded

ing work. But as it won him, out of hand, the Legion of Honor and commissions from the Government and the Municipality, with at least thirty flaming notices in the papers, I doubt if he can ever recover from that success."

"That is a verdict *à la* Bixiou," said Émile Blondet.

"So it is, and with good reason. Did you ever see the man?"

"No, he is seen nowhere."

"True, that is his favorite haunt. He is a bear, but a bear intentionally; out of affectation and deliberate purpose."

"I really cannot see," said Joseph Bridau, "that such a dislike to society is a bad frame of mind for an artist. What can a sculptor, especially, gain by frequenting drawing-rooms where men and women have got into the habit of wearing clothes?"

"Well, even a sculptor may get some amusement which saves him from monomania or brooding. And then he can see how the world wags—that 1839 is neither the fifteenth nor the sixteenth century."

"What!" said Blondet, "do you mean the poor fellow suffers from that delusion?"

"He!—he talks quite glibly of living the life of the artists of mediæval times, with all their universal studies and learning, and the terrific labors which he can conceive of in a society that was still semi-barbarous, but that has no place in ours. He is a guileless dreamer, and never perceives that civilization, by strangely complicating our social intercourse, devotes to business, interest, and pleasure thrice as much time as a less advanced social organization would spend on those objects. Look at the savage in his den! He has nothing to do; but we, with the Bourse, the opera, the newspapers, parliamentary debates, drawing-room meetings, elections, railways, the *Café de Paris,* and the National Guard—when, I ask you, are we to find time for work?"

"A splendid theory for idlers," said Émile Blondet, laughing.

"Not at all, my dear boy; it is perfectly true. The curfew

no longer rings at nine o'clock, I suppose! Well, and only last evening, if my door-porter Ravenouillet didn't give a party! Perhaps I committed a serious blunder by declining the indirect invitation he sent me."

"Still," said Joseph Bridau, "it is evident that a man who is not mixed up with the business interests or pleasures of his age may, out of his savings, accumulate a very pretty capital of time. Dorlange, I fancy, has a comfortable income irrespective of commissions: there is nothing to hinder him from living as he has a mind to live."

"And, as you see, he goes to the opera, since it was there he picked up his duel.—And, indeed, you have hardly hit the nail on the head by representing him as cut off from all contemporary interests, when I happen to know that he is on the point of taking them up on the most stirring and absorbing side of the social machine—namely, politics!"

"What! he thinks he can be a politician?" asked Émile Blondet scornfully.

"It is part, no doubt, of his famous scheme of universal efficiency, and you should see how logically and perseveringly he is carrying out the idea. Last year two hundred and fifty thousand francs fell on him from the sky, and my man purchased a house in the Rue Saint-Martin as a qualification; and then, as another little speculation, with the rest of the money he bought shares in the *National* newspaper, and I find him in the office whenever I am in the mood to have a laugh at the Republican Utopia. There he has his flatterers; they have persuaded him that he is a born orator and will make a sensation in the Chamber. There is, in fact, a talk of working up a constituency to nominate him, and on days when they are very enthusiastic they discover that he is like Danton."

"Oh, this is the climax of burlesque!" said Émile Blondet.

I do not know, my dear sir, whether you have ever observed that men of superior talent are always extremely indulgent. This was now proved in the person of Joseph Bridau.

"I agree with you," said he, "that if Dorlange starts on that track he is almost certainly lost to art. But, after all, why should he not be a success in the Chamber? He speaks with great fluency, and seems to be full of ideas. Look at Canalis; when he won his election: 'Faugh! a poet!' said one and another, which has not prevented his making himself famous as an orator and being made Minister."

"Well, the first point is to get elected," said Émile Blondet. "What place does Dorlange think of standing for?"

"For one of the rotten boroughs of the *National,* of course," remarked Bixiou. "However, I do not know that the place is yet decided on."

"As a general rule," said the man of the *Débats,* "to be returned as a member, even with the hottest support of your party, requires a somewhat extensive political notoriety, or else, at least, some good provincial status of family or of fortune. Does any one know whether Dorlange can command these elements of success?"

"As to family status, that would be a particular difficulty with him; his family is non-existent to a desperate extent."

"Indeed," said Blondet. "Then he is a natural son?"

"As natural as may be—father and mother alike unknown. But I can quite imagine his being elected; it is the rank and file of his political notions that will be so truly funny."

"He must be a Republican if he is a friend of the gentlemen on the *National,* and has a likeness to Danton."

"Evidently. But he holds his fellow-believers in utter contempt, and says that they are good for nothing but fighting, rough play and big talk. So provisionally he will put up with a monarchy bolstered up by republican institutions—though he asserts that this citizen-kingship must infallibly be undermined by the abuse of private interest which he calls corruption. This would tempt him to join the little Church of the Left Centre; but there again—there is always a but—he can discern nothing but a coalition of ambitious and emasculated men, unconsciously smoothing the way to a revolution which he sees already on the horizon; to his great regret, because in his opinion the masses are neither sufficiently prepared nor sufficiently intelligent to keep it from slipping through their fingers.

"As to Legitimism, he laughs at it; he will not accept it as a principle under any aspect. He regards it simply as a more definite and time-honored form of hereditary monarchy, allows it no other superiority than that of old wine over new. And while he is neither Legitimist, nor Conservative, nor Left Centre, but a republican who deprecates a republic, he stoutly sets up for being a Catholic and rides the hobby of that party —freedom in teaching; and yet this man, who wants freedom in teaching, is, on the other hand, afraid of the Jesuits, and still talks, as if we were in 1829, of the encroachments of the priestly party and the Congregation.

"And can you imagine, finally, the great party he proposes to form in the Chamber—himself, of course, its leader? That of justice, impartiality, and honesty: as if anything of the kind were to be found in the parliamentary pottage or as if every shade of opinion had not from time immemorial flourished that flag to conceal its ugly emptiness?"

"So that he gives up sculpture once and for all?" said Joseph Bridau.

"Not immediately. He is just finishing a statue of some female Saint, but he will not let anybody see it, and does not mean to exhibit it this year. He has notions of his own about that too."

"Which are——?" asked Émile Blondet.

"That religious works ought not to be displayed to the judgment of criticism and the gaze of a public cankered by scepticism; that, without confronting the turmoil of the world, they ought modestly and piously to take the place for which they were intended."

"Bless me!" exclaimed Blondet. "And such a fervent Catholic could fight a duel?"

"Oh, there is a better joke than that. Catholic as he is, he lives with a woman he brought over from Italy, a sort of goddess of Liberty, who is at the same time his model and his housekeeper."

"What a gossip—what a regular inquiry office that Bixiou is!" they said, as they divided.

They had just been asked by Madame de Montcornet to accept a cup of tea from her fair hands.

As you see, my dear sir, M. Dorlange's political aspirations are not regarded very seriously, most people thinking of them very much as I do myself. I cannot doubt that you will write to him at once to thank him for his zealous intervention to defend you against calumny. His brave devotion has, in fact, filled me with sympathy for him, and I should be really glad to see you making use of your old friendship for him to hinder him from embarking on the thankless track he is so eager to tread. I am not guided by the thought of the drawbacks attributed to him by M. Bixiou, who has a sharp and too ready tongue; like Joseph Bridau, I think little of them; but a mistake that every one must regret, in my opinion, would be to abandon a career in which he has already won a high position, to rush into the political fray. Sermonize him to this effect, and as much as you can, to induce him to stick to Art. Indeed, you yourself are interested in his doing so if you are still bent on his undertaking the work he has so far refused to accept.

In the matter of the personal explanation I advised you to have with him, I may tell you that your task is greatly facilitated. You are not called upon to enter into any of the details that might perhaps be too painful. Mme. de l'Estorade, to whom I have spoken of the mediator's part I proposed that she should play, accepts it with pleasure, and undertakes in half an hour's conversation to dissipate the clouds that may still hang between you and your friend.

While writing you this long letter, I sent to inquire for him: the report is as good as possible, and the surgeons are not in the least uneasy about him, unless some extraordinary and quite unforeseen complications should supervene. He is, it would seem, an object of general interest; for, according to my servant, people are standing in rows waiting to put their names down.

There is this also to be said—M. de Rhétoré is not liked. He is haughty, starch, and not clever. How different from her who dwells in our dearest memory! She was simple and kind, without ever losing her dignity, and nothing could compare with the amiability of her temper, unless it were the brightness of her wit.

The Comtesse de l'Estorade to Madame Octave de Camps.

PARIS, *February* 1839.

Nothing could be better than all you have written, dear madame: it was, in fact, highly probable that this annoying person would not think twice about speaking to me the next time we should meet. His heroism gave him a right to do so, and the most ordinary politeness made it incumbent on him. Unless he were content to pass for the clumsiest of admirers, he could not help asking me how Naïs and I had recovered from the effects of the accident he had been able to forefend. But if, contrary to all expectations, he should persist in not stepping out of his cloud, I was fully determined to act on your wise advice. If the mountain did not come to me, I would go to the mountain. Like *Hippolyte* in *Théramène's* tale, I would "thrust myself on the monster" and fire my gratitude in his teeth. Like you, my dear friend, I quite understood that the real danger of this persecution lay in its continuance, and the inevitable explosion that threatened me sooner or later; the fact that the servants, or the children, might at any moment detect the secret; that I should be exposed to the most odious inferences if it were suspected by others; and, above all, the idea that if this ridiculous mystery should be discovered by M. de l'Estorade and drive him to such lengths as his southern nature and past experience in the army made me imagine only too easily,—all this had spurred me to a point I cannot describe, and I might have gone further even than you advised.—I had not only recognized the necessity for being the first to speak; but under the pretext that my husband would call to thank him under his own roof, I meant to compel him to give me his name and address, and, supposing he were at all a possible acquaintance, to invite him forthwith to dinner, and thus entice the wolf into the sheepfold.

For, after all, what danger could there be? If he had but a shade of common-sense when he saw the terms I live on with M. de l'Estorade, and my *maniacal* passion for my children, as you call it, in short, the calm regularity of my home-life, would he not understand how vain was his pursuit? At any rate, whether he should persist or no, his vehemence would have lost its perilous out-of-door character. If I was to be persecuted, it would, at any rate, be under my own roof, and I should only have to deal with one of those common adventures to which every woman is more or less liable. And we can always get over such slippery places with perfect credit, so long as we have a real sense of duty and some little presence of mind.

Not, I must tell you, that I have come to this conclusion without a painful effort. When the critical moment should come, I was not at all sure that I should be cool enough to confront the situation with such a high hand as was indispensable. However, I had fully made up my mind; and— you know me—what I have determined on I do.

Well, my dear madame, all this fine scheme, all my elaborate courage, and your not less elaborate foresight, are entirely wasted. Since your last letter the doctor has let me out of his hands. I have been out several times, always majestically surrounded by my children, that their presence, in case I should be obliged to take the initiative, might screen the crudity of such a proceeding. But in vain have I scanned the horizon on all sides out of the corner of my eye, nothing, absolutely nothing, has been visible that bore the least resemblance to a deliverer or a lover. What, now, do you say to this new state of affairs? A minute since I spoke of thrusting myself on the monster. Was this gentleman bent on giving himself the airs of a monster, and of the most dangerous species? How was I to interpret this absence? Had he, with admirable perspicacity, scented the snare in which we meant to trap him, and was he prudently keeping out of the way? Or was there some deeper motive still? Did this man, in whom I had failed to discern the smallest sign of elegance, carry refinement and delicacy so far as to sacrifice his fancy to his fear of marring a generous action?

But if this were so, he would be really a man to think seriously about; my dear M. de l'Estorade, you must take care of yourself! For, do you know, the attentions of a man of such noble sentiments might prove to be more dangerous than was apparent at a first glance?

You see, my dear friend, I am trying to take the matter lightly, but in my heart of hearts I believe that I sing to keep my courage up. This skilful and unexpected strategy leaves me wondering; and my wonderment brings me back to some other ideas which at first I dismissed from my mind; now, however, I must trouble you with them, as the end of this little annoyance is beyond my ken.

As to my feeling for the man, you will not misunderstand that. He saved my little girl, it is true, but merely to lay me under an obligation. Meanwhile he has upset my pleasantest habits: I am obliged to send the poor children out without me; I cannot go to church as often as I please, since even before the altar he dares to come between me and God; in fact, he has upset that perfect equanimity of thought and feeling which till now has been the joy and the pride of my life. But though this persecution is odious and intolerable, the man has a sort of magnetic power over me that distresses me greatly. I can feel him near me before I see him. His gaze oppresses me without my meeting his eye. He is ugly; but there is something vigorous and strongly marked about him which leaves an impression on the mind; one fancies that he must have some powerful and dominating characteristics. So, do what I will, I cannot hinder his occupying my mind. Now, I feel as if I had got rid of him altogether.—Well, may I say it? I am conscious of a void. I miss him as the ear misses a sharp and piercing sound that has annoyed it for a long time.

What I am going to add will strike you as very childish, but can we control the mirage of our fancy?—I have often told you of my discussions with Louise de Chaulieu as to the way in which women should deal with life.   For my part, I always told her that the frenzy with which she never ceased to seek the Infinite was quite ill regulated, and fatal to happiness.   And she would answer: "You, my dearest, have never loved.   Love implies a phenomenon so rare, that we may live all our life without meeting the being on whom nature has bestowed the faculty of giving us happiness.   If on some glorious day that being appears to wake your heart from its slumbers, you will take quite another tone."

The words of those doomed to die are so often prophetic! Supposing this man should be the serpent, though late, that Louise seemed to threaten me with; good Heavens!   That he should ever represent a real danger, that he should ever be able to tempt me from my duty, there is certainly no fear. I am confidently strong as to any such extreme of ill.   But I did not—like you, my dear friend—marry a man who was the choice of my heart.   It was only by dint of patience, determination, and sense that I built up the austere but solid attachment that binds me to M. de l'Estorade.   Hence I cannot but be terrified at the mere idea of anything that might undermine that feeling; and the constant occupation of my mind by another man, even in the form of detestation, must be a real misery to me.

I say to you, as Monsieur, Louis XIV.'s brother, said to his wife when he brought her papers he had just written, for her to decipher them: "See clearly for me, dear madame, read my heart and brain; disperse the mists, allay the antagonistic impulses, the ebb and flow of will which these events have given rise to in my mind."   Was not my dear Louise mistaken?   Am I not one of those women on whom love, in her sense, has no hold?   The "Being who on some glorious day awoke my heart from its slumbers" was my Armand—my

René—my Naïs, three angels for whom and in whom I have
hitherto lived; and for me, I feel, there can never be any
other passion.

The Comtesse de l'Estorade to Madame Octave de Camps.

PARIS, March 1839.

In about the year 1820, two *new boys,* to use my son Armand's technical slang, joined the school at Tours in the same
week. One had a charming face; the other might have been
called ugly, but that health, honesty, and intelligence beamed
in his features and made up for their homeliness and irregularity.—And here you will stop me, dear madame, asking me
whether I have quite got over my absorbing idea, that I am
in the mood to write you a chapter of a novel? Not at all,
and this strange beginning, little as it may seem so, is only the
continuation and sequel of my adventure. So I beg you to
listen to my tale and not to interrupt. To proceed. Almost
from the first, the two boys formed a close friendship; there
was more than one reason for their intimacy. One of them—
the handsome lad—was dreamy, thoughtful, even a little sentimental; the other eager, impetuous, always burning for
action. Thus their two characters supplemented each other—
the best possible combination for any union that is to prove
lasting. Both, too, had the same stain on their birth. The
dreamy boy was the son of the notorious Lady Brandon, born
in adultery; he was known as Marie-Gaston, which can hardly
be called a name. The other, whose father and mother were
both unknown, was called Dorlange—which is not a name at
all.—Dorlange, Valmon, Volmar, Derfeuil, Melcourt, these
are all names adopted for the stage, and that only in the old-
fashioned plays, where they dwell now in company with
Arnolphe, Alceste, Clitandre, Damis, Éraste, Philinte, and
Arsinoë. So another reason why these unhappy no-man's-
sons should cling together for warmth was the cruel desertion
they both suffered from. During the seven mortal years of
their life at school, not once for a single day, even in holiday

time, did the prison doors open to let them out. At long intervals Marie-Gaston had a visitor in the person of an old nurse who had served his mother. Through this woman's hands came the quarterly payment for his schooling.

The money paid for Dorlange came with perfect regularity from some unknown source through a banker at Tours. One thing was observed—that this youth's weekly allowance was fixed at the highest sum permitted by the college rules, whence it was concluded that his anonymous parents were rich. Owing to this, but yet more to the generous use he made of his money, Dorlange enjoyed a certain degree of consideration among his companions, though he could in any case have commanded it by the prowess of his fist. At the same time, it was remarked, but not loud enough for him to hear, that no one had ever asked to see him in the parlor, nor had anybody outside the house ever taken the smallest interest in him.

These two boys, both destined to fame, were far from brilliant scholars. Though they were neither refractory nor idle, since they did not know any mother to be happy in their success, what could they care for rewards at the end of the year?

And they worked, each after his own fashion. At the age of fifteen, Marie-Gaston had produced a volume of verse: satires, elegies, meditations, to say nothing of two tragedies. As for Dorlange, his studies led him to steal firelogs; out of these, with his knife, he carved virgins, grotesques, schoolmasters and saints, grenadiers, and—in secret—figures of Napoleon.

In 1827 their school days ended; the friends left the Collège de Tours together, and both were sent to Paris. A place had already been secured for Dorlange in Bosio's studio, and thenceforward a certain amount of caprice was discernible in the occult Providence that watched over him. On arriving at the house to which the master of the college had directed him on leaving, he found pleasant rooms prettily furnished for him. Under the glass shade over the clock a large letter, addressed to him, had been so placed as to strike his eye at once. Within the envelope he found a note in these words:

"The day after your arrival in Paris, go, at eight in the morning precisely, to the Garden of the Luxembourg, Allée de l'Observatoire, the fourth bench on the right-hand side from the gate. This is imperative. Do not on any account fail."

Dorlange was punctual, as may be supposed, and had not waited long when he was joined by a little man, two feet high, who, with his enormous head and thick mop of hair, his hooked nose and chin and crooked legs, might have stepped out of one of Hoffmann's fairy tales. Without a word—for to his personal advantages, this messenger added that of being deaf and dumb—he placed in the youth's hands a letter and a purse. The letter said that Dorlange's family were much pleased to find that he had a disposition for the fine arts. He was urged to work hard and profit by the teaching of the great master under whose tuition he was placed. He would, it was hoped, be steady, and an eye would be kept on his behavior. On the other hand, he was not to forego the rational amusements suited to his age. For his needs and his pleasures he might count on a sum of twenty-five louis, which would be paid to him every three months at this same place, by the same messenger. With regard to this emissary, Dorlange was expressly forbidden to follow him when he departed after fulfilling his errand. In case of disobedience, either direct or indirect, the penalty was serious—no less, in fact, than the withdrawal of all assistance, and complete desertion.

Now, my dear friend, do you remember that in 1831 I carried you off to the École des Beaux-Arts, where, at that time, the exhibition used to be held of works competing for the first prize in sculpture? The subject set for the competition had appealed to my heart—Niobe weeping over her children. And do you remember my fury at the work sent in by one of the competitors, round which there was a crowd so dense that we could scarcely get near it? The insolent wretch had made game of the subject. His Niobe, indeed, as I could not but agree with you and the public, was most touching in her beauty and grief; but to have represented her children as so many monkeys, lying on the ground in the most various and grotesque attitudes—what a deplorable waste of talent! It was in vain that you insisted in pointing out how charming the monkeys were—graceful, witty—and that it was impossible to laugh more ingeniously at the blindness and idolatry of mothers who regard some hideous brat as a masterpiece of Nature's handiwork. I considered the thing a monstrosity; and the indignation of the older academicians, who demanded the solemn erasure of this impertinent work from the list of competing sculpture, was, in my opinion, wholly justified. Yielding, however, to public opinion and to the papers, which spoke of raising a subscription to send the sculptor to Rome if the *Grand Prix* were given to anybody else, the Academy did not agree with me and with its elders. The remarkable beauty of the Niobe outweighed all else, and this slanderer of mothers found his work crowned, though he had to take a pretty severe lecture which the secretary was desired to give him on the occasion. Unhappy youth! I can pity him now, for he never had known a mother.—He was Dorlange, the youth abandoned at the school at Tours, and Marie-Gaston's friend.

For four years, from 1827 till 1831, when Dorlange was sent to Rome, the two young men had never parted. Dorlange, with his allowance of two thousand four hundred francs, always punctually paid by the hand of the mysterious dwarf, was a sort of Marquis d'Aligre. Marie-Gaston, on the contrary, if left to his own resources, would have lived in great penury; but between persons who truly care for each other, a rarer case than is commonly supposed, on one side plenty, and on the other nothing, is a determining cause of their alliance. Without keeping any score, our two pigeons had everything in common—home, money, troubles, pleasures, and hopes; the two lived but one life. Unfortunately for Marie-Gaston, his efforts were not, like his friend's, crowned with success. His volume of verse, carefully recast and revised, with other poems from his pen and two or three dramas, all, for lack of goodwill on the part of stage-managers and publishers, remained in obscurity. At last the firm of two, by Dorlange's insistency, took strong measures: by dint of strict economy, the needful sum was saved to print and bring out a volume. The title—*Snowdrops*—was attractive; the binding was pearl-gray, the margins broad, and there was a pretty title-page designed by Dorlange. But the public was as indifferent as the publishers and managers—it would neither buy nor read; so much so, that one day when the rent was due, Marie-Gaston, in a fit of despair, sent for the old-book buyer, and sold him the whole edition for three sous a volume, whence a perfect crop of *Snowdrops* was ere long to be seen on every stall along the quays from the Pont Royal to the Pont Marie.

This wound was still bleeding in the poet's soul when it became necessary for Dorlange to set out for Rome. Life in common was no longer possible. Being informed by the mysterious dwarf that his allowance would be paid to him as usual in Rome, through Torlonia's bank, it occurred to Dorlange to offer Marie-Gaston the fifteen hundred francs a year granted him on the Royal scholarship for the five years while he should remain in Rome. But a heart noble enough to receive a favor is rarer even than that which can bestow one. Marie-Gaston, embittered by constant reverses, had not the necessary courage to meet this sacrifice half-way. The dissolution of partnership too plainly exposed the position of a dependent which he had hitherto accepted. Some trifling work placed in his hands by the great writer Daniel d'Arthez added to his little income would, he said, be enough to live on, and he peremptorily refused what his pride stigmatized as charity.

This misplaced pride led to a coolness between the friends. Their intimacy was kept alive till 1833 by a fairly brisk correspondence, but on Marie-Gaston's part there was a diminution of confidence and freedom. He was evidently hiding something. His haughty determination to be self-sufficing had led to bitter disappointment. His poverty increased day by day; and, prompted by inexorable necessity, he had drifted

into a most painful position. He had tried to release himself
from the constant pinch of want, which paralyzed his flight,
by staking everything for all or nothing. He imprudently
mixed himself up in the concerns of a newspaper, and then,
to obtain a ruling voice, took upon himself almost all the
expenses of the undertaking. Thus led into debt for a sum
of not less than thirty thousand francs, he saw nothing before
him but a debtor's prison opening its broad jaws to devour
him.

At this juncture he met Louise de Chaulieu. For nine
months, the blossoming time of their marriage, Marie-Gaston's letters were few and far between, and those he wrote
were high treason to friendship. Dorlange ought to have
been the first person told, and he was told nothing. That most
high and mighty dame, Louise de Chaulieu, Baronne de
Macumer, would have it so. When the day of the marriage
arrived, her passion for secrecy had reached a pitch bordering
on mania. I, her closest friend, was scarcely allowed to know
it, and no one was admitted to the ceremony. To comply
with the requirements of the law, witnesses were indispensable; but at the time when Marie-Gaston invited two friends
to do him this service, he announced that their relations must
be finally but amiably put an end to. His feelings towards
everybody but his wife, whom he exalted to a pure abstraction,
"would be," he wrote to Daniel d'Arthez, "friendship independent of the friend."

As for Louise, she, I believe, for greater security, would
have had the witnesses murdered on leaving the *Mairie,* but
for a wholesome fear of the public prosecutor!

Dorlange was still away, a happy excuse for telling him
nothing. Buried in a Trappist monastery, Marie-Gaston
could not have been more lost to him. By dint of writing to
other friends and asking for information, Dorlange at last
found out that Marie-Gaston no longer trod this lower earth;
that, like Tithonus, he had been translated by a jealous
divinity to a rural Olympus, which she had constructed on
purpose in the heart of the woods of Ville-d'Avray.

In 1836, when the sculptor came back from Rome, the sequestration of Marie-Gaston was closer and more unrelaxing than ever. Dorlange had too much spirit to steal or force his way into the sanctuary where Louise had sheltered her crazy passion, and Marie-Gaston was too desperately in love to break the spell and escape from Armida's garden. The friends, incredible as it must seem, never met, nor even exchanged notes. Still, on hearing of Madame Marie-Gaston's death, Dorlange forgot every slight and rushed off to Ville-d'Avray to offer what consolation he might. Vain devotion. Within two hours of the melancholy ceremony, Marie-Gaston was in a post-chaise flying south to Italy, with no thought for his friend, or a sister-in-law and two nephews, who were dependent on him. Dorlange thought this selfishness of grief rather too much to be borne; and he eradicated from his heart, as he believed, the last remembrance of a friendship which even the breath of sorrow had not revived.

My husband and I had loved Louise de Chaulieu too sincerely not to retain some feeling of affection for the man who, for three years, had been all in all to her. When leaving, Marie-Gaston had requested M. de l'Estorade to take entire charge of all his business matters, and he sent him a power of attorney to act for him in all particulars.

A few weeks since, his sorrow, still living and acute, suggested an idea to his mind. In the middle of the park at Ville-d'Avray there is a small lake, and in the middle of the lake an island which Louise was very fond of. To this island, a calm and shady retreat, Marie-Gaston wished to transfer his wife's remains, and he wrote us from Carrara to this effect. And then, remembering Dorlange, he begged my husband to call on him and inquire whether he would undertake to execute a monument. Dorlange at first affected not even to remember Marie-Gaston's name, and under a civil pretext refused the commission.

But here comes a startling instance of the strength of old association in an affectionate nature. On the evening of the day when he had shown out M. de l'Estorade, being at the opera, he overheard the Duc de Rhétoré speak slightingly of his old friend, and took the matter up with eager indignation. Hence a duel, in which he was wounded—and of which the news must certainly have reached you; so here is a man risking his life for an absentee whom he had strenuously denied in the morning.

How all this long story is directly connected with my own absurd adventure is what I would proceed to tell you if my letter were not already interminable. And, indeed, as I have called it the chapter of a novel, this, it will no doubt seem to you, is a favorable place for a break. I have, I flatter myself, excited your interest to such a pitch of curiosity as to have a right to refuse to satisfy it. To be continued, therefore, by the next post.

The Comtesse de l'Estorade to Madame Octave de Camps.

PARIS, *March* 1839.

I derived the main facts of the long biographical notice I sent you, my dear friend, from a recent letter written by M. Marie-Gaston. On hearing of the heroic devotion of which he had been the object, his first impulse was to hasten to Paris and see the friend who had made such a noble return for his faithlessness. Unluckily, the day before he should have started, a painful hindrance interfered. By a singular coincidence, while M. Dorlange was wounded in his behalf in Paris, he himself, visiting Savarezza—one of the finest marble quarries that are worked at Carrara—had a bad fall and sprained his leg. Being obliged to put off his journey, he wrote to M. Dorlange from his bed of suffering to express his gratitude.

By the same mail I also received a voluminous letter: M. Marie-Gaston, after telling me all the past history of their friendship, begged me to call on his old school-fellow and advocate his cause. In point of fact, he could not be satisfied with this convincing proof of the place he still held in M. Dorlange's affections. What he desires is to prove that, in spite of evidence to the contrary, he has never ceased to deserve it. This is a matter of some little difficulty, because he would not on any account consent to attribute the blame to the real author of the mischief. This, however, is the whole secret of his conduct to M. Dorlange. His wife was bent on having him entirely to herself, and insisted, with extraordinary perversity, on uprooting every other feeling. But nothing would persuade him to admit this, or the sort of moral mediocrity which such ill-regulated and frenzied jealousy denotes. To him Louise de Chaulieu is absolute perfection; even the most extravagant freaks of her imagination and temper were in his eyes adorable. The utmost he might concede would be that the character and the conduct of his beloved despot must not be weighed in the same scales as those of other women. He regards Louise as a glorious exception to her sex in general, and would allow that on those grounds indeed she may need explaining.

Who then better than I, from whom she had no secrets, could undertake this task? So I was requested to proceed to throw so much light as that on the matter for M. Dorlange's benefit; since if Madame Marie-Gaston's influence was justified and understood, her husband's conduct must be forgiven.

My first idea, to this end, was to write a note to his friend the sculptor and beg him to call on me. But, on second thoughts, he has hardly yet got over his wound, and besides, this kind of convocation with a definite object in view would give an absurd solemnity to my part as go-between. I thought of another plan. Anybody may visit an artist's studio: without any preliminary announcement I could call on M. Dorlange with my husband and Naïs, under pretence of reiterating the request already put to him to give us the benefit of his assistance. And by seeming to bring my feminine influence to bear on this matter, I had a bridge ready made to lead me to the true point of my visit.—Do you not approve?—and doesn't it seem to you that in this way everything was well prepared?

So, on the day after I had come to this happy conclusion, I and my escort, as proposed, found our way to a pleasant little house in the Rue de l'Ouest, behind the gardens of the Lux-embourg, one of the quietest parts of Paris. In the vestibule and passages, fragments of sculpture, bas-reliefs, and inscriptions, nicely arranged against the walls, showed the owner's good taste and betrayed his habitual interests.

We were met on the steps by a woman to whom M. de l'Estorade had already alluded. The Student from Rome, it would seem, could not come away from Italy without bringing some *souvenir*. This beautiful Italian, a sort of middle-class Galatea, sometimes housekeeper and sometimes a model, representing at once the Home and Art, fulfils in M. Dorlange's household—if scandal is to be trusted—the most perfect ideal of the "woman-of-all-work" so constantly advertised in newspapers.

At the same time, I must at once say plainly that there was absolutely nothing whatever in her appearance to lead me to imagine such a strange plurality of offices. She was gravely and rather coldly polite. Her large, velvety black eyes, somewhat tawny complexion, hair done in bands, and arranged in such broad, thick plaits as to show that it must be magnificently luxuriant, her rather large hands, well shaped and of an amber whiteness, that was conspicuous against her black dress; a very simple dress, but fitting so as to do justice to her splendid figure; and then an air of almost untamed pride pervading her whole person—the demeanor by which, as I have heard, you may always know a Roman *Trasteverina:* there you have the portrait of our guide who led us into a gallery crowded with works of art and opening into the studio.

While this handsome housekeeper announced M. le Comte and Mme. la Comtesse de l'Estorade, M. Dorlange, in a picturesque studio jacket, having his back to us, hastily drew a green baize curtain in front of the statue he was working on.

The instant he turned round, before I had had time to believe my eyes, imagine my astonishment at seeing Naïs rush up to him and almost into his arms, exclaiming with childish glee:

"Oh! you are the gentleman who saved me!"

What—the gentleman who had saved her? Why, then M. Dorlange must be that much-talked-of Unknown.

Yes, madame, and I at once saw, as Naïs did, that it was certainly he.

"Well, but if he is the Unknown, he is also the persecutor?"

Yes, madame; chance, often the most ingenious of romancers, willed that M. Dorlange should be all this; and my last letter, I fancy, must have suggested this to you, if only by the prolixity with which I enlarged on his previous history.

"And you, my dear Countess, rushing thus into his studio——?"

My dear madame, don't speak of it! Startled, trembling, red and white by turns, I must for a moment have looked an image of awkward confusion.

Happily, my husband launched at once into elaborate compliments as a happy and grateful father. I, meanwhile, had time to recover myself; and when it came to my turn to speak, I had composed my features to one of my finest expressions à l'Estorade, as you choose to call them; I then, as you know, register twenty-five degrees below zero, and should freeze the words on the lips of the most ardent adorer. I thus hoped to keep my artist friend at a distance, and hinder him if he should hope to make capital out of my stupid visit to his house. M. Dorlange himself seemed surprised rather than disconcerted by the meeting; and then, as if we were insisting on our gratitude too strongly for his modesty, to cut it short and suddenly change the subject, he began:

"Madame," said he, "since we are better acquainted than we had any reason to suppose, may I be permitted to indulge my curiosity——?"

I fancied I felt the cat's claw extended to play with the mouse, so I replied:

"Artists, if I am not mistaken, are sometimes very indiscreetly curious——"

And I emphasized my meaning with a marked severity

which I hoped would give it point. But my man was not abashed.

"I hope that will not prove to be the case with my inquiry," said he. "I only wanted to know if you have a sister?"

"Well done," thought I. "A way out of the difficulty! The game he means to play is to ascribe his persistent persecution to some fancied resemblance."

But though I should very willingly have given him that loophole in M. de l'Estorade's presence, I was not free to tell him a lie.

"No, monsieur," replied I, "I have no sister—at any rate, not to my knowledge."

And I said it with an air of superior cunning so as to make sure of not being taken for a dupe.

"At any rate," said M. Dorlange, "it was not impossible that my idea was a true one. The family, among whom I once met a lady strikingly like you, is involved in an atmosphere of mystery which allows every possible hypothesis."

"And am I indiscreet in asking their name?"

"Not in the least. They are people you may perhaps have known in Paris in 1829-30. They kept house in great style, and entertained magnificently. I met them in Italy."

"But their name?" said I, with a determination that was not prompted, I own, by any charitable motive.

"Lanty," said M. Dorlange, without any hesitation or embarrassment.

There was, in fact, a family of that name in Paris before I came to live here, and you, like me, may remember hearing some strange tales about them.

As he answered the question, the sculptor went up to the veiled statue.

"I have taken the liberty, madame, of giving you the sister you never had," he said, rather abruptly, "and I make so bold as to ask you if you do not yourself discern a family likeness?"

At the same time he pulled away the baize which hid the work, and then, my dear madame, I beheld myself, in the guise of a saint, crowned with glory. How, I ask you, could

I be angry? On seeing the startling likeness that really stared them in the face, my husband and Naïs exclaimed with admiration.

As for M. Dorlange, he proceeded without delay to explain this rather dramatic surprise.

"This statue," said he, "is a Saint Ursula, a commission from a convent in the country. In consequence of circumstances too long to relate, the features of the young lady I mentioned just now remained deeply stamped on my memory. I should have striven vainly to create, by the help of my imagination, any head that would more perfectly have represented my idea. I began, therefore, to model it from memory; but one day, madame, in the Church of St. Thomas d'Aquin, I saw you, and I was so superstitious as to believe that Providence had sent you to me as a duplicate for my benefit. From that time you were the model from which I worked; and as I could not think of asking you to come and sit to me in my studio, I availed myself, as far as possible, of every chance of meeting you. I also took particular care not to know your name or your social position: that would have been to vulgarize you, to bring you down from the ideal. If by any mischance you had happened to notice my persistency in crossing your path, you would have taken me for one of those idlers who hang about in hope of an adventure, and I was nothing worse than a conscientious artist, *prenant son bien où il le trouve,* like Molière, making the most of my chances, and trying to find inspiration in Nature alone, which always gives the best results."

"Oh, I had noticed you following us," said Naïs, with an all-knowing air.

Children! my dear madame—does any one understand them? Naïs had seen all; at the time of her accident it would have been natural that she should say something to her father or to me about this gentleman, whose constant presence had not escaped her notice—and yet, not a word. Brought up as she has been by me with such constant care, and hardly ever out of my sight, I am absolutely certain of her perfect innocence. Then it must be supposed that Nature alone can give a little girl of thirteen an instinctive knowledge of certain secrets. Is it not terrible to think of?

But husbands! my dear madame, husbands are what are so truly appalling when, at unexpected moments, we find them abandoned to a sort of blind predestination. Mine, for instance, as it seems to me, ought to have pricked up his ears as he heard this gentleman describe how he had dared to take me for his model. M. de l'Estorade is not considered a fool; on all occasions he has a strong sense of the proprieties; and if ever I should give the least cause, I believe him capable of being ridiculously jealous. And yet, seeing his *belle Renée,* as he calls me, embodied in white marble as a saint, threw him, as it seems, into such a state of admiration as altered him out of all knowledge!

He and Naïs were wholly absorbed in verifying the fidelity of the copy; that was quite my attitude, quite my eyes, my mouth, the dimples in my cheeks. In short, I found that I must take upon myself the part which M. de l'Estorade had quite forgotten, so I said very gravely to this audacious artist:

"Does it not occur to you, monsieur, that thus to appropriate without leave—in short, to put it plainly, thus to steal a stranger's features—might strike her, or him, as a rather strange proceeding?"

"Indeed, madame," replied he, very respectfully, "my fraudulent conduct would never have gone beyond the point you yourself might have sanctioned. Though my statue is doomed to be buried in a chapel for nuns, I should not have despatched it without obtaining your permission to leave it as it was. I could, when necessary, have ascertained your address; and while confessing the fascination to which I had succumbed, I should have requested you to come to see the work. Then, when you saw it, if a too exact likeness should have offended you, I would have said what I now say: with a few strokes of the chisel I will undertake to mislead the most practised eye."

Diminish the resemblance! That was no part of the programme! My husband, apparently, did not think it close enough, for at this moment he turned to M. Dorlange to say, with beatific blandness:

"Do not you think, monsieur, that Madame de l'Estorade's nose is just a little thinner?"

Thoroughly upset as I was by these unforeseen incidents, I should, I fear, have pleaded badly for M. Marie-Gaston; however, at my very first allusion to the subject:

"I know," said M. Dorlange, "all you could say in defence of the 'faithless one.' I do not forgive, but I will forget. As things have turned out, I was within an ace of being killed for his sake, and it would be really too illogical to owe him now a grudge on old scores. Still, as regards the monument at Ville-d'Avray, nothing will induce me to undertake it. As I have already explained to M. de l'Estorade, there is an obstacle in the way which grows more definite every day; I also consider it contemptible in Marie-Gaston that he should persist in chewing the cud of his grief, and I have written to him to that effect. He must show himself a man, and seek such consolation as may always be found in study and work."

The object of my visit was at an end, and for the moment I had no hope of penetrating the dark places, on which, however, I must throw some light. As I rose to leave, M. Dorlange said:

"May I hope, then, that you will not insist on any too serious disfigurement of my statue?"

"It is my husband rather than I who must answer that question. We can re-open it on another occasion, for M. de l'Estorade hopes you will do us the honor to return this call."

M. Dorlange bowed respectful acquiescence, and we came away. As he saw us to the carriage, not venturing to offer me his arm, I happened to turn round to call Naïs, who was rashly going up to a Pyrenean dog that lay in the forecourt. I then perceived the handsome housekeeper behind a window-curtain eagerly watching me. Finding herself caught in the act, she dropped the curtain with evident annoyance.

"Well," thought I, "now this woman is jealous of me! Is she afraid, I wonder, that I may become her rival, at least as a model?"

In fact, I came away in a perfectly vile temper. I was furious with Naïs and with my husband. I could have given him the benefit of a scene of which he certainly could have made neither head nor tail.

Now, what do you think of it all? Is this man one of the cleverest rogues alive, who all in a moment, to get himself out of a scrape, could invent the most plausible fiction? Or is he, indeed, an artist and nothing but an artist, who *artlessly* regarded me as the living embodiment of his ideal?—This is what I mean to find out within the next few days; for, more than ever now, I shall carry out my programme, and not later than to-morrow M. le Comte and Mme. la Comtesse de l'Estorade will have the honor of inviting M. Dorlange to dinner.

The Comtesse de l'Estorade to Madame Octave de Camps.

PARIS, *March* 1839.

DEAR MADAME,—M. Dorlange dined with us yesterday. My own notion had been to receive him *en famille,* so as to have him under my eye and catechise him at my ease. But M. de l'Estorade, to whom I did not communicate my disinterested purpose, pointed out that such an invitation, to meet nobody, might be taken amiss: M. le Comte de l'Estorade, Peer of France, might appear to regard the sculptor Dorlange as having no pretensions to mix with his society.

"We cannot treat him," my husband smilingly added, "as if he were one of our farmers' sons who came to display his sub-lieutenant's épaulette, and whom we should invite quite by himself because we could not send him to the kitchen."

So to meet our principal guest, we asked M. Joseph Bridau the painter; the Chevalier d'Espard, M. and Mme. de la Bastie, and M. de Ronquerolles. When inviting this last gentleman, my husband took care to ask him whether he would object to meeting M. de Rhétoré's adversary—for you know, no doubt, that the Duke chose for his seconds in the duel General de Montriveau and M. de Ronquerolles.

"Far from objecting," he replied, "I am delighted to seize an opportunity of improving my acquaintance with a clever man, whose conduct in the affair in which we were concerned was in all respects admirable."

And when my husband told him of the obligation we owe to M. Dorlange:

"Why, the artist is a hero!" he exclaimed. "If he goes on as he has begun, we shall not be able to reach to his knees."

In his studio, with his throat bare so as to give freedom to his head, which is a little large for his body, and dressed in a most becoming loose Oriental sort of garment, M. Dorlange was certainly better looking than in ordinary evening dress. At the same time, when he is talking with animation, his face lights up, and then his eyes seem to pour out a tide of that magnetic fluid of which I had been conscious at our previous meetings. Mme. de la Bastie was no less struck by it.

I forgot whether I told you of the object of M. Dorlange's ambition: he proposes to come forward as a candidate on the occasion of the next elections. This was his reason for declining the commission offered him by my husband as representing M. Marie-Gaston. This, which M. de l'Estorade and I had supposed to be a mere subterfuge or an empty dream, is, it would seem, a serious scheme. At dinner, being challenged by M. Joseph Bridau as to the reality of his parliamentary pretensions, M. Dorlange asserted and maintained them. As a result, almost all through the dinner, the conversation took an exclusively political turn. I expected to find our artist, if not an absolute novice, at least very moderately conversant with such matters, which hitherto must have lain quite outside his range. Not at all; on men and things, on the past and future history of party strife, he had really fresh views, evidently not borrowed from the daily cant of newspapers; and he spoke with lucidity, ease, and elegance—so much so, that, when he had left, M. de Ronquerolles and M. de l'Estorade expressed their amazement at the clear and powerful political intelligence that he had revealed to them. The admission is all the more striking because these two gentlemen, both by instinct and position, are staunch Conservatives, while M. Dorlange's proclivities tend very evidently to democratic ideas.

This quite unexpected intellectual superiority in my problematical admirer reassured me considerably. Politics, in fact, are an absorbing and dominating passion which can scarcely allow a second to flourish by its side. Nevertheless, I was bent on studying the situation to the bottom, and after dinner I insidiously drew my gentleman into one of those *tête-à-tête* chats which the mistress of a house can generally arrange. After speaking of M. Marie-Gaston, our friend in common, of my dear Louise's crazy flights, and my own constant but useless attempts to moderate them, after giving him every opportunity and facility for opening the battle, I asked him whether his Saint Ursula was to be sent off soon.

"It is quite ready to start, madame," said he. "But I wait for your permission, your *exeat;* for you to tell me, in short, whether or no I am to alter anything in the face."

"First tell me this," replied I. "Supposing I were to wish for any alteration, would such a change greatly injure the statue?"

"It probably would. However little you clip a bird's wings, it is always checked in its flight."

"One more question. Is your statue most like me or *the other* woman?"

"You, madame, I need hardly say. You are the present; she is the past."

"But to throw over the past in favor of the present is called, as you doubtless are aware, monsieur, by an ugly name. And you confess to this evil tendency with a frank readiness that is really quite startling."

"It is true that art can be brutal," said M. Dorlange, laughing. "Wherever it may find the raw material of a creation, it rushes on it with frenzy."

"Art," said I, "is a big word, under which a world of things find refuge!—The other day you told me that circumstances, too long to be related, had contributed to stamp on your mind, as a constant presence, the features of which mine are a reflection, and which have left such an impression on your memory. Was not this saying pretty plainly that it was not the sculptor alone who remembered them?"

"Indeed, madame, I had not time to explain myself more fully. And in any case, on seeing you for the first time, would you not have thought it extraordinary if I had assumed a confidential tone?——"

"But now?" said I audaciously.

"Even now, unless under very express encouragement, I should find it hard to persuade myself that anything in my past life could have a special interest for you."

"But why so? Some acquaintances ripen quickly. Your devotion to my Naïs is a long step forward in ours.—Besides," I added with affected giddiness, "I love a story beyond all things."

"Besides the fact that mine has no end, it has, even to me, remained a mystery."

"All the more reason——Between us, perhaps, we may be able to solve it."

M. Dorlange seemed to consider the matter; then, after a short silence, he said:

"It is very true; women are clever in discerning faint traces in facts or feelings where we men can detect none. But this revelation does not involve myself alone, and I must be allowed to beg that it remains absolutely between ourselves. I do not except even M. de l'Estorade; a secret ceases to exist when once it goes beyond the speaker and the recipient."

I really was desperately puzzled as to what was coming.

This last clause suggested the cautious preliminaries of a man about to trespass on another's property. However, I pursued my policy of impudence and encouragement.

"M. de l'Estorade," said I, "is so little accustomed to hear everything from me, that he never saw a single line of my correspondence with Madame Marie-Gaston."

At the same time I made a mental reservation with reference to you, my dear friend; for are you not the keeper of my conscience? And to a confessor one must confess all, if one is to be judiciously advised.

Till now M. Dorlange had been standing in front of the fireplace, while I sat at the corner. He now took a chair close to me, and by way of preamble he said:

"I spoke to you, madame, of the Lanty family——"

At this instant Mme. de la Bastie, as provoking as a shower at a picnic, came up to ask me whether I had seen Nathan's new play? Much I cared for anybody else's comedy when absorbed in this drama, in which it would seem I had played a pretty lively part! However, M. Dorlange was obliged to give up his seat by me, and it was impossible to have him to myself any more that evening.

As you see, nothing has come of all my forwardness and wiliness; no light has dawned on the matter; but in the absence of any advances from M. Dorlange, as I remember his manner, which I carefully studied, I am more and more inclined to believe in his perfect innocence.

Nor, in fact, is there anything in this interrupted tale to suggest that love played the part I had insinuated. There are plenty more ways of stamping a personality on one's memory; and if M. Dorlange did not love the woman of whom I reminded him, what grudge can he have against me who am but a sort of second edition? Nor must we overlook that very handsome housekeeper; for, granting that she is but a habit, adopted for reasons of common sense rather than a passion, the woman must still be, at any rate in some degree, a fence against me. Consequently, dear madame, all the alarms I have dinned into your ears would be ridiculous indeed; I should somewhat resemble Bélise in *Les Femmes Savantes,* who is haunted by the idea that every one who sees her must fall in love with her.

But I should be only too glad to come to this dull conclusion.

Lover or no, M. Dorlange is a man of high spirit and remarkable powers of mind; if he does not put himself out of court by any foolish aspirations, it will be an honor and a pleasure to place him on our list of friends. The service he did us predestines him to this, and I should really be sorry to seem hard on him. In that case, indeed, Naïs would quarrel with me, for she very naturally thinks everything of her rescuer.

In the evening, when he left:

"Mamma, how well M. Dorlange talks!" said she, with a most amusing air of approval.

Speaking of Naïs, this is the explanation she gives of the reserve that disturbed me so much.

"Well, mamma," said she, "I supposed that you would have seen him too. But after he stopped the horses, as you did not seem to know him, and as he is rather common-looking, I fancied he was a man——"

"A man—what do you mean?"

"Why, yes; the sort of man one takes no notice of. But how glad I was when I found that he was a gentleman! You heard me exclaim, *'Why, you are the gentleman who saved me.'*"

Though her innocence is perfect, there is in this explanation an ugly streak of pride, on which, you may be sure, I delivered a fine lecture. This distinction between the man and the gentleman is atrocious; but, on the whole, was not the child in the right? She only said with guileless crudity what even our democratic notions still allow us to carry out in practice, though they do not allow us to profess it. The famous Revolution of '89, at any rate, went so far as to establish this virtuous hypocrisy on a social footing. But here am I too drifting into politics; and if I carry my criticism any further, you will be telling me to beware, for that I am already catching it from M. Dorlange.

The Comtesse de l'Estorade to Madame Octave de Camps.

For nearly a fortnight, my dear madame, we heard no more of M. Dorlange. Not only did he not think proper to come and re-open the confidences so provokingly interrupted by Madame de la Bastie, but he did not seem aware that after dining with anybody, a card, at least, is due within a week.

Yesterday morning we were at breakfast, and I had just made a remark to this effect, without bitterness, and merely by way of conversation, when Lucas, who, as an old servant, is somewhat overbold and familiar, made some one throw open the door of the dining-room as if in triumph; and handing a note first to M. de l'Estorade, he set down in the middle of the table a mysterious object wrapped in tissue paper, which at first suggested a decorative dish of some kind.

"What in the world is that?" I asked Lucas, seeing in his face the announcement of a surprise. And I put out my hand to tear away the paper.

"Oh, madame, be careful!" cried he. "It is breakable."

My husband meanwhile had read the note, which he handed to me, saying, "M. Dorlange's apology."

This is what the artist wrote:—

"Monsieur le Comte, I fancied I could discern that Madame de l'Estorade gave me permission very reluctantly to take advantage of the audacious use I had made of my petty larceny. I have therefore bravely determined to alter my work and at the present moment hardly a likeness is discernible between 'the two sisters.' Still, I could not bear that all I had done should be lost to the world, so I had a cast taken of Saint Ursula's head before altering it, and made a reduced copy, placing it on the shoulders of a charming Countess, who is not yet canonized, thank Heaven!

"The mould was broken after the first copy was taken, and that only copy I have the honor to beg you to accept. This fact, which was only proper, gives the statuette rather more value.—Believe me, etc."

While I was reading, my husband, Lucas, Naïs, and René had been very busy extracting me from my wrappings; and behold, from a saint I had been converted into a lady of fashion, in the shape of a lovely statuette elegantly dressed. I thought that M. de l'Estorade and the two children would go crazy with admiration. The news of this wonder having spread through the house, all the servants—whom we certainly spoil—came in one after another, as if they had been invited, and each in turn exclaimed—"How like madame!" I quote only the leading theme, and do not remember every stupid variation.

I alone remained unaffected by the general enthusiasm. It seemed to me that to be the eternal subject of M. Dorlange's plastic efforts was not an enviably happy lot; and, for the reasons you know, I should have liked far better to be less frequently in his thoughts and under his chisel. As to M. de l'Estorade, after spending an hour in deciding on the place in his study where the great work would look best, he came to say:

"On my way to the Exchequer office I will look in on M. Dorlange. If he is disengaged this evening, I will ask him to dine here. Armand, whom he has not yet seen, will be at home; thus he will see all the family together, and you can express your thanks."

I did not approve of this family dinner; it seemed to me to place M. Dorlange on a footing of intimacy which this fresh civility again warned me might be dangerous. When I raised some little difficulty, M. de l'Estorade remarked:

"Why, my dear, the first time we invited him, you wanted to ask him only, which would have been extremely awkward, and now that it is perfectly suitable, you are making objections!"

To this argument, which placed me entirely in the wrong,

I could make no reply, excepting saying to myself that husbands are sometimes very clumsy.

M. Dorlange consented to join us. He may have found me a little cold in my expressions of gratitude. I even went so far as to say that I should not have asked him to alter the statue, which no doubt made him sorry he had done so, and implied that I did not particularly approve of the present he had sent us.

He also contrived to vex me on another point, on which, as you know, I am never amenable. At dinner, M. de l'Estorade reverted to the subject of the elections, disapproving more than ever of M. Dorlange as a candidate, though no longer thinking it ridiculous; this led to a political discussion. Armand, who is a very serious person, and reads the newspapers, joined in the conversation. Unlike most lads of the present day, he shares his father's opinions, that is to say, he is strongly Conservative—indeed, rather in excess of that wise moderation which is very rare, no doubt, at sixteen. He was thus tempted to contradict M. Dorlange, who, as I have told you, is a bit of a Jacobin. And really it did not appear to me that my little man's arguments were unsound or too virulently expressed.

Without being rude, M. Dorlange seemed to scorn the idea of discussing the matter with the poor boy, and he rather sharply reminded him of his school uniform; so much so, that I saw Armand ready to lose his temper and answer viciously. As he is quite well bred, I had only to give him a look, and he controlled himself; but seeing him turn crimson and shut himself up in total silence, I felt that his pride had been deeply wounded, and thought it ungenerous of M. Dorlange to have crushed him by his superiority. I know that in these days all children want to be of importance too soon, and that it does them no harm to interfere now and then and hinder them from being men of forty. But Armand really has powers of mind and reason beyond his age.

Do you want proof?

Until last year I would never part from him; he went

to the Collège Henri IV. as a day scholar. Well, it was he who, for the benefit of his studies, begged to be placed there as a boarder, since the constant to and fro inevitably interfered with his work; and to be allowed, as a favor, to shut himself up under the ferule of an usher, he exhausted more arguments, and wheedled me with more coaxing, than most boys would have used to obtain the opposite result. Thus the grown-up manner, which in many school-boys is intolerably absurd, in him is the evident result of natural precocity, and this precocity ought to be forgiven him, since it is the gift of God. M. Dorlange, owing to the misfortune of his birth, is less able than most men to enter into the feelings of boys, so, of course, he is deficient in indulgence.—But he had better be careful! This is a bad way of paying his court to me, even on the most ordinary footing of friendship.

Being so small a party, I could not, of course, revert to the history he had to tell me; but I did not think that he was particularly anxious to recur to the subject. In fact, he was less attentive to me than to Naïs, for whom he cut out black paper figures during an hour or more. It must also be said that Madame de Rastignac came in the way, and that I had to give myself up to her visit. While I was talking to her by the fire, M. Dorlange, at the other end of the room, was making Naïs and René stand for their portraits, and they presently came exultant to show me their profiles, wonderfully like, snipped out with the scissors.

"Do you know," said Naïs in a whisper, "M. Dorlange says he will make a bust of me in marble?"

All this struck me as in rather bad taste. I do not like to see artists who, when admitted to a drawing-room, still carry on the business, as it were. They thus justify the aristocratic arrogance which sometimes refuses to think them worthy to be received for their own sake.

M. Dorlange went away early; and M. de l'Estorade got on my nerves, as he has done so many times in his life, when he insisted on showing out his guest, who had tried to steal away unperceived, and I heard him desire him to repeat his visits less rarely, that I was always at home in the evening.

The result of this family dinner has been civil war among the children. Naïs lauding her dear deliverer to the skies, in which she is supported by René, who is completely won over by a splendid lancer on horseback, cut out for him by M. Dorlange. Armand, on the contrary, says he is ugly, which is indisputable; he declares he is just like the portraits of Danton in the illustrated history of the Revolution, and there is some truth in it. He also says that in the statuette he has made me look like a milliner's apprentice, which is not true at all. Hence endless squabbles among the dear creatures. Only just now I was obliged to interfere and tell them that I was tired of hearing of their M. Dorlange.

Will you not say the same of me, dear madame, when I have written so much about him and told you nothing definite after all?

Dorlange to Marie-Gaston.

PARIS, *April* 1839.

Why do I give up my art, and what do I expect to find in that "galley" called politics?

That is what comes, my dear fond lover, of shutting yourself up for years in conventual matrimony. The world, meanwhile, has gone on. Life has brought fresh combinations to those whom you shut out, and the less you know of them, the readier you are to blame those you have forgotten. Every one is clever at patching other folks' affairs.

You must know then, my inquisitive friend, that it was not of my own accord that I took the step for which you would call me to account. My unforeseen appearance in the electoral breach was in obedience to the desire of a very high personage. A father has at last allowed a gleam of light to shine in the eternal darkness; he has three parts revealed himself; and, if I may trust appearances, he fills a place in society that might satisfy the most exacting conceit. And, to be in keeping with the usual current of my life, this revelation was involved in circumstances singular and romantic enough to deserve telling in some detail.

Since for two years past you have been living in Italy and visiting the most interesting cities, I believe I need hardly tell you that the Café *Greco* is the general haunt of the art pupils from the Paris schools, and the artists of every nationality who are staying in Rome.

In Paris, Rue du Coq-Saint-Honoré, there is remote equivalent for this institution in a café that has long been known as the *Café des Arts.* I spend the evening there two or three times a week, and meet there several Roman students, my contemporaries. They have made me acquainted with some journalists and men of letters, agreeable and superior men, with whom it is both pleasant and profitable to exchange ideas. There is a particular corner where we congregate, and where every question of a serious character is discussed and thrashed out; but, as having the most living interests, politics especially give rise to the most impassioned arguments. In our little club democratic views predominate; they are represented in the most diverse shades, including the Utopia or phalanstery of workers. This will show you that the proceedings of the Government are often severely handled, and that unlimited freedom of language characterizes our verdicts.

Rather more than a year ago the waiter—the only waiter who is allowed the honor of supplying our wants—took me aside one day, having, as he declared, a communication of importance to make.

"You are watched by the police, sir," said he, "and you will be wise not to talk always open-mouthed like St. Paul."

"By the police, my good fellow! Why, what on earth can it find to watch? All I can say, and a great deal more, is printed every morning in the newspapers."

"That has nothing to do with it. They have an eye on you. I have seen it. There is a little old man who takes a great deal of snuff, and who always sits where he can hear you. When you are speaking he listens much more attentively than to any of the others, and I even caught him once writing something in his pocket-book in signs that were not the alphabet."

"Very good; the next time he comes, show him to me."

The next time was no further off than the morrow.

The man pointed out was small and gray-haired, untidy in his appearaance, and his face, deeply marked by the small-pox, was, I thought, that of a man of fifty. And he certainly very often took a pinch out of a large snuff-box, and seemed to honor my remarks with a degree of attention which I could, as I chose, regard as highly complimentary or extremely impertinent. But of the two alternatives I was inclined to the more charitable by the air of honesty and mildness that pervaded this supposed emissary of the police. When I remarked on this reassuring aspect to the waiter, who flattered himself that he had scented out a secret agent:

"Oh yes, indeed!" said he. "Those are the sweet manners they always put on to hide their game."

Two days after, one Sunday, at the hour of vespers, in the course of one of those long walks all across Paris, which you know I always loved, mere chance led me into the Church of Saint-Louis en l'Ile, the parish church of that God-forsaken quarter. The building is not particularly interesting, in spite of what some historians have said, and, following them, every *Stranger's Guide to Paris.* I should only have walked through it, but that the wonderful talent of the organist who was playing the service irresistibly held me. When I tell you that the performer came up to my ideal, you will know that is high praise; for you will, I daresay, remember that I draw a distinction between organ players and organists—a rank of the superior nobility to whom I grant the title only on the highest grounds.

When the service was over, I was curious to see the face of so remarkable an artist buried in such a corner. I took my stand at the door from the organ loft to be close to the player as he came out. I could have done no more for a crowned head! But are not great artists, after all, the real kings by divine right? Imagine my amazement when, after waiting a few minutes, instead of a perfectly strange face, I saw a man whom I at once vaguely recognized, and knew at

a second glance for my watchful listener of the *Café des Arts.*
Nor was this all: at his heels came a sort of spoilt attempt
at humanity; and in this misshapen failure, with crooked
legs and a thicket of unkempt hair, I discerned our old
quarterly providence, my banker, my money-carrier—in short,
our respected friend the mysterious dwarf.

I, you may be sure, did not escape his sharp eye, and I
saw him eagerly pointing me out to the organist. He instinctively, and not probably calculating all that would come
of it, turned quickly to look at me, and then, taking no further
notice of me, went on his way. The dwarf, meanwhile—whom
I might recognize as his master's servant by this single detail
—went familiarly up to the man who distributed holy water
and offered him a pinch of snuff; then he hobbled away,
never looking at me again, and vanished through a door in a
corner under one of the side aisles.

The care this man had taken to point me out to the organist was a revelation. The *Maestro* was evidently fully informed as to the strange means by which my allowance used
to reach me, and it had been regularly handed over to me
after my return from Rome, till I was placed above want by
receiving some commissions. It was not less probable that
the man who knew about this financial mystery was the de-
pository of other secrets; and I was all the more eager to
extract from him some explanation because, as I am now living
on the fruit of my own exertions, I had no fear of finding
my curiosity punished by the stoppage of supplies that had
formerly been threatened.

I acted on the spur of the moment and rushed after the
organist. By the time I had got out of the church door, he
was out of sight, but chance favored me and led me in the
direction he had taken; as I came out on the Quai de Béthune,
I saw him in the distance knocking at a door.

I boldly followed and said to the gate porter:
"Is the organist of Saint-Louis en l'Ile within?"
"M. Jacques Bricheteau?"
"Yes, M. Jacques Bricheteau; he lives here, I think?"

"On the fourth floor above the *entresol,* the door on the left. He has just come in; you may catch him up on the stairs."

Run as fast as I could, by the time I reached my man his key was in the lock.

"M. Jacques Bricheteau?" I hastily exclaimed. "I have the honor, I think——?"

"I know no such person," said he coolly, as he turned the key.

"I may be mistaken in the name; but M. the organist of Saint-Louis en l'Ile?"

"I never heard of any organist living in this house."

"I beg your pardon, monsieur: there certainly is, for the concierge has just told me so. Besides, you are undoubtedly the gentleman I saw coming out of the organ loft, accompanied by a man—I may say——"

But before I had finished speaking, this strange individual had balked me of his company and shut his door in my face.

For a moment I wondered whether I had been mistaken; but, on reflection, mistake was impossible. Had not this man already, and for years, proved his extravagant secretiveness? It was he certainly who persistently refused to have anything to say to me, and not I who had blundered. I proceeded to pull his bell with some energy, quite determined to persist till I knew the reason of this fixed purpose of ignoring me. For some little time the besieged party put up with the turmoil I was making; but I suddenly remarked that the bell had ceased to sound. It had evidently been muffled; the obstinate foe would not come to the door, and the only way of getting at him would be to beat it in. That, however, is not thought mannerly.

I went down again to the door-porter and told him of my failure, without saying anything about the reasons that had led to it; and I so far invited his confidence that I extracted some information concerning the impenetrable M. Jacques Bricheteau. But though it was given with all desirable willingness, it threw no light whatever on the situation.—M. Bricheteau was a quiet resident, polite but not communicative; punctual in paying his rent, but not in easy circumstances, for he kept no servant—not even a maid to clean for him, and he never took a meal at home. He was always out by ten in the morning, and never came in till the evening, and was probably a clerk in an office, or perhaps a music master giving lessons.

Only one fact in this heap of vague and useless information seemed to be of the slightest interest. For some months past M. Jacques Bricheteau had pretty frequently been the recipient of heavy letters, which, to judge by the cost of postage, were no doubt from some distant country; but, with the best will in the world, the worthy porter had never been able to decipher the postmark, and at any rate the name, which he had but guessed at, had quite escaped his memory; so for the moment this observation, which might have been of some use, was absolutely valueless.

On my return home I persuaded myself that a pathetic epistle addressed to my recalcitrant friend would induce him to admit me. Seasoning my urgent supplication with a spice of intimidation, I gave him to understand that I was immovably bent on penetrating, at any cost, the mystery of my birth, of which he seemed to be fully informed. Now that I had some clue to the secret, it would be his part to consider whether my desperate efforts, blindly rushing against the dark unknown, might not entail much greater trouble than the frank explanation I begged him to favor me with.

My ultimatum thus formulated, to the end that it should reach the hands of M. Jacques Bricheteau as soon as possible, on the following morning, before nine, I arrived at the door. But, in a frenzy of secrecy—unless he has some really inexplicable reason for avoiding me—at daybreak that morning, after paying the rent for the current term and for a term's notice, the organist had packed off his furniture; and it is to be supposed that the men employed in this sudden flitting were handsomely bribed for their silence, since the concierge

could not discover the name of the street whither his lodger
was moving. The men did not belong to the neighborhood,
so there was not a chance of unearthing them and paying
them to speak. The man, whose curiosity was at least as
eager as my own, had, to be sure, thought of a simple plan
for gratifying it. This, not indeed a very creditable one,
was to follow the van in which the musician's household goods
were packed. But the confounded fellow was prepared for
everything: he kept an eye on the over-zealous porter, and
remained on sentry duty in front of the house till his cargo
was too far on its way for any risk of pursuit.

Still, and in spite of the obstinacy and cleverness of this
unattainable antagonist, I would not be beaten. I felt there
was still a connecting thread between us in the organ of
Saint-Louis'; so on the following Sunday, before the end of
High Mass, I took up a post at the door of the organ loft,
fully determined not to let the sphinx go till I had made it
speak.—Here was a fresh disappointment: M. Jacques
Bricheteau was represented by one of his pupils, and for
three Sundays in succession it was the same. On the fourth
I ventured to speak to the substitute and ask him if the
maestro were ill.

"No, monsieur. M. Bricheteau is taking a holiday; he
will be absent for some time, and is away on business."

"Where then can I write to him?"

"I do not exactly know. Still, I suppose that you can
write to his lodgings, close at hand, Quai de Béthune."

"But he has moved. Did you not know?"

"No. Indeed! and where is he now living?"

I was out of luck—asking for information from a man
who, when I questioned him, questioned me. And as if to
drive me fairly beside myself, while investigating matters
under such hopeful conditions, I saw in the distance that confounded deaf and dumb dwarf, who positively laughed as he
looked at me.

Happily for my impatience and curiosity, which were enhanced by every defeat, and rising by degrees to an almost

intolerable pitch, daylight presently dawned. A few days after this last false scent, a letter reached me; and I, a better scholar than the concierge of the Quai de Béthune, at once saw that the postmark was Stockholm, Sweden, which did not excessively astonish me. When in Rome, I had the honor of being kindly received by Thorwaldsen, the great sculptor, and I had met many of his fellow-countrymen in his studio—some commission perhaps, for which he had recommended me—so imagine my surprise and emotion when, on opening it, the first words I read were:

"Monsieur mon fils."

The letter was long, and I had not patience enough to read it through before looking to see whose name I bore. So I turned at once to the signature. This beginning, *Monsieur mon fils,* which we often find in history as used by kings when addressing their scions, must surely promise aristocratic parentage!—My disappointment was great: there was no signature.

"Monsieur mon fils," my anonymous father wrote, "I cannot regret that your inveterate determination to solve the secret of your birth should have compelled the man who watched over your youth to come here and confer with me as to the steps to which we should be compelled by this dangerous and turbulent curiosity. I have for a long time cherished an idea which has now come to maturity, and it has been far more satisfactorily discussed in speech than it could have been by correspondence.

"Being obliged to leave France almost immediately after your birth, which cost your mother her life, I made a large fortune in a foreign land, and I now fill a high position in the Government of this country. I foresee a time when I may be free to give you my name, and at the same time to secure for you the reversion of the post I hold. But, to rise so high as this, the celebrity which, with my permission, you promise to achieve in Art would not be a sufficient recommendation. I therefore wish you to enter on a political career; and in that career, under the existing conditions in France, there are not two ways of distinguishing yourself —you must be elected a member of the Chamber. You are not yet, I know, of the required age, and you have not the necessary qualifications. But you will be thirty next year, and that is just long enough to enable you to become a landed proprietor and prove your possession for more than a twelve-month. On the day after receiving this you may call on the Brothers Mongenod, bankers, Rue de la Victoire; they will pay you a sum of two hundred and fifty thousand francs. This you must at once invest in the purchase of a house, and devote any surplus to the support of some newspaper which, in due course, will advocate your election—after another out-lay is met which I shall presently explain.

"Your aptitude for politics is vouched for by the friend who has watched over you in your deserted existence, with a zeal and disinterestedness that I can never repay. He has for some time followed you and listened to you, and he is con-vinced that you would make a creditable appearance in the Chamber. Your opinions—Liberal, and at once moderate and enthusiastic—meet my views, and you have, unconsciously, hitherto played into my hand very successfully.

"I cannot at present reveal to you the place of your proba-ble election. It is being prepared with a deep secrecy and skill which will be successful in proportion as they are wrapped in silence and darkness. However, your success may be, perhaps, partly insured by your carrying out a work which I commend to your notice, advising you to accept its apparent singularity without demur or comment. For the present you must still be a sculptor, and you are to employ the talent of which you have given evidence in the execution of a statue of Saint Ursula.—The subject does not lack poetry or in-terest; Saint Ursula, virgin and martyr, was, it is generally believed, the daughter of a prince of Great Britain. She was martyred in the fifth century at Cologne, where she had founded a convent of maidens known to popular supersti-tion as the Eleven Thousand Virgins. She was subsequently taken as the patron saint of the Ursuline Sisters who adopted her name; also of the famous House of the Sorbonne.

"An artist so clever as you are, may, it seems to me, make something of all these facts.

"Without knowing the name of the place you are to represent, it is desirable that you should at once make due profession of your political tendencies and proclaim your intention of standing for election. At the same time, I cannot too earnestly impress on you the need for secrecy as to this communication, and for patience in your present position. Leave my agent in peace, I beg of you, and setting aside a curiosity which, I warn you, will involve you in the greatest disasters, await the slow and quiet development of the splendid future that lies before you. By not choosing to conform to my arrangements, you will deprive yourself of every chance of being initiated into the mystery you are so eager to solve. However, I will not even suppose that you can rebel; I would rather believe in your perfect deference to the wishes of a father who feels that the happiest day of his life will be that when he is at last able to make himself known to you.

"*P.S.*—As your statue is intended for the chapel of an Ursuline convent, it must be in white marble. The height of the figure is to be 1.706 metre, or in other words, five feet three inches. As it will not stand in a niche, it must be equally well finished on all sides. The cost to be defrayed out of the two hundred and fifty thousand francs advised by the present letter."

The present letter left me cold and unsatisfied; it bereft me of a hope I had long cherished—that of some day knowing a mother as kind as yours, of whose adorable sweetness you often told me, my dear friend. This was, after all, no better than twilight in the thick fog of my life; it did not even tell me whether I had been born in wedlock or no. And it also struck me that, as addressed to a man of my age, there was a very imperious and despotic tone in the paternal instructions. Was it not a strange act to turn my life upside down

—just as, at school, we were made to wear our coats inside
out as a punishment? My first instinct was to address to
myself all the arguments that you or any other friend might
have found to deny my political vocation.

However, curiosity took me to the bankers; and on finding
at Messrs. Mongenod's, in hard and ready cash, the two hundred and fifty thousand francs promised me, I confess I
reasoned differently. It struck me that the determination
which began by advancing so large a sum must in fact be
serious; since that power knew all, and I knew nothing, it
seemed to me unreasonable and inopportune to attempt to
struggle. After all, had I any special dislike to the path
pointed out to me? No. Political matters have always interested me up to a certain point; and if my attempt to be
elected came to nothing, I could come back to my art, not
more ridiculous than a hundred other still-born ambitions
that see the light under every new administration.

I bought the house, I took shares in the *National,* and I
found ample encouragement in my political schemes, as well
as the certainty of a keen contest whenever I should reveal the
name of the place I meant to stand for—hitherto I have had
no difficulty in keeping that secret.

I also executed the "Saint Ursula," and I am now waiting
for further instructions, which certainly seem to me to be a
long time coming, now that I have loudly proclaimed my ambitions and that the stir of a general election is in the air—
a fight to which I am by no means equal. To obey the instructions of paternal caution I need not, I know, ask you
to be absolutely secret about all I confide to you. Reserve is
a virtue which I know you to have brought to such perfection
that I need not preach it to you. But I am wrong, my dear
friend, to allow myself any such malicious allusions to the
past, for at this moment I am under greater obligations to you
than you fancy. Partly out of interest in me, no doubt, and
to a great extent out of a very general aversion for your
brother-in-law's arrogance, when I was wounded, the democratic party came in a body to inquire for me, and the talk

about this duel, which has really helped to make me famous, has no doubt greatly improved my chances of election. So a truce to your perpetual thanks—do you not see that I have to thank you?

Dorlange to Marie-Gaston.

PARIS, *April* 1839.

MY DEAR FRIEND,—I am still playing my part as best I may of a candidate without a constituency. My friends are puzzled, and I must confess that I am worried, for there are but a few weeks now till the general election; and if all these mysterious preparations end in smoke, a pretty figure I shall cut in the eyes of M. Bixiou, whose spiteful comments you reported to me not long ago. Still, one thought supports me: It seems hardly likely that anybody should sow two hundred and fifty thousand francs in my furrow without the definite purpose of gathering some sort of crop. Possibly, indeed, if I could see the thing more clearly, this absence of hurry on the part of those who are working for me in such a deliberate and underground manner may, in fact, be the result of perfect confidence in my success. Be this as it may, I am being kept, in consequence, in a state of idle expectancy that is a burden to me; riding a-straddle, as it were, on two lives, one on which I have as yet no foothold, and one from which I am not yet quite free; I have not the spirit to start on any new work, and feel uncommonly like a traveler who has come much too early for his coach and does not know what to do with himself or where to pass the spare time.

You will not, I believe, be sorry that I should turn this *far niente* to account in favor of our correspondence; and, now I think of it, I will recur to two passages in your last letter to which at first I was not inclined to pay any particular attention. For one thing, you warned me that my political pretensions found no favor with M. Bixiou; and for another, you insinuated that I might find myself falling in love with Mme. de l'Estorade, if I had not done so already. First as to the Great Disapprobation of M. Bixiou—we used to say the Great Treason of M. de Mirabeau.

In one word I will paint the man—M. Bixiou is envious.
There was in him unquestionably the making of a great artist;
but in the economy of his individuality the stomach has killed
the heart and head, and by sheer subjection to sensuous appe-
tite he is now for ever doomed to remain no more than a caricaturist, a man, that is to say, who lives from hand to mouth,
discounts his talent in frittered work, real penal servitude
which enables the man to live jovially, but brings him no
consideration, and promises him no future; a man whose
talent is a mere feeble abortion; his mind as much as his face
is stamped with the perpetual, hopeless grimace which human
instinct has always ascribed to the fallen angels. And just
as the Prince of Darkness attacks by preference the greatest
saints, as reminding him most sternly of the angelic heights
from which he fell, so M. Bixiou sheds his venom on every
talent and every character in whose strength, and spirit, and
purpose he feels the brave resolve not to waste itself as his
has been wasted. But there is one thing which may reassure
you as to the outcome of his slander and his abuse—for from
M. de l'Estorade's report to you I perceive that he indulges
in both: namely, at the very time when he fancies he is most
successfully occupied in a sort of burlesque autopsy of my person, he is but a plastic puppet in my hands, a jumping-jack of
which I hold the string, and into whose mouth I can put what
words I please.

Feeling sure that a little advertisement should prepare the
way for my appearance as a statesman, I looked about me
for some public criers, deep-mouthed, as Mme. Pernelle would
say, and well able to give tongue. If among blatant trumpeters I could have found one more shrill, more deafeningly
persistent than the great Bixiou, I would have preferred him.
I took advantage of the malignant inquisitiveness that takes
that amiable pest into every studio in turn, to fill himself up
with information. I told him everything, of my good luck,
of the two hundred and fifty thousand francs, ascribing them
to a lucky turn on 'Change, of all my parliamentary schemes,
to the very number of the house I had purchased. And I am

much mistaken if that number is not written down somewhere in his notebook.

This, I fancy, is enough to reduce the admiration of his audience at the Montcornets', and prove that this formidable magpie is not quite so miraculously informed on all points.

As to my political horoscope, which he condescended to cast, I cannot say that his astrology, strictly speaking, is far from the truth. It is quite certain that by announcing my intention of never attempting to keep step with other men's opinions I shall attain to the position so clearly set forth by a pleader worthy to be the successor of M. de la Palisse: "What do you do, gentlemen, to a man whom you place in solitary confinement? You isolate him." Isolation, in fact, must at first be my lot; and the life of an artist, a solitary life, in which a man spins everything out of himself, has predisposed me to accept the situation. And if I find myself in consequence—especially as a beginner—exempt from all lobby and backstairs influences, this may do me good service as a speaker; for I shall be able to express myself with unbiased strength and freedom. Never being bound by any pledge, by any trumpery party interest, there will be nothing to hinder me from being myself, or from expressing in their sacred crudity any ideas I think wholesome and true.

I know full well that in the face of an assembled multitude these poor truths for truth's sake do not always get their chance of becoming infectious, or even of being respectfully welcomed. But have you not observed that by knowing how to snatch an opportunity we sometimes hit on a day which seems to be a sort of festival of sense and intelligence, when the right thing triumphs almost without an effort? On those days, in spite of the utmost prejudice in the hearers, the speaker's honesty makes them generous and sympathetic, at any rate for the moment, with all that is upright, true, and magnanimous. At the same time, I do not deceive myself; though this system of mine may win me some consideration and notoriety as an orator, it is of very little avail in the pursuit of office, nor will it gain me the reputation as a practical

man for which it is now the fashion to sacrifice so much. But
if my influence at arm's length should be inconsiderable, I
shall be heard at a distance, because I shall, for the most part,
speak out of the window—outside the narrow and suffocating
atmosphere of parliamentary life, and over the head of its
petty passions and mean interests.

This kind of success will be all I need for the purposes my
benevolent parent seems to have in view. What he appears
to aim at is that I should make a noise and be heard afar; and
from that side, political life has, I declare, its artistic aspect
which will not too monstrously jar with my past life.

Now, to come to another matter—that of my actual or
possible passion for Mme. de l'Estorade. This is your very
judicial epitome of the case:—In 1837, when you set out for
Italy, Mme. de l'Estorade was still in the bloom of her beauty.
Leading a life so calm, so sheltered from passion as hers has
always been, it is probable that the lapse of two years has left
no deep marks on her; and the proof that time has stood still
for that privileged beauty you find in my strange and audacious persistency in deriving inspiration from it. Hence, if
the mischief is not already done, at any rate you will give me
warning; there is but one step from the artist's admiration
to the man's, and the story of Pygmalion is commended to my
prudent meditation.

In the first place, most sapient and learned mythologist,
I may make this observation: The person principally interested in the matter, who is on the spot and in a far better
position than you to estimate the perils of the situation, has
no anxiety on the subject. M. de l'Estorade's only complaint
is that my visits are not more frequent, and my reticence is,
in his eyes, pure bad manners.—"To be sure!" you exclaim,
"a husband—any husband—is the last to suspect that his wife
is being made love to!"—So be it. But what about Mme. de
l'Estorade, with her high reputation for virtue, and the cold,
almost calculating reasonableness which she so often brought
to bear on the ardent and impassioned petulance of another
lady known to you? And will you not also allow that the

love of her children, carried to the last degree of fervor, I had almost said fanaticism, that we see in women, must in her be an infallible protection? So far, and for her, well and good.

But it is not her peace of mind, but mine, that concerns your friendship; for if Pygmalion had failed to animate his statue, much good his love would have done him! I might, in reply to your charitable solicitude, refer you to my principles—though the word and the thing alike are completely out of fashion—to a certain very absurd respect that I have always professed for conjugal fidelity, to the very natural obstacle to all such levity of fancy raised in my mind by the serious responsibilities on which I am embarking. And I might also say that, though not indeed by the superiority of my genius, at least by every tendency of mind and character, I am one of that earnest and serious school of a past time who, regarding Art as long, and Life as short—*Ars longa et vita brevis*—did not waste their time and their creative powers in silly, dull intrigues.

But I can do better still. Since M. de l'Estorade has spared you no detail of the really romantic circumstances under which his wife and I met, you know that it was a reminiscence which made me follow the steps of such a beautiful model. Well, that memory, while it attracted me in one sense to the fair Countess, is the very thing of all others to keep me at a distance. This, of course, seems to you very elaborate and enigmatical. But, patience—and I will explain. If you had not thought proper to cut the thread which for so many years connected our lives, I should not at this day have so much to work over again; since, however, you have made it necessary that I should pay up arrears, you must, my dear fellow, make the best of my long stories, and be a patient listener.

In 1835, the last year I spent in Rome, I was on terms of considerable intimacy with a French Academy student named Desroziers. He was a musician, a man of distinguished and observant mind, who would probably have made a mark in his art if he had not been carried off by typhoid fever the year after I left.

One day when we had taken it into our heads that we would travel as far as Sicily, an excursion allowed by the rules of the Academy, we found ourselves absolutely penniless, and we were wandering about the streets of Rome considering by what means we could repair the damage to our finances, when we happened to pass by the Braschi palace. The doors stood wide open, admitting an ebb and flow of people of all classes in an endless tide.

"By the Mass!" cried Desroziers, "this is the very thing for us!"

And without any explanation as to whither he was leading me, we followed in the stream and made our way into the palace.

After going up a magnificent marble staircase, and through a long suite of rooms, poorly enough furnished—as is usual in Roman palaces, where all the luxury consists in fine ceilings, pictures, statues, and other works of art—we found ourselves in a room hung with black and lighted with many tapers. It was, as you will have understood, a body lying in state. In the middle, on a raised bed covered with a canopy, lay the most hideous and grotesque *thing* you can conceive of. Imagine a little old man, with a face and hands withered to such a state of desiccation that a mummy by comparison would seem fat and well-looking. Dressed in black satin breeches, a violet velvet coat of fashionable cut, a white waistcoat embroidered with gold, and a full shirt frill of English point lace, this skeleton's cheeks were thickly coated with rouge, which enhanced the parchment yellow of the rest of the skin; and crowning a fair wig, tightly curled, it had a huge hat and feathers tilted knowingly over one ear, and making the most reverent spectator laugh in spite of himself. After glancing at this ridiculous and pitiable exhibition, the indispensable preliminary to a funeral according to the aristocratic etiquette of Rome:

"There you see the end," said Desroziers. "Now, come and look at the beginning."

So saying, and paying no heed to my questions, because he

wanted to give me a dramatic surprise, he led me off to the
Albani gallery, and placing me in front of a statue of Adonis
reclining on a lion's skin:

· "What do you think of that?" said he.

"That!" cried I at a first glance; "it is as fine as an antique."

"It is as much an antique as I am," replied Desroziers,
and he pointed to a signature on the plinth: *"Sarrasine,
1758."*

"Antique or modern, it is a masterpiece," I said, when I
had studied this delightful work from all sides. "But how are
this fine statue and the terrible caricature you took me to see
just now to help us on our way to Sicily?"

"In your place, I should have begun by asking who and
what was Sarrasine."

"That was unnecessary," replied I. "I had already heard
of this statue. I had forgotten it again, because when I came
to see it the Albani gallery was closed for repairs—as they
say of the theatres. Sarrasine, I was informed, was a pupil
of Bouchardon's, and, like us, a pensioner on the King of
Rome, where he died within six months of his arrival."

"But who or what caused his death?"

"Some illness probably," replied I, never dreaming that my
reply was prophetic of the end of the man I was addressing.

"Not a bit of it," said Desroziers. "Artists don't die in such
an idiotic way."

And he gave me the following details.

Sarrasine, a youth of genius, but of ungovernable passions,
almost as soon as he arrived in Rome, fell madly in love
with the principal soprano at the *Argentina,* whose name
was Zambinella. At that time the Pope would not allow
women to appear on the stage in Rome. The difficulty was
overcome by means well known, and imported from the East.
Sarrasine, in his fury at finding his love thus cheated, having
already executed an imaginary statue of this imaginary mistress, was on the point of killing himself. But the singer
was under the protection of a great personage, who, to be be-

forehand with him, had cooled the sculptor's blood by a few pricks of the stiletto. Zambinella had not approved of this violence, but nevertheless continued to sing at the *Argentina* and on every stage in Europe, amassing a splendid fortune.

When too old to remain on the stage, the singer shrank into a little old man, very vain, very shy, but as wilful and capricious as a woman. All the affection of which he was capable he bestowed on a wonderfully beautiful niece, whom he placed at the head of his household. She was the Madame Denis of this strange Voltaire, and he intended that she should inherit his vast wealth. The handsome heiress, in love with a Frenchman named the Comte de Lanty, who was supposed to be a highly skilled chemist, though, in fact, little was known of his antecedents, had great difficulty in obtaining her uncle's consent to her marriage with the man of her choice. And when, weary of disputing the matter, he gave in, it was on condition of not parting from his niece. The better to secure the fulfilment of the bargain, he gave her nothing on her marriage, parting with none of his fortune, which he spent liberally on all who were about him.

Bored wherever he found himself, and driven by a perpetual longing for change, the fantastic old man had at different times taken up his abode in the remotest parts of the world, always dragging at his heels the family party whose respect and attachment he had secured at least for life.

In 1829, when he was nearly a hundred years old, and had sunk into a sort of imbecility—though still keenly alive when he listened to music—a question of some interest to the Lantys and their two children brought them to settle in a splendid house in the Faubourg Saint-Honoré. They there received all Paris. The world was attracted by the still splendid beauty of Madame de Lanty, the innocent charm of her daughter Marianina, the really royal magnificence of their entertainments, and a peculiar flavor of mystery in the atmosphere about these remarkable strangers. With regard to the old man particularly, comments were endless; he was the object of so much care and consideration, but at the same time so like a petted captive, stealing out like a spectre into the midst of the parties, from which such obvious efforts were made to keep him away, while he seemed to find malicious enjoyment in scaring the company, like an apparition.

The gunshots of July 1830 put this phantom to flight. On leaving Paris, to the great annoyance of the Lantys, he insisted on returning to Rome, his native city, where his presence had revived the humiliating memories of the past. But Rome was his last earthly stage; he had just died there, and it was he whom we had seen so absurdly dressed out and lying in state in the Braschi palace—he also on whom we now looked, in all his youthful beauty, in the Albani collection.

These details, given me by Desroziers, were no doubt curious, and a more dramatic contrast was, in truth, inconceivable; still, how would it help us visit Sicily? That was the question.

"You have skill enough to make a copy of this statue, I suppose?" said Desroziers.

"At any rate, I like to think so."

"Well, I am sure of it. Get leave from the curator, and set to work forthwith. I know of a purchaser for such a copy."

"Why, who will buy it?"

"The Comte de Lanty, to be sure. I am giving his daughter lessons in harmony; and when I mention in his house that I know of a fine copy of this Adonis, they will never rest till it belongs to them."

"But does not this savor somewhat of extortion?"

"Not in the least. Some time since the Lantys had a painting done of it by Vien, as they could not purchase the marble; the Albani gallery would not part with it at any price. Various attempts have been made at reproducing it in sculpture, but all have failed. You have only to succeed, and you will be paid enough for forty trips to Sicily, for you will have gratified a whim which has become hopeless, and which, when the price is paid, will still think itself your debtor."

Two days later I had begun the work; and as it was quite
to my mind, I went on so steadily that, three weeks later, the
Lanty family, all in deep mourning, invaded my studio, under
Desroziers' guidance, to inspect a sketch in a forward stage of
completion. M. de Lanty seemed to know what he was about,
and he declared himself satisfied. Marianina, who, as her
grand-uncle's favorite, had been especially benefited under his
will, seemed delighted with what I had done.

Marianina was at that time one-and-twenty. I need not
describe her, since you know Mme. de l'Estorade, whom she
strikingly resembles. This charming girl, already an accomplished musician, had a remarkable talent for every form
of art. Coming from time to time to my studio to follow the
progress of my work—which, after all, was never finished, as
it happened—she, like Princess Marguerite d'Orleans, took
a fancy for sculpture, and until the family left Rome—some
months before I had come away—Mlle. de Lanty came to me
for lessons. Nothing could be further from my thoughts
than any idea of playing the part of Abélard or Saint-Preux,
but I may say I was most happy in my teaching. My pupil
was so intelligent, and so apt to profit by the slightest hint;
she had at once such a bright temper and such ripe judgment;
her voice, when she sang, went so straight to the heart; and I
heard so constantly from the servants, who adored her, of her
noble, generous, and charitable actions, that, but for my
knowing of her vast fortune, which kept me at a distance, I
might have run into the danger you are warning me to avoid
now.

Marianina on her part found my teaching luminous. I was
ere long received in the house on a somewhat familiar footing,
and I could easily see that my beautiful pupil took some
pleasure in my conversation. When the question arose of
the whole family returning to live in Paris, she suddenly
discovered that Rome was a delightful residence, and expressed real regret at leaving; nay, Heaven forgive me if,
when we parted, there was not the glitter of a tear in her eye.

On my return to Paris, my first visit was to the Hôtel
Lanty.

Marianina was too well bred, and too sweet by nature, ever to make herself disagreeable or to be scornful; but I at once perceived that a singularly cold reserve had taken the place of the gracious and friendly freedom of her manner. It struck me as probable that the liking she had shown me—not, indeed, for my person, but for my mind and conversation—had been commented on by her family. She had no doubt been lectured, and she seemed to me to be acting under strict orders, as I could easily conclude from the distant and repellent manner of M. and Mme. de Lanty.

A few months later, at the Salon of 1837, I fancied I saw a corroboration of my suspicions. I had exhibited a statue which made some sensation; there was always a mob round my Pandora. Mingling with the crowd I used to stand *incognito,* to enjoy my success and gather my laurels fresh. One Friday, the fashionable day, I saw from afar the approach of the Lanty family. The mother was on the arm of a well-known "buck," Comte Maxime de Trailles; Marianina was with her brother; M. de Lanty, who looked anxious, as usual, was alone; and, like the man in the song of Malbrouck, *"ne portait rien,"* carried nothing. By a crafty manœuvre, while the party were pushing their way through the crowd, I slipped behind them so as to hear what they thought, without being seen. *Nil admirari*—think nothing fine—is the natural instinct of every man of fashion; so, after a summary inspection of my work, M. de Trailles began to discover the most atrocious faults, and his verdict was pronounced in a loud and distinct voice, so that his dictum could not be lost on anybody for some little distance round. Marianina, thinking differently, listened to this profound critic with a shrug or two of her shoulders; then when he ceased:

"How fortunate it is!" said she, "that you should have come with us! But for your enlightened judgment I should have been quite capable, like the good-natured vulgar, of thinking this statue beautiful. It is really a pity that the sculptor should not be here to learn his business from you."

"But that is just where he is, as it happens, behind you,"

said a stout woman, with a loud shout of laughter—an old woman who kept carriages for hire, and to whom I had just nodded as the owner of the house in which I have my studio.

Instinct was prompter than reflection; Marianina involuntarily turned round. On seeing me, a faint blush colored her face. I hastily made my escape.

A girl who could so frankly take my part, and then betray so much confusion at being discovered in her advocacy, would certainly not be displeased to see me; and though at my first visit I had been so coldly received, having now been made Chevalier of the Legion of Honor, in recognition of my exhibited work, I determined to try again. The distinction conferred on me might possibly gain me a better reception from the haughty Comte de Lanty.

I was admitted by an old servant for whom Marianina had great regard.

"Ah, monsieur," said he, "terrible things have been happening here!"

"Why—what?" cried I anxiously.

"I will take in your name, sir," was his only reply.

A minute later I was shown into M. de Lanty's study.

The man received me without rising, and greeted me with these words:

"I admire your courage, monsieur, in showing yourself in this house!"

"But I have not been treated here, as yet, in a way that should make me need any great courage."

"You have come, no doubt," M. de Lanty went on, "to fetch the object you so clumsily allowed to fall into our hands. I will return you that elegant affair."

He rose and took out of his writing-table drawer a dainty little pocket-book, which he handed to me.

As I looked at it in blank amazement:

"Oh, the letters, to be sure, are not there," he said. "I supposed that you would allow me to keep them."

"This pocket-book—letters?—The whole thing is a riddle to me, monsieur."

At this moment Mme. de Lanty came in.

"What do you want?" asked her husband roughly.

"I heard that M. Dorlange was here," said she, "and I fancied that there might be some unpleasant passages between you and him. I thought it my duty, as a wife, to interpose."

"Your presence, madame," said I, "is not needed to impose perfect moderation on me; the whole thing is the result of some misunderstanding."

"Oh, this is really too much!" cried M. de Lanty, going again to the drawer from which he had taken the pocketbook. And rudely pushing into my hands a little packet of letters tied up with pink ribbon, he went on: "Now, I imagine the misunderstanding will be cleared up."

I looked at the letters; they had not been through the post, and were all addressed *"A Monsieur Dorlange,"* in a woman's writing perfectly unknown to me.

"Indeed, monsieur," said I coldly, "you are better informed than I am. You have in your possession letters which seem to belong to me, but which have never reached me."

"On my word!" cried M. de Lanty, "it must be confessed that you are an admirable actor. I never saw innocence and amazement more successfully assumed."

But, while he was speaking, Mme. de Lanty had cleverly contrived to place herself behind her husband; and by a perfectly intelligible pantomime of entreaty, she besought me to accept the situation I was so strenuously denying. My honor was too deeply implicated, and I really saw too little of what I might be doing, to feel inclined to surrender at once. So, with the hope of feeling my way a little, I said:

"But, monsieur, from whom are these letters? Who addressed them to me?"

"From whom are the letters?" exclaimed M. de Lanty, in a tone in which irony was merged in indignation.

"Denial is useless, monsieur," Madame de Lanty put in. "Marianina has confessed everything."

"Mademoiselle Marianina wrote those letters to me?" replied I. "Then there is a simple issue to the matter; confront her with me. From her lips I will accept the most improbable statements as true."

"The trick is gallant enough," retorted M. de Lanty. "But Marianina is no longer here; she is in a convent, sheltered for ever from your audacity and from the temptations of her ridiculous passion. If this is what you came to learn, now you know it.—That is enough, for I will not deny that my patience and moderation have limits, if your impudence knows none."

"Monsieur!" cried I, in great excitement.

But when I saw that Mme. de Lanty was ready to drop on her knees to entreat me, it struck me that perhaps Marianina's future fate might depend on my conduct now. Besides, M. de Lanty was slight and frail, he was near sixty years of age, and seemed thoroughly convinced of this imaginary outrage; so I said no more in reply to his insulting speech, and left without any further words.

I hoped that I might find the old servant who had given me warning of this scene, on my way as I went out, and obtain some explanation from him; but I did not see him, and was left, with no light whatever, to an indefinite variety of suppositions.

I was but just up next morning when I was told that M. l'Abbé Fontanon wished to see me. I desired that he should be shown in, and presently found myself face to face with a tall old man, of a bilious complexion, and a gloomy, stern expression, who, conscious perhaps of his forbidding appearance, tried to remedy it by the refinement of excessive politeness and an affectation of honeyed but frigid servility.

As soon as he was seated, he began:

"Monsieur, Mme. la Comtesse de Lanty does me the honor of accepting me as the keeper of her conscience. From her I have heard of a scene that took place yesterday between you and her husband. Prudence would not at the time allow of her giving some explanations to which you have an undoubted right, and I have undertaken to communicate them to you;—that is the reason of my presence here."

"I am listening, sir," was all I replied.

"Some weeks ago," the priest went on, "M. de Lanty purchased an estate in the neighborhood of Paris, and took advantage of the fine weather to go thither with his family. M. de Lanty sleeps badly; one night when he was lying awake in the dark, he fancied he heard footsteps below his window, which he at once opened, calling out, 'Who's there?' in emphatic tones, to the nocturnal visitor he suspected. Nor was he mistaken, there was somebody there—somebody who made no answer, but took to his heels, two pistol shots fired by M. de Lanty having no effect. At first it was supposed that the stranger was bent on robbery; this, however, did not seem likely; the house was not furnished, the owners had only the most necessary things for a short stay; thieves, consequently, who generally are well informed, could not expect to find anything of value; and besides, some information reached M. de Lanty which gave his suspicions another direction.—He was told that, two days after his arrival, a fine young man had taken a bedroom in an inn at the neighboring village; that this gentleman seemed anxious to keep out of sight, and had several times gone out at night; so not a robber evidently—but a lover."

"I have never met with a romancer, M. le Abbé," said I, "who told his story in better style."

By this not very complimentary insinuation, I hoped to induce the speaker to abridge his story; for, as you may suppose, I wanted to hear the end.

"My romance is, unfortunately, painful fact," replied he. "You will see.—M. de Lanty had for some time been watching his daughter, whose vehement passions must, he feared, ere long result in an explosion. You, yourself, monsieur, had in Rome given him some uneasiness——"

"Quite gratuitous, M. le Abbé," I put in.

"Yes. I know that in all your acquaintance with Mlle. de Lanty your behavior has been perfectly correct. And, indeed, their leaving Rome put an end to this first ground for uneasiness; but in Paris another figure seemed to fill her

young mind, and day after day M. de Lanty proposed coming
to some explanation with his daughter.   The man who seems
to have captured her is audacious, enterprising, quite capable
of running serious risks if he could but compromise an heiress.
But on being questioned as to whether by any levity of manner
she had encouraged or given cause for the daring invasion
of which they were seeking the perpetrator, Mlle. de Lanty's
manner showed her to be quite above suspicion."

"I could have sworn to it !" cried I.

"Wait a moment," said the Abbé.   "A maid was then accused, and desired to leave the house at once.   This woman's
father is a violent-tempered man, and if she returned home
charged with anything so disgraceful, she would meet with
ruthless severity of treatment.   Mlle. de Lanty—that much
justice I must do her—had a Christian impulse ; she could not
allow an innocent person to be punished in her stead ; she
threw herself at her father's feet, and confessed that the nocturnal visit had been for her ; and though she had not authorized it, she was not altogether surprised.

"M. de Lanty at once named the supposed culprit ; but she
would not admit that he had guessed rightly, though she refused to mention any other name instead.   The whole day
was spent in altercation ; M. de Lanty at last gave up the
struggle, desiring his wife to try what she could do where he
had failed.   He thought, and with reason, that there might be
more freedom and candor between the mother and daughter.

"In point of fact, alone with Mme. de Lanty, Marianina at
length confessed that her father's suspicions were correct.
At the same time, she gave a reason for her obstinate reserve,
which certainly deserved consideration.   The man whose audacity she had encouraged had fought and won in several duels.
By birth he is the equal of M. de Lanty and his son ; he moves
in the same society, and consequently they frequently meet.
Hence the greatest disasters might ensue.   How could the
father or brother endure the man's presence without demand-
ing satisfaction for conduct so insulting to the honor of the
family ?—What then was to be done ?   It was the imprudent

girl herself who suggested the idea of giving a name which, while justifying M. de Lanty's fury, would not cry to him for vengeance."

"I understand," I interrupted. "The name of a man of no birth, a person of no consequence, an artist perhaps, a sculptor, or some such low fellow——"

"I think, monsieur," said the Abbé, "that you are ascribing to Mademoiselle de Lanty a feeling to which she is quite a stranger. In my opinion her love of the arts is only too strongly pronounced, and that perhaps is what has led to this unfortunate laxity of imagination. The thing that made her take refuge in the use of your name from the risks she foresaw was her recollection of the suspicions M. de Lanty had already expressed; she thought of you as the most likely seeming accomplice, and I am sure I may say that she saw nothing beyond."

"And then, M. l'Abbé, what about the pocket-book—the letters—which played so strange a part in yesterday's scene?"

"That again was a device of Marianina's; and though, as it has turned out, the strange inventiveness of her wit has had a good result, it was this in her character which, if she had remained in the world, would have given cause for uneasiness. When once she and Mme. de Lanty had agreed that you were to be the night-prowler, the statement had to be supported by evidence to favor its success. Instead of words, this terrible young lady determined to act in that sense. She spent the night in writing the letters you saw. She used different kinds of paper, ink of which she altered the tone, and she carefully varied the writing; she forgot nothing. Having written them, she placed them in a pocket-book her father had never seen; and then, after having made a hunting dog smell it all over— a dog noted for its intelligence and allowed in the house— she threw the whole thing into a clump of shrubs in the park, and came back to endure her father's angry cross-examination.

"The same sharp contest had begun once more when the dog came in carrying the pocket-book to his young mistress. She acted agonized alarm; M. de Lanty pounced on the ob-

ject, and to him everything was clear—he was deluded as
had been intended."

"And all these details," said I, with no great air of credulity, "were reported to you by Mme. de Lanty?"

"Confided to me, monsieur, and you yourself had proof
yesterday of their exactitude. Your refusal to recognize the
situation might have undone everything, and that was why
Mme. de Lanty interposed. She desires me to thank you for
your connivance—passive connivance at any rate—in this
pious fraud. She thought she could do no less than show her
gratitude by putting you in possession of her secret and
trusting to your silence."

"And Mademoiselle Marianina?" I asked.

"As M. de Lanty told you, she was immediately sent away
to a convent in Italy. To avoid any scandal, she is said to
have had a sudden call to the religious life. Her future prospects will depend on the attitude she chooses to assume."

Even if my self-respect had not been so aggrieved by this
story—if it were true—I should have felt some doubts, for
does it not strike you as rather too romantic? However, an
explanation has since offered itself, which may afford a clue
to the facts. Not long ago Marianina's brother married into
the family of a German Grand-Duke. The Lantys must have
had to sacrifice immense sums to achieve such an alliance.
May not Marianina have paid the expenses of this royal alliance, since she, by her grand-uncle's will, had the bulk of his
fortune, and was disinherited by taking the veil? Or again,
may she not have really felt for me the affection expressed in
her letters, and have been childish enough to write them,
though she would not go so far as to send them? Some mischance may have led to their discovery, and then to punish
her—not for having written, but for having thought so—she
was shut up in a convent; and to disgust me with her, this
got-up story of another lover was invented for my benefit, in
which I am made to play the part of lightning-conductor.

I can believe anything of these Lantys. The head of the
family has always seemed to me a very deep and crafty char-

acter, capable at a pinch of the blackest designs; and then, if you remember that these people have all their lives slept, as it were, on the secret knowledge of a fortune so ignobly earned, is it not conceivable that they should be ripe for any kind of intrigues, or can you imagine them dainty in their choice of means to an end?

And I may add that the official intervention of the Abbé Fontanon justifies the worst imputations. I have made inquiries about him; he is one of those mischief-making priests who are always eager to have a finger in private family affairs; and it was he who helped to upset the home of M. de Granville, Attorney-General in Paris under the Restoration.

Whatever may be true or false in all my hypotheses, I have no means of knowing, and am not likely to learn, at any rate for a long time to come. But, as you may suppose, the thought of Marianina, like a vision floating above this chaos, is to me a spot of light which, in spite of myself, attracts my gaze. May I love her? Must I hate and despise her?—This is the question I ask myself daily; and under the shroud of such uncertainty the memory of a woman is, it seems to me, more likely to become permanent than to fade.

And is it not a really diabolical coincidence that my chisel should be called upon to execute a pale daughter of the cloister? Under these circumstances was not my imagination inevitably memory; could I invent any image but that which possesses my soul and is so deeply graven on my brain? And behold! a second Marianina rises up before me in the flesh; and when, for the better furtherance of the work, the artist takes advantage of this stroke of fortune, he must be supposed, forsooth, to have transferred his affections. Could that frigid Mme. de l'Estorade ever fill the place of my enchanting pupil with the added charm and halo of forbidden fruit and of mystery? In short, you must give up all your imaginings.

The other day I was within an ace of relating the whole romance of Mademoiselle de Lanty to her supposed rival. And if I really aspired to this woman's favor—but she can love no one but her children—a pretty way of courting her it would be, I may say, to tell her that little tale. And so, to return to our starting-point, I care no more for M. Bixiou's opinion than for last year's roses. And so, I really do not know whether I am in love with Marianina; but I am quite sure that I am not in love with Madame de l'Estorade. This, it seems to me, is a plain and honest answer.

Now, let us leave things to the Future, who is the master of us all.

The Comtesse de l'Estorade to Madame Octave de Camps.

PARIS, *April* 1839.

MY DEAR MADAME,—M. Dorlange came last evening to take leave of us. He is starting to-day for Arcis-sur-Aube, where he is to see his statue set up in its place. That also is the town where the Opposition are about to propose him as their candidate. M. de l'Estorade declares that no worse choice could have been made, and that he has not a chance of being elected;—but this is not what I have to write about.

M. Dorlange called early after dinner. I was alone, for M. de l'Estorade was dining with the Minister of the Interior; and the children, who had been on a long excursion in the afternoon, had of their own accord begged to go to bed before the usual hour. Thus the conversation previously interrupted by Madame de la Bastie was naturally re-opened; and I was about to ask M. Dorlange to finish the story, of which he had only given me a hint of the end, when old Lucas came in, bringing me a letter. It was from my Armand, to tell me that he had been in the sickroom all day, very unwell.

"I want the carriage," said I to Lucas, with such agitation as you may suppose.

"Well, madame, but monsieur ordered it to fetch him at half-past eight, and Tony is gone," replied Lucas.

"Then get me a hackney cab."

"I am sure I don't know whether I can find one," said the old man, who always raises difficulties. "It has just begun to rain."

Without noticing this objection, and quite forgetting M. Dorlange, whom I left somewhat embarrassed, not liking to leave without saying good-bye, I went to my room to put on my bonnet and shawl. Having done so in great haste, I returned to the drawing-room, where I still found my visitor.

"You must excuse me, monsieur," said I, "for leaving you so abruptly; I am hurrying off to the Collège Henri IV. I could not endure to spend the night in such anxiety as I am feeling in consequence of a note from my son, who tells me that he has been in the sickroom all day."

"But surely," said M. Dorlange, "you are not going alone in a hackney coach to such an out-of-the-way part of the town?"

"Lucas will come with me."

At this moment Lucas came in again. His words were fulfilled; there was not a cab to be had, and it was pouring in torrents. Time was flying; it was almost too late already to visit at the school, where everybody would be in bed by nine o'clock.

"I must go," said I to Lucas. "Go and put on your thick shoes, and we will go on foot with umbrellas."

I saw the man's face lengthen; he is no longer young; he likes his ease, and he complains of rheumatism in the winter. He suddenly found a number of objections; it was very late; we should *revolutionize* the school; I should certainly catch cold; M. Armand could not be very ill since he had written himself—my plan of campaign was evidently not at all to my old man's mind.

Then M. Dorlange very obligingly offered to go for me and come back to report the invalid, but such half-measures will not do for me—I wanted to see, and satisfy myself. So, with many thanks to him, I said to Lucas, in an authoritative tone:

"Come, go and get ready, and be quick, for one thing you have said that is perfectly true—it is growing late."

Thus nailed to the point, Lucas boldly hoisted the flag of rebellion.

"It is simply impossible, madame, that you should go out in such weather, and I do not want to get a scolding from the master for giving in to any such idea."

"Then you simply do not mean to obey me?"

"You know, madame, that for anything useful or reasonable I would do whatever you might order, even if it were to walk through fire."

"To be sure, warmth is good for the rheumatism, and rain is bad for it."

Then I turned to M. Dorlange without listening to the old rebel's reply, and said to him:

"Since you were good enough to offer to go alone on this errand, I venture to hope that you will not refuse me the support of your arm."

"Like Lucas," said he, "I do not see that this expedition is indispensable; however, as I have no fear of being scolded by M. de l'Estorade, I will, of course, have the honor of escorting you."

We set out; and as I went downstairs, I could not help thinking that life is full of singular coincidences. Here was a man whom I do not wholly trust, who, two months ago, manœuvred, like a pirate, to get sight of me, and to whom I had now entrusted myself with complete confidence, under conditions which the most favored lover would have hardly dared to dream of.

The weather really was horrible; we had not gone fifty yards when we were already drenched, in spite of Lucas' vast umbrella, held by M. Dorlange so as to shelter me by sacrificing himself. Then a new complication arose. A hackney cab went past; my companion hailed the driver; it was empty. To tell my escort that I could not allow him to get in with me was out of the question. Not only would such an implied doubt have been grossly uncivil, but it would have been derogatory to myself even to suggest it. And yet, you see, my dear friend, what slippery ways we tread, and how true it is that from the time of Dido and Æneas rain has always served the turn of lovers!

It is difficult to talk in a cab; the clatter of wheels and windows compels one to shout. M. Dorlange knew too that I was extremely uneasy, and he had the good taste to make no attempt at a prolonged conversation; just now and again he made some trivial remark to break the silence which otherwise would have been awkward under the circumstances.

When we reached the school, M. Dorlange, after handing me out, understood that he could not go in with me; he got into the coach again to wait for me.

Master Armand's indisposition was somewhat of a practical joke so far as I was concerned. His illness was no more than a headache, which since his note was written had completely disappeared. The doctor, who had seen him in the morning, to order something, had prescribed lime-flower tea, and told him he could return to the classroom next day. So I had taken a sledge-hammer to kill a flea, and committed a preposterous blunder in arriving at an hour when all the staff were in bed, to find my young gentleman still up and playing a game of chess with one of the attendants.

By the time I went out again the rain had ceased, and bright moonlight silvered the pavement, which the rain had so thoroughly washed that there was not a sign of mud. I was so oppressed and vexed that I longed for the fresh air. So I begged M. Dorlange to send away the coach, and we walked home. This was a fine chance for him; between the Panthéon and the Rue de Varenne there is time to say much. But M. Dorlange was so little inclined to avail himself of the situation, that, taking Master Armand's prank as his text, he expatiated on the mischief of spoiling children. The subject is one I have no liking for, and he might have discovered that from the dry reserve with which I took my part in the conversation.

"Come," thought I, "we must come to an end of this story, which is always interrupted, like the famous anecdote of Sancho's goatherd which could never be told."

So, cutting short his theories of education—

"It seems to me," said I to my earnest companion, "that

this would be a good opportunity for going on with the confidential narrative you were interrupted in. Here we are
quite safe from any intrusion."

· "I am afraid," said M. Dorlange, "that I am but a bad narrator. I exhausted all my genius the other day in communicating the history to Marie-Gaston."

"That," said I, with a laugh, "is against your principles of
secrecy, in which a third person is one too many."

"Oh, Marie-Gaston and I are but one person. Besides, I
had to give some answer to the odd fancies he had formed as
to you and me."

"What—as to me!"

"Yes. He opines that by staring too hard at the sun one
may be dazzled by its rays."

"Which, in less metaphorical language, means?——"

"That seeing how strange the circumstances were that led
to my having the honor of your acquaintance, I might possibly, madame, in your society, fail to preserve my common-
sense and self-possession."

"And your story answers this hypothesis of Marie-Gaston's?"

"You shall judge," said M. Dorlange.

And then, without further preamble, he told me a rather
long story, which I do not repeat to you, my dear madame,
because on the one hand it has really nothing to do with your
functions as keeper of my conscience, and on the other it is
mixed up with a family secret which demands more discretion
on my part than I could have anticipated.

The upshot of the matter is that M. Dorlange is in love
with the woman who had sat in his imagination for the Saint
Ursula. Still, as it must be said that she is apparently for
ever out of his reach, it did not seem to me quite impossible
that he might sooner or later transfer to me the feeling he
still preserves for her. Hence, when, having finished his narrative, he asked me whether I did not take it as a triumphant
refutation of our friend's absurd fears, I could but reply:

"Modesty makes it incumbent on me to share your confidence. At the same time, a cannon ball often kills by ricochet."

"And you believe me guilty of the audacity which Marie-Gaston fears may be so fatal to me?"

"I do not know that it would be audacity," said I, rather harshly; "but if you had such a fancy and took it to heart, I should, I own, think you greatly to be pitied."

His reply was a home-thrust:

"Well, madame, you need not pity me.—In my opinion, first love is a kind of vaccination which saves a man from catching the complaint a second time."

This closed the conversation; the story had been a long one, and we were at home. I asked M. Dorlange to come upstairs, a politeness he accepted, remarking that M. de l'Estorade had probably come in, and he could say good-bye to him.

My husband was in fact at home. I do not know whether Lucas, to anticipate the blame I should have cast on him, had done his best to misrepresent my proceedings, or whether my maternal exploit prompted M. de l'Estorade, for the first time in his life, to a spasm of jealousy of which he was unable to conceal the unfamiliar symptoms; at any rate, he received me with an indignant rating, saying that nothing was so unheard of as the idea of going out at this hour, and in such weather, to inquire after an invalid who, by announcing his illness himself, showed it was not in the least serious.

After allowing him to go on for some time in a highly unbecoming manner, I thought it was time to put an end to the scene.

"Well," said I sharply, "I wished to get some sleep to-night; I went to the school in pouring rain. Now I have come back in beautiful moonlight, and I beg to remind you that after kindly consenting to escort me, M. Dorlange, who leaves Paris to-morrow, came upstairs to bid you good-bye."

I have habitually too much influence over M. de l'Estorade for this call to order to fail of its effect; still, I could see that there was something of the aggrieved husband in his tone; for, having brought in M. Dorlange to divert his thoughts, I soon perceived that I had but made him a victim to my ogre's ill-temper, which was now vented on him.

After telling him that his nomination for election had been much discussed at the Minister's dinner-table, M. de l'Estorade, with evident satisfaction, told him all the reasons which must lead to his failing conspicuously; the constituency of Arcis-sur-Aube was one of those where the Ministry were most secure of the votes; a man of extraordinary ability had already been sent down there, and had for some days been *working up* the place, and he had sent the most flourishing reports to the Government. All this was dealing in generalities, and M. Dorlange replied with perfect modesty, and the manner of a man who has prepared himself beforehand for all the freaks of chance that may affect his return. But M. de l'Estorade had a last shaft to fling which certainly could not fail to prove effective, since with the same blow it would hit the candidate and the profligate—if profligate he were.

"Listen to me, my dear sir," said M. de l'Estorade to his victim, "when a man rushes into a parliamentary career, he must remember that he has to show every card—his public and his private life. His adversaries overhaul his past and present with merciless hands, and woe to him whose life has the shadow of a stain!—Well, I may tell you plainly, this evening a little scandal was raked up—a very little one in the life of an artist, but one which, as affecting a representative of the people, assumes far more serious proportions. You understand me. I am alluding to the handsome Italian woman who lives under your roof. Take care; you may be called to account by some puritan voter for the more or less doubtful morality of her connection with you."

M. Dorlange's reply was very dignified:

"I can have but one wish for those who choose to question me on that detail of my domestic life," said he, "and that is that they may have nothing worse to look back upon in theirs. —If I had not already bored Madame la Comtesse with one interminable story during our walk home, I would tell you that of the pretty Italian, and you would see that her presence in my house need deprive me of none of the esteem you have kindly honored me with."

"But indeed," said M. de l'Estorade, suddenly mollified by hearing that our long walk had been spent in narrating history, "you take my remarks far too seriously! As I said but just now, an artist needs a handsome model, nothing can be more natural; but it is a piece of furniture that is of no use to gentlemen engaged in politics."

"What appears to be of more use to them," retorted M. Dorlange, with some vivacity, "is the advantage that may be taken of a calumny greedily accepted with evil haste, and with no effort to verify it.—However, far from dreading an explanation on the subject you are pleased to discuss, I am eager for it; and the Ministry would be doing me a service by instructing so clever an inquisitor as they have put on my track to bring this delicate matter before my constituents."

"So you are going to-morrow?" asked M. de l'Estorade, finding that he had started on a path where, instead of bringing M. Dorlange to confusion, he had afforded him an opportunity of answering with no little haughtiness of tone and phrase.

"Yes, and early in the day, so that I will have the honor now of wishing you good-night, for I still have some packing to finish."

With these words M. Dorlange rose, and after bowing to me rather formally, he left the room, not shaking hands with my husband, who, indeed, did not offer him the opportunity.

M. de l'Estorade, to avoid the impending and inevitable explanation, at once exclaimed:

"Well, and what was the matter with Armand?"

"What was the matter with Armand matters little," replied I, "as you may suppose from my having returned without him and showing no anxiety; what is a far more interesting question is what is the matter with you, for I never saw you so out of tune, so bitter and cross-grained."

"What! Because I told that ridiculous candidate that he might go into mourning at once over his chances?"

"In the first place, it was not complimentary, and at any rate the time was ill-chosen, when my motherly alarms had just inflicted an odious amount of trouble on the man you attacked."

"I cannot stand officious people," retorted M. de l'Estorade, in a higher tone than he usually adopts with me. "And, after all, if this gentleman had not been on the spot to offer you his escort, you would not have set out on this unseemly expedition."

"You are mistaken. I should have gone in a still more unseemly manner; for I should have gone alone, as your servants are the masters here, and refused to escort me."

"But, after all, you must confess that if any one had met you at half-past nine at night, walking arm in arm with M. Dorlange, out by the Panthéon, it would have been thought strange, to say the least."

Then, affecting to have just discovered what I had known for an hour past:

"Bless me, monsieur!" cried I, "after fifteen years of married life are you doing me the honor of being jealous for the first time? Then, indeed, I can understand that, in spite of your regard for the proprieties, you took advantage of my being present to question M. Dorlange on the not very proper subject of the woman who is supposed to be his mistress. It was neither more nor less than very basely perfidious; you were trying to lower him in my eyes."

Thus riddled with shot, my hapless husband tried indeed to beat about the bush, and at last found no better alternative than to ring for Lucas, whom he lectured pretty sharply; and there the matter ended.

But although I had won an easy victory, the great little incidents of the evening left a most uncomfortable impression on my mind. I had come in quite satisfied, thinking that I now knew exactly *where to have* M. Dorlange. To be honest, at the moment when he uttered that magniloquent,

"Do not pity me," as a woman is always more or less a woman, my vanity felt a little shock; but as I came upstairs I reflected that the firm and simple tone in which he spoke commanded belief. It was undoubtedly a natural and frank outburst of genuine feeling, which was not aimed at me, but certainly intended for some one else. So I might be perfectly at my ease.

But, then, what is to be said of the conjugal tact which, while trying to make the man—of whom I had really been thinking too much—commit himself in my presence, gave him an opportunity of appearing in a better light than ever, and to the greatest advantage? For there is no doubt whatever that the indignation with which M. Dorlange retaliated on the malignancy of which he was the object was the answer of an easy conscience, sure, too, of being able to refute the calumny. What, my dear madame, I ask you, what is this man whose vulnerable point is not discoverable, whom we have seen on one or two occasions positively heroic—and that as if he himself did not perceive the fact, as if he never lived but in that high air, and greatness were his element? Is it possible that, all appearances to the contrary, this Italian woman is nothing to him?

Are there, then, in the midst of our small and colorless society still some characters so strongly tempered that they can walk on the very precipice of opportunity and never fall! What a nature must that be that can plunge through thorns and leave no wool! I had fancied I could make a friend of him!

Nay, I will not play at that game. Supposing this Dante Alighieri of the chisel to be convinced at last that his Beatrice will never return to him; supposing that he should again, as he has done once already, look round on me—what could I do? Is a woman ever safe against the powerful fascination that such a man must exert? As M. de Montriveau said to the poor Duchesse de Langeais, not only must *she never touch the axe,* but she must keep as far from it as she can, for fear that a beam reflected from such polished steel should dazzle her eyes.

Happily, M. de l'Estorade is already hostile to this dangerous man; but my husband may be quite easy, I shall take care to encourage and cultivate this germ of enmity. And besides this, if M. Dorlange should be elected, he and my husband will be in opposite camps; and political passions—thank Heaven!—have often cut short older and better established intimacies than this.

"But he saved your little girl," you will say; "you were afraid of his loving you, and he does not think of you at all; he is a man of cultivated intellect and magnanimous feeling, with whom there is not a fault to the found?——"

What arguments are these, my dear lady?—He frightens me, and that is enough. And when I am frightened, I neither argue nor reason; I only consider whether I have legs and breath, and simply run and run till I feel myself in safety.

Dorlange to Marie-Gaston.

PARIS, *April* 1839.

On coming in from taking leave of the Estorades, I find your letter, my dear friend, announcing your immediate arrival. I will wait here all to-morrow; but in the evening, without any further delay, I must set out for Arcis-sur-Aube, where, within a week, the end of my political struggle is to be fought out. What supporters and abettors I have in that town which—as I am informed—I am so anxious to represent; on whose help or opposition I am to build my hopes; in one word, who it is that is making this electoral bed for me to lie in,—of all this I know no more now than I did a year ago when I was first apprised of my parliamentary vocation.

Only a few days since did I receive a communication emanating from the paternal office, not from Stockholm this time, but with the Paris postmark. From the tenor of this document I should hardly be surprised to hear that the high functions fulfilled in the northern capital by the mysterious author of my being were simply those of a corporal in the Prussian army; for it is impossible to give instructions in a

more domineering and peremptory tone, or with more tiresome regard for the minutest details.

The note has a title or heading; as thus:

WHAT MY SON IS TO DO

On receipt of *these presents* I am to send off the "Saint
Ursula," to see it packed myself in a case, and address it,
by quick goods vans, to Mother Marie des Anges, Superior of
the House of the Ursuline Sisters at Arcis-sur-Aube, AUBE
—you understand?—In fact, but for this added information
I might have fancied that Arcis-sur-Aube was situated in
the department of the Gironde or of Finisterre.—I am there
to make an arrangement with the carrier's agents to insure
the delivery of the parcel—my "Saint Ursula" a parcel!—
at the door of the convent chapel.   I am then commanded
to start a very few days later, so as to reach the aforenamed
town of Arcis-sur-Aube by the second of May at latest.   You
see, these are military orders; so much so that I half thought
of taking out a soldier's pass instead or an ordinary permit to
travel, and of taking my journey at the regulation fare of
three sous per league.

The hotel I am to put up at is expressly mentioned:
I am to stay at the *Hôtel de la Poste;* hence, if I should
happen to prefer the *Three Blackamoors* or the *Silver Lion,*
which are to be found there, no doubt, as in every country
town, I must not indulge the fancy.   Finally, on the day
before I start, I am to announce, in any newspapers I can
work upon, the fact of my intending to stand as a candidate
for election in the electoral district of Arcis-sur-Aube (Aube),
but not to put forward any declaration of my political creed,
which would be useless and premature.   And the whole concludes with instructions—a little humiliating perhaps, but
giving me some faith in the progress of affairs—to call on
the morning of the day when I set out on Mongenod Brothers,
where I can again draw a sum of two hundred and fifty thousand francs, which ought to be lying there in my name.   "I

am to take the greatest care," the document goes on, "that in conveying this sum from Paris to Arcis-sur-Aube it is neither lost nor stolen."

What, my good sir, do you make of this last clause. The money *"ought* to be lying there"—then it may not be; and if not, what then? What am I to do with it at Arcis? Am I to work my election in the English fashion?—that, no doubt, is why a profession of faith would be "useless and premature." As to the advice not to lose the money or allow myself to be robbed—don't you think it makes me wonderfully young again? Since reading it I have quite longed to suck my thumb and get a padded cap.

However, as to my lord and father, though he puts my mind on the rack by all these queer ways of his, I could exclaim—but for the respect I owe him—like Don Basilio in speaking of Almaviva, "That devil of a man has his pockets full of irresistible arguments!"

So I shut my eyes and give myself up to the stream that is carrying me on; and in spite of the news of your early advent, I must call to-morrow morning on Mongenod Brothers and set forth with a brave heart, picturing to myself the amazement of the good folks of Arcis when they see me drop into their midst, as sudden and as startling an apparition as a Jack-in-the-box.

I have already made my mark in Paris. The *National* announced me as a candidate yesterday morning in the most flaming terms; and this evening it would seem that I was the subject of much discussion at the house of the Minister of the Interior, where M. de l'Estorade was dining. I must in honesty add that, according to M. de l'Estorade, the general impression was that I must inevitably fail. In the district of Arcis, it would seem, the worst the Government had to fear was a *Left-Centre* candidate; the democratic party, which I am by way of representing, can hardly be said to have any existence there. The *Left-Centre* candidate has already been brought to his senses by the dispatch of a particularly alert and skilful canvasser; and at his moment, when I am flinging my name to the winds, the election of the Conservative is already a certainty.

Added to these elements of inevitable failure, M. de l'Estorade was good enough to speak of a circumstance as to which, my dear fellow, I am surprised that you should never have given me a sermon, for it is one of the most pleasing of the calumnies set rolling in the Montcornet drawing-room by the honorable and highly honored Monsieur Bixiou. It has to do with a very handsome Italian woman whom I am supposed to have brought with me from Rome, and to be living with in most uncanonical relationship.

Pray tell me what has kept you from asking for explanations of the matter? Did you think the case so atrocious that you were shy of offending my sense of decency by alluding to it in any way? Or is it that you have such confidence in my high moral sense that you need no certificate on that point?—I had not time to go into the necessary explanations with M. de l'Estorade, nor have I time now to volunteer them to you. I mention the incident only to bring me to a remark which I believe to be true, and which I would beg you to verify when you come to Paris.

I have a strong notion that M. de l'Estorade would not be best pleased at my succeeding in this electoral campaign. He has never expressed much approbation of my plans, and has constantly done his utmost to divert me from them—always indeed by urging considerations in my own interest. But now that the idea has taken shape, and is even discussed in Ministerial circles, my gentleman has turned sour; and while finding malicious pleasure in promising me defeat, he brings up the pretty little activity under which he hopes to smother and bury me—as a friendly act. Now, why?

I will tell you. The fact is, that though he is under an obligation to me, the good man by his high social position feels himself my superior in a way which my election to the Chamber would nullify, and he does not like the notion of renouncing it. For, after all, what is an artist—even if he were a genius—in comparison with a Peer of France, a bigwig

who has a finger in the supreme direction of great political
and social questions—a man who can buttonhole the Ministers
and the King, who, if he were capable of such an audacious
flight, has a right to blackball the Budget? And is it conceivable that I, in my turn, should want to be such a
privileged person, with even greater importance and authority
as being a member of the elective body? Is it not a trying
piece of insolence and conceit? Hence is M. le Comte
furious!

Nor is this all. These politicians by right divine have
a fixed idea: they believe themselves to have been initiated by
long study into a science supposed to be very abstruse, which
they call Statecraft, and which they alone have a right to
know and practise, as none but physicians may practise
medicine. So they cannot endure that without having taken
out a license, any low fellow—such as a journalist, for
instance, or, lower still, an artist, an image-maker—should
dare to poach on their domain and speak as they do. A poet,
an artist, a writer may have great gifts—that they are ready
to grant; in fact, their business requires it; but they cannot
be statesmen. Chateaubriand himself, though naturally in
a position which justified him in making a place for himself
on the Olympus of Government, was nevertheless shown the
door, and one morning a very brief note, signed "Joseph
Villèle," sent him packing—as was but proper!—back to
René, Atala, and other literary trivialities.

I know that time, and that stalwart posthumous daughter
of us all whom we call Posterity, will in the long run do us
all full justice and put every man in his right place. In
2039, if the world holds out so long, most men will still
know who, in 1839, were Canalis, Joseph Bridau, Daniel
d'Arthez, Stidmann, and Léon de Lora; while only an infinitely small number will be aware that at the same time M.
le Comte de l'Estorade was a Peer of France and President of
the Court of Exchequer; that M. le Comte de Rastignac was
Minister of Public Works, and M. le Baron Martial de la
Roche-Hugon, his brother-in-law, a diplomatist and privy

councillor on special service more or less extraordinary. Still, pending this postponed resifting and far-off justice, I do not think it a bad thing that these great men in office should have a reminder to the effect that, short of being a Richelieu or a Colbert, they are subject to competition, and must take the consequences. Thus, merely out of this spirit of contrariness, I am bent on my project; and if I should be elected, unless you can assure me this evening that I have misunderstood l'Estorade's behavior, I shall find some opportunity for making him and some others feel that a man who has the will can step over the palings of their little enclosure and figure in it as their equal.

But I have talked too much of myself, my dear friend, without thinking of the painful feelings that must attend your return here. How will you bear it? And will you not, instead of setting your sorrows aside, rather go forth to meet them, and take a melancholy pleasure in reviving their bitterness? Well, I might say of such great griefs what I said just now of the great men in office: they must be regarded in their place in time and space, and then they are intangible, imperceptible, they are held of no more account in a man's life when his biography is written than the hairs he combs out of his head every morning. That charming lunatic with whom you spent three years of matrimonial ecstasy put out a hand, as she thought, where Death was—and Death, mocking at her schemes, her plans, at the refinement and graces she added to life, snatched at her suddenly and brutally. You remain: You, with youth on your side and the gifts of intellect, and with what is, believe me, an element of power—deep and premature disgust of things. Now, why not do as I am doing? Why not join me in the political arena? Then there would be two of us to carry out my plans, and the world would see what can be done by two determined and energetic men, yoked together as it were, and both pulling at the heavy collar of justice and truth.

But if you think that I am too much bent on becoming infectious, or inoculating all and sundry with my parliamentary yellow-fever, return at least to the world of letters where you have already made your mark, and exert your imagination to enable you to ignore your heart, which speaks too constantly of the past. I, for my part, will make as much stir for you as I can; and even if it should cost me part of my sleep to keep up our correspondence to divert your mind whether you will or no, I shall take care to keep you informed of all the vicissitudes of the drama I am about to play a part in.

Since, on your arrival in Paris, you will have no fixed habitation, I should take it very kindly, and feel you quite your old self, if you would but make yourself at home in my house instead of going on to Ville-d'Avray, which is a bad and dangerous place for you. Then you can judge of my handsome housekeeper, and see how she is slandered and misunderstood. You will be near to l'Estorade, who will, I expect, prove quite a comfort to you; and it will be an admirable way of expiating all the involuntary offences of which you have been guilty towards me. Just on the chance, I have given the necessary orders, and your room is ready for you. The quiet part of the town where I live will serve as a transition to the infernally noisy heart of Paris, which I doubt your ever again becoming accustomed to. I live at no great distance from the Rue d'Enfer, where we formerly were at home together, and where we were often so happy.

What dreams we dreamed, what schemes we laid, and how little life has realized of them all! Our commonest daydream was of glory, and that, the only one in which we might perhaps not have become bankrupt, we have voluntarily abandoned: you to suffer and weep, I to run after a will-o'-the-wisp relationship on which I may not after all have to congratulate myself!—The ever-changing current has carried everything before it—our dykes, our flower-gardens, our budding rose-trees, our country houses; one thing alone has hung by its anchor, our old and sacred friendship. Do nothing more to wreck it, I entreat, dear prodigal, nor run the risk of a quarrel with the Northern Court of which I may some day be the Suger or the Sully.

P.S.—You have not arrived, my dear friend, and I must close my letter, which will be handed to you by my* housekeeper when you call—for, of course, your first visit will be to me. Till then you cannot know that I am gone.

I went this morning to the bankers Mongenod: the two hundred and fifty thousand francs were ready, but with the most extraordinary directions—in the name of *M. le Comte de Sallenauve, known as Dorlange, sculptor, Rue de l'Ouest, No. 42.* And in spite of this designation, which has never been mine, the money was handed over to me without a demur. Under the eyes of the cashier I had presence of mind enough not to seem utterly amazed by my new name and title; but I had a private interview with M. Mongenod *senior,* a man of the highest character in the banking world, and to him I confessed my surprise, begging for any explanation he might be able to afford me. He could give me none: the money was forwarded to him through a Dutch bank, his correspondent at Rotterdam, and that is all he knows.

Bless me! what next I wonder? Am I now to be a nobleman? Has the moment arrived when my father will reveal himself?

I am just starting in a state of excitement and anxiety that you may imagine. Till further instructions I shall address to you at my house; if you will not consent to take up your abode there let me know of your whereabouts, for it strikes me that we shall have a great deal to say to each other. Not a word, I entreat you, to the Estorades—all this is strictly between ourselves.

Dorlange to Marie-Gaston.

ARCIS-SUR-AUBE, *May* 3, 1839.

MY DEAR OLD FRIEND,—Last evening, at seven o'clock, in the presence of Maître Achille Pigoult, notary to the King in the town of Arcis-sur-Aube, the obsequies were solemnized of Charles Dorlange, who, presently, like a butterfly emerging from the larva, fluttered out on the world under the name and person of Charles de Sallenauve, son of François-Henri-Pantaléon Dumirail, Marquis de Sallenauve. Hereinafter are set forth the recorded facts which preceded this great and glorious metempsychosis.

On the evening of May 1st I left Paris in all the official revelry of St. Philip's Day; and on the following afternoon, in obedience to paternal instructions, I made my entry into the good town of Arcis-sur-Aube. On getting out of the chaise my amazement was considerable, as you may imagine, on discerning, in the street where the diligence had just arrived, that evasive Jacques Bricheteau whom I had never seen since our strange meeting in the Ile Saint-Louis. But this time, instead of behaving like Jean de Nivelle, behold him coming towards me with a smile on his face; and holding out his hand, he said:

"At last, my dear sir, we are almost at an end of these mysteries, and you will soon, I hope, find no further reason to complain of me."

At the same time, with an air of anxious solicitude that was too much for him, he added:

"You have brought the money?"

"Yes," I replied. "Neither lost nor stolen," and I took out the pocket-book that contained the two hundred and fifty thousand francs in banknotes.

"That is well," said Jacques Bricheteau. "Now we will go to the *Hôtel de la Poste.*—You doubtless know who is waiting for you?"

"No, indeed," said I.

"Then you did not observe the name under which the money was made payable?"

"On the contrary—and anything so strange could not fail to strike me and set my imagination working."

"Well, presently the veil will be removed of which, so far, a corner has just been lifted that you might not be too suddenly startled by the great and happy event that is about to take place in your life."

"Is my father here?"

I asked the question eagerly, and yet without the deep emotion I should probably have felt at the thought of embracing my mother.

"Yes," replied Jacques Bricheteau. "But I think it well to warn you of a possible chill on your meeting. The Marquis has gone through much suffering. The Court life to which he has since been accustomed has made him unready to display any expression of feeling; besides, he has a perfect horror of anything suggesting *bourgeois* manners; so you must not be surprised at the aristocratically cold and dignified reception you may meet with. He is kind at heart, and you will appreciate him more as you know him better."

"These preliminaries are highly encouraging," thought I. And as I myself did not feel any very ardent predispositions, I augured that this first interview would be at a temperature of some degrees below zero.

On going into the room where the Marquis awaited me, I saw a very tall, very thin, very bald man, seated at a table on which he was arranging papers. On hearing the door open, he pushed his spectacles up on his forehead, rested his hands on the arms of his chair, and looking round at us he waited.

"Monsieur le Comte de Sallenauve," said Jacques Bricheteau, announcing me with the solemnity of an usher of ambassadors or a groom of the Chambers.

But in the presence of the man to whom I owed my life the ice in me was instantly melted; I stepped forward with an eager impulse, feeling the tears rise to my eyes. He did not move. There was not the faintest trace of agitation in his face, which had that peculiar look of high dignity that used to be called "the grand air"; he merely held out his hand, limply grasped mine, and then said:

"Be seated, monsieur—for I have not yet the right to call you my son."

When Jacques Bricheteau and I had taken chairs—

"Then you have no objection," said this strange kind of father, "to assuming the political position we are trying to secure for you?"

"None at all," said I. "The notion startled me at first, but I soon grew accustomed to it; and to insure success, I have punctually carried out all the instructions that were conveyed to me."

"Excellent," said the Marquis, taking up from the table a gold snuff-box which he twirled in his fingers.

Then, after a short silence, he added:

"Now I owe you certain explanations. Our good friend Jacques Bricheteau, if he will have the kindness, will lay them before you."—A sort of echo of the royal formula, *"My Chancellor will tell you the rest."*

"To begin at the beginning," said Jacques Bricheteau, accepting the task thus thrust upon him, "I ought to tell you, monsieur, that you are not a Sallenauve in the direct line. On his return from the Emigration, about the year 1808, M. le Marquis here present made the acquaintance of your mother, and you are the issue of that connection. Your mother, as you already know, died at your birth, and as a misfortune never comes single, shortly after this terrible sorrow M. de Sallenauve, being implicated in a plot against the Imperial throne, was obliged to fly the country. M. le Marquis, like myself, a native of Arcis, honored me with his confidence, and on the eve of this second exile he placed your young life in my charge. I accepted the responsibility, I will not say gladly, but with sincere gratitude."

At these words the Marquis held out his hand to Jacques Bricheteau, who was sitting near him, and after a silent pressure—which, I may say, did not seem to agitate them deeply —Jacques Bricheteau went on:

"The elaborate and mysterious precautions I so carefully contrived, in order to conceal the functions I had accepted, may be accounted for by many reasons. I might say that every change of government that we have lived under since your birth has indirectly reacted on you. While the Empire lasted,

I feared lest a power which was not reputed indulgent to those who attacked it might include you in your father's banishment, and that first suggested the idea of giving you a sort of anonymous identity. Under the Restoration, I had reason to fear another form of hostility. The Sallenauve family, of which M. le Marquis here present is the sole surviving representative, was then all-powerful. The circumstances of your birth had got wind, and it had not escaped their perspicacity that monsieur your father had taken care not to admit his paternity, so as to be able to leave you his whole fortune, of which, as a recognized natural child, the law would only have allowed a fixed portion.

"The obscurity that surrounded you seemed to me the best protection against the investigations of your money-seeking relations; and certain suspicious proceedings on their part to spy on me at different times showed that my anticipations were justified. Finally, after the Revolution of July, I was afraid for you of your connection with me. I had seen the change of dynasty with deep regret; and having allowed myself to become involved in some overt acts of rebellion, since I had no belief in its stability—for men are always ready to fight a government that is forced upon them, and to which they are averse—I found myself on the black list of the police——"

On this, remembering that at the *Café des Arts* Jacques Bricheteau had been the object of very different suspicions, I could not help smiling, and the *Chancellor* pausing, said with extreme solemnity:

"Do these details that I have the honor of giving you by any misfortune appear to you doubtful?"

When I had accounted for the expression of my face—

"The waiter," said Jacques Bricheteau, "was not altogether in the wrong. I have for many years been employed by the police in the public health department; but I am not a spy— on the contrary, I have more than once very nearly been a victim.—Now, to return to the secrecy I still preserved as to our connection, though I did not apprehend positive persecution as resulting to you from knowing me, it seemed to me that such an acquaintance might be detrimental to your career. 'Sculptors,' I reflected, 'cannot get on without the support of Government. I might possibly prevent his getting commissions.' I ought also to say that at the time when I gave you notice that your allowance was to cease, I had for some years lost track of Monsieur le Marquis. Of what use was it, then, to tell you the history of the past, since it apparently could have no effect on your future prospects?

"I decided that it was best to leave you in complete ignorance, and busied myself in inventing some fiction which might mislead your curiosity, and at the same time relieve me from the long privation I endured by avoiding any direct intercourse with you——"

"The man you employed as your representative," said I, interrupting him, "was well chosen, no doubt, from the point of view of secrecy, but you must admit that he is not attractive."

"Poor Gorenflot!' said the organist, laughing. "He is simply one of the parish bell-ringers, and I employ him to blow the organ. I do not know whether the author of *Notre-Dame de Paris* had ever seen him when he invented Quasimodo."

During this parenthesis an absurd sound fell on our ears; a distinct snore from my father gave us to understand that either he took very little interest in all these explanations given in his name, or that he thought them too prolix. Whether it was his conceit as an orator that was nettled, or what else it was that roused Jacques Bricheteau's temper, I know not, but he started to his feet with annoyance, and violently shook the sleeper's arm, exclaiming:

"What, Marquis!—if you sleep like this when sitting in Council, my word! the country must be well governed!"

M. de Sallenauve opened his eyes, shook himself, and speaking to me, he said:

"Excuse me, M. le Comte, but I have traveled post for ten days and nights without stopping, in order to be in time to meet you here; and though I spent last night in a bed, I am still rather tired."

He then rose, took a large pinch of snuff, and paced the room, while Jacques Bricheteau went on:

"It is rather more than a year since I first heard again from your father. He explained his long silence and his purposes for you, saying that, perhaps for some years to come, it was absolutely necessary that he should still maintain the strictest incognito. It was just then that chance threw you in my way. I found you prepared to rush into any folly to get to the bottom of the secret of which you could no longer doubt the existence——"

"You are good at a quick removal!" said I, with a laugh to the erewhile lodger of the Quai de Béthune.

"I did better than that. Tormented by the idea that, in spite of my efforts, you would succeed in piercing the darkness I had so elaborately left you in, and at the very moment when M. le Marquis might think it most indispensable——"

"You set out for Stockholm?"

"No, for your father's residence; but I posted at Stockholm the letter he gave me for you."

"But I do not quite understand——"

"Nothing can be simpler," said the Marquis decisively. "I do not live in Sweden, and we wished to put you off the scent."

"Would you wish to tell the rest of the story yourself?" said Jacques Bricheteau, though not seeming anxious to be superseded in his narrative; for, as you see, he has an easy and elegant flow of language.

"Not at all, not at all—go on," said the Marquis; "you are doing it admirably."

"The presence here of M. le Marquis," Jacques Bricheteau went on, "will not, as I must warn you, immediately clear up all the mysteries which have hitherto complicated your relations. For the furtherance of your future prospects, and of his own, he reserves the right of leaving you in ignorance for some time yet of the name of the country where he hopes to see you invited to succeed him, and of certain other details of his biography. In fact, he is here this day chiefly with a view to avoiding further explanations, and to renew the lease, so to speak, of your patient curiosity. Having observed that your equivocal family circumstances were likely to involve you in difficulties in the political career you are entering on, or, at least, in mortifications, on my making a remark to that effect in one of my letters, your father determined to delay no longer the legal and official recognition which the extinction of all his family made so desirable for you; and he set out from his distant residence to carry it into effect.

"The recognition and legitimization of a natural son is a serious matter, surrounded by legal complications. An authenticated affidavit must be taken in the presence of a notary; and even though the father's personal deposition can be represented by a specially prepared document, M. le Marquis thought that the formalities indispensable to make this power of attorney effective might divulge the secret of his identity, not only to your disadvantage, but in the foreign land where he is married, and to some extent naturalized; and that secret it is still incumbent on him to keep for a time. This decided him. He made an excuse to take a few weeks' absence, arrived, posting all the way, and taking me by surprise, arranged for our meeting here.

"In the course of such a long and hurried journey he feared that the considerable sum of money he is devoting to secure your election might not be quite safe in his keeping, and he therefore transmitted it through his bankers, to be drawn on a certain day. That is why, on your arrival, I asked you the question which may have surprised you.—Now I have to ask you another of far greater importance: Do you consent to take M. de Sallenauve's name and be acknowledged by him as his son?"

"I am no lawyer," said I; "but it seems to me that, even if I did not feel highly honored by it, it does not lie in my hands to decline such a recognition."

"I beg your pardon," said Jacques Bricheteau; "you might be the son of a very undesirable father, and find it to your interest to dispute the relationship; in the case as it stands you could plead, probably with success, to decline the favor proposed. I ought also to tell you—and I know that I am expressing the intentions of M. le Marquis—that if you do not think a man who has already spent half a million of francs out of pocket with a view to your election a father altogether to your mind, we leave you perfectly free, and have no wish to coerce you."

"Quite so, quite so," said M. de Sallenauve, in a short, sharp tone and the thin high pipe which is peculiar to these relics of the old aristocracy.

Mere politeness required me to say that I was only too happy to accept the parentage thus pressed on me; and in reply to the few words I spoke to that effect, Jacques Briche-teau went on:

"And we do not ask you to 'buy a *father* in a poke.'—Not so much with a view to command your confidence, which he believes he has won, as to enable you to judge of the family whose name you will bear, M. le Marquis will place before you all the title-deeds and parchments that are in his possession; and besides this, though it is a long time since he left France, he can prove his identity by the evidence of his still living contemporaries, which will serve to corroborate the validity of the act he will put his name to.—For instance, among the persons of unimpeachable honor who have already recognized him, I may mention the venerable Mother Superior of the Ursuline Sisters here, Mother Marie des Anges—for whom, I may add, you have executed a masterpiece."

"Yes, on my honor, a very pretty thing," said the Marquis. "If you are as strong in politics——"

"Well, then, Marquis," said Jacques Bricheteau, who seemed to me a little overbearing, "will you and our young friend proceed to verify those family papers?"

"It is quite unnecessary," said I.

And I must own that it did not seem to me that I was run-ning any great risk; for, after all, of what consequence were such papers in the hands of a man who might have forged or stolen them?

But my father would not let me off; for more than two hours he spread before me deeds, pedigrees, settlements, letters patent, a thousand documents, to prove that the Sallenauves are, with the exception of the Cinq-Cygnes, one of the oldest families in the Province of Champagne generally, and of the department of the Aube in particular. I may add that this display of archives had a running accompaniment of endless details in words, which certainly gave the identity of the last Marquis de Sallenauve a very convincing semblance of genuineness.

On all other subjects my father is apt to be laconic; his mind is not, I should say, remarkably open, and he is always ready to leave his Chancellor to speak for him. But on the subject of his family papers he was bewilderingly full of anecdotes, reminiscences, and heraldic information; in short, the complete gentleman of an older time, ignorant or superficial on most subjects, but a Benedictine for erudition on everything connected with his ancestors.

There we should have sat, I believe, till now but for Bricheteau's intervention: as he saw the Marquis preparing to complete his endless chronicle by reading aloud to me a voluminous memorial, intended to refute a certain passage in the *Historiettes* of Tallemant des Réaux, which was not written to the honor and glory of the Sallenauves, the judicious organist remarked that it was dinner-time if we meant to arrive punctually at seven at Maître Achille Pigoult's office, as had been arranged.

So we dined, not at the *table d'hôte,* but in a private room. There was nothing remarkable about the meal, unless it were the length of time it lasted in consequence of the absorbed silence and slowness of the Marquis' deglutition, in consequence of the loss of all his teeth.

So by seven o'clock we were at Maître Pigoult's——

But it is near on two in the morning, and I am dropping asleep; so, till to-morrow,—when, if I have time, I will go on with this letter and the circumstantial account of all that took place in the notary's office. However, you know the upshot of it all, like a man who turns to the page of a novel to see whether Evelina marries her Arthur, and you may let me off the details. As I step into bed, I shall say to myself: Good-night, M. de Sallenauve.

In fact, that old rascal Bricheteau was clumsy enough in foisting on me such a name as Dorlange; it was only fit for some hero of romance under the Empire, or one of the provincial tenors on the lookout for an engagement under the meagre shade of the Palais-Royal. You will owe me no grudge, I trust, for leaving you in favor of my bed, where I shall fall asleep to the soft murmurs of the Aube. In the unspeakable stillness of the night in a small country town, I can hear its ripples from this room.

May 4, five in the morning.

I had counted on slumbers gladdened by the fairest dreams; and I had not been asleep one hour when I woke, stung to the quick by a horrible thought. But before communicating it to you—for it really has no common-sense—I must tell you what took place last evening at the notary's. Some of the incidents of that scene may perhaps have had something to do with the phantasmagoria that have since danced through my brain. After Maître Pigoult's maid-servant, a country wench of the purest breed, had led us through an office of the most venerably antique type—where, however, no clerks were to be seen working in the evening, as in Paris—she showed us into her master's private room, a large room, cold and damp, and barely lighted by two composition candles on the desk. Notwithstanding a sharp north wind that was blowing, in honor of the poet's month of May and of the spring, as declared by law at this season of the year, there was no fire on the hearth, though the wood was laid for a cheerful blaze.

Maître Achille Pigoult, a feeble little man, much marked with small-pox, and afflicted with green spectacles, over which, however, he can flash a look of great keenness and intelligence, asked us if we found the room warm enough. On our replying in the affirmative—which he must have seen was a mere form of politeness—he had carried his incendiary purpose so far as to strike a match, when, from one of the darkest corners of the room, a broken and quavering voice, whose owner we had not yet discerned, opposed this lavish extravagance.

"No, no, Achille, do not light the fire," cried the old man. "There are five of us in the room; the candles give a good deal of heat, and we shall be suffocated before long."

To these words of this hot-blooded Nestor, the Marquis exclaimed:

"Why, it is worthy M. Pigoult, the old justice of the peace!"

The old man, thus recognized, rose and came up to my father, whom he examined narrowly.

"To be sure!" said he. "And I know you for a native of the province, of the old block; Achille told me the truth when he promised me that I should meet two old acquaintances. You," said he to the organist, "are little Bricheteau, nephew to the good Mother-Superior Marie des Anges. But that tall fellow, with his face like a duke—I cannot put a name to him —and you must not be too hard on my memory, for after eighty-six years of hard service—it has a right to be a little stiff in the joints."

"Now, then, grandfather," said Achille Pigoult, "try to furbish up your recollections—and you, gentlemen, not a word, not a hint.—I want to enlighten my faith. I have not the honor of knowing the client on whose behalf I am about to act, and, to be strictly regular, proof of his identity is required. The act of Louis XII., passed in 1498, and of François I. confirming it, in 1535, make this imperative on notaries —gardes-notes as they were called—to forefend any substitution of parties to such deeds. The law is too reasonable to have fallen into desuetude; and, for my part, I should not have the smallest respect for the validity of an act if it could be proved that such identification had been neglected."

While his son was speaking, old Pigoult had been racking his memory. My father, by good luck, has a queer nervous twitch of his features, which was naturally aggravated under the steady gaze of the certifier. On seeing this muscular movement, the old lawyer at last spotted his man.

"Ah, I have it !" he exclaimed. "Monsieur is the Marquis de Sallenauve—the man we used to call the *Grimacier*—who would, at this day, be the master of the Château d'Arcis if he had but married his pretty cousin, who had it for her marriage portion, instead of going off with the rest of the madmen as an *émigré.*"

"Still a bit of a *sans-culotte,* it would seem," said the Marquis, laughing.

"Gentlemen," said the notary impressively, "the test I had planned seems to me to be decisive. This evidence and the papers which M. le Marquis has been good enough to submit to me, leaving them in my hands, together with the certificate of identity forwarded to me by Mother Marie des Anges, who is prohibited by the rules of her house from coming to my office, certainly justify us in completing the deeds which I have already prepared. One of them requires the signature of two witnesses. For one, we have here M. Bricheteau ; for the other, my father, if you will accept him, and the honor, it seems to me, is his by right, for we may say he has won it at the point of his memory."

"Well, then, gentlemen, let us take our seats !" exclaimed Bricheteau enthusiastically.

The notary seated himself at his table ; we made a semicircle, and he began to read the deeds. The object in view was set forth—to authenticate the recognition by François-Henri-Pantaléon Dumirail, Marquis de Sallenauve, of his son, in my person ; but here a difficulty arose. Deeds under a notary's certificate must mention the place of residence of the contracting parties, otherwise they are void. Now, where did my father reside ? A blank space had been left by the notary, who wished to fill it up before proceeding any further.

"In the first place," said Pigoult, "it would seem that M. le Marquis has no place of residence in France, since, in fact, he does not reside in the country, and has for many years owned no land in it."

"That is true," said the Marquis, in a graver tone than the remark seemed to call for; "in France I am but a vagabond."

"Aha!" said Jacques Bricheteau, "but vagabonds like you, who can hand over on the nail such gifts to a son as the sum needed to purchase a mansion, are not beggars we need waste our pity on. At the same time, what you say is true—equally true in France or elsewhere—for with your mania for eternally wandering it seems to me pretty difficult to name your place of residence."

"Well, well," said Achille Pigoult, "we will not be brought to a standstill by such a trifle as that.—Monsieur," and he turned to me, "is now the owner of the Château d'Arcis, for an agreement to sell is equivalent to a sale when the parties are agreed as to the terms and price. Then, what can be more natural than that the father's domicile should be stated as at one of his son's estates; especially when it is family property recovered to the original owners by purchase for that son's benefit, though paid for by the father; when, moreover, that father was born in the place where the said residence or domicile is situated, and is known and recognized by residents of standing whenever, at long intervals, he chooses to visit it?"

"Quite right," said old Pigoult, yielding without hesitation to the argument set forth by his son, in that emphatic tone peculiar to men of business when they believe they have laid their finger on a conclusive opinion.

"Certainly," said Jacques Bricheteau, "if you think the thing can be worked so——"

"You see that my father, a man of great experience, does not hesitate to support my opinion.—So we will say," added the notary, taking up his pen: " 'François-Henri-Pantaléon Dumirail, Marquis de Sallenauve, residing with M. Charles de Sallenauve, his natural son legitimized by this act, in the house known as the Château d'Arcis in the district of Arcis-sur-Aube, department of the Aube.' "—And the rest of the deed was read without any hitch.

Then followed a very ridiculous little scene.

All having signed, while we were still standing there, Jacques Bricheteau said:

"Now, M. le Comte, embrace your father."

My father opened his arms with no small indifference, and I coldly fell into them, vexed with myself, however, for not being more deeply moved or feeling in my heart the glow of kindred blood.

Were this coldness and dryness the result of my rapid increase of fortune?—At any rate, immediately after, by another deed which we had to listen to, I became, in consideration of a sum of a hundred and eighty thousand francs in ready money, possessor of the Château d'Arcis, a fine large house which I had noticed from afar, lording it over the country with quite a feudal air, though the prophetic voice of the proprietor was no more heard within me than that of blood relationship. The importance of this property as bearing on my election, even if I had not been instinctively aware of it, would have been made clear to me by a few words that passed between the notary and Jacques Bricheteau. After the manner of sellers, who will still run up the value of their goods even after they have parted with them:

"You may think yourselves lucky," said Achille Pigoult; "you have got that estate for a mere song."

"Stuff and nonsense!" retorted Bricheteau. "How long have you had it on your hands? To anybody else your client would have sold it for fifty thousand crowns, but as a family property you made us pay for the chance of having it. We shall have to spend twenty thousand francs in making it habitable; the ground will hardly return four thousand francs a year; so our money, including expenses, will not bring in two and a half per cent."

"What have you to complain of?" replied the notary; "you will have to employ labor, and that is not bad luck for a candidate."

"Ah, that election," said Jacques Bricheteau. "We will talk that over to-morrow when we come to pay over the money for the house, and our debt to you."

Thereupon we came away, and returned to the *Hôtel de la Poste,* where, after saying good-night to my father and his mouthpiece, I retired to my room to chat with you.

And now for the dreadful idea which drove away sleep and made me take up my pen again; I must tell you what it was, though, having relieved myself a little by writing these two pages, it does not seem to me so pressingly evident as it did just now. One thing at least is certain—everything that has come into my life during the past year is prodigiously romantic. You will perhaps say that adventures seem to form the natural current of my life; that my birth, the coincidence that threw us together with a strange similarity of fate, my position with regard to Marianina, and my handsome housekeeper, even my meeting and acquaintance with Mme. de l'Estorade, seem to suggest that I was born under a whimsical star, and that I am even now living under the influence of one of its vagaries. Absolutely true. Still, if at the same time, and under the same influence, I should be involved, without knowing it, in some diabolical plot of which I am being made the passive tool!

To give my ideas some little order, I will begin at that half million of francs spent, as you must allow, on a somewhat nebulous dream—that of one day possibly seeing me a Minister to some imaginary court heaven knows where, the name being carefully concealed. And who is it that lavishes such fabulous sums on me? A father tenderly devoted to the child of a lost love?—No—a father whose demeanor is absolutely cold, who goes to sleep while the balance-sheet, as it were, of our reciprocal relations is being read to me; for whom I on my part, and more's the pity, have no sympathy, whom I should, in fact, describe as an old owl of an *émigré,* but for the filial respect and affection I try to feel.—But now, I say, supposing this man were not my father, were not even the Marquis de Sallenauve, as he assumes to be; supposing that, like that luckless Lucien de Rubempré—whose story made such a noise at the time—I were wrapped in the coils of some serpent of the type of the sham priest Carlos Herrera, and to wake presently to the frightful truth!

"What possible chance is there of that?" you will say. "Carlos Herrera had an object in fascinating Lucien de Rubempré; but what hold can any one have over you, a man of principle, who have never looked for luxury, who have led a life of study and hard work?—and above all, what is to be got out of you?"

Well and good. But is the professed and apparent object of these men any clearer? Why does the man who recognizes me as his son conceal the name of the place he lives in, and that by which he himself is known in the unknown northern land where he is said to hold office? Why so little confidence and so many sacrifices on my behalf?—And does it seem to you that, in spite of his lengthy explanations, Jacques Bricheteau has satisfactorily accounted for the mystery in which he has wrapped my life? Why his dwarf? Why his impudent denial of his own identity the first time I addressed him? Why that frantic flitting?

All this, my dear fellow, whirling in my brain and culminating in the five hundred thousand francs paid over to me by the brothers Mongenod, seems to lend substance to a queer notion, at which you will laugh perhaps, but which is not without foundation in the annals of crime. As I said at first, I was invaded by it, and its suddenness seems to give it the character of an instinctive apprehension. One thing is certain: If I had had the most distant inkling of it last evening, I would have had my hand cut off sooner than sign that deed, binding up my life and fortunes with those of a stranger whose destiny may be as dark as a canto of Dante's *inferno,* and who may drag me with him into the blackest depths.

In short, this idea—while I am making you beat about the bush, not liking to be frank with you—is in its blank crudity just this: I am afraid lest I am unwittingly the agent of one of those associations of coiners who, in order to put their spurious currency into circulation, have been frequently discovered by justice in the act of conspiracies and schemes quite as complicated and inextricable as this with which I am now mixed up. In these trials we constantly see that the accomplices make many and long journeys; they deal in bills drawn in remote spots on banks in important commercial centres, or in such capital cities as Stockholm, Rotterdam, or Paris. And we constantly find their unhappy dupes implicated in the case. Now in this man Bricheteau's mysterious proceedings, do you not detect a sort of imitation or mimicry of the manœuvres to which these ingenious criminals have recourse, using them with such talent and imaginative skill as romance-writers might long for?

As you may suppose, I have represented to myself every argument that can tell against this gloomy view of the case; and if I do not state them here, it is because I wish to have them from you, and so give them a value which they would cease to have if I had inspired them. Of one thing I am certain: I am living in an unwholesome atmosphere, thick and heavy; I want air, and I cannot breathe.

Still, if you can, reassure me, convince me; I shall be only glad, as you may well suppose, to find it all a bad dream. But, at any rate, no later than to-morrow I mean to have an explanation with both these men, and get a little more light on the subject than has as yet been vouchsafed me.

Here is a new aspect to the story. While I was writing I heard the clatter of horses in the street. Having grown distrustful, and inclined to take a serious view of every incident, I opened my window, and by the pale light of daybreak I saw at the inn door a post-chaise—horses, postilion, and all—ready to start, and Jacques Bricheteau talking to somebody inside, whose face was hidden by the peak of his traveling cap. I acted at once: I ran downstairs; but before I reached the bottom, I heard the dull clatter of wheels and the ringing cracks of the whip—a sort of parting song with all postilions.

At the foot of the stairs I stood face to face with Jacques Bricheteau.

Not in the least embarrassed, he said, with perfect simplicity: "What! up already, my dear boy?"

"Of course," said I, "the least I could do was to say good-bye to my most kind father."

"He did not wish it," said the confounded musician, with a cool solemnity that made me long to thrash him. "He was afraid of the agitation of a parting."

"He is in a devil of a hurry," said I, "if he could not spare one day to his brand-new paternity."

"What can I say? He is an oddity. He has done what he came to do, and he saw no reason to remain any longer."

"To be sure, the high functions he fulfils in that northern court——"

There could be no mistake as to the deeply ironical tone with which I spoke.

"Till now," said Bricheteau, "you have put more trust in us."

"Yes, but I confess that my confidence is beginning to be shaken by the ponderous mysteries that are so unmercifully and incessantly piled upon it."

"I should really be most distressed," said Jacques Bricheteau, "at seeing you give way, at this critical moment, to these doubts, which are certainly justified by the way you have been dealt with during so many years, if I had none but personal arguments or statements to countervail them. But you may remember that old Pigoult, last evening, spoke of an aunt of mine in these parts, and you will see before long that she is a person of considerable importance. I may add that her sacred dignity gives absolute authority to her word. I had arranged that we should see her in any case to-day; but give me only time to shave myself, and in spite of its being so early we will go at once to the Ursuline convent. You can then question Mother Marie des Anges, who is regarded as a saint throughout the department of the Aube, and by the end of the interview, I fancy, no cloud will hang between us."

All the time this strange man was talking his countenance was so unmistakably honest and benevolent; his language—always calm, elegant, and moderate—is so persuasive to his audience, that I felt the tide of my wrath ebbing and my confidence reviving.

In fact, the answer was final. The Ursuline convent, bless me! cannot be a mint for false coin; and if Mother Marie des Anges will answer for my father, as it would seem she has already done to the notary, I should be mad to feel any further doubts.

"Very well," said I, "I will go upstairs for my hat and wait for you on the bank of the river."

"Do so. And keep an eye on the door of the inn for fear I should make a bolt, as I did from the Quai de Béthune!"

The man is as clever as can be; he seems to read one's thoughts. I was ashamed of my distrust, and said that while waiting I would finish a letter.—This is it, my dear friend, and I must now close it and post it if it is to reach you in due time. Another day I will tell you of our visit to the convent.

Marie-Gaston to Madame la Comtesse de l'Estorade.

ARCIS-SUR-AUBE, *May* 6, 1839.

MADAME,—I should in any case have availed myself with pleasure of your commands that I should write to you during my stay here; but you have no idea how great was your kindness in grating me so precious a favor. But for you, madame, and the honor I may have of occasionally writing to you, what would become of me, a prey to the accustomed tyranny of my sad thoughts, in a town where there is no society, no commerce, no object of interest, no pretty environs, and where intellectual activity is limited to the production of pickled pork, soft soap, stockings, and cotton night-caps?

Dorlange, whom I shall not continue to call by that name— you shall presently learn why—is so much absorbed in the cares of his canvass that I scarcely ever see him. I told you, madame, that I was about to join our friend here in consequence of some disturbance of mind that I was aware of in a letter telling me of a great change in his life and prospects. I am now allowed to be more explicit on the subject—Dorlange at last knows his father. He is the natural son of the Marquis de Sallenauve, the last survivor of one of the oldest

families of this province. The Marquis, though giving no
explanation of the reasons that led to his keeping his son's
birth so profoundly secret, has just acknowledged him with
every legal formality. At the same time, he has purchased
for him an estate which had long since ceased to belong to the
Sallenauves, and which will now again be a family possession.
It is actually in Arcis, and it seems probable that it may be
advantageous to the electoral schemes just now under discussion.

These schemes had their beginnings longer ago than we
supposed, and they did not take their rise in Dorlange's brain.
The Marquis began his preparations above a year since, by
sending his son a large sum to enable him to acquire the necessary qualification by the purchase of a freehold; and it is
with a view to smoothing the way to political advancement
that he has given his son a name and title and property in
this town.

What the ultimate purpose may be of such considerable
expenditure the Marquis has never explained to Charles de
Sallenauve; and it was this still hazy horizon to his sky that
led the poor fellow to such apprehensions that, as a friend,
I could do no less than hasten to alleviate them. The Marquis, in fact, seems to be as eccentric as he is wealthy; instead of remaining at Arcis, where his presence and his name
might have contributed to the success he is so anxious for,
on the very day after carrying out all the formalities required by the law, he set out privily for some distant country
where he has, it would seem, some important function—not
even giving his son the opportunity of bidding him good-bye.
This coldness has a good deal embittered Charles' satisfaction;
however, fathers must be taken as we find them, for Dorlange
and I both live to prove that they are not to be had for the
wishing.

Another whim of my Lord Marquis is having selected as his
son's chief elector an old Ursuline nun, by a sort of bargain
in which subsequently you, madame, were a factor. Yes;
for the "Saint Ursula" for which you unawares were the

model will probably have no little influence over our friend's return to Parliament.

This is what happened. For many years Mother Marie des Anges, Superior of the Ursuline Sisters at Arcis-sur-Aube, had dreamed of erecting a statue of the patron saint in the convent chapel. But the Abbess, being a woman of taste and culture, would have nothing to do with the peddler's images of saints, sold ready-made by the dealers; on the other hand, she could not in conscience rob the poor of a sum so considerable as would pay for a work of art on commission. This excellent lady's nephew is an organist in Paris, and the Marquis de Sallenauve while he was traveling all over the world had confided his son to this man's care; for all these years his first object has been to keep the poor boy in absolute ignorance of his birth. When it occurred to him to make Sallenauve a deputy, Arcis was naturally thought of as the place where his family was still remembered, and every way and means was considered of making acquaintance, and utilizing all possible aids to his election.

Then the organist remembered his aunt's long-cherished ambition; he knew her to have influence in the district, where she is in great odor of sanctity, and also a touch of the spirit of intrigue, ever ready to rush into an affair that may be difficult and arduous. He went to see her with the Marquis de Sallenauve's concurrence, and told her that one of the most eminent of Paris sculptors was prepared to offer her a statue of the most masterly execution, if she, on her part, would undertake to secure his return as member for the district of Arcis at the next election.

The old Abbess did not think this at all beyond her powers. So now she is the proud possessor of the object of her pious ambition; it came safely to hand a few days since, and is already in its place in the convent chapel, where, ere long, it will be solemnly dedicated. Now it remains to be seen how the good Mother will perform her share of the bargain.

Well, madame, strange to say, all things weighed and con-

sidered, I should not at all wonder if this singular woman
were to succeed. From the description given me by Charles,
Mother Marie des Anges is a little woman, short but thick-
set, with a face that still contrives to be attractive in spite
of her wrinkles and the saffron-tinted pallor induced by time
and by the austerities of a cloister. She carries the burden
of a stout figure and seventy-six years with ease, and is as
quick, bright, and spirited as the youngest of us. A thoroughly
capable woman, she has governed her House for fifty years,
and it has always been the best regulated, the most efficient,
and at the same time the richest convent in the whole diocese
of Troyes. No less well qualified for educating girls—the
great end, as you know, of the Ursuline Sisterhoods—she has
for the same length of time, through varying fortunes, managed a lay school which is famous in the department and in
all the country round. Having thus presided over the education of almost all the daughters of the better families of the
province, it is easy to understand that she has ubiquitous influence in the aristocratic circles of Champagne, for a well-
conducted education always leads to permanent friendship
between teacher and pupils. She probably knows very well
how to turn these family connections to the best advantage in
the contest she has pledged herself to engage in.

It would seem, too, that on the other hand, this remarkable
woman can absolutely command all the democratic votes in
the district. So far, indeed, on the scene of the struggle, this
party has but a sickly and doubtful existence; still, it is by
nature active and busy, and it is under that flag, with some
little modifications, that our candidate comes forward. Hence,
any support from that side is useful and important. You,
madame, like me, will certainly admire the *bicephalous* powers, so to speak, of this old Abbess, who contrives at the same
time to be in good odor with the nobility and the secular
clergy, while wielding the conductor's stick for the radical
party, their perennial foes. As a woman of admirable charity
and enlightenment, regarded as a saint by the country folks,
and the object of bitter persecutions during the Revolution,

enduring them with immense fortitude, it is easy to understand the position she holds among the higher and Conservative circles; but that she should be no less welcome to democrats and destructives seems almost incredible.

Her great influence over the popular party is based on a little contest she once had with them. About the year '93 that amiable faction proposed to cut her head off. Turned out of her convent, and convicted for having sheltered a contumacious priest, she was imprisoned, brought before the revolutionary tribunal, and condemned to the guillotine. The thing came to Danton's knowledge; he was then a member of the Convention. Danton had been acquainted with Mother Marie des Anges; he believed her to be the most virtuous and enlightened woman he had ever seen. On hearing of her sentence, he flew into a terrific rage, wrote a letter from his *high horse* to the revolutionary municipality, and commanded a respite with such authority as no man in Arcis would have dreamed of disputing. He stood up in the Tribune that very day; and after alluding in general terms to certain *sanglants imbéciles* whose insane folly was damaging the prospects of the Revolution, he explained who and what Mother Marie des Anges was, spoke of her wonderful gifts for the training of the young, and laid before the meeting a sketch for a decree by which she was to be placed at the head of a Great National Gynecæum, the details to be regulated by subsequent enactment.

Robespierre, who would have regarded the Ursuline nun's superior intelligence as an additional qualification for the scaffold, was not that day present at the sitting; the motion was carried with enthusiasm. As Mother Marie des Anges could not possibly carry out the decree thus voted without a head on her shoulders, she was allowed to retain it, and the executioner cleared away his machinery. And though the former decree, authorizing the Grand National Gynecæum, was presently forgotten, the Convention having quite other matters to occupy it, the good Sister carried it out on her own lines; and instead of something Grand, Greek, and National, with the help of some of her former associates she started a simple lay school at Arcis, to which, as soon as order was to some degree restored in the land and in men's minds, pupils flocked from all the neighboring country.

Under the Emperor, Mother Marie des Anges reconstituted her House, and her first act of government was a signal piece of gratitude. She decided that on the 5th of April every year, the anniversary of Danton's death, Mass should be said in the convent chapel for the repose of his soul.

To some who objected to this service for the dead—

"Do you know many persons," she would reply, "for whom it is more necessary to implore Divine mercy?"

After the Restoration, the performance of this Mass became a matter of some little difficulty; but Mother Marie des Anges would never give it up, and the veneration with which she was regarded even by those who were most set against what they called a scandal, ended in their making the best of it. Under the July Revolution, as you may suppose, this courageous perversity had its reward. Mother Marie des Anges is now in high favor at Court; there is nothing she cannot obtain from the most august persons in command; still, it is but fair to add that she asks for nothing, not even to help the poor; she finds the means of supplying most of their wants by her judicious economy in dealing with the funds of the community. What is even more obvious is that her gratitude to the great revolutionary leader is a strong recommendation to that party; this, however, is not the whole secret of her influence with them. The representative in Arcis of the extreme Left is a wealthy miller, named Laurent Goussard, who owns two or three mills on the river Aube. It was this man, formerly a member of the revolutionary municipality of Arcis, and a particular friend of Danton's, who wrote to that terrible Cordelier to tell him of the axe that hung over the Ursuline prioress' head, though this did not hinder that worthy *sans-culotte* from purchasing a large part of the convent lands when they were sold as nationalized property.

Then, when Mother Marie des Anges was enabled to re-

constitute her Sisterhood, Laurent Goussard, who had not as
it happened found the estate very profitable, came to the
worthy Abbess and proposed to reinstate her in the former
possessions of the Abbey. Laurent Goussard, a man with a
keen eye to business, whose niece Mother Marie des Anges had
brought up gratuitously (the young lady died in Paris in
1809), affected to make this a point of honor, offering to restore to the community the lands he had bought for the price
he had paid for them. The good man was not making a bad
bargain; the mere difference of value between silver and the
assignats he had paid in was a handsome turn of profit. But
Mother Marie des Anges, who had not forgotten that but for
his intervention Danton could have known nothing, determined to do better than that for the man who had really
saved her life. The Ursuline Sisterhood, when Laurent
Goussard proposed this arrangement, was, financially speaking, in a flourishing position. Since its re-establishment it
had come in for some liberal donations, and the Mother Superior had put away a considerable sum during her long management of the lay school; this she generously handed over for
the use of the convent. Laurent Goussard was, no doubt,
somewhat amazed when she spoke to this effect:

"I cannot accept your offer; I cannot buy at the lowest
price; my conscience forbids it. Before the Revolution the
convent lands were valued at so much; this is the price I propose to pay, not that to which they were brought down as a
result of the general depreciation in value of all the nationalized lands. In short, my good sir, I mean to pay more—if
that meets your views."

Laurent Goussard thought at first that he misunderstood
her, or had been misunderstood; but when it dawned upon
him that the Mother Superior's scruples of conscience would
bring him a profit of about fifty thousand francs, he had no
wish to coerce so delicate a conscience, and pocketing this
godsend, which had really fallen from heaven, he made the
astonishing facts known far and wide; and this, as you may
suppose, madame, raised Mother Marie des Anges to such

estimation in the eyes of every buyer of nationalized lands, that she will never have anything to fear from any revolution. Personally, Laurent Goussard is her fanatical adorer; he never does a stroke of business or moves a sack of corn without consulting her; and, as she said jestingly the other day, if she had a mind to treat the Sous-préfet like John the Baptist, in a quarter of an hour Laurent Goussard would bring her that official's head in a sack. Does not that sufficiently prove, madame, that at a nod from our Abbess he will vote, and get all his friends to vote, for the candidate of her choice?

Mother Marie des Anges has, of course, a wide connection among the clergy, both by reason of her habit and her reputation for distinguished virtue; and among her most devoted allies may be numbered Monseigneur Troubert, the bishop of the diocese, who, though formerly an adherent of the *Congregation,* would, under the dynasty of July, put up with an archbishopric as preliminary to the cardinal's hat. Now if, to assist him in this ambition—justified, it must be said, by great and indisputable capabilities—Mother Marie des Anges were to write a few lines to the Queen, it is probable that his promotion would not be too long deferred. But it will be give and take. If the Ursuline Abbess works for the archbishopric, Monseigneur de Troyes will work the election. Nor will his share of the bargain be at all difficult, since the candidate in whom he is required to interest himself is a declared advocate of freedom in teaching, which is the only political principle for which the clergy care at this moment.

Winning the clergy almost certainly secures the Legitimist vote, for that party is no less passionately bent on freedom in teaching; and, out of hatred for the new (Orleans) dynasty, does not even take fright at seeing that principle in monstrous alliance with radical politics. The head of that party in this district is the family of Cinq-Cygne. The old Marquise, whose haughty temper and determined will are known to you, madame, never comes to the Château of Cinq-

Cygne without visiting Mother Marie des Anges, whose pupil her daughter Berthe formerly was—now the Duchesse de Maufrigneuse; as to the Duke, he will certainly support us, for, as you know, Daniel d'Arthez is a great friend of mine, and through Arthez we are certain to secure the interest of the Princesse de Cadignan, our handsome Duke's mother, so we may count on him.

If we now turn to a more obdurate party—the Conservatives, who must not be confounded with the Ministerialists—their leader is the Comte de Gondreville, your husband's colleague in the Upper Chamber. At his heels comes a very influential voter, his old friend, the former mayor and notary of Arcis, who in his turn drags in his train a no less important elector, Maître Achille Pigoult, to whom, on retiring, he sold his connection. But Mother Marie des Anges has a strong hold on the Comte de Gondreville through his daughter, the Maréchale de Carigliano. This great lady, who, as you are aware, is immensely devout, comes every year to the Ursuline Convent for a penitential retreat. Mother Marie des Anges says, moreover, though she gives no explanations, that she has a hold on the old Count through some circumstances known only to herself; and, in fact, this regicide's career—becoming a Senator, a Count of the Empire, and now a peer of France —must have led him through devious and subterranean ways, making it probable that there have been secret passages which he would not care to have brought to light. Now, Gondreville is one with Grévin, for fifty years his second self and active tool; and even supposing that by some impossible chance their long union should be severed, at least we should be sure of Achille Pigoult, Grévin's successor as notary to the Ursuline Sisterhood; indeed, at the time of the acquisition of the estate in Arcis by the Marquis de Sallenauve, which was effected through him, the purchaser took care to pay him a honorarium so large—so *electoral*—that he pledged himself merely by accepting it.

As to the ruck of the voters, our friend is certain to recruit a strong force, since he is about to give them employment on the important repairs he proposes to begin at once; for the château, of which he is now the proprietor, is, fortunately, falling into ruin in many places. We may trust also to the effect of a magniloquent profession of principles which Charles de Sallenauve has just had printed, setting forth in lofty terms that he will accept neither favors nor office from the Government. And then the oratorical display we may look for at the preliminary meeting, which is already fixed; the support of the opposition papers in Paris as well as here; the abuse and calumny with which the ministerial papers have already opened fire—everything combines to make me hopeful. And there is a further consideration which seems to me final: It would surely not be strange if the good folks of Champagne, with a view to counteracting their reputation as Bœotians, should be eager to elect a man distinguished in art, whose masterpiece they have under their very eyes, who has made himself their fellow-townsman by purchasing an estate which has for ten years been in the market, and who is now about to restore the house, one of the finest in the province, to its former splendor, with prodigal disregard of cost.

After this voluminous essay on our military resources and movements, it hardly beseems me, madame, to complain of any want of mental occupation. I know not whether it is in consequence of the interest I feel in my friend, but I really believe that I have caught a touch of the electoral fever which is raging here; you may even think that this letter, crammed with local details, in which your utmost kindness will scarcely enable you to feel much interest, is a symptom of a terribly bad attack. Again, will you thank me, I wonder, for representing this man as likely to be seen ere long through the halo of parliamentary glory, when, only the other day, you were saying that it was not safe to make a friend of him, in view of his superhuman, and consequently rather aggressive pre-eminence?

To be quite frank, madame, whatever successes may await Charles de Sallenauve in his political career, I fear he may some day regret the calmer glory he would have achieved in the realm of art, but neither he nor I was born under a tranquil star; we have paid dear for our very existence, and that you should not like us is doubly cruel. You have some kind feeling for me, because the fragrance still clings to me of our beloved Louise; have then some little regard for the man whom I have dared to speak of throughout this letter as *our* friend. If indeed, do what he will, he betrays a sort of insufferable greatness, should we not rather pity him than call him to a strict account? Do we not know, you and I, by cruel experience, that the noblest and most glorious lights are those which first sink into the extinction of eternal darkness?

Marie-Gaston to the Comtesse de l'Estorade.

ARCIS-SUR-AUBE, *May* 9, 1839.

MADAME,—You too have the election fever, and you have been good enough to transmit as a message from M. de l'Estorade a certain list of *discouragements,* which no doubt deserve consideration. I may however say at once that this communication does not seem to me to be so important as you perhaps think; and even before your official warning reached us, the difficulties in our course had not failed to occur to us. We knew already of the confidential mission undertaken by M. de Trailles, though for some days he tried, not very successfully, to disguise it under a pretence of commercial business. We even knew what you, madame, do not seem to have known, that this ingenious instrument of the ministerial mind had contrived to combine the care of his personal interests with that of party politics.

M. Maxime de Trailles, if we are correctly informed, was not long since on the point of sinking under the last and worst attack of a chronic malady from which he has long suffered. This malady is his Debt—for we do not speak of M. de Trailles' debts, but of his Debt, as of the National Debt of England. In *extremis,* the gentleman, bent on some desperate remedy, seems to have hoped for a cure in marriage— a marriage *in extremis,* as it might well be called, since he is

said to be very near fifty. Being well known—that is to say,
in his case, much depreciated—in Paris, like tradespeople
whose goods are out of date, he packed himself off to the country, and unpacked himself at Arcis-sur-Aube just as the fun
of the election was beginning, wisely supposing that the rather
uproarious tumult of this kind of political scrimmage might
favor the slightly shady character of his proceedings. He calculated well; the unlooked-for death of young Charles Keller,
who was first chosen as the ministerial candidate, threw the
whole electoral district into great perturbation. M. Maxime
de Trailles, fishing in these turbid waters, contrived to har-
poon a candidate recommended by two very dissimilar kinds
of merit and suitability.

From the point of view of public affairs, M. Beauvisage,
whose name, madame, you will certainly remember, has the
immense advantage of having thoroughly beaten and crushed
the nomination of a little attorney named Simon Giguet, who,
to the great indignation of the Government, wanted to take
his seat with the Left Centre. This ousting of a pert upstart
on the side of the Opposition was thought such an inestimable
boon, that it led folks to overlook the notorious and indisputable ineptitude of this Beauvisage, and the ridicule
which his return could not fail to bring on those who should
vote for his election. On the private side of the question—
that is to say, M. de Trailles' personal interest—M. Beauvisage has the great merit of owning an only daughter, tolerably pretty, who, without any exaggeration, it would seem,
will bring her husband a fortune of five hundred thousand
francs, amassed in the cotton night-cap trade, of which I
spoke in such ribald terms in my last letter. So now the wire-
pulling is all exposed to view. M. de Trailles had to ignite
and feed an ambition and hope of sitting in the Chamber
in the mind of a man who certainly would never have thought
of it unaided; to insinuate that, in return for his help and
disbursements, he meant, of course, to win the daughter and
the dowry; to dazzle her by a made-up semblance of youth,
by supreme elegance of manner, and by the title of Countess;

to begin carefully by seeming to hesitate between the daughter and the mother, and make a crowning display of disinterestedness and reformation by insisting that the settlements should protect the lady's fortune from his extravagance by every restriction the law can devise;—this was the task, the really herculean work, accomplished by M. de Trailles in less than a fortnight!

But then we appeared on the scene. We are of the province; Champenois by the name that dropped on us one morning from the skies; we make ourselves even more so by acquiring land in the district; and, as it happens, the country is bent at this election on sending no one to the Chamber but a specimen of its own vintage!—For that very reason you will say Beauvisage is certain to win; he is the purest and most unmitigated product of the soil.

So you might think, madame, but then we are not quite so idiotic as Beauvisage; we do not invariably make ourselves ridiculous; we do not indeed make cotton night-caps, but we make statues for which we have earned the Legion of Honor; religious statues, to be dedicated with much pomp in the presence of Monseigneur the Bishop, who will condescend to give an address, and of the municipal authorities; statues which the whole of the town—that part of it which is not admitted to the ceremony—is crowding to admire at the House of the Ursulines, who are vain enough of this magnificent addition to their gem of a chapel, and threw open their public rooms and oratory to all comers for the whole day—and this you may be sure tends to make us popular.

What contributes even better to this popularity is that we are not mean like Beauvisage, and do not hoard our income *sou* by *sou;* that we are employing thirty workmen at the château—painters, masons, glaziers, gardeners, trellis-makers; and that while the mayor of the town trudges shabbily on foot, we are to be seen driving through Arcis in an elegant open chaise with two prancing steeds, which our father—not in heaven, but in Paris—anxious to be even more delightful

at a distance than on the spot, sent hither post haste, with
a view, I believe, to snuffing out M. de Trailles' tilbury and
tiger. These, I may tell you, before our arrival were the
talk of the town.

This evening, madame, to crown the great occasion of the
dedication of the "Saint Ursula," we are giving a dinner to
fifty guests at our château; and we have been so clever as to
invite not only all the principal magnates of the neighborhood, but every official, permanent or temporary, without distinction. These last, now that we have announced our intention of standing for election, will, we know, certainly not
accept. So much the better! there will be more room for
those who do; and the defaulters, whose names will all be
known to-morrow, will be caught in the very act of such
flagrant servility and subserviency as will, we hope, strike a
fatal blow to their influence.

Yesterday, madame, we drove out in our chaise to the
Château of Cinq-Cygne, where Arthez introduced us to the
Princesse de Cadignan. That woman is really miraculously
preserved; she seems to have been embalmed by the happiness
of her *liaison* with the great writer. "They are the prettiest
picture of happiness ever seen," you said, I remember, of
M. and Mme. de Portenduère; and you might say the same
of Arthez and the Princess, altering the word "pretty" in
consideration of their Indian summer.

From what I knew of a scene that took place, long ago
now, at Mme. d'Espard's at the very beginning of that connection, I felt quite sure of not finding M. de Trailles in
high favor at Cinq-Cygne; for, on that occasion, he had
done his utmost to be offensive to Arthez; and Arthez, though
content with making him ridiculous, regarded him with contempt; and that lofty and noble spirit can never get over
that. On his first arrival here the ministerial envoy was met
with some civilities at Cinq-Cygne; but he was no more than
a floating stick—Arthez soon sent him to the bottom. One
man, who flattered himself that he should find a fulcrum for
intrigue at Cinq-Cygne, is now so entirely out of court that

it was from the Duc de Maufrigneuse—to whom M. de
Trailles was so imprudent as to detail his schemes, as having
known him at the Jockey Club—that I obtained the information set forth at the beginning of this letter, to be handed
on to M. de l'Estorade if you will undertake the commission.

Mme. de Maufrigneuse and the old Marquise de Cinq-
Cygne were wonderfully kind in their reception of Dorlange
—Sallenauve, I should say, but I find it difficult to remember;
as they are less humble than you are, they were not frightened
at any loftiness they might meet with in our friend, and he,
in an interview which was really rather difficult, behaved to
perfection. It is very strange that after living so much
alone, he should at once have turned out perfectly presentable.
Is it perhaps that the Beautiful, which has hitherto been the
ruling idea of his life, includes all that is pleasing, elegant,
and appropriate—things which are generally learned by practice as opportunity offers? But this cannot be the case, for
I have seen very eminent artists, especially sculptors, who,
outside their studios, were simply unendurable.

I must here make a break, madame; I am at an end of
my facts, and drifting into twaddle. To-morrow I shall have
to give you an account of the great banquet, which will be
more interesting than my reflections—philosophical and
moral.

May 10.

The dinner is over, dear madame; it was a magnificent
affair, and will, I fancy, be long talked of in Arcis. Sallenauve has in the organist—who, by the way, at the
ceremony of the statue yesterday, displayed his exquisite
talent on the good Sisters' organ—a sort of steward and
factotum transcending all the Vatels that ever lived. He is
not the man to fall on his sword because the fish is late.
Colored lamps, transparencies, garlands, and drapery to decorate the dining-room, even a little packet of fireworks which
had been stowed in the boot of the chaise by that surly and
invisible father—who has his good side however—nothing
was wanting to the festivities. They were kept up till a late

hour in the gardens of the château, to which the *plebs* were admitted to dance and drink copiously.

Almost all our guests appeared, excepting those whom we had asked merely to compromise them. The invitation was so short—a difficulty inevitable and pardonable under the circumstances—that it was quite amusing to see notes of excuse arriving up to the very dinner hour, for Sallenauve had ordered that they should all be brought to him as soon as they arrived. And as he opened each letter he took care to say quite audibly: "M. le Sous-préfet—M. le Procureur du Roi—The Deputy Judge—expresses his regrets at being unable to accept my invitation."

All these "refusals of support" were listened to with significant smiles and whispering; but when a note was brought from Beauvisage, and Dorlange read aloud that M. le Maire "found it impossible to *correspond* to his polite invitation," laughter was loud and long, as much at the matter as the manner of the refusal. It ended only on the arrival of a M. Martener, examining judge here, who showed the highest courage in accepting this dinner. At the same time, it may be noted that an examining judge is in his nature a divisible entity. As a judge he is a permanent official; all the change he can be subject to is that of his title, and the loss of the small additional salary he is allowed, with the right to issue summonses and catechize thieves, grand privileges of which he may be deprived by the fiat of the Keeper of the Seals. However, allowing that only half of M. Martener was bold, he was hailed like a "full moon."

In the presence of the Duc de Maufrigneuse, of Arthez, and, above all, of Monseigneur the Bishop, who is spending a few days at Cinq-Cygne, one absentee was much commented on, though his reply, sent early in the day, was not read to the company. This was the old notary Grévin. As to the Comte de Gondreville, also absent, nothing could be said; the recent death of his grandson Charles Keller prohibited his presence at this meeting; and Sallenauve, by making his invitation in some sort conditional, had been careful to suggest the excuse; but Grévin, the Comte de Gondreville's right hand, who has certainly made greater and more compromising efforts for his friend than that of dining out—Grévin's absence seemed to imply that his patron was still a supporter of Beauvisage, now almost deserted. And this influence—lying low, in sporting phrase—is really of no small importance to us. Maître Achille Pigoult, Grévin's successor, explained, it is true, that the old man lives in complete retirement, and can hardly be persuaded to dine even with his son-in-law two or three times a year; but the retort was obvious that when the Sous-préfet had lately given a dinner to introduce the Beauvisage family to M. Maxime de Trailles, Grévin had been ready to accept his invitation. So there will be some little pull from the Gondreville party, and Mother Marie des Anges will, I believe, have to bring her secret thrust into play.

The pretext for the dinner being the dedication of the "Saint Ursula," an event which the Sisterhood could not celebrate by a banquet, Sallenauve had a fine opportunity at dessert for proposing a toast:

"To the Mother of the poor; to the noble and saintly spirit which for fifty years has shone on our Province, and to whom is due the prodigious number of cultivated and accomplished women who adorn this beautiful land!"

If you, madame, knew this corner of Champagne as well as I do, you would, when you read this sentence which I have transcribed with tolerable exactitude, exclaim at Sallenauve for a contemptible wretch, and wonder that the passion for power should make any man capable of such horrible enormities. And is it worth a man's while—a man usually so self-respecting—to find courage to tell a lie so great as to be almost a crime, when a mere trifle of which he had never once thought, which is no merit of his own, and of which all the credit must be referred to the fortuitous concourse of linked atoms, recommended him to the sympathy of the voters better than all the speeches in the world?

You yourself mentioned to me that your son Armand saw

a strong resemblance in Sallenauve to the portraits of Danton; it would seem that the remark is true, for I heard it
on all sides, applied not to the portraits, but to the man himself, by guests who had known the great revolutionary well.
Laurent Goussard, as the head of a party, had of course been
invited. He was not only Danton's friend, he was in a way
his brother-in-law; Danton, who was a scapegrace wooer,
having paid his court for several years to one of the honest
miller's sisters. Well, the likeness must in fact be striking;
for after dinner, while we were drinking our coffee, the wine
of the country having mounted a little to the good man's
brain—for there had been no stint, as you may suppose—he
went up to Sallenauve and asked him point-blank if he could
by any chance be mistaken as to his father, and if he were
sure that Danton had had nothing to do with the begetting
of him.

Sallenauve laughed at the idea, and simply did a little
sum:

"Danton died on April 5, 1793. To be his son I must
have been born in 1794 at the latest, and should be five-
and-forty now. Now, as the register in which my birth was
entered—father and mother unknown—is dated 1809, that
—and I hope my face as well—prove me to be but just
thirty."

"Quite true," said Laurent Goussard, "the figures bowl me
over. Never mind; we will get you in all the same."

And I believe the man is right; this whimsical likeness
will be of immense weight in turning the scale of the election. And it must not be supposed that Danton is an object
of execration and horror to the citizens of Arcis, in spite of
the dreadful associations that surround his memory. In the
first place, time has softened them, and there yet remains the
recollection of a strong mind and great brain that they are
proud of owning in a fellow-countryman. At Arcis curiosities and notabilities are scarce; here the people speak of
Danton as at Marseilles they would speak of the Cannebière.
So good luck to this likeness to the demigod, whose worship

is not confined to the town only, but extends throughout the suburbs and district.

These voters, *extra muros,* are sometimes amusingly artless; a little contradiction does not stick in their throat. Some agents sent out into the neighboring country have already made good use of this resemblance; and as in canvassing the rustics it is more important to strike hard than to strike straight, Laurent Goussard's explanation, apocryphal as it is, has gone the round of the rural hamlets with a precision that has met with no contradiction. And while this revolutionary parentage, though purely imaginary, is serving our friend well, on the other hand we say to those worthy voters who are to be caught by something at once more accurate and not less striking:

"He is the gentleman who has just bought the Château d'Arcis."

And as the Château d'Arcis towers above the town and is known to everybody for miles round, it is a sort of landmark; and at the same time, with a perennial instinct of reversion to old world traditions, less dead and buried than might be supposed.

"Oho! he is the lord of the château," they say, a free but respectful version of the idea suggested to them.

So this, madame, saving your presence, is the procedure in the electoral kitchen, and the way to dress and serve up a Member of the Chamber.

Marie-Gaston to Madame de l'Estorade.

ARCIS-SUR-AUBE, *May* 11, 1839.

MADAME,—Since you do me the honor to say that my letters amuse you, I am bound not to be shy of repeating them. But is not this a little humiliating? and when I think of the terrible grief which was our first bond of union, is it possible that I should be an amusing man all the rest of my days? Here, as I have told you, I am in an atmosphere that intoxicates me. I have made a passion of Sallenauve's success, and being, as I am, of a gloomy and hopeless nature, an even greater passion perhaps of the wish to hinder the triumph of ineptitude and folly under the patronage of base interest and intrigue. Thank you, M. de Trailles, for the exhibition you have favored us with of your really burlesque father-in-law! For you have succeeded in interesting me in something; every now and then I laugh rather than rage; but at those moments, at any rate, I forget.

To-day, madame, the grotesque is paramount; we are on full parade. Notwithstanding M. de l'Estorade's discouraging warnings, we are led to suppose that the Ministry has not very exultant tidings from its agent; and this is what makes us think so: *We* are no longer at the *Hôtel de la Poste;* we have left it for our château. But, thanks to a long-standing rivalry between the two inns, *la Poste* and *le Mulet*—where M. de Trailles has his headquarters—we still have ample information from our former residence; and our host there is all the more zealous and willing because I strongly suspect that he had a hand, greatly to his advantage I should think, in arranging and furnishing the banquet of which I had the honor to send you full particulars.

From this man, then, we learn that immediately after our departure, a journalist from Paris put up at the hotel. This gentleman, whose name I have forgotten—which is well for him, considering how glorious a mission he bears—also announced that he came as a champion to lend the *vis* of his Parisian wit to the war of words to be opened on us by the local press, subsidized by the "office of public spirit." So far there is nothing very droll or very depressing in the proceedings; ever since the world began, Governments have been able to find pens for hire, and have never been shy of hiring them. Where the comedy begins is at the co-arrival at the *Hôtel de la Poste* of a damsel of very doubtful virtue, who is said indeed to have accompanied His Excellency the Ministerial newsmonger. The young lady's name, by the way, I happen to remember: she is designated on her passport as Mademoiselle Chocardelle, of independent means; but the journalist in speaking of her never calls her anything but Antonia, or, if he yearns to be respectful, Mademoiselle or *Miss* Antonia.

But what has brought Mlle. Chocardelle to Arcis? A little pleasure trip, no doubt; or perhaps to serve as an escort to monsieur the journalist, who is willing to give her a share in the credit account opened for him on the secret service fund for the daily quota of defamation to be supplied by contract? —No, madame, Mlle. Chocardelle has come to Arcis on business—to recover certain moneys. It would seem that before leaving for Africa, where he has met a glorious death, young Charles Keller signed a bill in favor of Mademoiselle Antonia, an order for ten thousand francs, *value received in furniture,* a really ingenious quibble, the furniture having obviously been *received* by Mademoiselle Chocardelle, who thus priced the sacrifice she made in accepting it at ten thousand francs. At any rate, the bill being nearly due, a few days after hearing of the death of her debtor Mlle. Antonia called at the Kellers' office to know whether it would be paid. The cashier, a rough customer, as all cashiers are, replied that he did not know how Mademoiselle Antonia could have the face to present such a claim; but that in any case the Brothers Keller, his masters, were at present at Gondreville, where all the family had met on hearing the fatal news, and that he should not pay without referring the matter to them.

"Very well, I will refer it myself," said the young lady, who would not leave her bill to run beyond its date.

Thereupon, just as she was arranging to set out alone for Arcis, the Government suddenly felt a call to abuse us, if not more grossly, at any rate more brilliantly than the provincials do; and the task of sharpening these darts was confided to a journalist of very mature youth, to whom Mlle. Antonia had been kind—in the absence of Charles Keller!

"I am off to Arcis!" the scrivener and the lady said at the same moment; the commonest and simplest lives offer such coincidences. So it is not very strange that, having set out together, they should have arrived together, and have put up at the same inn.

And now I would beg you to admire the concatenation of things. Mlle. Chocardelle, coming here with an eye solely to finance, the lady has suddenly assumed the highest political importance ! And, as you will see, her valuable influence will amply compensate for the stinging punishment to be dealt us by her gallant fellow-traveler.

In the first place, it appears that on learning that M. de Trailles was in Arcis, Mlle. Chocardelle's remark was:

"What ! he here—that horrid rip ?"

The expression is not parliamentary, and I blush as I write it. But it refers to previous relations—business relations again—between Mlle. Antonia and the illustrious confidant of the Ministerial party. M. de Trailles, accustomed as he is to pay his court only to ladies of position—who help to reduce his debt rather than to add to the burden—once in his life took it into his head to be loved not "for himself alone," and to be useful rather than expensive. He consequently bought a circulating library for Mademoiselle Antonia in the Rue Coquenard, where for some time she sat enthroned. But the business was not a success; a sale became necessary; and M. Maxime de Trailles, with an eye to business as usual, complicated matters by the purchase of the furniture, which slipped through his fingers by the cleverness of a rascal more rascally than himself. By these manœuvres Mlle. Antonia lost all her furniture, which the vans were waiting to remove; and another young lady—Hortense, also "of private means," and attached to old Lord Dudley—gained twenty-five louis by Antonia's mishap.

Of course, madame, I do not pretend to make all these details absolutely clear; they came to us only at second hand from the landlady of the *Poste,* to whom they were confided by Mademoiselle Antonia with more coherency and lucidity no doubt. At any rate, M. de Trailles and Mlle. Chocardelle parted on no friendly terms, and the young lady believes herself justified in speaking of him with the levity, the total absence of moderation, which will have struck you as it did me. In fact, since that first little outburst on her part, things seem to have come to such a pass that M. de Trailles, in consequence of this or of other similar remarks, considered himself seriously compromised, and desired the journalist—whom he frequently sees, of course—to give his ready-tongued companion a "talking to." She, however, cared not a jot, and by the constant dropping of her sarcasms and anecdotes she is producing the effect, I will not say of a countermine, but of a *counter-Maxime,* which is a paralyzing check on the poisonous malignity of our terrible foe. The matter of the bill meanwhile hangs fire: she has twice been out to Gondreville, but was not admitted.

The journalist has much to do: to write his articles in the first place, and to do various small jobs for M. de Trailles, at whose service he is to be. Hence Mlle. Antonia is often left to herself, and, idle and bored as she is, so bereft of any kind of Opera, Ranelagh, Boulevard des Italiens, she has found for herself a really desperate pastime. Incredible as it seems, this amusement is not, after all, utterly incomprehensible, as the device of a Parisienne of her class exiled to Arcis. Quite close to the *Hôtel de la Poste* is a bridge over the Aube. Below the bridge, down a rather steep slope, a path has been made leading to the water's edge, and so far beneath the highroad—which, indeed, is not much frequented—as to promise precious silence and solitude to those who choose to go there and dream to the music of the waters. Mlle. Antonia at first betook herself to sit there with a book; but perhaps, from a painful association with the remembrance of her reading-room, "books," as she says, "are not much in her line"; and at last the landlady of the inn, seeing how tired the poor soul was of herself, happily thought of offering her guest the use of a very complete set of fishing-tackle belonging to her husband, whose multifarious business compels him to leave it for the most part idle.

The fair exile had some luck with her first attempts, and took a great liking for the pastime, which is evidently very fascinating, since it has so many fanatical devotees; and now the few passers-by, who cross the bridge, may admire, on the banks of the Aube, a charming water-nymph in flounced skirts and a broad-brimmed straw hat, casting her line with the conscientious gravity of the most sportsman-like Paris arab, in spite of the changes of our yet unsettled temperature.

So far so good, and at present the lady's fishing has not much to do with our election; but if you should happen to remember in *Don Quixote*—a book you appreciate, madame, for the sake of the good sense and mirthful philosophy that abound in it—a somewhat unpleasant adventure that befalls Rosinante among the Muleteers, you will anticipate, before I tell you, the good luck to us that has resulted from Mademoiselle Antonia's suddenly developed fancy.   Our rival, Beauvisage, is not merely a hosier (retired) and an exemplary mayor, he is also a model husband, never having tripped in the path of virtue, respecting and admiring his wife.   Every evening, by her orders, he is in bed by ten o'clock, while Madame Beauvisage and her daughter go into what Arcis is agreed to call Society.   But stagnant waters are the deepest, they say, and nothing could be less chaste and well regulated than the calm and decorous Rosinante in the meeting I have alluded to.   In short, Beauvisage, making the rounds of *his* town—his laudable and daily habit—standing on the bridge, happened to remark the damsel, her arm extended with manly vigor, her figure gracefully balanced, absorbed in her favorite sport.   A bewitching, impatient jerk as the fair fisher-maiden drew up the line when she had not a nibble, was, perhaps, the electric spark which fired the heart of the hitherto blameless magistrate.   None, indeed, can tell how the matter came about, nor at what precise moment.

I may, however, observe that in the interval between his retirement from the cotton night-cap trade and his election as mayor, Beauvisage himself had practised the art of angling with distinguished skill, and would do so still but for his higher dignity, which—unlike Louis XIV.—keeps him from the shore.   It struck him, no doubt, that the poor girl, with more good-will than knowledge, did not set to work the right way ; and it is not impossible that, as she is temporarily under

Mlle. Antonia Chocardelle.

his jurisdiction, the idea of guiding her into the right way
was the origin of his apparent misconduct. This alone is
certain: crossing the bridge with her mother, Mlle. Beauvisage, like an *enfant terrible,* suddenly exclaimed:

"Why, papa is talking to that Paris woman!"

To make sure, by a glance, of the monstrous fact; to rush
down the slope; to face her husband, whom she found beaming with smiles and the blissful look of a sheep in clover; to
crush him with a thundering "Pray, what are you doing
here?" to leave him no retreat but into the river, and issue
her sovereign command that he should go—this, madame,
was the prompt action of Mme. Beauvisage *née* Grévin; while
Mlle. Chocardelle, at first amazed, but soon guessing what had
happened, went into fits of the most uncontrollable laughter.
And though these proceedings may be regarded as justifiable,
they cannot be called judicious, for the catastrophe was known
to the whole town by the evening, and M. Beauvisage, convicted of the most deplorable laxity, saw a still further thin-
ning of his reduced phalanx of followers.

However, the Gondreville-Grévin faction still held its own,
till—would you believe it?—Mlle. Antonia once more was the
means of overthrowing their last defences.

This is the history of the marvel. Mother Marie des
Anges wished for an interview with the Comte de Gondreville; but she did not know how to manage it, as she thought
it an ill-timed request. Having some severe remarks to make,
it would seem, she would not ask the old man to visit her
on purpose; it was too cruel an offence to charity. Besides,
comminations fired point-blank at the culprit miss their aim
quite as often as they frighten them; whereas observations
softly insinuated are far more certain to have the desired
effect. Still, time was fleeting; the election takes place to-
morrow—Sunday, and to-night the preliminary meeting is to
be held. The poor, dear lady did not know which way to turn,
when some information reached her which was not a little
flattering. A fair sinner, who had come to Arcis intending
to get some money out of Keller, Gondreville's son-in-law, had

heard of the virtues of Mother Marie des Anges, of her indefatigable kindness and her fine old age—in short, all that is said of her in the district where she is, next to Danton, the chief object of interest; and this minx's great regret was that she dared not ask to be admitted to her presence.

An hour later, this note was delivered at the *Hôtel de la Poste*:—

"MADEMOISELLE,—I am told that you wish to see me, and do not know how. Nothing can be easier: ring at the door of my solemn dwelling, ask the Sister who opens it for me, do not be overawed by my black dress and grave face, nor fancy that I force my advice on pretty girls who do not ask it, and may one day be better saints than I am.

"That is the whole secret of an interview with Mother Marie des Anges, who greets you in the Lord Jesus Christ. ✠"

As you may suppose, madame, there was no refusing so gracious an invitation, and before long Mlle. Antonia, in the soberest garb at her command, was on her way to the convent. I much wish I could give you authentic details of the meeting, which must have been a curious one; but nobody was present, nor have I been able to hear what report of it was given by the wandering lamb, who came away moved to tears.

When the journalist tried to make fun of her converted airs:

"There, hold your tongue!" said Mlle. Antonia. "You never in your life wrote such a sentence!"

"What was the sentence, come?"

"'Go, my child,' said the good old lady, 'the ways of God are beautiful and little known; there is more stuff to make a saint of in a Magdalen than in many a nun.'"

And I may add, madame, that as she repeated the words the poor girl's voice broke, and she put her handkerchief to her eyes. The journalist—a disgrace to the press, one of those wretches who are no more typical of the press than a bad priest is of religion—the journalist began to laugh, but scenting danger, he added, "And, pray, when do you mean really to go to Gondreville to speak to Keller, whom I shall certainly end by kicking—in a corner of some article—in spite of all Maxime's instructions to the contrary?"

"Am I going to meddle with any such dirty tricks?" asked Antonia, with dignity.

"What? So now you do not mean to present your bill!"

"I?" replied the devotee of Mother Marie des Anges, probably echoing her sentiments, but in her own words. "*I* try to blackmail a family in such grief? Why, the recollection of it would stab me on my deathbed, and I could never hope that God would have mercy upon me."

"Well, then, become an Ursuline and have done with it."

"If only I had courage enough, I should perhaps be happier; but, at any rate, I will not go to Gondreville.—Mother Marie des Anges will settle everything."

"Why, wretched child, you never left the bill with her!"

"I was going to tear it up, but she stopped me, and told me to give it to her, and that she would manage to pull me through by hook or by crook."

"Oh, very well! You were a creditor—you will be a beggar——"

"No, for I am giving alms. I told Madame the Abbess to keep the money for the poor."

"Oh, if you are going to be a benefactress to convents with your other vice of angling, you will be pleasant company!"

"You will not have my company for long, for I am off this evening, and leave you to your dirty job."

"Hallo! Going to be a Carmelite?"

"Carmelite is good," retorted Antonia sharply; "very good, old boy, when I am leaving a Louis XIV."

For even the most ignorant of these girls all know the story of la Vallière, whom they would certainly adopt as their patron saint, if Saint Louise of Mercy had ever been canonized.

Now, how Mother Marie des Anges worked the miracle

I know not, but the Comte de Gondreville's carriage was standing this morning at the convent gate; the miracle, be it understood, consisting not in having brought that old owl out, for he hurried off, you may be sure, as soon as he heard of ten thousand francs to be paid, though the money was not to come out of his purse but Keller's—it was the family's, and such misers as he have a horror of other folks spending when they do not think the money well laid out. But Mother Marie des Anges was not content with having got him to the convent; she did our business too. On leaving, the Peer drove to see his friend Grévin; and in the course of the day the old notary told a number of persons that really his son-in-law was too stupid by half, that he had got himself into ill odor through this affair with the Parisian damsel, and that nothing could ever be made of him.

Meanwhile, it was rumored that the priests of the two parishes had each received, by the hand of Mother Marie des Anges, a sum of a thousand crowns for distribution among the poor, given to her by a benevolent person who wished to remain unknown. Sallenauve is furious because some of our agents are going about saying that he is the anonymous benefactor, and a great many people believe it, though the story of Keller's bill has got about, and it would be easy to trace this liberality to the real donor. But when once the wind is favorable, it is difficult to trim the sails with mathematical exactitude, and you often get more way on than you wish.

M. Maxime de Trailles cannot get over it, and there is every probability that the defeat, which he must now see is inevitable, will wreck his prospects of marriage. All that can be said with regard to his overthrow is what we always say of an author who has failed—he is a clever man, and will have his revenge.

A very strange man, madame, is this organist, whose name, Bricheteau, is the same as that of one of our great physicians, though they are not related. It is impossible to have more energy, more presence of mind, more devotion and intelligence, and there are not two men in Europe who can play the organ

as he does.   You, who wish Naïs to be something better than
a *strummer,* should certainly get him to teach her.   He is a
man who would really teach her music, and he will not oppress
you with his superiority, for he is as modest as he is gifted.
He is Sallenauve's poodle—just as clever, just as faithful—I
might say just as ugly, if a man with so good and honest a
countenance could be anything but good-looking.

Marie-Gaston to the Comtesse de l'Estorade.

ARCIS-SUR-AUBE, *Sunday, May 12,* 1839.

MADAME,—Yesterday evening the preliminary meeting
was held, a somewhat ridiculous business, and uncommonly
disagreeable for the candidates; however, it had to be faced.
When people are going to pledge themselves to a representative for four or five years, it is natural that they should
wish to know something about him.   Is he intelligent?   Does
he really express the opinions of which he carries the ticket?
Will he be friendly and affable to those persons who may
have to commend their interests to his care?   Has he determination?   Will he be able to defend his ideas—if he has
any?   In a word, will he represent them worthily, steadily,
and truly?—This is the serious and respectable side of the
institution, which, not being enjoined in any code, must have
some good reason for its existence to have established itself so
firmly as a matter of custom.

But every medal has its reverse; and on the other side we
may see the voter at such meetings puffed up with arrogance,
eager to display the sovereign authority which he is about to
transfer to his deputy, selling it as dear as he is able.   From
the impertinence of some of the questions put to the candidate, might you not suppose that he was a serf, over whom
each voter had the power of life and death?   There is not a
corner of his private life which the unhappy mortal can be
sure of hiding from prying curiosity; as to merely stupid
questions, anything is conceivable—as "Does he prefer the
wines of Champagne to those of Bordeaux?"—At Bordeaux,

where wine is the religion, such a preference would prove a
lack of patriotism, and seriously endanger his return. Many
voters attend solely to enjoy the confusion of the nominees.
They cross-examine them, as they call it, to amuse themselves,
as children spin a cockchafer; or as of yore old judges watched
the torture of a criminal, and even nowadays young doctors
enjoy an autopsy or an operation. Many have not even so
refined a taste; they come simply for the fun of the hubbub,
the confusion of voices which is certain to arise under such
circumstances; or they look forward to an opportunity for displaying some pleasing accomplishment; for instance, at the
moment when—as the reports of the sittings in the Chamber
have it—the tumult is at its height, it is not uncommon to
hear a miraculously accurate imitation of the crowing of a
cock, or the yelping of a dog when his foot is trodden on.
Intelligence, which alone should be allowed to vote, having,
like d'Aubigné—Mme. de Maintenon's brother—taken its promotion in cash, we cannot be surprised to find stupid folks
among the electors, and indeed they are numerous enough in
this world to have a claim to be represented.

The meeting was held in a good-sized hall, where an eating-
house keeper gives a dance every Sunday. There is a raised
gallery for the orchestra, which was reserved as a sort of
platform, to which a few non-voters were admitted; I was
one of these privileged few.   Some ladies occupied front seats:
Mme. Marion, the aunt of Giguet the advocate, one of the
candidates; Mme. and Mlle. Mollot, the wife and daughter of
the clerk of assize, and a few others whose names and position
I have forgotten. Mme. and Mlle. Beauvisage, like Brutus
and Cassius, were conspicuous by their absence.

Before M. Beauvisage presented himself for election, M.
Simon Giguet, it would seem, was supposed to have a good
chance; now, the appearance in the field of our friend
Sallenauve, who in his turn has outstripped the mayor, leaves
the lawyer two rungs behind. His father, an old Colonel of
the Empire, is greatly respected in the neighborhood; and as
a testimony of their regret at not being able to elect his

son, they unanimously voted him into the president's chair.

Giguet was the first candidate to address the meeting; his speech was long, a medley of commonplace; very few questions were put to him to be recorded in this report. Every one felt that the real battle was not to be fought here.

Then M. Beauvisage was called for. Maître Achille Pigoult rose and begged to be allowed to speak, and said:

"M. le Maire has been very unwell since yesterday——"
Shouts and roars of laughter interrupted the speaker.

Colonel Giguet rang the bell with which he had been duly provided for a long time before silence was restored. At the first lull, Maître Pigoult tried again:

"As I had the honor of saying, gentlemen, M. le Maire, suffering as he is from an attack, which, though not serious——"

A fresh outbreak, more noisy than the first. Like all old soldiers, Colonel Giguet's temper is neither very long-suffering nor altogether parliamentary. He started to his feet, exclaiming:

"Gentleman, this is not one of Frappart's balls" (the name of the owner of the room); "I must beg you to behave with greater decency, otherwise I shall resign the chair."

It is to be supposed that a body of men prefer to be rough-ridden, for this exhortation was received with applause, and silence seemed fairly well restored.

"As I was saying, to my regret," Maître Achille began once more, varying his phrase each time, "having a tiresome indisposition which, though not serious, will confine him to his room for some days——"

"Loss of voice!" said somebody.

"Our excellent and respected Mayor," Achille Pigoult went on, heedless of the interruption, "could not have the pleasure of attending this meeting. However, Madame Beauvisage, whom I had the honor of seeing but just now, told me, and commissioned me to tell you, that for the present M. Beauvisage foregoes the honor of claiming your suffrages, begging

such gentlemen as had expressed their interest in his election
to transfer their votes to M. Simon Giguet."

This Achille Pigoult is a very shrewd individual, who had
very skilfully brought about the intervention of Mme. Beauvisage, thus emphasizing her conjugal supremacy. The assembly were, however, too thoroughly provincial to appreciate
this little dirty trick.   In the country women are constantly
mixed up with their husbands' concerns, even the most
masculine; and the old story of the priest's housekeeper, who
replied quite seriously, "We cannot say mass so cheap as
that," has to us a spice of the absurd which in many small
towns would not be recognized.

Finally, Sallenauve rose, and I was at once struck by the
calm ease and dignity of his demeanor on the platform. This
is a most reassuring promise for other and more serious occasions, for of one thing there can be no doubt—the character and quality of a man's audience have hardly anything to
do with his sensations. To the speaker who has fear at his
heels it is all the same whether he is addressing lords or
louts. They are eyes to stare at him, ears to hear him; what
he sees before him are not men, but one man—the meeting,
of whom he is conscious as a mass, not analyzing it into
elements.

After briefly enumerating the facts which tie him to the
district, and alluding with skill and dignity to his birth, as
not being the same as most people's, Sallenauve set forth his
political views. He esteems a republic as the best form of
government, but believes it impossible to maintain in France;
hence he cannot wish for it. He believes that really representative government, with the politics of the *camarilla* so
firmly muzzled that there is nothing to be feared from its
constant outbreaks and incessant schemes, may tend largely
to the dignity and prosperity of a nation. Liberty and
Equality, the two great principles which triumphed in '89,
have the soundest guarantees from that form of government.
As to the possible trickery that kingly power may bring to
bear against them, institutions cannot prevent it. Men and

the moral sense, rather than the laws, must be on the alert in such a case; and he, Sallenauve, will always be one of these living obstacles.—He expressed himself as an ardent supporter of freedom in teaching, said that in his opinion further economy might be brought to bear on the budget, that there were too many paid officials in the Chamber, and that the Court especially was too strongly represented.—The electors who should vote for him were not to expect that he would ever take any step in their behalf which was not based on reason and justice. It had been said that the word "impossible" was not French. Yet there was one impossibility that he recognized, and by which he should always feel it an honor to be beaten, namely, any infringement of justice or the least attempt to defeat the right. (Loud applause.)

Silence being restored, one of the electors spoke:

"Monsieur," said he, after due license from the chairman, "you have said that you will accept no office from the Government. Is not that by implication casting a slur on those who are in office? My name is Godivet; I am the town registrar; I do not therefore conceive myself open to the scorn of my respected fellow-citizens."

Said Sallenauve:

"I am delighted, monsieur, to hear that the Government has conferred on you functions which you fulfil, I am sure, with perfect rectitude and ability. But may I inquire whether you were from the first at the head of the office you manage?"

"Certainly not, monsieur. I was for three years supernumerary; I then rose through the various grades; and I may honestly say that my modest promotion was never due to favor."

"Well, then, monsieur, what would you say if I, with my title as deputy—supposing me to secure the suffrages of the voters in this district—I, who have never been a supernumerary, and have passed no grade, who should have done the Ministry no service but that of voting on its side— if I were suddenly appointed to be director-general of your department—and such things have been seen?"

"I should say—I should say, monsieur, that the choice was a good one, since the King would have made it."

"No, monsieur, you would not say so; or if you said it aloud, which I cannot believe possible, you would think to yourself that such an appointment was ridiculous and unjust. 'Where the deuce did the man learn the difficult business of an office when he has been a sculptor all his life?' you would ask. And you would be right not to approve of the royal caprice; for acquired rights, long and honorable service, and the regular progression of advancement would be nullified by this system of selection by the Sovereign's pleasure. And it is to show that I disapprove of the crying abuse I am denouncing; it is because I do not think it just, or right, or advantageous that a man should be thus raised over other men's heads to the highest posts in the public service, that I pledge myself to accept no promotion. And do you still think, monsieur, that I am contemning such functions? Do I not rather treat them with the greatest respect?"

M. Godivet expressed himself satisfied.

"But look here, sir," cried another elector, after requesting leave in a somewhat vinous voice, "you say you will never ask for anything for your electors; then what good will you be to us?"

"I never said, my good friend, that I would ask for nothing for my constituents; I said I would ask for nothing but what was just. That, I may say, I will demand with determination and perseverance, for justice ought always to be thus served."

"Not but what there are other ways of serving it," the man went on. "For instance, there was that lawsuit what they made me lose against Jean Remy—we had had words, you see, about a landmark——"

"Well," said Colonel Giguet, interposing, "you are not, I suppose, going to tell us the history of your lawsuit and speak disrespectfully of the magistrates?"

"The magistrates, Colonel? I respect them, which I was a member of the municipality for six weeks in '93, and I know the law.—But to come back to my point. I want to ask the gentleman, who is here to answer me just as much as the others, what is his opinion of the licensed tobacco jobs."

"My opinion of tobacco licenses? That would be a little difficult to state briefly. However, I may go so far as to say that, if I am correctly informed, they do not seem to me to be always judiciously granted."

"Well done you! You are a man!" cried the voter, "and I shall vote for you, for they won't make a fool of you in a hurry. I believe you; the tobacco licenses are given away anyhow. Why, there is Jean Remy's girl—a bad neighbor he was; he has never been a yard away from his plough tail, and he fights with his wife every day of the week, and——"

"But, my good fellow," said the chairman, interrupting him, "you are really encroaching on these gentlemen's patience——"

"No, no; let him speak!" was shouted on all sides.

The man amused them, and Sallenauve gave the Colonel to understand that he too would like to know what the fellow was coming to. So the elector went on:

"Then what I say is this, saving your presence, my dear Colonel, there was that girl of Jean Remy's—and I will never give him any peace, not even in hell, for my landmark was in its right place and your experts were all wrong—well, what does the girl do? There she leaves her father and mother, and off she goes to Paris: what is she up to in Paris? Well, I didn't go to see; but if she doesn't scrape acquaintance with a member of the Chamber, and at this day she has a licensed tobacco shop in the Rue Mouffetard, one of the longest streets in Paris; whereas, if I should kick the bucket to-day or to-morrow, there is my wife, the widow of a hardworking man, crippled with rheumatism all along of sleeping in the woods during the terror of 1815—and where's the tobacco license she would get, I should like to know!"

"But you are not dead yet," said one and another in reply to this wonderful record of service. And the Colonel, to put an end to this burlesque scene, gave the next turn to a little pastrycook, a well-known republican.

The new speaker asked Sallenauve in a high falsetto voice this insidious question, which at Arcis indeed may be called national.

"What, sir, is your opinion of Danton?"

"Monsieur Dauphin," said the President, "I must be allowed to point out to you that Danton is now a part of history."

"The Pantheon of History, Monsieur le Président, is the proper term."

"Well, well!—History, or the Pantheon of History—Danton seems to me to have nothing to do with the matter in hand."

"Allow me, Mr. President," said Sallenauve. "Though the question has apparently no direct bearing on the objects of this meeting, still, in a town which still rings with the fame of that illustrious name, I cannot shirk the opportunity offered me for giving a proof of my impartiality and independence by pronouncing on that great man's memory."

"Yes, yes! hear, hear!" cried the audience, almost unanimously.

"I am firmly convinced," Sallenauve went on, "that if Danton had lived in times as calm and peaceful as ours, he would have been—as indeed he was—a good husband, a good father, a warm and faithful friend, an attaching and amiable character, and that his remarkable talents would have raised him to an eminent position in the State and in Society."

"Hear, hear! bravo! capital!"

"Born, on the contrary, at a period of great troubles, in the midst of a storm of unchained and furious passions, Danton, of all men, was the one to blaze up in this atmosphere of flame. Danton was a burning torch, and his crimson glow was only too apt for such scenes of blood and horror as I will not now remind you of.

"But, it has been said, the independence of the nation had to be saved; traitors and sneaks had to be punished; in short, a sacrifice had to be consummated, terrible but necessary for the requirements of public safety.—Gentlemen, I do not accept this view of the matter. To kill wholesale, and, as has been proved twenty times over, without any necessity—to kill unarmed men, women, and prisoners is under any hypothesis an atrocious crime; those who ordered it, those who allowed it, those who did the deeds are to me included in one and the same condemnation!"

I wish, madame, that I could adequately describe Salle-nauve's tone and face as he pronounced this anathema. You know how his countenance is transfigured when a glowing thought fires it.—The audience sat in gloomy silence; he had evidently hit them hard, but under his strong hand the steed dared not rear.

"Still," he went on, "there are two possible sequels to a crime committed and irreparable—repentance and expiation. Danton expressed his repentance not in words, he was too proud for that—he did better, he acted; and at the sound of the knife of the head-cutting machine, which was working without pause or respite, at the risk of hastening his turn to lose his own, he ventured to move for a Committee of Clemency. It was an almost infallible way of expiation, and when the day of expiation came we all know that he did not shrink! By meeting his death as a reward for his brave attempt to stay the tide of bloodshed, it may be said, gentle-men, that Danton's figure and memory are purged of the crimson stain that the terrible September had left upon them. Cut off at the age of thirty-five, flung to posterity, Danton dwells in our memory as a man of powerful intellect, of fine private virtues, and of more than one generous action— these were himself; his frenzied crimes were the contagion of the age.

"In short, in speaking of such a man as he was, the jus-tice is most unjust which is not tempered with large allow-ances—and, gentlemen, there is a woman who understood and pronounced on Danton better than you or I, better than any orator or historian—the woman who, in a sublime spirit of charity, said to the relentless, 'He is with God! Let us pray for the peace of his soul!'"

The snare thus avoided by this judicious allusion to Mother Marie des Anges, the meeting seemed satisfied, and we might fancy that the candidate was at the end of his examination. The Colonel was preparing to call for a show of hands when several voters demurred, saying that there were still two matters requiring explanation by the nominee—Sallenauve had said that he would always stand in the way of any trickery attempted by the Sovereign authority against National Institutions. What were they to understand by resistance; did he mean armed resistance, riots, barricades?"

"Barricades," said Sallenauve, "have always seemed to me to be machines which turn and crush those who erected them; nay, we are bound to believe that it is in the nature of a rebellion to serve, ultimately, the purpose of the Government, since on every occasion the police is presently accused of beginning it.—The resistance I shall offer will always be legal, and carried on by lawful means—the press, speeches in the Chamber, and patience—the real strength of the oppressed and vanquished."

If you knew Latin, madame, I would say, *"In cauda venenum,"* that is to say, that the serpent's poison is in its tail—a statement of the ancients which modern science has failed to confirm.

M. de l'Estorade was not mistaken: Sallenauve's private life was made a matter of prying inquiry; and, under the inspiration, no doubt, of Maxime, the virtuous Maxime, who had flung out several hints through the journalist intrusted with his noble plot, our friend was at last questioned as to the handsome Italian he keeps "hidden" in his house in Paris. Sallenauve was no more put out of countenance than he was in your presence and M. de l'Estorade's; he merely wished to know in return whether the meeting thought proper to waste its time in listening to a romance worthy to fill the space at the bottom of a newspaper. When a body of men are assembled together, madame, as your husband may have told you, they are like grown-up children, who are only too glad to hear a long story——

But Sallenauve has come in, and he tells me that the committee chosen by the constituents is such as to make his election presumably certain. So I put the pen in his hands; he himself will tell you the story of which you were cheated at his last visit, and he will close this letter.

Sallenauve to Madame de l'Estorade.

Seven o'clock in the evening.

MADAME,—The rather abrupt manner of my leave-taking when I bid you and M. de l'Estorade farewell, that night after our excursion to the Collège Henri IV., is by now quite accounted for, no doubt, by the anxieties of every kind that were agitating me; Marie-Gaston, I know, has told you the result. I must own that in the state of uneasy excitement in which I then was, the belief which M. de l'Estorade seemed inclined to give to the scandal he spoke of caused me both pain and surprise. "What," thought I to myself, "is it possible that a man of so much moral and common sense as M. de l'Estorade can *à priori* suppose me capable of loose conduct, when on all points he sees me anxious to give my life such gravity and respectability as may command esteem? And if he has such an opinion of my libertine habits, it would be so amazingly rash to admit me on a footing of intimacy in his house with his wife, that his present politeness must be essentially temporary and precarious. The recollection of the service I had so recently done him may have made him think it necessary for the time being, but I shall be dropped at the first opportunity."—And it occurred to me, madame, that evening, that the places assigned to us, perhaps ere long in hostile political camps, might be the pretext on which M. de l'Estorade would dismiss me, as it were, to what he called my shameless connection.

An hour or so before I observed these distressing signs, I had given you my confidence concerning a matter which might, at any rate, have preserved me from the mortification of finding that you had as bad an impression of me as M.

de l'Estorade. I did not, therefore, see any immediate need for justifying myself, and two long stories in one evening seemed to me too severe a trial for your patience.

As to M. de l'Estorade, I was, I confess, nettled with him, finding him so recklessly ready to echo a calumny against which I thought he might have defended me, considering the nature of the acquaintance we had formed, so to him I would not *condescend* to explain: this I now withdraw, but at the time it was the true expression of very keen annoyance.

The chances of an election contest have necessitated my giving the explanation, in the first instance, to a public meeting, and I have been so happy as to find that men in a mass are more capable perhaps than singly of appreciating a generous impulse and the genuine ring of truth. I was called upon, madame, under circumstances so unforeseen and so strange as to trench very nearly on the ridiculous, to make a statement of almost incredible facts to an audience of a very mixed character. M. de l'Estorade, in his own drawing-room, might have accepted them only as pending further evidence; here, on the contrary, they met with trust and sympathy.

This is my story, very much as I told it to my constituents at their requisition:

Some months before I left Rome, we received a visit almost every evening in the café where the Academy pupils are wont to meet from an Italian named Benedetto. He called himself a musician, and was not at all a bad one; but we were warned that he was also a spy in the employment of the Roman police, which accounted for his constant regularity and his predilection for our company. At any rate, he was a very amusing buffoon; and as we cared not a straw for the Roman police, we were more than tolerant of the fellow; we tempted him to frequent the place—a matter of no great difficulty, since he had a passion for *zabajon, poncio spongato,* and *spuma di latte.*

One evening as he came in, he was asked by one of our party who the woman was with whom he had been seen walking that morning.

"My wife, signor!" said the Italian, swelling with pride.

"Yours, Benedetto? You the husband of such a beauty?"

"Certainly, by your leave, signor."

"What next! You are stumpy, ugly, a toper. And it is said that you are a police agent into the bargain; she, on the other hand, is as handsome as the huntress Diana."

"I charmed her by my musical gifts; she dies of love for me."

"Well, then, if she is your wife, you ought to let her pose for our friend Dorlange, who at this moment is meditating a statue of Pandora. He will never find such another model."

"That may be managed," replied the Italian.

And he went off into the most amusing tomfoolery, which made us all forget the suggestion that had been made.

I was in my studio next morning, and with me certain painters and sculptors, my fellow-pupils, when Benedetto came in, and with him a remarkably beautiful woman. I need not describe her to you, madame; you have seen her. A cheer of delight hailed the Italian, who said, addressing me:

"*Ecco la Pandora!*—Well, what do you think of her?"

"She is beautiful; but will she sit?"

"Peugh!" was Benedetto's reply, as much as to say, "I should like to see her refuse."

"But," said I, "so perfect a model will want high pay."

"No, the honor is enough. But you will make a bust of me—a terra-cotta head—and make her a present of it."

"Well, then, gentlemen," said I to the others, "you will have the goodness to leave us to ourselves."

No one heeded; judging of the wife by the husband, all the young scapegraces crowded rudely round the woman, who, blushing, agitated, and scared by all these eyes, looked rather like a caged panther baited by peasants at a fair. Benedetto went up and took her aside to explain to her in Italian that the French signore wanted to take her likeness at full length, and that she must dispense with her garments. She gave him one fulminating look and made for the door. Benedetto rushed forward to stop her, while my companions—the virtuous brood of the studio—barred the way.

A struggle began between the husband and wife; but as I saw that Benedetto was defending his side of the argument with the greatest brutality, I flew into a passion; with one arm, for I am luckily pretty strong, I pushed the wretch off, and turning to the youths with a determined air— "Come," said I, "let her pass!" I escorted the woman, still quivering with anger, to the door. She thanked me briefly in Italian, and vanished without further hindrance.

On returning to Benedetto, who was gesticulating threats, I told him to go, that his conduct was infamous, and that if I should hear that he had ill treated his wife, he would have an account to settle with me.

"Debole!" (idiot!) said the wretch with a shrug.

But he went, followed, as he had been welcomed, by a cheer.

Some days elapsed. We saw no more of Benedetto, and at first were rather uneasy. Some of us even tried to find him in the Trastevere suburb, where he was known to live; but research in that district is not easy; the French students are in ill odor with the Trasteverini, who always suspect them of schemes to seduce their wives and daughters, and the men are always ready with the knife. By the end of the week no one, as you may suppose, ever thought of the buffoon again.

Three days before I left Rome his wife came into my studio. She could speak a little bad French.

"You go to Paris," said she. "I come to go with you."

"Go with me?—And your husband?"

"Dead," said she calmly.

An idea flashed through my brain.

"And you killed him?" said I to the Trasteverina. She nodded:

"But I try to killed me too."

"How?" asked I.

"After he had so insult me," said she, "he came to our

house, he beat me like always, and then went out all day.
The night he came back and showed me a pistol-gun. I
snatch it away; he is drunk; I throw that *briccone* (wretch)
on his bed; and he go to sleep. Then I stuff up the door
and the window, and I put much charcoal on a *brasero,* and
I light it; and I have a great headache, and then I know
nothing till the next day. The neighbors have smell the charcoal, and have make me alive again—but he—he is dead before."

"And the police?"

"The police know; and that he had want to sell me to an
English. For that he had want to make me vile to you, then
I would not want to resist. The judge he tell me go—quite
right. So I have confess, and have absolution."

"But, *cara mia,* what can you do in France? I am not
rich as the English are."

A scornful smile passed over her beautiful face.

"I shall cost you nothing," said she. "On the contrary,
I shall save much money."

"How?" said I.

"I will be the model for your statues; yes, I am willing.
Benedetto used to say I was very well made and a very good
housewife. If Benedetto would have agreed, we could have
lived happily, *perche* I have a talent too."

And taking down a guitar that hung in a corner of my
studio, she sang a *bravura* air, accompanying herself with
immense energy.

"In France," she said when it was finished, "I shall have
lessons and go on the stage, where I shall succeed—that was
Benedetto's plan."

"But why not go on the stage in Italy?"

"Since Benedetto died, I am in hiding; the Englishman
wants to carry me off. I mean to go to France; as you see,
I have been learning French. If I stay here, it will be in
the Tiber."

M. de l'Estorade will admit that by abandoning such a
character to its own devices, I might fear to be the cause of

some disaster, so I consented to allow Signora Luigia to accompany me to Paris. She manages my house with remarkable ability and economy; she herself begged to stand as model for my Pandora; but you will believe me, madame, when I say that the corpse of Benedetto lay ever between his wife and me during this perilous test. I gave my housekeeper a singing master, and she is now ready to appear in public.

In spite of her dreams of the stage, she is pious, as all Italian women are; she has joined the fraternity of the Virgin at Saint-Sulpice, my parish church, and during the month of Mary, now a few days old, the good woman who lets chairs counts on a rich harvest from her fine singing. She attends every service, confesses and communicates frequently; and her director, a highly respectable old priest, came to me lately to beg that she might no longer serve as the model for my statues, saying that she would never listen to his injunctions on the subject, fancying her honor pledged to me. I yielded, of course, to his representations, all the more readily because in the event of my being elected, as seems extremely probable, I intend to part with this woman. In the more conspicuous position which I shall then fill, she would be the object of comments not less fatal to her reputation and prospects than to my personal dignity. I must be prepared for some resistance on her part, for she seems to have formed a sincere attachment to me, and gave me ample proof of it when I was wounded in that duel. Nothing could hinder her from sitting up with me every night, and the surgeon told me that even among the Sisters at his hospital he had never met with a more intelligent nurse or more fervid charity.

I have spoken with Marie-Gaston of the difficulty I anticipate in the way of this separation. He fears it, he says, even more than I. Hitherto, to this poor soul, Paris has been my house; and the mere idea of being cast alone into the whirlpool which she has never even seen, is enough to terrify her. One thing struck Marie-Gaston in this connection. He does not think that the intervention of the confessor can be of any use; the girl, he says, would rebel against the sacrifice if she thought it was imposed on her by rigorous devotion. Also the worthy man had failed in his authority on a point on which he had far more right to speak loudly and decisively; she would not submit till I had released her from what she thought a strange pledge of honor to me.

Marie-Gaston is of opinion that the intervention and counsels of a person of her own sex, with a high reputation for virtue and enlightenment, might in such a case be more efficacious, and he declares that I know a person answering to his description, who, at our joint entreaty, would consent to undertake this delicate negotiation. But, madame, I ask you what apparent chance is there that this notion should be realized? The lady to whom Marie-Gaston alludes is to me an acquaintance of yesterday; and one would hardly undertake such a task even for an old friend. I know you did me the honor to say some little while since that some acquaintanceships ripen fast. And Marie-Gaston added that the lady in question was perfectly pious, perfectly kind, perfectly charitable, and that the idea of being the patron saint of a poor deserted creature might have some attractions for her.—In short, madame, on our return we propose to consult you, and you will tell us whether it may be possible to ask for such valuable assistance.

In any case, I beg you will be my advocate with M. de l'Estorade, and tell him that I indulge a hope of seeing not a vestige of the little cloud that had come between us.

By this time to-morrow, madame, I shall have met with a repulse which will send me back, once for all, to my work as an artist, or I shall have my foot set on a new path. Need I tell you that I am anxious at the thought? The effect of the unknown, no doubt.

I had almost forgotten to tell you a great piece of news which will be a protection to you against the *ricochet* of certain projectiles. I confided to Mother Marie des Anges—of whom Marie-Gaston had told you wonders—all my suspicions as to some violence having been used towards **Mlle. Lanty,** and she is sure that in the course of no very long time she can discover the convent where Marianina is probably detained. The good woman, if she sets her heart upon it, is quite capable of success; and with this chance of rediscovering the original, the copy cannot surely fear my committing any misdemeanor!

I am not quite satisfied about Marie-Gaston; he seems to me to be in a state of feverish excitement as a consequence of the immense importance his friendship ascribes to my election. He is like an honest debtor who, having made up his mind to pay a sacred debt, puts everything aside, even his sorrows, till that is done. But I cannot but fear lest, after such an effort, he should have a relapse; his grief, though for the moment he suppresses it, has not really lost its poignancy. Have you not been struck by the light, sardonic tone of his letters, of which I have read portions? This is not natural. When he was happy he never had these bursts of turbulent gaiety. This cheerfulness is assumed for the occasion, and I greatly fear that when the electoral breeze dies away he will collapse into prostration, and slip through our fingers.

He has consented to stay with me on arriving in Paris, and not to go to Ville-d'Avray till I return, and in my society. Such prudence, though I begged it of him—with no hope of his consenting—alarms and troubles me. He is evidently afraid of the memories that await him there, and shall I be able to deaden the shock?—Old Philippe, whom he would not take with him to Italy, has been ordered to change nothing in the châlet, and from what I know of him, he is too well drilled a servant to fail in carrying out the order to the letter; thus the unhappy fellow, in the midst of all the objects that will speak of the past, will find himself back on the day after his wife's death. And there is a still more alarming fact! He has never once mentioned her to me, has never even allowed me to approach the subject. We can but hope that this is but a crisis to be got over, and that by uniting to do our best we may succeed in calming him.

Adieu, then, till we meet, dear madame.—Conquering or conquered, I am always your most devoted and respectful servant.

Marie Gaston to the Comtesse de l'Estorade.

ARCIS-SUR-AUBE, *May* 13, 1839.

We have had a narrow escape, madame, while sleeping. And those blundering rioters, of whose extraordinary outbreak we have news to-day by telegraph, for a moment imperiled our success. No sooner was the news of the rising in Paris yesterday known, through the bills posted by order of the Sous-préfet, than it was cleverly turned to account by the Ministerial party.

"Elect a democrat if you will!" they cried on all sides, "that his speeches may make the cartridges for insurgent muskets!"

This argument threw our phalanx into disorder and doubt. Fortunately, as you may remember, a question—not apparently so directly to the point—had been put to Sallenauve at the preliminary meeting, and there was something prophetic in his reply.

Jacques Bricheteau had the happy thought of getting a little handbill printed and widely distributed forthwith:

"A RIOT WITH HARD FIGHTING TOOK PLACE YESTERDAY IN PARIS.

"Questioned as to such criminal and desperate methods of opposition, one of our candidates, M. de Sallenauve, at the very hour when those shots were being fired, was using these words" —followed by some of Sallenauve's speech, which I reported to you. Then came, in large letters:

"THE RIOT WAS SUPPRESSED; WHO WILL BENEFIT BY IT?"

This little bill did wonders, and balked M. de Trailles' supreme efforts, though, throwing aside his incognito, he spent the day speechifying in white gloves in the market-place and at the door of the polling-room.

This evening the result is known:—Number of voters, 201.

Beauvisage, ...	2
Simon Giguet, ...	29
Sallenauve, ...	170

Consequently M. Charles de Sallenauve is elected

MEMBER FOR ARCIS.

PART III.

THE COMTE DE SALLENAUVE

On the evening of the day following the election that had ended so disastrously for his vanity, Maxime de Trailles returned to Paris.

On seeing him make a hasty toilet and order his carriage as soon as he reached home, it might have been supposed that he was going to call on the Comte de Rastignac, Minister of Public Works, to give an account of his mission and explain its failure; but a more pressing interest seemed to claim his attention.

"To Colonel Franchessini's," said he to the coachman.

When he reached the gate of one of the prettiest houses in the Bréda quarter, the concierge, to whom he nodded, gave M. de Trailles the significant glance which conveyed that "Monsieur was within." And at the same moment the porter's bell announced his arrival to the man-servant who opened the hall door.

"Is the Colonel visible?" said he.

"He has just gone in to speak to madame. Shall I tell him you are here, Monsieur le Comte?"

"No, you need not do that. I will wait in his study."

And, without requiring the man to lead the way, he went on, as one familiar with the house, into a large room with two windows opening on a level with the garden. This study, like the Bologna lute included in the *Avare's* famous inventory, was "fitted with all its strings, or nearly all"; in other words, all the articles of furniture which justified its designation, such as a writing-table, book-cases, maps, and globes, were there, supplemented by other and very handsome furniture; but the Colonel, an ardent sportsman, and one of the most energetic members of the Jockey Club, had

(275)

by degrees allowed this sanctuary of learning and science to be invaded by the appurtenances of the smoking-room, the fencing-school, and the harness-room. Pipes and weapons of every form, from every land, including the Wild Indian's club, saddles, hunting-crops, bits and stirrups of every pattern, fencing-gloves, and boxing-gloves, lay in strange and disorderly confusion. However, by thus surrounding himself with the accessories of his favorite occupations and *studies,* the Colonel showed that he had the courage of his opinions. In fact, in his opinion no reading was endurable for more than a quarter of an hour, unless indeed it were the *Stud-journal.*

It must be supposed, however, that politics had made their way into his life, devoted as it was to the worship of muscular development and equine science, for Maxime found strewn on the floor most of the morning's papers, flung aside with contempt when the Colonel had looked them through. From among the heap M. de Trailles picked up the *National,* and his eye at once fell on these lines, forming a short paragraph on the front page:

"Our side has secured a great success in the district of Arcis-sur-Aube. In spite of the efforts of local functionaries, supported by those of a special agent sent by the Government to this imperiled outpost, the Committee is almost entirely composed of the adherents of the most advanced Left. We may therefore quite confidently predict the election to-morrow of M. Dorlange, one of our most distinguished sculptors, a man whom we have warmly recommended to the suffrages of our readers. They will not be surprised at seeing him returned, not under the name of Dorlange, but as Monsieur Charles de Sallenauve.

"By an act of recognition, signed and witnessed on May 2nd, at the office of Maître Achille Pigoult, notary at Arcis, M. Dorlange is authorized to take and use the name of one of the best families in Champagne, to which he did not till then know that he belonged. But Dorlange or Sallenauve, the new member is one of Us, a fact of which the Government will ere long be made aware in the Chamber. As we read the eloquent utterances of this candidate when addressing the preliminary meeting, without flattery and quite apart from party feeling, we may predict his brilliant success on the parliamentary platform."

Maxime tossed the sheet aside with petulant annoyance and picked up another. This was an organ of the Legitimist party. In it he read under the heading of Elections:

"The staff of the National Guard and the Jockey Club, who had several members in the last Chamber of Deputies, have just sent one of their most brilliant notables to the newly-elected Parliament, of which the first session is about to open. Colonel Franchessini, so well known for his zealous prosecution of National Guards who shirk service, was elected almost unanimously for one of the rotten boroughs of the Civil List. It is supposed that he will take his seat with the phalanx of the Aides-de-Camp, and that in the Chamber, as in the office of the Staff, he will be a firm and ardent supporter of the policy of the *Status quo*."

As Maxime got to the end of this paragraph, the Colonel came in.

Colonel Franchessini, for a short time in the Imperial Army, had, under the Restoration, figured as a dashing officer; but in consequence of some little clouds that had tarnished the perfect brightness of his honor, he had been compelled to resign his commission, so that in 1830 he was quite free to devote himself with passionate ardor to the "dynasty of July." He had not, however, re-entered the service, because, not long after his little misadventure, he had found great consolation from an immensely rich Englishwoman who had allowed herself to be captivated by his handsome face and, figure, at that time worthy of Antinous, and had annexed him as her husband. He had ultimately resumed his epaulettes as

a member of the Staff of the Citizen Militia. He had revealed
himself in that position as the most turbulent and conten-
tious of swashbucklers, and by the aid of the extensive connections secured to him by his wealth and this influential position, he had now pushed his way—the news was correct—into
a seat in the Chamber.

Colonel Franchessini, like his friend Maxime de Trailles
nearly fifty years of age, had an air of second youth, for which
his lightly-knit frame and agile military figure promised
long duration. Though he had finally made up his mind to
iron-gray hair, concealing the silver sheen by keeping it cut
very short, he was less resigned to a white moustache; wearing
it turned up with a jaunty and juvenile curl, he did his best
to preserve its original hue by the use of *Pomade Hongroise*.
But those who try to prove too much prove nothing; and in
the application of this black dye, art exaggerating nature was
betrayed by an intensity and equality of hue too perfect to
be thought genuine. This gave his strongly marked countenance, with its dark complexion and conspicuous stamp of
the Italian origin indicated by his name, a strangely hard-
set expression, which was far from being corrected or softened
by angular features, piercing eyes, and a large nose like the
beak of a bird of prey.

"Well, Maxime," said he, holding out a hand to his ex-
pectant visitor, "where the devil do you come from? We have
not seen a sign of you at the club this fortnight past."

"Where have I come from?" repeated Monsieur de Trailles.
"I will tell you.—But first let me congratulate you."

"Yes," said the Colonel airily, "they took it into their heads
to elect me. On my word, I am very innocent of it all; if no
one had worked any harder for it than I——"

"My dear fellow, you are a man of gold for any district,
and if only the voters I have had to deal with had been equally
intelligent——"

"What, have you been standing for a place? But from the
state—the somewhat entangled state—of your finances I did
not think you were in a position——"

"No; and I was not working on my own account. Rastignac was worried about the voting in Arcis-sur-Aube, and asked me to spend a few days there."

"Arcis-sur-Aube! But, my dear fellow, if I remember rightly some article I was reading this morning in one of those rags, they are making a shocking bad choice—some plaster-cast maker, an image-cutter, whom they propose to send up to us?"

"Just so, and it is about that rascally business that I came to consult you. I have not been two hours in Paris, and I shall see Rastignac only as I leave this."

"He is getting on famously, that little Minister!" said the Colonel, interrupting the skilful modulation through which Maxime by every word had quietly tended to the object of his visit. "He is very much liked at the *Château*.—Do you know that little Nucingen girl he married?"

"Yes, I often see Rastignac; he is a very old friend of mine."

"She is a pretty little thing," the Colonel went on. "Very pretty; and when the first year of matrimony is dead and buried, I fancy that a mild charge in that quarter might be ventured on with some hope of success."

"Come, come!" said Maxime, "a man of position like you, a legislator! Why, after merely stirring the electoral pot for somebody else, I have come back quite a settled and reformed character."

"Then you went to Arcis-sur-Aube to hinder the election of this hewer of stone?"

"Not at all; I went there to scotch the wheels of a Left Centre candidate."

"Peugh! I am not sure that it is not as bad as the Left out and out.—But take a cigar; I have some good ones there—the same as the Princes smoke."

Maxime would have gained nothing by refusing, for the Colonel had already risen to ring for his valet, to whom he merely said: "Lights."

Their cigars fairly started, M. de Trailles anticipated another interruption by declaring, before he was asked, that he had never smoked anything so fine. The Colonel, lounging comfortably in his chair, and, so to say, ballasted by the occupation he had secured, seemed likely to give less volatile attention to the conversation. So M. de Trailles resumed:

"At first everything was going splendidly. To oust the candidate who had scared the Ministry—a lawyer, the very worst kind of vermin—I disinterred a retired hosier, the mayor of the town, idiot enough for anything, whom I persuaded to come forward. This worthy was convinced that he, like his opponent, belonged to the Opposition. That is the prevalent opinion in the whole district at the present time, so that the election, by my judicious manœuvring, was as good as won. And our man once safe in Paris, the great wizard at the Tuileries would have spoken three words to him, and this rabid antagonist, turned inside out like a stocking of his own making, would have been anything we wished."

"Well played," said the Colonel; "I see the hand of my Maxime in it all."

"You will see it yet plainer when he tells you that in this little arrangement, without taking toll from his employers, he expected to turn an honest penny. To engraft on that dull stock some sort of parliamentary ambition, I had to begin by making myself agreeable to his wife, a not unpalatable country matron, though a little past the prime——"

"Yes, yes; very good——" said Franchessini. "The husband a deputy—satisfied——?"

"You are not near it, my dear fellow. There is a daughter in the house, an only child, very much spoilt, nineteen, nicelooking, and with something like a million francs of her own."

"But, my dear Maxime, I passed by your tailor's yesterday and your coachmaker's, and I saw no illuminations."

"They would, I am sorry to say, have been premature.— But so matters stood: the two ladies crazy to make a move to Paris; full of overflowing gratitude to the man who could get them there through the door of the Palais Bourbon; the girl possessed with the idea of being a Countess; the mother transported at the notion of holding a political drawing-room—you see all the obvious openings that the situation afforded, and you know me well enough to believe that I was not behindhand to avail myself of such possibilities when once I had discerned them."

"I am quite easy on that score," said the Colonel, as he opened a window to let out some of the cigar smoke that by this time was filling the room.

"So I was fully prepared," Maxime went on, "to swallow the damsel and the fortune as soon as I had made up my mind to leap plump into this *mésalliance;* when, falling from the clouds, or to be accurate, shot up from underground, the gentleman with two names, of whom you read in the *National* this morning, suddenly came on the scene."

"By the way," said the Colonel, "what may this act of recognition be which enables a man to take a name he had never heard of only a day since?"

"The recognition of a natural son in the presence of a notary.—It is perfectly legal."

"Then our gentleman is of the interesting tribe of the nameless? Yes, yes, those rascals often have great luck. I am not at all surprised that this one should have cut the ground from under your feet."

"If we were living in the middle ages," said Maxime, "I should account for the unhorsing of my man and the success of this fellow by magic and witchcraft; for he will, I fear, be your colleague. How can you account for the fact that an old *tricoteuse,* formerly a friend of Danton's, and now the Mother Superior of an Ursuline convent, with the help of a nephew, an obscure Paris organist whom she brought out as the masculine figure-head of her scheme, should have hoodwinked a whole constituency to such a point that this stranger actually polled an imposing majority?"

"Well, but some one knew him, I suppose?"

"Not a soul, unless it were this old hypocrite. Till the moment of his arrival he had no fortune, no connections—not

even a father! While he was taking his boots off he was made
—Heaven knows how—the proprietor of a fine estate. Then,
in quite the same vein, a gentleman supposed to be a native
of the place, from which he had absented himself for many
years, presented himself with this ingenious schemer in a
notary's office, acknowledged him post-haste as his son,
and vanished again in the course of the night, no one knowing
by which road he went. This trick having come off all right,
the Ursuline and her ally launched their nominee; republicans, legitimists, and conservatives, the clergy, the nobility,
the middle classes—one and all, as if bound by a spell cast
over the whole land, came round to this favorite of the old
nun-witch; and, but for the sacred battalion of officials who,
under my eye, put a bold face on the matter, and did not
break up, there was nothing to hinder his being returned
unanimously, as you were."

"And so, my poor friend, good-bye to the fortune?"

"Well, not so bad as that. But everything is put off.—
The father complains that the blissful peace of his existence
is broken, that he has been made quite ridiculous—when
the poor man is so utterly ridiculous to begin with. The
daughter would still like to be a Countess, but the
mother cannot make up her mind to see her political
drawing-room carried down stream; God knows to what
lengths I may have to go in consolation! Then, I myself am
worried by the need for coming to an early solution of the
problem. There I was—there was the girl—I should have
got married; I should have taken a year to settle my affairs,
and then by next session, I should have made my respectable
father-in-law resign, and have stepped into his seat in the
Chamber.—You see what a horizon lay before me."

"But, my dear fellow, apart from the political horizon,
that million must not be allowed to slip."

"Oh well, so far as that goes, I am easy; it is only postponed. My good people are coming to Paris. After the
repulse they have sustained, Arcis is no longer a possible
home for them. Beauvisage particularly—I apologize for the

name, but it is that of my fair one's family—Beauvisage, like Coriolanus, is ready to put the ungrateful province to fire and sword.—And indeed the hapless exiles will have a place here to lay their heads, for they are the owners, if you please, of the Hôtel Beauséant."

"Owners of the Hôtel Beauséant!" cried the Colonel in amazement.

"Yes indeed; and, after all—Beauséant—Beauvisage; only the end of the name needs a change.—My dear fellow, you have no idea of what these country fortunes mount up to, accumulated sou by sou, especially when the omnipotence of thrift is supported by the incessant suction of the leech we call trade! We must make the best of it; the middle classes are rising steadily like a tide, and it is really very kind of them to buy our houses and lands instead of cutting our heads off, as they did in '93 to get them for nothing."

"But you, my dear Maxime, have reduced your houses and lands to the simplest expression."

"No—since, as you perceive, I am thinking of reinstating myself."

"The Hôtel Beauséant!" said the Colonel, calling up a long-buried reminiscence. "I have never set foot there since the last ball given by the Viscountess who then owned it, on the very evening when, in love and despair, she made up her mind to go and bury herself in Normandy on one of her estates. I was there with poor Lady Brandon, and the effect was startling; but I remember the splendor of the rooms; it was quite a royal residence."

"Happily, everything has been completely spoilt. It was let for years to some English people, and now extensive repairs are needed. This is a capital bond between me and my country friends, for without me they have no idea how to set to work. It is understood that I am to be director general of the works; but I have promised my future mother-in-law another thing, and I need your assistance, my dear fellow, to enable me to perform it."

"You do not want a license for her to sell tobacco and stamps?"

"No, nothing so difficult as that.—These confounded wo-men, when they are possessed by a spirit of hatred or revenge, have really wonderful instinct; and Madame Beauvisage, who roars like a lioness at the mere name of Dorlange, has taken it into her head that there must be some dirty intrigue wriggling at the bottom of his incomprehensible success. It is quite certain that the apparition and disappearance of this 'American' father give grounds for very odd surmises; and it is quite possible that if we pressed the button, the organist, who is said to have taken entire charge of this interesting bastard's education, and to know the secret of his parentage, might afford the most unexpected revelations.

"And thinking of this, I remembered a man over whom you have, I fancy, considerable influence, and who in this 'Dorlange hunt' may be of great use to us. You recollect the robbery of Jenny Cadine's jewels, which she lamented so bitterly one evening when supping with you at Véry's? You called to the waiter for paper and ink; and in obedience to a line from you, sent at three in the morning to M. de Saint-Estève, the police took up the matter so effectively that the thieves were caught and the jewels restored by the following evening."

"Yes," said the Colonel, "I remember very well. My au-dacity was lucky. But I may tell you frankly, that with more time for thought, I should not have dealt so cavalierly with Monsieur de Saint-Estève. He is a man to be approached with respect."

"Bless me! Why, is not he a retired criminal who has served his time on the hulks, and whose release you helped to obtain—who must have for you some such veneration as Fieschi showed to one of his protectors?"

"Very true. Monsieur de Saint-Estève, like his predecessor Bibi-Lupin, has had his troubles. But he is now at the head of the criminal police, with very important functions that he fulfils with remarkable address. If this were a matter strictly within his department, I should not hesitate to give you an introduction; but the affair of which you speak is a delicate business, and first and foremost I must feel my way to ascertain whether he will even discuss it with you."

"Oh, I fancied he was entirely at your commands. Say no more about it if there is any difficulty."

"The chief difficulty is that I never see him. I cannot, of course, write to him about such a thing; I lack opportunity—the chance of a meeting.—But why not apply to Rastignac, who would simply order him to take steps?"

"Rastignac, as you may understand, will not give me a very good reception. I had promised to succeed, and I have come back a failure; he will regard this side issue as one of those empty dreams a man clutches at to conceal a defeat. And, in any case, I should be glad to owe such a service solely to your tried friendship."

"It will not prove lacking," said the Colonel, rising. "I will do my best for you, only it will take time."

Maxime had paid a long visit, and took the hint to cut it short; he took leave with a shade of coolness, which did not particularly disturb the Colonel.

As soon as Monsieur de Trailles was gone, Franchessini took the knave of spades out of a pack of cards, and cut the figure out from the background. Placed between two thick folds of letter-paper, he tucked it into an envelope, which he addressed in a feigned hand to Monsieur de Saint-Estève, Petite Rue Sainte-Anne, Près du Quai des Orfèvres.

This done, he rang, countermanded his carriage, which he had ordered before Maxime's visit, and setting out on foot, posted the strange missive with his own hand in the first letter-box he came to. He took particular care to see that it was securely sealed.

At the close of the elections, which were now over, the Government, against all expectations, still had a majority in the Chamber, but a problematical and provisional majority, promising but a struggling and sickly existence to the Ministry in power. Still, it had won the numerical success which is held to be satisfactory by men who wish to remain in office at any price. Every voice in the Ministerial camp was raised in a *Te Deum,* which as often serves to celebrate a doubtful defeat as an undoubted victory.

On the evening of the day when Colonel Franchessini and Maxime de Trailles had held the conversation just recorded, the general result of the elections was known; the ministers living on the left bank of the Seine who held receptions that day saw their rooms mobbed; and at the house of the Minister of Public Works, the Comte de Rastignac, the throng was immense. Though not conspicuous as an orator, this diminutive statesman, by his dexterity, by the elegance of his manners, by his inexhaustible fund of resource, and, above all, by his complete devotion to personal policy, was sure to rise to a post of the first importance in a Cabinet which lived only by expedients.

Madame de l'Estorade, who was too much taken up by her children to be very punctual in her social duties, had long owed Madame de Rastignac a visit in return for that paid by the Minister's wife on the evening when the sculptor, now promoted to be deputy, had dined there after the famous occasion of the statuette, as related by her to Madame Octave de Camps. Monsieur de l'Estorade, a zealous Conservative, as we know, had insisted that, on a day when politics and politeness were both on the same side, his wife should discharge this debt already of long standing. Madame de l'Estorade had gone early to have done with the task as soon as possible, and so found herself at the upper end of the group of seated ladies; while the men stood about, talking. Her chair was next to Madame de Rastignac, who sat nearest to the fire. At official receptions this is usual, a sort of guide to the newcomers who know where to go at once to make their bow to the lady of the house.

But Madame de l'Estorade's hopes of curtailing her visit had not taken due account of the fascinations of conversation in which, on such an occasion, her husband was certain to be involved.

Monsieur de l'Estorade, though no great orator, was influ-

ential in the Upper Chamber, and regarded as a man of great
foresight and accurate judgment; and at every step he took as
he moved round the rooms, he was stopped either by some
political bigwig or by some magnate of finance, of diplomacy,
or merely of the business world, and eagerly invited to give
his opinion on the prospects of the opening session. To
every question, the President of the Court of Exchequer answered at more or less length, and now and again he had the
keen satisfaction of finding himself the centre of a group
who anxiously took note of his views.

This success made him quite indifferent to his wife's agitated signals; and she, keeping her eye on his various evolu-
tions, telegraphed to him whenever he came within her ken
that she wished to end the sitting. The little heed he paid
to her impatience was in itself a fact to be noted in the record
of the usually clear and serene sky that bent over the couple.
Ten years even after their marriage, Monsieur de l'Estorade,
who had been accepted by his wife with anything rather than
enthusiasm, would have been horrified at the idea of such
obviously slack obedience; but three lustres had now elapsed
since he had won the hand of the beautiful Renée de Mau-
combe; and though she had not yet lost any of her magnificent
beauty, he, on the contrary, had grown a good deal older.
The twenty years that lay between his age of fifty-two and
hers of thirty-two was all the more marked now because, even
at seven-and-thirty, when he had married and settled, his hair
was already gray and his health wrecked. A malady of the
liver from which he then suffered, after lying dormant for
some years, had of late seemed to assume an active form; and
while this morbid condition, a common one among statesmen
and ambitious workers, produced a stronger taste in him for
political interests, it no doubt made his mouth harder, so to
speak, to the matrimonial bit.

It is, however, quite possible that the absurd fit of jealousy
to which we once saw him yield was caused solely by the
obscure disorder which had already tinged his worn face with
the yellowish hue of pronounced liver-disease.

Monsieur de l'Estorade talked so long and so well, that at last the drawing-room was almost empty, and only a small circle was left of intimate friends, gathered round his wife and Madame de Rastignac. The Minister himself, as he returned from seeing off the last of his guests to whose importance such an attention was due, rescued Monsieur de l'Estorade from the clutches—as he thought somewhat peril-- ous—of a Wurtemberg Baron, the mysterious agent of some Northern Power, who, helped by his Orders and his gibberish, had the knack of acquiring rather more information about any given matter than his interlocutor intended to give him.

Hooking his arm confidentially through that of the guile- less Monsieur de l'Estorade, who was lending a gullible ear to the trans-Rhenish rhodomontade in which the wily Teuton carefully wrapped up the curiosity he dared not frankly avow:

"That man, you know, is a mere nobody," said Rastignac, as the foreigner made him a humbly obsequious bow.

"He does not talk badly," replied Monsieur de l'Estorade. "If it were not for his villainous accent——"

"That, on the contrary, is his strong point, as it is Nu- cingen's, my father-in-law. With their way of mutilating the French language, and always seeming to be in the clouds, these Germans have the cleverest way of worming out a secret——"

As they joined the group about Madame de Rastignac—

"Madame," said the Minister to the Countess, "I have brought you back your husband, having caught him red- handed in 'criminal conversation' with a man from the Zoll- verein who would probably not have released him this night."

"I was about to ask Madame de Rastignac if she could give me a bed, to set her free at any rate, for Monsieur de l'Estorade's interminable conversations have hindered me from leaving her at liberty."

Madame de Rastignac protested as to the pleasure it had been to enjoy Madame de l'Estorade's society as long as possi- ble, only regretting the necessity for frequent interruptions to respond to the civilities of the extraordinary looking newly-elected deputies who had come in an endless stream to make their bow to her.

"Oh, my dear!" cried Rastignac. "The session will open immediately; pray give yourself no scornful airs to the elect representatives of the nation!—Besides, you will get into Madame de l'Estorade's black books. One of our newly-made sovereigns is, I am told, high in her good graces."

"In mine?" said Madame de l'Estorade with a look of surprise, and she colored a little. Her complexion, still brilliantly clear, lent itself readily to this expression of emotion.

"To be sure! quite true," said Madame de Rastignac. "I had quite forgotten that artist who, on the last occasion of my seeing you at your own house, was cutting out such charming silhouettes for your children, in a corner. I must own that I was then far from supposing that he would become one of our masters."

"But even then he was talked of as a candidate," replied Madame de l'Estorade; "though, to be sure, it was not taken very seriously."

"Quite seriously by me," said Monsieur de l'Estorade, eager to add a stripe to his reputation as a prophet. "From the very first talk on political matters that I had with our candidate, I expressed my astonishment at his breadth of view—Monsieur de Ronquerolles is my witness."

"Certainly," said this gentleman, "he is no ordinary youth; still, I do not build much on his future career. He is a man of impulse, and, as Monsieur de Talleyrand well observed, the first impulse is always the best."

"Well, then, monsieur?" said Madame de l'Estorade innocently.

"Well, madame," replied Monsieur de Ronquerolles, who piqued himself on scepticism, "heroism is out of date; it is a desperately heavy and clumsy outfit, and sinks the wearer on every road."

"And yet I should have supposed that great qualities of heart and mind had something to do with the composition of a man of mark."

"Qualities of mind, yes—you are right there; but even so, on condition of their tendency in a certain direction. But qualities of heart—of what use, I ask you, can they be in a political career?—To hoist you on to stilts on which you walk far less firmly than on your feet, off which you tumble at the first push and break your neck."

"Whence we must conclude," said Madame de Rastignac, laughing, while her friend preserved a disdainful silence, "that the political world is peopled with good-for-nothings."

"That is very near the truth, madame; ask *Lazarille!*" And with this allusion to a pleasantry that is still famous on the stage, Monsieur de Ronquerolles laid his hand familiarly on the Minister's shoulder.

"In my opinion, my dear fellow, your generalizations are rather too particular," said Rastignac.

"Nay," said Monsieur de Ronquerolles, "come now; let us be serious.—To my knowledge, this Monsieur de Sallenauve —the name he has assumed, I believe, instead of Dorlange, which he himself said frankly enough was a name for the stage—has committed two very handsome deeds within a short time. In my presence, aiding and abetting, he was within an ace of being killed by the Duc de Rhétoré for a few unpleasant remarks made on one of his friends. Now he really need not have heard those remarks; and, having heard them, it was straining a point to consider that he had, I will not say a claim, but even a right to take up the quarrel."

"Ah!" said Madame de Rastignac, "it was he then who fought the duel with Monsieur de Rhétoré which was so much discussed?"

"Yes, madame, and I may add that he behaved at the meeting with splendid courage—and I know what I am talking about."

Before the other "handsome deed" could be brought into the discussion, at the risk of seeming rude by interrupting the course of the argument, Madame de l'Estorade rose and gave her husband an imperceptible nod to signify that she wished to leave.

Monsieur de l'Estorade took advantage of the slightness of the signal to ignore it, and remained immovable. Monsieur de Ronquerolles went on:

"His other achievement was to fling himself under the feet of some runaway horses and snatch Madame de l'Estorade's little daughter from certain death."

Everybody looked at Madame de l'Estorade, who this time blushed crimson; but at the same instant she found words, feeling that by some means she must keep her countenance, and she said with some spirit:

"It would seem, monsieur, that you wish to convey that Monsieur de Sallenauve was a great fool for his pains, since he risked his life, and would thus have cut short all his chances in the future. I may tell you, however, that there is one woman whom you would hardly persuade to share that opinion—and that is my child's mother."

As she spoke, Madame de l'Estorade was almost in tears. She warmly shook hands with Madame de Rastignac, and so emphatically made a move, that this time she got her fixture of a husband under way.

Madame de Rastignac, as she went with her friend to the drawing-room door, spoke in an undertone:

"I really thank you," said she, "for having boldly held your own against that cynic. Monsieur de Rastignac has some unpleasant allies left from his bachelor days."

As she returned to her seat, Monsieur de Ronquerolles was speaking:

"Aha," said he, "these life-preservers!—Poor l'Estorade is, in fact, as yellow as a lemon!"

"Indeed, monsieur, you are atrocious!" said Madame de Rastignac indignantly. "A woman whom calumny has never dared to blight, who lives solely for her husband and children, and who has tears in her eyes at the mere remote recollection of the danger that theatened one of them!"

"Bless me, madame," said Monsieur de Ronquerolles, heedless of this little lecture, "I can only tell you that your Newfoundland dog is a dangerous and unwholesome breed.—After all, if Madame de l'Estorade should think herself too seriously compromised, she has always this to fall back on—she can get him to marry the girl he saved."

Monsieur de Ronquerolles had no sooner spoken than he was conscious of the hideous blunder he had made by uttering such a speech in Augusta de Nucingen's drawing-room. It was his turn to redden—though he had lost the habit of it, and deep silence, which seemed to enfold him, put the crowning touch to his embarrassment.

"That clock is surely slow," said Rastignac, to make some sound of whatever words, and also to put an end to a sitting at which speech was so luckless.

"It is indeed," said Monsieur de Ronquerolles, after looking at his watch. "Just on a quarter-past twelve"—the hour was half-past eleven.

He bowed formally to the mistress of the house, and went, as did the rest of the company.

"You saw how distressed he was," said Rastignac to his wife, as soon as they were alone. "He was a thousand miles away from any malicious intent."

"No matter; as I was saying just now to Madame de l'Estorade, your bachelor life has left you heir to some odious acquaintances."

"But, my dear child, the King is civil every day to people he would be only too glad to lock up in the Bastille, if there still were a Bastille, and if the Charter would allow it."

Madame de Rastignac made no reply; she went up to her room without saying good-night.

Not long after, the Minister tapped at a side door of the room, and finding it locked:

"Augusta," said he, in the voice which the most ordinary *bourgeois* of the Rue Saint-Denis would have adopted under similar circumstances.

The only answer he heard was a bolt shot inside.

"There are some things in the past," said he to himself, with much annoyance, "that are quite unlike that door—they always stand wide open on the present."

"Augusta," he began again, "I wanted to ask you at what hour I might find Madame de l'Estorade at home. I mean to call on her to-morrow after what has happened——"

"At four o'clock," the lady called back, "when she comes in from the Tuileries, where she always walks with the children."

One of the questions which had been most frequently mooted in the world of fashion since Madame de Rastignac's marriage was this—"Does Augusta love her husband?"

Doubt was allowable; Mademoiselle de Nucingen's marriage had been the ill-favored and not very moral result of an intimacy such as is apt to react on the daughter's life when it has lasted in the mother's till the course of years and long staleness have brought it to a state of atrophy and paralysis. In such unions, where love is to be transferred to the next generation, the husband is usually more than willing, for he is released from joys that have turned rancid, and avails himself of a bargain like that offered by the magician in the *Arabian Nights* to exchange old lamps for new. But the wife is in the precisely opposite predicament; between her and her husband there stands an ever-present memory—which may come to life again. Even apart from the dominion of the senses, she must be conscious of an older power antagonistic to her newer influence; must she not almost always be a victim, and can she be supposed to feel impassioned devotion to the maternal leavings?—Rastignac had stood waiting outside the door for about as long as it has taken to give this brief analysis of a not uncommon conjugal situation.

"Well, good-night, Augusta," said he, preparing to depart.

As he piteously took his leave, the door was suddenly opened, and his wife, throwing herself into his arms, laid her head on his shoulder, sobbing.

The question was answered: Madame de Rastignac loved her husband.—And yet the distant murmuring of a nice little hell might be heard under the flowers of this paradise.

Rastignac was less punctual than usual next morning; and

by the time he went into his private office, the ante-room
beyond was already occupied by seven applicants armed with
letters of introduction, besides two peers and seven members
of the Lower Chamber.

A bell rang sharply, and the usher, with such agitation as
proved contagious among the visitors, hurried into the Minister's room. A moment later he reappeared with the stereo-
typed apology:

"The Minister is called to attend a Council. He will, however, have the honor of receiving the members of the Upper
and Lower Chambers. The rest of the gentlemen are requested to call again."

"But when—again?" asked one of the postponed victims.
"This is the third time I have called within three days, and
all for nothing."

The usher shrugged his shoulders, as much as to say, "That
is no fault of mine; I only obey orders." However, hearing
some murmurs as to the privilege accorded to the Honorable
Members:

"Those gentlemen," said he, with some pomposity, "come
to discuss matters of public interest."

The visitors having been paid in this false coin, the bell
rang again, and the usher put on his most affable smile.

By some obscure natural affinity the happier portion of
this little crowd had gravitated into one corner. Though they
had never met before, since most of them were the offspring
of the latest national travail, they had somehow recognized
each other by a *representative* manner, very difficult to define,
but quite unmistakable. It was to this upper side of the sieve,
so to speak, that the man directed his insinuating glance;
not daring to decide among so many great men, he mutely
suggested:

"Whom shall I have the honor of announcing first?"

"Gentlemen," said Colonel Franchessini, "I believe I have
seen you all come in?"

And he went towards the door which the usher threw open,
announcing in a loud, distinct voice:

"Monsieur le Colonel Franchessini."

"Ah, a good beginning this morning!" said the Minister, going forward a few steps and holding out his hand. "What do you want of me, my dear fellow? A railway, a canal, a suspension bridge——?"

"I have come, my dear friend, to trouble you about a little private affair—a matter that concerns both you and me?"

"That is not the happiest way of urging the question, for I must tell you plainly I hold no good recommendation to myself."

"You have had a visitor lately?" said the Colonel, proceeding to the point.

"A visitor? Dozens. I always have."

"Yes. But on the evening of Sunday the 12th—the day of the riot?"

"Ah! now I know what you mean.—But the man is going mad."

"Do you think so?" said the Colonel dubiously.

"Well, what am I to think of a sort of visionary who makes his way in here under favor of the relaxed vigilance which in a Ministerial residence always follows on musket-firing in the streets; who proceeds to tell me that the Government is undermined by the Republican party, at the very moment when the Staff-officers of the National Guard assure me that we have not had even a skirmish, and who finally suggests that he is himself the only man who can insure the future safety of the dynasty?"

"So that you did not welcome him very cordially?"

"So that I soon showed him out, and rather peremptorily, in spite of his persistency. At any time, and under any circumstances, he is a visitor I could never find agreeable; but when, on my pointing out to him that he holds a post for which he is admirably fitted, and which he fills with the greatest skill, so that it must be the utmost limit of his ambition, the maniac replies that unless his services are accepted France is on the brink of a precipice, you may suppose I had but one thing to say—namely, that we hope to save it without his help."

"Well, it is done!" said the Colonel. "But now, if you will allow me to explain matters——"

The Minister, sitting at his table with his back to the fire, leaned round to look at the clock.

"Look here, my dear fellow," said he, after seeing what the time was, "I have a suspicion that you will not be brief, and there is a hungry pack waiting outside that door; even if I could give you time, I could not listen properly. Be so kind as to go for an airing till noon, and come back to breakfast. I will introduce you to Madame de Rastignac, whom you do not know, I believe, and when we rise from table we will take a turn in the garden; there I shall be wholly at your service, and can give you all the time you need."

"That will suit me perfectly," said the Colonel, leaving. As he crossed the waiting-room:

"Well, gentlemen," said he, "I have not kept you long, have I?"

He shook hands with one and another, and went away.

Three hours later, when the Colonel appeared in Madame de Rastignac's drawing-room—where he was introduced to her—he found there Nucingen, the Minister's father-in-law, who came almost every day to breakfast there on his way to the Bourse; Émile Blondet, of the *Débats;* Messrs. Moreau (de l'Oise), Dionis, and Camusot, three fiercely Conservative members; and two of the newly elect, whose names it is not certain that Rastignac himself knew. Franchessini also recognized Martial de la Roche-Hugon, the Minister's brother-in-law; the inevitable des Lupeaulx, a Peer of France; and a third figure, who talked for a long time with Rastignac in a window recess. He, Émile Blondet explained in reply to the Colonel's inquiries, was a former functionary of the secret police, who still carried on his profession as an amateur, making the round of all the Government offices every morning, under every Ministry, with as much zeal and punctuality as if it still were his duty.

In consequence of the somewhat keen remarks that had passed between the Colonel and Maxime de Trailles as to the frame of mind in which Madame de Rastignac might find herself when marriage should have palled a little, he was bound to give some attention to the last and fourteenth person, a fresh-colored, rosy youth who was, he heard, the Minister's private secretary. It is well known that private secretaries, when they are caught young, if they are but zealous and guileless, have to some extent taken the place of the aides-de-camp of the past. However, as soon as he heard Madame de Rastignac address this young official with the familiar *tu*, asking him after his mother Madame de Restaud, he troubled himself no further. This was merely a little cousin, not a dangerous rival, whatever the playwrights may say, when a young wife has a due sense of her dignity. Monsieur de Rastignac had taken as his private secretary Félix Restaud, second son of his mother-in-law Madame de Nucingen's sister. Ernest, the elder, was pledged to the Legitimist party as having married Camille, daughter of the Vicomtesse de Grandlieu, who must not be confounded with the Duchess of the same name.

Madame de Rastignac, seen close, was fair but not lymphatic. She was strikingly like her mother, but with the shade of greater elegance, which in parvenu families grows from generation to generation as they get further from the source. The last drop of the original Goriot seemed to have evaporated in this lovely young woman, who was especially distinguished by the fine hands and feet, which show breeding, and of which the absence in Madame de Nucingen, in spite of her beauty, had always stamped her so distressingly as the vermicelli-maker's daughter.

The Colonel, as a man who might subsequently have ideas of his own, showed repressed eagerness in his attentions to Madame de Rastignac, with the gallantry, now rather out of date, which seems addressed to Woman rather than to the individual woman; idle men alone, especially if they have been soldiers, seem to preserve a reflection of this tradition. The Colonel, whose successes in the boudoir had been many, knew that this distant method of preparing the approaches is a very effective strategy in besieging a place. An air of adoration and worship, though so much out of fashion, never displeases a woman; and, with the exception of a few who are Voltairean sceptics as to love, regarding it as mere good-fellowship, and laughing at the respectful feeling of a man who hesitates to approach them with a cigar between his teeth, so to speak, most women are grateful to an adorer, particularly if he is not a Celadon, when he treats them with pious reverence and rather like sacred relics.

The Colonel, as he meant to be asked to the house again, took care to speak of his wife. "She lived," he said, "very much in the old English way, in her own home; but he would be happy to drag her out of her habitual retirement to introduce her to a lady of such distinguished merit as Madame de Rastignac, if indeed she would allow him to bring her. In spite of a wide difference in age between his wife and his friend the Minister's, they would find, he thought, one happy point of contact in a similar zeal for good works."

In fact, Franchessini had hardly entered the room when he found himself obliged to take from Madame de Rastignac a ticket for a ball of which she was a lady patroness, to be got up for the benefit of the victims of the recent earthquake in Martinique.

It was the fashion *then* among women to display in such acts of charity an audacity beyond all bounds; now, as it happened, Madame Franchessini was an Irishwoman of great piety, who spent in good works most of her spare time after superintending the management of her house, and a large part of the sums she reserved for her own use apart from her husband's. So the offer of an intimacy with a woman who would be so ready to give her money and her exertions when needed for a *crèche,* or infant schools, or children orphaned by the cholera, was a really skilful stroke of diplomacy; and it shows that the sportsman in the Colonel had not altogether killed the faculty of foresight.

Breakfast over, the guests left or withdrew to the drawing-room; and Franchessini, who had sat at Madame de Rastignac's right hand, continued his conversation with her.

While he, like Hercules at the feet of Omphale, devoted his anxious attention to the worsted work—for the benefit of the poor—which the Countess held in her pretty fingers, the Minister, in obedience to the proverb, "Give every dog his day," had taken Émile Blondet's arm—Blondet of the *Débats* —and made a couple of rounds of the grass plot that lay outside the glass doors of the drawing-room. As he parted from him he gave him this final hint:

"You understand? We do not want to drive a bargain; however, the majority is ours."

"Now for you and me, my friend!" said he to the Colonel, and they went into the garden.

"I, less fortunate than you," said Franchessini, taking up his story at the point where it had been interrupted a few hours previously, "have kept up communications with the man we spoke of—not constant, indeed; but a sort of evil concatenation of contact. To avoid ever having him in my house, we agreed that whenever he wanted to speak to me he should write to me without any signature and tell me where to meet him. In the almost impossible event of my wishing to see him, I was to send a playing card figure cut out to his den in the Rue Sainte-Anne, and he would notify the spot where we might meet undisturbed. He may be trusted for a clever choice of a suitable place; no man knows his Paris better, or the ways of moving about *underground*."

"High political qualifications!" said Rastignac sarcastically.

"I tell you the whole truth, you see," replied the Colonel, "to prove to you that, in my opinion, this is a man to be treated with respect; and, at the same time, that you may not suppose that I am showing you a mere phantasmagoria with a view to persuading you into doing a thing quite contrary to your first intentions."

"Pray go on," said Rastignac, pausing to gather a full-blown China rose—by way, perhaps, of showing his perfect openness of mind.

"On the evening of the very day when you had given him

so rough a reception, and my election was already known by telegraph and announced in an evening paper, I received a note from him, a thing that had not happened for the last eighteen months—very short and concise:—'To-morrow morning, six o'clock—Redoute de Clignancourt.' "

"Like a challenge," observed Rastignac.

"A reminder of one, certainly; for, as you may remember, it was at Montmartre that, in that unfortunate duel—with my own hands—about 1820—poor young Taillefer!—Sometimes, at dusk, I think of that luckless fellow, though the wound, as you know, was honestly given——"

"Ay, one of those ugly stories," said Rastignac, "which save us from regretting our young days when such things were done."

"The man whom you call a visionary," Franchessini went on, "was, when I joined him, sitting on a knoll, his head between his hands. When he heard me, and as I went close to him, he rose in a state of high excitement, took me by the hand, led me to the spot—very little altered—where the duel took place, and in the strident voice you know so well: 'What did you do here, nearly five-and-twenty years ago?' said he.— 'A thing,' said I, 'of which, on my honor, I repent.'—'And I too.—And for whom?' As I made no reply, he went on: 'For a man whose fortune I wanted to make. You killed the brother to please me, that the sister might be a rich heiress for him to marry——' "

"But it was all done without my knowledge," Rastignac hastily put in; "and I did everything in my power to prevent it."

"So I told him," said the Colonel, "and he paid no heed to the remark, but only grew more frantic, exclaiming: 'Well, and when I go to that man's house, not to ask him a favor, but to offer him my services, he shows me the door! And does he think I am going to overlook it?' "

"He is remarkably touchy," said Rastignac quietly. "I did not show him the door. I only rather roughly cut short his boasting and exaggeration."

"He then went on," said the Colonel, "to relate his interview with you the previous evening; the proposal he had made to give up his place in the criminal police in favor of a post as superintendent—far more needed, in his opinion—of political malefactors. 'I am sick,' said he, 'of liming twigs to catch thieves, such an idiotic kind of game-bird that all their tricks are stale to me. And, then, what interest can I find in nabbing men who would steal a silver mug or a few banknotes, when there are others only waiting for a chance to grab at the crown?'"

"Very true," said Rastignac, with a smile, "if it were not for the National Guard, and the army, and the two Chambers, and the King who can ride."

"He added," said Franchessini, "that he was not appreciated, and, with a reminiscence of the lingo of the past, that he was fagged out over mere child's play; that he had in him very powerful qualities adapted to shine in a higher sphere; that he had trained a man to take his place; that I must positively see and talk to you; and that now I was a member, I had a right to speak and impress on you the possible results of a refusal."

"My dear fellow," said Rastignac decisively, "I can but say, as I did at the beginning of our conversation, the man is a lunatic, and I have never been afraid of a madman, whether a cheerful or furious one."

"I do not deny that I myself saw great difficulties in the way of satisfying his demand. However, I tried to soothe him by promising to see you, pointing out to him that nothing could be done in a hurry, and in point of fact, but for an accessory circumstance, I should probably not have mentioned the matter for some long time to come."

"And that circumstance——?" asked the Minister.

"Yesterday morning," replied the Colonel, "I had a visit from Maxime, who had just returned from Arcis-sur-Aube——"

"I know," said Rastignac. "He mentioned the matter to me—an idea devoid of common-sense. Either the man on

whom he wants to set your bloodhound is good for something
—or he is not. If he is not, it is perfectly useless to employ
a dangerous and suspected instrument to destroy the thing
that does not exist. If, on the other hand, we have to do
with a good man in the right place, he has, on the platform
of the Chamber, and in the newspapers, every means, not only
of parrying such blows as we may be able to strike with
muffled swords, but of turning them against ourselves.—Take
it as a general rule, in a country like ours, crazy for publicity,
wherever the hand of the police is seen, even if it were to un-
veil the basest turpitude, you may be sure that there will be
an outcry against the Government. Opinion in such a case
behaves like the man to whom some one sang an air by Mozart
to prove how great a composer he was. The hearer, conquered
by the evidence, said at last to the singer, 'Well, Mozart may
be a great musician, but you, my good friend, may congratulate yourself on having a great cold!' "

"Indeed, there is much truth in your remark," said
Franchessini. "Still, the man Maxime wants to unmask can
only be of respectable mediocrity; and without being able to
lunge with such force as you suppose, he may nevertheless
tease you a good deal. The most dangerous adversaries are
not all giants of formidable eloquence."

"I expect to ascertain the true worth of your new colleague
ere long from a quarter where I may count on better information than Monsieur de Trailles can command. On this occasion he has let himself in, and is trying to make up for
lack of skill by vehemence. As to your incubus—whom I
should not, in any case, employ to carry out Maxime's dream
—as he seems not altogether useless, at least from the point
of view of your connection with him, just to give him an
answer I should say——"

"Well, what?" said Franchessini, with increased attention.

"I should tell him that, quite apart from his criminal experience, which, as soon as he heads the political ranks, might
expose him to serious outrages that would recoil on us, there
are in his past life some very ugly records——"

"But records only," replied Franchessini. "For you understand that when he ventured into your presence it was, so to speak, in a new skin."

"I know all," said Rastignac. "You do not suppose that he is the only police spy in Paris.—After his visit I made inquiries, and I heard that since 1830, when he was placed at the head of his department, he had lived a middle-class life of the strictest respectability; the only fault I have to find with it is that it is too perfect a disguise."

"Nevertheless——" said the Colonel.

"He is rich," Rastignac went on; "his salary is twelve thousand francs a year from the Government; with three hundred thousand he inherited from Lucien de Rubempré, and the profits from a patent-leather factory which he has near Gentilly, and which is paying very well. His aunt Jacqueline Collin, who keeps house with him, still dabbles in certain dirty jobs, from which, of course, she derives large profits; and I have strong reason to believe that they have both gambled successfully on the Bourse. The deuce is in it, my dear fellow, if, under such circumstances, a man cannot whitewash himself and turn over a new leaf. In the age in which we live, luxury is a power; it does not, indeed, secure consideration and respect, but it presents their counterfeit, which comes to much the same thing. Just set some great financiers or statesmen I could name in a garret, or going about on foot —why, the street boys would run after them and hoot them like drunkards or carnival guys!—And your man, who, to escape tramping the mud, wanted to perch his life on a pedestal, could find no better plan than to get himself suddenly transferred to the furthest social pole from his own. Every evening now, in a café close to the Préfecture, at the foot of the Pont Saint-Michel, he sits down sociably to his game of dominoes; and on Sundays he goes with a party of retired tradesmen to spend the day in philosophical retirement in a shanty he has bought not far from the woods of Romainville in the Prés Saint-Gervais; there he tries to grow blue dahlias, and was talking last year of crowning a rose-queen!

"Now all this, my dear Colonel, is too bucolic to lead up to the superintendence of the political police. Let him bestir himself a little—this old *Germeuil,* fling a little money about, give some dinners!—Why, the executioner could get men to dine with him if he wished it."

"I quite agree with you," said Franchessini. "I think that he keeps himself too much curled up for fear of attracting notice."

"Tell him, on the contrary, to uncurl; and, since he wants to have a finger in public business, he should find some creditable opportunity for being talked about. Does he fancy that, hide in what corner he will, the press will not know where to find him? Let him do as the niggers do; they do not try to wash themselves white, but they have a passion for bright colors, and dress in scarlet coats covered with gold braid.— I know what I should do in his place: to appear thoroughly cleaned, I should take up with some actress, some one very notorious, conspicious, before the public. I do not say that I would ruin myself, but I would seem to ruin myself for her, with all the airs of one of those frenzied passions for which the public is always indulgent, if not sympathetic. I should display all my luxury on this idol's account; people would come, not to my house, but to hers. Then, thanks to my mistress, I should be endured at my own table, and by degrees I should make a connection. All the leading men in our sphere of life gather round a famous actress as inevitably as moths round a candle; the men who can make or unmake, or —which is the crowning feat of art—can remake a reputation. Politicians, men on 'Change, journalists, artists, men of letters, I would harness them all to drag me out of the mud, while feeding them well, and showing myself ever ready with my sympathy, and yet more with my money, to help them in a hundred little ways.

"All this, my dear fellow, will not, of course, make him a Saint Vincent de Paul—though he too had been on the galleys—but it would get him classed among the third or fourth rate notabilities—a man possible to deal with. The road thus laid, Monsieur de Saint-Estève might prove 'ne-gotiable'; and if he then came to me, and I were still in power, I might be able to listen to him."

"There is certainly something to be said for this plan," replied Franchessini. But in his own mind he reflected that his friend the Minister had made great strides since the days of the Pension Vauquer, and that he and Vautrin—as Saint-Estève was then called—had exchanged parts.

"But at any rate," added Rastignac, going up the steps to return to the drawing-room, "make him clearly understand that he misinterpreted my way of receiving him. That even-ing I was naturally absorbed in anxious reflections."

"Be quite easy," said Franchessini, "I will talk to him in the right way; for, as I must repeat, he is not a man to drive to extremities; there have been incidents in our past which cannot be wiped out."

And as the Minister made no reply, it was sufficiently obvious that he appreciated the observation at its true value.

"You will be here for the King's speech, I hope," said Ras-tignac to the Colonel; "we want a little enthusiasm."

Franchessini, before leaving, asked Madame de Rastignac to name a day when he might have the honor of bringing his wife to call.

"Any day," replied Augusta, "but more especially any Friday."

At the hour when Rastignac, by his wife's instructions, thought himself sure to find Madame de l'Estorade, he did not fail to call. Like all who had been present at the little scene to which Monsieur de Ronquerolles' remarks had given rise, the Minister had been struck by the Countess' agitation; and without concerning himself to gauge the nature or depth of her feelings towards the man who had saved her child, he was convinced that she was at least greatly interested by him.

The unexpected feat of winning his election attracted the attention of the Government to Sallenauve, all the more because at first his nomination had hardly been taken seriously. It was known, too, that at the preliminary meeting on the eve of the election he had shown himself a clever man. He might easily become a fairly resonant voice, speaking for a dangerous and restless party, represented in the Chamber by an almost imperceptible minority. His fortune, whatever its origin, would enable him to dispense with Ministerial favors, and all the information obtainable represented him as a man not easily turned from the path he had chosen, and characterized by a certain gravity of demeanor and purpose. On the other hand, the obscurity that hung over his history might at any moment serve to extinguish him.

Rastignac, while affecting to discard with vehemence the idea of an attack from that side, in his own mind did not altogether renounce the possibility of using means which he foresaw would be difficult to handle; he would fall back on them only if it were obviously necessary. In this state of things Madame de l'Estorade might be useful in two ways: through her it seemed easy to arrange an *accidental* meeting with the new deputy, so as to study him at ease and ascertain whether there were any single point at which he might prove accessible to terms. And since this, it would seem, was improbable, it would at any rate be easy, by confiding to Madame de l'Estorade in a friendly but official way the underhand plotting that was going on against Sallenauve, to warn him to be cautious, and consequently less aggressive.

And all this would follow naturally from the step the Minister was now taking. By seeming to call on purpose to apologize for Monsieur de Ronquerolles' mode of speech, he would allude in the most natural manner possible to the man who had been the occasion and the object of it; and the conversation once started on these lines, he must be clumsy indeed if he could not achieve one or the other, or possibly both, of the results he aimed at.

Monsieur de Rastignac's plan of action was, however, destined to be modified. The servant, who happened to be speaking to the gate keeper, had just informed the visitor that

Madame de l'Estorade was not at home, when Monsieur de l'Estorade came in on foot, and seeing the Minister's carriage, rushed forward. However well a man may stand with the world, it always seems a pity to dismiss a visitor of such importance; and the accountant-general was not the man to resign himself to such a misfortune without a struggle.

"But my wife will soon be in," he insisted as he saw his house threatened with the loss of such a piece of good fortune. "She is gone to Ville-d'Avray with her daughter, and Monsieur and Madame Octave de Camps. Monsieur Marie-Gaston, a great friend of ours—the charming poet, you know, who married Louise de Chaulieu—has a house there, where his wife died. He has never till now set foot in it since that misfortune. These ladies were so charitable as to accompany him, so as to break the shock of his return; and a little out of curiosity too, for the villa is said to be one of the most perfect retreats ever imagined."

"But in that case Madame de l'Estorade's visit may last till late," said Rastignac. "It was to her, and not to you, my dear Count, that I came to offer my apologies for the little scene last evening, which seemed to annoy her a good deal.—Will you kindly express to her from me——"

"I will stake my head on it, my dear sir, that by the time you turn the street corner, my wife will be here; she is absolutely punctual in everything she does, and to me it is simply miraculous that she should be even a few minutes late."

Seeing him so bent on detaining him, Rastignac feared to be disobliging, and made up his mind to be dragged out of his carriage, and await the Countess' return in her drawing-room; for, often enough, for less than this a faithful voter has been lost.

"So Madame Octave de Camps is in Paris?" said he, for the sake of saying something.

"Yes, she made her appearance unexpectedly without letting my wife know, though they are in constant correspondence. Her husband has, I think, some request to make to you. You have not seen him?"

"No; but I think I remember seeing his card."

"It is some mining business he is projecting; and as I have your ear, allow me to tell you something about it."

"Mercy!" thought Rastignac, "I am very kind, I am sure, to have come here merely to stand a fire of recommendations, point-blank."

So, cutting short the explanation l'Estorade had already begun, and seeing no reason why he should not quite unceremoniously ask the husband one of the things which he had proposed to ask the wife:

"Excuse my interrupting you," said he, "we will return to the subject; but at this moment I am in some uneasiness."

"How is that?"

"Your friend Sallenauve's election has made a devil of a rumpus. The King was speaking of him to me this morning, and he was not particularly delighted when I communicated to him the opinion you expressed only last evening as to our new adversary."

"Bless me! But, as you know, the tribune is a rock on which many a ready-made reputation is wrecked. And I am sorry too that you should have spoken of Sallenauve to the King as a friend of ours. It is not I who direct the elections. You should appeal to the Minister of the Interior. I can only say that I tried fifty ways to hinder the tiresome man from standing."

"But you must see that the King can owe you no grudge because you happen to know a candidate so absolutely undreamed of——"

"No. But last evening in your own drawing-room you remarked to my wife that she seemed greatly interested in him. I could not contradict before others, because it is monstrous to deny knowledge of a man to whom we lie under so serious an obligation. But, in fact, my wife especially has felt that obligation a burden since the day when he went off to stand for election. Though she never troubles her head about politics, she prefers the society of those who swim in our own waters, and she probably foresees that an intimacy with a man whose daily business it is to attack our side may be difficult and very moderately pleasant. She even said to me the other day that he was an acquaintance to be quietly dropped——"

"Not, I hope," interrupted Rastignac, "before you have done me the service I came to ask."

"At your service, my dear Minister, whatever it may be."

"To plunge in head foremost, then: before seeing this man in the Chamber I want to take his measure, and for that purpose I want to meet him. To invite him to dine with us would be useless; under the eye of his party he would not dare to accept, even if he wished it. Besides, he would be on his guard, and I should not see him as he is. But if we came across each other by chance, I should find him, as it were, in undress, and could feel my way to discover if he has a weak spot."

"If I asked him to meet you at dinner here, there would be the same difficulty.—Supposing I were to find out some evening that he intended to call, and sent you word in the course of the day?"

"We should be too small a party," said Rastignac, "and then a separate conversation between two is hard to manage; the meeting is so intimate that any *tête-à-tête* betrays the aggravating circumstance of premeditated arrangement——"

"Stay!" cried Monsieur de l'Estorade, "I have a bright idea——"

"If the idea is really bright," thought the Minister, "I shall have gained by not finding the lady in, for she certainly would not have been so anxious to carry out my wishes."

"One day soon," l'Estorade went on, "we are giving a little party, a children's dance. It is a treat my wife, tired of refusing, has promised our little girl, in fact as a festival to celebrate our joy at still having her with us. The Preserver, as you perceive, is an integral and indispensable item, and I think I may promise you noise enough to enable you to take your man aside without any difficulty, while at a party of that kind premeditation can hardly be suspected."

"The idea is certainly a good one—probability alone is wanting."

"Probability?"

"Certainly. You forgot that I have been married scarcely a year, and that I have no contingent to account for my presence that evening among your party."

"That is true. I had not thought of that."

"But let me consider," said the Minister. "Among your guests will there be the little Roche-Hugons?"

"No doubt; the children of a man I should esteem most highly even if he had not the honor of so near a relationship to you."

"Well, then, all is plain sailing. My wife will come with her sister-in-law, Madame de la Roche-Hugon, to see her nieces dancing—nothing is more complimentary on such occasions than to drop in without the formality of an invitation; and I, without saying anything to my wife, am gallant enough to come to take her home."

"Admirable!" said Monsieur de l'Estorade, "and we by this little drama gain the delightful reality of your presence here!"

"You are too kind," said Rastignac, shaking hands cordially. "But I believe it will be well to say nothing to Madame de l'Estorade. Our puritan, if he got wind of the plan, is the man to stay away. It will be better that I should pounce on him unexpectedly like a tiger on its prey."

"Quite so.—A surprise for everybody!"

"Then I am off," said Rastignac, "for fear I should drop a word to Madame de l'Estorade. I shall be able to amuse the King to-morrow by telling him of our little plot and the education of children to be political go-betweens."

"Well, well," said Monsieur de l'Estorade philosophically, "is not this the whole history of life: great effects from small causes?"

Rastignac had only just left when Madame de l'Estorade, her daughter Naïs, and her friends Monsieur and Madame Octave de Camps came into the drawing-room where the conspiracy had been laid against the new member's independence —a plot here recorded at some length as a specimen of the thousand-and-one trivialities to which a constitutional minister not unfrequently has to attend.

"And do you not smell the smell of a Minister here?" said Monsieur de l'Estorade.

"Not such a very delicious scent, I am sure," replied Monsieur de Camps, who, as a Legitimist, belonged to the Opposition.

"That is a matter of taste," said the Peer.—"My dear," he went on, addressing his wife, "you have come so late that you have missed a distinguished visitor."

"Who is that?" the Countess asked indifferently.

"The Minister of Public Works, who came to offer you an apology. He had noted with regret the unpleasant impression made upon you by the theories put forward by that wretched Ronquerolles."

"That is disturbing himself for a very small matter," replied Madame de l'Estorade, who was far from sharing her husband's excitement.

"At any rate," replied he, "it was very polite of him to have noticed the matter."

Madame de l'Estorade, without seeming to care much, asked what had passed in the course of the visit.

"We discussed indifferent subjects," said Monsieur de l'Estorade craftily. "However, I took the opportunity of getting a word in on the subject of Monsieur de Camps' business."

"Much obliged," said Octave, with a bow. "If only you could have persuaded the gentleman to grant me a sight of his private secretary, who is as invisible as himself, between them they might arrange to give me an interview."

"You must not be annoyed with him," said Monsieur de l'Estorade. "Though his office is not strictly political, Rastignac has, of course, been much taken up with election matters. Now that he is freer, we will, if you like, call on him together one morning."

"I hesitate to trouble you about a matter that ought to go smoothly of itself; I am not asking a favor. I never will ask one of this Government; but since Monsieur de Rastignac is the dragon in charge of the metallic treasures of the soil, I am bound to go through the regular channel and apply to him."

"We can settle all that, and I have started the thing in the right direction," replied Monsieur de l'Estorade.

Then, to change the conversation, he said to Madame de Camps:

"Well, and the chalet, is it really such a marvel?"

"Oh," said Madame Octave, "it is a fascinating place; you can have no idea of such elegant perfection and such ideal comfort."

"And Marie-Gaston?" asked Monsieur de l'Estorade, much as Orgon asks, "And Tartuffe?"—but with far less anxious curiosity.

"He was—I will not say quite calm," replied Madame de l'Estorade, "but certainly quite master of himself. His behavior was all the more satisfactory because the day began with a serious disappointment."

"What happened?" asked Monsieur de l'Estorade.

"Monsieur de Sallenauve could not come with him," cried Naïs, making it her business to reply.

She was one of those children brought up in a hot-house who intervene rather oftener than they ought in matters that are discussed in their presence.

"Naïs," said her mother, "go and ask Mary to put your hair up."

The child perfectly understood that she was sent away to her English nurse for having spoken out of season, and she went off with a little pout.

"This morning," said Madame de l'Estorade, as soon as Naïs had closed the door, "Monsieur Marie-Gaston and Monsieur de Sallenauve were to have set out together for Ville-d'Avray, to receive us there, as had been arranged; last evening they had a visit from the organist who was so active in promoting Monsieur de Sallenauve's election—he came to hear the Italian housekeeper sing and decide as to whether she were fit to appear in public."

"To be sure!" said Monsieur de l'Estorade. "Now we have ceased to make statues, we must quarter her somewhere!"

"As you say," answered his wife, rather tartly. "Monsieur de Sallenauve, to silence slander, was anxious to enable her to follow out her own idea of going on the stage; but he wished first to have the opinion of a judge who is said to be remarkably competent. The two gentlemen went with the organist to Saint-Sulpice, where the handsome Italian sings every evening in the services for the month of Mary. After hearing her: 'That contralto has at least sixty thousand francs in her throat!' the organist remarked."

"Just the income I derive from my forges!" remarked Octave de Camps.

"On returning home," Madame de l'Estorade went on, "Monsieur de Sallenauve told his housekeeper of the opinion pronounced on her performance, and with the utmost circumspection he insinuated that she must now soon be thinking of making her living, as she always intended. 'Yes, I think the time is come,' said Signora Luigia. Then she closed the conversation, saying, 'We will speak of it again.'—This morning at breakfast they were much surprised at having seen nothing of the Signora, who was habitually an early riser. Fancying she must be ill, Monsieur de Sallenauve sent a woman who comes to do the coarser cleaning to knock at her door. No answer. More and more anxious, the two gentlemen went themselves to find out what was happening.

"After knocking and calling in vain, they determined to turn the key and go in. In the room—nobody; but instead, a letter addressed to Monsieur de Sallenauve. In this letter the Italian said that, knowing herself to be in his way, she was retiring to the house of a woman she knew, and thanked him for all his kindness to her."

"The bird had felt its wings!" said Monsieur de l'Estorade. "It had flown away."

"That was not Monsieur de Sallenauve's idea," said the Countess. "He does not for an instant suspect her of an impulse of ingratitude.—Before explaining to the meeting of voters the relation in which they stood, Monsieur de Sallenauve, having ascertained that he would be questioned about it, had with great delicacy written to ask her whether this public avowal would not be too painful to her. She replied that she left it entirely to him. At the same time, he noticed on his return that she was out of spirits, and treated him with more than usual formality; whence he now concludes that, fancying herself a burden to him, in one of those fits of folly and temper of which she is peculiarly capable, she has thought it incumbent on her to leave his house without allowing him in any way to concern himself with providing for her in the future."

"Well, well," said Monsieur de l'Estorade, "luck go with her!—A good riddance."

"Neither Monsieur de Sallenauve nor Monsieur Marie-Gaston takes such a stoical view of the matter. Knowing the woman's determined and headstrong nature, they fear lest she should have laid violent hands on her life—an idea which her previous history justifies. Or else they fear that she has been ill advised. The under-servant I mentioned had observed that while the gentlemen were in the country, Signora Luigia two or three times had a mysterious visitor in the person of a middle-aged lady, handsomely dressed, who came in a carriage, but whose appearance was singular, and who made a great show of secrecy about their interviews."

"Some charitable visitor," said Monsieur de l'Estorade, "since the runaway is one of the very devout."

"At any rate, that must be ascertained; and it was to discover what has become of the luckless creature that Monsieur de Sallenauve, by Monsieur Marie-Gaston's earnest desire, spent the day in the search instead of accompanying him to Ville-d'Avray.

"I adhere to my opinion," replied Monsieur de l'Estorade.

"And in spite of immaculate virtue on both sides, I maintain that he has been caught by her."

"At any rate," remarked Madame de l'Estorade, emphasizing the word, "it does not seem that she *has been caught.*"

"I do not agree with you," said Madame de Camps. "Flying from a person is often a proof of very true love."

Madame de l'Estorade looked at her friend with some vexation, and a faint color flushed her cheeks. But this no one noticed, the servant having thrown the double doors open and announced that dinner was served.

After dinner, they proposed to go to the play; it is one of the amusements that Parisians most miss in the country; and Monsieur Octave de Camps, whose odious ironworks, as Madame de l'Estorade called them, had made him a sort of "Wild Man of the Woods," had come to town eager for this diversion, for which his wife, a serious and stay-at-home woman, was far from sharing his taste.

So when Monsieur de Camps spoke of going to the Porte Saint-Martin to see a fairy piece that was attracting all Paris, his wife replied:

"Neither I nor Madame de l'Estorade have any wish to go out. We are very tired with our expedition, and will give up our places to Naïs and René, who will enjoy the marvels of the *Rose-fairy* far more than we should."

The two children awaited the ratification of this plan with such anxiety as may be imagined. Their mother made no objection; and thus, a few minutes later, the two ladies, who since Madame de Camps' arrival in Paris had not once been able to escape from their surroundings for a single chat, found themselves left to an evening of confidential talk.

"Not at home to anybody," said Madame de l'Estorade to Lucas, when the party were fairly off.

Then, taking as her starting-point the last words spoken by Madame de Camps before dinner:

"You really have, my dear friend," said she, "a stock of the sharpest little arrows, which go as straight to their mark as so many darts."

"Now that we are alone," replied Madame Octave, "I am going to deal you blows with a bludgeon; for, as you may suppose, I have not traveled two hundred leagues and abandoned the care of our business, which Monsieur de Camps has trained me to manage very competently when he is absent, only to tell you sugared truths."

"I am willing to hear anything from you," said Madame de l'Estorade, pressing her friend's hand—her dear conscience-keeper, as she called her.

"Your last letter simply frightened me."

"Why? Because I myself told you that this man frightened me, and that I would find some means of keeping him at a distance?"

"Yes. Until then I had doubted what my advice ought to be; but from that moment I became so uneasy about you, that, in spite of all Monsieur de Camps' objections to my making the journey, I was determined to come—and here I am."

"But, I assure you, I do not understand——"

"Well, supposing Monsieur de Camps, Monsieur Marie-Gaston—or even Monsieur de Rastignac, though his visits intoxicate your husband with delight—were either of them to get into the habit of calling, would it disturb you as much?"

"No, certainly not; but neither of these men has any such claim on me as this man has."

"Do you believe, tell me truly, that Monsieur de Sallenauve is in love with you?"

"No. I believe, I am perfectly certain, that he is not; but I also believe that on my part——"

"We will come to that presently. What I want to know now is whether you wish that Monsieur de Sallenauve should fall in love with you?"

"God forbid!"

"Well, an excellent way of drawing him to your heel is to hurt his conceit, to be unjust and ungrateful—to compel him, in short, to think about you."

"But is not that a rather far-fetched notion, my dear?"

"Why, my dear child, have you never observed that men, if they have any subtlety of feeling, are more readily caught by severity than by softness; that we plant ourselves most solidly in their minds by a stern attitude; that they are very like those little lap-dogs who never want to bite till you snatch away your hand?"

"If that were the case, every man we scorn and never even think of glancing at would be a lover!"

"Now, my dear, do not put nonsense into my mouth. It is self-evident that in order to catch fire a man must be predisposed to combustion; that, to go to a man's head there must be some beginnings of a fancy on both sides; and it seems to me that between you and Monsieur de Sallenauve there has been ample introduction! Though he may not love you, he loves your semblance; and, as you said the other day, wittily enough, what is there to prevent him, now that the other is evidently lost beyond recall, from a *ricochet* into love for you?"

"But, on the contrary, he has better hopes than ever of finding the lady, by the help of a very clever seeker who is making inquiry."

"Well and good; but supposing he should not find her for a long time to come, are you to spend the time in getting him on your hands?"

"Dear Dame Morality, I do not at all accept your theory, at any rate so far as he is concerned: he will be very busy; he will be far more devoted to the Chamber than to me; he is a man of high self-respect, who would be disgusted by such mean behavior on my part, and think it supremely unjust and ungrateful; and if I try to put two feet of distance between us, he will put four, you may be quite certain."

"But you, my dear?" said her friend.

"How—I?"

"Yes—you who are not so busy, who have not the Chamber to absorb you, who have—I will allow—plenty of self-respect, but who know as much about affairs of the heart as a school-girl or a wet-nurse—what is to become of you under the perilous regimen you propose to follow?"

"I !—If I do not love him when I see him, I shall still less love him when he is absent."

"So that if you found him accepting this ostracism with indifference, your woman's pride would not be in the least shocked?"

"Of course not; it is that I aim at."

"And supposing, on the other hand, that he complains of your behavior, or without complaining, suffers acutely, will your conscience have really nothing to say to you?"

"It will say that I have acted for the best—that I could not do otherwise."

"And if his success is so great that it comes to your ears, if his name fills all the hundred mouths of Fame, you will still forget his existence?"

"I shall think of him as I do of Monsieur Thiers or Monsieur Berryer."

"And Naïs, who dreams only of him, and who will say even more emphatically than on the day when he first dined with you, 'How well he talks, mamma!'"

"Oh! if you take a child's silly chatter into account——"

"And Monsieur de l'Estorade, who annoys you already when, in his blind devotion to party spirit, he utters some ill-natured insinuation about Monsieur de Sallenauve—will you silence him on every occasion when he is perpetually talking about this man, denying his talents, his public spirit?—You know the verdict men always pronounce on those who do not agree with their opinions."

"In short," said Madame de l'Estorade, "you mean to say that I shall never be so much tempted to think of him as when he has gone quite out of my ken?"

"What has happened to you once, my dear, when he followed you about, and his sudden disappearance surprised you, like the silence when a drum that has been deafening you for an hour on end abruptly stops its clatter."

"In that there was reason.   His absence upset a plan."

"Listen to me, my dear," said Madame de Camps gravely; "I have read and re-read your letters.   In them you were more natural and less argumentative; and they left me one clear impression—that Monsieur de Sallenauve had certainly touched your heart if he had not invaded it."

At a gesture of denial from Madame de l'Estorade, her strenuous Mentor went on:

"I know you have fortified yourself against such a notion. And how could you admit to me what you have so carefully concealed from yourself? But the thing that is, *is*. You cannot feel the magnetic influence of a man; you cannot be aware of his gaze—even without meeting his eyes; you cannot exclaim, 'You see, madame, I am invulnerable to love,' without having been more or less hit already."

"But so many things have happened since I wrote those preposterous things!"

"It is true, he was only a sculptor, and now, in the course of time, he may possibly be in the Ministry, like—I will not say Monsieur de Rastignac, for that is not saying much, but like Canalis the great poet."

"I like a sermon to have some conclusion," said Madame de l'Estorade pettishly.

"You say to me," replied Madame de Camps, "exactly what Vergniaud said to Robespierre on the 31st of May, for in the solitude of our wilderness I have been reading the history of the French Revolution; and I reply in Robespierre's words, 'Yes, I am coming to the conclusion'—a conclusion against your pride as a woman, who having reached the age of two-and-thirty without suspecting what love might be even in married life, cannot admit that at so advanced an age she should yield to the universal law; against the memory of all your sermons to Louise de Chaulieu, proving to her that there is no misfortune so great as a passion that captures the heart—very much as if you were to argue that an inflammation of the lungs was the worst imprudence a sick man could commit; against your appalling ignorance, which conceives that merely saying '*I will not*' in a resolute tone is stronger than an inclination complicated by a concurrence of circumstances from which the cleverest woman, my cousin the

Princesse de Cadignan let us say, could scarcely shake herself free."

"But the practical conclusion?" said Madame de l'Estorade, impatiently patting her knee with her pretty hand.

"My conclusion is this," replied her friend. "I do not really see any danger of your drowning unless you are so foolish as to try to stem the stream. You are firm-tempered, you have good principles, and are religious; you worship your children, and for their sakes you esteem their father Monsieur de l'Estorade, who has now for more than fifteen years been the companion of your life. With so much ballast you will not upset, and, believe me, you are well afloat."

"Well, then?" said Madame de l'Estorade.

"Well, then, there is no necessity for violent efforts, with very doubtful results, in my opinion, to preserve an unmoved attitude under impossible conditions, when you have already to a great extent abandoned it. You are quite sure that Monsieur de Sallenauve will never think of inviting you to take a step further; you have said that he is leagues away from thinking of such a thing. Keep still then where you are; make no barricades when nobody it attacking you; do not excite yourself over a useless defence which would only involve you in painful tempests of feeling and conscience, while endeavoring to pacify your conscience and bring peace to your heart just rippled by a breath of wind.

"The bond of friendship between man and woman always, no doubt, bears some hue of the usually warmer sentiments that exist between the two sexes; but it is not a mere empty illusion, nor an ever-yawning gulf. If Louise de Chaulieu and her adorable first husband had lived, were you not already on such a footing of intimacy with him as never existed between you and any other man? And now, with her second husband, Monsieur Marie-Gaston, are you not on quite exceptional terms in memory of the friend you have lost? And even with the escort of your little girl, my husband, and myself, would you have thought of paying the kindly visit we carried out to-day to the first comer, just anybody, without some previous knowledge and recommendation?"

"Then I am to make a friend of Monsieur de Sallenauve?" said Madame de l'Estorade pensively.

"Yes, my dear, to save yourself from his becoming a fixed idea—a regret—a remorse—three things which poison life."

"With the world looking on; with my husband, who has already had one fit of jealousy!"

"My dear, you may compromise yourself just as much or more in the eyes of the world by your efforts to mislead it as by the liberty you frankly allow yourself. Do not imagine, for instance, that your abrupt departure last evening from the Rastignacs', in order to avoid any discussion of your obligations to Monsieur de Sallenauve, can have escaped observation. And would not calmer demeanor have more effectually disguised the sense of indebtedness which you displayed, on the contrary, by so much agitation?"

"In that you are quite right.—But some people's impudence when they talk has the gift of putting me beside myself——"

"Your husband is, I think, somewhat altered, and not for the better. What used to be attractive in him was the perfect respect, the unlimited deference he showed for your person, your ideas, your impressions, everything about you; that sort of dog-like submissiveness gave him a dignity he had no idea of, for there is real greatness in knowing how to obey and to admire. I may be mistaken, but I think politics have spoilt him; as you cannot fill his seat in the Upper Chamber, it has dawned on his mind that he could quite well live without you. In your place I should keep a sharp eye on such fancies for independence; and since this question is the order of the day, I should make it a cabinet question on the point of Monsieur de Sallenauve."

"But do you know, my dear friend," said Madame de l'Estorade, laughing, "that you are delightfully pestilential, and that if I acted on your advice I should bring down fire and sword?"

"Not at all, my child; I am simply a woman of five-and-forty, who has always looked on things in their practical aspect; and I did not marry my husband, to whom I am passionately attached, till I was well assured, by putting him to a severe test, that he also was worthy of my esteem. It is not I who make life what it is; I take it as I find it, trying to bring order and *possibility* into the incidents that may occur. I am not frantic passion like Louise de Chaulieu, nor am I exaggerated good sense like Renée de l'Estorade. I am a sort of Jesuit in petticoats, convinced that rather wide sleeves are more serviceable than sleeves that are too tight about the wrists; and I never set my heart on the Quest of the Absolute."

At this moment Lucas opened the drawing-room door and announced Monsieur de Sallenauve. As his mistress gave the old man a look as much as to ask him how he dared take so little account of her orders, Lucas replied with a shrug, which seemed to say that this visitor was an article he could not have supposed would be included in the code of prohibition.

As Sallenauve took his seat in a chair the man pushed forward for him:

"You see," Madame de Camps whispered to her friend, "the servants even have an instinctive idea that he is not a mere *anybody*."

Madame de Camps, who had never met the new deputy, devoted her whole attention to studying him, and saw no reason to repent of preaching that he was not to be outraged. Sallenauve accounted for his visit by his anxious curiosity to know how matters had gone off at Ville-d'Avray; if he should hear that Marie-Gaston had been too much upset, he was quite prepared, though it was already late, to set out at once and join him.

As to the business that had occupied his day, he had as yet had no form of success. He had availed himself of his title of Deputy, a sort of universal pass-key, to interview the prefect of police, who had referred him to Monsieur de Saint-Estève of the detective department. Sallenauve, knowing, as all Paris knew, the past history of this man, was amazed to find him an official of good manners. But the great detective had not given him much hope.

"A woman hidden in Paris," said he, "is literally an eel hidden in the deepest hole."

He himself, with the help of Jacques Bricheteau, meant to continue the search during the whole of the next day; but if, by the evening, neither he nor the great official inquisitor had discovered anything, he was determined to go then to Ville-d'Avray to be with Marie-Gaston, concerning whom he was far more uneasy than Madame de l'Estorade was.

As he said good-night, before the return of Monsieur de l'Estorade and Monsieur de Camps—who was to call for his wife:

"Do not forget," said Madame de l'Estorade, "that Naïs' party is on the evening after to-morrow. You will offend her mortally if you fail to appear. Try to persuade Marie-Gaston to come with you; it will be a little diversion at any rate."

On coming in from the theatre, Monsieur Octave de Camps declared that it would be many a long day before he would ever go to another fairy extravaganza. Naïs, on the contrary, still bewitched by the marvels she had seen, began to give an eager report of the play, which showed how deeply it had struck her young imagination.

As Madame de Camps went away with her husband, she remarked:

"That little girl would make me very anxious; she reminds me of Moïna d'Aiglemont. Madame de l'Estorade has brought her on too fast, and I should not be surprised if in the future she gave them some trouble."

It is difficult to fix the exact date in the history of modern manners, when a sort of new religion had its rise which may be called the worship of children. Nor would it be any easier to determine what the influence was under which this cultus acquired the extensive vogue it has now attained. But while

it remains inexplicable, the fact exists, and must be recorded
by every faithful chronicler of the greater and minor impulses
of social life.

Children now fill the place in the family which was held
among the ancients by the household gods; and the individual
who should fail to share this devotion would be thought not
so much a fractious and cross-grained person, perverse and
contradictory, as simply an atheist. The influence of Rousseau, however—who for a while persuaded all mothers to
suckle their infants—has now died out; still, he must be
a superficial observer who would find a contradiction in this
to the next remark. Any one who has ever been present at the
tremendous deliberations held over the choice of a wet nurse
to live in the house, and understood the position this queen
of the nursery at once takes up in the arrangements of the
household, may be quite convinced that the mother's renunciation of her rights is on her part only the first of many acts
of devotion and self-sacrifice. The doctor and the accoucheur,
whom she does not try to influence, declare that she is not
equal to the task; and it is an understood thing that, solely
for the sake of the being she has brought into the world, she
resigns herself to the inevitable. But, then, having secured
for the child what schoolmasters describe as excellent and
abundant board, what frantic care and anxiety surround it!
How often is the doctor called up at night to certify that the
mildest indigestion is not an attack of much-dreaded croup!
How often is he snatched away from the bedside of the dying,
and urgently plied with agonized questions by a mother in
tears, who fancies that her cherub looks *peeky* or *pasty,* or
has not soiled its napkins quite as usual!

At last the baby has got over this first difficult stage; released from the wet nurse's arms, it no longer wears a Henri
IV. hat, bedizened with plumes and tufts like an Andalusian
mule; but then the child, and its companions, still remind us
of Spain: dedicated to the Virgin and arrayed in white, they
might be taken for young statues of the *Commendatore* in the
opera of *Don Giovanni.* Others, reminding us of Walter

Scott and the "White Lady," look as if they had come down from the Highlands, of which they display the costume—the short jacket and bare knees.

More often the sweet idols supply in their dress what M. Ballanche would have called a palingenesis of national history. As we see, in the Tuileries, hair cut square *à la* Charles VI., the velvet doublets, lace and embroidered collars, the Cavalier hats, short capes, ruffles and shoes with roses, of Louis XIII. and Louis XIV., we can go through a course of French history related by tailors and dressmakers with stricter exactitude than by Mézeray and President Hénault.

Next come anxieties, if not as to the health, at any rate as to the constitution of our little household gods—for they are always so delicate; and to strengthen them, a journey every year to the sea, or the country, or the Pyrenees, is imperatively ordered. And, of course, during the five or six months spent by the mother in these hygienic wanderings, the husband, if he is detained in Paris, must make the best of his widowhood, of his empty and dismantled house, and the upheaval of all his habits.

Winter, however, brings the family home again; but do you suppose that these precious darlings, puffed up with precocity and importance, can be amused, like the children born in the ages of heartless infanticide, with rattles, dolls, and twopenny Punches? What next, indeed! The boys must have ponies, cigarettes, and novels; the little girls must be allowed to play on a grand scale at being grown-up mistress of the house; they give afternoon dances, and evening parties with the genuine *Guignol* puppets from the Champs-Élysées, or Robert Houdin promised on the invitation card; nor are these like Lambert and Molière, you may depend on it; once on the programme, they are secured.

Finally, now and again these little autocrats, like Naïs de l'Estorade, get leave to give a party on a sufficiently grown-up scale to make it necessary to engage a few police to guard the door; while at Nattier's, at Delisle's, and at Prévost's the event casts its shadow before in the purchase of silks, artificial flowers, and real bouquets for the occasion. From what we have seen of Naïs, it will be understood that no one was more capable than she of filling the part and the duties that devolved on her by her mother's temporary abdication in her favor of all her power and authority.

This abdication had dated from some days before the evening now arrived; for it was Mademoiselle Naïs de l'Estorade who, in her own name, had requested the guests to do her the honor of spending the evening with her; and as Madame de l'Estorade would not carry the parody to such a length as to allow the cards to be printed, Naïs had spent several days in writing these invitations, taking care to add in the corner the sacramental formula *"Dancing."*

Nothing could be stranger, or, as Madame Octave de Camps would have said, more alarming than the perfect coolness of this little girl of thirteen, standing, as she had seen her mother do on similar occasions, at the drawing-room door, and toning the warmth of her welcome to the finest shades as she received her guests, from the most affectionate cordiality to a coolness verging on disdain. With her bosom friends she warmly shook hands *à l'Anglaise;* for others, she had smiles graduated for different degrees of intimacy; a bow or nod to those whom she did not know or care for; and from time to time the most amusing little motherly air and pet words for the tiny ones who are necessarily included in these juvenile routs, difficult and perilous as such company is to manage.

To the fathers and mothers of her guests, as the party was not given for them, and she was acting strictly on the Evangelical precept, *Sinite parvulos venire ad me,* Naïs aimed at distant but respectful politeness. But when Lucas, reversing the usual order of things, in obedience to her instructions, announced, "Mesdemoiselles de la Roche-Hugon, Madame la Baronne de la Roche-Hugon, and Madame la Comtesse de Rastignac," the cunning little puss abandoned this studied reserve; she rushed forward to meet the Minister's wife, and, with the prettiest possible grace, she seized her hand and kissed it.

Monsieur and Madame de l'Estorade also pressed forward to welcome their unexpected visitor; and without allowing her to make any apology as to the liberty she had taken in coming with her sister-in-law without an invitation, they led her to a good seat, whence she could have a complete view of the proceedings, by this time of a very lively character.

Naïs could not accept every invitation to dance which the elegant little dandies vied with each other in pressing on her, and, indeed, she got a little confused over the order of her engagements. In spite of the famous *"entente cordiale,"* her heedlessness was near causing a revival of the perennial rivalry of France and perfidious Albion. A quadrille promised twice over, to a young English nobleman, aged ten, and a boy from a preparatory naval school—Barniol's school—was about to result in something more than railing accusations, for the young heir to the English peerage had already doubled his fist in attitude to box.

This squabble being settled, another disaster befel: a very small boy, seeing the servant bring in a tray of cakes and cooling drinks after a polka, which had made him very hot, was anxious to refresh himself; but as he was too short to reach the level at which the objects of his desire were held by the footman, he unfortunately tried clinging to the rim of the tray to bring it within reach; the tray tilted, lost its balance, and one of its corners serving as a gutter, there flowed, as from the urn of a mythological river-god, a sort of cascade of mingled orgeat, currant-syrup, and capillaire, of which the fountain-head was the overturned glasses. It would have been well if only the rash infant himself had suffered from the sudden sticky torrent; but in the confusion caused by the catastrophe, ten innocent victims were severely splashed, among them five or six infant bacchantes, who, enraged at seeing their garments stained, seemed ready to make a second Orpheus of the luckless blunderer.

While he was rescued with difficulty from their hands, and delivered over to those of a German governess, who had hastened to the scene of the uproar:

"What could Naïs be thinking of," said a pretty, fair-haired little girl to a youthful Highlander with whom she had been dancing all the evening, "to invite little children no bigger than that?"

"Oh, I quite understand," said the Highlander; "he is a little boy belonging to the Accountant Office people; Naïs was obliged to ask him on account of his parents; it was a matter of civility."

At the same time putting his hand through a friend's arm:

"I say, Ernest," he went on, "I could smoke a cigar! Suppose we try and find a corner out of all this riot."

"I cannot, my dear fellow," replied Ernest mysteriously. "You know that Léontine always makes a scene when she finds out that I have been smoking. She is in the sweetest mood to-night. There, look what she has just given me!"

"A horse-hair ring, with two flaming hearts!" said the Highlander scornfully. "Why, every schoolboy makes them!"

"Then, pray, what have you to show?" retorted Ernest, much nettled.

"Oh!" said the Highlander, "better than that."

And with a consequential air he took out of the sporran, which formed part of his costume, a sheet of scented blue paper.

"There," said he, holding it under Ernest's nose, "just smell that."

Ernest, with conspicuous lack of delicacy, snatched at the note and got possession of it; the Highlander, in a rage, struggled to get it back. Then Monsieur de l'Estorade intervened, and having not the remotest suspicion of the cause of the fray, separated the combatants, so that the spoiler could enjoy the fruits of his crime unmolested in a corner. The paper was blank. The young rascal had stolen the sheet of scented paper that morning from his mamma's blotting-book—she perhaps would have made some less immaculate thing of it.

Ernest presently returned it to the Highlander:

"Here; I give you back your letter," said he, in a tone of derision. "It is desperately compromising!"

"Keep it, sir," replied the other. "I will ask you for it to-morrow under the chestnut-trees in the Tuileries. Meanwhile, you must understand that we can have nothing more to say to each other!"

Ernest's demeanor was less chivalrous. His only reply was to put the thumb of his right hand to his nose, spreading his fingers, and turning an imaginary handle—an ironical demonstration which he had learned from seeing it performed by his mother's coachman. Then he went off to find his partner for a quadrille that was being formed.

But why are we wasting time over such trivialities when we know that interests of a superior order are obscurely working themselves out beneath this childish surface?

Sallenauve, who had returned at about four in the afternoon from spending two days at Ville-d'Avray, could not give Madame de l'Estorade a good report of his friend. Under a mask of cold resignation, Marie-Gaston was in deep dejection; and the most serious cause of anxiety, because it was so unnatural, was that he had not yet been to visit his wife's grave; it was as though he foresaw the risk of such agitation as he really dared not face. This state of mind had so greatly disturbed Sallenauve, that, but for fear of really distressing Naïs by not appearing at her ball, he would not have left his friend, who was by no means to be persuaded to come to Paris with him.

It really seemed as though Marie-Gaston had expended his remaining powers in the perfervid enthusiasm and cheerfulness to which he had wound himself up during the Arcis election, and that now the most disastrous prostration had set in as a reaction from the excitement of which his letters to Madame de l'Estorade were but a faint reflection. One thing, however, had made Sallenauve feel that his patient was safe during the few hours of his absence; before he had fully decided to come away, an English gentleman had been announced whom Marie-Gaston had known in Florence, and whose arrival he hailed with apparent joy. So some happy effect might perhaps be hoped for from this unforeseen visit.

To divert Sallenauve's mind from these anxieties—and, in fact, she thought them exaggerated—Madame de l'Estorade at once made him acquainted with Monsieur Octave de Camps, who had expressed a strong wish to know him; and by the time the deputy had been conversing a quarter of an hour with the ironmaster, he had quite won this gentleman's good opinion by the extent of his knowledge in metallurgy.

It may be remembered that one of Bixiou's chief grievances against Dorlange had been the sculptor's ambition, if not indeed to know everything, at any rate to examine everything. During the last year especially Sallenauve, having spent no time in his art but what was needed for the "Saint Ursula," had been at leisure to devote himself to the scientific studies which justify a parliamentary representative in speaking with authority when they can serve to support or illustrate his political views.

Hence, though in talking to Monsieur Godivet, the Registrar of Taxes at Arcis, he had modestly expressed himself as ignorant of the details of that official's functions, he had given his attention to the various elements on which they bore —the customs, conveyancing-fees, stamps, and direct or indirect taxes. Then, in turning to the science—so problematical, and yet so self-confident that it has assumed a name— Political Economy, Sallenauve had studied with no less care the various sources which contribute to form the mighty river of the nation's wealth; and the branch of the subject relating to mines, the matter just now of preponderating interest to Monsieur de Camps, had not been neglected. The ironmaster had been so exclusively interested in the question of iron ores, that he had much to learn in the other branches of metallurgy, and his delight may be imagined on hearing from the newly-made deputy a sort of *Arabian Nights'* tale of the riches of the land, though, certified by science, there could be no doubt of the facts.

"Do you mean, monsieur," cried Monsieur de Camps, "that besides our coal and iron mines we have deposits of copper, lead, and even of silver?"

"If you will only consult some specialist, he will tell you that the famous mines of Bohemia and Saxony, of Russia and of Hungary, are not to be compared to those that exist in the Pyrenees; in the Alps from Briançon to the Isère; in the Cevennes, especially about the Lozère; in the Puy-de-Dôme; in Brittany and in the Vosges. In the Vosges, not far from the town of Saint-Dié, I can tell you of a single vein of silver ore that runs with a width of from fifty to eighty mètres for a distance of about eight miles."

"How is it, then, that this mineral wealth has never been worked?"

"It was, at one time," said Sallenauve, "at a distant period, especially during the Roman dominion in Gaul. These mines were abandoned at the fall of the Roman Empire, but worked again during the Middle Ages by the clergy and the lords of the soil; then, during the struggle between the feudal nobles and the sovereign, and the long civil wars which devastated the country, the working was given up, and no one has taken it up since."

"And you are sure of the facts?"

"Ancient writers, Strabo and others, all speak of these mines; the tradition of their working survives in the districts where they lie; imperial decrees and the edicts of kings bear witness to their existence and to the value of their output; and in some places there is still more practical evidence in excavations of considerable length and depth, shafts and caverns hewn out of the living rock, and all the traces which bear witness to the vast undertakings that immortalized Roman enterprise. To this may be added the evidence of modern geological science, which has everywhere confirmed and amplified these indications."

Monsieur de Camps' imagination had been sufficiently fired by the prospects of a mere iron-mine to bring him to Paris as a petitioner to a Government he despised, and at the suggestion of all this buried wealth it positively blazed; he was about to ask his informant what his ideas might be as to the process of extracting the treasure that was so strangely neglected, when, by a coincidence for which the reader is prepared, Lucas threw open the drawing-room door, and announced in his loudest and most impressive tones, "Monsieur the Minister of Public Works."

The effect on the assembly was electrical; it even broke in on the *tête-à-tête* of the two new friends.

"Let us have a look at this little Rastignac who has blossomed into a public personage," said Monsieur de Camps disdainfully, as he rose.

But in his heart it struck him that this was an opportunity of getting hold of the inaccessible Minister; in virtue of the sound principle that a bird in hand is worth two in the bush, he left the hidden fortune revealed to him by Sallenauve to rest in peace, and went back to his iron-mine. Sallenauve, on his part, foresaw an introduction to be inevitable; it seemed to him impossible but that Monsieur de l'Estorade's Conservative zeal would contrive to bring it about.

And what would his allies of the Opposition say to the news, which would certainly be reported on the morrow, that a representative of the Extreme Left had been seen in a drawing-room in conversation with a Minister so noted for his ardor and skill in making political proselytes? Sallenauve had already had a taste of his party's ideas of tolerance in the office of the *National;* he had heard it insinuated that the affectation of moderation promised by his profession of political faith was not to be taken literally as to his parliamentary conduct; that, in fact, he would soon find himself deserted if he should attempt to make his practice agree with his theories.

Anxious as he was, too, about Marie-Gaston, having put in an appearance at Naïs' party, he was eager now to return to Ville-d'Avray, and for all these reasons he determined to profit by the general excitement and beat a retreat. By quiet and simple tactics he got round to the door, and hoped to escape without being observed. But he had reckoned without Naïs, to whom he had promised a quadrille. The instant he laid his hand on the door-handle the little girl sounded the alarm, and Monsieur de l'Estorade, with what precipitancy may be imagined, took her part to detain the deserter. Seeing that his ruse had failed, Sallenauve dared not commit himself to a retreat which would have been in bad taste by assuming an importance suggestive of political priggishness; so he took his chance of what might happen, and allowing himself to be reinstated on Naïs' list of partners, he remained.

Monsieur de l'Estorade knew Sallenauve to be too clever a man to become the dupe of any finessing he might attempt to throw him in the Minister's way. He therefore acted with perfect simplicity; and a quarter of an hour after Monsieur de Rastignac's arrival, they came to the deputy arm in arm, the host saying:

"Monsieur de Rastignac, Minister of Public Works, has desired me before the battle begins to introduce him to one of the generals of the hostile force."

"Monsieur le Ministre does me too much honor," said Sallenauve ceremoniously. "Far from being a general, I am but one of the humblest and least known of the rank and file."

"Nay!" said the Minister, "the fight at Arcis-sur-Aube was no small victory; you sent our men pretty smartly to the right about, monsieur."

"There was nothing very astonishing in that, monsieur; as you may have heard, we had a Saint on our side."

"At any rate," replied Rastignac, "I prefer such an issue to that which had been planned for us by a man whom I had believed to be more capable, and whom we sent down to the scene of action. That Beauvisage would seem to be hopelessly stupid; he would have reflected on us if we had got him in; and, after all, he was only Left Centre, like that lawyer Giguet. Now the Left Centre is in fact our worst enemy, because, while traversing our politics, it aims principally at getting into office."

"Oh!" said Monsieur de l'Estorade, "from what you were told of the man, he would have been whatever he was bidden to be."

"No, no, my dear fellow, don't fancy that. Fools often cling more closely than you might believe to the flag under which they have enlisted. Going over to the enemy implies a choice, and that means a rather complicated mental process; obstinacy is far easier."

"I quite agree with the Minister," said Sallenauve; "the extremes of innocence and cunning are equally proof against being talked over."

"You kill your man kindly," said Monsieur de l'Estorade, patting Sallenauve on the shoulder.

Then seeing, or pretending to see, in the mirror over the chimney-shelf by which they stood, a signal that he was wanted:

"Coming," said he over his shoulder, and having thus thrown the foes together, he went off, as if he were required for some duty as host.

Sallenauve was determined not to look like a school-girl frightened out of her wits at the notion of being left alone with a gentleman; since they had met, he would put a good face on the matter, and, speaking at once, he asked whether the Ministry had any large number of bills to lay before the Houses, which would meet a few days hence.

"No, very few," replied Rastignac. "We honestly did not expect to remain in office; we appealed to an election because in the confusion of public opinion forced on by the Press, we felt it our duty to bring it to its bearings, and compel it to know its own mind by requiring it to declare itself. We had no hope of the result proving favorable to ourselves; and the victory, it must be confessed, finds us quite unprepared."

"Like the peasant," said Sallenauve, laughing, "who, expecting the end of the world, did not think it worth while to sow his field."

"Oh!" said Rastignac modestly, "we did not regard our retirement as the end of the world. We believe that there will be men after us, and many of them, perfectly able to govern; only, in that temporary sojourn known as office, as we expected to give very few performances, we did not unpack our scenery and dresses. The session was not in any case to be one of business; the question now to be decided is between what is called the Château, the personal influence of the sovereign, and parliamentary supremacy. This question will inevitably come to the front when we are required to ask for the secret service fund. When it has been settled one way or the other, when the budget is passed, and a few acts of minor importance, Parliament will have got through its task with credit, for it will have put an end to a heartbreaking struggle, and the country will know once for all to which of the two powers it is to look with assurance for the promotion of its prosperity."

"Then you think," said Sallenauve, "that this is a very useful question to settle in the economy of a constitutional government?"

"Well, it was not we who raised it," said Rastignac. "It is perhaps the outcome of circumstances; and, to a great extent, of the impatience of some ambitious men, and of party tactics."

"So that, in your opinion, sir, one of those powers is in no respect to blame, and has nothing whatever to repent of?"

"You are a Republican," replied Rastignac, "and consequently à priori an enemy of the dynasty. It would be, I conceive, pure waste of time on my part to try to rectify your ideas as to the course of conduct of which you accuse it."

"You are quite mistaken," said the supporter of the theoretical, imaginable future republic. "I have no preconceived hatred of the reigning dynasty. I even think that in its past history, variegated, if I may say so, with royal relationship and revolutionary impulses, there are all the elements that should commend it to the liberal and monarchical instincts of the people. At the same time, you will fail to convince me that the present head of the royal family is untainted by those extravagant notions of personal prerogative which, in the long run, must undermine, disfigure, and wreck the most admirable and the strongest institutions."

"Yes," said Rastignac sarcastically, "their salvation is to

be found in the famous saying of the member for Sancerre, 'The King reigns; he does not govern!' "

Whether it was that he was tired of standing, or that he wished to show that he was quite at his ease in avoiding the pitfall that had so evidently been laid for him, Sallenauve, before he answered, pulled forward an armchair for the Minister, and, after seating himself, replied:

"Will you allow me, monsieur, to quote the example of another royal personage?—a Prince who was not thought to be indifferent to the prerogatives of his crown, and who certainly was not ignorant of constitutional procedure. In the first place, because, like our present King, he was not ignorant on any subject whatever; and, in the second place, because he himself had introduced the constitutional system into our country."

"Louis XVIII.," said Rastignac, "or, as the newspapers have it, 'The illustrious author of the Charter'?"

"Just so," said Sallenauve. "Now, let me ask you, where did he die?"

"At the Tuileries, of course."

"And his successor?"

"In exile.—I see your point."

"My point is not, in fact, very difficult to discern. But have you observed, sir, the inference to be drawn from that royal career—for which I, for my part, profess entire respect? Louis XVIII. was not a citizen king. He vouchsafed the Charter; it was not wrung from him. He was born nearer to the throne than the King whose unfortunate tendencies I have mentioned, and was bound to inherit a larger share of the ideas, infatuations, and prejudices of Court life. His person was laughable—and this in France means degeneracy; he had to make the best of a new régime following a government which had intoxicated the people with that fine gilded smoke called glory; also, if he was not actually brought in by foreigners, he at least came in at the heels of an invasion by Europe in arms. And now, shall I tell you why, in spite of his own original sin, and in spite of a standing conspiracy against his rule, he was allowed to die in peace under his canopy at the Tuileries?"

"Because he was constitutional?" said Rastignac, with a shrug. "But can you say that we are not?"

"In the letter you are; in the spirit, no.—When Louis XVIII. placed his confidence in a prime minister, it was complete and entire; he played no underhand game, but supported him to the utmost. Witness the famous edict of the 5th of September, and the dismissal of the undiscoverable Chamber, which was more royalist than himself—a thing he was well advised enough to disapprove. Later, a revulsion of opinion shook the Minister who had prompted him to this action. That Minister was his favorite—his child, as he called him. No matter; yielding to constitutional necessity, after wrapping him in orders and titles, and everything that could deaden the shock of a fall, he courageously sent him abroad; and then he did not dig mines, or set watch, or try to make opportunities for surreptitiously recalling him to power. That Minister never held office again."

"For a man who does not hate Us," said Rastignac, "you are pretty hard upon Us. We are little short of forsworn to the constitutional compact, and Our policy, by your account, is ambiguous, and tortuous, and suggests a certain remote likeness to M. Doublemain, the clerk in the *Mariage de Figaro.*"

"I would not say that the evil lay so deep, or came from so far," replied Sallenauve. "We are perhaps merely a busybody—only in the sense, of course, of loving to have a finger in everything."

"Well, monsieur, but if We were the cleverest politician in the kingdom!"

"That does hinder the kingdom—which is all the world—from having the luck now and again of being as clever as We are."

"On my word!" said Rastignac, in the tone which seems to emphasize the climax of a conversation, "I wish I could realize a dream——"

"Of what?" said Sallenauve.

"Of seeing you face to face with that meddlesome cleverness which you seem to me to hold so cheap."

"You know, monsieur, that three-quarters of every man's life are spent in imagining the impossible."

"Impossible! Why? Would you be the first Opposition member ever seen at the Tuileries?—And an invitation to dinner—quite publicly and ostensibly given—that would bring you near to what you judge so hardly from a distance——?"

"I should do myself the honor of refusing it, monsieur," and he accentuated *the honor* in such a way as to give his own meaning to the word.

"That is just like you, all you men of the Opposition," cried Rastignac, "refusing to see the light when the occasion offers —incapable of seeing it, in fact!"

"Do you see the light to any particular advantage, monsieur, when, in the evening, as you pass a druggist's shop, you get full in your eyes a glare from those gigantic glass jars which seem to have been invented expressly to blind people?"

"You are not afraid of Our beams, but of the dark lantern of your colleagues making their rounds."

"There is perhaps some truth in that, Monsieur le Ministre. A party, and the man who craves the honor of representing it, are like a married couple, who, if they are to get on together, must treat each other with mutual consideration, sincerity, and fidelity, in fact as well as in form."

"Then try to be moderate! Your dream, indeed, is far more impossible to realize than mine; you will have some experience yet of the consideration shown you by your chaste spouse."

"If there was any misfortune I might be certain of, it was that, no doubt."

"You think that! And you with the noble and generous feeling that is evident in you—can you even endure unmoved the slander which is perhaps already sharpening its darts?"

"Have you yourself, monsieur, never felt its sting? or, if

you have, did it turn you aside from the road you were following?"

"But if I were to tell you," said Rastignac, lowering his voice, "that I have already had occasion to decline certain officious proposals to stir the depths of your private life, on a side, which, being a little less open to daylight than the others, has seemed particularly adapted for the setting of a snare?"

"I will not thank you, sir, for merely doing yourself justice by scorning the attempts of these meddlers, who are neither of your party nor of mine—whose only party is that of their own low greed and interest. But even if by some impossible chance they had found a loophole through which to approach you, believe me, that any purpose sanctioned by my conscience would not have been in the least affected."

"Still, do but consider the constituent elements of your party: a rabble of disappointed schemers, of envious brutality, base imitators of '93, despots disguised as devotees of liberty."

"My party has not, and wants to *have*. Yours calls itself Conservative—and with good reason—its principal aim being to keep power, places, fortune, everything it has, in its clutches. But at bottom, monsieur, the cooking is the same: eat, but do not see the process; for, as la Bruyère says, 'If you see a meal anywhere but on a well-laid table, how foul and disgusting it is!'"

"But, at any rate, monsieur, We are not a blind alley—We lead to something. Now, the more you rise by superior character and intelligence, the less will you be allowed to get through with your horde of democrats in your train, for its triumph would mean not a mere change of policy, but a revolution."

"But who says that I want to get through, to arrive anywhere?"

"What, merely march without trying to attain!—A certain breadth of faculty not only gives a man the right to aim at the conduct of affairs, it makes it his duty."

"To keep an eye on those who conduct them is surely a useful function too, and, I may add, a very absorbing one."

"You do not imagine, my dear sir," said Rastignac, "that I should have taken so much trouble to convince Beauvisage; to be sure, it must be said that with him I should have had an easier task."

"One happy result will ensue from the introduction which chance has brought about," said Sallenauve. "We shall feel that we know each other, and in our future meetings shall be pledged to courtesy—which will not diminish the strength of our convictions."

"Then I am to tell the King, for I had special instructions from his Majesty——"

Rastignac could not finish the sentence which was his last cartridge, as it were; for, as the band played the introductory bars of a quadrille, Naïs rushed up to him, and, with coquettish courtesy, said:

"Monsieur le Ministre, I am very sorry, but you have taken possession of my partner, and you must give him up to me. I have his name down for the eleventh quadrille, and if I miss a turn it makes such dreadful confusion!"

"You will excuse me, monsieur," said Sallenauve, laughing. "You see I am not a very red Republican."

And he went with Naïs, who dragged him away by the hand.

Madame de l'Estorade had had a kindly thought. It had occurred to her that Sallenauve's good-natured consent to humor Naïs might cost his dignity a prick, so she had contrived that some papas and mammas should join in the quadrille he had been drawn into; and she herself, with the young Highlander, the hero of the blank billets-doux—who, little as she suspected it, was quite capable of making mischief for her—took the place of *vis-à-vis* to the little girl.

Naïs was beaming with pride and delight; and at a moment, when in the figure of the dance she had to take her mother's hand:

"Poor mamma," said she, giving it an ecstatic clutch, "but for *him* you would not have me here now!"

The sudden and unexpected impression of this reminiscence so startled Madame de l'Estorade that she was seized with a return of the nervous spasm that had attacked her at the sight of the child's narrow escape. She was obliged to take a seat, and seeing her turn pale, Sallenauve, Naïs, and Madame de Camp all three came up to know if she was ill.

"It is nothing," said Madame de l'Estorade, as she turned to Sallenauve—"only this child reminded me of our immense obligation to you. 'But for him,' she said to me, 'you would not have me here, poor mamma!'—And it is true, monsieur, but for your magnanimous courage, where would she be now?——"

"Come, come, be calm," said Madame Octave, hearing that her friend's voice was broken and hysterical. "Have you no sense that you can be so upset by a little girl's speech?"

"She has more feeling than we have," replied Madame de l'Estorade, throwing her arms round Naïs, who, with the rest, was saying, "Come, mamma, be calm."

"There is nothing in the world that she thinks more of than her preserver—while her father and I—we have hardly expressed our gratitude."

"Why, you have overwhelmed me, madame," said Sallenauve politely.

"Overwhelmed?" said Naïs, shaking her pretty head dubiously. "If any one had saved my daughter, I should treat him very differently!"

"Naïs," said Madame de Camps severely, "little girls should be seen and not heard when their opinion is not asked."

"What is the matter?" said Monsieur de l'Estorade, who now joined the group.

"Nothing," said Madame de Camps. "Dancing made Renée a little giddy."

"And is she all right again?"

"Yes, I have quite recovered," replied Madame de l'Estorade.

"Then come to say good-night to Madame de Rastignac; she is just going."

In his eagerness to attend the Minister's wife, Monsieur de l'Estorade did not think of giving his arm to his own wife. Sallenauve offered her his. As they crossed the room, Monsieur de l'Estorade leading the way so that he could not hear, his wife said to Sallenauve:

"You were talking to Monsieur de Rastignac for a long time. He tried, no doubt, to convert you?'

"Do you think he has succeeded?" asked Sallenauve.

"No; but these attempts at inveiglement are always unpleasant. I can only beg you to believe that I was no party to the conspiracy. I am not such a frenzied Ministerialist as my husband."

"Nor am I such a rabid revolutionary as seems to be supposed."

"I only hope that these vexatious politics, which will bring you more than once into antagonism with Monsieur de l'Estorade, will not sicken you of including us among your friends."

"Nay, madame, that is an honor I can be only happy in."

"It is not honor but pleasure that I would have you look for," said Madame de l'Estorade eagerly. "I must parody Naïs—'If I had saved anybody's daughter, I should be less ceremonious.'"

And having said this, without waiting for a reply, she released her hand from Sallenauve's arm, and left him not a little surprised at her tone.

My readers will hardly be surprised to find Madame de l'Estorade so entirely obedient to Madame Octave's advice, ingenious perhaps rather than judicious. In fact, they must long since have suspected that the unimpressionable Countess had yielded to a certain attraction towards the man who had not only saved her child's life, but also appealed to her imagination through such singular and romantic accessory facts. No one but herself, it is quite certain, had been deluded into security by a conviction of Sallenauve's perfect indifference. The certainty of his not caring for her was, in fact, the only snare into which she could trip; as a declared lover he would have been infinitely less dangerous.

On closer acquaintance, Madame de l'Estorade was far from being one of those imperturbable natures which can withstand every contagion of love outside the family circle. Her beauty was almost of the Spanish type, with eyes, of which her friend Louise de Chaulieu used to say that they ripened the peaches when they looked at them; her coldness, then, was not what medical men term congenital; it was acquired self-control. Married, and not for love, to a man whose intellectual poverty has been seen, she had, in opposition to an axiom of the comic opera, forced her contempt to take the form of affection; and by means of a certain atrophy of the heart into which she had drilled herself, she had succeeded till the present time, without ever stumbling, in making Monsieur de l'Estorade the happiest of husbands. To the same end she had fostered her maternal feeling to a hardly credible fervency, thus cheating her other instincts.

But in considering the success that had hitherto crowned her stern task, one of the first elements to be reckoned with was the *circumstance* of Louise de Chaulieu. To her that poor reasonless woman had been like the drunken slaves, by whose example the Spartans were wont to give a living lesson to their children, and a sort of tacit wager had existed between the two friends. Louise de Chaulieu having thrown herself into the part of unchecked passion, Renée had assumed that of sovereign reason; and to gain the stakes, she had exerted such brave good sense and prudence as, but for this incitement, would perhaps have seemed a far greater sacrifice. At the age she had now attained, with such confirmed habits of self-control, it is quite intelligible that if she had seen, advancing down the highroad, the temptation to love against which she had so loudly preached, she would at once have recognized and dismissed it. But here was a man who cared not for her, though he thought her beauty ideal, who perhaps loved another woman; a man who, after snatching her child from death, looked for no reward; who was dignified, reserved, and absorbed in quite other interests—how, when he came into her life by a side path, was she to think of him as dangerous, or to refuse him from the first the calm cordiality of friendship?

Sallenauve, meanwhile, was on his way to Ville-d'Avray, whither he had set out in spite of the lateness of the hour, possessed by his fears for his friend. And this was what he was thinking about:

As he looked back on the incidents of the evening, the deputy, as may be supposed, attached no great importance either to Rastignac's attempts at gaining him, or to Naïs' impassioned demonstrations, which indeed could have no result but that of making him ridiculous; but he was far from being so indifferent to Madame de l'Estorade's effusive burst of gratitude; it was this perfervid expression of thanks that occupied his mind. Without having anything definite to complain of in the Countess' attitude, Sallenauve had certainly never found her at all warm in her regard, and he had formed the same estimate of her temper and character as the rest of the world around her. He had seen her as a woman of remarkable intellectual gifts, but paralyzed as to her heart, by her absorbing and exclusive passion for her children. "The ice-bound Madame de l'Estorade," Marie-Gaston had once called her, and it was correct if he had ever thought of making a friend of her—that is to say, of becoming her lover.

Nor was it only as regarded Madame de l'Estorade, but as regarded her husband too, that Sallenauve had doubted the future permanency of their alliance. "We shall quarrel over politics," he had told himself a dozen times, and the reader may remember one of his letters in which he had contemplated this conclusion with some bitterness. So when Madame de l'Estorade had seemed to encourage him to take up an attitude of more effusive intimacy with her, what had most surprised him was the marked distinction she had drawn between her husband's probable demeanor and her own. Before a woman would say with such agitation as she had put into the inviting words, "I only hope that these vexatious politics will not disgust you with us as friends," she must have, Sallenauve thought, to speak so warmly, a warmer heart than she was generally credited with; and this profession of alliance was not, he felt sure, to be taken as a mere drawing-room civility, or the thoughtless utterance of a transient and shallow impulse, as the little nervous attack had been which had led to it all.

Having thus analyzed this somewhat serious flirtation, to repay Madame de l'Estorade's politeness the statesman did not scorn to descend to a remark, which was illogical, it must be owned, as regards his usual reserve, and certain memories of his past life. He recollected that more than once, at Rome, he had seen Mademoiselle de Lanty dance, and comparing the original with the duplicate, he could assure himself that, notwithstanding the difference in their age, the girl had not a more innocent air, nor had she struck him as more elegant and graceful.

And in view of this fact, will not the clear-sighted reader—who may some time since have begun to suspect that these two natures, apparently so restrained, so entrenched in their past experiences, might ultimately come into closer contact—discern a certain convergence of gravitation though hitherto scarcely perceptible? It was, if you please, solely out of deference to Madame de Camps' advice that Madame de l'Estorade had so completely modified her austere determination; still, short of admitting some slight touch of the sentiment her friend had hinted at, is it likely that she would have given such singular vehemence to her expression of grateful regard, or that a mere remark from a child would have strung her nerves up to such a point as to surprise her into the outburst?

On his part, not having taken advantage of the privileged position thus recklessly thrown open to him, our deputy was tempted to think, with a persistency which, if not very imprudent, was at least very unnecessary, of these superficial graces. Madame de Camps had spoken truly: "Friendship between a man and woman is neither an impossible dream nor an ever-yawning gulf." But in practice, it must be said, that this sentiment, by which we delude ourselves, proves to be a very narrow and baseless bridge across a torrent, needing in those who hope to cross it without difficulty much presence of mind on both sides and nerves less sensitive than Madame de l'Estorade's; while it is a necessary precaution never to look to right and left, as Sallenauve had just been doing.

From this elaborate observation, subtle as it may appear, there is, it would seem, a conclusion to be drawn: namely, that there would presently be a rise of temperature between these two whose affinities were as yet so negative and so slow to develop.

However, on arriving at Ville-d'Avray, Sallenauve found himself face to face with a strange event; and who does not know how, in spite of our determination, events often disperse our maturest plans?.

Sallenauve had not been mistaken in his serious anxiety as to his friend's mental condition.

When Marie-Gaston abruptly fled after his wife's death from the spot where that cruel parting had occurred, he would have been wise to pledge himself never to see it again. Nature and Providence have willed it that in presence of the stern decrees of Death he who is stricken through the person of those he loves, if he accepts the stroke with the resignation demanded under the action of every inevitable law, does not for long retain the keen stamp of the first impression. In his famous letter against suicide, Rousseau says: "Sadness, weariness, regret, despair are but transient woes which never take root in the soul, and experience exhausts the feeling of bitterness which makes us think that our sorrow must be eternal."

But this is no longer true for those rash beings who, trying to escape from the first grip of the jaws of grief, evade it either by flight or by some immoderate diversion. All mental suffering is a kind of illness for which time is a specific, and which presently wears itself out, like everything violent. If, on the contrary, instead of being left to burn itself out slowly on the spot, it is fed by change of scene or other extreme measures, the action of Nature is hampered. The sufferer deprives himself of the balm of comparative forgetfulness promised to those who can endure; he merely transforms into a chronic disease, less visible perhaps, but more deeply seated, an acute attack, thrown in by checking its healthy crisis. The imagination sides with the heart, and, as the heart is by nature limited while the fancy is boundless, there is no possibility of calculating the violence of the excesses by which a man may be carried away under its ere long absolute dominion.

Marie-Gaston, as he wandered through this home where he had believed that after the lapse of two years he should find only the pathos of remembrance, had not taken a step, had not met with an object in his path that could fail to revive all his happiest days and at the same time the disaster that had ended them. The flowers his wife had loved, the lawns and trees—verdurous under the soft breath of spring, while she who had formed the lovely spot lay under the cold earth— all the dainty elegance brought together to decorate this exquisite nest for their love, combined to sing a chorus of lamentation, a long drawn wail of anguish in the ears of him who dared to breathe the dangerous atmosphere. Terrified when half-way by the overwhelming sorrow that had seized on him, Marie-Gaston, as Sallenauve had observed, had not dared accomplish the last station of his Calvary. In absence, he had calmly busied himself with drawing up an estimate for the private tomb he had intended to build for the remains of his beloved Louise; but here he could not endure even to do them pious homage in the village graveyard where they were laid.

The worst, in short, might be feared from a sorrow which, instead of being soothed by the touch of time, was, on the contrary, aggravated by duration, having as it seemed found fresh poison for its sting.

As Sallenauve approached this melancholy dwelling, thinking less of himself and of the joys or disappointments possibly in store for him, he was more and more vaguely anxious, and two or three times he urged the coachman to whip up his horses and get on faster.

The door was opened by Philippe, the old man who in Madame Marie-Gaston's time had been the house steward.

"How is your master?" asked Sallenauve.

"He is gone, sir," replied Philippe.

"Gone—where?"

"Yes, sir, with the English gentleman who was here when you left."

"But without a word for me, without telling you where they are gone?"

"After dinner, when all was well, my master suddenly said that he wanted a few things packed for a journey, and he saw to them himself. At the same time, the Englishman, after saying he would walk in the park and smoke a cigarette, mysteriously asked me where he could write a letter without being seen by my master. I took him into my own room, but I dared not ask him anything about this journey, for I never saw any one less communicative or open. When he had written the letter everything was ready; and then, without a word of explanation, the two gentlemen got into the English gentleman's chaise, and I heard them tell the coachman to drive to Paris——"

"But the letter?" said Sallenauve.

"It is addressed to you, sir, and the Englishman gave it me in secret, as he had written it."

"Then give it me, my good man!" cried Sallenauve; and without going any further than the hall where he had stood questioning Philippe, he hastily read it.

His features, as the man studied them, showed great distress.

"Tell them not to take the horses out," said he. And he read the letter through a second time.

When the old servant came back from delivering the order:

"At what hour did they start?" Sallenauve inquired.

"At about nine o'clock."

"They have three hours' start," said he to himself, looking at his watch, which marked some minutes past midnight.

He turned to get into the carriage that was to take him

away again. Just as he was stepping into it, the steward ventured to ask, "There is nothing alarming, I hope, in that letter, sir?"

"No, nothing. But your master may be absent some little time; take care to keep the house in good order."

And then, like the two who had preceded him, he said: "To Paris."

Next morning, pretty early, Monsieur de l'Estorade was in his study very busy in a strange way. It may be remembered that Sallenauve had sent him a statuette of Madame de l'Estorade; he had never been able to find a place where the work stood to his mind in a satisfactory light. But ever since the hint given him by Rastignac that his friendship with the sculptor might serve him but ill at court, he had begun to agree with his son Armand that the artist had made Madame de l'Estorade look like a milliner's apprentice; and now, when by his obduracy to the Minister's inveiglements, Sallenauve had shown himself irreclaimably opposed to the Government, the statuette—its freshness a little dimmed, it must be owned, by the dust—no longer seemed presentable, and the worthy peer was endeavoring to discover a corner, in which it would be out of sight, so that he might not be required to tell the name of the artist, which every visitor asked, without making himself ridiculous by removing it altogether. So he was standing on the top step of a library ladder with the sculptor's gift in his hands and about to place it on the top of a tall cabinet. There the hapless sketch was to keep company with a curlew and a cormorant, shot by Armand during his last holidays. They were the first fruits of the young sportsman's prowess, and paternal pride had decreed them the honors of stuffing.

At this juncture Lucas opened the door to show in: "Monsieur Philippe."

The worthy steward's age, and the confidential position he held in Marie-Gaston's household, had seemed to the l'Estorades' factotum to qualify him for the title of *Monsieur* — a civility to be, of course, returned in kind.

The master of the house, descending from his perch, asked Philippe what had brought him, and whether anything had happened at Ville-d'Avray. The old man described his master's strange departure, followed by the no less strange disappearance of Sallenauve, who had fled as if he were at the heels of an eloping damsel, and then he went on:

"This morning, as I was putting my master's room tidy, a letter fell out of a book, addressed to Madame la Comtesse. As it was sealed and ready to be sent off, I thought that, perhaps in the hurry of packing, my master had forgotten to give it me to post. At any rate, I have brought it; Madame la Comtess may, perhaps, finds that it contains some explanation of this unexpected journey—I have dreamed of nothing else all night."

Monsieur de l'Estorade took the letter.

"Three black seals!" said he, turning it over.

"It is not the color that startles me," said Philippe. "Since madame died, monsieur uses nothing but black; but I confess the three seals struck me as strange."

"Very good," said Monsieur de l'Estorade; "I will give the letter to my wife."

"If there should be anything to reassure me about my master," said Philippe wistfully, "would you let me know, Monsieur le Comte?"

"You may rely on it, my good fellow.—Good-morning."

"I humbly beg pardon for having an opinion to offer," said the old servant, without taking the hint thus given him; "but for fear of there being any bad news in the letter, do not you think, Monsieur le Comte, that it would be well to know it, so as to prepare Madame la Comtesse?"

"Why! What! Do you suppose?——" Monsieur de l'Estorade began, without finishing his question.

"I do not know. My master has been very much depressed these last few days."

"It is always a very serious step to open a letter not addressed to oneself," said the Accountant-General. "This case is peculiar—the letter is addressed to my wife, but in fact was never sent to her—it is really a puzzling matter——"

"Still, if by reading it you could prevent something dreadful——"

"Yes—that is just what makes me hesitate."

Madame de l'Estorade settled the question by coming into the room. Lucas had told her of old Philippe's arrival.

"What can be the matter?" she asked, with uneasy curiosity. All Sallenauve's apprehensions of the night before recurred to her mind.

When the steward had repeated the explanations he had already given to Monsieur de l'Estorade, she unhesitatingly broke the seals.

"I know so much now," she said to her husband, who tried to dissuade her, "that the worst certainty would be preferable to the suspense we should be left in."

Whatever the contents of this alarming epistle, the Countess' face told nothing.

"And you say that your master went off accompanied by this English gentleman," said she, "and not under any compulsion?"

"On the contrary, madame, he seemed quite cheerful."

"Well, then, there is nothing to be frightened about. This letter has been written a long time; and, in spite of the three black seals, it has no bearing on anything to-day."

Philippe bowed and departed. When the husband and wife were alone:

"What does he say?" asked Monsieur de l'Estorade, and he put out his hand for the letter his wife still held.

"No. Do not read it," said the Countess, not surrendering it.

"Why not?"

"It will pain you. It is quite enough that I should have had the shock, and in the presence of the old steward, before whom I had to control myself."

"Does it speak of any purpose of suicide?"

Madame de l'Estorade did not speak, but she nodded affirmatively.

"But a definite, immediate purpose?"

"The letter was written yesterday morning; and to all appearance, but for the really providential presence of this stranger, last evening, during Monsieur de Sallenauve's absence, the wretched man would have carried out his fatal purpose."

"The Englishman has, no doubt, carried him off solely to hinder it. That being the case, he will not lose sight of him."

"We may also count on Monsieur de Sallenauve's intervention," observed Madame de l'Estorade. "He has probably followed them."

"Then there is nothing so very alarming in the letter," said her husband. And again he held out his hand for it.

"But when I entreat you not to read it," said Madame de l'Estorade, holding it back. "Why do you want to agitate yourself so painfully? It is not only the idea of suicide—our unhappy friend's mind is completely unhinged."

At this instant piercing shrieks were heard, uttered by René, the youngest of the children, and this threw his mother into one of those maternal panics of which she was quite unable to control the expression.

"Good God! What has happened?" she cried, rushing out of the room.

Monsieur de l'Estorade, less easily perturbed, only went as far as the door to ask a servant what was the matter.

"It is nothing, Monsieur le Comte. Monsieur René in shutting a drawer pinched the tip of his finger."

The Peer of France did not think it necessary to proceed to the scene of the catastrophe; he knew that in these cases he must leave his wife to give free course to her extravagant motherly solicitude, or take a sharp *wigging*. As he returned to his seat by the table he felt a paper under his foot; it was the famous letter, which Madame de l'Estorade had dropped as she flew off without observing its fall.

Opportunity and a sort of fatality that frequently rules

human affairs, prompted Monsieur de l'Estorade, who could not understand his wife's objections; he hastened to gratify his curiosity.

Marie-Gaston wrote as follows:

"MADAME,—This letter will not be so amusing as those I wrote you from Arcis-sur-Aube. But you must not be frightened by the determination I have come to. I am simply going to join my wife, from whom I have been too long parted, and to-night, soon after midnight, I shall be with her, never to leave her again. You and Sallenauve have, no doubt, remarked that it is strange that I should not yet have been to visit her tomb; two of my servants were saying so the other day, not knowing that I could overhear them. But I should have been a great fool to go to a graveyard and stare at a block of stone that cannot speak to me, when every night as midnight strikes, I hear a little tap at my bedroom door, which I open at once to our dear Louise, who is not altered at all; on the contrary, I think she is fairer and lovelier. She has had great difficulty in getting my discharge from this world from Mary the Queen of the Angels; but last night she brought me my papers properly made out, sealed with a large seal of green wax, and at the same time she gave me a tiny phial of hydrocyanic acid. One drop sends me to sleep, and when I wake I am on the other side.

"Louise also gave me a message for you; to tell you that Monsieur de l'Estorade has a liver complaint and cannot live long; and that when he is dead you are to marry Sallenauve, because over there you are always restored to the husband you loved; and she thinks our party of four will be much pleasanter with you and me and Sallenauve than with your Monsieur de l'Estorade, who is enough to bore you to death, and whom you married against your will.

"My message delivered, I have only to wish you good patience, madame, during the time you have still to spend down here, and to subscribe myself your affectionate humble servant."

If, on finishing this letter, it had occurred to Monsieur de l'Estorade to look at himself in a glass, he would have seen in the sudden crestfallen expression of his features the effects of the unavowed but terrible blow he had dealt himself by his luckless curiosity. His feelings, his mind, his self-respect had all felt one and the same shock; and the quite obvious insanity revealed in the prediction of which he was the subject only made it seem more threatening. Believing, like the Mussulmans, that madmen are gifted with a sort of second sight, he gave himself over at once, felt a piercing pain in his diseased liver, and was seized with a jealous hatred of Salle-nauve, his designate successor, such as must cut off any kind of friendly relations between them.

At the same time, as he saw how ridiculous, how absolutely devoid of reason, was the impression that had taken posses-sion of him, he was terrified lest any one should suspect its existence; and with the instinctive secretiveness which always prompts the mortally sick to hide the mischief, he began to consider how he could keep from his wife the foolish act that had blighted his whole existence. It would seem incredible that lying under his very eye the fatal letter should have escaped his notice; and from this to the suspicion that he had read it the inference was only too plain.

He rose, and softly opening the door of his room, after making sure that there was nobody in the drawing-room be-yond, he went on tiptoe to throw the letter on the floor at the furthest side of the room, where Madame de l'Estorade would suppose that she had dropped it. Then, like a schoolboy who had been playing a trick, and wishes to put the authorities off the scent by an affectation of studiousness, he hastily strewed his table with papers out of a bulky official case, so as to seem absorbed in accounts when his wife should return.

Meanwhile, as need scarcely be said, he listened in case any-body but Madame de l'Estorade should come into the outer room where he had laid his trap; in that case he would have intervened at once to hinder indiscreet eyes from investigating the document that held such strange secrets.

Madame de l'Estorade's voice speaking to some one, and her appearance in his room a few minutes after with Monsieur Octave de Camps, showed that the trick had succeeded. By going forward as his visitor came in, he could see through the half-open door the spot where he had left the letter. Not only was it gone, but he could detect by a movement of his wife's that she had tucked it into her morning gown in the place where Louis XIII. dared not seek the secrets of Mademoiselle de Hautefort.

"I have come to fetch you to go with me to Rastignac, as we agreed last evening," said de Camps.

"Quite right," said his friend, putting up his papers with a feverish haste that showed he was not in a normal frame of mind.

"Are you ill?" said Madame de l'Estorade, who knew her husband too well not to be struck by the singular absence of mind he betrayed; and at the same time, looking him in the face, she observed a strange change in his countenance.

"You do not look quite yourself, indeed," said Monsieur de Camps. "If you had rather, we will put off this visit."

"Not at all," said Monsieur de l'Estorade; "I have worried myself over this work, and want pulling together—But what about René?" said he to his wife, whose inquisitive eye oppressed him. "What was the matter that he screamed so loud?"

"A mere trifle!" said Madame de l'Estorade, still studying his face.

"Well, then, my dear fellow," said her husband, assuming as indifferent a manner as he could command, "I have only to change my coat and I am yours."

When the Countess was alone with Monsieur de Camps:

"Does it not strike you," said she, "that Monsieur de l'Estorade seems quite upset this morning?"

"As I said just now, he is not at all himself. But the explanation is perfectly reasonable; we disturbed him in the middle of his work. Office work is unhealthy; I never in my life was so well as I have been since I took over the ironworks you so vehemently abuse."

"To be sure," said Madame de l'Estorade, with a deep sigh; "he needs exercise, an active life; there can be no doubt that he has some incipient liver disease."

"Because he looks yellow? But he has looked so ever since I have known him."

"Oh! monsieur, I cannot be mistaken. There is something seriously wrong, and you would do me the greatest service——"

"Madame, you have only to command me."

"When Monsieur de l'Estorade comes back, we will speak of the little damage René has done to his finger. Tell me that trifling accidents, if neglected, may lead to serious mischief—that gangrene has been known to supervene and make amputation necessary. That will give me an excuse for sending for Dr. Bianchon."

"Certainly," said Monsieur de Camps. "I do not think medical advice very necessary; but if it will reassure you——"

At this moment Monsieur de l'Estorade came back; he had almost recovered his usual looks, but a strong smell of Eau de Mélisse des Carmes proved that he had had recourse to that cordial to revive him. Monsieur de Camps played his part as Job's comforter to perfection; as to the Countess, she had no need to affect anxiety; her make-believe only concerned its object.

"My dear," said she to her husband, after listening to the ironmaster's medical discourse, "as you come home from the Minister's I wish you would call on Dr. Bianchon."

"What next!" said he, shrugging his shoulders, "call out such a busy man for what you yourself say is a mere trifle."

"If you will not go, I will send Lucas. Monsieur de Camps has quite upset me."

"If you choose to be ridiculous," said her husband sharply, "I know no means of preventing it; but one thing I may remind you, and that is, that if you send for a medical man when there is nothing the matter, under serious circumstances you may find that he will not come."

"And you will not go?"

"I will certainly not," said Monsieur de l'Estorade; "and if I had the honor of being master in my own house, I should forbid your sending any one in my stead."

"My dear, you are the master, and since you refuse so emphatically we will say no more about it. I will try not to be too anxious."

"Are you coming, de Camps?" said Monsieur de l'Estorade, "for at this rate I shall be sent off directly to order the child's funeral."

"But, my dear, are you ill," said the Countess, taking his hand, "that you can say such shocking things in cold blood? It is not like your usual patience with my little motherly fussiness—nor like the politeness on which you pride yourself—to everybody, including your wife."

"No, but the truth is," said Monsieur de l'Estorade, irritated instead of soothed by this gentle and affectionate remonstrance, "your motherly care is really becoming a monomania; you make life unbearable to everybody but your children. Deuce take it all! if they are our children, I am their father; and if I am not adored as they are, at any rate I have the right to expect that my house may not be made uninhabitable!"

While he poured out this jeremiad, striding up and down the room, the Countess was gesticulating desperately to Monsieur de Camps as if to ask him whether he did not discern a frightful symptom in this scene.

To put an end to this painful contest, of which he had so involuntarily been the cause, he now said:

"Are we going?"

"Come along," said Monsieur de l'Estorade, leading the way, without taking leave of his wife.

"Oh, I was forgetting a message for you," added the ironmaster, turning back. "Madame de Camps will call for you at about two o'clock to choose some spring dress stuffs; she has settled that we shall all four go on afterwards to the flower-show. When we leave Rastignac, l'Estorade and I will come back to fetch you, and if you are not in we will wait."

The Countess scarcely heeded this programme; a flash of light had come to her. As soon as she was alone, she took out Marie-Gaston's letter, and finding it folded in the original creases:

"Not a doubt of it!" she exclaimed. "I remember replacing it in the envelope folded inside out. The unhappy man has read it."

Some hours later Madame de l'Estorade and Madame de Camps were together in the drawing-room where only a few days since Sallenauve's cause had been so warmly argued.

"Good heavens! what is the matter with you?" cried Madame de Camps, on finding her friend in tears as she finished writing a letter.

The Countess told her of all that had passed, and read her Marie-Gaston's letter. At any other time the disaster it so plainly betrayed would have greatly grieved her friend; but the secondary misfortune which it had apparently occasioned absorbed all her thoughts.

"And are you quite sure that your husband mastered the contents of that ill-starred letter?" she asked.

"How can I doubt it?" replied Madame de l'Estorade. "The paper cannot have turned itself inside out; and besides, when I recall it all, I fancy that at the moment when I flew off to René I let something drop. As ill-luck would have it, I did not stop to look."

"But very often, when you rack your memory, you remember things that did not happen."

"But, my dear friend, the extraordinary change that so suddenly took place in Monsieur de l'Estorade could only be due to some overpowering shock. He looked like a man struck by lightning."

"Very well; but then if it is to be accounted for by a painful surprise, why do you insist on regarding it as the result of a liver complaint."

"Oh, that is no new thing to me," said Madame de l'Estorade. "Only, when sick people make no complaints one is

apt to forget.—Look here, my dear," she went on, pointing
to a volume that lay open near her, "just before your arrival
I was reading in this medical dictionary that persons with
liver disease become gloomy, restless, and irritable. And for
some little time past I have noticed a great change in my husband's temper; you yourself remarked on it the other day; and
this little scene, at which Monsieur de Camps was present—
unprecedented, I assure you, in our married life—seems to
me a terrible symptom."

"My dear, good child, you are like all people when they
are bent on worrying themselves. In the first place, you
study medical books, which is the most foolish thing in the
world. I defy you to read the description of a disease without fancying that you can identify the symptoms in yourself
or in some one you care for. And besides, you are mixing
up things that are quite different: the effects of a fright with
those of a chronic complaint—they have nothing on earth
in common."

"No, no, I am not confusing them; I know what I am talking about. Do not you know that in our poor human machinery, if any part is already affected, every strong emotion
attacks that spot at once?"

"At any rate," said her friend, to put an end to the medical
question, "if that unhappy madman's letter is likely to have
some ulterior influence on your husband's health, it threatens
far more immediately to imperil your domestic peace. That
must be considered first."

"There is no alternative," said the Countess. "Monsieur
de Sallenauve must never again set foot in the house."

"There is a good deal to be said on that point, and it is
just what I want to talk over with you.—Do you know that
yesterday I found you lacking in that moderation which has
always been a prominent trait in your character——"

"When was that?" asked Madame de l'Estorade.

"At the moment when you favored Monsieur de Sallenauve
with such a burst of gratitude. When I advised you not to
avoid him for fear of tempting him to seek your company, I

certainly did not advise you to fling your kindness at his head, so as to turn it! As the wife of so zealous an adherent of the reigning dynasty, you ought to know better what is meant by *Le Juste Milieu*" (the happy medium).

"Oh, my dear, no witticisms at my husband's expense!"

"I am not talking of your husband, but of you, my dear. You amazed me so much last night, that I felt inclined to recall all I had said on my first impulse. I like my advice to be followed—but not too much followed."

"At any other moment I would ask you to tell me wherein I so far exceeded your instructions; but now that fate has settled the question, and Monsieur de Sallenauve must be simply cleared out of the way, of what use is it to discuss the exact limit-line of my behavior to him?"

"Well," said Madame de Camps, "to tell you the whole truth, I was beginning to think the man a danger to you on quite another side."

"Which is?——"

"Through Naïs. That child, with her passion for her preserver, really makes me very anxious."

"Oh," said the Countess, with a melancholy smile, "is not that ascribing too much importance to a child's nonsense?"

"Naïs is a child, no doubt, but who will be a woman sooner than most children. Did you not yourself write to me that she had intuitions on some subjects quite beyond her years?"

"That is true. But in what you call her passion for Monsieur de Sallenauve, besides its being quite natural, the dear child is so frank and effusive that the feeling has a genuinely childlike stamp."

"Well—trust me, and do not trust to that; not even when this troublesome person is out of the way! Think, if when the time came to arrange for her marriage this liking had grown up with her—a pretty state of things!"

"Oh, between this and then—thank Heaven!——" said the Countess incredulously.

"Between this and then," replied Madame de Camps, "Monsieur de Sallenauve may have achieved such success that his name is in everybody's mouth; and with her lively imagination, Naïs would be the first to be captivated by such brilliancy."

"But still, my dear, the difference of age——"

"Monsieur de Sallenauve is thirty; Naïs is nearly thirteen. The difference is exactly the same as between your age and Monsieur de l'Estorade's, and you married him."

"Quite true; you may be right," said Madame de l'Estorade; "what I did as a matter of good sense, Naïs might insist on passionately. But be easy; I will so effectually shatter her idol——"

"That again, like the hatred you propose to act for your husband's benefit, requires moderation. If you do not manage it gradually, you may fail of your end. You must allow .it to be supposed that circumstances have brought about a feeling which should seem quite spontaneous."

"But do you suppose," cried Madame de l'Estorade excitedly, "that I need act aversion for this man? Why, I hate him! He is our evil genius!"

"Come, come, my dear, compose yourself! I really do not know you. You who used to be unruffled reason!"

Lucas at this moment came in to ask the Countess if she could see a Monsieur Jacques Bricheteau.

Madame de l'Estorade looked at her friend, saying:

"The organist who was so helpful to Monsieur de Sallenauve at the time of his election. I do not know what he can want of me."

"Never mind; see him," said her friend. "Before opening hostilities, it is not amiss to know what is going on in the enemy's camp."

"Show him in," said the Countess.

Jacques Bricheteau came in. So sure had he been, on the other hand, of being among friends, that he had given no special attention to his toilet. A capacious chocolate-brown overcoat, whose cut it would have been vain to assign to any date of fashion; a checked waistcoat, gray and green, buttoned to the throat; a black cravat, twisted to a rope, and

worn without a collar, while it showed an inch of very doubtful clean shirt front; yellow drab trousers, gray stockings,
and tied shoes—this was the more than careless array in
which the organist ventured into the presence of the elegant
Countess.

Scarcely bidden to take a seat:

"Madame," said he, "I have perhaps taken a liberty in presenting myself to you, unknown; but Monsieur Marie-Gaston
spoke to me of your possibly wishing that I should give some
lessons to mademoiselle your daughter. I told him at first
that there might be some little difficulty, as all my time was
filled up; but the Préfet of Police has just set me at leisure
by dismissing me from a post I held in his department, so I
am happy to be able to place myself entirely at your service."

"And has your dismissal, monsieur, been occasioned by the
part you played in Monsieur de Sallenauve's election?" asked
Madame de Camps.

"As no reason was assigned, it seems probable; all the more
so that, in the course of twenty years' service, this discharge
is the very first hitch that has ever arisen between me and
my superiors."

"It cannot be denied," said Madame de l'Estorade, sharply
enough, "that you very seriously interfered with the intentions
of the Government."

"Yes, madame; and I accepted my dismissal as a disaster
I was quite prepared for. After all, what was the loss of
my small appointment in comparison with the election of
Monsieur de Sallenauve?"

"I am really distressed," the Countess went on, "to make
no better return for the eagerness you are good enough to
express; but I may as well tell you that I have no fixed purpose as to choosing a master for my daughter, and in spite
of the immense talent for which the world gives you credit,
I should be afraid of such serious teaching for a little girl of
thirteen."

"Quite the reverse, madame," replied the organist. "Nobody credits me with talent. Monsieur de Sallenauve and

Monsieur Marie-Gaston have heard me two or three times, but apart from that, I am a mere unknown teacher, and perhaps you are right—perhaps a very tiresome one. So, setting aside the question of lessons to mademoiselle your daughter, let me speak of the thing that has really brought me here—Monsieur de Sallenauve."

"Did Monsieur de Sallenauve charge you with any message to my husband?" said Madame de l'Estorade, with marked coldness.

"No, madame, he has, I grieve to say, charged me with nothing. I went to call on him this morning, but he was absent. I went to Ville-d'Avray, where I was told that I should find him, and learned that he had started on a journey with Monsieur Marie-Gaston. Then, thinking that you might possibly know the object of this journey, and how long he would be away——"

"Nothing of the kind," said Madame de l'Estorade, interrupting him in a hard tone.

"I had a letter this morning," Jacques Bircheteau went on, "from Arcis-sur-Aube. My aunt, Mother Marie des Anges, warns me, through Monsieur de Sallenauve's notary, that a base conspiracy is being organized, and our friend's absence complicates matters very seriously. I cannot understand what put it into his head to vanish without warning anybody who takes an interest——"

"That he should not have given you notice," said Madame de l'Estorade, in the same tone, "may possibly surprise you. But so far as my husband and I are concerned, there is nothing to be astonished at."

The significance of this uncivil distinction was too clear to be misunderstood. Jacques Bircheteau looked at the Countess, and her eyes fell; but the whole expression of her face, set due North, confirmed the meaning which it was impossible to avoid finding in her words.

"I beg your pardon, madame," said he, rising. "I did not know—I could not have supposed that you were so utterly indifferent to Monsieur de Sallenauve's prospects and honor.

But a minute ago, in the ante-room, when your servant was in doubt about announcing me, mademoiselle your daughter, on hearing that I was a friend of his, eagerly took my part; and I was so foolish as to conclude that she represented the general good feeling of the family."

After pointing this distinction, which was quite a match for Madame de l'Estorade's, thus paying her back in her own coin, Jacques Bircheteau bowed ceremoniously, and was about to leave.

The two ladies exchanged a glance, as if to ask each other whether it would be well to let this man depart thus after shooting so keen a parting dart.

In fact, a crushing contradiction was at this instant given to the Countess' assumption of indifference: Naïs came flying in.

"Mamma!" she cried exultantly, "a letter from Monsieur de Sallenauve!"

The Countess blushed purple.

"What manners are these, bouncing in like a mad thing?" said she severely. "And how do you know that the letter is from that gentlemen?"

"Oh!" said Naïs, turning the blade in the wound, "when he wrote to you from Arcis, I got to know his writing."

"You are a silly, inquisitive child," said her mother, roused out of her usual indulgence by so many luckless speeches. "Go to nurse."

Then to give herself some countenance:

"Allow me, monsieur," said she to Jacques Bricheteau, as she opened the letter so inappropriately delivered.

"Nay, Madame la Comtesse," replied the organist, "it is I who crave your permission to wait till you have read your letter. If by any chance Monsieur de Sallenauve should give you any account of his movements, you would perhaps have the kindness to give me the benefit of it——"

Having looked through the letter:

"Monsieur de Sallenauve," said the Countess, "desires me to tell my husband that he is on his way to England—Hanwell, in the county of Middlesex. He is to be addressed under cover to Doctor Ellis."

Jacques Bricheteau again bowed with due formality, and left the room.

"Naïs has just treated you to a taste of her girl-in-love tricks," said Madame de Camps. "But you had well earned it. You had behaved to that poor man with a hardness that deserved a severer sally than his parting retort. He seems to have a ready wit of his own; and *'If by any chance'* Monsieur de Sallenauve had given you any information, was rather neat under the circumstances."

"What is to be done?" said her friend; "the day began badly; all the rest is to match."

"What about the letter?"

"It is heartbreaking.—Read it."

"MADAME" (Sallenauve wrote),—"I succeeded in overtaking Lord Lewin a few leagues beyond Paris—he is the Englishman of whom I spoke to you, and Providence sent him to spare us a terrible catastrophe. Possessed of a large fortune, he, like many of his countrymen, is liable to attacks of depression, and only his strength of mind has saved him from the worst results of the malady. His indifference to life, and the cool stoicism with which he speaks of voluntary death, won him at Florence, where they met, our unhappy friend's confidence. Lord Lewin, who is interested in the study of vehement emotions, is intimately acquainted with Dr. Ellis, a physician famous for his treatment of the insane, and his Lordship has often spent some weeks at the Hanwell Asylum for Lunatics in Middlesex. It is one of the best managed asylums in England, and Dr. Ellis is at the head of it.

"Lord Lewin, on arriving at Ville-d'Avray, at once discerned in Marie-Gaston the early symptoms of acute mania. Though not yet obvious to superficial observers, they did not escape Lord Lewin's practised eye. 'He picked and hoarded,' said he, in speaking of our poor friend; that is to say, as they walked about the park Marie-Gaston would pick up such rubbish as straws, old bits of paper, and even rusty nails, putting them carefully in his pocket; and this, it would seem, is a symptom familiar to those who have studied the progress of mental disease. Then, by recurring to the discussions they had held at Florence, Lord Lewin had no difficulty in discovering his secret purpose of killing himself. Believing that his wife visited him every evening, the poor fellow had determined—on the very night of your little dance—to follow his adored Louise, as he said. So, you see, my fears were not exaggerated, but were the outcome of an instinct.

"Lord Lewin, instead of opposing his resolution, affected to participate in it.

" 'But men like us,' said he, 'ought not to die in any vulgar way, and there is a mode of death of which I had thought for myself, and which I propose that we should seek in common.—In South America, not far from Paraguay, there is one of the most tremendous cataracts in the world, known as the Falls of Gayra. The spray that rises from the abyss is to be seen for many leagues, and reflects seven rainbows. A vast volume of water, spreading over a breadth of more than twelve thousand feet, is suddenly pent up in a narrow channel, and falls into a gulf below with a sound more deafening than a hundred thunderclaps at once.—That is where I have always dreamed of dying.'

" 'Let us be off,' said Marie-Gaston.

" 'This very minute,' said Lord Lewin. 'Pack your things; we will sail from England, and be there in a few weeks.'

"And in this way, madame, the clever foreigner succeeded in putting our friend off from his dreadful purpose. As you may understand, he is taking him to England to place him in Dr Ellis' care, since he—Lord Lewin says—has not his match in Europe for treating the very sad case that is to be confided to him. If I had been present, I should have concurred entirely in this arrangement, which has this advantage, that in the event of his recovery our friend's attack will remain unknown.

"Informed by a letter left for me by Lord Lewin at Ville-d'Avray, I immediately set out in pursuit; and at Beauvais, whence I am writing, I came up with them in a hotel, where Lord Lewin had put up to enable the patient to benefit by sleep, which had happily come over him in the carriage, after weeks of almost total insomnia. Lord Lewin looks upon this as a very favorable symptom, and he says that the malady thus treated, as it will be, from the beginning, has the best possible chance of cure.

"I shall follow them closely to Hanwell, taking care not to be seen by Marie-Gaston, since, in Lord Lewin's opinion, my presence might disturb the comparative tranquillity of mind that he has derived from the thought of the pompous end he is going to find. On reaching the asylum, I shall wait to hear Dr. Ellis' verdict.

"The session opens so soon that I fear I may not be back in time for the first sittings; but I shall write to the President of the Chamber, and if it should happen that any difficulty arose as to the leave of absence for which I must petition, I venture to rely on Monsieur de l'Estorade's kindness to certify the absolute necessity for it. At the same time, I must beg him to remember that I cannot authorize him on any consideration to reveal the nature of the business which has compelled me to go abroad. However, the mere statement of a fact by such a man as M. de l'Estorade must be enough to secure its acceptance without any explanation.

"Allow me, madame, to remain, etc."

As Madame de Camps finished reading, carriage wheels were heard.

"There are our gentlemen back again," said the Countess. "Now, shall I show this letter to my husband?"

"You cannot do otherwise. There would be too great a risk of what Naïs might say. Besides, Monsieur de Sallenauve writes most respectfully; there is nothing to encourage your husband's notions."

As soon as Monsieur de l'Estorade came in, his wife could

see that he had recovered his usual looks, and she was about to congratulate him, when he spoke first.

"Who is the man of very shabby appearance," asked Monsieur de l'Estorade, "whom I found speaking to Naïs on the stairs?"

As his wife did not seem to know what he was talking about, he went on. "A man very much marked by the small-pox, with a greasy hat and a brown overcoat?"

"Oh!" said Madame de Camps to her friend, "our visitor! Naïs could not resist the opportunity of talking about her idol."

"But who is the man?"

"Is not his name Jacques Bricheteau?" said the Countess, "a friend of Monsieur de Sallenauve's."

Seeing a cloud fall on her husband's countenance, Madame de l'Estorade hurriedly explained the two objects of the organist's visit, and she gave the Member's letter to Monsieur de l'Estorade.

While he was reading it:

"He seems better, do you think?" the Countess asked Monsieur de Camps.

"Oh, he is perfectly right again," said the ironmaster. "There is not a sign of what we saw this morning. He had worried himself over his work; exercise has done him good; and yet it is to be observed that he had an unpleasant shock just now at the Minister's."

"Why, what happened?" asked Madame de l'Estorade.

"Your friend Monsieur de Sallenauve's business seems to be in a bad way."

"Thank you for nothing!" said Monsieur de l'Estorade, returning the letter to his wife. "I shall certainly not do anything he asks me."

"Then have you heard anything against him?" said she, trying to appear perfectly indifferent as she asked the question.

"Yes; Rastignac told me that he had letters from Arcis; some very awkward discoveries have been made there."

"Well, what did I tell you?" cried Madame de l'Estorade.

"What did you tell me?"

"To be sure. Did I not give you a hint some time ago that Monsieur de Sallenauve was a man to be let drop? Those were the very words I used, as I happen to remember."

"But was it I who brought him here?"

"You can hardly say that it was I.—Only just now, before knowing anything of the distressing facts you have just learned, I was speaking to Madame de Camps of another reason which should make us anxious to put an end to the acquaintance."

"Very true," said Madame de Camps. "Your wife, but a minute ago, was talking of the sort of frenzy that possesses Naïs with regard to her preserver, and she foresaw great difficulties in the future."

"It is an unsatisfactory connection in every way," said Monsieur de l'Estorade.

"It seems to me," said Monsieur de Camps, who was not behind the scenes, "that you are rather in a hurry. Some compromising discoveries are said to have been made with reference to Monsieur de Sallenauve, but what is the value of these discoveries? Wait before you hang him, at least till he has been tried."

"My husband can do what he thinks proper," said the Countess. "For my part, I do not hesitate to throw him over at once. My friends, like Cæsar's wife, must be above suspicion."

"The awkward thing," said Monsieur de l'Estorade, "is that we are under such an annoying obligation to him——"

"But, really," exclaimed Madame de l'Estorade, "if a convict had saved my life, should I be obliged to receive him in my drawing-room?"

"Indeed, my dear, you are going too far," said Madame de Camps.

"Well, well," said Monsieur de l'Estorade, "there is no occasion to raise a scandal; things must be allowed to take their course. The dear man is abroad now; who knows if he will ever come back?"

"What, he has fled at a mere rumor?" said Monsieur de Camps.

"Not precisely on that account," replied the Count. "He had a pretext—but once out of France——"

"As to that conclusion," said Madame de l'Estorade, "I do not for a moment believe in it. His pretext is a good reason, and as soon as he hears from his friend the organist he will hurry back. So, my dear, you must take your courage in both hands and cut the intimacy short at a blow if you do not intend it to continue."

"And that is really your meaning?" said Monsieur de l'Estorade, looking keenly at his wife.

"I?—I would write to him without any sort of ceremony, and tell him that he will oblige us by calling here no more. At the same time, as it is a little difficult to write such a letter, we will concoct it together if you like."

"We will see," said her husband, beaming at the suggestion; "the house is not falling yet. The most pressing matter at the moment is the flower-show we are to go to together. It closes, I think, at four o'clock, and we have but an hour before us."

Madame de l'Estorade, who had dressed before Madame de Camps' arrival, rang for the maid to bring her bonnet and shawl.

As she was putting them on in front of a glass:

"Then you really love me, Renée?" said her husband in her ear.

"Can you be so silly as to ask?" replied she, giving him her most affectionate look.

"Well, I have a confession to make to you—I read the letter Philippe brought."

"Then I am no longer surprised at the change that came over you. I too must tell you something. When I proposed that we should concoct Monsieur de Sallenauve's dismissal between us, I had already written it—directly after you went out; and you can take it out of my blotting-book and post it if you think it will do."

Quite beside himself with joy at finding that his hypothetical successor had been so immediately sacrificed, Monsieur de l'Estorade threw his arms round his wife and kissed her effusively.

"Well done!" cried Monsieur de Camps. "This is better than this morning!"

"This morning I was a fool," said the Count, as he turned over the blotting-book to find the letter, which he might have taken his wife's word for.

"Say no more," said Madame de Camps in an undertone to her husband. "I will explain all this pother to you presently."

Younger again by ten years, the Count offered his arm to Madame de Camps, while his wife took the ironmaster's.

"And Naïs?" said Monsieur de l'Estorade, seeing the little girl looking forlorn as they went. "Is not she coming too?"

"No," said her mother; "I am not pleased with her."

"Pooh!" said the father, "I proclaim an amnesty.—Run and put your bonnet on," he added to the child.

Naïs looked at her mother for the ratification which she thought necessary under the hierarchy of power as it existed in the l'Estorade household.

"Go," said the Countess, "since your father wishes it."

While they waited for the little girl:

"To whom are you writing, Lucas?" asked the Count of the man-servant, who had begun a letter on the table by which he stood.

"To my son," said Lucas, "who is very anxious to get his sergeant's stripes. I am telling him that you promised me a note to his colonel, Monsieur le Comte."

"Perfectly true, on my honor; and I had quite forgotten it. Remind me to-morrow morning; I will write it the first thing when I get up."

"You are very good, sir——"

"Here," said Monsieur de l'Estorade, putting his fingers

in his waistcoat pocket and taking out three gold pieces, "send these to the corporal from me, and tell him to get his men to drink to his stripes."

Lucas was amazed; he had never known his master so genial and liberal.

When Naïs was ready, Madame de l'Estorade, proud of having had the courage to leave her in disgrace for half an hour, hugged her as if she had not seen her for two years; then they all set out for the Luxembourg, where the Horticultural Society at that time held its shows.

Towards the end of the interview which Monsieur Octave de Camps, under the auspices of Monsieur de l'Estorade, had at last been able to get with Rastignac, the Minister's usher had come in to give him the cards of Monsieur le Procureur-Général Vinet and Monsieur Maxime de Trailles.

"Very well," said the Minister. "Tell the gentlemen I will see them in a few minutes."

Soon after, the ironmaster and Monsieur de l'Estorade rose to leave; and it was then that Rastignac had briefly told the Count of the danger looming on the parliamentary horizon of his friend Sallenauve. At the word "friend," Monsieur de l'Estorade had protested.

"I do not know, my dear Minister," said he, "why you persist in giving that name to a man who is really no more than an acquaintance, I might say a provisional acquaintance, if the reports you have mentioned should prove to have any foundation."

"I am delighted to hear you say so," replied Rastignac. "For in the thick of the hostilities which seem likely to arise between that gentleman and our side, I confess that the warm feeling I imagined you to have towards him would somewhat have fettered me."

"I am grateful for your consideration," replied the Count; "but pray understand that I give you a free hand. It is a matter entirely at your discretion to treat Monsieur de Sallenauve as a political foe, without any fear that the blows you deal him will at all hurt me."

Thereupon they left, and Messieurs Vinet and de Trailles had been shown in.

Vinet, the Attorney-General, and father of Olivier Vinet, whom the reader already knows, was one of the warmest champions and most welcome advisers of the existing Government. Designate as the Minister of Justice at the next shuffling of the Cabinet, he was behind the scenes of every ambiguous situation; and in every secret job nothing was concocted without his co-operation, in the plot at least, if not in the doing.

The electoral affairs of Arcis had a twofold claim on his interference: First, because his son held a position among the legal magnates of the town; secondly, because as connected through his wife with the Chargebœufs of la Brie, the Cinq-Cygnes of Champagne being a younger branch of that family, this aristocratic alliance made him think it a point of honor to assert his importance in both districts, and never to miss a chance of interfering in their affairs.

So, that morning, when Monsieur de Trailles had called on the Minister armed with a letter from Madame Beauvisage, full of compromising scandal concerning the new Member for Arcis:

"Find Vinet, as coming from me," said Rastignac, without listening to any explanations, "and try to bring him here as soon as possible."

At Maxime's bidding—who offered to fetch him in his carriage—Vinet was quite ready to go to Rastignac; and now that he has made his way to the Minister's private room, we shall be better informed as to the danger hanging over Sallenauve's head, of which Jacques Bricheteau and Monsieur de l'Estorade have given us but a slight idea.

"Then you mean, my dear friends," said the Minister as soon as they had settled to their talk, "that we may get some hold on this political purist!—I met him yesterday at l'Estorade's, and he struck me as most undauntedly hostile."

Maxime, whose presence was in no sense official, knew better than to answer this remark. Vinet, on the contrary, almost insolently conscious of his political importance, Public Prosecutor as he was, had too much of the advocate in his composition to miss a chance of speaking.

"When, only this morning, monsieur"—and he bowed to Maxime—"did me the honor to communicate to me a letter he had received from Madame Beauvisage, I had just had one from my son, in which he gave me, with slight variations, the same information. I agree with him that the matter looks ugly for our adversary—but it will need nice management."

"I really hardly know what the matter is," said the Minister. "As I particularly wished for your opinion on the case, my dear Vinet, I begged Monsieur de Trailles to postpone the details till we were all three together.

This was authorizing Maxime to proceed with the narrative, but Vinet again seized the opportunity for hearing his own voice.

"This," said he, "is what my son Olivier writes to me, confirming Madame Beauvisage's letter—she, I may say incidentally, would have made a famous Member of Parliament, my dear sir.—On a market day not long since, Pigoult the notary, who has the management of all the new Member's business matters, received a visit, it would seem, from a peasant woman from Romilly, a large village not far from Arcis. To hear the Marquis de Sallenauve, who has so suddenly reappeared, you would think that he was the only existing scion of the Sallenauve family; but this did not prevent this woman from displaying some papers in due form, proving that she too is a living Sallenauve, in the direct line, and related nearly enough to claim her part in any heritable property."

"Well," said Rastignac, "but did she know no more of the Marquis' existence than he knew of hers?"

"That did not plainly appear from her statements," said Vinet; "but that very confusion seems to me most convincing, for, as you know, between relations in such different positions great difficulties are apt to arise."

"Kindly proceed with the story," said the Minister. "Before drawing conclusions, we must hear the facts—though, as you know by experience, that is not the invariable practice in Parliament."

"Not always to the dissatisfaction of the Ministers," said Maxime, laughing.

"Monsieur is right," said Vinet; "all hail to a successful muddler!—But to return to our peasant woman, who, in consequence of the ruin of the Sallenauve family, has fallen into great poverty and a station far beneath her birth; she first appeared as a petitioner for money, and it seems probable that prompt and liberal generosity would have kept her quiet. But it is also likely that she was but ill pleased by Maître Achille Pigoult's reception of her demands; for on leaving his office she went to the market square, and seconded by a neighbor, a lawyer from the village, who had come with her, she disburdened herself of various statements relating to my highly-esteemed fellow-member which were not very flattering to his character; declaring that the Marquis de Sallenauve was not his father; and again, that there was no Marquis de Sallenauve in existence. And at any rate, she concluded, this newly-made Sallenauve was a heartless wretch who would have nothing to say to his relations. But, she added, she could make him disgorge, and, with the help of the clever man who had come with her to support her by his advice, Monsieur le Député might be sure that they 'would make him jump to another tune.'"

"I have not the slightest objection," said Rastignac. "But the woman has, I suppose, some proof in support of her statements?"

"That is the weak point of the matter," replied Vinet. "But let me go on.—At Arcis, my dear sir, the Government has a remarkably devoted and intelligent servant in the head of the police. Moving about among the people, which is his practice on market-days, he picked up some of the woman's vicious remarks, and going off at once to the Mayor's house, he asked to see, not the Mayor himself, but Madame Beauvisage, to whom he told what was going on."

"Then is the candidate whom you had chosen for a crowning treat a perfect idiot?" Rastignac asked Maxime.

"The very man you wanted," replied Monsieur de Trailles, "imbecile to a degree! There is nothing I would not do to reverse this vexatious defeat."

"Madame Beauvisage," Vinet went on, "at once thought she would like to talk to this woman of the ready tongue; and to get hold of her, it was not a bad idea to desire Groslier, the police sergeant, to go and fetch her with a sternly threatening air, as if the authorities disapproved of her levity in using such language with regard to a member of the National Chamber, and to bring her forthwith to the Mayor's house."

"And it was Madame Beauvisage, you say, who suggested this method of procedure?" said Rastignac.

"Oh yes, she is a very capable woman," said Maxime.

"Driven hard," continued the speaker, "by Madame the Mayoress, who took care to secure her husband's presence at the cross-examination, the woman proved to be anything rather than coherent. How she had ascertained that the Member could not be the Marquis' son; and her confident assertion, on the other hand, that the Marquis did not even exist, were not by any means conclusively proved. Hearsay, vague reports, inferences drawn by her village attorney were the best of the evidence she could bring."

"Well, then," said Rastignac, "what is the upshot of it all?"

"*Nil* from the legal point of view," replied Vinet. "For even if the woman could prove that it is a mere whim on the part of the Marquis de Sallenauve to recognize the man Dorlange as his son, she would have no ground for an action in disproof. According to section 339 of the Civil Code, a positive and congenital right alone can give grounds for disputing the recognition of a natural child; in other words, there must be a direct claim on the property in which the child whose birth is disputed is enabled to claim a share."

"Your balloon collapsed!" observed the Minister.

"Whereas, on the other hand, if the good woman chooses

to dispute the existence of the Marquis de Sallenauve, she would disinherit herself, since she certainly has no claim on the estate of a man who would then be no relation of hers; besides, it is the duty of the crown, and not her part at all, to prosecute for the assumption of a false identity; the utmost she could do would be to bring the charge."

"Whence you conclude?" said Rastignac, with the sharp brevity which warns a too diffuse talker to abridge his story.

"Whence I conclude, legally speaking, that this Romilly peasant, by taking up either charge as the basis for an action, would find it a bad speculation, since in one case she must obviously lose, and in the other—which, in fact, she cannot even bring—she would get nothing out of it. But, politically speaking, it is quite another story."

"Let us see the political side then," said Rastignac; "for, so far, I can make nothing of it."

"In the first place," replied the lawyer, "you will agree with me that it is always possible to fight a bad case?"

"Certainly."

"And, then, I do not suppose that you would care whether this woman fights an action which would only end in her having to pay a lawyer's bill."

"No; I confess it is a matter to me of perfect indifference."

"And if you had cared, I should, all the same, have advised you to let matters take their course; for the Beauvisages have undertaken all the costs, including a visit to Paris for this woman and her legal adviser."

"Well, well—the action brought, what comes of it?" said Rastignac, anxious to end.

"What comes of it?" cried the lawyer, warming to the subject. "Why, everything you can manage to make of it, if, before it is argued, you can work up comments in the papers and insinuations from your friends.—What comes of it? Why, the utmost discredit for our antagonist, if he is suspected of having assumed a name he has no right to.—

What comes of it? Why, an opportunity for a fulminating speech in the Chamber——"

"Which you, no doubt, will undertake?" asked Rastignac.

"Oh, I do not know. The case must be thoroughly studied; I must see what turn it is likely to take."

"Then for the moment," the Minister observed, "it is all reduced to an application, hit or miss, of Basile's famous theory of calumny—that it is always well to keep it stirred, and that something will stick."

"Calumny? Calumny?" replied Vinet. "That we shall see; it may be no more than honest evil-speaking. Monsieur de Trailles, here, knows what went on much better than we do. He will tell you that all through the district the father's disappearance as soon as he had legally acknowledged his son had the very worst effect; that everybody retained a vague impression of mysterious complications to favor the election of this man we are talking about.

"You have no idea, my dear fellow, what can be got out of a lawsuit cleverly kept simmering, and in my long and busy career as a pleader I have seen miracles worked by such means. A parliamentary struggle is quite another matter. There proof is not needed; you may kill your man with nothing but hypotheses and asseverations if you stick to them defiantly enough."

"Well, to sum up," said Rastignac, speaking as a man of method, "how do you recommend that the affair should be managed?"

"In the first place," replied the lawyer, "I should allow the Beauvisages—since they have a fancy for it—to pay all the expenses of moving the peasant woman and her friend, and subsequently the costs of the action."

"Do I make any objection?" said the Minister. "Have I either the right or the means?"

"The case," Vinet went on, "must be put into the hands of a wily and clever lawyer: Desroches, for instance, Monsieur de Trailles' lawyer. He will know how to fill out the body of a case which, as you justly observe, is very thin."

"I certainly should not say to Monsieur de Trailles, 'I forbid you to allow anybody you please to secure the services of your solicitor,' " said Rastignac.

"Then we want an advocate who can talk with an air of 'The Family' as a sacred and precious thing; who will wax indignant at the surreptitious intrigues by which a man may scheme to insinuate himself within its holy pale."

"Desroches can find your man; and again, the Government is not likely to hinder a pleader from talking, or from being transported with indignation!"

"But, Monsieur le Ministre," Maxime put in, startled out of his attitude of passive attention by Rastignac's indifference, "is non-interference all the support to be hoped for from the Government in this struggle?"

"I hope you did not think that we should take up the action on our own acccunt?"

"No, of course not; but we had a right to imagine that you would take some interest in it."

"How—in what way?"

"How can I tell? As Monsieur Vinet was saying just now, by tuck of drum in the subsidized newspapers—by getting your supporters to spread the gossip—by using the influence which men in power always have over the Bench."

"Thank you for nothing," said the Minister. "When you want to secure the Government as an accomplice, my dear Maxime, you must have a rather more solidly constructed scheme to show. Your air of business this morning made me think you really had a strong hand, and I have troubled our excellent friend the Public Prosecutor, who knows how high a value I set on his learning and advice; but really your plot strikes me as too transparent, and the meshes so thin that I can see through them an inevitable defeat. If I were a bachelor and wanted to marry Mademoiselle Beauvisage, I daresay I might be bolder, so I leave it to you to carry on the action in any way you please. I will not say that Government will not watch your progress with its best wishes; but it certainly will not tread the path with you."

"Well, well," said Vinet, hindering Maxime's reply, which would, no doubt, have been a bitter one, "but supposing we take the matter into court; supposing that the peasant woman, prompted by the Beauvisages, should denounce the man who was identified before the notary as being a spurious Sallenauve; then the Member is guilty of conspiracy, and for that we have him before the superior court."

"But, again, where are your proofs?" asked Rastignac. "Have you a shadow of evidence?"

"You admitted just now," observed Maxime, "that a bad case may be fought out."

"A civil action, yes; a criminal charge is quite another matter. And this would break down, for it means disputing the validity of an act drawn up by a public official, and without a particle of proof. A pretty piece of work! The case would be simply dismissed before it came to be argued in court. If we wanted to perch our enemy on a pedestal as high as the column of July, we could not go about it more effectually."

"So that in your opinion there is nothing to be done?" asked Maxime.

"By us—nothing.—But you, my dear Maxime, who have no official position, and can at a pinch use your pistol in support of the attack on Monsieur de Sallenauve's character —there is nothing to hinder you from trying your luck in the contest."

"Yes," said Maxime petulantly, "I am a sort of 'condottiere!'"

"Not at all; you are a man with an instinctive conviction of certain facts that cannot be legally proved, and you would not be afraid to stand at the judgment seat of God."

Monsieur de Trailles rose, considerably annoyed. Vinet also rose, and giving Rastignac his hand as he took leave:

"I cannot deny," said he, "that your conduct is dictated by great prudence; and I will not say but that in your place I should do the same."

"No ill-feeling, at any rate, Maxime," said the Minister, and Maxime bowed with icy dignity.

When the two conspirators were in the outer room alone:

"Do you understand what this prudery means?" asked Maxime.

"Perfectly," said Vinet, "and for a clever man you seem to me easily taken in."

"No doubt—making you lose your time, besides losing my own to have the pleasure of hearing a man lay himself out for the reward of virtue——"

"It is not that. I think you very guileless to believe in the refusal of support that had vexed you so much."

"What? You think——"

"I think that the business is a toss-up. If the plan succeeds, the Government, sitting with its arm folded, will get all the benefit; if, on the contrary, success is not for us, it would, as soon as not, keep out of the risk of defeat. But, take my word for it, I know Rastignac; looking quite impassive, and without compromising himself at all, he will perhaps serve us better than by outspoken connivance.—Just reflect: Did he say a single word against the moral side of the attack? Did he not repeat again and again—'I make no objection. I have no right to hinder you.' And what fault had he to find with the snake's venom? That its action was not deadly enough! The fact is, my dear sir, that there will be a sharp tug of war, and it will take all Desroches' skill to put a good face on the business."

"Then you think I had better see him?"

"Do I think so?—Why, this moment, when we part."

"Do not you think it would be well that he should go and talk matters over with you?"

"No, no, no!" said Vinet. "I may be the man to do the talking in the Chamber. Desroches might be seen at my house, and I must seem immaculate."

Thereupon he bowed to Maxime, and left him in some haste, excusing himself by having to go to the Chamber and hear what was going on.

"And if I," said Maxime, running after him as he left, "if I should need your advice?"

"I am leaving Paris this evening to look after my court in the country before the session opens."

"And the question in the Chamber that you may be called upon to ask?"

"Oh, if it is not I, it will be some one else. I shall return as soon as possible; but you will understand that I must set my shop in order before I come away for at least five or six months."

"Then *Bon voyage,* monsieur," said Maxime sarcastically, and parting from him at last.

Monsieur de Trailles, left to himself, stood a little disconcerted as he fancied that here were two political Bertrands, each intending that he should snatch the chestnuts from the fire.

Rastignac's behavior especially nettled him when he looked back on their first meeting, just twenty years ago, at Madame de Restaud's. He, then already a formed man holding the sceptre of fashion, and Rastignac a poor student, not knowing how to enter or leave a room, and dismissed from the door of that handsome house when he called after his first visit, in the course of which he had contrived to commit two or three incongruous blunders!—And now Rastignac was a Peer of France and in office; while he, Maxime, no more than his tool, was obliged to listen with grounded arms when he was told that his man-traps were too artless, and that if he fancied them, he must work them alone.

But this prostration was but a lightning flash.

"Well, then!" he said to himself. "Yes, I will try the game single-handed. My instinct assures me that there is something in it.

"What next! A Dorlange, a nobody, is to keep me in check, Comte Maxime de Trailles, and make my defeat a stepping-stone? There are too many dark places in that rogue's past life for it not to be possible sooner or later to open one to the light of day——"

"To the lawyer's," said he to the coachman as he opened his carriage door.

And when he was comfortably seated on the cushions:

"After all, if I cannot succeed in overthrowing this upstart, I will put myself in the way of his insulting me; I shall have the choice of weapons, and will fire first. I will do better than the Duc de Rhétoré, my insolent friend! I will kill you, never fear!"

It may be observed that Monsieur Maxime de Trailles had been quite upset by the mere idea of being taken for a *condottiere*.

Desroches was at home, and Monsieur de Trailles was at once shown in to his private room.

Desroches was an attorney who, like Raphael, had had many manners. Having in the first instance taken over an office without a connection, he had left no stone unturned, taking every case that offered, and had found himself in very poor esteem in court. But he was hard-working, well up in all the tricks and windings of legal technicalities, an acute observer and keen reader of every impulse of the human heart; thus he had finally made a very good connection, had married a woman with a fine fortune, and had given up all pettifogging double-dealing as soon as he could make his way without it.

By 1839 Desroches was an honest attorney in good practice; that is to say, he conducted his clients' business with zeal and skill; he never would countenance any underhand proceedings, much less would he have lent them a hand. As to the fine bloom of delicate honesty which existed in Derville and some other men of that stamp, besides the impossibility of preserving it from rubbing off in the world of business—in which, as Monsieur de Talleyrand said, "Business means other people's money"—it can never be the second development of any life. The loss of that down of the soul, like that of anything virginal, is irreparable; so Desroches had made no attempt to restore it. He would have nothing to say to what was ignoble or dishonest; but the above-board tricks allowed by the Code of Procedure, the recognized sur-

prises and villainies to steal a march on an adversary, he was
ready to allow.

Then, Desroches was an amusing fellow; he liked good
living; and, like all men who are incessantly absorbed by
the imperious demands of hard thinking, he felt a craving
for highly-spiced enjoyments snatched in haste, and strong to
the palate. So, while he had by degrees cleansed his ways
as a lawyer, he was still the favorite attorney of men of
letters, artists, and actresses, of popular courtesans and dandy
bohemians such as Maxime; because he was content to live
their life, all these people attracted him, and all relished his
society. Their slang and wit, their rather lax moral views,
their somewhat *picaresque* adventures, their expedients, their
brave and honorable toil—in short, all their greatness and all
their misery were perfectly understood by him, and like an
ever-indulgent providence, he gave them advice and help
whenever they asked for them.

But to the end that his serious and paying clients should
not discover what might be somewhat compromising in his
intimacy with these clients of his heart, he had days when
he was the husband and father—more especially Sundays.
Rarely did he fail to be seen in his quiet little carriage, in
the Bois de Boulogne, his wife by his side—the largeness of
her fortune stamped in her ugliness. On the opposite seat
were the three children in a group, all unfortunately like
their mother. This family picture, these virtuous Sunday
habits, were so unlike the week-day Desroches, dining in any
pot-house with all the fastest men and women of the day,
that Malaga, a circus-rider, famous for her fun and smart
sayings, said that attorneys ought not to be allowed to play
such improbable pranks, and cheat the public by showing off
papier-maché children.

So it was to this relatively honest lawyer that Monsieur
de Trailles had come for advice, as he never failed to do in
every more or less tight place in his career. Desroches, as
had long been his habit, listened without interrupting him
to the long statement of the case as it was unfolded to him,

including the scene that had just taken place at Rastignac's. As Maxime had no secrets from this confessor, he gave all his reasons for owing Sallenauve an ill turn, and represented him, with perfect conviction, as having stolen the name under which he would sit in the Chamber. His hatred appeared to him in the light of positive evidence of a felony that was hardly probable or possible. In the bottom of his heart Desroches had no wish to undertake a case in which he at once foresaw not the smallest chance of success; and his lax honesty was shown in his talking to his client as if it were a quite ordinary legal matter, and in not telling him point-blank his opinion of an action which was simply an intrigue.

The amount of wrong that is done by such verbal connivance, that never goes so far as active complicity, is really incalculable.—"What concern is it of mine? Let them fight it out! Why should I set up for being the bashful knight of virtue?" This is what men of Desroches' nature are apt to think, and it would be hard to guess at their number in a somewhat advanced state of civilization.

"To begin with, my dear sir," said the attorney, "a civil action is not to be thought of: if your Romilly peasant had her pockets full of proofs, her application would be refused because, so far, she can have no direct interest in disputing the affiliation of the opposing party."

"Yes, that is what Vinet said just now."

"As to a criminal prosecution, that, of course, you might bring about by lodging an information of false personation."

"Vinet seemed in favor of that course," said Maxime.

"Well, but there are many objections to this method of procedure. In the first place, merely to get the information heard, you must have something resembling proof; next, if the information is lodged and the Crown decides to prosecute, to get a verdict there must be far stronger evidence of the felony; and if, after all, the crime were proved against the self-styled Marquis de Sallenauve, how are you to show that his self-styled son is in the conspiracy, since he may have been deceived by an impostor."

"But what motive could that impostor have," said Maxime, "for giving this Dorlange all the advantages that accrue to him from being recognized as the Marquis de Sallenauve's son?"

"Oh, my dear fellow," replied Desroches, "when you come to State questions, any eccentricity is possible. No sort of trials or actions has furnished so many romances to the compilers of *causes célèbres* or to novelists. But there is another point: the assumption of a false identity is not in itself a crime in the eye of the law."

"How is that?" cried Maxime. "Impossible!"

"Look here, my lord," said Desroches, taking down the *Five Codes,* "have the kindness to read section 145 of the Penal Code—the only one which seems to lend an opening to the action you propose to bring, and see whether the misdemeanor we are discussing is contemplated."

Maxime read aloud section 145, as follows:

"Any functionary or public officer who shall have committed forgery in the exercise of his functions—either by forged signatures, or by defacing and altering deeds, documents, or signatures—or by assuming a false identity——"

"There, you see," said Maxime, "false identity——"

"Read to the end," said Desroches.

"Or by altering or adding to a register or any other public document, after it has been legally attested and sealed, is liable to penal servitude for life."

Monsieur de Trailles rolled the words unctuously on his tongue as a foretaste of the fate in store for Sallenauve.

"My dear Count," said Desroches, "you read as the parties to a suit always do; they never study a point of law but from their own side of the case. You fail to observe that, in this section, mention is made only of 'functionaries and public officers'; it has no bearing on the false identity of any other class of person."

Maxime re-read the paragraph, and saw that Desroches was right.

"Still," he remarked, "there must be something elsewhere to that effect?"

"Nothing of the kind; take my word for it as a lawyer; the Code is absolutely silent on that point."

"Then the crime we should inform against has the privilege of impunity?"

"That is to say," replied Desroches, "that its punishment is doubtful at best. A judge sometimes by induction extends the letter of the law——" He paused to turn over a volume of leading cases.

"Here, you see, reported in Carnot's *Commentaries on the Penal Code,* two judgments delivered at Assizes—one of July 7, 1814, and the other of April 24, 1818, both confirmed in the Court of Appeal, which condemned certain individuals who were neither functionaries nor public officers for assuming false names and identity; but these two verdicts, exceptional in every way, are based on a section in which this particular misdemeanor is not even mentioned, and it was only by very recondite argument that it was brought to bear on the cases. So you will understand that the outcome of such an action must always be doubtful, since, in the absence of any positive rule, it is impossible to say what the judges' decision may be."

"Consequently, it is your opinion, as it is Rastignac's, that we may send our countrywoman back to Romilly, and that there is nothing to be done?"

"There is always something to be done," replied Desroches, "when you know how to set about it. There is a further complication which does not seem to have occurred to you or Monsieur de Rastignac, or even to Monsieur Vinet; and that is that, apart from the legal point, you need authority from the Chamber before you can prosecute a member of the representative body in a criminal court."

"That is true," said Maxime; "but how does a further complication help us out of our difficulty?"

"You would not be sorry, I fancy," said the lawyer, laughing, "to send your enemy to the hulks?"

"A scoundrel," said Maxime, with a droll twinkle, "who has perhaps caused me to miss a good marriage, who sets up for austere virtue, and allows himself such audacious tricks——!"

"Well; you must, nevertheless, put up with some less showy revenge. If you create a scandal, throw utter discredit on your man—that, I suppose, would, to some extent, achieve your end?"

"No doubt; half a loaf is better than no bread."

"Your ideas thus reduced, this is what I should advise: Do not urge your woman to bring an action against this gentleman who annoys you so much, but get her to place a petition for authority to prosecute in the hands of the President of the Chamber. She will most probably not obtain it, and the affair will collapse at that stage; but the fact of the application will be rumored in the Chamber, the papers will have every right to mention it, and the Government will be free, behind the scenes, to add venom to the imputation by the comments of its supporters."

"*Peste!*" exclaimed Maxime, enchanted at seeing an outlet for his instincts of aversion, "you are a clever fellow—far cleverer than all your self-styled statesmen. But as to this petition for leave to prosecute, who can draw that up?"

"Not I," replied Desroches, who did not care to go any further in such dirty work. "What you want is not a judicial document, but a weapon, and that is no part of my business. But there are dozens of attorneys without clients who are always ready to put a finger into a political pie—Massol, for instance, will do your job as well as any man. But I particularly beg that you will not mention me as having originated the idea."

"Not a word," said Maxime. "I will take the responsibility, and in that shape, perhaps, Rastignac may at last swallow the scheme."

"Mind you do not make an enemy of Vinet, for he will think you have taken a great liberty in having thought of a thing that ought at once to have occurred to such a practised parliamentary tactician as he is."

"Oh, before very long," said Maxime, rising, "I hope that Vinet, Rastignac, and the rest well have to reckon with me. —Where are you dining to-night?" he added.

It is a question which one "man about town" often asks another.

"In a cave," said Desroches, "with the banditti."

"Where is it?"

"Why, in the course of your erotic experiences you have, no doubt, had recourse to the good offices of an old wardrobe-buyer named Madame de Saint-Estève?"

"No," said Maxime; "I always manage my own business."

"Ah, I was not thinking," said the lawyer. "You have always been a conqueror in high life, where such go-betweens are not employed. However, the woman's name is not unknown to you?"

"Quite true. Her shop is in the Rue Saint-Marc. It was she who brought about the meeting between Nucingen and that little slut Esther, who cost him something like five hundred thousand francs. She must be related to a villain of the same kidney who is at the head now of the detective force, and goes by the same name."

"That I do not know," replied Desroches. "But I can tell you this much: she made a fortune by her trade as dresser (*appareilleuse*, as it was called at a time when the world was less prudish than it is now), and to-day the worthy lady is magnificently housed in the Rue de Provence, where she is at the head of a matrimonial agency."

"And you are dining there?"

"Yes, my dear sir, with the manager of the Opera House in London, with Émile Blondet, Andoche Finot, Lousteau, Félicien Vernou, Théodore Gaillard, Hector Merlin, and Bixiou, who was instructed to invite me, because my experience and great knowledge of business are to be called into play."

"Bless me! is there some great financial enterprise at the back of that dinner?"

"A joint-stock undertaking, my dear friend, and a theatrical engagement, and I am to read through the two agreements. As regards the last, you understand that the distinguished guests invited to meet me will proceed to blow the trumpet as soon as the deed is signed."

"And who is the star whose engagement needs so much ceremony."

"Oh, a star who may look forward, it would seem, to European glory! An Italian woman discovered by a great Swedish nobleman, Count Halphertius, through the ministrations of Madame de Saint-Estève. To have her brought out on the opera stage in London, the illustrious stranger becomes a sleeping partner with the *Impresario* to the tune of a hundred thousand crowns."

"So the Swedish Count is marrying her?"

"H'm," said Desroches, "I have not as yet been asked to draw up the settlements. Madame de Saint-Estève, as you may suppose, still has some connection with the 'thirteenth *arrondissement*' in her agency business."

"Well, my good fellow, I hope you will enjoy the party," said Maxime, leaving. "If your star is a success in London, we shall probably see her in Paris this winter. I will be off to put a spoke, if I can, in the chariot wheels of the rising sun of Arcis.—By the way, where does Massol live?"

"On my word, I cannot tell you. I have never taken him a brief; I have no use for pleaders who meddle in politics; but you can send for his address to the office of the *Gazette des Tribunaux;* he writes for it, I know."

Maxime himself went to the office to ask where Massol lived; but the office-boy had strict orders not to give his address to anybody, probably with a view to the calls of duns; and in spite of his hectoring tone, Monsieur de Trailles had wasted his time, and could not obtain the information he had come for. He fortunately remembered that Massol rarely missed a performance at the Opera, and he felt tolerably certain of finding him in the lounging-room after dinner.

Before dinner, he went to call at some little furnished lodgings where he had housed the peasant woman and her lawyer, who had already come to Paris. He found them at table, and enjoying a capital dinner at the Beauvisages' expense. He desired them to come to him before breakfast, between eleven and twelve next morning. In the evening he met Massol, as he expected, at the Opera. Addressing him with his usual rather haughty politeness:

"I should like to talk with you, monsieur," said he, "over a partly legal and partly political matter. If it were not necessary to observe the strictest secrecy in every way, I would have had the honor of calling at your office, but I believe we shall discuss it in greater privacy at my house, where I can put you into direct communication with two interested persons. May I hope that you will give me the pleasure of taking a cup of tea with me to-morrow morning soon after eleven?"

If Massol had in fact boasted of an office, for the dignity of his robe he would perhaps not have consented to reverse the usual order of things by going to a client instead of receiving him at home. But as he perched rather than lodged in his room, he was glad of an arrangement which preserved the *incognito* of his residence.

"I shall have the honor of waiting on you to-morrow at the hour you name," he eagerly replied.

"You know," said Maxime, "the Rue Pigalle?"

"Perfectly," replied Massol, "close to the Rue de la Rochefoucauld."

On the evening when Sallenauve, Marie-Gaston, and Jacques Bricheteau had gone together to Saint-Sulpice to hear Signora Luigia sing, a little incident had occurred in the church which had scarcely been noticed. Through the little-used door, opening on the Rue Palatine, opposite the Rue Servandoni, a fair-haired youth hastily came in. He seemed so agitated and hurried that he even forgot to take off a cap of shiny leather, shaped like those worn by the students at German universities. As he pushed forward to where the crowd was thickest, he felt himself gripped by the arm, and his face, which was florid and rosy, turned lividly pale; but on turning round he saw that he had been alarmed without cause. It was only the *Suisse,* or beadle, who said in impressive tones:

"Young man, is your cap nailed to your head?"

"I beg pardon, monsieur," said the youth. "It was an oversight."

And after obeying this lesson in reverence, human and divine, he lost himself in the densest part of the crowd, through which he roughly made his way with his elbows, getting a few blows in return, about which he did not trouble himself. Having reached an open space, he looked round with a hasty, anxious eye; then leaving by the door on the side to the Rue Garancière, almost opposite to that he had come in by, he flew off at a great pace, and vanished down one of the deserted streets that lie about the Marché Saint-Germain.

A few seconds after the irruption of this strange worshiper, in at the same door came a man with a deeply-seamed face framed in white whiskers; thick hair, also white, but somewhat rusty, and falling to his shoulders, gave him the look of some old member of the Convention, or of Bernardin de Saint-Pierre after having the smallpox. The age of his face and hair was well past sixty; but his robust frame, the vigorous energy of his movements, and, above all, the piercing sharpness of the look he flashed all round the church as he came in, showed a strongly-knit nature, on which the advance of years had told but little.

He obviously was bent on following the light-haired youth, but he was not so clumsy as to rush after him through the mass of people in front of the high altar, in which, as he understood, the fugitive had tried to be lost. So, working round the building close to the wall, in a contrary direction, he had every chance of reaching the other door as soon as his prey; but, as has happened to many another, his cleverness played him a trick. As he passed a confessional, he perceived a kneeling form very like that of the man he was chasing. Attributing to him an ingenuity that would, no doubt, have been his in similar circumstances, it struck him that, to put him off the scent, his escaped victim had suddenly thrown himself on the penitential tribunal. In the time it took him to make sure of the man's identity, which as we know was not confirmed, he was outstripped. So practised a hunter at once gave up the useless chase; he understood that the game was up for to-day, and he had missed his chance.

He too was about to leave the church, when, after a brief prelude on the organ, Signora Luigia's contralto voice in a few deep notes began the glorious melody to which the *Litanies to the Virgin* are sung. The beauty of her voice, the beauty of the strain, the beauty of the words of that sacred hymn, which her admirable style gave out with perfect distinctness, seemed to impress this strange man deeply. Far from leaving, as he had intended, he took his stand in the shadow of a pillar, not looking for a seat; but at the moment when the last notes of the canticle died away, he had fallen on his knees, and any one looking at his face would have seen that two large tears were trickling down his cheeks.

The *Benedicite* having been pronounced, and the greater part of the crowd having left the church:

"What a fool I am!" said he, as he rose and wiped his eyes.

He went out by the same door as he had come in by, turning up the Rue Servandoni, paused for a moment in front of a closed shop, went on to the Place Saint-Sulpice, and getting into one of the hackney cabs that stood there, he said to the driver:

"Rue de Provence, and look sharp, my good fellow. It will be worth your while."

On reaching the house where he stopped the coach, he ran past the gatekeeper's lodge and made for the backstairs, not wishing to be seen; but the porter, who was conscientious in the discharge of his duty, came to his door and called after him:

"Pray, where are you going, sir?"

"To Madame de Saint-Estève," replied the visitor in a tone of annoyance.

Immediately after he rang at a back door, which was opened by a negro.

"Is my aunt in?" he asked.

"Oh yes, Missy at home," replied the black man, putting on the most gracious smile he could command, which made him look like an ape cracking nuts.

Making his way along the passages, which gave an idea of the extent of the apartments, the newcomer reached the drawing-room door; the negro threw it open, announcing "Monsieur Saint-Hèsteve," with a violent aspirate.

The head of the detective police went into a room remarkable for it magnificence, but yet more so for the extraordinary bad taste of the furniture. Three women of venerable antiquity were sitting at a round table, solemnly playing dominoes. Three glasses, a silver bowl drained empty, and a vinous perfume that was unpleasantly conspicuous on coming into the room, showed that the worship of the double-sixes was not the only cultus solemnized there.

"Good-evening, ladies," said the great man, taking a chair, "I am glad to find you all together, for I have something to say to each of you."

"We will listen presently," said his aunt; "let us finish the game. I am playing for fours."

"Double-blank," said one of the antiquities.

"Domino!" cried Madame de Saint-Estève, "and game. You two must certainly have four points between you, and all the blanks are out."

So speaking, she put out a bony hand to take the punch-ladle and fill the glasses; but finding the bowl empty, instead of rising to pull the bell, she rang a peal with the spoon in the silver bason. The negro came in.

"Have something put into that," said she, handing it to him; "and bring a glass for monsieur."

"Thanks; I will take nothing," said Saint-Estève.

"I have had a sufficiency," said one of the old ladies.

"And I have been put upon milk," said the other, "by the doctor, on account of my gastripes."

"You are all milksops together," said the mistress of the house.—"Here, clear all this away," said she to the negro; "and, above all, don't let me catch you listening at the door! You remember the clawing you got?"

"Oh yes—I 'member," said the man, his shoulders shaking with laughter—"me got no ears now."

And he went away.

"Well, Tommy, it is your turn now," said the old aunt to Saint-Estève, after a stormy settlement of accounts between the three witches.

"You, Madame Fontaine," said the head detective, turning to one of them, who by her fly-away looks, her disorderly gray hair and her frightfully crooked green silk bonnet, might have been taken for a blue-stocking in labor with an article on the fashions, "you forget yourself too much; you never send us in any report, while, on the contrary, we hear too many reports about you. Monsieur le Préfet does not at all care for establishments of your class. I only keep you going for the sake of the services you are supposed to do us; but without pretending, as you do, to look into the future, I can positively predict that if you continue to afford us so little information, your fortune-telling shop will be shut before long."

"There you go!" retorted the pythoness. "You prevented my taking the rooms Mademoiselle Lenormand had in the Rue de Tournon. Who do you suppose will come to me in the Rue Vieille-du-Temple? Poor clerks, cooks, laborers, and apprentice girls! And you want me to go tattling to you of what I pick up from such folks? You should have let me work on a large scale, and you would have got more information."

"Madame Fontaine, you didn't ought to say that," said Madame de Saint-Estève; "why, I send some of my customers to you most days."

"Not more than I send you mine!"

"And not above four days since," the matrimonial agent went on, "that Italian woman went to you from me. She is not a milliner's apprentice, she is not; and she lives with a deputy who is against the Government! You might have reported that. But you do not care to use your pen; and since you quarreled with your little counter-jumper for having too many waistcoats from the tailor, no more writing for you!"

"There is one thing in particular," said the detective, "which is constantly mentioned in the reports that reach me about you—that foul creature you make use of in your divinations——"

"Who? Ashtaroth?" asked Madame Fontaine.

"Yes; that batrachian, that toad, to speak plainly, whom you pretend to consult. A little while since it would seem a woman was so upset by his horrible appearance that she——"

"There, there," the fortune-teller broke in, "if I am to do nothing now but read the cards, you may as well ruin me at once—cut my throat and have done with it! Because a woman has a still-born child, are you going to get rid of toads altogether in this world? If so, what did God create them for?"

"My dear madame," said the man, "there was a time when you would have been less partial to such help. In 1617 a philosopher named Vanini was burned at Toulouse solely because he kept a toad in a bottle."

"Ay, but we live in an age of enlightenment," said Madame Fontaine cheerfully, "and the police are not so hard upon us."

"You, Madame Nourrisson," said the detective, turning to the other old woman, "pick the fruit too green, I am told. Having kept shop so long as you have, you must be well aware of the laws and regulations, and I am surprised at having to remind you that morals must be respected—under one-and-twenty."

Madame Nourrisson had, in fact, been, under the Empire, what Parent du Châtelet (whose work is such a curious study of the great plague of prostitution) euphemistically called a *Dame de Maison*. She had afterwards set up in the Rue Neuve-Saint-Marc the shop for buying and selling old clothes, where the business of Esther had been managed, to which Maxime de Trailles had referred as having cost Nucingen the banker more than five hundred thousand francs. But on that occasion Madame Nourrisson had screened herself behind Madame Saint-Estève; and she, advised by Vautrin in conducting the affair, had for the time used the old clothes-dealer's shop as the headquarters of her operations. Between persons who have memories of such complicity, extreme familiarity is a foregone conclusion; so it is not surprising that Madame Nourrisson should retort on Saint-Estève for the lecture he had given her:

"And you, you great bully, you respected morality, I supposed when, in 1809, you placed that girl of seventeen from Champagne in my care——!"

"If it is thirty years since that folly was committed in my name," replied the man, "that is thirty years' record in my favor; for it was the last into which I was ever drawn by a petticoat. However, dear ladies, you can make such use as you please of my warnings. If mischief overtakes you, you cannot now complain that you had not due notice.

"As to you, my little aunt, what I have to say to you is private and confidential."

At this hint the other two prepared to leave.

"Shall I send for a cab for you?" Madame de Saint-Estève asked Madame Fontaine.

"No, indeed," said the fortune-teller. "I am going to walk; I am told to take exercise. I told my forewoman, Ma'am Jamouillot, to come for me."

"And you, Madame Nourrisson?"

"That's a good 'un!" said the woman. "A cab to go from the Rue de Provence to the Rue Neuve-Saint-Marc! Why, we are quite near neighbors."

In point of fact, the old-clothes woman had come in every-day attire: a white cap with yellow ribbons, a patent front of jet black curls, a black silk apron, and a cotton print gown with a dark blue ground; and, as she said facetiously, it was most unlikely that any one should want to run away with her.

Before reporting the interview now about to take place between Monsieur de Saint-Estève and his aunt, some explanations must find a place here.

In this public protector, who on the evening of the outbreak on the 12th of May had offered his services to Rastignac, every reader will have recognized the notorious Jacques Collin, *alias* Vautrin, one of the most familiar and elaborately drawn figures of the HUMAN COMEDY.

A little while before the revolution of 1830, this hero of the hulks, very hard hit by the death of a friend, lost heart to carry on the struggle he had maintained for five-and-twenty years against society, and had given in his resignation, so to speak, to Monsieur de Granville, the Attorney-General, under somewhat dramatic circumstances. Since that time he had succeeded the famous Bibi-Lupin as head of the detective police force, under the name of Monsieur de Saint-Estève; he was now the terror of those who had formerly been his accomplices; and by the unrelenting persecution by which he harried them, he had acquired a reputation for skill and energy which remains unmatched in the annals of the criminal police.

But, as he had told his old friend Colonel Franchessini, he was tired of this perpetual thief-hunting; there was no longer any hazard or anything unforeseen in the game; and, like a too experienced gambler, he had ceased to take an interest in it. For some years there had been still some spice in the business, and that had given him endurance from the endless attacks and ambushes planned against him by his old *chums* on the hulks, who were furious at what they called his treason; but by this time his cleverness and his good luck, which had always protected him from their conspiracies, had discouraged his foes, and they had laid down their arms. Since then his duties had lost all their charm; he was anxious to change his sphere of employment and transfer his marvelous instincts as a spy and his indefatigable energy to that of politics.

Colonel Franchessini had taken care to see him again after his visit to Rastignac; and his old fellow-boarder at Madame Vauquier's was not the man to underestimate the purport of the Minister's views as to the luxury of such a plain citizen life as he had suggested to cast oblivion on the odious past that weighed on him.

"Haha!" said he, "the pupil then has outstripped his master! His advice deserves consideration; I will think about it."

In fact, he had thought about it, and it was under the influence of much meditation and careful examination of the scheme proposed to him that he had now come to see his aunt Jacqueline Collin—otherwise known as Madame de Saint-Estève—an *alias* they had agreed to adopt, which, while masking the past history of this formidable pair, marked their close relationship.

Jacqueline Collin herself, besides taking an active part in many of her nephew's enterprises, had led an adventurous life; and on one of the many occasions when Vautrin found himself at variance with the law, an examining judge had thus summed up the antecedent history of this much-respected aunt, from certain data furnished by the police, of which there is no reason to doubt the accuracy:—

"She is, it would seem, an extremely cunning receiver of stolen goods—for no proof can be brought against her. She is said to have been Murat's mistress, and after his death she lived with a chemist, executed in the year VIII. (1799) as a false coiner. She was witness at the trial. While with him she acquired much dangerous knowledge of poisons. From the year IX. till 1805, she dealt in old clothes. She was in prison for two years, 1807-8, for entrapping girls under age.

"You, Jacques Collin, were at that time on your trial for forgery; you had left the banking house where your aunt had apprenticed you as clerk under favor of the education you had received and the influence she could wield over persons for whose depravity she had entrapped victims."

Since the time when this edifying biography had been placed in her nephew's hands, Jacqueline Collin, without falling again into the clutches of the public prosecutor, had enlarged her borders; and when Vautrin renounced the ways of wickedness, she was far from assuming an equally immaculate garb of innocence. But having—as he had—made a great deal of money, she would now pick and choose; she had kept at a safe distance from the arm of the law; and under the pretence of a more or less decent line of business, she had carried on certain underground practices, to which she devoted really diabolical intelligence and energy.

We have already learned from Desroches that the more or less matrimonial agency managed by Madame de Saint-Estève was situated in the Rue de Provence; and we may add that it was carried on on an extensive scale, occupying all the first floor of one of the enormous houses which Paris builders raise from the earth as if by magic. They are scarcely finished, and never free from debt, when they are filled with tenants, at any price, while waiting for a buyer to whom they are sold out of hand. If the builder finds a fool to deal with, he does a fine stroke of business; if, on the other hand, the purchaser is a tough customer, the builder has to be content with recovering his outlay, with a few thousand francs as interest; unless, while the work is going on, the speculation has been hampered by one of those bankruptcies which in the building trade are among the commonest and most familiar complications.

Women of the town, business agents, still-born insurance companies, newspapers fated to die young, the offices of impossible railway companies, discount brokers who borrow instead of lending, advertisement agents, who lack the publicity they profess to sell; in short, all descriptions of shy or doubtful enterprise and trade combine to provide the temporary inhabitants of these republics.

They are built merely for show, *run up* with perfect in-difference to the fact that in the course of a few months settlement will hinder the windows from opening, warping will split the doors, the seams of the flooring will yawn, the drains, gutter-pipes, and sinks will leak, and the whole card-board structure be uninhabitable. That is the purchaser's business; and he, after patching the house up, is at liberty to be more fastidious in the choice of his tenants, and to raise the rents.

Madame de Saint-Estève having taken possession of her first floor before the stage of early decay had set in, had se-cured a very comfortable tenement at a low rent; and the best success, to say nothing of her profits from other unconfessed sources, crowned the efforts of her skilful management. It need hardly be said that Madame de Saint-Estève, regarding the display of advertisement as beneath her notice, left it to her rivals, and never flaunted her *office* on the fourth page of a newspaper. This haughtiness, which, in view of the dark passages of her early life, was but prudent, had led to her discovering some other ingenious and less vulgar methods for attracting attention to her *agency*. In the country, and even abroad, she would employ certain clever commercial travelers, who cautiously distributed a circular drawn up by Gaudissart, one of the most remarkable puff-writers of mod-ern times.

The ostensible object of this document was to offer the as-sistance of a strictly commercial agency through which, on the most moderate terms, wedding outfits and presents could be procured from Paris, suitable to every fortune or sum in set-tlement. It was only as a modest *N.B.*, after an estimate of cost of the objects commonly included in such lists, divided, somewhat like an undertaker's prospectus, into first, second, third, and fourth classes, that Madame de Saint-Estève hinted at her "being enabled, through her high social con-nections, to facilitate introductions between persons wishing to marry."

In Paris the lady herself appealed to public credulity, and

her means were as ingenious as they were various. She made a bargain with a job-master, who sent two or three decent-looking carriages to stand for hours at her door. Then, in her waiting-room, supposed clients of both sexes, well dressed, and affecting great impatience, took it in turns to come in and out, so as to suggest a constant crowd; and, as may be supposed, the conversation of these confederates—who pretended not to know each other—expatiated in suitable terms on the merits and superior adroitness of Madame de Saint-Estève.

The ingenious adventuress, by some donations to the poor, and to the charities of Notre-Dame de Lorette, her parish, got an occasional call from a priest, which was at once a voucher of respectability and of the genuineness of her matrimonial undertakings. Another of her ingenious tricks was to keep herself supplied by the market-woman with lists of all the fashionable weddings in Paris, and to be seen in the church very handsomely dressed, arriving in a carriage with men-servants, so as to allow it to be inferred that she had had something to do with bringing about the union she had honored with her presence.

On one occasion, however, a not very tolerant family objected to the idea of serving her purpose of advertisement, and had treated her with contumely; so she was now cautious as to how she tried this plan for which she had substituted a system of rumor less compulsory and far less dangerous. Having known Madame Fontaine for many years—for there is a natural affinity among all these underground traffickers—she had plotted with her for a sort of reciprocal insurance company for working on the credulity of the Parisians; and between these two hags the terms were thus arranged: when a woman goes to have her fortune told, at least eight times out of ten her curiosity turns on the question of marriage. So when the sorceress announced to one of her fair clients in time-honored phraseology, that she would ere long meet her fate in the person of a light-haired or a dark-haired man, she took care to add: "But the union can only be brought about through the agency of Madame de Saint-Estève, a very rich and highly respectable woman, living in the Rue de Provence Chaussée-d'Antin, who has a passion for match-making." While Madame de Saint-Estève on her part, when she proposed a match, if she thought there was any chance of thus promoting its success, would say: "But go at any rate and consult the famous Madame Fontaine as to the outcome of the negotiation—Rue Vieille-du-Temple—her reputation as a fortune-teller by the cards is European; she never makes a mistake; and if she tells you that I have made a good hit, you may conclude the bargain in perfect confidence."

It may easily be understood that the Numa of the Rue Sainte-Anne should have taken so resourceful a woman for his Egeria.

Rastignac's informant had not been quite correct in saying that the aunt and nephew lived together; but it was perfectly true that Vautrin, when business allowed of it, never passed a day without coming, as mysteriously as possible, to visit his respectable relation. For many years, if any serious incident occurred in his life, Jacqueline Collin had a finger in it as his adviser, and often as his active assistant.

"My dear granny!" said Vautrin, to begin the conversation for which he had come, "I have so many things to tell you that I do not know where to begin."

"I believe you—why, I have not seen you for nearly a week."

"To begin with, I may as well tell you that I just missed a splendid stroke of business."

"What sort?" asked Jacqueline Collin.

"Oh, all in the way of my vile trade. But this time the game was worth the trouble.—Do you remember that little Prussian engraver about whom I sent you to Berlin?"

"Who forged the Vienna banknotes in such an astounding manner?" said the aunt, finishing the story.

"Well, not an hour ago in the Rue Servandoni, where I had been to see one of my men who is on the sick list, passing by a greengrocer's shop, I fancied I recognized my man buying a slice of Brie cheese. which was being wrapped in paper."

"It would seem that he is not much the richer then, for all he knows so much about banknotes——"

"My first thought," Vautrin went on, "was to rush into the shop—the door was shut—and to collar my rogue; but, not having seen his face very close, I was afraid of being mistaken. He, it would seem, had kept a lookout; he saw some one spying him through the window, and presto! he vanished into the back-shop, and I saw him no more——"

"Then, old boy, that is what comes of wearing long hair and a beard all round your chin. The game scents you a hundred yards away!"

"But then, as you know, my fancy for being easily recognized is what most impresses my customers. 'He must be jolly well sure of himself,' they say, 'never to want any disguise!'—Nothing has done so much to make me popular."

"Well," said Jacqueline, "so your man was in the back-shop."

"I hastily took stock of the premises," Vautrin went on. "The shop was on one side of an arched entry; at the bottom of the entry the door was open to a courtyard, into which there would be a door from the back-shop; consequently, unless the fellow lived in the house, I was in command of all the exits. I waited about a quarter of an hour; it is a long time when you are waiting. I looked into the shop in vain, no sign of him. Three customers went in; the woman served them without seeming to be aware of any one keeping an eye on her, she never gave a glance one way or the other, or seemed at all on the watch. 'Well!' said I to myself at last, 'he must be a lodger; if not, the woman would certainly have been more puzzled at his going out the back way.' So I determined to drop in and ask a question or two. Pff! I had scarcely crossed the threshold when I heard steps in the street—the bird had flown."

"You were in too great a hurry, my dear. And yet, only the other day you said to me—'Police spells patience.'"

"Without waiting for further information," said Vautrin, "I was off in pursuit. Exactly facing the Rue Servandoni—

the name of the architect who built Saint Sulpice—there is
a door into the church, which was open because of the month
of Mary, service being held there every afternoon. My rascal
having the advantage of me, flew through this door, and was
so effectually lost in the crowd, that when I went in I could
nowhere find him."

"Well," said the woman, "I cannot be sorry that the rascal
stole a march on you. I always feel some interest in a
smasher. Coining is a neat sort of crime, and clean; no
blood spilt, no harm done but to that mean hunks the Government."

"And the Frankfort house that was ruined by his for-
geries."

"You may say what you like; it is better form than your
Lucien de Rubempré, who ate us out of house and home.
Now, if you had but had a lad like this under your thumb
in our best days!——"

"In spite of your admiration, you will have to go to-morrow and pick up some information from the greengrocer
woman, who must certainly know him, since she winked at
his escape. When I went back to the shop I found shutters
and doors all shut up. I had lost some time in the
church——"

"Listening to a singer, I bet," interrupted the aunt.

"Quite true. How did you know?"

"Why, all Paris is crowding to hear her," replied Jacqueline
Collin, "and I know her too, in my own little way."

"What! That voice that touched me so deeply, that took
me back fifty years to my first communion under the good
Oratorian fathers, who brought me up—that woman who
made me cry, and transformed me for five minutes into a
saint—and you have her on your books——?"

"Yes," said Madame de Saint-Estève carelessly, "I have a
transaction on hand for her: I am getting her on to the stage."

"Aha! So you are a dramatic agent too? Matrimony is
not enough?"

"This is the case in two words, my boy. She is an Italian,

as handsome as can be, come from Rome with an idiot of a
sculptor, whom she worships without his suspecting it. Indeed, this Joseph cares so little about her, that after using her
as his model for a statue, he has never yet been at the pains
to be more than civil."

"That is a man who ought to do well in his art," remarked
Jacques Collin, "with such a contempt for women and so
much strength of mind."

"And the proof of that," replied Jacqueline, "is that he has
just given his art up to become a member of the Chamber.
It was about him that I said to old Fontaine that she might
have found something to write to you. I sent my Italian to
her, and she told the cards as regards this ice-bound lover."

"And how did you come to know the woman?"

"Through old Ronquerolles. Having gone to see the
sculptor one day, in the matter of a duel in which he was
second, he saw this jewel of a woman, and became quite Nucingen about her."

"And you undertook the negotiations?"

"As you say. It was above a month ago, and the poor man
had had all his pains for nothing. Now I, having the matter
in hand, made inquiries; I found out that the beauty was a
member of the Sisters of the Virgin; thereupon I called on
her as a *Dame de Charité,* and imagine what luck for me as
a beginning—the sculptor was in the country getting himself
elected——"

"I have no fears about you; at the same time, a lady of
charity who undertakes a theatrical agency——!"

"By the time I had seen her twice she had told me all her
little secrets," the old woman went on. "That she could no
longer bear life with that man of marble; that she was determined to owe nothing to him; and that having studied for the
stage, if she could only secure an engagement, she would run
away. So one day I went off to her and arrived quite out of
breath to tell her that a friend of mine—a great lord, highly
respectable, old, virtuous—to whom I had spoken of her,
would undertake to get her an opening, and I asked her to let
me take him to see her."

"A word and a blow!" said Jacques Collin.

"Yes; but she, a devil for suspiciousness, and less bent on deserting her sculptor than she had thought, kept me, shilly-shally, from day to day. So at last, to give her a shove, I hinted that she should go to consult old Fontaine, as indeed she was ready enough to do. But even now, in spite of the cards, she is still very wide awake, and the job is spoiling, I fear, for she has seen her man again; he has come back elected.

"It is of no use to talk; I must proceed with caution. If he should make difficulties about our enticing away the woman, whom he would perhaps think he wanted as soon as she ceased to want him, he would hold a very strong hand. And that selfish old brute Ronquerolles, who is only a member of the Upper House, would not be much protection against a deputy of the Chamber——"

"That old rip Ronquerolles is not the man for that woman," said Jacques Collin. "If she is an honest woman, we must keep her so. I know a really respectable man who will get her on to the stage on honorable terms, and secure her a splendid position without asking for anything in return."

"What! you know of any such phenomenon? I should be truly glad to have his address; I would leave a card on him."

"All right—Petite Rue Sainte-Anne, Quai des Orfèvres; you will find a man there of your acquaintance."

"Are you guying me?" cried the woman, who in her astonishment fell back on the low slang which she had spoken so fluently of yore.

"No, I am quite serious. That woman touched me; she interests me; and I have another reason——"

Vautrin then related his proceedings with regard to Rastignac, Colonel Franchessini's intervention, the Minister's reply, and his transcendental theories of social reorganization.

"And that little ape thinks he can teach us!" exclaimed the aunt.

"He is in the right," said Vautrin, "only the woman was wanting; you have found her for me."

"Yes, but it will be sheer ruination."

"And for whom are we saving? We have no heirs, and I do not suppose you feel urgently drawn to found a hospital, or prizes for distinguished merit?"

"I am not such a softhead," replied the woman. "Besides, as you know, my Jacques, I have never kept an account against you. Still, I foresee one difficulty: this woman is as proud as a Roman—which she is, and your confounded duties——"

"There, you see," Jacques Collin eagerly put in, "I must at any price escape from a life where one is liable to such insults. But be easy; I can avert this particular offence. My business justifies me in playing every part in turn; and, as you will remember, I am not a bad actor. I may put a whole rainbow of orders in my button-hole to-morrow and take a house in any aristocratic name I may choose to assume. The fun of the carnival lasts all the year round for a detective.

"I had already hit on a plan. I know the man I mean to be. You may tell your Italian that Count Halphertius—a great Swedish lord, crazy about music and philanthropy—takes a great interest in her advancement. In point of fact, I will furnish a house for her; I will strictly observe the virtuous disinterestedness to which you may pledge me; in short, I will be her recognized patron. As to the engagement she wishes for, I wish it too; for my own future purpose I want her to be glorious and brilliant; and we are not Jacques and Jacquelin Collin if, with her gifts and our gold and determination, we fail in making her so."

"But then comes the question whether Rastignac will think you have won; it was Monsieur de Saint-Estève, the head of the detective police, that he told you to whitewash."

"Not at all, old lady. There is no such person as Saint-Estève, no Jacques Collin, no Vautrin, no Trompe-la-Mort, no Carlos Herrera; there is a remarkably powerful mind, strong and vigorous, offering its services to the Government. I am bringing it from the North, and christening it with a foreign name, and this makes me all the better fitted for the political and diplomatic police whose functions I henceforth intend to exercise."

"You forge ahead! it is wonderful. But first we must catch the jewel who is to make such a show for you, and we have not got her yet."

"That is no difficulty; I have seen you at work, and when you will you can."

"I will try," said Jacqueline Collin diffidently. "Come and see me again to-morrow night, at any rate; perhaps I may have something to show."

"And meanwhile do not forget the greengrocer's shop in the Rue Servandoni, No. 12, where you are to make inquiries. That capture, as being important to a foreign government, has a political air about it that would be of service towards helping me to my end."

"I will give you a good account of the shopwoman, never fear," said Jacqueline. "But the other affair is rather more ticklish; we must not handle it roughly."

"You have a free hand," replied Vautrin. "I have always found you equal to any undertaking, however difficult. So good-bye till to-morrow."

On the following day Vautrin was sitting in his office in the Petite Rue Sainte-Anne when he received the following note:

"You are not much to be pitied, old boy; everything is working out as you want it. Early this morning I was told that a lady wished to speak to me. Who should come in but our Italian, to whom I had given my address in case she should need me in a hurry. Her Joseph having spoken last evening, in cheerful terms, of his intention that they should part company, the poor dear had not closed her eyes all night, and her little brain is in such a pother that she came straight to me, begging me to introduce her to my respectable friend, in whose hands she is prepared to place herself if he is to be trusted, because she feels it a point of honor to owe nothing more to that icicle who can disdain her.—So come at once in the new skin you have chosen, and then it is your business to make your way to the charmer's good graces.

"Your affectionate aunt,

"J. C. DE SAINT-ESTÈVE."

Vautrin replied:

"I will be with you this evening at nine. I hope the change in my decorative treatment will be so handsome that if I had not told you the name I shall assume, you would find it difficult to recognize me. I have already taken steps in the matter of the engagement, and can speak of it in such a way that the charmer will form a good idea of her *Papa's* influence.

"Sell some stock out in the course of the day for a rather considerable sum; we must have ready money; I, on my part, will do the same.—Till this evening,

"Your nephew and friend,

"SAINT-ESTÈVE."

That evening, punctual to the hour he had fixed, Vautrin went to his aunt's rooms. On this occasion he went up the main staircase, and was announced as Monsieur le Comte Halphertius by the negro, who did not recognize him.

Warned though she was of his metamorphosis, Jacqueline stood in amazement at this really great actor, who was altogether another man. His long hair, *à la* Franklin, was now short and curled and powdered; his eyebrows and whiskers, cutlet-shaped, in the style of the Empire, were dyed dark brown, in strong contrast with the powdered wig; and a false moustache of the same hue gave his not naturally noble features a stamp of startling originality, which might, by a stretch of imagination, be called distinction. A black satin stock gave deportment to his head. He wore a blue tail-coat, buttoned across, and in one button-hole an inch of ribbon displayed the colors of half the orders of Europe. A nankeen waistcoat, visible below the coat-front, effected a harmonious transition to pearl-gray trousers; patent leather boots and lemon kid gloves completed the "get-up," which aimed at careless elegance. The powder, of which the last wearers could now easily be counted, gave the crowning touch to an old foreign diplomate, and a very happy sobriety to a costume which, but for that corrective, might have appeared too juvenile.

After giving a few minutes to admiration of his disguise, Vautrin asked his aunt:

"Is she here?"

"Yes," said Jacqueline. "The angel retired to her room half an hour ago to tell her beads, now that she is deprived of attending the services of the month of Mary. But she impatiently awaits your visit, seeing how I have sung your praises all day."

"And what does she think of your house? Does she repent of the step she has taken?"

"Her pride would in any case be too great to allow of her showing such a feeling. Besides, I have cleverly won her confidence, and she is one of those persons who are determined never to look back when once they have started."

"The best of the joke," said Vautrin, "is that her Deputy, who is worried about her, was sent to me by Monsieur le Préfet that I might help him to find her."

"He wants her, then?"

"He is not in love with her, you understand, but he considered her as being in his care, and he was afraid that she might have taken it into her head to kill herself, or might have fallen into the hands of some intriguing woman. And you know that, but for my fatherly intervention, he would have laid his finger on the spot."

"And what did you say to your flat?"

"Oh, of course I allowed him to hope, but really and truly I was sorry not to be able to do what he asked me. I took a fancy to him at once; he has a pleasant way with him, energetic and clever, and it strikes me that our friends the Ministry will find him a pretty tough customer."

"So much the worse for him; he should not have driven the dear child to extremities," said the aunt. "And the engagement, for which you said you had the irons in the fire?"

"You know what a queer thing luck is, my beauty," replied Vautrin, taking out a newspaper. "Good or bad, it always comes in squalls. This morning, after receiving your letter, which brought me such good news, I opened this theatrical journal and read this paragraph: 'The Italian opera season in London, which began so badly by the lawsuit that brought to light the pecuniary difficulties under which Sir Francis Drake's management is struggling, seems still further embarrassed by the serious illness of la Serboni, necessitating her absence from the stage for an indefinite period. Sir Francis arrived yesterday at the *Hôtel des Princes,* Rue de Richelieu, having come in search of two *desiderata*—a prima donna and some funds. But the hapless impresario is moving in a vicious circle; for without money no prima donna, and without a prima donna no money.

"'We may hope, however, that he will escape from this deadlock; for Sir Francis Drake has a character for being honest and intelligent, and with such a reputation he will surely not find every door closed against him.'"

"Men of the world are your journalists!" said the old aunt with a knowing air. "Is every door to be thrown open because a man is honest and intelligent?"

"In the present case," said Vautrin, "the phrase is not so far wrong; for the moment I had read the article I figged myself out, as you see, took a private fly, and went off to the address given.

"'Sir Francis Drake?' I ask.

"'I do not know whether he can see you, sir,' says the gentleman's gentleman, coming forward; he was there, I strongly suspect, to give the same answer to any one who might call. 'He is with the Baron de Nucingen.'

"I made believe to look through a pocket-book well stuffed with banknotes for a card, which, of course, I had not got.

"'Well,' said I, with a slight German accent and a sprinkling of Germanisms, 'I am Count Halphertius, a Swedish gentleman. Tell Sir Francis Drake I had come for to discuss some business. I shall go to the Bourse, where I give some orders to my broker, and I shall come back after a half-hour.'

"Saying this in the most lordly tone, I went back to my carriage. I had hardly set foot on the step when the lackey, running after me, said he had made a mistake; that Monsieur de Nucingen was gone, and his master could see me at once."

"Trying their games on us!" said Jacqueline Collin, with a shrug.

"Sir Francis Drake," Vautrin went on, "is a regular Englishman, very bald, with a red nose, and large prominent yellow teeth. He received me with frigid politeness, and asked me in good French what my business was.

" 'Just now,' said I, 'at the Café de Paris, I read this,' and I handed him the paper, pointing to the place.

" 'It is inconceivable,' said he, returning me the newspaper, 'that a man's credit should be thus cried down publicly.'

" 'The journalist is wrong? You have no want of money?'

" 'You may imagine, monsieur, that I should not in any case try to obtain it through the medium of a theatrical journal.'

" 'Very good! Then have we nothing to talk about?' said I, rising. 'I come to put some money in your business.'

" 'I would rather you had a prima donna to offer me!' said he.

" 'I offer you both,' said I, sitting down again. 'One not without the other.'

" 'A well-known talent?' asked the impresario.

" 'Not at all known,' replied I. 'Never seen yet at any theatre.'

" 'Hum—risky,' said the gentleman with a cunning look. 'The protectors of youthful talent often make great mistakes.'

" 'But I offer you a hundred thousand crowns—as an investment—for you only for to listen to my nightingale.'

" 'That would be a large sum for so little trouble, and but a small one as a help to my management if it were in such difficulties as your paper says.'

" 'Well, then, hear us for nothing; if we are what you want, and you make a handsome offer, I will put down twice so much.'

" 'You speak with a freedom that invites confidence; from what country is your young *prima?'*

" 'Roman—of Rome—a pure-bred Italian, and very handsome. You may believe if I am interested in her; I went mad about her, only for that I had heard her a long way off in a church. I did not see her till afterwards.'

" 'But it strikes me,' said the Englishman, 'that women do not sing in church in Italy.' "

"Well!" said Madame de Saint-Estève, "are there churches nowhere but in Italy?"

"Precisely," said Vautrin. "I felt that to give some appearance of reality to my disguise and my proceedings, I must assume some suspicion of eccentricity; so seizing the opportunity of getting up a German quarrel:

" 'I beg to remark, monsieur,' said I in a very pugnacious tone, 'that you have done me the honor to give me the lie.'

" 'What!' said the Englishman in amazement, 'nothing could be further from my thoughts.'

" 'It is plainly so, all the same,' said I. 'I tell you, I heard the signora in church; you say, "Women do not sing in church in Italy"—that is so much as to say I shall not have heard her.'

" 'But you *may* have heard her in another country.'

" 'You should have thought of that,' said I, in the same quarrelsome tone, 'before you made that remark—extraordinary remark. At any rate, I see we shall not agree. The signora can wait till the Italian Opera opens in Paris in October. Artists get much better known here. So, Monsieur Drake, I wish you a good-morning.' And I really seemed about to leave."

"Well played!" said his aunt.

In all the most risky affairs undertaken by them in common, they had always duly considered the artistic side.

"Well, to make a long story short," said Vautrin, "having thus brought my man to the sticking-point, we parted on these terms—I am to put down a hundred thousand crowns in money, the signora gets fifty thousand francs for the remainder of the season, supposing her voice is satisfactory; and, to judge of her quality, we are to meet to-morrow at two o'clock at Pape's, where Sir Francis Drake will have brought two or three friends to assist him, to whose presence I have consented. We are to be supposed to have gone to choose a piano. I said, just to keep up the game, that the lady might be terrified at the solemnity of a formal hearing, and that we are more sure in this way of knowing what she can really do."

"But I say, old boy," said Jacqueline, "a hundred thousand crowns is a lot of money!"

"Just the sum that I inherited from that poor boy Lucien de Rubempré," said Vautrin carelessly. "However, I have gone into the matter. Sir Francis Drake, with some one to back him, may have a very good season.—There is my secretary, Théodore Calvi, who is mine for life or death. He is very alert on all questions of interest. I have secured him the place of cashier, and he will keep an eye on the partner's profits. Now, there is but one thing that I am anxious about. Signora Luigia moved me deeply, but I am no connoisseur; artists may not think of her as I do."

"Artists have pronounced on her, my ducky; her sculptor never thought of giving her the key of the fields till she had been heard by a certain Jacques Bricheteau, an organist and a first-rate musician. They were at Saint-Sulpice the very evening of your pious fit, and the organist declared that the woman had sixty thousand francs in her voice whenever she pleased—those were his words."

"Jacques Bricheteau!" said Vautrin; "why, I know the man. There is a fellow of that name employed in one of the police departments."

"Well, then," said his aunt, "it is your nightingale's good fortune to be under the protection of the police!"

"No, I remember," said Vautrin. "This Jacques Bricheteau was an inspector of nuisances, who has just been dismissed for meddling in politics. Well, now, suppose you were to effect the introduction. It is late."

Jacqueline Collin had hardly left the room to go for Luigia, when there was a great commotion in the ante-room leading to it. Immediately after, the door was thrown open, and in spite of a desperate resistance on the part of the negro, who had been expressly ordered to admit nobody whatever, in came a personage whose advent was, to say the least, inopportune, if not altogether unexpected. In spite of an insolently aristocratic demeanor, the newcomer, caught in his violence by a stranger, was for a moment disconcerted, and Vautrin was malicious enough to intensify the situation by saying with Teutonic bluntness:

"Monsieur is an intimate friend of Madame de Saint-Estève's?"

"I have something of importance to say to her," replied the intruder, "and that servant is such an ass that he cannot tell you plainly whether his mistress is at home or out."

"I can bear witness that she is out," replied the supposed Count Halphertius. "For more than an hour I have wait for to see her, by her own appointment. She is a flighty thing, and I believe she is gone to the theatre, for what her nephew have sent her a ticket, the negro told me."

"At whatever hour she may come in I must see her," said the newcomer, taking an easy-chair, into which he settled himself.

"For me, I wait no longer," replied Vautrin.

And, having bowed, he prepared to leave. Then Madame de Saint-Estève appeared on the scene. Warned by the negro, she had put on a bonnet and thrown a shawl over her shoulders, to appear as if she had just come in.

"Gracious!" she exclaimed, with well-feigned surprise. "Monsieur de Ronquerolles, here, at this hour!"

"Devil take you! what do you mean by shouting out my name?" said her customer in an undertone.

Vautrin, entering into the farce, turned back, and coming up with an obsequious bow:

"Monsieur le Marquis de Ronquerolles?" said he, "Peer of France, formerly her ambassador. I am glad to have spent a minute with a statesman so well known—a so perfect diplomate!"

And with a respectful flourish he went to the door.

"What, Baron, going so soon?" said the old woman, trying to assume the tone and accent of a dowager of the Faubourg Saint-Germain.

"Yes. Monsieur le Marquis has much to talk to you. I shall return back to-morrow at eleven—and be punctual."

"Very well; to-morrow at eleven," said his aunt. "But I may tell you everything is going on swimmingly; the lady thinks you will be all she could wish."

Another bow, and Vautrin was gone.

"Who in the world is that strange creature?" asked Ronquerolles.

"A Prussian Baron for whom I am finding a wife," replied the woman "Well," she went on, "is there anything new that you so pressingly want to speak to me?"

"Yes. And something which you ought to have known! The fair one left the sculptor's house this morning."

"Pooh!" said Jacqueline. "Who told you that?"

"My man, who has seen the maid-of-all-work."

"Hah!—Then you keep several irons hot!" said she, glad of an excuse for a quarrel.

"My good woman, you were making no way at all, and the matter has been in hand a month——"

"You seem to think that all you want is to be had ready-made, and that an Italian is the same soft tinder as your Paris sluts!—And then you are so liberal!"

"Why, you have extracted more than three banknotes for a thousand francs already for your sham expenses."

"A perfect fortune! And what about the engagement you undertook to arrange?"

"Can I open the Italian Opera expressly for that woman? If she would have sung at the French house——"

"There is Italian Opera in London though not in Paris for the moment, and the manager, as it happens, is over here in search of a prima."

"So I saw in the papers, of course; but what good could I do by trying to deal with a bankrupt?"

"Why, that is your best chance. You bolster up the man, and then, out of gratitude——"

"Oh, certainly!" said the Marquis, shrugging his shoulders. "A mere trifle of five hundred thousand francs—what *la Torpille* cost Nucingen!"

"My good man, you want the woman or you don't. Esther had tried the streets. This Italian is at least as handsome, *and* virtuous—green seal! Then she has a glorious voice. You have forked out three thousand-franc notes; what is that, pray, to make such a noise about?"

"Did you or did you not undertake the business?"

"I did. And I ought to have it left entirely to me; and if I had supposed that I was going to be checked off by your man-servant, I would have asked you to apply elsewhere. I do not care to have a partner in the game."

"But, you conceited old thing, but for that fellow, would you have known what I have just told you?"

"And did he tell you the rest of the story?"

"The rest of the story? What?" said the Marquis eagerly.

"Certainly. Who got the bird out of its nest, and in what cage it may be at this present speaking."

"Then you know?" cried Ronquerolles.

"If I do not know, I can make a guess."

"Then, tell me," said he, in great excitement.

"You, who know every queer specimen, old or young, in the Paris menagerie, must certainly have heard of Count Halphertius, a Swede—enormously rich, and just arrived."

"I never heard his name till this moment."

"You had better ask your servant; he can tell you."

"Come, come; do not try finessing. This Count Halphertius, you say——?"

"Is music-mad—and as woman-mad as Nucingen."

"And you think that la Luigia will have flown that way?"

"I know that he was hovering round her; he even charged me to make her splendid offers, and if I had not pledged myself to you——"

"Oh, I daresay; you are a dame of such lofty virtue!"

"Is that the way you take it?" said Jacqueline Collin, putting her hand in her pocket and pulling out a purse fairly well filled with notes. "You can take your money back, my boy, and I only beg you to trouble me no further."

"Get along, you wrong-headed creature," replied the Marquis, seeing three thousand-franc notes held out to him. "What I have given, you know I never take back."

"And I never keep what I have not earned.—You are done, Monsieur le Marquis. I am working for Count Halphertius; I brought away the lady; she is hidden here, in my rooms, and to-morrow morning she and the Swede set out for London, where a splendid engagement is waiting for her!"

"No, no, I do not believe that you would cheat me," said Ronquerolles, fancying that the fact thus fired at him point-blank was really the sarcasm it appeared. "We are old friends, you know; pocket those banknotes, and tell me honestly what you think of this rich foreigner as a rival."

"Well, I have told you. He is enormously rich; he will stick at no sacrifice; and I know that he has had several talks with Madame Nourrisson."

"Then you learned all those facts from that old carrion?"

"Madame Nourrisson is my friend," said Madame de Saint-Estève, with much dignity. "We may be competing to gain the same prize, but that is no reason for her being evil-spoken of in my presence."

"Did she tell you at least where this Count Halphertius is living?"

"No. But I know that he was to start for London yesterday. That is why I ran alongside before I put the flea in your ear."

"It is very evident the Italian woman is gone off to join him."

"You may very likely be right."

"A pretty mess you have made of it!" said Ronquerolles as he rose.

"Indeed!" said Jacqueline insolently. "And were you never checkmated in your diplomatic business?"

"Do you suppose you will get any more exact information?"

"We will see," said she. It was her formula for promising her assistance.

"But no underhand tricks," cried the Marquis. "You know I do not understand a joke."

"Will the case be brought before the Chamber of Peers?" said Madame de Saint-Estève, who was not a woman to be easily daunted.

Without answering this piece of insolence, Ronquerolles only remarked:

"You might perhaps desire your nephew to help in your inquiries."

"Yes," said Jacqueline; "I think it would not be amiss to tell him something about the matter—without naming you, of course."

"And if at any time I can be of use to him with his chief, you know, I am as staunch a friend as I am a dangerous foe."

Thereupon Madame de Saint-Estève and her client parted, and as soon as the enemy's coach-wheels were heard in the distance, the virtuous matron had no occasion to go in search of her nephew. He had gone round by a back passage, and come to wait in the room behind the drawing-room, whence he had overheard everything.

"You tricked him neatly!" said Vautrin. "We will contrive by little scraps of information to keep his head in the trough for a few days longer; but now go at once and fetch our 'Helen,' for unless it is too late you ought to introduce us."

"Be easy; I will settle that," said his aunt, who a minute later came back with the handsome housekeeper.

"Signora Luigia—Monsieur le Comte Halphertius," said she, introducing them to each other.

"Signora," said Vautrin in the most respectful tone, "my friend Madame de Saint-Estève tells me you will permit me to take some interest for your affairs——"

"Madame de Saint-Estève," replied Luigia, who had learned to speak French perfectly, "has spoken of you as a man with a great knowledge of art."

"That is to say, I am passionately devoted to it, and my fortune allows me to do all I can to encourage it. You, madame, have a splendid gift."

"That remains to be proved, if I am so fortunate as to get a chance of being heard."

"You may come out when you choose. I have seen the manager of the Italians theatre in London; he shall hear you to-morrow—it is settled."

"I am deeply grateful for the trouble you have been so good as to take; but before accepting your kind offices, I wish to come to a clear understanding."

"I love to be frank," said Vautrin.

"I am poor and alone in the world," said Luigia; "I am considered good-looking, and at any rate I am young. It behooves me, therefore, to be circumspect in accepting the eager benevolence that is shown me. In France, I am told, it is rarely disinterested."

"Disinterestedness," said Vautrin, "I shall promise. But as to hindering tongues of talking—I shall not promise."

"Oh! as for talk," said his aunt, "that you may make up your mind to. Monsieur le Comte's age even will not stop their wagging—for, in fact, a younger man is more likely to devote himself to a woman without any idea of—— In Paris your old bachelors are all reprobates!"

"I shall not have ideas," said Vautrin. "If I am so happy to be of use for the signora, which I admire her talent so much, she shall let me be her friend; but if I fail in my respect to her, she shall be independent for that talent, and she shall turn me out of her door like a servant that shall rob her."

"And I hear, Monsieur le Comte, that you have already been kind enough to inquire about an engagement for me?"

"It is almost settle," said Vautrin. "To-morrow you shall sing; and if your voice shall satisfy the manager of the Italians in London, it is fifty thousand francs for the rest of the season."

"It is a dream," said Luigia. "And, perhaps, when he shall have heard me——"

"He will be of the same opinion as that Monsieur Jacques Bricheteau," replied Jacqueline. "He said you had sixty thousand francs in your voice—so you are still robbed of ten thousand francs."

"Oh! as to his promise to pay fifty thousand francs as soon as he has heard you," said Vautrin, "I have no fear. Then to pay them—that is another thing. He wants money, they say. But we will have the agreement made by some clever man, Madame de Saint-Estève shall find him; and the signora shall not have to think about the money—that is her friends' concern. She shall think only of her parts."

Vautrin, as he said, "Then to pay them—that is another thing——" had managed to touch his aunt's foot with his own. She understood.

"On the contrary," said she, "I believe he will pay very punctually. He will not care to quarrel with us, my dear Count. It is not every day that you come across a man who, to secure an engagement, is ready to risk a sum of a hundred thousand crowns."

"What, monsieur! you are prepared to make such a sacrifice for my sake!—I can never allow it——"

"My good Madame de Saint-Estève," said Vautrin, "you are a tell-tale. I am risking nothing; I have looked into the matter, and at the end of the season I shall have my benefits; besides, I am v-e-ery rich, I am a widower, I have not children; and if part of that money shall be lost, I shall not for that hang myself."

"Nevertheless, monsieur, I will not permit such a piece of folly."

"Then you do not want me for your friend, and you are afraid you shall be compromised if I help you?"

"In Italy, monsieur, such a protector is quite recognized; and so long as there is nothing wrong, nobody cares for appearances; but I cannot entertain the idea of allowing you to risk so large a sum on my account."

"If it were a risk, no. But the risk is so small that your engagement and the hundred thousand crowns are two separate things, and I shall enter into partnership with the director even if you refuse."

"Come, come, pretty one," said Jacqueline, "you must make up your mind to owing this service to my friend Halphertius; you know that if I thought it was likely to carry you further than you think quite right, I should have nothing to do with it. Talk it over with your confessor, and you will see what he says about it."

"I would in Italy; but in France I should not consult him about a theatrical engagement."

"Well, then, signora," said Vautrin, in the kindest way, "consider your career as an artist. It lies before you, a splendid road! And when every paper in Europe is full of the *Diva Luigia,* there will be a good many people greatly vexed to think that they failed to recognize so great an artist, and to keep on friendly terms with her."

Vautrin knew men's minds too well not to have calculated the effect of this allusion to the secret sorrow of the Italian girl's heart. The poor woman's eyes flashed, and she gasped for breath.

"Monsieur le Comte," said she, "may I really trust you?"

"Undoubtedly; and all the more so, because if I spend the money, I expect to get some little return."

"And that is——?" said Luigia.

"That you show me some kind feeling; that the world shall believe me to be happier than I really shall be; and that you do nothing to deprive me of that little sop to my pride, with which I promise to be content."

"I do not quite understand," said the Italian, knitting her brows.

"And yet nothing can be plainer," said Madame de Saint-Estève. "My friend here does not wish to look a fool; and if while he is visibly your protector you were to take up with your deputy again, or fall in love with somebody else, his part, as you may understand, would not be a handsome one."

"I shall never be anything to the Count but a grateful and sincere friend," said Luigia. "But I shall be no more for any other man—especially for the man of whom you speak. I did not break up my life, dear madame, without due consideration."

"But you see, my dear," said the old woman, thus showing a profound knowledge of the human heart, "that the men of whom we declare that we have washed our hands are often just the most dangerous."

"You speak as a Frenchwoman, madame," said the Italian.

"Then to-morrow," said Vautrin, "I have your permission to come for you and take you to meet this manager? Of course, you know many of the parts in stock opera?"

"I know all the parts taken by Malibran and Pasta," said Luigia, who had been studying indefatigably for two years past.

"And you will not change your mind in the course of the night?" said Vautrin insinuatingly.

"Here is my hand on it," said Luigia, with artless frankness. "I do not know whether bargains are ratified so in France."

"Ah, Diva, Diva!" cried Vautrin, with the most burlesque caricature of dilettante admiration; and he lightly touched the fair hand he held with his lips.

When we remember the terrible secret of this man's past life, it must be admitted that the Human Comedy—nay, I should say, Human Life—has some strange doublings.

The success of the singer's trial was far beyond Vautrin's expectations. The hearers were unanimously in favor of Luigia's engagement. Nay, if they had listened to Sir Francis Drake, it would have been signed then and there, and the singer would have set out the same day for London, where, owing to La Serboni's illness, Her Majesty's Theatre was in great straits.

But Vautrin, when once that side of the question was settled, wished to make further inquiries as to the money to be invested; and instead of Signora Luigia, it was he, attended by his secretary, who accompanied the *impresario* to England with a view to looking into matters. In the event of finding the position altogether untenable, he was quite prepared to withdraw his offer with cool faithlessness, as the *diva's* engagement no longer depended on the advance of capital which he had at first been prepared to risk.

As he was starting, he said to his aunt:

"To-day is the 17th of May; at seven in the evening on the 21st, I shall be back in Paris with Sir Francis Drake. Meanwhile, take care that our protégée is provided with a suitable outfit. No absurd magnificence, as if you were dressing up a courtesan, but handsome things in the best style, not loud or too startling to the signora's good taste. In short, just what you would buy for your daughter, if you had one, and she were going to be married.

"For that same day, the 21st, order a dinner for fifteen from Chevet. The party will consist of the leaders of the press; your client Bixiou will get them together. You, of course, as mistress of the house, but I entreat you, dress quietly—nothing to scare the guests. Then I must have a clever man of business to look through the papers before we sign, and a pianist to accompany the *Diva,* who shall sing us something after dinner. You must prepare her to give a taste of her best quality to all those trumpeters of fame. Sir Francis Drake and I make the party up to fifteen. I need not say that it is your friend Count Halphertius who gives the dinner at your house, because he has none of his own in Paris; and everything is to be of the best, elegant and refined, that it may be talked about everywhere."

After giving these instructions, Vautrin got into a post-chaise, knowing Jacqueline Collin well enough to feel sure that his orders would be carried out with intelligence and punctuality.

When Vautrin had mentioned Bixiou as the recruiting-sergeant of his company, this was what he had meant by calling him her "client."

Among the various secret sources of wealth that helped to swell the ever-increasing fortune which Rastignac had scented under Saint-Estève's social status, usury, of course, had not been disdained. Though economists have gone so far as to maintain that money is a form of merchandise of which the price is wrongfully fixed by law, for consciences as broad as those of Vautrin and his aunt the provisions of the penal code were an obstacle only in so far as they failed to elude them—but who is the fool who allows himself to be caught in the clutches of the code? Unless he has never read Molière's *Avare,* he cannot help being aware of the *Maître Simon,* who, from time immemorial, has stood as a screen between the extortionate money-lender's transactions and the vexations of the law.

Now, Master Bixiou, whose extremely free-and-easy life frequently compelled him to have recourse to his credit, had, through an intermediary, found himself in business relations with Jacqueline Collin; and by his monkey-skill in worming out mysteries, especially such as might interest himself, in spite of the queer disguises in which she involved herself, he had succeeded in getting face to face with his creditor. Then, one day, being quite unable to meet a bill which would fall due on the morrow, he had boldly attacked the ogress, to work the miracle of extracting a renewal on favorable terms. The woman liked a man of spirit, and, like all wild beasts, she had her intervals of ruth. It need hardly be said that Bixiou had done his utmost to propitiate her; he was witty under his reverses, full of dazzling paradox and theories of jovial immorality, which so effectually bewildered the money-lender, that not only did she renew the bill, but she had even lent him a further sum; and this sum, to crown the marvel, he had actually repaid her.

Hence, between the artist and the "matrimonial agent" there arose a certain friendly feeling. Bixiou, not knowing what the terrible creature was with whom he rubbed shoulders, flattered himself that it was his cleverness that made her laugh, and now and then, when he was at his wits' end, enabled him to soften her to the extent of a few napoleons; he did not know that he was the dog of the raree show in the lion's den; and that this woman, in whose past life there had been incidents *à la* Brinvilliers, was not incapable of making him pay with his life for his insolent familiarity, to say nothing of the interest on her loans.

Meanwhile, and pending this fatal termination, which was not very probable, Jacqueline Collin did not hesitate to employ this jovial gossip in the ferreting he practised so successfully; indeed, she not unfrequently gave him, without his knowing it, a part to play in the shady imbroglios that were the occupation of her life.

In the affair of Luigia, the caricaturist was wonderfully useful; through him she could insure publicity for the rumor of Count Halphertius' appearance on the Parisian horizon, his passion for the singer, and the immense sums he was prepared to put down in her behalf. And it must be said that his universal acquaintance with the writing, singing, painting, eating, rollicking, swarming world of Paris, made him capable above other men of recruiting the full complement of celebrity-makers that Vautrin required.

On the 21st, at seven o'clock precisely, all the guests, of whom Desroches had given Bixiou the list, and Desroches himself, were assembled in the drawing-room in the Rue de Provence when the negro announced Sir Francis Drake and Count Halphertius, who had insisted on not being named first. The Swedish gentleman's dress was admirably correct: a black suit, white waistcoat, and white tie, over which the ribbon of a fancy order hung round his neck. His other decorations were fastened at his button-hole by little chains, but he had not dared to flaunt a star sewn to his coat.

As he glanced at the assembled circle, Vautrin was annoyed to perceive that his aunt's habits and instincts had proved stronger than his special and express injunctions, and a sort of turban, green and yellow, would have put him seriously out of temper, but that the skill she had shown in carrying out all his other wishes won forgiveness for her head-dress. As for Luigia, dressed, as usual, in black, having had the wisdom to refuse the assistance of a hairdresser who had vainly attempted to reduce what he called the disorder of her hair, she was supremely beautiful; and an air of melancholy gravity stamped on all her person compelled a feeling of respect, which surprised these men, to whom Bixiou had spoken of her as awaiting their verdict.

The only person who was specially introduced to Vautrin was Desroches, whom Bixiou brought up to him with this jovially emphatic formula:

"Maître Desroches, the most intelligent attorney of modern times."

As to Sir Francis Drake, if he seemed a shade less scornful than he had intended to be of the influence of journalism as affecting the supply of capital, it was because he happened to be acquainted with Félicien Vernou and Lousteau, two writers for the journalistic press, with whom he shook hands warmly.

Before dinner was announced, Count Halphertius thought it his part to make a little speech; and after a few minutes' conversation with Signora Luigia, to whom he had good taste enough not to speak till he had been in the room a short while, he ostensibly addressed Madame de Saint-Estève, but loud enough to be heard by all who were present.

"My dear madame," said he to his aunt, "you are really a wonderful woman. The first time I find myself in a Paris drawing-room, and you make me to meet all that is most distinguished in literature, in arts, and in the world of business. I, what am only a northern barbarian, though my country has its famous men—Linnæus, Berzelius, the great Thorvaldsen, Tegner, Franzen, Geier, and our charming novelist, Frédérica Bremer—I am here astonished and timid, and I do not know how to say to you that I am so extraordinary obliged."

"Well, through Bernadotte," said the lady, whose erudition took her so far as that, "France and Sweden clasped hands."

"It is quite certain," said Vautrin, "that our beloved sovereign Charles XIV.——"

He was interrupted by a butler, who threw open the doors and announced dinner.

Madame de Saint-Estève took Vautrin's arm, and whispered as they went:

"Don't you think it all very well done?"

"Yes," said Jacques Collin, "it is very well got up. Nothing is wrong but your diabolical parrot-colored turban, which startled me a good deal."

"No, no," said Jacqueline, "with my Javanese phiz" (she was born, in fact, in Java) "something Oriental carries it off."

She placed Sir Francis Drake to her right, and next to him Desroches; Vautrin, opposite to her at the other end of the table, was supported by Émile Blondet of the *Débats* and Luigia, next to whom sat Théodore Gaillard; the twenty-five thousand subscribers to the paper edited by this practised craftsman well earned him this distinction. The other guests seated themselves as they pleased.

The dinner was not, on the whole, particularly lively. The "Human Comedy" has more than once had occasion to include a picture of the cheerful race who were here present in force, under the brilliant light of the *triclinium;* but then they had not been muzzled as they were at this banquet. Bixiou, as a message from Madame de Saint-Estève, had particularly impressed on all the guests that they were to say nothing that could distress the chaste ears of the pious Italian. So these men, forced to be cautions, all men of wit and feeling—more or less, as a famous critic said, had lost their spirit; and falling back on the dinner, which was excellent, they murmured in undertones, or reduced the conversation to commonplace remarks.   In short, they ate and they drank under protest, so to speak; but they did not really dine.

Bixiou, to whom such a state of things was quite unendurable, was bent on making some break in this monotony. The intimacy between a foreign nobleman and their hostess had given him food for thought; he had also been struck by a certain inefficiency in the Amphitryon; and had said to himself that a genuine nobleman would at a smaller cost have succeeded ·in putting some life into the party.   So, in order to feel his way, it occurred to him to test the Count by speaking of Sweden, and· at the beginning of the second course he asked him all across the table:

"Monsieur le Comte, you are too young, I imagine, to have known Gustavus III., whom Scribe and Auber have set in an opera, and who in France has given his glorious name to a *galop.*"

"I beg your pardon," replied Vautrin, seizing the opportunity thus offered to him; "I am very nearly sixty, which would make me thirteen in 1792, when our beloved sovereign was killed by the assassin Anckastroem; so I can remember those times."

Having said this, by the help of a volume called *Caractères et Anecdotes de la cour de Suède* (published by Arthus Bertrand in 1808 without the author's name), which he had picked up at a bookstall since his incarnation as a Swede, Vautrin was in a position to defy pitfalls.   He improved the occasion; like a speaker who only waits to be started on a familiar text to display his powers to the best advantage, no sooner was the tap turned on than he flowed with such erudition and pertinence on all the great men of his country, gave so many circumstantial details, related so many curious and secret facts, especially with regard to the famous *Coup d'État,* by which Gustavus III. emancipated the Crown in 1772; in short, was so precise and so interesting, that as they rose from table, Émile Blondet said to Bixiou:

"I was like you—a foreign Count, introduced by this

matchmonger, at first struck me as suspicious. But not only was the dinner really princely; this man knows his Swedish Court in a way that is not to be got out of books. He is undoubtedly a man of good family; and if only I had time, I could make a very interesting pamphlet out of all he has told us."

When they had had coffee, Sir Francis Drake, Vautrin, and Desroches went into an adjoining room, where they talked over the deed of partnership and the engagement of the prima donna. All the terms being finally settled, Vautrin called in the *Diva* to sign.

"He is a very cunning fox," said Desroches to Bixiou as they came back to the drawing-room. "He must be enormously rich; he paid the Englishman a hundred thousand crowns down in banknotes on the spot; and when I wanted to insert a rather stringent clause in the agreement as to the payment of the lady's salary—for Sir Francis Drake has not a reputation for paying *on the tail,* as Léon de Lora would say—our gentleman would allow no written expression of distrust—whence I conclude that the fair Italian keeps him at arm's length, and that he is not sorry to have some hold over her through arrears of pay."

"And your fees," said Bixiou. "Did he happen to mention them? I told old Saint-Estève that she must not expect a man of your consequence to put himself out of the way for soup and beef—that they must be garnished with parsley."

"Here you are!" said Desroches, taking out of his pocket a gold box, oval in shape, and very handsomely chased. "Just now, while I was reading the indentures, I had laid my snuff-box of Irish horn—worth about ten francs perhaps—on the table by my side. Our friend interrupted me to ask me for a pinch. When I had done reading and wanted it, in the place of my box, which had vanished, I found this gem."

"Your 'uncle,'" said Bixiou, "would lend you three or four hundred francs on it, which would mean a value of about a thousand."

"As I protested against such an exchange," Desroches went

on, " 'I am the gainer by it,' says he. 'I have a relic of the Napoleon of attorneys.' "

"Mighty genteel!" said Bixiou, "and please God and the old woman I will cultivate his acquaintance.—I say, supposing I were to sketch him in an early number of the *Charivari?*"

"First we must find out whether he has enough French wit in him to be pleased to see himself caricatured."

At this moment a chord on the piano announced that the Signora Luigia was about to face the enemy. She sang the "Willow Song" with a depth of expression which touched her audience, though the trial was held by an areopagus who was digesting a dinner of no sparing character. Émile Blondet, a dogmatic politician rather than a man of imagination, was surprised into beating time in the fervor of his enthusiasm. He beat out of time, it is true, but the emotion was not the less evident.

The song ended, Vernou and Lousteau, going up to Sir Francis Drake, said, with an assumption of indignation as flattering to his skill as to his hopes as a manager:

"What a mean wretch you must be to have secured such an artist for fifty thousand francs—a mere song!"

Luigia then sang an air from *Nina,* by Paesiello, and in this light and vivacious character revealed a gift of impersonation at least equal to her talents as a singer.

"She startled me!" said the old aunt to Vautrin. "I fancied I saw Peyrade's daughter."

This was an allusion to a dreadful incident connected with Baron Nucingen's story, in which this formidable foe had played the chief part. She had driven an unhappy girl out of her mind by getting her into a house of ill-fame, in pursuance of an atrocious scheme of vengeance.

What crowned Luigia's success, and recommended her especially to her reporters, was her modesty—a sort of ignorance of her wonderful gifts in the midst of the praises that were showered on her. This little crowd of journalists, accustomed to the extravagant vanity and insolent assumption of the smallest stage queens, could not get over the humility and artlessness of this Empress of Song, who seemed quite surprised at the effect she had produced.

A few words skilfully whispered at parting to each of these great men, and a card left at their lodgings next day by Count Halphertius, secured for his protégée, at any rate for the moment, a chorus of admiration which would echo across the Channel, and be almost as good as a brilliant *début* at the Italian opera house in Paris.

The signora's departure was fixed for the morrow; she was to travel, escorted by Sir Francis Drake. To avoid a *tête-à-tête,* Madame de Saint-Estève had taken the precaution of engaging a maid, and, against her practice when she meddled with servants, she took care to secure an honest woman.

Count Halphertius gave proof of his disinterestedness in a way that was thoroughly appreciated. He said, which was perfectly true, that business detained him in Paris, reserving the right, if he should be so fortunate as to bring it to a conclusion in about a month or six weeks, to run over to London and enjoy the triumph, of which he no longer felt a doubt, and which he was so happy as to have been able to prepare.

Some days before Luigia's journey, the Boulogne boat carried another person of this drama to England.

As soon as he had ascertained where he could find Sallenauve, to give him the information he thought so urgent, Jacques Bricheteau abandoned the idea of writing to him. He thought it simpler and safer to go to see him.

On reaching London, the traveler was somewhat surprised to learn that Hanwell was one of the most famous lunatic asylums in the three kingdoms. If he had but remembered the apprehensions his friend had felt at the state of Marie-Gaston's brain, he would have guessed the truth; but he was quite at sea when he was further informed that this asylum, maintained by the rates, was open only to mad people of

the lower classes, and not to paying patients. However,
Jacques Bricheteau was not so foolish as to waste time in
vain conjectures. We have already seen that he was prompt
and determined; and he now set off without delay to Hanwell, and as the place is only about nine miles from London,
he was soon there.

Hanwell is a large building of not unhandsome appearance;
the front, nine hundred and ninety-six feet in length, is
broken by three octagonal towers, three stories high—one at
each end, and one in the middle; the monotony is thus relieved, though the melancholy purpose of the building necessitated a very moderate use of ornament.

The asylum is pleasantly situated at the foot of a hill on
the borders of Jersey (*sic*)* and Middlesex. The extensive,
grounds, gardens, and farms lie between the Uxbridge road,
the river Brent, and the Grand Junction Canal; nine hundred
patients can be accommodated and treated there. As it is
well known that manual labor is one of the most valuable
elements of the cure, the house contains workshops for car-
pentry, smiths' work, painting, glazing, and brushmaking;
cotton is spun, shoes, baskets, strawberry pottles, and straw
hats are made, and other light work for women. The finer
qualities of work are sold to visitors in a bazaar, and bring
in a considerable profit.

Such patients as are incapable of learning a trade work
in the garden and farm, which supply many of the wants of
the establishment; bread and beer are made on the premises;
all the necessary linen is made up and washed by means of
a steam engine, which also heats every part of the building.
A chapel with a fine organ, a library, and a concert-room—
the salutary effect of music on the patients being amply proved
—show that, hand in hand with intelligent care given to
physical suffering, the needs of the spiritual and intellectual
man are not neglected.

Finally, as Lord Lewin had told Sallenauve in his letter,
the superintendent and director was Dr. Ellis, a distinguished

* This curious mistake seems to have arisen from the proximity of Osterley Park,
Lord Jersey's residence.

physician to whom we owe a valuable treatise on the development and therapeutics of mental disease. In his treatment of these maladies this learned man does not despise the aid of phrenology.

On being shown into the doctor's room, the organist asked him whether a Frenchman named Sallenauve were not staying for a time at Hanwell. Here, again, Bricheteau paid the penalty of his neglected and shabby appearance; without vouchsafing any inquiries or explanations, Dr. Ellis shortly replied that he had never even heard Monsieur de Sallenauve's name. This, after all, was very probable; so Jacques Bricheteau withdrew, much disappointed; and fancying that Madame de l'Estorade had misread, or he himself had mistaken, the name of Hanwell, he spent some days in running about the county of Middlesex visiting every spot of which the name ending in *ell* invited his attention.

All his inquiries having ended in nothing, as he rarely allowed his persevering and resourceful spirit to be beaten in anything he undertook, Jacques Bricheteau resolved to make another attempt on Hanwell by letter, thinking, very rightly, that a letter sometimes got in where a man was barred out. In point of fact, on the evening of the day when he posted his letter he received a reply from Sallenauve, inviting him to call at the asylum, where he was promised a cordial welcome.

Dr. Ellis' conduct was accounted for when Jacques Bricheteau learned the extent of the disaster that had befallen Marie-Gaston. Discretion is, of course, one of the most indispensable virtues in the Head of an asylum for the insane; since every day, by his position, he becomes the depositary of secrets which affect the honor of whole families. To admit that the nearest friend of Marie-Gaston—whose deep melancholy was known to all—was then staying at Hanwell, would have been to put the inquirer, whoever he might be, in possession of the fact of his insanity, and thus the secret they had agreed to keep as to his state, which they still liked to believe would be temporary and curable, would have inevitably become known.

When Bricheteau arrived at the asylum, and was introduced by Sallenauve as his friend, he was heartily welcomed. Dr. Ellis made every apology; and having on various occasions in the course of his practice found really wonderful benefit derived from music, he said that he regarded the organist's arrival as quite a godsend, since his great talent might be of immense use as a means towards curing the patient.

Since leaving Ville-d'Avray, Marie-Gaston's state had unfortunately become seriously complicated. Until he reached England he had been comparatively cheerful and docile to Lord Lewin's advice; they might have been supposed to be friends traveling together for pleasure. But when, instead of embarking at once for South America, Lord Lewin, under the pretext of business to transact in the neighborhood of London, proposed to Marie-Gaston to accompany him, the madman began to suspect some snare into which he had been wheedled. He allowed himself, nevertheless, to be driven to Hanwell, represented by Lord Lewin as one of the royal residences; he had not even resisted when invited to cross the threshold of his prison; but once in the presence of Dr. Ellis, who had been forewarned by a letter from Lord Lewin, a sort of instinct, of which the insane are very capable, seemed to tell the unhappy man that his freedom was in danger.

"I do not like that man's face," he said aloud to Lord Lewin. "Let us go."

The doctor had tried to laugh off the remark; but Marie-Gaston, getting more and more excited, exclaimed:

"Hold your tongue! Your laughter is intolerable. You look just like an executioner."

And it is possible that the deep attention with which mad doctors must study the countenance of a patient, added to the stern fixed gaze by which they are often compelled to control a maniac, may at last give their features an expression of inquisitorial scrutiny. This, no doubt, has a highly irritating effect on the overstrung nervous sensibilities of the unhappy creatures brought within their ken.

"You will not deprive me, I hope," said the doctor, "of the pleasure of keeping you and my friend Lord Lewin to dinner?"

"I! Dine with you?" cried Marie-Gaston vehemently. "What—that you may poison me!"

"Well, but poison is just what you want, surely?" said Lord Lewin quickly. "Were you not talking the other day of a dose of prussic acid?"

Lord Lewin was not, as might perhaps be supposed, merely rash in making this pointed speech; he had studied mad persons, and he discerned that a deeply hostile aversion for the doctor was seething in Marie-Gaston's mind; so, being strong and active, he intended to divert on himself the storm that was about to burst. It fell out as he had expected.

"Vile scoundrel!" cried Marie-Gaston, seizing him by the throat, "you are in collusion with the other, and selling my secrets!"

It was with some difficulty, and the help of two warders; that Lord Lewin had shaken off his desperate clutch; the poor man had developed raving mania.

The paroxysm, after lasting some days, had yielded to care and treatment; the patient was now gentle and quiet, and showed some hopeful symptoms; but Sir William Ellis hoped to induce a final crisis, and he was considering the way and means to this end when Jacques Bricheteau arrived.

As soon as Sallenauve found himself alone with the organist, he questioned him as to the motives that had prompted him to follow him, and it was not without indignation that he heard of the intrigue which Maxime and the Beauvisages seemed to be plotting against him. His old suspicions revived:

"Are you quite certain," he asked, "that the man I but just saw was in fact the Marquis de Sallenauve?"

"Mother Marie des Anges and Achille Pigoult," replied Bricheteau, "who warned me of this plot, have no more doubt of the Marquis' identity than I have. And in all the gossip which they are trying to work up into a scandal, one thing

alone seems to me at all serious, and that is, that by your
absence you leave the field free to your enemies."

"But the Chamber will not condemn me unheard," replied
the member. "I wrote to the President to ask leave of
absence; and in the event of its being refused, which is most
improbable, I have asked l'Estorade, who knows my reasons
for being here, to answer for me."

"You also wrote to madame his wife?"

"I wrote only to his wife," replied Sallenauve. "I announced to her the misfortune that has overtaken our friend,
and at the same time begged her to explain to her husband
the good offices I requested of him."

"If that is the case," said Jacques Bricheteau, "do not depend for anything on the l'Estorades. A rumor of the
blow about to be dealt you had no doubt already reached
them."

And after telling him of the reception he had met with,
as well as the unkind speeches made by Madame de l'Estorade, Jacques Bricheteau drew the conclusion that in the
impending struggle no help could be hoped for from that
quarter.

"I have some right to be surprised at such a state of
things," said Sallenauve, "after Madame de l'Estorade's
pressing assurances of unfailing goodwill; however," he added
with a shrug, "nothing is impossible, and calumny has ere
now undermined closer friendship."

"So now, as you must understand," said the organist, "we
must set out for Paris without delay: all things considered,
your presence here is really far less necessary."

"On the contrary," replied Sallenauve, "only this morning
the doctor was congratulating himself on my having decided
on coming, saying that at the right moment my intervention
might be invaluable. In fact, I have not yet been allowed
to see Marie-Gaston, reserving my appearance as a surprise
at need."

"The usefulness of your presence," replied Jacques Bricheteau, "is nevertheless problematical; while, by remaining here

for an indefinite period, you are most certainly imperiling your political future, your social position, everything of which the most ardent friendship has no right to demand the sacrifice."

"We will go and talk it over with the doctor," said Sallenauve at length, for he could not fail to see that Jacques Bricheteau's importunity was justified.

On being asked whether Marie-Gaston's stay in the asylum was liable to be prolonged:

"Yes, I think so," said the doctor; "I have just seen our patient, and the cerebral irritation, which must give way to the material action of medicines before we can attempt to bring any moral influence to bear, seems to me most unfortunately on the highway to a fresh outbreak."

"Still," said Sallenauve anxiously, "you have not lost all hope of a cure?"

"Far from it; I believe firmly in a favorable termination. But these dreadful disorders often present frequent alternations of aggravation and improvement; and I am beginning to foresee that the case will be a longer one than I had at first hoped."

"I have but just been elected a member of the Lower Chamber," said Sallenauve, "and the opening of the session demands my return to Paris. It is no less required by urgent private matters which Monsieur Bricheteau came expressly to discuss. So unless I thought that my presence here would be immediately needed——"

"Go," said the doctor; "it may be a very long business. If the patient's condition had not shown a relapse, I had intended to arrange some startling scene with your help and that of Monsieur Bricheteau's music, aided too by a young lady, a relation of my wife's, who on various occasions has seconded me very intelligently—a little dramatic shock from which I hoped for good results. But, in the first place, my young relation is absent, and for the moment nothing can be done but by medical agents. So, for the moment, go! The patient is a man in whom it is impossible not to take a great interest; you may leave him in perfect confidence to me and Lord Lewin. I will even go so far as to say that I shall pride myself on achieving the cure, and I know no better warrant to offer you than this from a doctor's lips."

Sallenauve gratefully pressed the doctor's hand, seeing his eager wish to reassure him. He then took leave of Mrs. Ellis, who promised no less warmly than her husband the devoted care of a mother's watchfulness. As to Lord Lewin, Sallenauve's character had won his most friendly esteem, and his conduct in the past was a guarantee for all that might be expected of him now and in the future. So Bricheteau had no difficulty about getting off without any further delay.

They reached London at about five in the afternoon, and would have gone on to Paris the same evening but for a surprise which awaited them. Their eyes fell immediately on enormous posters, on a scale which only English "puff" can achieve, announcing at the corner of every street the appearance that same evening of SIGNORA LUIGIA at Her Majesty's Theatre. The name alone was enough to arrest the travelers' attention; but the papers to which they had recourse for information, supplied them, in the English fashion, with so many circumstantial facts as to the débutant's career, that Sallenauve could not doubt the transformation of his late housekeeper into one of the brightest stars that had risen for a long time above the horizon of England. If he had listened to Jacques Bricheteau, he would have been content to hail from afar the triumph of the handsome Italian, and have gone on his way. But having calculated that one evening spent in London would make no serious delay in his arrival, Sallenauve was bent on judging for himself, by his own eyes and ears, what the enthusiasm was worth which was expressed on all sides for the new prima donna.

Sallenauve went off at once to the box office, which he found closed, but he was enabled to perceive that the singer's success was immense. Every seat had been sold by two in the afternoon, and he thought himself lucky to secure two stalls at a private ticket office for the sum of five pounds.

The London opera-house had never perhaps held a more brilliant assembly; and it is impossible not to be struck by the capricious vicissitudes of human life, when we reflect that all this concourse of the English aristocracy was brought about originally by the ambition of a man who had been a felon on the hulks, to rise, as a member of the police, to a rather better rank in its hierarchy.

By a no less singular coincidence the piece announced was Paesiello's *Nina, o la Pazza per Amore* (mad for love), from which Luigia had sung an air after the dinner given by Madame de Saint-Estève.

When the curtain rose, Sallenauve, having spent nearly a week at Hanwell in the midst of mad people, could all the better appreciate the prodigious gifts as an actress displayed by his former housekeeper in the part of *Nina;* and in the face of her heartrending imitation, he went through a renewal of all the distress of mind he had just gone through while watching the dreadful reality of Marie-Gaston's insanity.

Bricheteau, in spite of his annoyance at first at Sallenauve's dawdling, as he called it, finally fell under the spell of the singer's power; and at last, seeing the whole house frantic with enthusiasm, and the stage strewn with bouquets, he said:

"On my word, I can wish you nothing better than a success in any degree like this on another stage!" and then he rashly added, "But there are no such triumphs in politics! Art alone is great——"

"And la Luigia is its prophet!" replied Sallenauve, smiling through the tears that admiration had brought to his eyes.

On coming out of the theatre, Bricheteau looked at his watch; it was a quarter to eleven, and by making great haste there was still time to get on board the packet starting at eleven. But when the organist looked round to urge this on Sallenauve, who was to follow him through the crowd, he no longer saw his man: the Député had vanished.

A quarter of an hour later Luigia's dresser came into a room where her mistress was receiving the compliments of the greatest names in England, introduced to her by Sir Francis Drake. She gave the signora a card. The prima donna as she read it changed color, and whispered a few words to the maid. And she then showed such obvious anxiety to be rid of her throng of admirers, that some budding adorers could not help betraying their surprise.

However, an artist who is the rage has many privileges; and the fatigue of a part into which the *Diva* had thrown her whole soul was so good an excuse for her want of cordiality, that her court dispersed without too much demur. Nay, her curtness, regarded as a whim, was taken as a very original proceeding, and recommended her to some incipent fancies.

As soon as she was alone, she hastily resumed her ordinary dress; the manager's carriage had soon conveyed her to the hotel where she had been living since her arrival; and on entering her sitting-room, she found Sallenauve, who had got there before her.

"You here, monsieur!" said she. "It is a dream!"

"Especially to me," replied Sallenauve, "since I find you in London after having sought you in vain in Paris."

"You took so much trouble—but why?"

"You left us in so strange a manner, your moods are so hasty, you knew so little of Paris, and so many dangers might await your inexperience, that I feared everything for you."

"What harm could come to me?" said she. "And I was neither your wife, nor your sister, nor your mistress; I was only your——"

"I had believed," Sallenauve eagerly put in, "that you were my friend."

"I was your debtor," said Luigia. "I saw that I was a trouble to you in your new position. Could I do otherwise than relieve you of my presence?"

"Pray, who had impressed you with that intolerable conviction? Had I said or hinted anything to that effect? Was it impossible to discuss a plan of life for you without so far offending your susceptibilities?"

"I feel what I feel," said the Italian. "I myself was conscious that you wished me anywhere rather than in your house. You had afforded me the means of having no fears for the future; indeed, as you see, it promises to be anything rather than alarming."

"On the contrary, it promises to be so brilliant that but for the fear of seeming too presuming, I should make so bold to ask from whose hand, happier than mine, you have obtained such prompt and efficient help."

"A great Swedish nobleman," replied Luigia without hesitation, "who spends part of an immense fortune in the encouragement of art, procured me this engagement at Her Majesty's; the kind indulgence of the public did the rest."

"Your talent, you should say. I heard you this evening."

"And were you pleased with your humble servant?" said the singer, with a coquettish courtesy.

"Your musical achievements did not surprise me; I knew your gifts already, and an infallible judge had answered for them; but your flights of dramatic passion, your acting, at once so strong and so sure of itself—that indeed amazed me."

"I have suffered much," said the Italian, "and grief is a great master."

"Suffered!" said Sallenauve; "in Italy, yes. But since you came to France, I like to flatter myself——"

"Everywhere," said Luigia in a broken voice. "I was not born under a happy star."

"That 'Everywhere' has to me a touch of reproach. It is late, indeed, to be telling me of any wrong I may have done you."

"You have not done me the smallest wrong. The mischief was there!" said Luigia, laying her hand on her heart. "I alone was in fault."

"From some fancy, I dare say, as foolish as your notion

that it was a point of honor that you should quit my house?"

"Oh, I was not dreaming then," said the Italian. "How well I knew what lay at the bottom of your mind! If it were only in return for all you had done for me, I ought to long for your esteem, and yet I was forbidden even to aspire to it."

"But, my dear Luigia, there is no word for such ideas. Did I ever fail in consideration and respect? And besides, has not your conduct always been exemplary?"

"Yes. I have tried never to do anything that could make you think ill of me. But I was Benedetto's widow, all the same."

"What! Do you fancy that that disaster, the outcome of just revenge——"

"Nay. It was not the man's death that could lower me in your eyes; quite the contrary. But I had been the wife of a buffoon, of a police spy, of a wretch always ready to sell me to any buyer——"

"While you were in that position, I felt that you were to be pitied; but scorned? Never!"

"Well," said the Italian, "we had lived together, alone, under the same roof, for nearly two years."

"Certainly; and to me it had become a delightful habit."

"Did you think me ugly?"

"You know I did not, since I took you for the model of my best statue."

"A fool?"

"A woman cannot be a fool who puts so much soul into a part."

"Well then; it is evident that you despised me!"

Sallenauve was utterly amazed at this prompt logic; he thought himself clever to reply:

"It seems to me that if I had behaved differently, I should have given greater proof of contempt."

But he had to deal with a woman who in all things—in her friendships and aversions, in act as well as in word—went straight to the mark.

She went on as if she were afraid that he had not understood her.

"At this day, monsieur, I can say everything, for I am talking of the past, and the future is no longer in my hands. Since the day when you were kind to me, and when by your generous protection I was rescued from an outrageous insult, my heart has been wholly yours."

Sallenauve, who had never suspected the existence of this feeling, and who, above all, could not conceive of its avowal, made with such artless crudity, did not know what to say.

"I was well aware," the strange creature went on, "that I should have much to do to raise myself from the base condition in which you had seen me at our first meeting. If even at the moment when you consented to take me with you I had seen any signs of gallantry in your behavior, any hint that you might take advantage of the dangerous position in which I had placed myself by my own act, my heart would have shrunk into itself, you would have been but an ordinary man, and to rehabilitate me after Benedetto it was not enough——"

"And so," said Sallenauve, "to love you would have been an insult, and not to love was cruelty. What a woman! How is it possible to avoid offending you?"

"I did not want you to love me when you did not know me," said the singer, "when I had scarcely shaken off the mire, for then it would have been only the love of the eye and of the taste, which it is never wise to trust. But when, after living in your house for two years, you could know by my conduct that I was worthy of your esteem; when, without ever craving a single pleasure, and devoted to the care of your house, with no relaxation but the study which was to raise me to the dignity of an artist like yourself, I could, merely for the happiness of seeing you create a masterpiece, sacrifice the womanly modesty which on another occasion you had seen me defend with vehemence—then you were cruel not to understand; and your imagination can never, never picture what I have suffered, or how many tears I have shed!"

"But, my dear Luigia, you were my guest; even if I could have suspected what you now reveal to me, my duty as a man of honor required me to see nothing, understand nothing, but on the plainest evidence."

"And was not my perpetual melancholy proof enough? If my heart had been free, should I not have been less reserved and more familiar? No—the case is plain enough: you could see nothing; your fancy was fixed elsewhere."

"Well, and if it were?"

"It ought not to have been," said the Italian stringently. "That woman was not free; she had a husband and children; and, though you chose to make a saint of her, even if I had no advantage over her excepting in youth—though that is, of course, quite absurd—it seems to me that she was not to compare with me."

Sallenauve could not help smiling. However, he replied quite gravely:

"You are altogether mistaken as to your rival. Madame de l'Estorade has never been anything to me but a head to study, and even so, of no interest whatever but for her likeness to another woman. That woman I knew at Rome before I ever saw you. She had beauty, youth, and a great talent for Art. At this day she is captive in a convent; so, like you, she has paid tribute to sorrow; as you see, all your perfections——"

"What! Three love stories, and all ending in air!" said Luigia. "You were born under a strange star indeed! Of course when I was so misunderstood, it was only because I was under its maleficent influence, and in that case you must be forgiven."

"Then, since you admit me to mercy, pray allow me to return to my former question. The future, you tell me, is no longer in your hands; the astounding frankness of your avowals leads me to infer that, to give you such boldness, a very solid barrier must have been raised between you and me. Then what is the power by which, at one leap, you have sprung so high? Have you made a bargain with the devil?"

"Perhaps so," said Luigia, laughing.

"Do not laugh," said Sallenauve. "You chose to face the hell of Paris alone; it would not at all surprise me to hear that you met with some dangerous acquaintance at starting. I know the difficulties that the greatest artists have to surmount before they can get a hearing. Do you know who the foreign gentleman is who has leveled every road before you?"

"I know that he has put down a fabulous sum to secure my engagement; that I am to be paid fifty thousand francs; and that he did not even accompany me to London."

"Then all this devotion is free, gratis?"

"Not at all. My patron has reached the age at which a man no longer loves, but has a great deal of conceit. So his protection is to be widely proclaimed, and I have pledged myself to do nothing, say nothing, that may give the lie to his fictitious happiness. To you alone did I owe the truth; but I know you to be trustworthy, and I entreat you to keep it absolutely secret."

"And it does not seem improbable to you that this state of things should last?—But how and where did you make acquaintance with this man whom you think you can for ever feed on air?"

"Through a *Dame de Charité* who came to see me while you were away. She had been struck by my voice at Saint-Sulpice during the services of the month of Mary, and she wanted to bribe me away to sing at her parish church, Notre-Dame de Lorette."

"What was the lady's name?"

"Madame de Saint-Estève."

Though he did not know all the depths of Jacqueline Collin's existence, Sallenauve had heard of Madame de Saint-Estève as a money-lender and go-between; he had heard Bixiou speak of her.

"That woman," said he, "has a notoriously bad reputation in Paris. She is an agent of the lowest intrigues."

"So I suspected," said Luigia, "but what does that matter to me?"

"If the man she has introduced to you——"

"Were such another as herself?" interrupted the singer. "But that is not likely. The hundred thousand crowns he has placed in the manager's hands have floated the theatre again."

"He may be rich and yet be scheming against you. The two are not incompatible."

"He may have schemes against me," said Luigia, "but they will not be carried out. Between them and me—*I* stand."

"But your reputation?"

"That I lost when I left your house. I was generally supposed to be your mistress; you had to give your own explanation to your constituency; and you contradicted the report, but do you imagine that you killed it?"

"And my esteem, on which you set such value?"

"I no longer need it. You did not love me when I wanted it; you will not love me when I no longer care."

"Who can tell?" said Sallenauve.

"There are two reasons against it," replied the Italian. "In the first place, it is too late; and in the second, we no longer tread the same road."

"What do you mean?"

"I am an artist, you have ceased to be one. I am rising, you are going down."

"You call it going down to rise perhaps to the highest dignities of State?"

"Whether you rise or no," cried Luigia ecstatically, "you will be beneath your past self and the splendid future that lay before you. Indeed, I believe I have deceived you; I believe if you had still been a sculptor, I should yet for some time have endured your coldness and disdain; at any rate, I should have waited till after my first trials in my art, hoping that the halo which lends glory to a woman on the stage might at last perhaps have made you aware of my existence—there—at your side. But from the day of your apostasy, I could no longer persist in my humiliating sacrifice. There is no future in common for us."

"What!" said Sallenauve, holding out his hand, which Luigia did not take, "are we not even to remain friends?"

"A friend—a man friend—you have already. No, it is all over and done with. We shall hear of each other; and from afar as we cross in life we shall wave each other a greeting, but nothing more."

"And this is how all is to end between you and me!" said Sallenauve sadly.

The singer looked at him for a moment, and tears sparkled in her eyes.

"Listen," said she, in a sincere and resolute tone, "this much is possible. I have loved you, and after you no man will find a place in the heart you scorned. You will be told that I have lovers: the old man whom I am pledged to own to, and others after him perhaps; but you will not believe it, remembering the woman that I am. And, who knows? By and by your life may be swept clear of the other affections which barred the way for mine, and the freedom, the eccentricity of the avowal I have just made will perhaps remain stamped on your memory—then it is not altogether impossible that after such long wandering you may at last want me. If that should happen—if, as the result of bitter disappointments, you should be brought back to the belief in Art—well, then, if time has not made love a too ridiculous dream for us, remember this night.

"Now we must part, for it is late for a *tête-à-tête,* and it is the semblance of fidelity to my elderly protector that I am pledged to preserve."

So speaking, she took up a candle and vanished into the adjoining room, leaving Sallenauve in a state of mind that may be imagined after the surprises of every kind that this interview had brought him.

On returning to the hotel whither he had taken his things on arriving from Hanwell, he found Bricheteau waiting for him at the door.

"Where the devil have you been?" cried the organist, frantic with impatience. "We might have got off by to-night's boat."

"Well, well," said Sallenauve carelessly, "I shall have a few more hours for playing truant."

"And meanwhile the enemy is pushing forward the mine!"

"What do I care? In that cave called political life must we not be prepared for whatever happens?"

"I suspected as much," said Bricheteau. "You have been to see la Luigia; her success has turned your head, and the statuary is breaking out through the Member."

"You yourself an hour since said Art alone is great."

"But the orator too is an artist," said Bricheteau, "and the greatest of all; for other artists appeal to the intellect and the feelings, he alone addresses the conscience and the will. Besides, this is not the time to look back; you have a duel to fight with your opponents. Are you a man of honor or a rogue who has stolen a name? That is the question which is perhaps being discussed and answered in your absence in the full light of the Chamber."

"I am sadly afraid that you have misled me; I had a jewel in my hands, and have flung it at my feet——"

"That," retorted the organist, "is happily a vapor that will vanish with the night. To-morrow you will remember your promises to your father and the splendid future that lies before you."

The Chambers were opened; Sallenauve had not been present at the royal sitting, and his absence had not failed to cause some sensation in the democratic party. At the office of the *National* especially there had been quite a commotion. It seemed only natural to expect that, as part owner of the paper and often to be seen at the office before the elections, having indeed contributed to its pages, he should, after being returned, have appeared there to get news when Parliament opened.

"Now he is elected," said some of the editors, commenting on the new member's total disappearance, "does my gentleman think he is going to play the snob? It is rather a common trick with our lords and masters in Parliament to pay us very obsequious court as long as they want supporters, and let us severely alone, like their old coats, as soon as they have climbed the tree. But we cannot allow this gentleman to play that game; there are more ways than one of turning the tables on a man."

The chief editor, less easily disturbed, had tried to soothe this first ebullition; but Sallenauve's non-appearance at the opening of the session had, nevertheless, struck him as strange.

On the following day, when the government officials were to be appointed—the presidents and secretaries—a business which is not unimportant, because it affords a means of estimating the majority, Sallenauve's absence was of more real consequence. In the office to which fate had attached him, the election of the head was carried by the Ministerialists by only one vote; thus the presence of the Member for Arcis would have turned the scale in favor of the Opposition. Hence the expression of strong disapproval in the organs of that party, explaining its defeat by this unforeseen defection, of which they spoke with some acrimonious surprise. They applied no epithets to the absentee's conduct, but they spoke of it as "quite inexplicable."

Maxime on his part kept a sharp lookout; he was only waiting till the official ranks of the Chamber should be filled to lay before the House, in the name of the Romilly peasant woman, a petition to prosecute. This document had been drawn up by Massol, and under his practised pen, the facts he had undertaken to set forth had assumed the air of probability which attorneys contrive to give to their statements and depositions even when furthest from the truth. And now, when Sallenauve's absence was so prolonged as to seem scandalous, he went once more to call on Rastignac; and availing himself of the ingenious plan of attack suggested by Desroches, he asked the Minister if he did not think that the moment had come when he, Rastignac, should abandon the attitude of passive observation which he had hitherto chosen to maintain.

Rastignac was, in fact, far more explicit. Sallenauve in a foreign land figured in his mind as a man conscience-stricken, who had lost his balance. He therefore advised Monsieur de Trailles to bring forward the preliminaries of the action that very day, and no longer hesitated to promise his support for the success of a scheme which now looked so hopeful, and from which a very pretty scandal might reasonably be looked for.

The effects of this underground influence were obvious on the very next day. The order of the day in the Lower Chamber was the verification of the returns. The member whose duty it was to report on the election at Arcis-sur-Aube happened to be a trusty Ministerialist, and, acting on the private instructions that had reached him, he took this view of the case:—

The constituents of Arcis had elected their member according to law. Monsieur de Sallenauve had, in due course, submitted to the examining committee all the documents needed to prove his eligibility, and there was no apparent difficulty in the way of his taking his seat. But reports of a strange character had arisen, even at the time of the election, as to the new deputy's identification, and in further support of those rumors a petition had now been presented to the house to authorize a criminal prosecution. This petition set forth a very serious accusation: Monsieur de Sallenauve was said to have assumed the name he bore without any right, and this assumption being certified on an official document, was indictable as a forgery committed for the purpose of false personation. "A circumstance much to be regretted," the speaker went on, "was Monsieur de Sallenauve's absence; instead of appearing to contradict the extraordinary accusation lodged against him, he had remained absent from the sittings of the House ever since the opening of the session, and nobody had seen him. Under these circumstances could his election be officially ratified? The committee had thought not, and proposed that a delay should be granted."

Daniel d'Arthez, a member of the Legitimist Opposition, who, as we saw at Arcis, was in favor of Sallenauve's return, at once rose to address the Chamber, and begged to point out how completely out of order such a decision would be.

"The legality of the election was beyond dispute. No irregularity had been proved. Hence, the Chamber had no alternative; they must put the question to the vote, and recognize the election as regular and valid, since there was nothing to invalidate it. To confuse with that issue the question as to a petition to prosecute, would be an abuse of power, because, by hindering any preliminary discussion of that question, and relieving the indictment of the usual formalities before its acceptance or rejection, it would assume a singular and exceptional character—that, namely, of a suspension of the mandate granted to their member by the sovereign power of the electors. And who," added the orator, "can fail to perceive that by giving effect to this petition for authority to prosecute, in any form whatever, we prejudge its justification and importance; whereas the presumption of innocence, which is the prerogative of every accused person, ought to be especially extended to a man whose honesty has never been open to doubt, and who has so lately been honored by the suffrages of his fellow-citizens."

A prolonged discussion followed, the Ministerial speakers naturally taking the opposite view; then a difficulty arose. The President for the time being, in right of seniority—for the Chamber had not yet elected its chief—was a weary old man, who, in the complicated functions so suddenly conferred on him by his register of birth, was not always prompt and competent. Sallenauve's application for leave of absence had reached him the day before; and if it had occurred to him to announce it to the Chamber at the beginning of the sitting—as he ought to have done—the discussion would probably have been nipped in the bud. But there is luck and ill-luck in parliamentary business; and when the House learned from this letter, at last communicated, that Charles de Sallenauve was abroad, and had no ground to offer for this application for unlimited leave but the vague common-place of "urgent private affairs," the effect was disastrous.

"It is self-evident," said all the Ministerialists, like Ras-tignac, "he is in England, where every form of failure takes refuge. He is afraid of the inquiry; he knows he will be unmasked."

This opinion, apart from all the political feeling, was shared by some of the sterner spirits, who could not conceive that a man should not appear to defend himself against so gross an accusation. In short, after a very strong and skilful speech from Vinet the public prosecutor, who had found courage in the absence of the accused, the confirmation of the election was postponed, though by a very small majority; at the same time, a week's leave of absence was voted to the accused member.

On the day after these proceedings, Maxime wrote as fol-lows to Madame Beauvisage:—

"MADAME,—The enemy met with a terrible reverse yester-day; and in the opinion of my friend Rastignac, a very expe-rienced and intelligent judge of parliamentary feeling, Dor-lange, whatever happens, cannot recover from the blow thus dealt him. If we should fail to procure any positive proof in support of our worthy countrywoman's charge, it is possible that the scoundrel, by sheer audacity, may finally be accepted by the Chamber, if, indeed, he dares show his face in France. But even then, after dragging on a sordid existence utterly unrecognized, he will inevitably ere long be driven to resign; then M. Beauvisage will be elected beyond doubt, for the constituency, ashamed of having been taken in by an adven-turer, will be only too happy to reinstate themselves by a choice that will do them honor, besides having been their first instinctive selection.

"This result, madame, will be due to your remarkable sagacity; for, but for the sort of second sight which enabled you to divine the precious truth hidden under the peasant-woman's story, we should have overlooked that valuable instrument. I may tell you, madame, even if it should inflate your pride, that neither Rastignac nor Vinet, the public prosecutor, understood the full importance of your discovery; indeed, I myself, if I had not been so happy as to know you, so as to be able to appreciate the value attaching to any idea of yours, might very probably have shared the indifference of these two statesmen as to the useful weapon you were putting into our hands. But, as the gift came from you, I at once understood its importance; and while pointing out to Rastignac the means of utilizing it, I succeeded in making my friend the Minister an eager partner in the plot, and, at the same time, a sincere admirer of the skill and perspicacity of which you had given proof.

"Thus, madame, if I should ever be so happy as to be connected with you by the bond of which we have already spoken, I shall not need to initiate you into political life; you have found the path so well unaided.

"Nothing new can happen within the next week, the length of leave granted to our man. If after that date the absentee does not appear, there is, I think, no doubt that the election will be pronounced null and void; for yesterday's vote, which you will have read in the papers, is a positive summons to him to appear in his place. You may be very sure that between this and his return—if he should return—I shall not fail to devote myself to fomenting the antagonistic feeling of the Chamber both by the press and by private communications. Rastignac has also issued orders to this end, and it is safe to conclude that the foe will find public opinion strongly prejudiced against him.

"Allow me, madame, to beg you to remember me to Mademoiselle Cécile, and accept for yourself and Monsieur Beauvisage the expression of my most respectful regard."

A few words of instruction to the Ministerial press had, in fact, begun to surround the name of Sallenauve with a sort of atmosphere of disrespect and ridicule; the most insulting innuendoes ascribed to his absence the sense of a retreat from his foes. The effect of these repeated attacks was all the more inevitable because Sallenauve was but feebly defended by the politicians of his own party.

Nor was this lukewarm feeling at all surprising. Not knowing how to account for his conduct, the Opposition papers, while they felt it their duty to defend him, were afraid of saying too much in favor of a man whose future grew more doubtful every day; for might he not at any moment give the lie to the certificate of high morals which had been so rashly given?

On the day when his week's leave ended, Sallenauve, not having yet returned, a second-rate Ministerial paper published, under the heading of "Lost, a deputy!" an insolent and witty article which made a considerable sensation.

That evening Madame de l'Estorade called on Madame de Camps, and found her alone with her husband. She was greatly excited, and exclaimed as she went in:

"Have you read that infamous article?"

"No," said Madame de Camps. "But my husband has told me about it; it is really disgraceful that the Ministry should order, or at least encourage, anything so atrocious."

"I am half crazed by it," said Madame de l'Estorade, "for it is all our doing."

"That is carrying conscientious scruples too far," said Madame de Camps.

"Not at all," said the ironmaster. "I agree with madame. All the venom of this attack would be dispersed by a single step on l'Estorade's part; and by refusing to take it, if he is not the originator, he is at least the abettor of the scandal."

"Then you have told him——?" asked the Countess reproachfully.

"Why, my dear," replied Madame Octave, "though we have our little women's secrets, I could not but explain to my husband what had given rise to the sort of monomania that possesses Monsieur de l'Estorade. It would have been such a distrust of my second self as would have hurt him deeply; and such explanations as I felt bound to give him have not, I think, made me a faithless depositary of any secret that concerns you personally."

"Ah, you are a happy couple!" said Madame de l'Estorade, with a sigh. "However, I am not sorry that Monsieur de Camps should have been admitted to our confidence; the point is, to find some way out of the difficult position in which I am struggling, and two opinions are better than one."

"Why, what has happened?" asked Madame de Camps.

"My husband's head is quite turned," replied the Countess. "He seems to me to have lost every trace of moral sense. Far from perceiving that he is, as Monsieur de Camps said just now, the abettor of the odious contest now going on, without having—as those who had started it—the excuse of ignorance, he seems to exult in it. He brought me that detestable paper with an air of triumph, and I found him quite ready to take offence because I did not agree with him in thinking it most amusing and witty."

"That letter," said Madame Octave, "was a terrible blow to him; it hit him body and soul at once."

"That I grant," cried the ironmaster. "But deuce take it! If you are a man, you take a lunatic's words for what they are worth."

"Still, it is very strange," said his wife, "that Monsieur de Sallenauve does not come back; for, after all, that Jacques Bricheteau to whom you gave his address must have written to him."

"What is to be done!" exclaimed the Countess. "There has been a fatality over the whole business. To-morrow the question is to be discussed in the Chamber as to whether or no Monsieur de Sallenauve's election is to be ratified; and if he should not then be in his place, the Ministry hopes to be able to annul it."

"But it really is atrocious!" said Monsieur de Camps; "and though my position hardly justifies me in taking such a step, a very little would make me go straight to the President of the Chamber and tell him a few home truths——"

"I would have begged you to do so, I think, even at the risk of my husband's detecting my intervention, but for one consideration—it would distress Monsieur de Sallenauve so greatly that his friend's unhappy state should be made public."

"Certainly," said Madame Octave. "Such a line of defence would evidently be contrary to his intentions; and, after all, he may yet arrive in time. Besides, the decision of the Chamber still remains problematical, while, Monsieur Marie-Gaston's madness once known, he can never get over the blow."

"And then," added Madame de l'Estorade, "all the odious part that my husband has taken so far in this dreadful business is as nothing in comparison with a really diabolical idea which he communicated to me just now before dinner."

"What can that be?" asked Madame de Camps anxiously.

"His idea is that to-morrow I am to go with him to the gallery reserved for the peers to hear the question discussed."

"Really, he is losing his wits!" said Monsieur de Camps. "It is quite like Diafoirus the younger, who offers his bride elect the diversion of seeing a dissection——"

Madame de Camps shook her head meaningly at her husband, as much as to say, "Do not pour oil on the flames." She merely asked the Countess if she had not shown Monsieur de l'Estorade how monstrous such a proceeding would appear.

"At the very first word I spoke to that effect, he flew into a rage," said Madame de l'Estorade, "telling me that I was apparently only too glad to perpetuate a belief in our intimacy with *this man,* since, on an opportunity when I could so naturally proclaim our rupture to the public I so resolutely declined it."

"Well, then, my dear, you must go," said Madame Octave, "Domestic peace before all things. Besides, after all, your presence at the sitting may equally well be regarded as a proof of kindly interest."

"For fifteen years," said the ironmaster, "you have reigned

and ruled at home, and this is a revolution which seriously shifts the focus of power."

"But, monsieur, I beg you to believe that I should never have made such use of the sovereignty, which indeed I have always tried to conceal."

"Do I not know it?" replied Monsieur de Camps warmly, as he took Madame de l'Estorade's hands in his own. "But I agree with my wife—this cup must be drained."

"I shall die of shame as I listen to the infamous charges the Ministerial party will bring! I shall feel as if they were murdering a man under my own eyes, whom I could save by merely putting my hand out—and I cannot do it——"

"Yes, it is so," said Monsieur de Camps. "And a man, too, who has done you signal service; but would you rather bring hell into your house, and aggravate your husband's unhealthy state?"

"Listen, my dear," said Madame de Camps. "Tell Monsieur de l'Estorade that I also wish to go to this sitting; that it will give less cause for comment if you are seen there with a person who is uninterested and merely curious; and on that point do not give way. Then, at any rate, I shall be there to keep your head straight on your shoulders and preserve you from yourself."

"I should not have dared to ask it of you," replied Madame de l'Estorade, "for one does not like to ask any one to assist in evil-doing; but since you are so generous as to offer it, I feel I am a degree less wretched.—Now, good-night, for my husband must not find me out when he comes in. He was to dine with Monsieur de Rastignac, and no doubt they have plotted great things for to-morrow."

"Go then; and in an hour or so I will send you a note, as though I had not seen you, to ask if you have any power to admit me to the Chamber to-morrow, as the meeting promises to be interesting."

"Oh! To be brought so low as to plot and contrive——" said Madame de l'Estorade, embracing her friend.

"My dear child," replied Madame de Camps, "it is said

that the life of the Christian is a warfare; but that of a
woman married to a certain type of man is a pitched battle.
Be patient and take courage."

And so the friends parted.

At about two o'clock on the following day Madame de
l'Estorade, with her husband and Madame de Camps, took her
seat in the peers' gallery; she looked ill, and returned the
bows that greeted her from various parts of the House with
cool indifference. Madame de Camps, who had never before
found herself in the parliamentary Chamber, made two observations: In the first place, she exclaimed at the slovenly
appearance of so many of the honorable members; and then
she was struck by the number of bald heads which, as she
looked down on them from the gallery that gave her a bird's-
eye view of the assembly, surprised her greatly.

She then listened while Monsieur de l'Estorade named the
notabilities present; first all the bigwigs, who need not be
mentioned here, since their names dwell in everybody's memory; then Canalis, the poet, who had, she thought, an Olympian air; d'Arthez, whose modest demeanor greatly attracted
her; Vinet, who, as she said, was like a viper in spectacles;
Victorin Hulot, one of the orators of the Left Centre. It
was some little time before she could get accustomed to the
hum of conversation all round her, comparing it to the noise
of a swarm of bees buzzing about a hive. But what chiefly
amazed her was the general aspect of the assembly; the
strange free-and-easiness and total absence of dignity did not
in the least suggest that it was representative of a great
nation.

It was written by the finger of fate that Madame de l'Estorade should be spared no form of annoyance. Just as the
sitting was about to open, the Marquise d'Espard, escorted
by Monsieur de Ronquerolles, came into the gallery, and took
a seat close to her. Though they met in society, the two
women could not endure each other. Madame de l'Estorade
scorned the spirit of intrigue, the total want of principle, and

the spiteful, bitter temper which the Marquise concealed under the most elegant manners; while Madame d'Espard had
even deeper contempt for what she called the "pot-boiling"
virtues of the Countess. It must be added that Madame de
l'Estorade was two-and-thirty, and of a type of beauty that
time had spared; while Madame d'Espard was forty-four,
and in spite of the arts of the toilet, her looks were altogether past.

"Do you often come here?" she said to the Countess, after
a few indispensable civilities as to the pleasure of meeting
her.

"Never," said Madame de l'Estorade.

"I am a constant visitor," said Madame d'Espard.

Then, with the air of making a discovery:

"To be sure," she added, "you have a special interest in the
meeting to-day. Some one you know, I believe, is on his
trial."

"Yes, Monsieur de Sallenauve has visited at my house."

"It is most distressing," said the Marquise, "to see a man
who, as Monsieur de Ronquerolles assures me, was quite a
hero in his way thus called to account by the police."

"His chief crime, so far, is his absence," said the Countess
drily.

"And he is consumed by ambition, it would seem," Madame
d'Espard went on. "Before this attempt to get into Parliament he had matrimonial projects, as you no doubt know,
and had tried to marry into the Lanty family—a scheme
which, so far as the handsome heiress was concerned, ended
in her retirement to a convent."

Madame de l'Estorade was not astonished to find that this
story, which Sallenauve had believed to be a perfect secret,
was known to the Marquise; she was one of the best-informed
women in Paris. An old Academician had called her drawing-room, in mythological parlance, "The Temple of Fame."

"They are about to begin, I think," said the Countess, who,
always expecting to feel Madame d'Espard's claws, was not
sorry to close the conversation.

The President had in fact rung his bell, the members were settling into their places, the curtain was about to rise.

To give the reader a faithful account of the sitting, we think it will be at once more exact and more convenient to copy the report as printed in one of the papers of the day.

CHAMBER OF DEPUTIES

MONSIEUR COINTET (Vice President) in the Chair.

May 23rd.

The President took the chair at two o'clock.

On the Ministers' bench were the Keeper of the Seals, the Minister of the Interior, and the Minister of Public Works.

The report of the last meeting was read and passed.

The order of the day was to discuss the validity of the election of the member returned by the borough of Arcis-sur-Aube.

The President—The representative of the Commission of Inquiry will read his report.

The Reporter—Gentlemen, the strange and unsatisfactory position in which Monsieur de Sallenauve has thought proper to place himself has not ended as we had reason to hope. Monsieur de Sallenauve's leave of absence expired yesterday, and he still remains away from the sittings of the Chamber; nor has any letter from him applying for further extension reached the President's hands. This indifference as to the functions which Monsieur de Sallenauve had sought, it would seem, with unusual eagerness (murmurs from the Left), would under any circumstances be a serious defection; but when it is coupled with the prosecution now threatened, does it not assume a character highly damaging to his reputation? (Murmurs from the Left. Applause from the Centre.) Your Commissioners, compelled to seek the solution of a question which may be said to be unexampled in parliamentary annals, when considering the steps to be taken, were divided by two opposite opinions. The minority, of which I am the sole representative—the Commissioners being but three—thought that a plan should be laid before you which I may call radical in its character, and which aims at settling the difficulty by submitting it to its natural judges. Annul M. de Sallenauve's election *hic et nunc,* and send him back to the constituency which returned him, and of which he is so faithless a representative: this is the first alternative I have to offer you. (Excitement on the Left.) The majority, on the contrary, pronounced that the electors' vote must be absolutely respected, and the shortcomings of a man honored by their confidence must be overlooked to the utmost limits of patience and indulgence. Consequently, the Commission requires me to propose that you should officially extend M. de Sallenauve's leave of absence to a fortnight from this date— (murmurs from the Centre. "Hear, hear," from the Left)— with the full understanding that if by the end of that time M. de Sallenauve has given no sign of life, he is to be regarded as simply having resigned his seat without entangling this House in any irritating and useless discussion of the matter. (Excitement on all sides.)

M. le Colonel Franchessini, who, during the reading of the report, had been engaged in earnest conversation with the Minister of Public Works on the Ministers' bench, anxiously begged to be heard.

The President—M. de Canalis wishes to speak.

M. de Canalis—Gentlemen, M. de Sallenauve is one of those bold men who, like me, believe that politics are not a forbidden fruit to any intelligent mind; but that the stuff of which a statesman is made may be found in a poet or an artist quite as much as in a lawyer, an official, a doctor, or a land-owner. In virtue, then, of our common origin, M. de Sallenauve has my fullest sympathy, and no one will be surprised to see me mount this tribune to support the recommendation of the Commission. Still, I cannot agree to their final decision; for the idea of our colleague being regarded, by the mere fact of his prolonged absence beyond the limit of leave, as having resigned his seat, is repugnant both to my conscience and my reason. You have heard it remarked that M. de Sallenauve's carelessness as to his duties is all the less excusable because he lies under a serious charge; but, supposing, gentlemen, that this charge were the actuating cause of his absence. (Laughter from the Centre.) Allow me—I am not so guileless as the laughers seem to fancy. It is my good fortune, by nature, that base suggestions do not occur to me; and that M. de Sallenauve, with the high position he had achieved as an artist, should plot to take his seat in this Chamber by means of a crime, is a theory I refuse to admit. Two foul spiders are ever ready to spin their web about a man with such a stain on his birth—Chicanery and Intrigue. But I, far from admitting that he would have fled before the charge brought against him, I say, suppose that at this moment, abroad, he were collecting the evidence for his defence? ("Hear, hear; well said!" from the Left.) In this belief,—a very plausible one, as it seems to me—far from being justified in requiring a strict account of his absence, ought we not rather to regard it as a proof of respect for this House, as feeling himself unworthy to take his place in it till he was in a position to defy his accusers?

A Voice—Ten years' leave of absence, like Telemachus, to look for his father. (General laughter.)

M. de Canalis—I did not expect so romantic an interruption! But since we are referred to the Odyssey, I may remind you that Ulysses, after suffering every outrage, at last drew his bow, very much to the discomfiture of the suitors. (Loud murmurs from the Centre.) I vote for a fortnight's further leave, and a reopening of the question at the end of that time.

M. le Colonel Franchessini—I do not know whether the last speaker intended to intimidate the Chamber; for my part, such arguments affect me very little, and I am always prepared to return them to those who utter them. ("Ordeɪ, ordeɾ," from the Left.)

M. le Président—No personalities, Colonel.

M. le Colonel Franchessini—At the same time, I am so far of the same opinion as the last speaker that I do not believe that the delinquent has fled from the charge brought against him. Neither that accusation, nor the effect it may have on your minds or on others, nor even the annulling of his election, has any interest for him at present. Do you wish to know what M. de Sallenauve is doing in England? Then read the English papers. They have for some days been full of the praises of a prima donna who has just come out at Her Majesty's Theatre. (Groans and interruptions.)

A Voice—Such gossip is unworthy of this House.

M. le Colonel Franchessini—Gentlemen, I am more accustomed to the blunt speech of camps than to the proprieties of the Chamber; I am perhaps rash in thinking aloud. The honorable gentleman who spoke last said that he believed that M. de Sallenauve had gone in search of evidence for his defence. I say—not I believe, but I know, that a wealthy foreigner has extended his protection to a handsome Italian who was formerly honored by that of our colleague Phidias. (Fresh interruptions. "Order, order; this is not to be allowed!")

A Voice—Monsieur le Président, will you not silence this speaker?"

Colonel Franchessini, folding his arms, waited till silence should be restored.

M. le Président—I must request the speaker to adhere to the question.

M. le Colonel Franchessini—I have never deviated from it; however, as the Chamber refuses to hear me, I can but say that I vote with the minority. It seems to me a very natural course to send Monsieur de Sallenauve back to his constituency, and to ascertain whether they meant to elect a deputy or a lover. ("Order, order!" A great commotion; excitement at the highest pitch.)

M. de Canalis hastily tried to mount the tribune.

M. le Président—The Minister of Public Works wishes to speak, and as one of the King's Ministry, he has always a right to be heard.

M. de Rastignac—It is no fault of mine, gentlemen, that

you have not been saved from this scandal in the Chamber. I tried, out of regard for my old friendship with Colonel Franchessini, to persuade him not to speak on so delicate a matter, since his inexperience of parliamentary rule, aggravated by his ready wit and fluency, might betray him into some regrettable extravagance. It was to this effect that I advised him in the course of the short conversation we held at my seat before he addressed the House; and I myself asked to be heard after him expressly to correct any idea of my collusion in the indiscretion he has committed—in my opinion —by descending to the confidential details he has thought proper to trouble you with. However, as against my intention, and so to say, against my will, I have mounted the tribune, though no ministerial interest detains me here, may I be allowed to make a few brief remarks? ("Speak, speak!" from the Centre.)

The Minister of Public Works proceeded to show that the absent member's conduct was characterized by marked contempt for the Chamber. He had treated it with cavalier indifference. He had indeed asked leave of absence; but how? By writing from abroad. That is to say, he first took leave, and then asked for it. Had he, as was customary, assigned any reason for the request? Not at all. He simply announced that he was compelled to be absent on urgent private business, a trumpery pretext which might at any time reduce the assembly by half its members. But supposing that M. de Sallenauve's business were really urgent, and that it were of a nature which he thought it undesirable to explain in a letter to be made public, why could he not have laid it in confidence before the President, or even have requested one of his friends of such standing as would secure credit for his mere word, to answer for the necessity for his absence without any detailed explanation?

At this moment the Minister was interrupted by a bustle in the passage to the right; several of the members left their places; others standing on the seats and craning their necks were looking at something. The Minister, after turning to the President, to whom he seemed to appeal for an explanation, went down from the tribune and returned to his seat, when he was immediately surrounded by a number of deputies from the Centre, among whom M. Vinet was conspicuous by his gesticulations. Other groups formed in the arena; in fact, the sitting was practically suspended.

In a few minutes the President rang his bell.

The ushers—Take your seats, gentlemen.

The members hastily returned to their places.

M. le Président—M. de Sallenauve will now speak.

M. de Sallenauve, who had been talking to M. d'Arthez and M. de Canalis since his arrival had suspended business, went up to the tribune. His manner was modest, but quite free from embarrassment. Everybody was struck by his resemblance to one of the most fiery of the revolutionary orators.

A Voice—Danton minus the smallpox.

M. de Sallenauve (deep silence)—Gentlemen, I am under no illusion as to my personal importance, and do not imagine that I myself am the object of a form of persecution, which would rather seem to be directed against the opinions I have the honor to represent. However that may be, my election seems to have assumed some importance in the eyes of the Ministry. To contest it, a special agent and special press writers were sent to Arcis; and a humble servant of the Government, whose salary, after twenty years of honorable service, had reached the figure of fifteen hundred francs a year, was suddenly dismissed from his post for being guilty of contributing to my success. (Loud murmurs from the Centre.) I can only thank the gentlemen who are interrupting me, for I suppose their noisy disapprobation is meant for this singular dismissal, and not to convey a doubt of the fact, which is beyond all question. (Laughter from the Left.) So far as I am concerned, as I could not be turned out, I have been attacked with another weapon; judicial calumny combined with my opportune absence——

The Minister of Public Works—It was the Ministry evidently that procured your extradition to England?

M. de Sallenauve—No, Monsieur le Ministre, I do not ascribe my absence either to your influence or to your suggestions; it was an act of imperative duty, and the result of no one's bidding; but as regards your share in the public accusations brought against me, I shall proceed to lay the facts before this assembly, and leave the matter to their judgment. (A stir of interest.) The law which, in order to protect the independence of a member of this Chamber, lays down the rule that a criminal prosecution cannot be instituted against any member without the preliminary authority of the Chamber, has been turned against me, I must say with consummate skill. The indictment, if presented to the Attorney-General in Court, would have been at once dismissed, for it stands alone without the support of any kind of proof; and, so far as I know, the Ministry of this nation is not in the habit of prosecuting anybody on the strength of the allegation of the first comer. I cannot, therefore, but admire the remarkable acumen which discerned that by appealing to this Chamber, the charge would have all the advantages of a political attack, though it had not the elements of the simplest criminal case. (Murmurs.) And then, gentlemen, who is the skilful parliamentary campaigner to be credited with this masterly device? As you know, it is a woman, a peasant, claiming only the humble rank of a hand-worker; whence we must infer that the countrywomen of Champagne can boast of an intellectual superiority of which hitherto you can surely have had no conception. (Laughter.) It must, however, be added that before setting out for Paris to state her grievance, my accuser would seem to have had an interview, which may have thrown some light on her mind, with the Mayor of Arcis, my ministerial opponent for election; and it is furthermore to be supposed that this magistrate had some interest in the prosecution to be instituted, since he thought it his duty to pay the traveling expenses both of the plaintiff and of the village lawyer who accompanied her. ("Ha-ha!" from the Left.) This remarkably clever woman having come to Paris, on whom does she first call? Well, on that very gentleman who had been sent to Arcis by the Government as a special agent to insure the success of the ministerial candidate. And who then made it his business to apply for authority to prosecute? Not indeed that same special agent, but a lawyer directed by him, after a breakfast to which the peasant woman and her rustic adviser were invited, to supply the necessary grounds. (Much excitement and a long buzz of talk.)

The Minister of Public Works, from his bench—Without discussing the truth of facts of which I personally have no knowledge, I may state on my honor that the Government was absolutely unaware of all the intrigues described, and repudiates and blames them in unqualified terms.

M. de Sallenauve—After the express denial which I have been so fortunate as to elicit, I feel, gentlemen, that it would be ungracious to insist on foisting on the Government the responsibility for these proceedings; but that I should have made the mistake will seem to you quite natural if you remember that at the moment when I entered this hall the Minister for Public Works was speaking from the tribune and taking part in a very unusual way in a discussion bearing on the rules of this Chamber, while trying to convince you that I had treated its members with irreverent contumely.

The Minister for Public Works made some remark which was not heard; there was a long burst of private discussion.

M. Victorin Hulot—I would beg the President to desire the Minister for Public Works not to interrupt. He will have the opportunity of replying.

M. de Sallenauve—According to M. de Rastignac, I failed in respect to this Chamber by applying from abroad for the leave of absence which I had already taken before obtaining the permission I affected to ask. But, in his anxiety to prove me in the wrong, the Minister overlooks the fact that at the time when I set out the session had not begun, and that by addressing such a request to the President of the Chamber I should have appealed to a pure abstraction. ("Quite true," from the Left.) As to the inadequacy of the reasons assigned for my absence, I regret to say that I was unable to be more explicit; that if I should reveal the true cause of my journey, I should betray a secret that is not mine. At the same time I was fully aware that by this reserve—which I must even now maintain—I exposed my actions to monstrous misinterpretation, and might expect to see a mixture of the burlesque and the offensive in the explanations that would be given as a substitute for the facts. (Excitement.) In reality, I was so anxious not to pretermit any of the formalities required by my position, that I, like the Minister himself, had thought of the arrangement by which I fancied I had put everything in order. A man of the highest honor, and, like myself, in possession of the secret that compelled me to travel, had been requested by me to guarantee to the President of this Chamber the imperative necessity to which I had yielded. But calumny had, no doubt, so far done its work that this honorable gentleman feared to compromise himself by affording the signal protection of his name and word to a man threatened with a criminal action. Although at this moment danger seems to be receding from me, I shall not destroy the incognito in which he has thought it proper and wise to shroud his defection. The less I was prepared for this egotistic prudence, the more have I the right to be surprised and pained by it; but the more careful shall I be to let this breach of friendship remain a secret between myself and his conscience, which alone will blame him.

At this stage there was a great commotion in the gallery reserved for the Peers of the Upper House, everybody crowding to help a lady who had a violent attack of hysterics. Several members hurried to the spot, and some, doctors no doubt, left the Chamber in haste. The sitting was interrupted for some minutes.

The President—Ushers, open the ventilators. It is want of air that has led to this unfortunate incident. M. de Sallenauve, be so good as to go on with your speech.

M. de Sallenauve—To resume, briefly: The application for authority to prosecute, of which you have heard, has now, no doubt, lost much of its importance in the eyes of my colleagues, even of the more hostile. I have here a letter in which the peasant-woman, my relation, withdraws her charge and confirms the statements I have had the honor of laying before you. I might read the letter, but I think it better simply to place it in the President's hands. ("Quite right, quite right!") As regards the illegality of my absence, I returned to Paris this morning; and by being in my place at the opening of this sitting, I could have been in my seat in Parliament within the strict limits of the time so generously granted me by this Chamber. But, as M. de Canalis suggested to you, I was determined not to appear here till the cloud that hung over my character could be cleared off. This task filled up the morning.—Now, gentlemen, it is for you to decide whether one of your colleagues is to be sent back to his constituents, for a few hours' delay in coming to claim his seat in this Chamber. After all, whether I am to be regarded as a forger, a desperate lover, or merely as a careless representative, I am not uneasy as to what their verdict will be; and after the lapse of a few weeks, the probable result, as I believe, will be that I shall come back again.

On all sides cries of "Divide."

On descending from the tribune, M. de Sallenauve was warmly congratulated.

The President—I put it to the vote: Whether or no the election of M. de Sallenauve, returned as Member for Arcis, is or is not valid?

Almost every member present rose to vote in favor of the admission of the new member; a few deputies of the Centre abstained from voting on either side.

M. de Sallenauve was admitted and took the oaths.

M. le Président—The order of the day includes the first reading of the Address, but the Chairman of the Committee informs me that the draft will not be ready to be laid before this Chamber till to-morrow. Business being done, I pronounce the sitting closed.

The Chamber rose at half-past four.

NOTE.—Balzac left "The Member for Arcis" unfinished. See introduction.

J. W. M.

THE SEAMY SIDE OF HISTORY

AND OTHER STORIES

INTRODUCTION

It would be difficult to find another book, composed of two parts by the same author, which offers more remarkable variations and contrasts than the volume which contains *L'Envers de l'Histoire Contemporaine* and *Z. Marcas.* And in certain respects it must be said that the contrast of the longer and later story with the earlier and shorter one is not such as to inspire us with any great certainty that, had Balzac's comparatively short life been prolonged, we should have had many more masterpieces. It is true that, considering the remarkable excellence of the work (*Les Parents Pauvres*) which immediately preceded *L'Envers de l'Histoire,* it is not possible to say with confidence that the inferiority of the present book is anything more than one of the usual phenomena of *maxima* and *minima*—of ups and downs—which present themselves in all human affairs.

At the same time, there is in *L'Envers de l'Histoire Contemporaine* an ominous atmosphere of flagging, combined with a not less ominous return to a weaker handling of ideas and schemes which the author had handled more strongly earlier. We have seen that the secret-society craze—a favorite one with most Frenchmen, and closely connected with their famous panic-terror of being "betrayed" in war and politics—had an especially strong hold on this most typical of French novelists. He had almost begun his true career with the notion of a league of *Dévorants,* of persons banded, if not exactly against society, at any rate for the gratifying of their own desires and the avenging of their own wrongs, with an utter indifference to social laws and arrangements. He ended it, or nearly so, with the idea of a contrary league of Consolation, which should employ money, time, pains, and combination to supply the wants and heal the wounds which Society either directly causes or more or less callously neglects.

The later idea is, of course, a far nobler one than the earlier; it shows a saner, healthier, happier state of imagination; it coincides rather remarkably with an increasing tendency of the age ever since Balzac's time. Nay, more, the working out of it contains none of those improbabilities and childishnesses which, to any but very youthful tastes and judgments, mar the *Histoire des Treize*. And it is also better written. Balzac, with that extraordinary "long development" of his, as they say of wines, constantly improved in this particular; and whatever may be the doubts on the point referred to above, we may say with some confidence that had he lived, he would have written, in the mere sense of *writing,* even better and better. Yet again, we catch quaint and pleasant echoes of youth in these pages, and are carried back nearly fifty years in nominal date, and more than twenty in dates of actual invention, by such names as Montauran and Pille-Miche and Marche-à-Terre.

But when all this is said, it cannot, I think, be denied that a certain dulness, a heaviness, does rest on Madame de la Chanterie and L'Initié. The very reference to the *Médecin de Campagne,* which Balzac with his systematizing mania brings in, calls up another unlucky contrast. There, too, the benevolence and the goodness were something fanciful, not to say fantastic; but there was an inspiration, a vigor, to speak vulgarly, a "go," which we do not find here. Balzac's awkward and inveterate habit of parenthetic and episodic narratives and glances backward is not more obvious here than in many other pieces; but there is not, as in some at least of these other pieces, strength enough of main interest to carry it off. The light is clear, it is religious and touching in its dimness; but the lamp burns low.

Z. Marcas, on the other hand, written a good deal earlier in the author's public career, at that quaint and tumbledown residence of Les Jardies, where he did some of his very best work, has all the verve and vigor which its companion or companions lack. Numerous and often good as are the stories by all manner of hands, eminent and other, of the strange neighbors and acquaintance which the French habit of living in apartments brings about, this may vie with almost the best of them for individuality and force. Of course, it may be said that its brevity demanded no very great effort; and also, a more worthy criticism, that Balzac has not made it so very clear after all why the political ingratitude of those for whom Marcas labored made it impossible for him to gain a living more amply and comfortably than by copying. The former carp needs no answer; the sonnet *is* the equal of the long poem if it is a perfect sonnet. The latter, more respectable, is also more damaging. But it is a fair, if not quite a full, defence to say that Balzac is here once more exemplifying his favorite notion of the *maniaque* in the French sense—of the man with one idea, who is incapable not only of making a dishonorable surrender of that idea, but of entering into even the most honorable armistice in his fight for it. Not only will such a man not bow in the House of Rimmon, but the fullest liberty to stay outside will not content him—he must force himself in and be at the idol. The external as well as the internal portraiture of *Z. Marcas* is also as good as it can be: and it cannot but add legitimate interest to the sketch to remember, first, that Balzac attributes to Marcas his own favorite habits and times of work; and secondly, that, like some other men of letters, he himself was an untiring, and would fain have been an influential, politician.

"*Un Episode sous la Terreur* is one of the brilliant things in a small way, which the author did not attempt afterwards to expand at the obvious risk of weakening. It is compressed into compass commensurate with its artistic limits, and, thus preserved, it displays all the strength and vivacity which the plot demands. When Balzac was thus content to leave a 'skit' of this sort, or when he condensed as only Balzac could condense—as in the case of *La Maison du Chat-qui-Pelote*—the result was a story the like of which could scarcely be duplicated in the whole range of French literature. As for the sinister side of *Un Episode sous la Terreur*, it is well known how great was the attraction with the author for things of this kind. And that he treated them vigorously and well, this story will witness."

Un Episode sous la Terreur, together with the two stories just noted, forms a part of the limited *Scènes de la Vie Politique.*

L'Envers de l'Histoire Contemporaine, as above stated, was, in part, one of the very latest of Balzac's works, and was actually finished during his residence at Vierzschovnia. *Madame de la Chanterie,* however, was somewhat earlier, part of it having been written in 1842. It appeared in a fragmentary and rather topsy-turvy fashion, with separate titles, in the *Musée des Familles,* from September in the year just named to November 1844, and was only united together in the first edition of the *Comédie* two years later, though even after this it had a separate appearance with some others of its author's works in 1847. *L'Initié,* or, as it was first entitled, *Les Frères de la Consolation,* was not written till this latter year, and appeared in 1848 in the *Spectateur Republicain,* but not as a book till after the author's death. In both cases there was the usual alternation of chapter divisions, with headings and none.

Z. Marcas, written in 1840, appeared in the *Revue Parisienne* for July of that year, made its first book appearance in a miscellany by different hands called *Le Fruit Défendu* (1841), and five years later took rank in the *Comédie.*

The other stories included here for the sake of convenience may be located readily by reference to the Balzacian scheme, all being from *Scènes de la Vie Parisienne.*

A Prince of Bohemia, the first of the short stories which Balzac originally chose as make-weights to associate with the long drama of *Splendeurs et Misères des Courtisanes,* is one of the few things that, both in whole and in part, one would much rather he had not written. Its dedication to Heine only brings out its shortcomings. For Heine, though he would certainly be as spiteful and unjust as Balzac here shows himself, never failed to carry the laugh on his side. You may wish him, in his lampoons, better morals and better taste, but you can seldom wish him better literature. Had he made this attack on Sainte-Beuve, we should certainly not have yawned over it; and it is rather amusing to think of the sardonic smile with which the dedicatee must have read Balzac's comfortable assurance that he, Heinrich Heine, would understand the *plaisanterie* and the *critique* which *Un Prince de la Bohème* contains. Heine "understood" most things; but if understanding, as is probable, here includes sympathetic enjoyment, we may doubt.

It was written at the same time, or very nearly so, as the more serious attack on Sainte-Beuve in August 1840, and, like that, appeared in Balzac's own *Revue Parisienne,* though it was somewhat later. The thread, such as there is, of interest is two-fold—the description of the Bohemian *grand seigneur* Rusticoli or La Palférine, and the would-be satire on Sainte-Beuve. It is difficult to say which is least well done. Both required an exceedingly light hand, and Balzac's hand was at no time light. Moreover, in the sketch of La Palférine he commits the error—nearly as great in a book as on the stage, where I am told it is absolutely fatal—of delineating his hero with a sort of sneaking kindness which is neither dramatic impartiality nor satiric raillery. La Palférine as portrayed is a "raff," with a touch of no aristocratic quality except insolence. He might have been depicted with cynically concealed savagery, as Swift would have done it; with humorous ridicule, as Gautier or Charles de Bernard would have done it; but there was hardly a third way. As it is, the sneaking kindness above referred to is one of the weapons in the hands of those who—unjustly if it be done without a great deal of limitation—contend that Balzac's ideal of a gentleman was low, and that he had a touch of snobbish admiration for mere insolence.

Here, however, it is possible for a good-natured critic to put in the apology that the artist has tried something unto which he was not born, and failing therein, has apparently committed faults greater than his real ones. This kindness is impossible in the case of the parodies, which are no parodies, of Sainte-Beuve. From the strictly literary point of view, it is disastrous to give as a parody of a man's work, with an intention of casting ridicule thereon, something which is not in the least like that work, and which in consequence only casts ridicule on its author. To the criticism which takes in life as well as literature, it is a disaster to get in childish rages with people because they do not think your work as good as you think it yourself. And it is not known that Balzac had to complain of Sainte-Beuve in any other way than this, though he no doubt read into what Sainte-Beuve wrote a great deal more than Sainte-Beuve did say. There is a story (I think unpublished) that a certain very great English poet of our times once met an excellent critic who was his old friend (they are both dead now). "What do you mean by calling —— vulgar?" growled the poet.—"I didn't call it vulgar," said the critic.—"No; but you meant it," rejoined the bard. On this system of interpretation it is of course possible to accumulate crimes with great rapidity on a censor's head. But it cannot be said to be a critical or rational proceeding. And it must be said that if an author does reply, against the advice of Bacon and all wise people, he should reply by something better than the spluttering abuse of the *Revue Parisienne* article or the inept and irrelevant parody of this story.

Un Homme d'Affaires, relieved of this unlucky weight, is better, but it also, in the eyes of some readers, does not stand very high. La Palférine reappears, and that more exalted La Palférine Maxime de Trailles, "Balzac's pet scoundrel," as some one has called him, though not present, is the hero of the tale, which is artificial and slight enough.

Gaudissart II. is much better. Of course, it is very slight, and the "Anglaise" is not much more like a human being than most "Anglaises" in French novels till quite recently. But the anecdote is amusing enough, and it is well and smartly told.

"*Sarrasine* presents two points of divergence from other Balzacian stories: It contains no feminine characters, although the pro- and epilogue introduce two of the 'stock' women personages of the *Comédie*. It is a story within a story, which is no infrequent thing, but, unlike others, the conteur is unknown. While not dealing with a theme the most pleasant, *Sarrasine* will appeal by its clear-cut style; it is one of the cleverest of the shorter tales. Considering the species of singer referred to, the personnel of the Italian operatic stage was well known as far back as the days of Addison and Steele. In France also its customs were freely discussed. Granted, however, that such was the case, the story is open to criticism on this account. It seems hardly possible that a well-informed man of the time should have been entirely ignorant of the fact that the Italians allowed no women to sing in public; and that this man, a sculptor by profession, should have been deceived by the figure of a eunuch so frankly displayed in the glare of the footlights. He studied every line of every limb. He noted the well-formed shoulders and the poise of the head. He reproduced the contour of the form in marble. Yet he was deluded openly and hoaxed without mercy. But, aside from this possible defect in plot, the story presents a striking contrast in the figures of the passionate, obstinate, hot-headed man, and the shrinking, irresolute, sexless creature."

Facino Cane did not originally rank in the Parisian Scenes at all, but was a *Conte Philosophique*. It is slight and rather fanciful, the chief interest lying in Balzac's unfailing fellow-feeling for all those who dream of millions, as he himself did all his life long, only to exemplify the moral of his own *Peau de Chagrin*.

Un Prince de la Bohème, in its *Revue Parisienne* appearance, bore the title of *Les Fantaisies de Claudine,* but when, four years later, it followed *Honorine* in book form, it took the present label. The *Comédie* received it two years later. *Gaudissart II.* was written for a miscellany called *Le Diable à Paris;* but as this delayed its appearance, it was first inserted in the *Presse* for October 12, 1844, under a slightly different title, which it kept in the *Diable*. Almost immediately, however, it joined the *Comédie* under its actual heading. *Un Homme d'Affaires* appeared in the *Siècle* for September 10, 1845, and was then called *Les Roueries d'un Créancier.* It entered the *Comédie* almost at once, but made an excursion therefrom to join, in 1847, *Ou mènent les mauvais chemins* and others as *Un Drame dans les Prisons.*

Facino Cane is earlier than these, having first seen the light in the *Chronique de Paris* of March 17, 1836. Next year it became an *Étude Philosophique*. It had another grouped appearance (with *La Muse du Département* and *Albert Savarus*) in 1843, and entered the *Comédie* the year after.

Sarrasine was published by Werdet in October 1838, being included in a volume with *Les Secrets de la Princesse de Cadignan, Les Employés, Facino Cane* and *La Maison Nucingen,* the latter of which was the title story. It was included in its present place in the *Comédie* in 1844.

THE SEAMY SIDE OF HISTORY

FIRST EPISODE

MADAME DE LA CHANTERIE

ONE fine September evening, in the year 1836, a man of about thirty was leaning over the parapet of the quay at a point whence the Seine may be surveyed up stream from the Jardin des Plantes to Notre-Dame, and down in grand perspective to the Louvre.

There is no such view elsewhere in the Capital of Ideas (Paris). You are standing, as it were, on the poop of a vessel that has grown to vast proportions. You may dream there of Paris from Roman times to the days of the Franks, from the Normans to the Burgundians, through the Middle Ages to the Valois, Henri IV., Napoleon, and Louis Philippe. There is some vestige or building of each period to bring it to mind. The dome of Sainte-Geneviève shelters the *Quartier Latin*. Behind you rises the magnificent east end of the Cathedral. The Hotel de Ville speaks of all the revolutions, the Hôtel Dieu of all the miseries of Paris. After glancing at the splendors of the Louvre, take a few steps, and you can see the rags that hang out from the squalid crowd of houses that huddle between the Quai de la Tournelle and the Hôtel Dieu; the authorities are, however, about to clear them away.

In 1836 this astonishing picture inculcated yet another lesson. Between the gentleman who leaned over the parapet and the cathedral, the deserted plot, known of old as le Terrain, was still strewn with the ruins of the Archbishop's palace. As we gaze there on so many suggestive objects, as the mind takes in the past and the present of the city of Paris, Religion seems

to have established herself there that she might lay her hands
on the sorrows on both sides of the river, from the Faubourg
Saint-Antoine to the Faubourg Saint-Marceau.

It is to be hoped that these sublime harmonies may be completed by the construction of an Episcopal palace in a Gothic
style to fill the place of the meaningless buildings that now
stand between the Island, the Rue d'Arcole, and the Quai de
la Cité.

This spot, the very heart of old Paris, is beyond anything
deserted and melancholy.   The waters of the Seine break
against the wall with a loud noise, the Cathedral throws its
shadow there at sunset.   It is not strange that vast thoughts
should brood there in a brain-sick man.   Attracted perhaps
by an accordance between his own feelings at the moment and
those to which such a varied prospect must give rise, the loiterer folded his hands over the parapet, lost in the twofold contemplation of Paris and of himself!   The shadows spread,
lights twinkled into being, and still he did not stir; carried
on as he was by the flow of a mood of thought, big with the
future, and made solemn by the past.

At this instant he heard two persons approaching, whose
voices had been audible on the stone bridge where they had
crossed from the Island of the Cité ,to the Quai de la Tournelle.   The two speakers no doubt believed themselves to be
alone, and talked somewhat louder than they would have
done in a more frequented place, or if they had noticed the
propinquity of a stranger.   From the bridge their tones betrayed an eager discussion, bearing, as it seemed, from a few
words that reached the involuntary listener, on a loan of
money.   As they came closer, one of the speakers, dressed as
a working man, turned from the other with a gesture of despair.   His companion looked round, called the man back, and
said:

"You have not a sou to pay the bridge-toll.   Here!"—and
he gave him a coin—"and remember, my friend, it is God
Himself who speaks to us when a good thought occurs to us."

The last words startled the dreamer.   The man who spoke

had no suspicion that, to use a proverbial expression, he was killing two birds with one stone; that he spoke to two unhappy creatures—a workman at his wits' end, and a soul without a compass; a victim of what Panurge's sheep call Progress, and a victim of what France calls equality.

These words, simple enough in themselves, acquired grandeur from the tone of the speaker, whose voice had a sort of magical charm. Are there not such voices, calm and sweet, affecting us like a view of the distant ocean?

The speaker's costume showed him to be a priest, and his face, in the last gleam of twilight, was pale, and dignified, though worn. The sight of a priest coming out of the grand Cathedral of Saint Stephen at Vienna to carry extreme unction to a dying man, persuaded Werner, the famous tragic poet, to become a Catholic. The effect was much the same on our Parisian when he saw the man who, without intending it, had brought him consolation; he discerned on the dark line of his horizon in the future a long streak of light where the blue of heaven was shining, and he followed the path of light, as the shepherds of the Gospel followed the voice that called to them from on high, "Christ the Lord is born!"

The man of healing speech walked on under the cathedral, and by favor of Chance—which is sometimes consistent—made his way towards the street from which the loiterer had come, and whither he was returning, led there by his own mistakes in life.

This young man's name was Godefroid. As this narrative proceeds, the reader will understand the reasons for giving to the actors in it only their Christian names.

And this is the reason why Godefroid, who lived near the Chausée d'Antin, was lingering at such an hour under the shadow of Notre-Dame.

He was the son of a retail dealer, who, by economy, had made some little fortune, and in him centered all the ambitions of his parents, who dreamed of seeing him a notary in Paris. At the early age of seven he had been sent to a school, kept by the Abbé Liautard, where he was thrown together with the children of certain families of distinction, who had selected this establishment for the education of their sons, out of attachment to religion, which, under the emperor, was somewhat too much neglected in the Lycées, or public schools. At that age social inequalities are not recognized between school-fellows; but in 1821, when his studies were finished, Godefroid, articled to a notary, was not slow to perceive the distance that divided him from those with whom he had hitherto lived on terms of intimacy.

While studying the law, he found himself lost in the crowd of young men of the citizen class, who, having neither a ready-made fortune nor hereditary rank, had nothing to look to but their personal worth or persistent industry. The hopes built upon him by his father and mother, who had now retired from business, stimulated his conceit without giving him pride. His parents lived as simply as Dutch folks, not spending more than a quarter of their income of twelve thousand francs; they intended to devote their savings, with half their capital, to the purchase of a connection for their son. Godefroid, reduced also to live under the conditions of this domestic thrift, regarded them as so much out of proportion to his parents' dreams and his own, that he felt disheartened. In weak characters such discouragement leads to envy. While many other men, in whom necessity, determination, and good sense were more marked than talent, went straight and steadfastly onward in the path laid down for modest ambitions, Godefroid waxed rebellious, longed to shine, insisted on facing the brightest light, and so dazzled his eyes. He tried to "get on," but all his efforts ended in demonstrating his incapacity. At last, clearly perceiving too great a discrepancy between his desires and his prospects, he conceived a hatred of social superiority; he became a Liberal, and tried to make himself famous by a book; but he learned, to his cost, to regard talent much as he regarded rank. Having tried by turns the profession of notary, the bar, and literature, he now aimed at the higher branch of the law.

At this juncture his father died. His mother, content in

her old age with two thousand francs a year, gave up almost her whole fortune to his use. Possessor now, at five-and-twenty, of ten thousand francs a year, he thought himself rich, and he was so as compared with the past. Hitherto his life had been a series of acts with no will behind them, or of impotent willing; so, to keep pace with the age, to act, to become a personage, he tried to get into some circle of society by the help of his money.

At first he fell in with journalism, which has always an open hand for any capital that comes in its way. Now, to own a newspaper is to be a Personage; it means employing talent and sharing its successes without dividing its labors. Nothing is more tempting to second-rate men than thus to rise by the brains of others. Paris has had a few *parvenus* of this type, whose success is a disgrace both to the age and to those who have lent a lifting shoulder.

In this class of society Godefroid was soon cut out by the vulgar cunning of some and the extravagance of others, by the money of ambitious capitalists or the manœuvring of editors; then he was dragged into the dissipations that a literary or political life entails, the habits of critics behind the scenes, and the amusements needed by men who work their brains hard. Thus he fell into bad company; but he there learned that he was an insignificant-looking person, and that he had one shoulder higher than the other without redeeming this malformation by any distinguished ill-nature or wit. Bad manners are a form of self-payment which actors snatch by telling the truth.

Short, badly made, devoid of wit or of any strong bent, all seemed at an end for a young man at a time when for success in any career the highest gifts of mind are as nothing without luck, or the tenacity which commands luck.

The revolution of 1830 poured oil on Godefroid's wounds; he found the courage of hope, which is as good as that of despair. Like many another obscure journalist, he got an appointment where his Liberal ideas, at loggerheads with the demands of a newly-established power, made him but a refractory instrument. Veneered only with Liberalism, he did not know, as superior men did, how to hold his own. To obey the Ministry was to him to surrender his opinions. And the Government itself seemed to him false to the laws that had given rise to it. Godefroid declared in favor of *movement* when what was needed was tenacity; he came back to Paris almost poor, but faithful to the doctrines of the opposition.

Alarmed by the licentiousness of the press, and yet more by the audacity of the republican party, he sought in retirement the only life suited to a being of incomplete faculties, devoid of such force as might defy the rough jolting of political life, weary too of repeated failures, of suffering and struggles which had won him no glory; and friendless, because friendship needs conspicuous qualities or defects, while possessing feelings that were sentimental rather than deep. Was it not, in fact, the only prospect open to a young man who had already been several times cheated by pleasure, and who had grown prematurely old from friction in a social circle that never rests nor lets others rest?

His mother, who was quietly dying in the peaceful village of Auteuil, sent to her son to come to her, as much for the sake of having him with her as to start him in the road where he might find the calm and simple happiness that befits such souls. She had at last taken Godefroid's measure when she saw that at eight-and-twenty he had reduced his whole fortune to four thousand francs a year; his desires blunted, his fancied talents extinct, his energy nullified, his ambition crushed, and his hatred for every one who rose by legitimate effort increased by his many disappointments.

She tried to arrange a marriage for Godefroid with the only daughter of a retired merchant, thinking that a wife might be a guardian to his distressful mind, but the old father brought the mercenary spirit that abides in those who have been engaged in trade to bear on the question of settlements. At the end of a year of attentions and intimacy, Godefroid's suit was rejected. In the first place, in the opinion of these case-hardened traders, the young man must necessarily have retained a deep-dyed immorality from his former pursuits; and then, even during this past year, he had drawn upon his capital both to dazzle the parents and to attract the daughter. This not unpardonable vanity gave the finishing touch; the family had a horror of unthrift; and their refusal was final when they heard that Godefroid had sacrificed in six years a hundred and fifty thousand francs of his capital.

The blow fell all the harder on his aching heart because the girl was not at all good-looking. Still, under his mother's influence, Godefroid had credited the object of his addresses with a sterling character and the superior advantages of a sound judgment; he was accustomed to her face, he had studied its expression, he liked the young lady's voice, manners, and look. Thus, after staking the last hope of his life on this attachment, he felt the bitterest despair.

His mother dying, he found himself—he whose requirements had always followed the tide of fashion—with five thousand francs for his whole fortune, and the certainty of never being able to repair any future loss, since he saw himself incapable of the energy which is imperatively demanded for the grim task of *making a fortune*.

But a man who is weak, aggrieved, and irritable cannot submit to be extinguished at a blow. While still in mourning, Godefroid wandered through Paris in search of something to "turn up"; he dined in public rooms, he rashly introduced himself to strangers, he mingled in society, and met with nothing but opportunities for expenditure. As he wandered about the Boulevards, he was so miserable that the sight of a mother with a young daughter to marry gave him as keen a pang as that of a young man going on horseback to the Bois, of a *parvenu* in a smart carriage, or of an official with a ribbon in his buttonhole. The sense of his own inadequacy told him that he could not pretend even to the more respectable of second-class positions, nor to the easiest form of office-work. And he had spirit enough to be constantly vexed, and sense enough to bewail himself in bitter self-accusation.

Incapable of contending with life, conscious of certain superior gifts, but devoid of the will that brings them into play, feeling himself incomplete, lacking force to undertake any great work, or to resist the temptations of those tastes he had acquired from education or recklessness in his past life, he was a victim to three maladies, any one of them enough to disgust a man with life when he has ceased to exercise his religious faith. Indeed, Godefroid wore the expression so common now among men, that it has become the Parisian type: it bears the stamp of disappointed or smothered ambitions, of mental distress, of hatred lulled by the apathy of a life amply filled up by the superficial and daily spectacle of Paris, of satiety seeking stimulants, of repining without talent, of the affectation of force; the venom of past failure which makes a man smile at scoffing, and scorn all that is elevating, misprize the most necessary authorities, enjoy their dilemmas, and disdain all social forms.

This Parisian disease is to the active and persistent coalition of energetic malcontents what the soft wood is to the sap of a tree; it preserves it, covers it, and hides it.

Weary of himself, Godefroid one morning resolved to give himself some reason for living. He had met a former schoolfellow, who had proved to be the tortoise of the fable while he himself had been the hare. In the course of such a conversation as is natural to old companions while walking in the sunshine on the Boulevard des Italiens, he was amazed to find that success had attended this man, who, apparently far less gifted than himself with talent and fortune, had simply resolved each day to do as he had resolved the day before. The brain-sick man determined to imitate this simplicity of purpose.

"Life in the world is like the earth," his friend had said; "it yields in proportion to our labors."

Godefroid was in debt. As his first penance, his first duty, he required himself to live in seclusion and pay his debts out of his income. For a man who was in the habit of spending six thousand francs when he had five, it was no light thing to reduce his expenses to two thousand francs. He read the advertisement-sheets every morning, hoping to find a place of refuge where he might live on a fixed sum, and where he might enjoy the solitude necessary to a man who wanted to study and examine himself, and discern a vocation. The manners and customs of the boarding-houses in the Quartier Latin were an offence to his taste; a private asylum, he thought, would be unhealthy; and he was fast drifting back into the fatal uncertainty of a will-less man, when the following advertisement caught his eye:

"Small apartments, at seventy francs a month; might suit a clerk in orders. Quiet habits expected. Board included; and the rooms will be inexpensively furnished on mutual agreement. Inquire of M. Millet, grocer, Rue Chanoinesse, by Notre-Dame, for all further particulars."

Attracted by the artless style of this paragraph, and the aroma of simplicity it seemed to bear, Godefroid presented himself at the grocer's shop at about four in the afternoon, and was told that at that hour Madame de la Chanterie was dining, and could see no one at meal-times. The lady would be visible in the evening after seven, or between ten and twelve in the morning. While he talked, Monsieur Millet took stock of Godefroid, and proceeded to put him through his first examination—"Was monsieur single? Madame wished for a lodger of regular habits. The house was locked up by eleven at latest."

"Well," said he in conclusion, "you seem to me, monsieur, to be of an age to suit Madame de la Chanterie's views."

"What age do you suppose I am?" asked Godefroid.

"Somewhere about forty," replied the grocer.

This plain answer cast Godefroid into the depths of misanthropy and dejection. He went to dine on the Quai de la Tournelle, and returned to gaze at Notre-Dame just as the fires of the setting sun were rippling and breaking in wavelets on the buttresses of the great nave. The quay was already in shadow, while the towers still glittered in the glow, and the contrast struck Godefroid as he tasted all the bitterness which the grocer's brutal simplicity had stirred within him.

Thus the young man was oscillating between the whisperings of despair and the appealing tones of religious harmony aroused in his mind by the cathedral bells, when, in the darkness, and silence, and calm moonshine, the priest's speech fell on his ear. Though far from devout—like most men of the century—his feelings were touched by these words, and he went back to the Rue Chanoinesse, where he had but just decided not to go.

The priest and Godefroid were equally surprised on turning into the Rue Massillon, opposite the north door of the cathedral, at the spot where it ends by the Rue de la Colombe, and is called Rue des Marmousets. When Godefroid stopped under the arched doorway of the house where Madame de la Chanterie lived, the priest turned round to examine him by the light of a hanging oil-lamp, which will, very likely, be one of the last to disappear in the heart of old Paris.

"Do you wish to see Madame de la Chanterie, monsieur?" asked the priest.

"Yes," replied Godefroid. "The words I have just heard you utter to that workman prove to me that this house, if you dwell in it, must be good for the soul."

"Then you witnessed my failure," said the priest, lifting the knocker, "for I did not succeed."

"It seems to me that it was the workman who failed. He had begged sturdily enough for money."

"Alas!" said the priest, "one of the greatest misfortunes attending revolutions in France is that each, in its turn, offers a fresh premium to the ambitions of the lower classes. To rise above his status and make a fortune, which, in these days, is considered the social guarantee, the workman throws himself into monstrous plots, which, if they fail, must bring those who dabble in them before the bar of human justice. This is what good-nature sometimes ends in."

The porter now opened a heavy gate, and the priest said to Godefroid:

"Then you have come about the rooms to let?"

"Yes, monsieur."

The priest and Godefroid then crossed a fairly wide court-yard, beyond which stood the black mass of a tall house, flanked by a square tower even higher than the roof, and amazingly old. Those who know the history of Paris are aware that the old soil has risen so much round the cathedral, that there is not a trace to be seen of the twelve steps which originally led up to it. Hence what was the ground floor of this house must now form the cellars. There is a short flight of outer steps to the door of the tower, and inside it an ancient *Vise* or stairs, winding in a spiral round a newell carved to imitate a vine-stock. This style, resembling that of the Louis XII. staircases at Blois, dates as far back as the fourteenth century.

Struck by these various signs of antiquity, Godefroid could not help exclaiming:

"This tower was not built yesterday!"

"It is said to have withstood the attacks of the Normans and to have formed part of a primeval palace of the kings of Paris; but according to more probable traditions, it was the residence of Fulbert, the famous Canon, and the uncle of Héloïse."

As he spoke the priest opened the door of the apartment, which seemed to be the ground floor, and which, in fact, is now but just above the ground of both the outer and the inner courtyard—for there is a small second court.

In the first room a servant sat knitting by the light of a small lamp; she wore a cap devoid of any ornament but its gauffered cambric frills. She stuck one of the needles through her hair, but did not lay down her knitting as she rose to open the door of a drawing-room looking out on the inner court. This room was lighted up. The woman's dress suggested to Godefroid that of some Gray Sister.

"Madame, I have found you a tenant," said the priest, showing in Godefroid, who saw in the room three men, sitting in armchairs near Madame de la Chanterie.

The three gentlemen rose; the mistress of the house also; and when the priest had pushed forward a chair for the stranger, and he had sat down in obedience to a sign from Madame de la Chanterie and an old-fashioned bidding to "Be seated," the Parisian felt as if he were far indeed from Paris, in remote Brittany, or the backwoods of Canada.

There are, perhaps, degrees of silence. Godefroid, struck already by the tranquillity of the Rue Massillon and Rue Chanoinesse, where a vehicle passes perhaps twice in a month, struck too by the stillness of the courtyard and the tower, may have felt himself at the very heart of silence, in this drawing-room, hedged round by so many old streets, old court-yards, and old walls.

This part of the Island, called the Cloister, preserves the character common to all cloisters; it is damp, and cold, and monastic; silence reigns there unbroken, even during the noisiest hours of the day. It may also be remarked that this part of the Cité, lying between the body of the Cathedral and the river, is to the north and under the shadow of Notre-Dame. The east wind loses itself there, unchecked by any obstacle, and the fogs from the Seine are to some extent en-trapped by the blackened walls of the ancient metropolitan church.

So no one will be surprised at the feeling that came over Godefroid on finding himself in this ancient abode, and in the presence of four persons as silent and as solemn as every-thing around them. He did not look about him; his curiosity centered in Madame de la Chanterie, whose name even had al-ready puzzled him.

This lady was evidently a survival from another century, not to say another world. She had a rather sweet face, with a soft, coldly-colored complexion, an aquiline nose, a benign brow, hazel eyes, and a double chin, the whole framed in curls of silver hair. Her dress could only be described by the old name of *fourreau* (literally, a sheath, a tightly-fitting dress), so literally was she cased in it, in the fashion of the eighteenth century. The material—silk of carmelite gray, finely and

closely striped with green—seemed to have come down from
the same date; the body, cut low, was hidden under a man-
tilla of richer silk, flounced with black lace, and fastened at
the bosom with a brooch containing a miniature. Her feet,
shod in black velvet boots, rested on a little stool. Madame de
la Chanterie, like her maid-servant, was knitting stockings,
and had a knitting pin stuck through her waving hair under
her lace cap.

"Have you seen Monsieur Millet?" she asked Godefroid
in the head voice peculiar to dowagers of the Faubourg Saint-
Germain, as if to invite him to speak, seeing that he was almost thunderstruck.

"Yes, madame."

"I am afraid the rooms will hardly suit you," she went on,
observing that her proposed tenant was dressed with elegance
in clothes that were new and smart.

Godefroid, in fact, was wearing patent leather boots, yellow gloves, handsome shirt-studs, and a neat watch chain
passed through the buttonhole of a black silk waistcoat
sprigged with blue.

Madame de la Chanterie took a small silver whistle out of
her pocket and blew it. The woman servant came in.

"Manon, child, show this gentleman the rooms. Will you,
my dear friend, accompany him?" she said to the priest.
"And if by any chance the rooms should suit you," she added,
rising, and looking at Godefroid, "we will afterwards discuss the terms."

Godefroid bowed and went out. He heard the iron rattle
of a bunch of keys which Manon took out of a drawer, and
saw her light a candle in a large brass candlestick.

Manon led the way without speaking a word. When he
found himself on the stairs again, climbing to the upper floors,
he doubted the reality of things; he felt dreaming though
awake, and saw the whole world of fantastic romance such as
he had read of in his hours of idleness. And any Parisian
dropped here, as he was, out of the modern city with its luxurious houses and furniture, its glittering restaurants and

theatres, and all the stirring heart of Paris, would have felt
as he did. The single candle carried by the servant lighted
the winding stair but dimly; spiders had hung it with their
dusty webs.

Manon's dress consisted of a skirt broadly pleated and made
of coarse woolen stuff; the bodice was cut square at the neck,
behind and before, and all her clothes seemed to move in a
piece. Having reached the second floor, which had been the
third, Manon stopped, turned the springs of an antique lock,
and opened a door painted in coarse imitation of knotted mahogany.

"There!" said she, leading the way.

Who had lived in these rooms? A miser, an artist who
had died of want, a cynic indifferent to the world, or a pious
man who was alien to it? Any one of the four seemed possible, as the visitor smelt the very odor of poverty, saw the
greasy stains on wall-papers covered with a layer of smoke,
the blackened ceilings, the windows with their small dusty
panes, the brown-tiled floor, the wainscot sticky with a deposit of fog. A damp chill came down the fireplaces, faced
with carved stonework that had been painted, and with mir-
rors framed in the seventeenth century. The rooms were at
the angle of a square, as the house stood, enclosing the inner
courtyard, but this Godefroid could not see, as it was dark.

"Who used to live here?" Godefroid asked of the priest.

"A Councillor to the Parlement, Madame's grand-uncle, a
Monsieur de Boisfrelon. He had been quite childish ever
since the Revolution, and died in 1832 at the age of ninety-
six; Madame could not bear the idea of seeing a stranger in
the rooms so soon; still, she cannot endure the loss of
rent . . ."

"Oh, and Madame will have the place cleaned and furnished, to be all monsieur could wish," added Manon.

"It will only depend on how you wish to arrange the rooms,"
said the priest. "They can be made into a nice sitting-room
and a large bedroom and dressing-room, and the two small
rooms round the corner are large enough for a spacious study.

That is how my rooms are arranged below this, and those on the next floor."

"Yes," said Manon; "Monsieur Alain's rooms are just like these, only that they look out on the tower."

"I think I had better see the rooms again by daylight," said Godefroid shyly.

"Perhaps so," said Manon.

The priest and Godefroid went downstairs again, leaving Manon to lock up, and she then followed to light them down. Then, when he was in the drawing-room, Godefroid, having recovered himself, could, while talking to Madame de la Chanterie, study the place, the personages, and the surroundings.

The window-curtains of this drawing-room were of old red satin; there was a cornice-valance, and the curtains were looped with silk cord; the red tiles of the floor showed beyond an ancient tapestry carpet that was too small to cover it entirely. The woodwork was painted stone-color. The ceiling, divided down the middle by a joist starting from the chimney, looked like an addition lately conceded to modern luxury; the easy-chairs were of wood painted white, with tapestry seats. A shabby clock, standing between two gilt candlesticks, adorned the chimney-shelf. An old table with stag's feet stood by Madame de la Chanterie, and on it were her balls of wool in a wicker basket. A clockwork lamp threw light on the picture.

The three men, sitting as rigid, motionless, and speechless as Bonzes, had, like Madame de la Chanterie, evidently ceased speaking on hearing the stranger return. Their faces were perfectly cold and reserved, as befitted the room, the house, and the neighborhood.

Madame de la Chanterie agreed that Godefroid's observations were just, and said that she had postponed doing anything till she was informed of the intentions of her lodger, or rather of her boarder; for if the lodger could conform to the ways of the household, he was to board with them—but their ways were so unlike those of Paris life! Here, in the Rue Chanoinesse, they kept country hours; every one, as a rule, had to be in by ten at night; noise was not to be endured; neither women nor children were admitted, so that their regular habits might not be interfered with. No one, perhaps, but a priest could agree to such a rule. At any rate, Madame de la Chanterie wished for some one who liked plain living and had few requirements; she could only afford the most necessary furniture in the rooms. Monsieur Alain was satisfied, however—and she bowed to one of the gentlemen—and she would do the same for the new lodger as for the old.

"But," said the priest, "I do not think that monsieur is quite inclined to come and join us in our convent."

"Indeed; why not?" said Monsieur Alain. "We are all quite content, and we all get on very well."

"Madame," said Godefroid, rising, "I will have the honor of calling on you again to-morrow."

Though he was but a young man, the four old gentlemen and Madame de la Chanterie stood up, and the priest escorted him to the outer steps. A whistle sounded, and at the signal the porter appeared, lantern in hand, to conduct Godefroid to the street; then he closed the yellow gate, as heavy as that of a prison, and covered with arabesque ironwork, so old that it would be hard to determine its date.

When Godefroid found himself sitting in a hackney cab and being carried to the living regions of Paris, where light and warmth reigned, all he had just seen seemed like a dream; and as he walked along the Boulevard des Italiens, his impressions already seemed as remote as a memory. He could not help saying to himself:

"Shall I find those people there to-morrow, I wonder?"

On the following day, when he woke in the midst of the elegance of modern luxury and the refinements of English comfort, Godefroid recalled all the details of his visit to the Cloister of Notre-Dame, and came to some conclusions in his mind as to the things he had seen there. The three gentlemen, whose appearance, attitude, and silence had left an impression on him, were no doubt boarders, as well as the priest.

Madame de la Chanterie's gravity seemed to him to be the result of the reserved dignity with which she had endured some great sorrows. And yet, in spite of the explanations he gave himself, Godefroid could not help feeling that there was an air of mystery in these uncommunicative faces. He cast a glance at his furniture to choose what he could keep, what he thought indispensable; but, transporting them in fancy to the horrible rooms in the Rue Chanoinesse, he could not help laughing at the grotesque contrast they would make there, and determined to sell everything, and pay away so much as they might bring; leaving the furnishing of the rooms to Madame de la Chanterie. He longed for a new life, and the objects that could recall his old existence must be bad for him. In his craving for transformation—for his was one of those natures which rush forward at once with a bound, instead of approaching a situation step by step as others do —he was seized, as he sat at breakfast, by an idea: he would realize his fortune, pay his debts, and place the surplus with the banking firm his father had done business with.

This banking house was that of Mongenod and Co., established in Paris since 1816 or 1817, a firm whose reputation had never been blown on in the midst of the commercial depravity which at this time had blighted, more or less, several great Paris houses. Thus, in spite of their immense wealth, the houses of Nucingen and du Tillet, of Keller Brothers, of Palma and Co., suffer under a secret disesteem whispered, as it were, between lip and ear. Hideous transactions had led to such splendid results; and political successes, nay, monarchical principles, had overgrown such foul beginnings, that no one in 1834 thought for a moment of the mud in which the roots were set of such majestic trees—the upholders of the State. At the same time, there was not one of these bankers that did not feel aggrieved by praises of the house of Mongenod.

The Mongenods, following the example of English bankers, make no display of wealth; they do everything quite quietly, and carry on their business with such prudence, shrewdness, and honesty as allow them to operate with certainty from one end of the world to the other.

The present head of the house, Frédéric Mongenod, is brother-in-law to the Vicomte de Fontaine. Thus his numerous family is connected, through the Baron de Fontaine, with Monsieur Grossetête, the Receiver-General (brother to the Grossetête and Co. of Limoges), with the Vandenesses, and with Planat de Baudry, another Receiver-General. This relationship, after being of the greatest service to the late Mongenod *senior* in his financial operations at the time of the Restoration, had gained him the confidence of many of the old nobility, whose capital and vast savings were intrusted to his bank. Far from aiming at the peerage, like Keller, Nucingen, and du Tillet, the Mongenods kept out of political life, and knew no more of it than was needed for banking business.

Mongenod's bank occupies a magnificent house in the Rue de la Victoire, with a garden behind and a courtyard in front, where Madame Mongenod resided with her two sons, with whom she was in partnership. Madame la Vicomtesse de Fontaine had taken out her share on the death of the elder Mongenod in 1827. Frédéric Mongenod, a handsome fellow of about five-and-thirty, with a cold manner, as silent and reserved as a Genevese, and as neat as an Englishman, had acquired under his father all the qualifications needed in his difficult business. He was more cultivated than most bankers, for his education had given him the general knowledge which forms the curriculum of the École Polytechnique; and, like many bankers, he had an occupation, a taste, outside his regular business, a love of physics and chemistry. Mongenod *junior,* ten years younger than Frédéric, filled the place, under his elder brother, that a head-clerk holds under a lawyer or a notary; Frédéric was training him, as he himself had been trained by his father, in the scientific side of banking, for a banker is to money what a writer is to ideas—they both ought to know everything.

Godefroid, as he mentioned his family name, could see how

highly his father had been respected, for he was shown through the offices at once to that next to Mongenod's private room. This room was shut in by glass doors, so that, in spite of his wish not to listen, Godefroid overheard the conversation going on within.

"Madame, your account shows sixteen hundred thousand francs on both sides of the balance sheet," Mongenod the younger was saying. "I know not what my brother's views may be; he alone can decide whether an advance of a hundred thousand francs is possible. You lacked prudence. It is not wise to put sixteen hundred thousand francs into a business——"

"Too loud, Louis!" said a woman's voice. "Your brother's advice is never to speak but in an undertone. There may be some one in the little waiting-room."

At this instant Frédéric Mongenod opened the door from his living rooms to his private office; he saw Godefroid, and went through to the inner room, where he bowed respectfully to the lady who was talking to his brother.

He showed Godefroid in first, saying as he did so, "And whom have I the honor of addressing?"

As soon as Godefroid had announced himself, Frédéric offered him a chair; and while the banker was opening his desk, Louis Mongenod and the lady, who was none else than Madame de la Chanterie, rose and went up to Frédéric. Then they all three went into a window recess, where they stood talking to Madame Mongenod, who was in all the secrets of the business. For thirty years past this clever woman had given ample proofs of her capacity, to her husband first, now to her sons, and she was, in fact, an active partner in the house, signing for it as they did. Godefroid saw in a pigeonhole a number of boxes labeled "La Chanterie," and numbered 1 to 7.

When the conference was ended by a word from the Senior to his brother, "Well, then, go to the cashier," Madame de la Chanterie turned round, saw Godefroid, restrained a start of surprise, and then asked a few whispered questions of Mongenod, who replied briefly, also in a low voice.

Madame de la Chanterie wore thin prunella shoes and gray silk stockings; she had on the same dress as before, and was wrapped in the Venetian cloak that was just coming into fashion again. Her drawn bonnet of green silk, *à la bonne femme,* was lined with white, and her face was framed in flowing lace. She stood very erect, in an attitude which bore witness, if not to high birth, at any rate to aristocratic habits. But for her extreme affability, she would perhaps have seemed proud. In short, she was very imposing.

"It is not so much good luck as a dispensation of Providence that has brought us together here, monsieur," said she to Godefroid. "I was on the point of declining a boarder whose habits, as I fancied, were ill suited to those of my household; but Monsieur Mongenod has just given me some information as to your family which is——"

"Indeed, madame—monsieur——" said Godefroid, addressing the lady and the banker together, "I have no longer any family, and I came to ask advice of my late father's banker to arrange my affairs in accordance with a new plan of life."

Godefroid told his story in a few words, and expressed his desire of leading a new life.

"Formerly," said he, "a man in my position would have turned monk; but there are now no religious Orders——"

"Go to live with Madame, if she will accept you as a boarder," said Frédéric Mongenod, after exchanging glances with Madame de la Chanterie, "and do not sell your investments; leave them in my hands. Give me the schedule of your debts; I will fix dates of payment with your creditors, and you can draw for your own use a hundred and fifty francs a month. It will take about two years to pay everything off. During those two years, in the home you are going to, you will have ample leisure to think of a career, especially as the people you will be living with can give you good advice."

Louis Mongenod came back with a hundred thousand-franc notes, which he gave to Madame de la Chanterie. Godefroid offered his arm to his future landlady, and took her to her hackney-coach.

"Then we shall meet again presently," said she in a kind tone.

"At what hour shall you be at home, madame?" said Godefroid.

"In two hours' time."

"I have time to get rid of my furniture," said he, with a bow.

During the few minutes while Madame de la Chanterie's arm had lain on his as they walked side by side, Godefroid could not see beyond the halo cast about this woman by the words, "Your account stands at sixteen hundred thousand francs," spoken by Louis Mongenod to a lady who buried her life in the depths of the Cloître de Notre-Dame.

This idea, "She must be rich!" had entirely changed his view of things. "How old is she, I wonder?"

And he had a vision of a romance in his residence in the Rue Chanoinesse.

"She looks like an aristocrat; does she dabble in banking affairs?" he asked himself.

And in our day nine hundred and ninety-nine men out of a thousand would have thought of the possibility of marrying this woman.

A furniture-dealer, who was also a decorator, but chiefly an agent for furnished flats, gave about three thousand francs for all that Godefroid wished to dispose of, leaving the things in his rooms for the few days needed to clean and arrange the dreadful rooms in the Rue Chanoinesse.

Thither the brain-sick youth at once repaired; he called in a painter, recommended by Madame de la Chanterie, who undertook for a moderate sum to whitewash the ceilings, clean the windows, paint the wainscoting like gray maple, and color the floors, within a week. Godefroid measured the rooms to carpet them all alike with green drugget of the cheapest description. He wished everything to be uniform and as simple as possible in his cell.

Madame de la Chanterie approved of this. With Manon's assistance she calculated how much white dimity would be needed for the window curtains and for a simple iron bedstead; then she undertook to procure the stuff and to have them made for a price so small as to amaze Godefroid. With the new furniture he would send in, his apartments would not cost him more than six hundred francs.

"So I can take about a thousand to Monsieur Mongenod."

"We here lead a Christian life," said Madame de la Chanterie, "which is, as you know, quite out of keeping with much superfluity, and I fear you still preserve too many."

As she gave her new boarder this piece of advice, she glanced at the diamond that sparkled in a ring through which the ends of Godefroid's blue necktie were drawn.

"I only mention this," she added, "because I perceive that you are preparing to break with the dissipated life of which you spoke with regret to Monsieur Mongenod."

Godefroid gazed at Madame de la Chanterie, listening with delight to the harmony of her clear voice; he studied her face, which was perfectly colorless, worthy to be that of one of the grave cold Dutch women so faithfully depicted by the painters of the Flemish school, faces on which a wrinkle would be impossible.

"Plump and fair!" thought he, as he went away. "Still, her hair is white——"

Godefroid, like all weak natures, had readily accustomed himself to the idea of a new life, believing it would be perfect happiness, and he was eager to settle in the Rue Chanoinesse; nevertheless, he had a gleam of prudence—or, if you like, of suspicion. Two days before moving in he went again to Monsieur Mongenod to ask for further information concerning the household he was going to join. During the few minutes he had spent now and then in his future home, to see what alterations were being made, he had observed the going and coming of several persons whose appearance and manner, without any air of mystery, suggested that they were busied in the practice of some profession, some secret occupation with the residents in the house. At this time many plots were afoot to help the elder branch of Bourbons to remount the throne, and Godefroid believed there was some conspiracy here.

But when he found himself in the banker's private room and under his searching eye, he was ashamed of himself as he formulated his question and saw a sardonic smile on Frédéric Mongenod's lips.

"Madame la Baronne de la Chanterie," he replied, "is one of the obscurest but one of the most honorable women in Paris. Have you any particular reason for asking for information?"

Godefroid fell back on flat excuses—he was arranging to live a long time with these strangers, and it was as well to know to whom he was tying himself, and the like. But the banker's smile only became more and more ironical, and Godefroid more and more ashamed, till he blushed at the step he had taken, and got nothing by it; for he dared ask no more questions about Madame de la Chanterie or his fellow-boarders.

Two days later, after dining for the last time at the Café Anglais, and seeing the first two pieces at the *Variétés,* at ten o'clock on a Monday night he came to sleep in the Rue Chanoinesse, where Manon lighted him to his room.

Solitude has a charm somewhat akin to that of the wild life of savages, which no European ever gives up after having once tasted it. This may seem strange in an age when every one lives so completely in the sight of others that everybody is inquisitive about everybody else, and that privacy will soon have ceased to exist, so quickly do the eyes of the Press—the modern Argus—increase in boldness and intrusiveness; and yet the statement is supported by the evidence of the first six Christian centuries, when no recluse ever came back to social life again. There are few mental wounds that solitude cannot cure. Thus, in the first instance, Godefroid was struck by the calm and stillness of his new abode, exactly as a tired traveler finds rest in a bath.

On the day after his arrival as a boarder with Madame de la Chanterie, he could not help cross-examining himself on

finding himself thus cut off from everything, even from Paris,
though he was still under the shadow of its Cathedral. Here,
stripped of every social vanity, there would henceforth be no
witnesses to his deeds but his conscience and his fellow-
boarders. This was leaving the beaten high-road of the world
for an unknown track; and whither would the track lead him?
To what occupation would he find himself committed?

He had been lost in such reflections for a couple of hours,
when Manon, the only servant of the establishment, knocked
at his door and told him that the second breakfast was served;
they were waiting for him. Twelve was striking.

The new boarder went downstairs at once, prompted by
his curiosity to see the five persons with whom he was thenceforth to live. On entering the drawing-room, he found all
the residents in the house standing up and dressed precisely
as they had been on the day when he had first come to make
inquiries.

"Did you sleep well?" asked Madame de la Chanterie.

"I did not wake till ten o'clock," said Godefroid, bowing
to the four gentlemen, who returned the civility with much
gravity.

"We quite expected it," said the old man, known as Monsieur Alain, and he smiled.

"Manon spoke of the second breakfast," Godefroid went on.
"I have, I fear, already broken one of your rules without intending it.—At what hour do you rise?"

"We do not get up quite by the rule of the monks of old,"
replied Madame de la Chanterie graciously, "but, like workmen, at six in winter and at half-past three in summer. We
also go to bed by the rule of the sun; we are always asleep by
nine in winter, by half-past eleven in summer. We drink
some milk, which is brought from our own farm, after prayers, all but Monsieur l'Abbé de Vèze, who performs early
Mass at Notre-Dame—at six in summer, at seven in winter—
and these gentlemen as well as I, your humble servant, attend that service every day."

Madame de la Chanterie finished this speech at table, where
her five guests were now seated.

The dining-room, painted gray throughout, and decorated with carved wood of a design showing the taste of Louis XIV., opened out of the sort of ante-room where Manon sat, and ran parallel with Madame de la Chanterie's room, adjoining the drawing-room, no doubt. There was no ornament but an old clock. The furniture consisted of six chairs, their oval backs upholstered with worsted-work evidently done by Madame de la Chanterie, of two mahogany sideboards, and a table to match, on which Manon placed the breakfast without spreading a cloth. The breakfast, of monastic frugality, consisted of a small turbot with white sauce, potatoes, a salad, and four dishes of fruit: peaches, grapes, strawberries, and green almonds; then, by way of *hors d'œuvre,* there was honey served in the comb as in Switzerland, besides butter, radishes, cucumber, and sardines. The meal was served in china sprigged with small blue cornflowers and green leaves, a pattern which was no doubt luxuriously fashionable in the time of Louis XVI., but which the increasing demands of the present day have made common.

"It is a fast day!" observed Monsieur Alain. "Since we go to Mass every morning, you may suppose that we yield blindly to all the practices of the Church, even the strictest."

"And you will begin by following our example," added Madame de la Chanterie, with a side-glance at Godefroid, whom she had placed by her side.

Of the four boarders, Godefroid already knew the names of the Abbé de Vèze and Monsieur Alain; but he yet had to learn those of the other two gentlemen. They sat in silence, eating with the absorbed attention that the pious seem to devote to the smallest details of their meals.

"And does this fine fruit also come from your farm, madame?" Godefroid inquired.

"Yes, monsieur," she replied. "We have our little model farm, just as the Government has; it is our country house, about three leagues from hence, on the road to Italy, near Villeneuve-Saint-Georges."

"It is a little estate that belongs to us all, and will be the property of the last survivor," said the worthy Monsieur Alain.

"Oh, it is quite inconsiderable," added Madame de la Chanterie, who seemed afraid lest Godefroid should regard this speech as a bait.

"There are thirty acres of arable land," said one of the men unknown to Godefroid, "six acres of meadow, and an enclosure of about four acres of garden, in the midst of which our house stands; in front of it is the farm."

"But such an estate must be worth above a hundred thousand francs," observed Godefroid.

"Oh, we get nothing out of it but our produce," replied the same speaker.

He was a tall man, thin and grave. At a first glance he seemed to have served in the army; his white hair showed that he was past sixty, and his face revealed great sorrows and religious resignation.

The second stranger, who appeared to be a sort of compound of a master of rhetoric and a man of business, was of middle height, stout but active, and his face bore traces of a joviality peculiar to the notaries and attorneys of Paris.

The dress of all four men was marked by the extreme neatness due to personal care; and Manon's hand was visible in the smallest details of their raiment. Their coats were perhaps ten years old, and preserved, as a priest's clothes are preserved, by the occult powers of a housekeeper and by constant use. These men wore, as it were, the livery of a system of life; they were all the slaves of the same thought, their looks spoke the same word, their faces wore an expression of gentle resignation, of inviting tranquillity.

"Am I indiscreet, madame," said Godefroid, "to ask the names of these gentlemen? I am quite prepared to tell them all about myself; may I not know as much about them as circumstances allow?"

"This," said Madame de la Chanterie, introducing the tall, thin man, "is Monsieur Nicolas; he is a retired Colonel of the Gendarmerie, ranking as a Major-General.—And this gentleman," she went on, turning to the little stout man, "was formerly Councillor to the Bench of the King's Court in Paris; he retired from his functions in August 1830; his name is Monsieur Joseph. Though you joined us but yesterday, I may tell you that in the world Monsieur Nicolas bore the name of Marquis de Montauran, and Monsieur Joseph that of Lecamus, Baron de Tresnes; but to us, as to the outer world, these names no longer exist. These gentlemen have no heirs; they have anticipated the oblivion that must fall on their families; they are simply Monsieur Nicolas and Monsieur Joseph, as you will be simply Monsieur Godefroid."

As he heard these two names—one so famous in the history of Royalism from the disaster which put an end to the rising of the Chouans at the beginning of the Consulate, the other so long respected in the records of the old *Parlement*—Godefroid could not repress a start of surprise; but when he looked at these survivors from the wreck of the two greatest institutions of the fallen monarchy, he could not detect the slightest movement of feature or change of countenance that betrayed a worldly emotion. These two men did not or would not remember what they once had been. This was Godefroid's first lesson.

"Each name, gentlemen, is a chapter of history," said he respectfully.

"The history of our own time," said Monsieur Joseph, "of mere ruins."

"You are in good company," said Monsieur Alain, smiling. He can be described in two words: he was a middle-class Paris citizen; a worthy man with the face of a calf, dignified by white hairs, but insipid with its eternal smile.

As to the priest, the Abbé de Vèze, his position was all sufficient. The priest who fulfils his mission is recognizable at the first glance when his eyes meet yours.

What chiefly struck Godefroid from the first was the profound respect shown by the boarders to Madame de la Chanterie; all of them, even the priest, notwithstanding the sacred dignity conferred by his functions, behaved to her as to a queen. He also noted the temperance of each guest; they ate solely for the sake of nourishment. Madame de la Chanterie, like the rest, took but a single peach and half a bunch of grapes; but she begged the newcomer not to restrict himself in the same way, offering him every dish in turn.

Godefroid's curiosity was excited to the highest pitch by this beginning. After the meal they returned to the drawing-room, where he was left to himself; Madame de la Chanterie and her four friends held a little privy council in a window recess. This conference, in which no animation was displayed, lasted for about half an hour. They talked in undertones, exchanging remarks which each seemed to have thought out beforehand. Now and again Monsieur Alain and Monsieur Joseph consulted their pocket-books, turning over the leaves.

"You will see to the Faubourg," said Madame de la Chanterie to Monsieur Nicolas, who went away.

These were the first words Godefroid could overhear.

"And you to the Quartier Saint-Marceau," she went on, addressing Monsieur Joseph.

"Will you take the Faubourg Saint-Germain and try to find what we need?" she added to the Abbé de Vèze, who at once went off.—"And you, my dear Alain," she added with a smile, "look into matters.—To-day's business is all settled," said she, returning to Godefroid.

She sat down in her armchair, and took from a little work-table some under-linen ready cut out, on which she began to sew as if working against time.

Godefroid, lost in conjectures, and seeing in all this a Royalist conspiracy, took the lady's speech as introductory, and, seating himself by her side, watched her closely. He was struck by her singular skill in stitching; while everything about her proclaimed the great lady, she had the peculiar deftness of a paid seamstress; for every one can distinguish, by certain tricks of working, the habits of a professional from those of an amateur.

"You sew," said Godefroid, "as if you were used to the business."

"Alas!" she said, without looking up, "I have done it ere now from necessity——"

Two large tears rose to the old woman's eyes, and rolled down her cheeks on to the work she held.

"Pray, forgive me, madame!" cried Godefroid.

Madame de la Chanterie looked at her new inmate, and saw on his features such an expression of regret, that she nodded to him kindly. Then, after wiping her eyes, she recovered the composure that characterized her face, which was not so much cold as chilled.

"You here find yourself, Monsieur Godefroid—for, as you know already, you will be called only by your Christian name—amid the wreckage from a great storm. We have all been stricken and wounded to the heart through family interests or damaged fortunes, by the forty years' hurricane that overthrew royalty and religion, and scattered to the winds the elements that constituted France as it was of old. Words which seem but trivial bear a sting for us, and that is the reason of the silence that reigns here. We rarely speak of ourselves; we have forgotten what we were, and have found means of substituting a new life for the old life. It was because I fancied, from your revelation to the Mongenods, that there was some resemblance between your situation and our own, that I persuaded my four friends to receive you among us; in fact, we were anxious to find another recluse for our convent. But what do you propose to do? We do not enter on solitude without some stock of moral purpose."

"Madame, as I hear you speak, I shall be too happy to accept you as the arbiter of my destiny."

"That is speaking like a man of the world," said she. "You are trying to flatter me—a woman of sixty!—My dear boy," she went on, "you are, you must know, among people who believe firmly in God, who have all felt His hand, and who have given themselves up to Him almost as completely as do the Trappists. Have you ever observed the assurance of a true priest when he has given himself to the Lord, when he hearkens to His voice and strives to be a docile instrument under the

fingers of Providence? He has shed all vanity, all self-consciousness, all the feelings which cause constant offences to
the worldly; his quiescence is as complete as that of the fatal-
ist, his resignation enables him to endure all things. The
true priest—an Abbé de Vèze—is like a child with his mother;
for the Church, my dear sir, is a good mother. Well, a man
may be a priest without a tonsure; not all priests are in orders. If we devote ourselves to doing good, we imitate the
good priest, we obey God!—I am not preaching to you; I do
not want to convert you; I am only explaining our life."

"Instruct me, madame," said Godefroid, quite conquered.
"I would wish not to fail in any particular of your rules."

"You would find that too much to do; you will learn by degrees. Above all things, never speak here of your past misfortunes, which are mere child's play as compared with the
terrible catastrophes with which God has stricken those with
whom you are now living——"

All the time she spoke, Madame de la Chanterie went on
pulling her thread through with distracting regularity; but
at this full stop, she raised her head and looked at Godefroid;
she saw that he was spellbound by the thrilling sweetness of
her voice, which had indeed a sort of apostolic unction. The
young sufferer was gazing with admiration at the really extraordinary appearance of this woman, whose face was radiant.
A faint flush tinged her wax-white cheeks, her eyes sparkled,
a youthful soul gave life to the wrinkles that had acquired
sweetness, and everything about her invited affection. Godefroid sat measuring the depth of the gulf that parted this
woman from vulgar souls; he saw that she had attained to an
inaccessible height, whither religion had guided her; and he
was still too much of the world not to be stung to the quick,
not to long to go down into that gulf and climb to the sharp
peak where Madame de la Chanterie stood, and to stand by
her side. While he gave himself up to a thorough study of
this woman, he related to her all the mortifications of his life,
all he could not say at Mongenod's, where his self-betrayal had
been limited to a statement of his position.

"Poor child!"

This motherly exclamation, dropping from the lips of Madame de la Chanterie, fell, from time to time, like healing balm, on the young man's heart.

"What can I find to take the place of so many hopes deceived, of so much disappointed affection?" said he at last, looking at the lady, who seemed lost in reverie. "I came here," he went on, "to reflect and make up my mind. I have lost my mother—will you take her place——"

"But," said she, "will you show me a son's obedience?"

"Yes, if you can show me the tenderness that exacts it."

"Very well; we will try," said she.

Godefroid held out his hand to take that which the lady offered him, and raised it reverently to his lips. Madame de la Chanterie's hands were admirably formed—neither wrinkled, nor fat, nor thin; white enough to move a young woman to envy, and of a shape that a sculptor might copy. Godefroid had admired these hands, thinking them in harmony with the enchantment of her voice and the heavenly blue of her eye.

"Wait here," said Madame de la Chanterie, rising and going into her own room.

Godefroid was deeply agitated, and could not think to what he was to attribute the lady's departure: he was not left long in perplexity, for she returned with a book in her hand.

"Here, my dear boy," said she, "are the prescriptions of a great healer of souls. When the things of everyday life have failed to give us the happiness we looked for, we must seek in a higher life, and here is the key to that new world. Read a chapter of this book morning and evening; but give it your whole attention; study every word as if it were some foreign tongue. By the end of a month you will be another man. For twenty years now have I read a chapter every day, and my three friends, Nicolas, Alain, and Joseph, would no more omit it than they would miss going to bed and getting up again; imitate them for the love of God—for my sake——" she said, with divine serenity and dignified confidence.

Godefroid turned the book round and read on the back

Imitation of Jesus Christ. The old lady's artlessness and youthful candor, her certainty that she was doing him good, confounded the ex-dandy. Madame de la Chanterie had exactly the manner, the intense satisfaction, of a woman who might offer a hundred thousand francs to a merchant on the verge of bankruptcy.

"I have used this book," she said, "for six-and-twenty years. God grant that its use may prove contagious! Go and buy me another copy, for the hour is at hand when certain persons are coming here who must not be seen."

Godefroid bowed and went up to his rooms, where he tossed the book on a table, exclaiming:

"Poor, dear woman! There——"

The book, like all that are constantly used, fell open at a particular place. Godefroid sat down to arrange his ideas a little, for he had gone through more agitation that morning than he had in the course of the most stormy two months of his life; his curiosity especially had never been so strongly excited. His eyes wandered mechanically, as happens with men when their minds are absorbed in meditation, and fell on the two pages that lay facing him. He read as follows:—

"CHAPTER XII.

"On the Royal Road of the Holy Cross."

He picked up the volume, and this paragraph of that grand book captivated his eyes as though by words of fire:

"He has gone before you carrying His cross, and died for you, that you too might have strength to carry your cross, and be willing to die upon the Cross. . . .

"Go where you will, try what you will, you will not find a grander way, or a safer way, than the way of the Holy Cross. Arrange and order all your life as you like or think fit, still you will find that you will always have something to suffer, by your own choice or by necessity; and so you will always find a cross. For either you will have bodily pain to bear, or some trouble of the spirit.

"Sometimes God will leave you to yourself, sometimes you will be vexed by your neighbor, and, what is harder than all, you will often be weary of yourself, and there is no remedy or solace by which you can be delivered or relieved. You will have to bear your trouble as long as God decrees. For He wishes you to learn to suffer trial without consolation, to yield humbly to His will, and to become humbler by means of tribulations."

"What a book!" said Godefroid to himself, as he turned over the pages.

And he came upon these words:

"When you have come to feel all trouble sweet and pleasant for the love of Christ, then indeed you may say that all is well with you; you have made for yourself a heaven on earth."

Irritated by this simplicity, characteristic of strength, and enraged at being vanquished by this book, he shut it; but on the morocco cover he saw this motto, stamped in letters of gold:

"Seek only that which is eternal."

"And have they found it here?" he wondered.

He went out to purchase a handsome copy of the *Imitation of Christ,* remembering that Madame de la Chanterie would want to read a chapter that evening. He went downstairs and into the street. For a minute or two he remained standing near the gate, undecided as to which way he would go, and wondering in what street, and at what bookseller's he might find the book he needed; and he then heard the heavy sound of the outer gate shutting.

Two men had just come out of the Hôtel de la Chanterie—for the reader, if he has understood the character of the old house, will have recognized it as an ancient family mansion. Manon, when she had called Godefroid to breakfast, had asked him how he had slept the first night at the Hôtel de la Chanterie, laughing as she spoke.

Godefroid followed the two men, with no idea of spying on them; and they, taking him for an indifferent passer-by, talked loud enough for him to hear them in those deserted streets. The men turned down the Rue Massillon, along by the side of Notre-Dame, and across the Cathedral Square.

"Well, old man, you see how easy it is to get the coppers out of 'em! You must talk their lingo, that is all."

"But we owe the money."

"Who to?"

"To the lady——"

"I should like to see myself sued for debt by that old image! I would——"

"You would what?—You would pay her, I can tell you."

"You're right there, for if I paid I could get more out of her afterwards than I got to-day."

"But wouldn't it be better to take their advice and set up on the square?"

"Get out!"

"Since she said she could find some one to stand security?"

"But we should have to give up life——"

"I am sick of 'life'—it is not life to be always working in the vineyards——"

"No; but didn't the Abbé throw over old Marin the other day. He wouldn't give him a thing."

"Ay, but old Marin wanted to play such a game as no one can win at that has not thousands at his back."

At this moment the two men, who were dressed like working foremen, suddenly doubled, and retraced their steps to cross the bridge by the Hôtel-Dieu to the Place Maubert; Godefroid stood aside; but seeing that he was following them closely, the men exchanged looks of suspicion, and they were evidently vexed at having spoken out so plainly.

Godefroid was indeed all the more interested in the conversation because it reminded him of the scene between the Abbé de Vèze and the workman on the evening of his first call.

"What goes on at Madame de la Chanterie's?" he asked himself once more.

As he thought over this question, he made his way to a bookshop in the Rue Saint-Jacques, and returned home with a very handsome copy of the best edition of *The Imitation* that has been published in France.

As he walked slowly homewards to be punctual to the dinner-hour, he went over in his mind all his experience of the morning, and found his soul singularly refreshed by it. He was possessed indeed by intense curiosity, but that curiosity paled before an indefinable wish; he was attracted by Madame de la Chanterie, he felt a vehement longing to attach himself to her, to devote himself for her, to please her and deserve her praise; in short, he was aware of a Platonic passion; he felt that there was unfathomed greatness in that soul, and that he must learn to know it thoroughly. He was eager to discover the secrets of the life of these pure-minded Catholics. And then, in this little congregation of the Faithful, practical religion was so intimately allied with all that is most majestic in the Frenchwoman, that he resolved to do his utmost to be admitted to the fold. Such a vein of feeling would have been sudden indeed in a man of busy life; but Godefroid, as we have seen, was in the position of a shipwrecked wretch who clings to the most fragile bough, hoping that it may bear him, and his soul was ploughed land, ready to receive any seed.

He found the four gentlemen in the drawing-room, and he presented the book to Madame de la Chanterie, saying:

"I would not leave you without a copy for this evening."

"God grant," said she, looking at the splendid volume, "that this may be your last fit of elegance!"

And seeing that the four men had reduced the smallest details of their raiment to what was strictly decent and useful, noticing too that this principle was rigorously carried out in every detail of the house, Godefroid understood the purpose of this reproof so delicately expressed.

"Madame," said he, "the men you benefited this morning

are monsters. Without intending it, I overheard what they were saying as they went away, and it was full of the blackest ingratitude."

"The two iron-workers from the Rue Mouffetard," said Madame de la Chanterie to Monsieur Nicolas, "that is your concern——"

"The fish gets off the hook more than once before it is caught," said Monsieur Alain, laughing.

Madame de la Chanterie's entire indifference on hearing of the immediate ingratitude of the men to whom she had certainly given money amazed Godefroid, who became thoughtful.

Monsieur Alain and the old lawyer made the dinner a cheerful meal; but the soldier was constantly grave, sad, and cold; his countenance bore the ineradicable stamp of a bitter sorrow, a perennial grief. Madame de la Chanterie was equally attentive to all. Godefroid felt that he was watched by these men, whose prudence was not less than their piety, and vanity led him to imitate their reserve, so he measured his words carefully.

This first day, indeed, was far more lively than those which came after. Godefroid, finding himself shut out from all serious matters, was obliged, during the early morning and the evening when he was alone in his rooms, to read *The Imitation of Christ,* and he finally studied it as we must study a book when we are imprisoned with that one alone. We then feel to the book as we should towards a woman with whom we dwelt in solitude; we must either love or hate the woman; and in the same way we must enter into the spirit of the author or not read ten lines of his work.

Now it is impossible not to be held captive by *The Imitation,* which is to dogma what action is to thought. The Catholic spirit thrills through it, moves and works in it, struggles in it hand to hand with the life of man. That book is a trusty friend. It speaks to every passion, to every difficulty, even to the most worldly; it answers every objection, it is more eloquent than any preacher, for it speaks with your own voice—a voice that rises from your own heart and that you hear with your soul. In short, it is the Gospel interpreted and adapted to all times and seasons, controlling every situation. It is strange indeed that the Church should not have canonized Gerson, for the Holy Spirit certainly guided his pen.

To Godefroid the Hôtel de la Chanterie contained a woman as well as a book; every day he was more and more bewitched by her. In her he found flowers buried under the snow of many winters; he had glimpses of such a sacred friendship as religion sanctions, as the angels smile on—as bound those five, in fact—and against which no evil could prevail. There is a sentiment superior to all others, an affection of soul for soul which resembles those rare blossoms that grow on the loftiest peaks of the earth. One or two examples are shown us in a century; lovers are sometimes united by it; and it accounts for certain faithful attachments which would be inexplicable by the ordinary laws of the world. In such an attachment there are no disappointments, no differences, no vanities, no rivalries, no contrasts even, so intimately fused are two spiritual natures.

It was this immense and infinite feeling, the outcome of Catholic charity, that Godefroid was beginning to dream of. At times he could not believe in the spectacle before his eyes, and he sought to find reasons for the sublime friendships between these five persons, wondering to find true Catholics, Christians of the most primitive type, in Paris, and in 1836.

A week after entering the house, Godefroid had seen such a number of people come and go, he had overheard fragments of conversation in which such serious matters were discussed, that he understood that the existence of this council of five was full of prodigious activity. He noticed that not one of them slept more than six hours at most. Each of them had, as it were, lived through a first day before they met at the second breakfast. Strangers brought in or carried away sums of money, sometimes rather considerable. Mongenod's cashier came very often, always early in the morning, so that his work in the bank should not be interfered with by this business, which was independent of the regular affairs of the House.

One evening Monsieur Mongenod himself called, and Godefroid observed a touch of filial familiarity in his tone to Monsieur Alain, mingled with the deep respect he showed to him, as to Madame de la Chanterie's three other boarders.

That evening the banker only asked Godefroid the most ordinary questions: Was he comfortable? Did he mean to stay? and so forth, advising him to persevere in his determination.

"There is but one thing wanting to make me happy," said Godefroid.

"And what is that?" said the banker.

"An occupation."

"An occupation!" cried the Abbé de Vèze. "Then you have changed your mind; you came to our retreat in search of rest."

"But without prayer, which gives life to the cloister; without meditation, which peoples the desert, rest becomes a disease," said Monsieur Joseph sententiously.

"Learn bookkeeping," said Mongenod, smiling. "In the course of a few months you may be of great use to my friends here——"

"Oh, with the greatest pleasure," exclaimed Godefroid.

The next day was Sunday. Madame de la Chanterie desired her boarder to give her his arm and to escort her to High Mass.

"This," she said, "is the only thing I desire to force upon you. Many a time during the week I have been moved to speak to you of your salvation; but I do not think the time has come. You would have plenty to occupy you if you shared our beliefs, for you would also share our labors."

At Mass, Godefroid observed the fervency of Messieurs Nicolas, Joseph, and Alain. Having, during these few days, convinced himself of the superior intellect of these three men, their perspicacity, extensive learning, and lofty spirit, he concluded that if they could thus abase themselves, the Catholic religion must contain mysteries which had hitherto escaped his ken.

"And, after all," said he to himself, "it is the religion of Bossuet, of Pascal, of Racine, of Saint-Louis, of Louis XVI., of Raphael, Michael Angelo, and Ximenes, of Bayard and du Guesclin—and how should such a poor creature as I compare myself with these great brains, statesmen, poets, warriors——?"

Were it not that a great lesson is to be derived from these trivial details, it would be foolish in such times as these to dwell on them; but they are indispensable to the interest of this narrative, which the readers of our day will, indeed, find it hard to believe, beginning as it does by an almost ridiculous incident—the influence exerted by a woman of sixty over a young man who had tried everything and found it wanting.

"You did not pray," said Madame de la Chanterie to Godefroid as they came out of Notre-Dame. "Not for any one, not even for the peace of your mother's soul!"

Godefroid reddened, but said nothing.

"Do me the pleasure," Madame de la Chanterie went on, "to go to your room, and not to come down to the drawing-room for an hour. And for the love of me, meditate on a chapter of the *Imitation*—the first of the Third Book, entitled 'ON CHRIST SPEAKING WITHIN THE FAITHFUL SOUL.'"

Godefroid bowed coolly, and went upstairs.

"The Devil take 'em all!" he exclaimed, now really in a rage. "What the deuce do they want of me here? What game are they playing? Pshaw! Every woman, even the veriest bigot, is full of tricks, and if Madame" (the name the boarders gave their hostess) "does not want me downstairs, it is because they are plotting something against me."

With this notion in his head, he tried to look out of his own window into that of the drawing-room, but the plan of the building did not allow of it. Then he went down one flight, but hastily ran up again; for it struck him that in a house where the principal inhabitants held such strict principles, an act of espionage would lead to his immediate dismissal. Now, to lose the esteem of those five persons seemed to him as serious a matter as public dishonor.

He waited about three-quarters of an hour, resolved to take Madame de la Chanterie by surprise, and to go down a little before the time she had named. He intended to excuse himself by a fib, saying that his watch was in fault, and twenty minutes too fast. He went down cautiously, without a sound, and on reaching the drawing-room door opened it suddenly.

He saw a man, still young but already famous, a poet whom he had often met in society, Victor de Vernisset, kneeling on one knee before Madame de la Chanterie and kissing the hem of her gown. The sky falling in splinters as if it were made of crystal, as the ancients believed, would have amazed Godefroid less than this sight. The most shocking ideas besieged his brain, and the reaction was even more terrible when, just as he was about to utter the first sarcasm that rose to his lips, he saw Monsieur Alain standing in a corner, counting thousand-franc notes.

In an instant Vernisset had started to his feet. Good Monsieur Alain stared in astonishment. Madame de la Chanterie flashed a look that petrified Godefroid, for the doubtful expression in the new boarder's face had not escaped her.

"Monsieur is one of us," she said to the young author, introducing Godefroid.

"You are a happy man, my dear fellow," said Vernisset. "You are saved!—But, madame," he went on, turning to Madame de la Chanterie, "if all Paris could have seen me, I should be delighted. Nothing can ever pay my debt to you. I am your slave for ever! I am yours, body and soul. Command in whatever you will, I will obey; my gratitude knows no bounds. I owe you my life—it is yours."

"Come, come," said the worthy Alain, "do not be rash. Only work; and, above all, never attack religion in your writings.—And remember you are in debt."

He handed him an envelope bulging with the banknotes he had counted out. Victor de Vernisset's eyes filled with tears. He respectfully kissed Madame de la Chanterie's hand, and went away after shaking hands with Monsieur Alain and with Godefroid.

"You did not obey Madame," said the good man solemnly; and his face had an expression of sadness, such as Godefroid had not yet seen on it. "That is a capital crime. If it occurs again, we must part.—It would be very hard on you, after having seemed worthy of our confidence——"

"My dear Alain," said Madame de la Chanterie, "be so good, for my sake, as to say nothing of this act of folly. We must not expect too much of a newcomer who has had no great sorrows, who has no religion—who has nothing, in fact, but great curiosity concerning every vocation, and who as yet does not believe in us."

"Forgive me, madame," replied Godefroid. "From this moment I will be worthy of you; I submit to every test you may think necessary before initiating me into the secret of your labors; and if Monsieur the Abbé will undertake to enlighten me, I give myself up to him, soul and reason."

These words made Madame de la Chanterie so happy that a faint flush rose to her cheeks, she clasped Godefroid's hand and pressed it, saying, with strange emotion, "That is well!"

In the evening, after dinner, Godefroid saw a Vicar-General of the Diocese of Paris, who came to call, two canons, two retired mayors of Paris, and a lady who devoted herself to the poor. There was no gambling; the conversation was general, and cheerful without being futile.

A visitor who greatly surprised Godefroid was the Comtesse de Saint-Cygne, one of the loftiest stars of the aristocratic spheres, whose drawing-room was quite inaccessible to the citizen class and to parvenus. The mere presence of this great lady in Madame de la Chanterie's room was sufficiently amazing; but the way in which the two women met and treated each other was to Godefroid quite inexplicable, for it bore witness to an intimacy and constant intercourse which proved the high merit of Madame de la Chanterie. Madame de Saint-Cygne was gracious and friendly to her friend's four friends, and very respectful to Monsieur Nicolas.

As may be seen, social vanity still had a hold on Godefroid, who, hitherto undecided, now determined to yield, with or without conviction, to everything Madame de la Chanterie and her friends might require of him, to succeed in being affiliated by them to their Order, or initiated into their secrets, promising himself that until then he would not definitely commit himself.

On the following day, he went to the bookkeeper recommended by Madame de la Chanterie, agreed with him as to the hours when they were to work together, and so disposed of all his time; for the Abbé de Vèze was to catechize him in the morning, he spent two hours of every day learning bookkeeping, and between breakfast and dinner he worked at the exercises and imaginary commercial correspondence set him by his master.

Some few days thus passed, during which Godefroid learned the charm of a life of which every hour has its employment. The recurrence of the same duties at fixed hours, and perfect regularity, sufficiently account for many happy lives, and prove how deeply the founders of religious orders had meditated on human nature. Godefroid, who had made up his mind to learn of the Abbé de Vèze, had already begun to feel qualms as to his future life, and to discover that he was ignorant of the importance of religious matters.

Finally, day by day, Madame de la Chanterie, with whom he always sat for about an hour after the second breakfast, revealed some fresh treasures of her nature; he had never conceived of goodness so complete, so all-embracing. A woman as old as Madame de la Chanterie seemed to be has none of the triviality of a young woman; she is a friend who may offer you every feminine dainty, who displays all the grace and refinement with which Nature inspires woman to please man, but who no longer asks for a return; she may be execrable or exquisite, for all her demands on life are buried beneath the skin—or are dead; and Madame de la Chanterie was exquisite. She seemed never to have been young; her looks never spoke of the past. Far from allaying his curiosity, Godefroid's increased intimacy with this beautiful character, and the discoveries he made day by day, increased his desire to know something of the previous history of the woman he now saw as a saint. Had she ever loved? Had she been married? Had she been a mother? There was nothing in her suggestive of the old maid; she had all the elegance of a woman of birth; and her strong health, and the extraordinary charm of her conversation, seemed to reveal a heavenly life, a sort of ignorance of the world. Excepting the worthy and cheerful Alain, all these persons had known suffering; but Monsieur Nicolas himself seemed to give the palm of martyrdom to Madame de la Chanterie; nevertheless, the memory of her sorrows was so entirely suppressed by Catholic resignation, and her secret occupations, that she seemed to have been always happy.

"You are the life of your friends," said Godefroid to her one day. "You are the bond that unites them; you are the housekeeper, so to speak, of a great work; and as we are all mortal, I cannot but wonder what would become of your association without you."

"Yes, that is what they fear; but Providence—to whom we owe our bookkeeper," said she with a smile—"will doubtless provide. However, I shall think it over——"

"And will your bookkeeper soon find himself at work for your business?" asked Godefroid, laughing.

"That must depend on him," she said with a smile. "If he is sincerely religious, truly pious, has not the smallest conceit, does not trouble his head about the wealth of the establishment, and endeavors to rise superior to petty social considerations by soaring on the wings God has bestowed on us——"

"Which are they?"

"Simplicity and purity," replied Madame de la Chanterie.

"Your ignorance proves that you neglect reading your book," she added, laughing at the innocent trap she had laid to discover whether Godefroid read the *Imitation of Christ*. "Soak your mind in Saint Paul's chapter on Charity. It is not you who will be devoted to us, but we to you," she said with a lofty look, "and it will be your part to keep account·of the greatest riches ever possessed by any sovereign; you will have the same enjoyment of them as we have; and let me tell you, if you remember the Thousand and One Nights, that the treasures of Aladdin are as nothing in comparison with ours. Indeed, for a year past, we have not known what to do; it was too much for us. We needed a bookkeeper."

As she spoke she studied Godefroid's face; he knew not what to think of this strange confidence; but the scene between Madame de la Chanterie and the elder Madame Mongenod had often recurred to him, and he hesitated between doubt and belief.

"Yes, you would be very fortunate!" said she.

Godefroid was so consumed by curiosity, that from that instant he resolved to undermine the reserve of the four friends, and to ask them about themselves. Now, of all Madame de la Chanterie's boarders, the one who most attracted Godefroid, and who was the most fitted in all ways to invite the sympathy of people of every class, was the kindly, cheerful, and unaffected Monsieur Alain. By what means had Providence guided this simple-minded being to this secular convent, where the votaries lived under rules as strictly observed, in perfect freedom and in the midst of Paris, as though they were under the sternest of Priors? What drama, what catastrophe, had made him turn aside from his road through the world to take a path so hard to tread across the troubles of a great city?

One evening Godefroid determined to call on his neighbor, with the purpose of satisfying a curiosity which was more excited by the incredibility of any catastrophe in such a man's

" Come in "

life than it could have been by the expectation of listening to some terrible episode in the life of a pirate.

On hearing the reply, "Come in," in answer to two modest raps on the door, Godefroid turned the key, which was always in the lock, and found Monsieur Alain seated in his chimney corner, reading a chapter of the *Imitation* before going to bed by the light of two wax candles with green shades, such as whist-players use. The worthy man had on his trousers and a dressing-gown of thick gray flannel; his feet were raised to the level of the fire on a hassock worked in cross-stitch—as his slippers were also—by Madame de la Chanterie. His striking old head, with its circlet of white hair, almost resembling that of an old monk, stood out, a lighter spot against the brown background of an immense armchair.

Monsieur Alain quietly laid his book, with its worn corners, on the little table with twisted legs, while with the other hand he waved the young man to the second armchair, removing his glasses, which nipped the end of his nose.

"Are you unwell, that you have come down so late?" he asked.

"Dear Monsieur Alain," Godefroid frankly replied, "I am a prey to curiosity which a single word from you will prove to be very innocent or very indiscreet, and that is enough to show you in what spirit I shall venture to ask a question."

"Oh, ho! and what is it?" said he, with an almost mischievous sparkle in his eye.

"What was the circumstance that induced you to lead the life you lead here? For to embrace such a doctrine of utter renunciation, a man must be disgusted with the world, must have been deeply wounded, or have wounded others."

"Why, why, my boy?" replied the old man, and his full lips parted in one of those smiles which made his ruddy mouth one of the most affectionate that the genius of a painter could conceive of. "May he not feel touched to the deepest pity by the sight of the woes to be seen within the walls of Paris? Did Saint Vincent de Paul need the goad of remorse or of wounded vanity to devote himself to foundling babes?"

"Such an answer shuts my mouth all the more effectually, because if ever a soul was a match for that of the Christian hero, it is yours," replied Godefroid.

In spite of the thickening given by age to his yellow and wrinkled face, the old man colored crimson, for he might seem to have invited the eulogium, though his well-known modesty forbade the idea that he had thought of it. Godefroid knew full well that Madame de la Chanterie's guests had no taste for this kind of incense. And yet good Monsieur Alain's guilelessness was more distressed by this scruple than a young maid would have been by some evil suggestion.

"Though I am far from resembling him in spirit," replied Monsieur Alain, "I certainly am like him in appearance——"

Godefroid was about to speak, but was checked by a gesture from the old man, whose nose had in fact the bulbous appearance of the Saint's, and whose face, much like that of some old vinedresser, was the very duplicate of the coarse, common countenance of the founder of the Foundling Hospital. "As to that, you are right," he went on; "my vocation to this work was the result of an impulse of repentance in consequence of an adventure——"

"An adventure! You!" said Godefroid softly, who at this word forgot what he had been about to say.

"Oh, the story I have to tell will seem to you a mere trifle, a foolish business; but before the tribunal of conscience it looked different. If, after having heard me, you persist in your wish to join in our labors, you will understand that feelings are in inverse proportion to our strength of soul, and that a matter which would not trouble a Freethinker may greatly weigh on a feeble Christian."

After this prelude, the neophyte's curiosity had risen to an indescribable pitch. What could be the crime of this good soul whom Madame de la Chanterie had nicknamed her *Paschal Lamb?* It was as exciting as a book entitled *The Crimes of a Sheep.* Sheep, perhaps, are ferocious to the grass and flowers. If we listen to one of the mildest republicans of our day, the best creatures living are cruel to something. But good Monsieur Alain! He, who, like Sterne's Uncle Toby, would not crush a fly when it had stung him twenty times! This beautiful soul—tortured by repentance!

These reflections filled up the pause made by the old man after he had said, "Listen, then!" and during which he pushed forward the footstool under Godefroid's feet that they might share it.

"I was a little over thirty," said he; "it was in the year '98, so far as I recollect, a time when young men of thirty had the experience of men of sixty. One morning, a little before my breakfast hour at nine o'clock, my old housekeeper announced one of the few friends left to me by the storms of the Revolution. So my first words were to ask him to breakfast. My friend, whose name was Mongenod, a young fellow of eight-and-twenty, accepted, but with some hesitancy. I had not seen him since 1793——"

"Mongenod!" cried Godefroid, "the——?"

"If you want to know the end of the story before the beginning," the old man put in with a smile, "how am I to tell it?"

Godefroid settled himself with an air that promised perfect silence.

"When Mongenod had seated himself," the good man went on, "I observed that his shoes were dreadfully worn. His spotted stockings had been so often washed, that it was hard to recognize that they were of silk. His knee-breeches were of nankeen-colored kerseymere, so faded as to tell of long wear, emphasized by stains in many places, and their buckles, instead of steel, seemed to me to be of common iron; his shoe-buckles were to match. His flowered white waistcoat, yellow with long use, his shirt with its frayed pleated frill, revealed extreme though decent poverty. Finally, his coat—a *houppelande,* as we called such a coat, with a single collar like a very short cape—was enough to assure me that my friend had fallen on bad times. This coat of nut-brown cloth, extremely threadbare, and brushed with excessive care, had a rim of grease or powder round the collar, and buttons off which the plating had worn to the copper. In fact, the whole outfit was so wretched, that I could not bear to look at it. His crush hat—a semicircular structure of beaver, which it was then customary to carry under one arm instead of wearing it on the head—must have survived many changes of government.

"However, my friend had no doubt just spent a few sous to have his head dressed by a barber, for he was freshly shaved, and his hair, fastened into a club with a comb, was luxuriously powdered, and smelled of pomatum. I could see two chains hanging parallel out of his fobs, chains of tarnished steel, but no sign of the watches within. It was winter, but Mongenod had no cloak, for some large drops of melting snow fallen from the eaves under which he had walked for shelter lay on the collar of his coat. When he drew off his rabbit-fur gloves and I saw his right hand, I could perceive the traces of some kind of hard labor.

"Now, his father, an advocate in the higher court, had left him some little fortune—five or six thousand francs a year. I at once understood that Mongenod had come to borrow of me. I had in a certain hiding-place two hundred louis in gold, an enormous sum at that time, when it represented I know not how many hundred thousand francs in paper *assignats*.

"Mongenod and I had been schoolfellows at the Collège des Grassins, and we had been thrown together again in the same lawyer's office—an honest man, the worthy Bordin. When two men have spent their boyhood together and shared the follies of their youth, there is an almost sacred bond of sympathy between them; the man's voice and look stir certain chords in your heart, which never vibrate but to the particular memories that he can rouse. Even if you have some cause to complain of such a comrade, that does not wipe out every claim of friendship, and between us there had not been the slightest quarrel.

"In 1787, when his father died, Mongenod had been a richer man than I; and though I had never borrowed from him, I had owed to him certain pleasures which my father's strictness would have prohibited. But for my friend's generosity, I should not have seen the first performance of the *Marriage of Figaro*.

"Mongenod was at that time what was called a finished gentleman, a man about town and attentive to 'the ladies.' I constantly reproved him for his too great facility in making friends and obliging them; his purse was constantly open, he lived largely, he would have stood surety for you after meeting you twice.—Dear me, dear me! You have started me on reminiscences of my youth!" cried Monsieur Alain, with a bright smile at Godefroid as he paused.

"You are not vexed with me?" said Godefroid.

"No, no. And you may judge by the minute details I am giving you how large a place the event filled in my life.— Mongenod, with a good heart and plenty of courage, something of a Voltairean, was inclined to play the fine gentleman," Monsieur Alain went on. "His education at the Grassins, where noblemen's sons were to be met, and his adventures of gallantry, had given him the polish of men of rank, in those days termed Aristocrats. So you may imagine how great was my consternation at observing in Mongenod such signs of poverty as degraded him in my eyes from the elegant young Mongenod I had known in 1787, when my eyes wandered from his face to examine his clothes.

"However, at that time of general public penury, some wily folks assumed an appearance of wretchedness; and as others no doubt had ample reasons for assuming a disguise, I hoped for some explanation, and invited it.

"'What a plight you are in, my dear Mongenod!' said I, accepting a pinch of snuff, which he offered me from a box of imitation gold.

"'Sad enough!' replied he. 'I have but one friend left— and you are that friend. I have done everything in the world to avoid coming to this point, but I have come to ask you to lend me a hundred louis. It is a large sum,' said he, noticing my surprise, 'but if you lend me no more than fifty, I shall never be able to repay you; whereas, if I should fail in what

I am undertaking, I shall still have fifty louis to try some other road to fortune, and I do not yet know what inspiration despair may bring me.'

" 'Then, have you nothing?' said I.

" 'I have,' said he, hiding a tear, 'just five sous left out of my last piece of silver. To call on you, I had my boots cleaned and my head dressed. I have the clothes on my back.—But,' he went on, with a desperate shrug, 'I owe my landlady a thousand crowns in assignats, and the man at the cookshop yesterday refused to trust me. So I have nothing—nothing.'

" 'And what do you propose to do?' said I, insistently meddling with his private affairs.

" 'To enlist if you refuse to help me.'

" 'You, a soldier! You—Mongenod!'

" 'I will get killed, or I will be General Mongenod.'

" 'Well,' said I, really moved, 'eat your breakfast in peace; I have a hundred louis——'

"And here," said the good man, looking slily at Godefroid, "I thought it necessary to tell a little lender's fib.

" 'But it is all I have in the world,' I said to Mongenod. 'I was waiting till the funds had gone down to the lowest mark to invest my money, but I will place it in your hands, and you may regard me as your partner; I leave it to your conscience to repay me the whole in due time and place. An honest man's conscience,' I added, 'is the best possible security.'

"Mongenod looked hard at me as I spoke, seeming to stamp my words on his heart. He held out his right hand, I gave him my left, and we clasped hands—I, greatly moved, and he, without restraining two tears which now trickled down his thin cheeks— The sight of those tears wrung my heart; and I was still more unnerved when, forgetful of everything in such a moment, Mongenod, to wipe them away, pulled out a ragged bandana.

" 'Wait here,' said I, running off to my hidden store, my heart as full as though I had heard a woman confess that she loved me. I returned with two rolls of fifty louis each.

" 'Here—count them.'

"But he would not count them; he looked about him for a writing-table in order, as he said, to give me a receipt. I positively refused to have one.

" 'If I were to die,' said I, 'my heirs would worry you. This is a matter between you and me.'

"Finding me so true a friend, Mongenod presently lost the haggard and anxious expression he had worn on entering, and became cheerful. My housekeeper gave us oysters, white wine, an omelette, kidneys *à la brochette,* and the remains of a pâté de Chartres sent me by my mother; a little dessert, coffee, and West Indian liqueur. Mongenod, who had fasted for two days, was the better for it. We sat till three in the afternoon talking over our life before the Revolution, the best friends in the world.

"Mongenod told me how he had lost his fortune. In the first instance, the reduction of the dividends on the Hôtel de Ville had deprived him of two-thirds of his income, for his father had invested the larger part of his fortune in municipal securities; then, after selling his house in the Rue de Savoie, he had been obliged to accept payment in *assignats;* he had then taken it into his head to run a newspaper, *La Sentinelle,* and at the end of six months was forced to fly. At the present moment all his hopes hung on the success of a comic opera called *Les Péruviens.* This last confession made me quake. Mongenod, as an author, having spent his all on the *Sentinelle,* and living no doubt at the theatre, mixed up with Feydeau's singers, with musicians, and the motley world behind the curtain, did not seem to me like the same, like my Mongenod. I shuddered a little. But how could I get back my hundred louis? I could see the two rolls, one in each fob like the barrel of a pistol.

"Mongenod went away. When I found myself alone, no longer face to face with his bitter and cruel poverty, I began to reflect in spite of myself; I was sober again. 'Mongenod,' thought I to myself, 'has no doubt sunk as low as possible; he has acted a little farce for my benefit!' His glee when he saw me calmly hand over so vast a sum now struck me as that of a stage rascal cheating some Géronte. I ended where I ought to have begun, resolved to make some inquiries about my friend Mongenod, who had written his address on the back of a playing-card.

"A feeling of delicacy kept me from going to see him the next day; he might have ascribed my haste to distrust of him. Two days after I found my whole time absorbed by various business; and it was not, in fact, till a fortnight had elapsed that, seeing no more of Mongenod, I made my way from La Croix-Rouge, where I then lived, to the Rue des Moineaux, where he lived.

"Mongenod was lodged in a furnished house of the meanest description; but his landlady was a very decent woman, the widow of a farmer-general who had died on the scaffold. She, completely ruined, had started with a few louis the precarious business of letting rooms. Since then she has rented seven houses in the neighborhood of Saint-Roch and made a fortune.

" 'Citizen Mongenod is out,' said she. 'But there is some one at home.'

"This excited my curiosity. I climbed to the fifth floor. A charming young woman opened the door! Oh! A person of exquisite beauty, who, looking at me doubtfully, stood behind the partly opened door.

" 'I am Alain,' said I, 'Mongenod's friend.'

"At once the door was wide open, and I went into a horrible garret, which the young woman had, however, kept scrupulously clean. She pushed forward a chair to the hearth piled with ashes, but with no fire, where in one corner I saw a common earthenware fire-pan. The cold was icy.

" 'I am glad indeed, monsieur,' said she, taking my hands and pressing them warmly, 'to be able to express my gratitude, for you are our deliverer. But for you I might never have seen Mongenod again. He would have—God knows— have thrown himself into the river. He was desperate when he set out to see you.'

"As I looked at the young lady I was greatly astonished

to see that she had a handkerchief bound about her head; and below its folds at the back and on the temples there was a sort of black shadow. Studying it attentively, I discovered that her head was shaved.

" 'Are you ill?' I asked, noticing this strange fact.

"She glanced at herself in a wretched dirty pier-glass, and colored, while tears rose to her eyes.

" 'Yes, monsieur,' said she hastily; 'I had dreadful head-aches; I was obliged to cut off my hair, which fell to my heels——'

" 'Have I the honor of speaking to Madame Mongenod?' I asked.

" 'Yes, monsieur,' said she, with a really heavenly expression.

"I made my bow to the poor little lady, and went down-stairs, intending to make the landlady give me some informa-tion, but she was gone out. It struck me that the young wo-man had sold her hair to buy bread. I went off at once to a wood merchant, and sent in half a load of wood, begging the carter and the sawyers to give the lady a receipted bill to the name of Mongenod.

"And there ends the phase of my life which I long called my foolish stage," said Monsieur Alain, clasping his hands and uplifting them a little with a repentant gesture.

Godefroid could not help smiling; but he was, as will be seen, quite wrong to smile.

"Two days later," the good man went on, "I met one of those men who are neither friends nor strangers—persons whom we see from time to time, in short, an acquaintance, as we say—a Monsieur Barillaud, who, as we happened to speak of *Les Péruviens,* proclaimed himself a friend of the author's.

" 'Thou know'st Citizen Mongenod?' said I—for at that time we were still required by law to address each other with the familiar *tu*," said he to Godefroid in a parenthesis.

"The citizen looked at me," said Monsieur Alain, resum-ing the thread of his story, "and exclaimed:

" 'I only wish I had never known him, for he has borrowed

money of me many a time, and is so much my friend as not to return it. He is a queer fellow! the best old boy alive, but full of illusions?—An imagination of fire.—I will do him justice; he does not mean to be dishonest, only as he is always deceiving himself about a thousand things, he is led into conduct that is not altogether straight.'

" 'How much does he owe you?'

" 'Oh, a few hundred crowns. He is a regular sieve. No one knows where his money goes, for he perhaps does not know that himself.'

" 'Has he any expedients?'

" 'Oh, dear, yes!' said Barillaud, laughing. 'At this moment he is talking of buying up land among the wild men in the United States.'

"I went away with this drop of vitriol shed by slander on my heart to turn all my best feelings sour. I went to call on my old master in the law, who was always my counselor. As soon as I had told him the secret of my loan to Mongenod, and the way in which I had acted:

" 'What,' cried he, 'is it a clerk of mine that can behave so? You should have put him off a day and have come to me. Then you would have known that I had shown Mongenod the door. He has already borrowed from me in the course of a year more than a hundred crowns in silver, an enormous sum! And only three days before he went to breakfast with you, he met me in the street and described his misery in such desperate language that I gave him two louis.'

" 'Well, if I am the dupe of a clever actor, so much the worse for him rather than for me!' said I. 'But what is to be done?'

" 'At any rate, you must try to get some acknowledgment out of him, for a debtor however worthless may recover himself, and then you may be paid.'

"Thereupon Bordin took out of one of the drawers of his table a wrapper on which was written the name of Mongenod; he showed me three acknowledgments, each for a hundred livres.

" 'The first time he comes,' said he, 'I shall make him add on the interest and the two louis I gave him, and whatever money he asks for; and then he must sign an acceptance and a statement, saying that interest accrues from the first day of the loan. That, at any rate, will be all in order; I shall have some means of getting paid.'

" 'Well, then,' said I to Bordin, 'cannot you put me as much in order as yourself? For you are an honest man, and what you do will be right.'

" 'In this way I remain the master of the field,' replied the lawyer. 'When a man behaves as you have done, he is at the mercy of another who may simply make game of him. Now I don't choose to be laughed at. A retired Public Prosecutor of the Châtelet! Bless me, what next!—Every man to whom you lend money as recklessly as you lent it to Mongenod, sooner or later thinks of it as his own. It is no longer your money; it is his money; you are his creditor, a very inconvenient person. The debtor then tries to be quit of you by a compromise with his conscience, and seventy-five out of every hundred will try to avoid meeting you again to the end of his days——'

" 'Then you look for no more than twenty-five per cent of honest men?'

" 'Did I say so?' said he, with an ironical smile. 'That is a large allowance!'

"A fortnight later I had a note from Bordin desiring me to call on him to fetch my receipt. I went.

" 'I tried to snatch back fifty louis for you,' said he.—I had told him all about my conversation with Mongenod.— 'But the birds are flown. You may say good-bye to your yellow-boys! Your canary-birds have fled to warmer climes. We have a very cunning rascal to deal with. Did he not assure me that his wife and his father-in-law had set out for the United States with sixty of your louis to buy land, and that he intended to join them there? To make a fortune, as he said, so as to return to pay his debts, of which he handed me the schedule drawn out in due form; for he begged me to

keep myself informed as to what became of his creditors.
Here is the schedule,' added Bordin, showing me a wrapper
on which was noted the total. 'Seventeen thousand francs
in hard cash! With such a sum as that a house might be
bought worth two thousand crowns a year.'

"After replacing the packet, he gave me a bill of exchange
for a sum equivalent to a hundred louis in gold, stated in
assignats, with a letter in which Mongenod acknowledged the
debt with interest on a hundred louis d'or.

" 'So now I am all safe?' said I to Bordin.

" 'He will not deny the debt,' replied my old master. 'But
where there are no effects, the King—that is to say, the Di-
rectoire—has no rights.'

"I thereupon left him. Believing myself to have been
robbed by a trick that evades the law, I withdrew my esteem
from Mongenod, and was very philosophically resigned.

"It is not without a reason that I dwell on these commonplace and apparently unimportant details," the good man
went on, looking at Godefroid. "I am trying to show you
how I was led to act as most men act, blindly, and in contempt
of certain rules which even savages do not disregard in the
most trifling matters. Many men would justify themselves
by the authority of Bordin; but at this day I feel that I had
no excuse. As soon as we are led to condemn one of our fellows, and to refuse him our esteem for life, we ought to rely
solely on our own judgment—and even then!—Ought we to
set up our own feelings as a tribunal before which to arraign
our neighbor? Where would the law be? What should be
our standard of merit? Would not a weakness in me be
strength in my neighbor? So many men, so many different
circumstances would there be for each deed; for there are no
two identical sets of conditions in human existence. Society
alone has the right of reproving its members; for I do not
grant it that of punishing them. A mere reprimand is sufficient, and brings with it cruelty enough.

"So as I listened to the haphazard opinions of a Parisian,
admiring my former teacher's acumen, I condemned Monge-

nod," the good man went on, after drawing from his narrative this noble moral.

"The performance of *Les Péruviens* was announced. I expected to have a ticket for the first night; I conceived myself in some way his superior. As a result of his indebtedness, my friend seemed to me a vassal who owed me many things besides the interest on my money. We are all alike!

"Not only did Mongenod send me no ticket, but I saw him at a distance coming along the dark passage under the Théâtre Feydeau, well dressed—nay, almost elegant; he affected not to see me; then, when he had passed me, and I thought I would run after him, he had vanished down some cross passage. This irritated me extremely; and my annoyance, far from being transient, increased as time went on.

"This was why. A few days after this incident I wrote to Mongenod much in these words:

" 'MY FRIEND,—You should not regard me as indifferent to anything that can happen to you, whether for good or ill. Does the *Péruviens* come up to your expectations? You forgot me—you had every right to do so—at the first performance, when I should have applauded you heartily! However, I hope, all the same, that you may find Peru in the piece, for I can invest my capital, and I count on you when the bill falls due.—Your friend, ALAIN.'

"After waiting for a fortnight and receiving no answer, I called in the Rue des Moineaux. The landlady told me that the little wife had, in fact, set out with her father, at the date named by Mongenod to Bordin. Mongenod always left his garret early in the morning, and did not come in till late at night. Another fortnight passed; I wrote another letter in these terms:

" 'MY DEAR MONGENOD,—I see nothing of you; you do not answer my notes; I cannot at all understand your conduct; and if I were to behave so to you, what would you think of me?'

"I did not sign myself 'Your friend.' I wrote 'With best regards.'

"A month slipped by; no news of Mongenod. The *Péruviens* had not obtained so great a success as Mongenod had counted on. I paid for a seat at the twentieth performance, and I found a small house. And yet Madame Scio was very fine in it. I was told in the *foyer* that there would be a few more performances of the piece. I went seven times to call on Mongenod; he was never at home, and each time I left my name with the landlady. So then I wrote again:

" 'Monsieur, if you do not wish to lose my respect after forfeiting my friendship, you will henceforth treat me as a stranger—that is to say, with civility—and you will tell me whether you are prepared to pay me when your note of hand falls due. I shall act in accordance with your reply.—Yours faithfully.   ALAIN.'

"No reply. It was now 1799; a year had elapsed all but two months.

"When the bill fell due I went to see Bordin. Bordin took the note of hand, and then took legal proceedings. The reverses experienced by the French armies had had such a depressing effect on the funds that five francs a year could be purchased for seven francs. Thus, for a hundred louis in gold, I might have had nearly fifteen hundred francs a year. Every morning, as I read the paper over my cup of coffee, I would exclaim:

"Confound that Mongenod! But for him, I could have a thousand crowns a year!'

"Mongenod had become my chronic aversion; I thundered at him even when I was walking in the street.

" 'Bordin is after him!' said I to myself. 'He will catch him—and serve him right!'

"My rage expended itself in imprecations; I cursed the man; I believed him capable of any crime. Yes! Monsieur Barillaud was quite right in what he said.

"Well, one morning my debtor walked in, no more disconcerted than if he had not owed me a centime; and I, when I saw him, I felt all the shame that should have been his. I was like a criminal caught in the act; I was quite ill at ease. The 18th of Brumaire was past, everything was going on well, and Bonaparte had set out to fight the battle of Marengo.

" 'It is unlucky, monsieur,' said I, 'that I should owe your visit solely to the intervention of a bailiff.'

"Mongenod took a chair and sat down.

" 'I have come to tell you,' said he, with the familiar *tu,* 'that I cannot possibly pay you.'

" 'You have lost me the chance of investing my money before the arrival of the First Consul—at that time I could have made a little fortune——'

" 'I know it, Alain,' said he; 'I know it. But what will you get by prosecuting me for debt and plunging me deeper by loading me with costs? I have letters from my father-in-law and my wife; they have bought some land and sent me the bill for the necessaries of the house; I have had to spend all I had in those purchases. Now, and nobody can hinder me —I mean to sail by a Dutch vessel from Flushing, whither I have sent all my small possessions. Bonaparte has won the battle of Marengo, peace will be signed, and I can join my family without fear—for my dear little wife was expecting a baby.'

" 'And so you have sacrificed me to your own interests?' cried I.

" 'Yes,' said he; 'I thought you my friend.'

"At that moment I felt small as compared to Mongenod, so sublime did that speech seem to me, so simple and grand.

" 'Did I not tell you so,' he went on; 'was I not absolutely frank with you—here, on this very spot? I came to you, Alain, as being the only man who would appreciate me.— Fifty louis would be wasted, I told you; but if you lent me a hundred, I would repay them. I fixed no date, for how can I tell when my long struggle with poverty will come to an end?— You were my last friend. All my friends, even our old master Bordin, despised me simply because I wanted to borrow money of them. Oh! Alain, you can never know the dreadful feelings that grip the heart of an honest man fighting misfortune when he goes into another man's house to ask for help! —and all that follows!—— I hope you may never know them; they are worse than the anguish of death!

" 'You have written me certain letters which, from me under similar circumstances, would have struck you as odious. You expected things of me that were out of my power. You are the only man to whom I attempt to justify myself. In spite of your severity, and though you ceased to be my friend and became only my creditor from the day when Bordin asked me for an acknowledgment of your loan, thus discrediting the handsome agreement we ourselves had come to, here, shaking hands on it with tears in our eyes!—Well, I have forgotten everything but that morning's work.

" 'It is in memory of that hour that I have come now to say, "You know not what misfortune is; do not rail at it!— I have not had an hour, not a second, to write to you in reply! Perhaps you would have liked me to come and pay you compliments?—You might as well expect a hare, harassed by dogs and hunters, to rest in a clearing and crop the grass!— I sent you no ticket! No; I had not enough to satisfy those on whom my fate depended. A novice in the theatrical world, I was the prey of musicians, actors, singers, the orchestra. To enable me to join my family over seas, and buy what they need, I sold the *Péruviens* to the manager with two other pieces I had in my desk. I am setting out for Holland without a sou. I shall eat dry bread on my journey till I reach Flushing. I have paid my passage, and have nothing more. But for my landlady's compassion, and her trust in me, I should have had to walk to Flushing with a knapsack on my back. And so, in spite of your doubting me, as, but for you, I could not have sent my father-in-law and my wife to New York, I am entirely grateful."—No, *Monsieur* Alain, I will not forget that the hundred louis you lent me might at this time be yielding you an income of fifteen hundred francs.'

" 'I would fain believe you, Mongenod,' said I, almost convinced by the tone in which he poured out this explanation.

" 'At any rate, you no longer address me as monsieur,' said he eagerly, and looking at me with emotion. 'God knows I should quit France with less regret if I could leave one man behind me in whose eyes I was neither half a rogue, nor a spendthrift, nor a victim to illusions. A man who can love truly, Alain, is never wholly despicable.'

"At these words I held out my hand; he took it and pressed it.

" 'Heaven protect you!' said I.

" 'We are still friends?' he asked.

" 'Yes,' I replied; 'it shall never be said that my schoolfellow, the friend of my youth, set out for America under the ban of my anger!——'

"Mongenod embraced me with tears in his eyes, and rushed off to the door.

"When I met Bordin a few days afterwards, I told him the story of our interview, and he replied with a smile:

" 'I only hope it was not all part of the performance!—He did not ask you for anything?'

" 'No,' said I.

" 'He came to me too, and I was almost as weak as you; but he asked me for something to get food on the way. However, he who lives will see!'

"This remark of Bordin's made me fear lest I had yielded stupidly to an impulse of feeling.

" 'Still, he too, the Public Prosecutor, did the same,' said I to myself.

"It is unnecessary, I think, to explain to you how I lost all my fortune excepting the other hundred louis, which I invested in Government securities when prices had risen so high that I had barely five hundred francs a year to live upon by the time I was four-and-thirty. By Bordin's interest I obtained an appointment at eight hundred francs a year in a branch of the *Mont-de-Piété,* Rue des Petits Augustins. I lived in the humblest way; I lodged on the third floor of a house in the Rue des Marais in an apartment consisting of two rooms and a closet for two hundred and fifty francs. I went out to dinner in a boarding-house where there was an open table, and for this I paid forty francs a month. In the evening I did some copying. Ugly as I am, and very poor, I had to give up all ideas of marriage——"

As he heard this verdict pronounced on himself by poor Alain in a tone of angelic resignation, Godefroid gave a little start, which proved better than any speech could have done the similarity of their fate; and the good man, in reply to this eloquent gesture, seemed to pause for his hearer to speak.

"And no one ever loved you?" asked Godefroid.

"No one," he replied, "excepting Madame, who returns to all of us alike our love for her—a love I might almost call divine.—You must have seen it: we live in her life, as she lives in ours; we have but one soul among us; and though our enjoyments are not physical, they are none the less very intense, for we live only through the heart.—How can we help it, my dear boy? By the time women are capable of appreciating moral qualities they have done with externals, and are growing old.—I have suffered much, I can tell you!"

"Ah! that is the stage I am at——" said Godefroid.

"Under the Empire," the old man went on, bowing his head, "dividends were not very punctually paid; we had to be prepared for deferred payment. From 1802 to 1814 not a week passed that I did not ascribe my difficulties to Mongenod: 'But for Mongenod,' I used to think, 'I might have been married. But for him I should not be obliged to live in privation.'—But sometimes, too, I would say to myself, 'Perhaps the poor man is pursued by ill-luck out there!'

"In 1806, one day when I found my life a heavy burden to bear, I wrote him a long letter that I despatched *via* Holland. I had no answer; and for three years I waited, founding hopes on that reply which were constantly deceived. At last I resigned myself to my fate. To my five hundred francs of dividends, and twelve hundred francs of salary from the Mont-de-Piété, for it was raised, I added five hundred for my work as bookkeeper to a perfumer, Monsieur Birotteau. Thus I not only made both ends meet, but I saved eight hundred francs a year. By the beginning of 1814, I was able to invest nine thousand francs of savings in the funds, buying at forty; thus I had secured sixteen hundred francs a year for my old age. So then, with fifteen hundred francs a year from the Mont-de-Piété, six hundred as a bookkeeper, and sixteen hundred in dividends, I had an income of three thousand seven hundred francs. I took rooms in the Rue de Seine, and I lived in rather more comfort.

"My position brought me into contact with many of the very poor. For twelve years I have known, better than any one, what the misery of the world is; once or twice I have helped some poor creatures; and I felt the keenest pleasure when, out of ten that I had assisted, one or two families were rescued from their difficulties.

"It struck me that true beneficence did not consist in throwing money to the sufferers. Being charitable, in the common phrase, often appeared to me to be a sort of premium on crime. I set to work to study this question. I was by this time fifty years old, and my life was drawing to a close.

"'What good am I in the world?' I asked myself. 'To whom can I leave my money? When I shall have furnished my rooms handsomely, have secured a good cook, have made my life suitably comfortable, what am I to do with my time?'

"For eleven years of revolutions and fifteen years of poverty had wasted the happiest part of my life, had consumed it in labors that were fruitless, or devoted solely to the preservation of my person! At such an age no one can make an obscure and penurious youth the starting-point to reach a brilliant position; but every one may make himself useful. I understood, in short, that a certain supervision and much good advice would increase tenfold the value of money given, for the poor always need guidance; to enable them to profit by the work they do for others, it is not the intelligence of the speculator that is wanting.

"A few happy results that I achieved made me extremely

proud. I discerned both an aim and an occupation, to say nothing of the exquisite pleasure to be derived from playing the part of Providence, even on the smallest scale."

"And you now play it on a large scale?" said Godefroid eagerly.

"Oh, you want to know too much!" said the old man. "Nay, nay.—Would you believe it," he went on after a pause, "the smallness of the means at my command constantly brought my thoughts back to Mongenod?

"'But for Mongenod I could have done so much more,' I used to reflect. 'If a dishonest man had not robbed me of fifteen hundred francs a year,' I often thought, 'I could have helped this or that family.'

"Thus excusing my inability by such an accusation, those to whom I gave nothing but words to comfort them joined me in cursing Mongenod. These maledictions were balm to my heart.

"One morning, in January 1816, my housekeeper announced—whom do you think?—Mongenod.—Monsieur Mongenod. And who should walk in but the pretty wife, now six-and-thirty, accompanied by three children; then came Mongenod, younger than when he left, for wealth and happiness shed a glory on those they favor. He had gone away lean, pale, yellow, and haggard; he had come back fat and well-liking, as flourishing as a prebendary, and well dressed. He threw himself into my arms, and finding himself coldly welcomed, his first words were:

"'Could I come any sooner, my friend? The seas have only been open since 1815, and it took me eighteen months to realize my property, close my accounts, and call in my assets. I have succeeded, my friend! When I received your letter in 1806, I set out in a Dutch vessel to bring you home a little fortune; but the union of Holland to the French Empire led to our being taken by the English, who transported me to the coast of Jamaica, whence by good luck I escaped.

"'On my return to New York I was a victim to bankruptcy; for Charlotte, during my absence, had not known how to be on her guard against swindlers. So I was compelled to begin again to accumulate a fortune.

" 'However, here we are at last. From the way the children look at you, you may suppose that they have often heard of the benefactor of the family.'

" 'Yes, indeed,' said pretty Madame Mongenod, 'we never passed a day without speaking of you. Your share has been allowed for in every transaction. We have longed for the happiness we enjoy at this moment of offering you your fortune, though we have never for a moment imagined that this "rector's tithe" can pay our debt of gratitude.'

"And as she spoke, Madame Mongenod offered me the beautiful casket you see there, which contained a hundred and fifty thousand-franc notes.

" 'You have suffered much, my dear Alain, I know; but we could imagine all your sufferings, and we craked our brains to find means of sending you money; but without success,' Mongenod went on. 'You tell me you could not marry; but here is our eldest daughter. She has been brought up in the idea that she should be your wife, and she has five hundred thousand francs——'

" 'God forbid that I should wreck her happiness!' cried I, as I beheld a girl as lovely as her mother had been at her age; and I drew her to me, and kissed her forehead.

" 'Do not be afraid, my pretty child,' said I. 'A man of fifty and a girl of seventeen—and so ugly an old fellow as I ! —Never!'

" 'Monsieur,' said she, 'my father's benefactor can never seem ugly in my eyes.'

"This speech, made with spontaneous candor, showed me that all Mongenod had told me was true. I offered him my hand, and we fell into each other's arms once more.

" 'My friend,' said I, 'I have often abused you, cursed you——'

" 'You had every right, Alain,' replied he, reddening. 'You were in poverty through my fault——'

5

"I took Mongenod's papers out of a box and restored them to him, after cancelling his note of hand.

" 'Now you will all breakfast with me,' said I to the family party.

" 'On condition of your dining with my wife as soon as we are settled,' said Mongenod, 'for we arrived only yesterday. We are going to buy a house, and I am about to open a bank in Paris for North American business to leave to that youngster,' he said, pointing to his eldest son, a lad of fifteen.

"We spent the afternoon together, and in the evening we all went to the theatre, for Mongenod and his party were dying to see a play. Next day I invested in the funds, and had then an income of about fifteen thousand francs in all. This released me from bookkeeping in the evening, and allowed me to give up my appointment, to the great satisfaction of all my subordinates.

"My friend died in 1827, after founding the banking house of Mongenod and Co., which made immense profits on the first loans issued at the time of the Restoration. His daughter, to whom he subsequently gave about a million of francs, married the Vicomte de Fontaine. The son whom you know is not yet married; he lives with his mother and his younger brother. We find them ready with all the money we may need.

"Frédéric—for his father, in America, had named him after me—Frédéric Mongenod, at seven-and-thirty, is one of the most skilful and respected bankers in Paris.

"Not very long since Madame Mongenod confessed to me that she had sold her hair for two crowns of six livres to be able to buy some bread. She gives twenty-four loads of wood every year, which I distribute among the poor, in return for the half-load I once sent her."

"Then this accounts for your connection with the house of Mongenod," said Godefroid. "And your fortune——"

The old man still looked at Godefroid with the same expression of mild irony.

"Pray go on," said Godefroid, seeing by Monsieur Alain's manner that he had more to say.

"This conclusion, my dear Godefroid, made the deepest impression on me. Though the man who had suffered so much, though my friend had forgiven me my injustice, I could not forgive myself."

"Oh!" said Godefroid.

"I determined to devote all my surplus income, about ten thousand francs a year, to acts of rational beneficence," Monsieur Alain calmly went on. "At about that time I met an Examining Judge of the department of the Seine named Popinot, whose death we mourned three years ago, and who for fifteen years practised the most enlightened charity in the Saint-Marcel quarter. He, in concert with the venerable vicar of Notre-Dame and with Madame, planned the work in which we are all engaged, and which, since 1823, has secretly effected some good results.

"This work has found a soul in Madame de la Chanterie; she is really the very spirit of the undertaking. The vicar has succeeded in making us more religious than we were at first, demonstrating the necessity for being virtuous ourselves if we desire to inspire virtue—for preaching, in fact, by example. And the further we progress in that path, the happier we are among ourselves. Thus it was my repentance for having misprized the heart of my boyhood's friend which led me to the idea of devoting to the poor, through myself, the fortune he brought home to me, which I accepted without demurring to the vast sum repaid to me for so small a loan; the application of it made it right."

This narrative, devoid of all emphasis, and told with touching simplicity of tone, gesture, and expression, would have been enough to make Godefroid resolve on joining in this noble and saintly work, if he had not already intended it.

"You know little of the world," said Godefroid, "if you had such scruples over a thing which would never have weighed on any other conscience."

"I know only the wretched," replied the good man. "I have no wish to know a world where men misjudge each other with so little compunction.—Now, it is nearly midnight, and I have to meditate on my chapter of the *Imitation.*—Good-night."

Godefroid took the kind old man's hand and pressed it with an impulse of genuine admiration.

"Can you tell me Madame de la Chanterie's history?" asked Godefroid.

"It would be impossible without her permission, for it is connected with one of the most terrible incidents of imperial politics. I first knew Madame through my friend Bordin; he knew all the secrets of that beautiful life; and it was he who led me, so to speak, to this house."

"At any rate, then," said Godefroid, "I thank you for having told me your life; it contains a lesson for me."

"Do you discern its moral?"

"Nay, tell it me," said Godefroid; "for I might see it differently to you——"

"Well, then," said the good man, "pleasure is but an accident in the life of the Christian; it is not his aim and end—and we learn this too late."

"What then happens when we are converted?" asked Godefroid.

"Look there!" said Alain, and he pointed to an inscription in letters of gold on a black ground, which the newcomer had not seen before, as this was the first time he had ever been into his companion's rooms. He turned round and read the words, "TRANSIRE BENEFACIENDO."

"That, my son, is the meaning we then find in life. That is our motto. If you become one of us, that constitutes your brevet. We read that text and take it as our counsel at every hour of the day, when we rise, when we go to bed, while we dress. Oh! if you could but know what infinite happiness is to be found in carrying out that device!"

"In what way?" said Godefroid, hoping for some explanations.

"In the first place, we are as rich as Baron de Nucingen.—But the *Imitation* prohibits our calling anything our own; we are but stewards; and if we feel a single impulse of pride, we are not worthy to be stewards. That would not be *transire benefaciendo;* it would be enjoyment in thought. If you say to yourself, with a certain dilation of the nostrils, 'I am playing the part of Providence'—as you might have thought this morning, if you had been in my place, giving new life to a whole family, you are a Sardanapalus at once—and wicked! Not one of our members ever thinks of himself when doing good. You must cast off all vanity, all pride, all self-consciousness; and it is difficult, I can tell you."

Godefroid bid Monsieur Alain good-night, and went to his own rooms, much moved by this story; but his curiosity was excited rather than satisfied, for the chief figure in the picture of this domestic scene was Madame de la Chanterie. This woman's history was to him so supremely interesting that he made the knowledge of it the first aim of his stay in the house. He understood that the purpose for which these five persons were associated was some great charitable endeavor; but he thought much less of that than of his heroine.

The neophyte spent some days in studying these choice spirits, amid whom he found himself, with greater attention than he had hitherto devoted to them; and he became the subject of a moral phenomenon which modern philanthropists have overlooked, from ignorance perhaps. The sphere in which he lived had a direct influence on Godefroid. The law which governs physical nature in respect to the influence of atmospheric conditions on the lives of the beings subject to them, also governs moral nature; whence it is to be inferred that the collecting in masses of the criminal class is one of the greatest social crimes, while absolute isolation is an experiment of which the success is very doubtful. Condemned felons ought, therefore, to be placed in religious institutions and surrounded with prodigies of goodness instead of being left among marvels of evil. The Church may be looked to for perfect devotion to this cause; for if She is ready to send missionaries to barbarous or savage nations, how gladly would She charge her religious Orders with the mission of rescuing and instructing the savages of civilized life! Every criminal is an atheist—often without knowing it.

Godefroid found his five companions endowed with the qualities they demanded of him; they were all free from pride or vanity, all truly humble and pious, devoid of the pretentiousness which constitutes *devoutness* in the invidious sense of the word. These virtues were contagious; he was filled with the desire to imitate these obscure heroes, and he ended by studying with ardor the book he had at first scorned. Within a fortnight he had reduced life to its simplest expression, to what it really is when regarded from the lofty point of view to which the religious spirit leads us. Finally, his curiosity, at first purely worldly and roused by many vulgar motives, became rarefied. He did not cease to be curious; it would have been difficult to lose all interest in the life of Madame de la Chanterie; but, without intending it, he showed a reserve which was fully appreciated by these men, in whom the Holy Spirit had developed wonderful depths of mind, as happens, indeed, with all who devote themselves to a religious life. The concentration of the moral powers, by whatever means or system, increases their scope tenfold.

"Our young friend is not yet a convert," said the good Abbé de Vèze; "but he wishes to be."

An unforeseen circumstance led to the revelation of Madame de la Chanterie's history, so that his intense interest in it was soon satisfied.

Paris was just then engrossed by the investigation of the case of the Barrière Saint-Jacques, one of those hideous trials which mark the history of our assizes. The trial derived its interest from the criminals themselves, whose daring and general superiority to ordinary culprits, with their cynical contempt for justice, really appalled the public. It was a noteworthy fact that no newspaper ever entered the Hôtel de la Chanterie, and Godefroid only heard of the rejection of the appeal to the Supreme Court from his master in bookkeeping; the trial had taken place long before he came to Madame de la Chanterie.

"Do you ever meet with such men as these atrocious scoundrels?" he asked his new friends. "Or, when you do, how do you deal with them?"

"In the first place," said Monsieur Nicolas, "there is no such thing as an atrocious scoundrel; there are mad creatures fit only for the asylum at Charenton; but with the exception of those rare pathological exceptions, what we find are simply men without religion, or who argue falsely, and the task of the charitable is to set souls upright and bring the erring into the right way."

"And to the apostle all things are possible," said the Abbé de Vèze; "he has God on his side."

"If you were sent to these two condemned men," said Godefroid, "you could do nothing with them."

"There would not be time," observed Monsieur Alain.

"As a rule," said Monsieur Nicolas, "the souls handed over to be dealt with by the Church are in utter impenitence, and the time is too short for miracles to be wrought. The men of whom you are speaking, if they had fallen into our hands, would have been men of mark; their energy is immense; but when once they have committed murder, it is impossible to do anything for them; human justice has taken possession of them——"

"Then you are averse to capital punishment?" said Godefroid.

Monsieur Nicolas hastily rose and left the room.

"Never speak of capital punishment in the presence of Monsieur Nicolas. He once recognized in a criminal, whose execution it was his duty to superintend, a natural child of his own——"

"And who was innocent!" added Monsieur Joseph.

At this moment Madame de la Chanterie, who had not been in the room, came in.

"Still, you must allow," Godefroid went on, addressing Monsieur Joseph, "that society cannot exist without capital punishment, and that these men, whose heads——"

Godefroid felt his mouth suddenly closed by a strong hand, and the Abbé de Vèze led away Madame de la Chanterie, pale and half dead.

"What have you done?" cried Monsieur Joseph. "Take him

away, Alain," he said, removing the hand with which he had gagged Godefroid; and he followed the Abbé de Vèze into Madame's room.

"Come with me," said Alain to Godefroid. "You have compelled us to tell you the secrets of Madame's life."

In a few minutes the two friends were together in Monsieur Alain's room, as they had been when the old man had told Godefroid his own history.

"Well," said Godefroid, whose face sufficiently showed his despair at having been the cause of what might be called a catastrophe in this pious household.

"I am waiting till Manon shall have come to say how she is going on," replied the good man, as he heard the woman's step on the stairs.

"Monsieur, Madame is better. Monsieur l'Abbé managed to deceive her as to what had been said," and Manon shot a wrathful glance at Godefroid.

"Good Heavens!" exclaimed the unhappy young man, his eyes filling with tears.

"Come, sit down," said Monsieur Alain, seating himself. Then he paused to collect his thoughts.

"I do not know," said the kind old man, "that I have the talent necessary to give a worthy narrative of a life so cruelly tried. You must forgive me if you find the words of so poor a speaker inadequate to the magnitude of the events and catastrophes. You must remember that it is a very long time since I was at school, and that I date from a time when thoughts were held of more importance than effect—from a prosaic age, when we knew not how to speak of things except by their names."

Godefroid bowed with an expression of assent, in which his worthy old friend could discern his sincere admiration, and which plainly said, "I am listening."

"As you have just perceived, my young friend, it would be impossible for you to remain one of us without learning some of the particulars of that saintly woman's life. There are certain ideas, allusions, words, which are absolutely prohibited in this house, since they inevitably reopen wounds, of which the anguish might kill Madame if it were once or twice revived——"

"Good Heavens!" exclaimed Godefroid, "what have I done?"

"But for Monsieur Joseph, who happily interrupted you just as you were about to speak of the awful instrument of death, you would have annihilated the poor lady.—It is time that you should be told all; for you will be one of us, of that we are all convinced."

"Madame de la Chanterie," he went on after a short pause, "is descended from one of the first families of Lower Normandy. Her maiden name was Mademoiselle Barbe-Philiberte de Champignelles—of a younger branch of that house; and she was intended to take the veil unless a marriage could be arranged for her with the usual renunciations of property that were commonly required in poor families of high rank. A certain Sieur de la Chanterie, whose family had sunk into utter obscurity, though dating from the time of Philippe-Auguste's crusade, was anxious to recover the rank to which so ancient a name gave him a claim in the province of Normandy. But he had fallen quite from his high estate, for he had made money—some three hundred thousand francs—by supplying the commissariat for the army at the time of the war with Hanover. His son, trusting too much to this wealth, which provincial rumor magnified, was living in Paris in a way calculated to cause the father of a family some uneasiness.

"Mademoiselle de Champignelles' great merits became famous throughout the district of le Bessin; and the old man, whose little feof of la Chanterie lay between Caen and Saint-Lô, heard some expressions of regret that so accomplished a young lady, and one so capable of making a husband happy, should end her days in a convent. On his uttering a wish to seek her out, some hope was given him that he might obtain the hand of Mademoiselle Philiberte for his son if he were content to renounce any marriage portion. He went to

Bayeux, contrived to have two or three meetings with the Champignelles family, and was fascinated by the young lady's noble qualities.

"At the age of sixteen, Mademoiselle de Champignelles gave promise of what she would become. She evinced well-founded piety, sound good sense, inflexible rectitude—one of those natures which will never veer in its affections even if they are the outcome of duty. The old nobleman, enriched by his somewhat illicit gains, discerned in this charming girl a wife who might keep his son in order by the authority of virtue and the ascendency of a character that was firm but not rigid; for, as you have seen, no one can be gentler than Madame de la Chanterie. Then, no one could be more confiding; even in the decline of life she has the candor of innocence; in her youth she would not believe in evil; such distrust as you may have seen in her she owes to her misfortunes. The old man pledged himself to the Champignelles to give them a discharge in full for the portion legitimately due to Mademoiselle Philiberte on the signing of the marriage-contract; in return, the Champignelles, who were connected with the greatest families, promised to have the feof of la Chanterie created a barony, and they kept their word. The bridegroom's aunt, Madame de Boisfrelon, the wife of the councillor to the Parlement who died in your rooms, promised to leave her fortune to her nephew.

"When all these arrangements were completed between the two families, the father sent for his son. This young man, at the time of his marriage, was five-and-twenty, and already a Master of Appeals; he had indulged in numerous follies with the young gentlemen of the time, living in their style; and the old army contractor had several times paid his debts to a considerable amount. The poor father, foreseeing further dissipation on the son's part, was only too glad to settle a part of his fortune on his daughter-in-law; but he was so cautious as to entail the estate of la Chanterie on the heirs male of the marriage——"

"A precaution," added Monsieur Alain in a parenthesis, "which the Revolution made useless."

"As handsome as an angel, and wonderfully skilled in all athletic exercises, the young Master of Appeals had immense powers of charming," he went on. "So Mademoiselle de Champignelles, as you may easily imagine, fell very much in love with her husband. The old man, made very happy by this promising beginning, and hoping that his son was a reformed character, sent the young couple to Paris. This was early in 1788. For nearly a year they were perfectly happy. Madame de la Chanterie was the object of all the little cares, the most delicate attentions that a devoted lover can lavish on the one and only woman he loves. Brief as it was, the honeymoon beamed brightly on the heart of the noble and unfortunate lady.

"As you know, in those days mothers all nursed their infants themselves. Madame de la Chanterie had a daughter. This time, when a wife ought to be the object of double devotion on her husband's part, was, on the contrary, the beginning of dreadful woes. The Master of Appeals was obliged to sell everything he could part with to pay old debts which he had not confessed, and more recent gambling debts. Then, suddenly, the National Assembly dissolved the Supreme Council and the Parlement, and abolished all the great law appointments that had been so dearly purchased. Thus the young couple, with the addition of their child, had no income to rely on but the revenues from the entailed estate, and from the portion settled on Madame de la Chanterie. Twenty months after their marriage this charming woman, at the age of seventeen and a half, found herself reduced to maintaining herself and the child at her breast by the work of her hands, in an obscure street where she hid herself. She then found herself absolutely deserted by her husband, who fell step by step into the society of the very lowest kind. Never did she blame her husband, never did she put him in the least in the wrong. She has told us that all through the worst time she prayed to God for her dear Henri.

"The rascal's name was Henri," remarked Monsieur Alain. "It is a name that must never be spoken here, any more than that of Henriette.—To proceed:

"Madame de la Chanterie, who never quitted her little room in the Rue de la Corderie-du-Temple unless to buy food or fetch her work, kept her head above water, thanks partly to an allowance of a hundred francs a month from her father-in-law, who was touched by so much virtue. However, the poor young wife, foreseeing that this support might fail her, had taken up the laborious work of a staymaker, and worked for a famous dressmaker. In fact, ere long the old contractor died, and his estate was consumed by his son under favor of the overthrow of the Monarchy.

"The erewhile Master of Appeals, now one of the most savage of all the presidents of the revolutionary tribunal, had become a terror in Normandy, and could indulge all his passions. Then, imprisoned in his turn on the fall of Robespierre, the hatred of the department condemned him to inevitable death. Madame de la Chanterie received a farewell letter announcing her husband's fate. She immediately placed her little girl in the care of a neighbor, and went off to the town where the wretch was in confinement, taking with her a few louis, which constituted her whole fortune. This money enabled her to get into the prison. She succeeded in helping her husband to escape, dressing him in clothes of her own, under circumstances very similar to those which not long after favored Madame de la Valette. She was condemned to death, but the authorities were ashamed to carry out this act of revenge, and she was secretly released with the connivance of the Court over which her husband had formerly presided. She got back to Paris on foot without any money, sleeping at farmhouses, and often fed by charity."

"Good Heavens!" exclaimed Godefroid.

"Wait," said the old man, "that was nothing.—In the course of eight years the poor woman saw her husband three times. The first time the gentleman spent twenty-four hours in his wife's humble lodgings, and went away with all her money, after heaping on her every mark of affection, and leading her to believe in his complete reformation.—'For I could not resist,' said she, 'a man for whom I prayed every day, and who filled my thoughts exclusively.'—The second time Monsieur de la Chanterie came in a dying state, and from some horrible disease! She nursed him, and saved his life; then she tried to reclaim him to decent feeling and a seemly life. After promising everything this angel begged of him, the revolutionary relapsed into hideous debaucheries, and in fact only escaped prosecution by the authorities by taking refuge in his wife's rooms, where he died unmolested.

"Still, all this was nothing!" said Alain, seeing dismay in Godefroid's face.

"No one in the world he had mixed with had known that the man was married. Two years after the miserable creature's death, she heard that there was a second Madame de la Chanterie, widowed and ruined like herself. The bigamous villain had found two such angels incapable of betraying him.—Towards 1803," the old man went on after a pause, "Monsieur de Boisfrelon, Madame de la Chanterie's uncle, having his name removed from the list of proscribed persons, came back to Paris and paid over to her two hundred thousand francs that the old Commissariat contractor had placed in his keeping, with instructions to hold it in trust for his niece. He persuaded the widow to return to Normandy, where she completed her daughter's education, and, by the advice of the old lawyer, purchased back one of the family estates under very favorable conditions."

"Ah!" sighed Godefroid.

"Oh! all this was nothing!" said Monsieur Alain. "We have not yet come to the hurricane.—To proceed. In 1807, after four years of peace, Madame de la Chanterie saw her only daughter married to a gentleman whose piety, whose antecedents, and fortune seemed a guarantee from every point of view; a man who was reported to be the 'pet lamb' of the best society in the country-town where Madame and her daughter spent every winter. Remark: this society consisted of seven or eight families belonging to the highest French nobility—the d'Esgrignons, the Troisvilles, the Casterans, the Nouâtres, and the like.

"At the end of eighteen months this man deserted his wife and vanished in Paris, having changed his name. Madame de la Chanterie could never discover the cause of this separation till the lightning flash showed it in the midst of the storm. Her daughter, whom she had brought up with the greatest care and the purest religious feelings, preserved absolute silence on the subject.

"This lack of confidence was a great shock to Madame de la Chanterie. Many times already she had detected in her daughter certain indications of the father's adventurous spirit, strengthened by an almost manly determination of character. The husband had departed without let or hindrance, leaving his affairs in the utmost disorder. To this day Madame de la Chanterie is amazed at this catastrophe, which no human power could remedy. All the persons she privately consulted had assured her before the marriage that the young man's fortune was clear and unembarrassed, in land unencumbered by mortgages, when, at that very time, the estate had, for ten years, been loaded with debt far beyond its value. So everything was sold, and the poor young wife, reduced to her own little income, came back to live with her mother.

"Madame de la Chanterie subsequently learned that this man had been kept going by the most respectable persons in the district for their own benefit, for the wretched man owed them all more or less considerable sums of money. Indeed, ever since her arrival in the province, Madame de la Chanterie had been regarded as a prey.

"However, there were other reasons for this climax of disaster, which you will understand from a confidential communication addressed to the Emperor.

"This man had long since succeeded in winning the good graces of the leading Royalists of the Department by his devotion to the cause during the stormiest days of the Revolution. As one of Louis XVIII.'s most active emissaries, he had, since 1793, been mixed up in every conspiracy, always withdrawing at the right moment, and with so much dexterity as to give rise at last to suspicions of his honor. The King dismissed him from service, and he was excluded from all further scheming, so he retired to his estate, already deeply involved. All these antecedents, at that time scarcely known —for those who were initiated into the secrets of the Cabinet did not say much about so dangerous a colleague—made him an object almost of worship in a town devoted to the Bourbons, where the cruelest devices of the Chouans were regarded as honest warfare. The Esgrignons, the Casterans, the Chevalier de Valois, in short, the Aristocracy and the Church, received the Royalist with open arms, and took him to their bosom. This favor was supported by his creditors' earnest desire to be paid.

"This wretch, a match for the deceased la Chanterie, was able to keep up his part for three years; he affected the greatest piety, and subjugated his vices. During the first few months of his married life he had some little influence over his wife; he did his utmost to corrupt her by his doctrines, if atheism may be called a doctrine, and by the flippant tone in which he spoke of the most sacred things.

"This backstairs diplomate had, on his return to the country, formed an intimacy with a young man, over head and ears in debt, like himself, but attractive, in so far that he had as much courage and honesty as the other had shown hypocrisy and cowardice. This guest at his house—whose charm and character could not fail to impress a young woman, to say nothing of his adventurous career—was a tool in the husband's hands which he used to support his infamous principles. The daughter never confessed to her mother the gulf into which circumstances had thrown her—for human prudence is no word for the caution exercised by Madame de la Chanterie when seeking a husband for her only child. And this last blow, in a life so devoted, so guileless, so religious as hers, tested as she had been by every kind of misfortune,

filled Madame de la Chanterie with a distrust of herself which
isolated her from her daughter; all the more so because her
daughter, in compensation for her ill-fortune, insisted on
perfect liberty, overruled her mother, and was sometimes very
rough with her.

"Thus wounded in every feeling, cheated alike in her devotion and her love for her husband—to whom she had sacrificed
her happiness, her fortune, and her life, without a murmur;
cheated in the exclusively religious training she had given her
daughter; cheated by the world, even in the matter of that
daughter's marriage, and meeting with no justice from the
heart in which she had implanted none but right feelings, she
turned more resolutely to God, clinging to Him whose hand
lay so heavy on her. She was almost a nun; she went to mass
every morning, carried out monastic discipline, and saved in
everything to be able to help the poor.

"Has any woman ever known a more saintly or more severely tried life than this noble creature, so mild to the unfortunate, so brave in danger, and always so perfect a Christian?" said the worthy man, appealing to Godefroid. "You
know Madame, you know whether she is deficient in sense,
judgment, and reflection. She has all these qualities in the
highest degree. Well, and still all these misfortunes, which
surely were enough to qualify any life as surpassing all others
in adversity, were a trifle compared with what God had yet in
store for this woman.—We will speak only of Madame de la
Chanterie's daughter," said Monsieur Alain, going on with his
narrative.

"At the age of eighteen, when she married, Mademoiselle
de la Chanterie had an extremely delicate complexion, rather
dark, with a brilliant color, a slender form, and charming
features. An elegantly formed brow was crowned by the most
beautiful black hair, that matched well with bright and lively
hazel eyes. A peculiar prettiness and a childlike countenance
belied her real nature and masculine decisiveness. She had
small hands and feet; in all her person there was something
tiny and frail, which excluded any idea of strength and wil-

fulness. Never having lived away from her mother, her mind was absolutely innocent, and her piety remarkable.

"This young lady, like Madame de la Chanterie, was fanatically devoted to the Bourbons, and hated the Revolution; she regarded Napoleon's empire as a plague inflicted on France by Providence, as a punishment for the crimes of 1793. Such a conformity of opinion between the lady and her son-in-law was, as it always must be in such cases, a conclusive reason in favor of the marriage, in which all the aristocracy of the province took the greatest interest.

"This wretched man's friend had at the time of the rebellion in 1799 been the leader of a troop of Chouans. It would seem that the Baron—for Madame de la Chanterie's son-in-law was a Baron—had no object in throwing his wife and his friend together but that of extracting money from them. Though deeply in debt, and without any means of living, the young adventurer lived in very good style, and was able, no doubt, to help the promoter of royalist conspiracies.

"Here you will need a few words of explanation as to an association which made a great noise in its day," said Monsieur Alain, interrupting his narrative. "I mean that of the raiders known as the *Chauffeurs*. These brigands pervaded all the western provinces more or less; but their object was not so much pillage as a revival of the Royalist opposition. Advantage was taken of the very general resistance of the people to the law of conscription, which, as you know, was enforced with many abuses. Between Mortagne and Rennes, and even beyond, as far as the Loire, nocturnal raids were frequent, commonly to the injury of those who held national lands. These bands of destroyers were the terrors of the country. I am not exaggerating when I tell you that in some Departments the arm of Justice was practically paralyzed. Those last thunders of civil war did not echo so far as you might suppose, accustomed as we now are to the startling publicity given by the press to the most trivial acts of political and private life. The Censor allowed nothing to appear in print that bore on politics, unless it were accomplished fact, and even that was

6

distorted. If you will take the trouble to look through old
files of the *Moniteur* and other newspapers, even those issued
in the western provinces, you will find not a word concerning
the four or five great trials which brought sixty or eighty of
these rebels to the scaffold. *Brigands,* this was the name given
under the Revolution to the Vendéans, the Chouans, and all
who took up arms for the house of Bourbon; and it was still
given in legal phraseology under the Empire to the Royalists
who were victims to sporadic conspiracies. For to some vehement souls the Emperor and his government were 'the
Enemy,' and everything seemed good that was adverse to him.
—I am explaining the position, not justifying the opinions,
and I will now go on with my story.

"So now," he said, after a pause, such as must occur in a
long story, "you must understand that these Royalists were
ruined by the war of 1793, though consumed by frantic passions; and if you can conceive of some exceptional natures
consumed also by such necessities as those of Madame de la
Chanterie's son-in-law and his friend the Chouan leader, you
will see how it was that they determined to commit, for their
private advantage, acts of robbery which their political opinions would justify, against the Imperial government for the
advantage of the Cause.

"The young leader set to work to fan the ashes of the
Chouan faction, to be ready to act at an opportune moment.
There was, soon after, a terrible crisis in the Emperor's affairs when he was shut up in the island of Lobau, and it
seemed that he must inevitably succumb to a simultaneous
attack by England and by Austria. The victory of Wagram
made the internal rebellion all but abortive. This attempt
to revive the fires of civil war in Brittany, la Vendée, and part
of Normandy, was unfortunately coincident with the Baron's
money difficulties; he had flattered himself that he could
contrive a separate expedition, of which the profits could be
applied solely to redeem his property. But his wife and
friend, with nobler feeling, refused to divert to private uses
any sums that might be snatched at the sword's point from

the State coffers; these were to be distributed to the rebel conscripts and Chouans, and to purchase weapons and ammunition to arm a general rising.

"At last, when after heated discussions the young Chouan, supported by the Baroness, positively refused to retain a hundred thousand francs in silver crowns which was to be seized from one of the Government Receivers' offices in the west to provide for the Royalist forces, the husband disappeared, to escape the execution on his person of several writs that were out against him. The creditors tried to extract payment from his wife, but the wretched man had dried up the spring of affection which prompts a woman to sacrifice herself for her husband.

"All this was kept from poor Madame de la Chanterie, but it was a trifle in comparison with the plot that lay behind this merely preliminary explanation.

"It is too late this evening," said the good man, looking at the clock, "and there is too much still to tell, to allow of my going on with the rest of the story. My old friend Bordin, who was made famous as a Royalist by his share in the great Simeuse trial, and who pleaded in the case of the *Chauffeurs* of Mortagne, gave me when I came to live here two documents which, as he died not long after, I still have in my possession. You will there find the facts set forth much more concisely than I could give them. The details are so complicated that I should lose myself in trying to state them, and it would take me more than two hours, while in these papers you will find them summarized. To-morrow morning I will tell you what remains to be told concerning Madame de la Chanterie, for when you have read these documents you will be sufficiently informed for me to conclude my tale in a few words."

He placed some papers, yellow with years, in Godefroid's hands; after bidding his neighbor good-night, the young man retired to his room, and before he went to sleep read the two documents here reproduced:

"BILL OF INDICTMENT.

"Court of Criminal and Special Justice for the Department of the Orne.

"The Public Prosecutor to the Imperial Court of Justice at Caen, appointed to carry out his functions to the Special Criminal Court sitting by the Imperial decree of September 1809, in the town of Alençon, sets forth to the Court the following facts, as proved by the preliminary proceedings, to-wit:

"That a conspiracy of brigands, hatched for a long time with extraordinary secrecy, and connected with a scheme for a general rising in the western departments, has vented itself in several attempts on the lives and property of citizens, and more especially in the attack with robbery, under arms, on a vehicle conveying, on the — of May, 18—, the Government moneys collected at Caen. This attack, recalling in its details the memories of the civil war now so happily at an end, showed deep-laid designs of a degree of villainy which cannot be excused by the vehemence of passion.

"From its inception to the end, the plot is extremely complicated, and the details numerous. The preliminary examinations lasted for more than a year, but the evidence forthcoming at every stage of the crime throws full light on the preparations made, on its execution, and results.

"The first idea of the plot was conceived by one Charles-Amédée-Louis-Joseph Rifoël, calling himself the Chevalier du Vissard, born at le Vissard, a hamlet of Saint-Mexme by Ernée, and formerly a leader of the rebels.

"This man, who was pardoned by His Majesty the Emperor at the time of the general peace and amnesty, and whose ingratitude to his sovereign has shown itself in fresh crimes, has already suffered the extreme penalty of the law as the punishment for his misdeeds; but it is necessary here to refer to some of his actions, as he had great influence over some of the accused now awaiting the verdict of justice, and he is concerned in every circumstance of the case.

"This dangerous agitator, who bore an alias, as is common with these rebels, and was known as *Pierrot,* used to wander about the western provinces enlisting partisans for a fresh rebellion; but his safest lurking-place was the château of Saint-Savin, the home of a woman named Lechantre and her daughter named Bryond, a house in the hamlet of Saint-Savin and in the district of Mortagne. This spot is famous in the most horrible annals of the rebellion of 1799. It was there that a courier was murdered, and his chaise plundered by a band of brigands under the command of a woman, helped by the notorious Marche-à-Terre. Hence brigandage may be said to be endemic in this neighborhood.

"An intimacy for which we seek no name had existed for more than a year between the woman Bryond and the above-named Rifoël.

"It was close to this spot that, in the month of April 1808, an interview took place between Rifoël and one Boislaurier, a superior leader, known in the more serious risings in the west by the name of Auguste, and he it was who was the moving spirit of the rising now under the consideration of the Court.

"This obscure point, namely, the connection of these two leaders, is plainly proved by the evidence of numerous witnesses, and also stands as a demonstrated fact by the sentence of death carried out on Rifoël. From the time of that meeting, Boislaurier and Rifoël agreed to act in concert.

"They communicated to each other, and at first to no one else, their atrocious purpose, founded on his Royal and Imperial Majesty's absence, in command, at the time, of his forces in Spain; and then, or soon after, they must have plotted to capture the State moneys in transit, as the base for further operations.

"Some time later, one Dubut of Caen despatched a messenger to the château of Saint-Savin, namely, one Hiley, known as le Laboureur, long known as a robber of the diligences; he was charged with information as to trustworthy accomplices. And it was thus, by Hiley's intervention, that the plot secured the co-operation from the first of one Herbomez, called Général-Hardi, a pardoned rebel of the same stamp as Rifoël, and, like him, a traitor to the amnesty.

"Herbomez and Hiley recruited in the neighboring villages seven banditti, whose names must at once be set forth as follows:

"1. Jean Cibot, called Pille-Miche, one of the boldest brigands of a troop got together by Montauran in the year VII., and one of the actors in the robbery and murder of the Mortagne courier.

"2. François Lisieux, known as Grand-Fils, a rebel-conscript of the department of the Mayenne.

"3. Charles Grenier, or Fleur-de-Genet, a deserter from the 69th half-brigade.

"4. Gabriel Bruce, known as Gros-Jean, one of the fiercest Chouans of Fontaine's division.

"5. Jacques Horeau, called Stuart, ex-lieutenant of that brigade, one of Tinténiac's adherents, and well known by the share he took in the Quiberon expedition.

"6. Marie-Anne Cabot, called Lajeunesse, formerly huntsman to the Sieur Carol of Alençon.

"7. Louis Minard, a rebel conscript.

"These, when enrolled, were quartered in three different hamlets in the houses of Binet, Mélin, and Laravinière, inn or tavern-keepers, all devoted to Rifoël.

"The necessary weapons were at once provided by one Jean-François Léveillé, a notary, and the incorrigible abettor of the brigands, serving as a go-between for them with several leaders in hiding; and, in this town, by one Felix Courceuil, called the Confesseur, formerly surgeon to the rebel army of la Vendée; both these men are natives of Alençon. Eleven muskets were concealed in a house belonging to Bryond in a suburb of Alençon; but this was done without his knowledge, for he was at that time living in the country on his estate between Alençon and Mortagne.

"When Bryond left his wife to go her own way in the fatal road she had set out on, these muskets, cautiously removed from the house, were carried by the woman Bryond in her own carriage to the château of Saint-Savin.

"It was then that the Department of the Orne and adjacent districts were dismayed by acts of highway robbery that startled the authorities as much as the inhabitants of those districts which had so long enjoyed quiet; and these raids prove that the atrocious foes of the Government and the Empire had been kept informed of the secret coalition of 1809 by means of communications from abroad.

"Léviellé the notary, the woman Bryond, Dubut of Caen, Herbomez of Mayenne, Boislaurier of le Mans, and Rifoël were the ringleaders of the association, which was also joined by those criminals who have been already executed under the sentence passed on them with Rifoël, by those accused under this trial, and by several others who have escaped public vengeance by flight, or by the silence of their accomplices.

"It was Dubut who, as a resident near Caen, gave notice to Léveillé of the despatch of the money. Dubut made several journeys between Caen and Mortagne, and Léveillé also was often on the roads. It may here be noted that, at the time when the arms were moved, Léveillé, who came to visit Bruce, Grenier, and Cibot at Mélin's house, found them arranging the muskets in an inside shed, and helped them himself in doing so.

"A general meeting was arranged to take place at Mortagne at the *Écu de France* inn. All the accused were present in various disguises. It was on this occasion that Léviellé, the woman Bryond, Dubut, Herbomez, Boislaurier, and Hiley, the cleverest of the subordinate conspirators, of whom Cibot is the most daring, secured the co-operation of one Vauthier, called Vieux-Chêne, formerly a servant to the notorious Longuy, and now a stableman at the inn. Vauthier agreed to give the woman Bryond due notice of the passing of the chaise conveying the Government moneys, as it commonly stopped to bait at the inn.

"The opportunity ere long offered for assembling the brigand recruits who had been scattered about in various lodgings with great precaution, sometimes in one village, and sometimes in another, under the care of Courceuil and of

Léveillé. The assembly was managed by the woman Bryond, who afforded the brigands a new hiding-place in the uninhabited parts of the château of Saint-Savin, at a few miles from Mortagne, where she had lived with her mother since her husband's departure. The brigands established themselves there with Hiley at their head, and spent several days there. The woman Bryond, with her waiting-maid Godard, took care to prepare with her own hands everything needed for lodging and feeding these guests. To this end she had trusses of hay brought in, and went to see the brigands in the shelter she had arranged for them, going to and fro with Léveillé. Provisions and victuals were procured under the orders and care of Courceuil, who took his orders from Rifoël and Boislaurier.

"The principal feat was decided on and the men fully armed; the brigands stole out of Saint-Savin every night; pending the transit of the Government chest, they carried out raids in the neighborhood, and the whole country was in terror under their repeated incursions. There can be no doubt that the robberies committed at La Sartinière, at Vonay, and at the château of Saint-Seny were the work of this band; their daring equaled their villainy, and they contrived to terrify their victims so effectually that no tales were told, so that justice could obtain no evidence.

"While levying contributions on all who held possession of the nationalized land, the brigands carefully reconnoitred the woods of Le Chesnay, which they had chosen to be the scene of their crime.

"Not far away is the village of Louvigny, where there is an inn kept by the brothers Chaussard, formerly gamekeepers on the property of Troisville, and this was to be the brigands' final rendezvous. The two brothers knew beforehand the part they were to play; Courceuil and Boislaurier had long before sounded them, and revived their hatred of the government of our august Emperor; and had told them that among the visitors who would drop in on them would be some men of their acquaintance—the formidable Hiley and the not less formidable Cibot.

"In fact, on the 6th the seven highwaymen, under the leadership of Hiley, arrived at the brother Chaussards' inn and spent two days there. On the 8th the chief led out his men, saying they were going three leagues away, and he desired the innkeepers to provide food, which was taken to a place where the roads met, a little way from the village. Hiley came home alone at night.

"Two riders—who were probably the woman Bryond and Rifoël, for it is said that she accompanied him in his expeditions, on horseback, and dressed as a man—arrived that evening and conversed with Hiley. On the following day Hiley wrote to Léveillé the notary, and one of the Chaussard brothers carried the letter and brought back the answer. Two hours later Bryond and Rifoël came on horseback to speak with Hiley.

"The upshot of all these interviews and coming and going was that a hatchet was indispensable to break open the cases. The notary went back with the woman Bryond to Saint-Savin, where they sought in vain for a hatchet.

"Thereupon he returned to the inn and met Hiley half-way, to whom he was to explain that no hatchet was to be found. Hiley made his way back and ordered supper at the inn for ten persons; he then brought in the seven brigands all armed. Hiley made them pile arms like soldiers. They all sat down and supped in haste, Hiley ordering a quantity of food to be packed for them to take away with them. Then he led the elder Chaussard aside and asked for a hatchet. The innkeeper, much astonished, by his own account, refused to give him one. Courceuil and Boislaurier presently came in, and the three men spent the whole night pacing up and down the room and discussing their plan. Courceuil, nicknamed the Confessor, the most cunning of the band, took possession of a hatchet, and at about two in the morning they all went out by different doors.

"Every minute was now precious; the execution of the crime was fixed for that day. Hiley, Courceuil, and Boislaurier placed their men. Hiley, with Minard, Cabot, and

Bruce, formed an ambush to the right of the wood of Le Chesnay. Boislaurier, Grenier, and Horeau occupied the centre. Courceuil, Herbomez, and Lisieux stood by the ravine under the fringe of the wood. All these positions are indicated on the subjoined plan to scale, drawn by the surveyor to the Government.

"The chaise, meanwhile, had started from Mortagne at about one in the morning, driven by one Rousseau, who was so far inculpated by circumstantial evidence as to make it seem desirable to arrest him. The vehicle, driving slowly, would reach the wood of Le Chesnay by about three. It was guarded by a single gendarme; the men were to breakfast at Donnery. There were three travelers, as it happened, besides the gendarme.

"The driver, who had been walking with them very slowly, on reaching the bridge of Le Chesnay, whipped the horses to a speed and energy that the others remarked upon, and turned into a cross-road known as the Senzey road. The chaise was soon lost to sight; the way it had gone was known to the gendarme and his companions only by the sound of the horses' bells; the men had to run to come up with it. Then they heard a shout: 'Stand, you rascals!' and four shots were fired.

"The gendarme, who was not hit, drew his sword and ran on in the direction he supposed the driver to have taken. He was stopped by four men, who all fired; his eagerness saved him, for he rushed past to desire one of the young travelers to run on and have the alarm bell tolled at Le Chesnay, but two of the brigands took steady aim, advancing towards him; he was forced to draw back a few steps; and just as he was about to turn the wood, he received a ball in the left armpit, which broke his arm; he fell, and found himself completely disabled.

"The shouting and shots had been heard at Donnery. The officer in command at this station hurried up with one of his gendarmes; a running fire led them away to the side of the wood furthest from the scene of the robbery. The single gendarme tried to intimidate the brigands by a hue and cry, and to delude them into the belief that a force was at hand.

" 'Forward!' he cried. 'First platoon to the right! now we have them! Second platoon to the left!'

"The brigands on their side shouted, 'Draw! This way, comrades! Send up the men as fast as you can!'

"The noise of firing hindered the officer from hearing the cries of the wounded gendarme, and helping in the manœuvre by which the other was keeping the robbers in check; but he could hear a clatter close at hand, arising from splitting the cases open. He advanced towards that side; four armed men took aim at him, and he called out, 'Surrender, villains!'

"They only replied, 'Stand, or you are a dead man!'

"He rushed forward; two muskets were fired, and he was hit, one ball going through his left leg into his horse's flank. The brave man, bleeding profusely, was forced to retire from the unequal struggle, shouting, but in vain, 'Help—come on —the brigands are at Le Chesnay.'

"The robbers, left masters of the field by superiority of numbers, pillaged the chaise which had been intentionally driven into a ravine. They blindfolded the driver, but this was only a feint. The chests were forced open, and bags of money strewed the ground. The horses were unharnessed and loaded with the coin. Three thousand francs' worth of copper money was scornfully left behind; three hundred thousand francs were carried off on four horses. They made for the village of Menneville adjacent to the town of Saint-Savin.

"The horde and their booty stopped at a solitary house belonging to the Chaussard brothers, inhabited by their uncle, one Bourget, who had been in their confidence from the first. This old man, helped by his wife, received the brigands, warned them to be silent, unloaded the beasts, and then fetched up some wine. The wife remained on sentry by the château. The old man led the horses back to the wood and returned them to the driver; then he released the two young men who had been gagged as well as the accommodating driver. After refreshing themselves in great haste, the brigands went on their way. Courceuil, Hiley, and Boislaurier reviewed their party, and after bestowing on each a trifling recompense, sent off the men, each in a different direction.

"On reaching a spot called le Champ-Landry, these malefactors, obeying the prompting which so often leads such wretches into blunders and miscalculations, threw their muskets away into a field of standing corn. The fact that all three did so at the same time is a crowning proof of their collusion. Then, terrified by the boldness and success of their crime, they separated.

"The robbery having been committed, with the additional features of violence and attempt to murder, the chain of subsidiary events was already in preparation, and other actors were implicated in receiving and disposing of the stolen property. Rifoël, hidden in Paris, whence he pulled all the wires of the plot, sent an order to Léveillé to forward to him immediately fifty thousand francs. Courceuil, apt at the management of such felonies, had sent off Hiley to inform Léveillé of their success and of his arrival at Mortagne, where the notary at once joined them.

"Vauthier, to whose fidelity they believed they might trust, undertook to find the Chaussards' uncle; he went to the house, but was told by the old man that he must apply to the nephews, who had given over large sums to the woman Bryond. However, he bid Vauthier wait for him on the road, and he there gave him a bag containing twelve hundred francs, which Vauthier took to the woman Lechantre for her daughter.

"By Léveillé's advice Courceuil then went to Bourget, who sent him direct to his nephews. The elder Chaussard led Vauthier to the wood and showed him a tree beneath which a bag of a thousand francs was found buried. In short, Léveillé, Hiley, and Vauthier went to and fro several times, and each time obtained a small sum, trifling in comparison with the whole amount stolen.

"These moneys were handed over to the woman Lechantre

at Mortagne; and, in obedience to a letter from her daughter, she carried them to Saint-Savin, whither the said Bryond had returned.

"It is not immediately necessary to inquire whether this woman Lechantre had any previous knowledge of the plot. For the present it need only be noted that she had left Mortagne to go to Saint-Savin the day before the crime was committed in order to fetch away her daughter; that the two women met half-way, and returned to Mortagne; that, on the following day, the notary, being informed of this by Hiley, went from Alençon to Mortagne, and straight to their house, where he persuaded them to transport the money, obtained with so much difficulty from the Chaussards and from Bourget, to a certain house in Alençon, presently to be mentioned as belonging to one Pannier, a merchant there. The woman Lechantre wrote to the man in charge at Saint-Savin to come to Mortagne and escort her and her daughter by cross-roads to Alençon. The money, amounting to twenty thousand francs in all, was packed into a vehicle at night, the girl Godard helping to dispose of it.

"The notary had planned the way they were to travel. They reached an inn kept by one of their allies, a man named Louis Chargegrain, in the hamlet of Littray. But in spite of the notary's precautions—he riding ahead of the chaise—some strangers were present and saw the portmanteaus and bags taken out which contained the coin.

"But just as Courceuil and Hiley, disguised as women, were consulting, in the market place at Alençon, with the aforenamed Pannier—who since 1794 had been the rebels' treasurer, and who was devoted to Rifoël—as to the best means of transmitting the required sum to Rifoël, the terror occasioned by the arrests and inquiries already made was so great that the woman Lechantre, in her alarm, set off at night from the inn where they were, and fled with her daughter by country byways, leaving Léveillé behind, and took refuge in the hiding-places known to them in the château Saint-Savin. The same alarm came over the other criminals. Courceuil, Boislaurier, and his relation Dubut exchanged two thousand francs in silver for gold at a dealer's, and fled across Brittany to England.

"On arriving at Saint-Savin, the mother and daughter heard that Bourget was arrested with the driver and the runaway conscripts.

"The magistrates, the police, and the authorities acted with so much decision, that it was deemed necessary to protect the woman Bryond from their investigations, for all these felons were devotedly attached to her, and she had won them all. So she was removed from Saint-Savin, and hid at first at Alençon, where her adherents held council and succeeded in concealing her in Pannier's cellars.

"Hereupon fresh incidents occurred. After the arrest of Bourget and his wife, the Chaussards refused to give up any more money, saying they had been betrayed. This unexpected defection fell out at the very moment when all the conspirators were in the greatest need of supplies, if only as a means of escape. Rifoël was thirsting for money. Hiley, Cibot, and Léveillé now began to doubt the honesty of the two Chaussards. This led to a fresh complication which seems to demand the intervention of the law.

"Two gendarmes, commissioned to discover the woman Bryond, succeeded in getting into Pannier's house, where they were present at a council held by the criminals; but these men, false to the confidence placed in them, instead of arresting Bryond, were enslaved by her charms. These rascally soldiers —named Ratel and Mallet—showed the woman every form of interest and devotion, and offered to escort her to the Chaussards' inn and compel them to make restitution. The woman went off on horseback, dressed as a man, and accompanied by Ratel, Mallet, and the maid-servant Godard. She set out at night, and on reaching the inn she and one of the Chaussard brothers had a private but animated interview. She had a pistol, and was resolved to blow her accomplice's brains out in case of his refusal; in fact, he led her to the wood, and she brought back a heavy sack. In it she found copper coin and twelve-sou pieces to the value of fifteen hundred francs.

"It was then suggested that as many of the conspirators as could be got together should take the Chaussards by surprise, seize them, and put them to torture. Pannier, on hearing of this disappointment, flew into a rage and broke out in threats; and though the woman Bryond threatened him in return with Rifoël's vengeance, she was compelled to fly.

"All these facts were confessed by Ratel.

"Mallet, touched by her position, offered the woman Bryond a place of shelter; they all set off together and spent the night in the wood of Troisville. Then Mallet and Ratel, with Hiley and Cibot, went by night to the Chaussards' inn, but they found that the brothers had left the place, and that the remainder of the money had certainly been removed.

"This was the last attempt on the part of the conspirators to recover the stolen money.

"It is now important to define more accurately the part played by each of the criminals implicated in this affair.

"Dubut, Boislaurier, Gentil, Herbomez, Courceuil, and Hiley are all leaders, some in council, and some in action. Boislaurier, Dubut, and Courceuil, all three contumacious deserters, are habitual rebels, stirring up troubles, the implacable foes of Napoleon the Great, of his successes, his dynasty, and his government, of our new code of laws and of the Imperial constitution. Herbomez and Hiley, as their right-hand men, boldly carried out what the three others planned. The guilt of the seven instruments of the crime is beyond question—Cibot, Lisieux, Grenier, Bruce, Horeau, Cabot, and Minard. It is proved by the depositions of those who are now in the hands of justice: Lisieux died during the preliminary inquiry, and Bruce has evaded capture.

"The conduct of the chaise-driver Rousseau marks him as an accomplice. The slow progress on the highroad, the pace to which he flogged the horses on reaching the wood, his persistent statement that his head was muffled, whereas, by the evidence of the young fellow-travelers, the leader of the brigands had the handkerchief removed and ordered him to recognize the men,—all contribute to afford presumptive evidence of his collusion.

"As to the woman Bryond and Léveillé the notary, their complicity was constant and continuous from the first. They supplied funds and means for the crime; they knew of it and abetted it. Léveillé was constantly traveling to and fro. The woman Bryond invented plot upon plot; she risked everything—even her life—to secure the money. She lent her house, her carriage, and was concerned in the plot from the beginning, nor did she attempt to persuade the chief leader to desist from it when she might have exerted her evil influence to hinder it. She led the maid-servant Godard into its toils. Léveillé was so entirely mixed up in it, that it was he who tried to procure the hatchet needed by the robbers.

"The woman Bourget, Vauthier, the Chaussards, Pannier, the woman Lechantre, Mallet, and Ratel were all incriminated in various degrees, as also the innkeepers Mélin, Binet, Laravinière, and Chargegrain.

"Bourget died during the preliminary inquiry, after making a confession which leaves no doubt as to the part taken by Vauthier and the woman Bryond; and though he tried to mitigate the charge against his wife and his nephews the Chaussards, the reasons for his reticence are self-evident.

"But the Chaussards certainly knew that they were supplying provisions to highway robbers; they saw that the men were armed and were informed of all their scheme; they allowed them to take the hatchet needed for breaking open the chests, knowing the purpose for which it was required. Finally, they received wittingly the money obtained by the robbery, they hid it, and in fact made away with the greater part of it.

"Pannier, formerly treasurer to the rebel party, concealed the woman Bryond; he is one of the most dangerous participators in the plot of which he was informed from its origin. With regard to him we are in the dark as to some circumstances as yet unknown, but of which justice will take cog-

nizance. He is Rifoël's immediate ally and in all the secrets
of the ante-revolutionary party in the West; he greatly regretted the fact that Rifoël should have admitted the women
into the plot or have trusted them at all. He forwarded money
to Rifoël and received the stolen coin.

"As to the two gendarmes, Ratel and Mallet, their conduct
deserves the utmost rigor of the law. They were traitors to
their duty. One of them, foreseeing his fate, committed
suicide after making some important revelations. The other,
Mallet, denied nothing, and his confession removes all doubt.

"The woman Lechantre, in spite of her persistent denials,
was informed of everything. The hypocrisy of this woman,
who attempts to shelter her professed innocence under the
practice of assumed devotion, is known by her antecedents to
be prompt and intrepid in extremities. She asserts that she
was deceived by her daughter, and believed that the money in
question belonged to the man Bryond. The trick is too transparent. If Bryond had had any money, he would not have fled
from the neighborhood to avoid witnessing his own ruin. Lechantre considered that there was no harm in the robbery
when it was approved of by her ally Boislaurier. But how,
then, does she account for Rifoël's presence at Saint-Savin,
her daughter's expeditions and connection with the man, and
the visit of the brigands who were waited on by the women
Godard and Bryond? She says she sleeps heavily, and is in
the habit of going to bed at seven o'clock, and did not know
what answer to make when the examining Judge observed that
then she must rise at daybreak, and could not have failed to
discern traces of the plot and of the presence of so many men,
or to be uneasy about her daughter's nocturnal expeditions.
To this she could only say that she was at her prayers.

"The woman is a model hypocrite. In fact, her absence
on the day when the crime was committed, the care she took
to remove her daughter to Mortagne, her journey with the
money, and her precipitate flight when everything was discovered, the care with which she hid herself, and the circumstances of her arrest, all prove her complicity from an early

stage of the affair. Her conduct was not that of a mother anxious to explain the danger to her daughter and to save her from it, but that of a terrified accomplice; and she was an accessory, not out of foolish affection, but from party spirit inspired by hatred, as is well known, for his Imperial Majesty's government. Maternal weakness indeed could not excuse her, and it must not be forgotten that consent, long premeditated, is an evident sign of her complicity.

"Not the crime alone, but its moving spirits, are now known. We see in it the monstrous combination of the delirium of faction with a thirst for repine; murder prompted by party spirit, under which men take shelter, and justify themselves for the most disgraceful excesses. The orders of the leaders gave the signal for the robbery of State moneys to pay for subsequent violence; base and ferocious hirelings were found to do it for wretched pay, and fully prepared to murder; while the agitators to rebellion, not less guilty, helped in dividing and concealing the booty. What society can allow such attempts to go unpunished? The law has no adequate punishment.

"The Bench of this Criminal and Special Court, then, will be called upon to decide whether the afore-named Herbomez, Hiley, Cibot, Grenier, Horeau, Cabot, Minard, Mélin, Binet, Laravinière, Rousseau, the woman Bryond, Léveillé, the woman Bourget, Vauthier, the elder Chaussard, Pannier, the widow Lechantre, and Mallet, all hereinbefore described and in presence of the Court, and the afore-named Boislaurier, Dubut, Courceuil, Bruce, Chaussard the younger, Chargegrain, and the girl Godard, being absent or having fled, are or are not guilty of the acts described in this bill of indictment.

"Given in to the Court at Caen the 1st of December, 180—

"(*Signed*)   BARON BOURLAC."

This legal document, much shorter and more peremptory than such bills of indictment are in these days, so full of detail and so complete on every point, especially as to the previous career of the accused, excited Godefroid to the utmost. The bare, dry style of an official pen, setting forth, in red ink, as it were, the principal facts of the case, was enough to set his imagination working. Concise, reserved narrative is to some minds a problem in which they lose themselves in exploring the mysterious depths.

In the dead of night, stimulated by the silence, by the darkness, by the dreadful connection hinted at by Monsieur Alain of this document with Madame de la Chanterie, Godefroid concentrated all his intelligence on the consideration of this terrible affair.

The name of Lechantre was evidently the first name of the la Chanterie family, whose aristocratic titular name had of course been curtailed under the Republic and the Empire.

His fancy painted the scenery where the drama was played out, and the figures of the accomplices rose before him. Imagination showed him, not indeed "the afore-named Rifoël," but the Chevalier du Vissard, a youth resembling Walter Scott's Fergus—in short, a French edition of the Jacobite. He worked out a romance on the passion of a young girl grossly betrayed by her husband's infamy—a tragedy then very fashionable—and in love with a young leader rebelling against the Emperor; rushing headlong, like Diana Vernon, into the toils of a conspiracy, fired with enthusiasm, and then, having started on the perilous descent, unable to check her wild career.—Had she ended it on the scaffold?

The whole world seemed to rise before Godefroid. He was wandering through the groves of Normandy; he could see the Breton gentleman and Madame Bryond in the copse; he dwelt in the old château of Saint-Savin; he pictured the winning over of so many conspirators—the notary, the merchant, and the bold Chouan leaders. He could understand the almost unanimous adhesion of a district where the memory was still fresh of the famous Marche-à-Terre, of the Comtes de Bauvan and de Longuy, of the massacre at la Vivetière, and of the death of the Marquis de Montauran, of whose exploits he had heard from Madame de la Chanterie.

This vision, as it were, of men and things and places, was but brief. As he realized the fact that this story was that of the noble and pious old lady whose virtues affected him to the point of a complete metamorphosis, Godefroid, with a thrill of awe, took up the second document given to him by Monsieur Alain, which bore the title:

"AN APPEAL ON BEHALF OF MADAME HENRIETTE BRYOND DES TOURS-MINIÉRES, *née* LECHANTRE DE LA CHANTERIE."

"That settles it," thought Godefroid.
The paper ran as follows:

"We are condemned and guilty; but if ever the Sovereign had cause to exercise his prerogative of mercy, would it not be under the circumstances herein set forth?

"The culprit is a young woman, who says she is a mother, and is condemned to death.

"On the threshold of the prison, and in view of the scaffold, this woman will tell the truth. That statement will be in her favor, and to that she looks for pardon.

"The case, tried in the Criminal Court of Alençon, presents some obscure features, as do all cases where several accused persons have combined in a plot inspired by party feeling.

"His Imperial and Kingly Majesty's Privy Council are now fully informed as to the identity of a mysterious personage, known as *le Marchand,* whose presence in the department of the Orne was not disputed by the public authorities in the course of the trial, though the pleader for the Crown did not think it advisable to produce him in Court, and the defendants had no right to call him, nor, indeed, power to produce him.

"This man, as is well known to the Bench, to the local authorities, to the Paris police, and to the Imperial and Royal Council, is Bernard-Polydor Bryond de la Tour-Miniéres, who, since 1794, has been in correspondence with the Comte de Lille; he is known abroad as the Baron des Tours-Miniéres, and in the records of the Paris police as Contenson.

"He is a very exceptional man, whose youth and rank were stained by unremitting vice, such utter immorality and such criminal excesses, that so infamous a life would inevitably have ended on the scaffold but for the skill with which he played a double part under shelter of his two names. Still, as he is more and more the slave of his passions and insatiable necessities, he will at last fall below infamy, and find himself in the lowest depths in spite of indisputable gifts and an extraordinary mind.

"When the Comte de Lille's better judgment led to his forbidding Bryond to draw money from abroad, the man tried to get out of the blood-stained field on to which his necessities had led him. Was it that this career no longer paid him well enough? Or was it remorse or shame that led the man back to the district where his estates, loaded with debt when he went away, could have but little to yield even to his skill? This it is impossible to believe. It seems more probable that he had some mission to fulfil in those departments where some sparks were still lingering of the civil broils.

"When wandering through the provinces, where his perfidious adhesion to the schemes of the English and of the Comte de Lille gained him the confidence of certain families still attached to the party that the genius of our immortal Emperor has reduced to silence, he met one of the former leaders of the Rebellion—a man with whom he had had dealings as an envoy from abroad at the time of the Quiberon expedition, during the last rising in the year VII. He encouraged the hopes of this agitator, who has since paid the penalty of his treasonable plots on the scaffold. At that time, then, Bryond was able to learn all the secrets of the incorrigible faction who misprize the glory of His Majesty the Emperor Napoleon I., and the true interests of the country as represented by his sacred person.

"At the age of five-and-thirty, this man, who affected the deepest piety, who professed unbounded devotion to the interests of the Comte de Lille, and perfect adoration for the rebels of the West who perished in the struggle, who skilfully disguised the ravages of a youth of debauchery, and whose personal appearance was in his favor, came, under the protection of his creditors, who told no tales, and of the most extraordinary good-nature on the part of all the *ci-devants* of the district, to be introduced with all these claims on her regard to the woman Lechantre, who was supposed to have a very fine fortune. The scheme in view was to secure a marriage between Madame Lechantre's only daughter, Henriette, and this *protégé* of the Royalist party.

"Priests, ex-nobles, and creditors, all from different motives, conspired to promote the marriage between Bernard Bryond and Henriette Lechantre.

"The good judgment of the notary who took charge of Madame Lechantre's affairs, and his shrewd suspicions, led perhaps to the poor girl's undoing. For Monsieur Chesnel, a notary at Alençon, settled the lands of Saint-Savin, the bride's sole estate, on her and her children, reserving a small charge on it and the right of residence to the mother for life.

"Bryond's creditors, who, judging from her methodical and economical style of living, had supposed that Madame Lechantre must have saved large sums, were disappointed in their hopes, and believing that she must be avaricious, they sued Bryond, and this led to a revelation of his impecuniosity and difficulties.

"Then the husband and wife quarreled violently, and the young woman came to full knowledge of the dissipated habits, the atheistical opinions both in religion and in politics, nay, I may say, the utter infamy, of the man to whom fate had irrevocably bound her. Then Bryond, being obliged to let his wife into the secret of the atrocious plots against the Imperial Government, offered an asylum under his roof to Rifoël du Vissard.

"Rifoël's character, adventurous, brave, and lavish, had an extraordinary charm for all who came under his influence; of this there is abundant proof in the cases tried in no less than three special criminal courts.

"The irresistible influence, in fact the absolute power, he acquired over a young woman who found herself at the bottom of a gulf, is only too evident in the catastrophe of which the horror brings her as a suppliant to the foot of the throne. And His Imperial and Kingly Majesty's Council will have no difficulty in verifying the infamous collusion of Bryond, who, far from doing his duty as the guide and adviser of the girl intrusted to his care by the mother he had deceived, condoned and encouraged the intimacy between his wife Henriette and the rebel leader.

"This was the plan imagined by this detestable man, who makes it his glory that he respects nothing, and that he never considers any end but the gratification of his passions, while he regards every sentiment based on social or religious morality as a mere vulgar prejudice. And it may here be remarked that such scheming is habitual to a man who has been playing a double part ever since 1794, who for eight years has deceived the Comte de Lille and his adherents, probably deceiving at the same time the superior police of the Empire—for such men are always ready to serve the highest bidder.

"Bryond, then, was urging Rifoël to commit a crime; he it was who insisted on an armed attack and highway robbery of the State treasure in transit, and on heavy contributions to be extorted from the purchasers of the national land, by means of atrocious tortures which he invented, and which carried terror into five Departments. He demanded no less than three hundred thousand francs to pay off the mortgages on his property.

"In the event of any objection on the part of Rifoël or Madame Bryond, he intended to revenge himself for the contempt he had inspired in his wife's upright mind, by handing them both over to be dealt with by the law as soon as they should commit some capital crime.

"As soon as he perceived that party spirit was a stronger motive than self-interest in these two whom he had thus thrown together, he disappeared; he came to Paris, armed with ample information as to the state of affairs in the western departments.

"The Chaussard brothers and Vauthier were, it is well known, in constant correspondence with Bryond.

"As soon as the robbery on the chests from Caen was accomplished, Bryond, assuming the name of le Marchand, opened secret communications with the préfet and the magistrates. What was the consequence? No conspiracy of equal extent, and in which so many persons in such different grades of the social scale were involved, has ever been so immediately divulged to justice as this, of which the first attempt was the robbery of the treasure from Caen. Within six days of the crime, all the guilty parties had been watched and followed with a certainty that betrays perfect knowledge of the persons in question, and of their plans. The arrest, trial, and execution of Rifoël and his companions are a sufficient proof, and mentioned here only to demonstrate our knowledge of this fact, of which the Supreme Council knows every particular.

"If ever a condemned criminal might hope for the clemency of the Sovereign, may not Henriette Lechantre?

"Carried away by a passion and by rebellious principles imbibed with her mother's milk, she is, no doubt, unpardonable in the eye of the law; but in the sight of our most magnanimous Emperor, may not the most shameless betrayal on one hand, and the most vehement enthusiasm on the other, plead her cause?

"The greatest of Generals, the immortal genius who pardoned the Prince of Hatzfeld, and who, like God Himself, can divine the arguments suggested by a blind passion, may, perhaps, vouchsafe to consider the temptations invincible in the young, which may palliate her crime, great as it is.

"Twenty-two heads have already fallen under the sword of justice and the sentence of the three courts. One alone remains—that of a young woman of twenty, not yet of age. Will not the Emperor Napoleon the Great grant her time for repentance? Is not that a tribute to the grace of God?

"For Henriette Lechantre, wife of Bryond des Tour-Minières,

"BORDIN,

"Retained for the defence, Advocate in the Lower
Court of the Department of the Seine."

This terrible tragedy haunted the little sleep Godefroid was able to get. He dreamed of decapitation, as the physician Guillotin perfected it with philanthropic intentions. Through the hot vapors of a nightmare he discerned a beautiful young woman, full of enthusiasm, undergoing the last preparations, drawn in a cart, and mounting the scaffold with a cry of "Vive le Roi!"

Godefroid was goaded by curiosity. He rose at daybreak, dressed, and paced his room, till at length he posted himself at the window, and mechanically stared at the sky, reconstructing the drama, as a modern romancer might, in several volumes. And always against the murky background of Chouans, of country folks, of provincial gentlemen, of rebel leaders, police agents, lawyers and spies, he saw the radiant figures of the mother and daughter; of the daughter deceiving her mother, the victim of a wretch, and of her mad passion for one of those daring adventurers who were afterwards regarded as heroes—a man who, to Godefroid's imagination, had points of resemblance to Georges Cadoudal and Charette, and the giants of the struggle between the Republic and the Monarchy.

As soon as Godefroid heard old Alain stirring, he went to his room; but on looking in through the half-opened door, he shut it again, and withdrew. The old man, kneeling on his prie-Dieu, was saying his morning prayers. The sight of that white head bent in an attitude of humble piety recalled Godefroid to a sense of duty, and he prayed too, with fervency.

"I was expecting you," said the good man when, at the end of a quarter of an hour, Godefroid entered his room. "I anticipated your impatience, and rose earlier than usual."

"Madame Henriette?——" Godefroid began, with evident agitation.

"Was Madame's daughter," replied Alain, interrupting him. "Madame's name is Lechantre de la Chanterie. Under the Empire old titles were not recognized, nor the names added to the patronymic or first surname. Thus the Baronne des Tours-Minières was 'the woman Bryond'; the Marquis d'Esgrignon was called Carol—Citizen Carol, and afterwards the Sieur Carol; the Troisvilles were the Sieurs Guibelin."

"But what was the end? Did the Emperor pardon her?"

"No, alas!" said Alain. "The unhappy little woman perished on the scaffold at the age of twenty-one.—After reading Bordin's petition, the Emperor spoke to the Supreme Judge much to this effect:

"'Why make an example of a spy? A secret agent ceases to be a man, and ought to have none of a man's feelings; he is but a wheel in the machine. Bryond did his duty. If our instruments of that kind were not what they are—steel bars, intelligent only in behalf of the Government they serve—government would be impossible. The sentences of Special Criminal Courts must be carried out, or my magistrates would lose all confidence in themselves and in me. And besides, the men who fought for these people are executed, and they were less guilty than their leaders. The women of the western provinces must be taught not to meddle in conspiracies. It is because the victim of the sentence is a woman that the law must take its course. No excuse is available as against the interests of authority.'

"This was the substance of what the Supreme Judge was so obliging as to repeat to Bordin after his interview with the Emperor. To re-establish tranquillity in the west, which was full of refractory conscripts, Napoleon thought it needful to produce a real 'terror.' The Supreme Judge, in fact, advised the lawyer to trouble himself no further about his clients."

"And the lady?" said Godefroid.

"Madame de la Chanterie was condemned to twenty-two years' imprisonment," replied Alain. "She had already been transferred to Bicêtre, near Rouen, to undergo her sentence, and nothing could be thought of till her Henriette was safe; for after these dreadful scenes, she was so wrapped up in her daughter that, but for Bordin's promise to petition for the mitigation of the sentence of death, it was thought that Madame would not have survived her condemnation. So they deceived the poor mother. She saw her daughter after the execution of the men who had been sentenced to death, but did not know that the respite was granted in consequence of a false declaration that her daughter was expecting her confinement."

"Ah, now I understand everything!" cried Godefroid.

"No, my dear boy. There are some things which cannot be guessed.—For a long time after that, Madame believed that her daughter was alive."

"How was that?"

"When Madame des Tours-Minières heard through Bordin that her appeal was rejected, the brave little woman had enough strength of mind to write a score of letters dated for several months after her execution to make her mother believe that she was still alive, but gradually suffering more and more from an imaginary malady, till it ended in death. These letters were spread over a period of two years. Thus Madame de la Chanterie was prepared for her daughter's death, but for a natural death; she did not hear of her execution till 1814.

"For two years she was kept in the common prison with the most infamous creatures of her sex, wearing the prison dress; then, thanks to the efforts of the Champignelles and the Beauséants, after the second year she was placed in a private cell, where she lived like a cloistered nun."

"And the others?"

"The notary Léveillé, Herbomez, Hiley, Cibot, Grenier, Hureau, Cabot, Minard, and Mallet were condemned to death, and executed the same day; Pannier, with Chaussard and Vauthier, was sentenced to twenty years' penal servitude; they were branded and sent to the hulks; but the Emperor pardoned Chaussard and Vauthier. Mélin, Laravinière, and Binet had five years' imprisonment. The woman Bourget was imprisoned for twenty-two years. Chargegrain and Rousseau were acquitted. Those who had got away were all sentenced to death, with the exception of the maid-servant Godard, who, as you have guessed, is none other than our good Manon."

"Manon!" exclaimed Godefroid in amazement.

"Oh, you do not yet know Manon," replied the worthy man. "That devoted soul, condemned to twenty-two years' imprisonment, had given herself up to justice that she might be with Madame de la Chanterie in prison. Our beloved vicar is the priest from Mortagne who gave the last sacrament to Madame des Tours-Minières, who had the fortitude to escort her to the scaffold, and to whom she gave her last farewell kiss. The same brave and exalted priest had attended the Chevalier du Vissard. So our dear Abbé de Vèze learned all the secrets of the conspirators."

"I see now when his hair turned white," said Godefroid.

"Alas!" said Alain.—"He received from Amédée du Vissard a miniature of Madame des Tours-Minières, the only likeness of her that exists; and the Abbé has been a sacred personage to Madame de la Chanterie ever since the day when she was restored triumphant to social life."

"How was that?" asked Godefroid in surprise.

"Well, on the restoration of Louis XVIII. in 1814, Boislaurier, who was the younger brother of Monsieur de Boisfrelon, was still under the King's orders to organize a rising in the West—first in 1809, and afterwards in 1812. Their name is Dubut; the Dubut of Caen was related to them. There were three brothers: Dubut de Boisfranc, President of the Court of Subsidies; Dubut de Boisfrelon, Councillor at Law; and Dubut-Boislaurier, a Captain of Dragoons. Their father had given each the name of one of his three several estates to give them a title and status (*savonnette à la vilain*, as it was called), for their grandfather was a linen merchant. Dubut of Caen, who succeeded in escaping, was one of the branch who had stuck to trade; but he hoped, by devoting himself to the Royal cause, to be allowed to succeed to Monsieur de Boisfranc's title. And in fact Louis XVIII. gratified the wish of his faithful adherent, who, in 1815, was made Grand Provost, and subsequently became a Public Prosecutor under the name of Boisfranc; he was President of one of the Higher Courts when he died. The Marquis du Vissard, the unhappy Chevalier's elder brother, created peer of France, and loaded with honors by the King, was made Lieutenant of the Maison Rouge, and when that was abolished became Préfet. Monsieur d'Herbomez had a brother who was made a Count and Receiver-General. The unfortunate banker Pannier died on the hulks of a broken heart. Boislaurier died childless, a Lieutenant-General and Governor of one of the Royal residences.

"Madame de la Chanterie was presented to His Majesty by Monsieur de Champignelles, Monsieur de Beauséant, the Duc de Verneuil, and the Keeper of the Seals.—'You have suffered much for me, Madame la Baronne,' said the King; 'you have every claim on my favor and gratitude.'

"'Sir,' she replied, 'your Majesty has so much to do in comforting the sufferers, that I will not add the burden of an inconsolable sorrow. To live forgotten, to mourn for my daughter, and do some good—that is all I have to live for. If anything could mitigate my grief, it would be the graciousness of my Sovereign, and the happiness of seeing that Providence did not suffer so much devoted service to be wasted.' "

"And what did the King do?" asked Godefroid.

"He restored to Madame de la Chanterie two hundred thousand francs in money," said the good man, "for the estate of Saint-Savin had been sold to make good the loss to the treasury. The letters of pardon granted to Madame la Baronne and her woman express the Sovereign's regret for all they had endured in his service, while acknowledging that the zeal of his adherents had carried them too far in action; but the thing that will seem to you most horrible of all is, that throughout his reign Bryond was still the agent of his secret police."

"Oh, what things kings can do!" cried Godefroid.—"And is the wretch still living?"

"No. The scoundrel, who at any rate concealed his name, calling himself Contenson, died at the end of 1829, or early in 1830. He fell from a roof into the street when in pursuit of a criminal.—Louis XVIII. was of the same mind as Napoleon as regards police agents.

"Madame de la Chanterie, a perfect saint, prays for this monster's soul, and has two masses said for him every year.

"Though her defence was undertaken by one of the famous pleaders of the day, the father of one of our great orators, Madame de la Chanterie, who knew nothing of her daughter's risks till the moment when the money was brought in— and even then only because Boislaurier, who was related to her, told her the facts—could never establish her innocence. The Président du Ronceret, and Blondet, Vice-President of the Court at Alençon, vainly tried to clear the poor lady; the influence of the notorious Mergi, the Councillor to the Supreme Court under the Empire, who presided over these trials —a man fanatically devoted to the Church and Throne, who afterwards, as Public Prosecutor, brought many a Bonapartist head under the axe—was so great at this time over his two colleagues that he secured the condemnation of the unhappy Baronne de la Chanterie. Bourlac and Mergi argued the case with incredible virulence. The President always spoke of the Baronne des Tours-Minières as the woman Bryond, and of Madame as the woman Lechantre. The names of all the accused were reduced to the barest Republican forms, and curtailed of all titles.

"There were some extraordinary features of the trial, and I cannot recall them all; but I remember one stroke of audacity, which may show you what manner of men these Chouans were.—The crowd that pressed to hear the trials was beyond anything your fancy can conceive of; it filled the corridors, and the square outside was thronged as if on market days. One morning at the opening of the Court, before the arrival of the judges, Pille-Miche, the famous Chouan, sprang over the balustrade into the middle of the mob, made play with his elbows, mixed with the crowd, and fled among the terrified spectators, 'butting like a wild boar,' as Bordin told me. The gendarmes and the people rushed to stop him, and he was caught on the steps just as he had reached the market-place. After this daring attempt, they doubled the guard, and a detachment of men-at-arms was posted on the square, for it was feared that there might be among the crowd some Chouans ready to aid and abet the accused. Three persons were crushed to death in the crowd in consequence of this attempt.

"It was subsequently discovered that Contenson—for, like my old friend Bordin, I cannot bring myself to call him Baron des Tours-Minières, or Bryond, which is a respectable old name—that wretch, it was discovered, had made away with sixty thousand francs of the stolen treasure. He gave ten thousand to the younger Chaussard, whom he enticed into the police and inoculated with all his low tastes and vices; but all his accomplices were unlucky. The Chaussard who escaped was pitched into the sea by Monsieur de Boislaurier, who understood from something said by Pannier that Chaussard had turned traitor. Contenson indeed had advised him to join the fugitives in order to spy upon them. Vauthier was killed in Paris, no doubt by one of the Chevalier du Vissard's obscure but devoted followers. The younger Chaussard too was finally murdered in one of the nocturnal raids conducted by the police; it seems probable that Contenson took this means of ridding himself of his demands or of his remorse by sending him to sermon, as the saying goes.

"Madame de la Chanterie invested her money in the funds, and purchased this house by the particular desire of her uncle, the old Councillor de Boisfrelon, who in fact gave her the money to buy it. This quiet neighborhood lies close to the Archbishop's residence, where our beloved Abbé has an appointment under the Cardinal. And this was Madame's chief reason for acceding to the old lawyer's wish when his income, after twenty-five years of revolutions, was reduced to six thousand francs a year. Besides, Madame wished to close a life of such terrible misfortunes as had overwhelmed her for six-and-twenty years in almost cloistered seclusion.

"You may now understand the dignity, the majesty, of this long-suffering woman—august indeed, as I may say——"

"Yes," said Godefroid, "the stamp of all she has endured has given her an indefinable air of grandeur and majesty."

"Each blow, each fresh pang, has but increased her patience

and resignation," Alain went on. "And if you could know her as we do, if you knew how keen her feelings are, and how active is the spring of tenderness that wells up in her heart, you would be afraid to take count of the tears she must shed, and her fervent prayers that ascend to God. Only those who, like her, have known but a brief season of happiness can resist such shocks. Hers is a tender heart, a gentle soul clothed in a frame of steel, tempered by privation, toil, and austerity."

"Such a life as hers explains the life of hermits," said Godefroid.

"There are days when I wonder what can be the meaning of such an existence. Is it that God reserves these utmost, bitterest trials for those of His creatures who shall sit on His right hand on the day after their death?" said the good old man, quite unaware that he was artlessly expressing Swedenborg's doctrine concerning the angels.

"What!" exclaimed Godefroid, "Madame de la Chanterie was mixed up with——?"

"Madame was sublime in prison," Alain said. "In the course of three years the story of the Vicar of Wakefield came true, for she reclaimed several women of profligate lives. And in the course of her imprisonment, as she took note of the conduct of those confined with her, she learned to feel that great pity for the misery of the people which weighs on her soul, and has made her the queen of Parisian charity. It was in the horrible Bicêtre at Rouen that she conceived of the plan which we devote ourselves to carry out. It was, as she declared, a dream of rapture, an angelic inspiration in the midst of hell; she had no thought of ever seeing it realized.

"But here, in 1819, when peace seemed to be descending on Paris, she came back to her dream. Madame la Duchesse d'Angoulême, the Dauphiness, the Duchesse de Berri, the Archbishop, and then the Chancellor and some pious persons contributed very liberally to the first necessary expenses. The fund was increased by what we could spare from our income, for each of us spends no more than is absolutely necessary."

Tears rose to Godefroid's eyes.

"We are the faithful priesthood of a Christian idea, and belong body and soul to this work, of which Madame de la Chanterie is the founder and the soul—that lady whom you hear us respectfully designate as Madame."

"Ah, and I too am wholly yours!" cried Godefroid, holding out his hands to the worthy man.

"Now, do you understand that there are subjects of conversation absolutely prohibited here, never even to be alluded to?" Alain went on. "Do you appreciate the obligation of reticence under which we all feel ourselves to a lady whom we reverence as a saint? Do you understand the charm exerted by a woman made sacred by her misfortunes, having learned so many things, knowing the inmost secret of every form of suffering—a woman who has derived a lesson from every grief, whose every virtue has the twofold sanction of the hardest tests and of constant practice, whose soul is spotless and above reproach; who has known motherhood only through its sorrows, and conjugal affection only through its bitterness; on whom life never smiled but for a few months—for whom Heaven no doubt keeps a palm in store as the reward of such resignation and gentleness amid sorrows? Is she not superior to Job in that she has never murmured?

"So you need never again be surprised to find her speech so impressive, her old age so fresh, her spirit so full of communion, her looks so persuasive; she has had powers extraordinary bestowed on her as a *confidante* of the sorrowing, for she has known every sorrow. In her presence smaller griefs are mute."

"She is the living embodiment of charity," cried Godefroid with enthusiasm. "May I become one of you?"

"You must pass the tests, and above all else, *Believe!*" said the old man with gentle excitement. "So long as you have not hold on faith, so long as you have not assimilated in your heart and brain the divine meaning of Saint Paul's epistle on Charity, you can take no part in our work."

PARIS, 1843-1845.

SECOND EPISODE

INITIATED

WHAT is nobly good is contagious, as evil is. And by the time Madame de la Chanterie's boarder had dwelt for some months in this silent old house, after the story told him by Monsieur Alain, which filled him with the deepest respect for the half-monastic life he saw around him, he became conscious of the ease of mind that comes of a regular life, of quiet habits and harmonious tempers in those we live with. In four months Godefroid, never hearing an angry tone or the least dispute, owned to himself that since he had come to years of discretion he did not remember ever being so completely at peace—for he could not say happy. He looked on the world from afar, and judged it sanely. At last the desire he had cherished these three months past to take his part in the deeds of this mysterious association had become a passion; and without being a very profound philosopher, the reader may imagine what strength such a passion may assume in seclusion.

So one day—a day marked as solemn by the ascendency of the Spirit—Godefroid, after sounding his heart and measuring his powers, went up to his good friend Alain—whom Madame de la Chanterie always called her lamb—for of all the dwellers under that roof he had always seemed to Godefroid the most accessible and the least formidable. To him, then, he would apply, to obtain from the worthy man some information as to the sort of priesthood which these Brethren in God exercised in Paris. Many allusions to a period of probation suggested to him that he would be put to initiatory tests of some kind. His curiosity had not been fully satisfied by what the venerable old man had told him of the reasons why he had joined Madame de la Chanterie's association; he wanted to know more about this.

At half-past ten o'clock that evening Godefroid found himself for the third time in Monsieur Alain's rooms, just as the old man was preparing to read his chapter of *The Imitation*. This time the mild old man could not help smiling, and he said to the young man, before allowing him to speak:

"Why do you apply to me, my dear boy, instead of addressing yourself to Madame? I am the most ignorant, the least spiritual, the most imperfect member of the household.—For the last three days Madame and my friends have seen into your heart," he added, with a little knowing air.

"And what have they seen?" asked Godefroid.

"Oh," said the good man, with perfect simplicity, "they have seen a guileless desire to belong to our community. But the feeling is not yet a very ardent vocation. Nay," he replied to an impulsive gesture of Godefroid's, "you have more curiosity than fervor. In fact, you have not so completely freed yourself from your old ideas but that you imagine something adventurous, something romantic, as the phrase goes, in the incidents of our life——"

Godefroid could not help turning red.

"You fancy that there is some resemblance between our occupations and those of the Khalifs in the *Arabian Nights*, and you anticipate a kind of satisfaction in playing the part of the good genius in the idyllic beneficences of which you dream! Ah, ha! my son, your smile of confusion shows me that we were not mistaken. How could you expect to conceal your thoughts from us, who make it our business to detect the hidden impulses of the soul, the cunning of poverty, the calculations of the needy; who are honest spies, the police of a merciful Providence, old judges whose code of law knows only absolution, and physicians of every malady whose only prescription is a wise use of money? Still, my dear boy, we do not quarrel with the motives that bring us a neophyte if only he stays with us and becomes a brother of our Order. We shall judge you by your works. There are two kinds of curiosity—one for good, and one for evil. At this moment your curiosity is for good. If you are to become a laborer in our vineyard, the juice of the grapes will give you perpetual thirst for the divine fruit. The initiation looks easy, but is difficult, as in every natural science. In well-doing, as in poetry, nothing can be easier than to clutch at its semblance; but here, as on Parnassus, we are satisfied with nothing short of perfection. To become one of us, you must attain to great knowledge of life—and of such life. Good God! Of that Paris life which defies the scrutiny of the Chief of the Police and his men. It is our task to unmask the permanent conspiracy of evil, and detect it under forms so endlessly changing that they might be thought infinite. In Paris, Charity must be as omniscient as Sin, just as the police agent must be as cunning as a thief. We have to be at once frank and suspicious; our judgment must be as certain and as swift as our eye.

"As you see, dear boy, we are all old and worn out; but then we are so well satisfied with the results we have achieved, that we wish not to die without leaving successors, and we hold you all the more dear because you may, if you will, be our first disciple. For us there is no risk, we owe you to God! Yours is a sweet nature turned sour, and since you came to live here the evil leaven is weaker. Madame's heavenly nature has had its effect on you.

"We held council yesterday; and as you have given me your confidence, my good brothers decided on making me your instructor and guide.—Are you satisfied?"

"Oh, my kind Monsieur Alain, your eloquence has aroused——"

"It is not I that speak well, my dear boy, it is that great deeds are eloquent.—We are always sure of soaring high if we obey God and imitate Jesus Christ so far as lies in man aided by faith."

"This moment has decided my fate; I feel the ardor of the neophyte!" cried Godefroid. "I too would fain spend my life in well-doing——"

"That is the secret of dwelling in God," replied the good man. "Have you meditated on our motto, *Transire bene-faciendo? Transire* means to pass beyond this life, leaving a long train of good actions behind you."

"I have understood it so, and I have written up the motto of the order in front of my bed."

"That is well.—And that action, so trivial in itself, is of great value in my eyes.—Well, my son, I have your first task ready for you, I will see you with your foot in the stirrup. We must part.—Yes, for I have to leave our retreat and take my place in the heart of a volcano. I am going as foreman in a large factory where all the workmen are infected with communistic doctrines—and dream of social destruction, of murdering the masters, never seeing that this would be to murder industry, manufacture, and commerce.

"I shall remain there—who knows—a year, perhaps, as cashier, keeping the books, and making my way into a hundred or more humble homes, among men who were misled by poverty, no doubt, before they were deluded by bad books. However, we shall see each other here every Sunday and holiday; as I shall live in the same quarter of the town we may meet at the Church of Saint-Jacques du Haut-Pas; I shall attend mass there every morning at half-past seven. If you should happen to meet me elsewhere, you must never recognize me, unless I rub my hands with an air of satisfaction. That is one of our signals.—Like the deaf-mutes, we have a language by signs, of which the necessity will soon be more than abundantly evident to you."

Godefroid's expression was intelligible to Monsieur Alain, for he smiled and went on:

"Now for your business. We do not practise either beneficence or philanthropy as they are known to you, under a variety of branches which are preyed upon by swindlers, just like any other form of trade. We exercise charity as it is defined by our great and sublime master Saint Paul; for it is our belief, my son, that such charity alone can heal the woes of Paris. Thus, in our eyes, sorrow, poverty, suffering, trouble, evil—from whatever cause they may proceed and in whatever class of society we find them—have equal claims upon us. Whatever their creed or their opinions, the unfortunate are, first and foremost, unfortunate; we do not try to persuade them to look to our Holy Mother the Church till we have rescued them from despair and starvation. And even then we try to convert them by example and kindness, for thus we believe that we have the help of God. All coercion is wrong.

"Of all the wretchedness in Paris, the most difficult to discover and the bitterest to endure is that of the respectable middle-class, the better class of citizens, when they fall into poverty, for they make it a point of honor to conceal it. Such disasters as these, my dear Godefroid, are the object of our particular care. Such persons, when we help them, show intelligence and good feeling; they return us with interest what we may lend to them; and in the course of time their repayments cover the losses we meet with through the disabled, or by swindlers, or those whom misfortune has stultified. Sometimes we get useful information from those we have helped; but the work has grown to such vast dimensions, and its details are so numerous, that it is beyond our powers. Now, for the last seven or eight months, we have a physician in our employment in each district of the city of Paris. Each of us has four *arrondissements* (or wards) under his eye; and we are prepared to pay to each three thousand francs a year to take charge of our poor. He is required to give up his time and care to them by preference, but we do not prevent his taking other patients. Would you believe that we have not in eight months been able to find twelve such men, twelve good men, in spite of the pecuniary aid offered by our friends and acquaintance? You see, we needed men of absolute secrecy, of pure life, of recognized abilities, and with a love of doing good. Well, in Paris there are perhaps ten thousand men fit for the work, and yet in a year's search the twelve elect have not been found."

"Our Lord found it hard to collect His apostles," said Godefroid, "and there were a traitor and a disbeliever among them after all!"

"At last, within the past fortnight, each *arrondissement* has been provided with a *visitor,*" said the old man, smiling—"for so we call our physicians—and, indeed, within that fortnight there has been a vast increase of business. However, we have worked all the harder. I tell you this secret of our infant fraternity because you must make acquaintance with the physician of your district, all the more so because we depend on him for information. This gentleman's name is Berton— Doctor Berton—and he lives in the Rue de l'Enfer.

"Now for the facts. Doctor Berton is attending a lady whose disease seems in some way to defy science. That indeed does not concern us, but only the Faculty; our business is to find out the poverty of the sick woman's family, which the doctor believes to be frightful, and concealed with a determination and pride that baffle all our inquiries. Hitherto, my dear boy, this would have been my task; but now the work to which I am devoting myself makes an assistant necessary in my four districts, and you must be that assistant. The family lives in the Rue Notre-Dame des Champs, in a house looking out over the Boulevard du Mont-Parnasse. You will easily find a room to let there, and while lodging there for a time you must try to discover the truth. Be sordid as regards your own expenses, but do not trouble your head about the money you give. I will send you such sums as we consider necessary, taking all the circumstances of the case into consideration. But study the moral character of these unfortunate people. A good heart and noble feelings are the security for our loans. Stingy to ourselves and generous to suffering, we must still be careful and never rash, for we dip into the treasury of the poor.—Go to-morrow, and remember how much power lies in your hands. The Brethren will be on your side."

"Ah!" cried Godefroid, "you have given me so much pleasure in trusting me to do good and be worthy of some day being one of you, that I shall not sleep for joy."

"Stay, my boy, one last piece of advice. The prohibition to recognize me unless I make the sign concerns the other gentlemen and Madame, and even the servants of the house. Absolute incognito is indispensable to all our undertakings, and we are so constantly obliged to preserve it that we have made it a law without exceptions. We must be unknown, lost in Paris.

"Remember, too, my dear Godefroid, the very spirit of our Order, which requires us never to appear as benefactors, but to play the obscure part of intermediaries. We always represent ourselves as the agents of some saintly and beneficent personage—are we not toiling for God?—so that no gratitude may be considered due to ourselves, and that we may not be supposed to be rich. •True, sincere humility, not the false humility of those who keep in the shade that others may throw a light on them, must inspire and govern all your thoughts.— You may rejoice when you succeed; but so long as you feel the least impulse of vanity, you will be unworthy to join the Brotherhood. We have known two perfect men. One, who was one of our founders, Judge Popinot; the other, who was known by his works, was a country doctor who has left his name written in a remote parish. He, my dear Godefroid, was one of the greatest men of our day; he raised a whole district from a savage state to one of prosperity, from irreligion to the Catholic faith, from barbarism to civilization. The names of those two men are graven on our hearts, and we regard them as our examples. We should be happy indeed if we might one day have in Paris such influence as that country doctor had in his own district.

"But here the plague-spot is immeasurable, and, so far, quite beyond our powers. May God long preserve Madame, and send us many such helpers as you, and then perhaps we may found an Institution that will lead men to bless His holy religion.

"Well, farewell. Your initiation now begins.

"Bless me! I chatter like a Professor, and was forgetting the most important matter. Here is the address of the family I spoke of," he went on, handing a scrap of paper to Godefroid. "And I have added the number of Monsieur Berton's house in the Rue de l'Enfer.—Now, go and pray God to help you."

Godefroid took the good old man's hands and pressed them affectionately, bidding him good-night, and promising to forget none of his injunctions.

"All you have said," he added, "is stamped on my memory for life."

Alain smiled with no expression of doubt, and rose to go and kneel on his prie-Dieu. Godefroid went back to his own room, happy in being at last allowed to know the mysteries of this household, and to have an occupation which, in his present frame of mind, was really a pleasure.

At breakfast next morning there was no Monsieur Alain, but Godefroid made no remark on his absence. Nor was he questioned as to the mission given him by the old man; thus he received his first lesson in secrecy.· After breakfast, however, he took Madame de la Chanterie aside, and told her that he should be absent for a few days.

"Very well, my child," replied Madame de la Chanterie. "And try to do your sponsor credit, for Monsieur Alain has answered for you to his brethren."

Godefroid took leave of the other three men, who embraced him affectionately, seeming thus to give him their blessing on his outset in his laborious career.

Association—one of the greatest social forces which was the making of Europe in the Middle Ages—is based on feelings which have ceased, since 1792, to exist in France, where the individual is now supreme over the State. Association requires, in the first place, a kind of devotedness which is not understood in this country; a simplicity of faith which is contrary to the national spirit; and finally, a discipline against which everything rebels, and which nothing but the Catholic faith can exact. As soon as an Association is formed in France, each member of it, on returning home from a meeting where the finest sentiments have been expressed, makes a bed for himself of the collective devotion of this combination of forces, and tries to milk for his own benefit the cow belonging to all, till the poor thing, inadequate to meet so many individual demands, dies of attenuation.

None can tell how many generous emotions have been nipped, how many fervid germs have perished, how much resource has been crushed and lost to the country by the shameful frauds of the French secret Societies, of the patriotic fund for the Champs d'Asile (emigration to America), and other political swindles, which ought to have produced great and noble dramas, and turned out mere farces of the lower police courts.

It was the same with industrial as with political associations. Self-interest took the place of public spirit. The Corporations and Hanseatic Guilds of the Middle Ages, to which we shall some day return, are as yet out of the question; the only Societies that still exist are religious institutions, and at this moment they are being very roughly attacked, for the natural tendency of the sick is to rebel against the remedies and often to rend the physician. France knows not what self-denial means. Hence no Association can hold together but by the aid of religious sentiment, the only power that can quell the rebellion of the intellect, the calculations of ambition, and greed of every kind. Those who are in search of worlds fail to understand that Association has worlds in its gift.

Godefroid, as he made his way through the streets, felt himself a different man. Any one who could have read his mind would have wondered at the curious phenomenon of the communication of the spirit of union. He was no longer one man, but a being multiplied tenfold, feeling himself the representative of five persons whose united powers were at the back of all he did, and who walked with him on his way. With this strength in his heart, he was conscious of a fulness of life, a lofty power that uplifted him. It was, as he afterwards owned, one of the happiest moments of his life, for he rejoiced in a new sense—that of an omnipotence more absolute than that of despots. Moral force, like thought, knows no limits.

"This is living for others," said he to himself, "acting with others as if we were but one man, and acting alone as if we were all together! This is having Charity for a leader, the fairest and most living of all the ideals that have been created of the Catholic virtues.—Yes, this is living!—Come, I must subdue this childish exultation which Father Alain would laugh to scorn.—Still, is it not strange that it is by dint of trying to annul my Self that I have found the power so long wished for? The world of misfortune is to be my inheritance."

He crossed the precincts of Notre-Dame to the Avenue de l'Observatoire in such high spirits that he did not heed the length of the walk.

Having reached the Rue Notre-Dame des Champs, at the end of the Rue de l'Ouest, he was surprised to find such pools of mud in so handsome a quarter of the town, for neither of those streets was as yet paved. The foot-passenger had to walk on planks laid close to the walls of the marshy gardens, or creep by the houses on narrow side-paths, which were soon swamped by the stagnant waters that turned them into gutters.

After much seeking, he discovered the house described to him, and got to it, not without some difficulty. It was evidently an old manufactory which had been abandoned. The building was narrow, and the front was a long wall pierced with windows quite devoid of any ornament; but there were none of these square openings on the ground floor—only a wretched back-door.

Godefroid supposed that the owner had contrived a number of rooms in this structure to his own profit, for over the door there was a board scrawled by hand to this effect: *Several rooms to let.* Godefroid rang, but no one came; and as he stood waiting, a passer-by pointed out to him that there was another entrance to the house from the boulevard, where he would find somebody to speak to.

Godefroid acted on the information, and from the boulevard he saw the front of the house screened by the trees of a small garden-plot. This garden, very ill-kept, sloped to the house, for there is such a difference of level between the boulevard and the Rue Notre-Dame des Champs as to make the garden a sort of ditch. Godefroid went down the path, and at the bottom of it saw an old woman whose dilapidated garb was in perfect harmony with the dwelling.

"Was it you who rang in the Rue Notre-Dame?" she asked.

"Yes, madame.—Is it your business to show the rooms?"

On a reply in the affirmative from this portress, whose age it was difficult to determine, Godefroid inquired whether the house was tenanted by quiet folk; his occupations required peace and silence; he was a bachelor, and wished to arrange with the doorkeeper to cook and clean for him.

On this hint the woman became gracious, and said:

"Monsieur could not have done better than to hit on this house; for excepting the days when there are doings at the *Chaumière,* the boulevard is as deserted as the Pontine Marshes——"

"Do you know the Pontine Marshes?" asked Godefroid.

"No, sir; but there is an old gentleman upstairs whose daughter is always in a dying state, and he says so.—I only repeat it. That poor old man will be truly glad to think that you want peace and quiet, for a lodger who stormed around would be the death of his daughter.—And we have two writers of some kind on the second floor, but they come in for the day at midnight, and then at night they go out at eight in the morning. Authors, they say they are, but I do not know where or when they work."

As she spoke, the portress led Godefroid up one of those horrible stairs built of wood and brick, in such an unholy alliance that it is impossible to say whether the wood is parting from the bricks or the bricks are disgusted at being set in the wood; while both materials seem to fortify their disunion by masses of dust in summer and of mud in winter. The walls, of cracked plaster, bore more inscriptions than the Academy of Belles-lettres ever invented.

The woman stopped on the first floor.

"Now, here, sir, are two very good rooms, opening into each other, and on to Monsieur Bernard's landing. He is the old gentleman I mentioned—and quite the gentleman. He has the ribbon of the Legion of Honor, but he has had great troubles, it would seem, for he never wears it.—When first they came they had a servant to wait on them, a man from the country, and they sent him away close on three years ago. The lady's young gentleman—her son—does everything now; he manages it all——"

Godefroid looked shocked.

"Oh!" said the woman, "don't be uneasy, they will say nothing to you; they never speak to anybody. The gentleman has been here ever since the revolution of July; he came in 1831.—They are some high provincial family, I believe, ruined by the change of government; and proud! and as mute as fishes.—For four years, sir, they have never let me do the least thing for them, for fear of having to pay.—A five-franc piece on New Year's day, that's every sou I get out of them.— Give me your authors! I get ten francs a month, only to tell everybody who comes to ask for them that they left at the end of last quarter."

All this babble led Godefroid to hope for an ally in this woman, who explained to him, as she praised the airiness of the two rooms and adjoining dressing-closets, that she was not the portress, but the landlord's deputy and housekeeper, managing everything for him to a great extent.

"And you may trust me, monsieur, I promise you! Madame Vauthier—that's me—would rather have nothing at all than take a sou of anybody else's."

Madame Vauthier soon came to terms with Godefroid, who wished to take the rooms by the month and ready furnished. These wretched lodgings, rented by students or authors "down on their luck," were let furnished or unfurnished, as might be required. The spacious lofts over the whole house were full of furniture. But Monsieur Bernard himself had furnished the rooms he was in.

In getting Madame Vauthier to talk, Godefroid discovered that her ambition was set up in a *pension bourgeoise;* but in the course of five years she had failed to meet with a single boarder among her lodgers. She inhabited the ground floor, on the side towards the boulevard; thus she was herself the doorkeeper, with the help of a big dog, a sturdy girl, and a boy who cleaned the boots, ran errands, and did the rooms, two creatures as poor as herself, in harmony with the squalor of the house and its inhabitants, and the desolate, neglected appearance of the garden in front.

They were both foundlings, to whom the widow Vauthier gave no wages but their food—and such food! The boy, of whom Godefroid caught a glimpse, wore a ragged blouse, list slippers instead of shoes, and sabots to go out in. With a shock of hair, as touzled as a sparrow taking a bath, and blackened hands, as soon as he had done the work of the house, he went off to measure wood logs in a woodyard hard by, and when his day was over—at half-past four for wood-sawyers—he returned for his occupations. He fetched water for the household from the fountain by the Observatory, and the widow supplied it to the lodgers, as well as the faggots which he chopped and tied.

Népomucène—this was the name of the widow Vauthier's slave—handed over his earnings to his mistress. In summer-time the unhappy waif served as waiter in the wineshops by the barrière on Sundays and Mondays. Then the woman gave him decent clothes.

As for the girl, she cooked under the widow's orders, and helped her in her trade work at other times, for the woman plied a trade; she made list slippers for peddlers to sell.

All these details were known to Godefroid within an hour, for Madame Vauthier took him all over the house, showing him how it had been altered. A silkworm establishment had been carried on there till 1828, not so much for the production of silk as that of the eggs—the seed, as it is called. Eleven acres of mulberry-trees at Mont-Rouge, and three acres in the Rue de l'Ouest, since built over, had supplied food for this nursery for silkworms' eggs.

Madame Vauthier was telling Godefroid that Monsieur Barbet, who had lent the capital to an Italian named Fresconi to carry on this business, had been obliged to sell those three acres to recover the money secured by a mortgage on the land and buildings, and was pointing out the plot of ground, lying on the other side of the Rue Notre-Dame des Champs, when a tall and meagre old man, with perfectly white hair, came in sight at the end of the street where it crosses the Rue de l'Ouest.

"In the very nick of time!" cried Madame Vauthier. "Look, that is your neighbor, Monsieur Bernard.—Monsieur Bernard," cried she, as soon as the old man was within hearing, "you will not be alone now; this gentleman here has just taken the rooms opposite yours——"

Monsieur Bernard looked up at Godefroid with an apprehensive eye that was easy to read; it was as though he had said, "Then the misfortune I have so long feared has come upon me!"

"What, monsieur," said he, "you propose to reside here?"

"Yes, monsieur," said Godefroid civilly. "This is no home for those who are lucky in the world, and it is the cheapest lodging I have seen in this part of the town. Madame Vauthier does not expect to harbor millionaires.—Good-day, then, Madame Vauthier; arrange things so that I may come in at six o'clock this evening. I shall return punctually."

And Godefroid went off towards the Rue de l'Ouest, walking slowly, for the anxiety he had read in the old man's face led him to suppose that he wanted to dispute the matter with him. And, in fact, after some little hesitation, Monsieur Bernard turned on his heel and walked quickly enough to come up with Godefroid.

"That old wretch! he wants to hinder him from coming back," said Madame Vauthier to herself. "Twice already he has played me that trick.—Patience! His rent is due in five days, and if he does not pay it down on the nail, out he goes! Monsieur Barbet is a tiger of a sort that does not need much lashing, and—I should like to know what he is saying to him—Félicité! Félicité! you lazy hussy, will you make haste?" cried the widow in a formidable croak, for she had assumed an affable piping tone in speaking to Godefroid.

The girl, a sturdy, red-haired slut, came running out.

"Just keep a sharp eye on everything for a few seconds, do you hear? I shall be back in five minutes."

And the widow Vauthier, formerly cook to the bookseller's shop kept by Barbet, one of the hardest money-lenders on short terms in the neighborhood, stole out at the heels of her two lodgers, so as to watch them from a distance and rejoin Godefroid as soon as he and Monsieur Bernard should part company.

Monsieur Bernard was walking slowly, like a man in two minds, or a debtor seeking for excuses to give to a creditor who has left him to take proceedings.

Godefroid, in front of this unknown neighbor, turned round to look at him under pretence of looking about him. And it was not till they had reached the broad walk in the Luxembourg Gardens that Monsieur Bernard came up with Godefroid and addressed him.

"I beg your pardon a thousand times, monsieur," said he, bowing to Godefroid, who returned the bow, "for stopping you, when I have not the honor of knowing you; but is it your firm intention to live in the horrible house where I am lodging?"

"Indeed, monsieur——"

"I know," said the old man, interrupting Godefroid with a commanding air, "that you have a right to ask me what concern of mine it is to meddle in your affairs, to question you. —Listen, monsieur; you are young, and I am very old; I am older than my years, and they are sixty-six—I might be taken for eighty!—Age and misfortune justify many things, since the law exempts septuagenarians from various public duties; still, I do not dwell on the privileges bestowed by white hairs; it is you whom I am concerned for. Do you know that the part of the town in which you think of living is a desert by eight in the evening, and full of dangers, of which being robbed is the least? Have you noticed the wide plots where there are no houses, the waste ground and market gardens?—You will, perhaps, retort that I live there; but I, monsieur, am never out of doors after six in the evening. Or you will say that two young men are lodgers on the second floor, above the rooms you propose to take; but, monsieur, those two unhappy writers are the victims of writs out against them; they are pursued by their creditors; they are in hiding, and go out all day to come in at midnight; and as they always keep together and carry arms, they have no fear of being robbed.—I myself obtained permission from the chief of the police for them each to carry a weapon."

"Indeed, monsieur," said Godefroid, "I have no fear of robbers, for the same reasons as leave these gentlemen invulnerable, and so great a contempt for life, that if I should be murdered by mistake, I should bless the assassin."

"And yet you do not look so very wretched," said the old man, who was studying Godefroid.

"I have barely enough to live on, to give me bread, and I chose that part of town for the sake of the quiet that reigns there.—But may I ask, monsieur, what object you can have in keeping me out of the house?"

The old man hesitated; he saw Madame Vauthier in pursuit. Godefroid, who was examining him attentively, was surprised at the excessive emaciation to which grief, and perhaps hunger, or perhaps hard work, had reduced him; there were traces of all these causes of weakness on the face where the withered skin looked dried on to the bones, as if it had been exposed to the African sun. The forehead, which was high and threatening, rose in a dome above a pair of steel-blue eyes, cold, hard, shrewd, and piercing as those of a savage, and set in deep, dark, and very wrinkled circles, like a bruise round each. A large, long, thin nose, and the upward curve of the chin, gave the old man a marked likeness to the familiar features of Don Quixote; but this was a sinister Don Quixote, a man of no delusions, a terrible Don Quixote.

The old man, in spite of his look of severity, betrayed nevertheless the timidity and weakness that poverty gives to the unfortunate. And these two feelings seemed to have graven lines of ruin on a face so strongly framed that the destroying pickaxe of misery had rough hewn it. The mouth was expressive and grave. Don Quixote was crossed with the Président de Montesquieu.

The man's dress was of black cloth throughout, but utterly threadbare; the coat, old-fashioned in cut, and the trousers showed many badly-executed patches. The buttons had been recently renewed. The coat was fastened to the chin, showing no linen, and a rusty-black stock covered the absence of a collar. These black clothes, worn for many years, reeked of poverty. But the mysterious old man's air of dignity, his gait, the mind that dwelt behind that brow and lighted up those eyes, seemed irreconcilable with poverty. An observer would have found it hard to class this Parisian.

Monsieur Bernard was so absent-minded that he might have been taken for a professor of the college-quarter, a learned man lost in jealous and overbearing meditation; and Godefroid was filled with excessive interest and a degree of curiosity to which his beneficent mission added a spur.

"Monsieur," said the old man presently, "if I were assured that all you seek is silence and privacy, I would say, 'Come and live near me.' Take the rooms," he went on in a louder voice, so that the widow might hear him, as she passed them, listening to what they were saying. "I am a father, monsieur, I have no one belonging to me in the world but my daughter and her son to help me to endure the miseries of life; but my daughter needs silence and perfect quiet.—Every one who has hitherto come to take the rooms you wish to lodge in has yielded to the reasoning and the entreaties of a heart-broken father; they did not care in which street they settled of so desolate a part of the town, where cheap lodgings are plenty and boarding-houses at very low rates. But you, I see, are very much bent on it, and I can only beg you, monsieur, not to deceive me; for if you should, I can but leave and settle beyond the barrier.—And, in the first place, a removal might cost my daughter her life," he said in a broken voice, "and then, who knows whether the doctors who come to attend her—for the love of God—would come outside the gates?——"

If the man could have shed tears, they would have run down his cheeks as he spoke these last words; but there were tears in his voice, to use a phrase that has become commonplace, and he covered his brow with a hand that was mere bone and sinew.

"What, then, is the matter with madame, your daughter?" asked Godefroid in a voice of ingratiating sympathy.

"A terrible disease to which the doctors give a variety of names—or rather, which has no name.—All my fortune went——"

But he checked himself, and said, with one of those movements peculiar to the unfortunate:

"The little money I had—for in 1830, dismissed from a high position, I found myself without an income—in short, everything I had was soon eaten up by my daughter, who had already ruined her mother and her husband's family. At the present time the pension I draw hardly suffices to pay for necessities in the state in which my poor saintly daughter now is.—She has exhausted all my power to weep.

"I have endured every torment, monsieur; I must be of granite still to live—or rather, God preserves the father that his child may still have a nurse or a providence, for her mother died of exhaustion.

"Ay, young man, you have come at a moment when this old tree that has never bent is feeling the axe of suffering, sharpened by poverty, cutting at its heart. And I, who have never complained to anybody, will tell you about this long illness to keep you from coming to the house—or, if you insist, to show you how necessary it is that our quiet should not be disturbed.

"At this moment, monsieur, day and night, my daughter barks like a dog!"

"She is mad, then?" said Godefroid.

"She is in her right mind, and a perfect saint," replied Monsieur Bernard. "You will think I am mad when I have told you all. My only daughter is the child of a mother who enjoyed excellent health. I never in my life loved but one woman—she was my wife. I chose her myself, and married for love the daughter of one of the bravest colonels in the Imperial guard, a Pole formerly on the Emperor's staff, the gallant General Tarlovski. In the place I held strict morality was indispensable; but my heart is not adapted to accommodate my fancies—I loved my wife faithfully, and she deserved it. And I am as constant as a father as I was as a husband; I can say no more.

"My daughter never left her mother's care; no girl ever led a chaster or more Christian life than my dear child. She was more than pretty—lovely; and her husband, a young man of whose character I was certain, for he was the son of an old friend, a President of the Supreme Court, I am sure was in no way contributory to his wife's malady."

Monsieur Bernard and Godefroid involuntarily stood still a moment looking at each other.

"Marriage, as you know, often changes a woman's constitution," the old man went on. "My daughter's first child was safely brought into the world, a son—my grandson, who lives with us, and who is the only descendant of either of the united families. The second time my daughter was expecting an infant, she had such singular symptoms that the physicians, all puzzled, could only ascribe them to the singular conditions which sometimes occur in such cases, and which are recorded in the memoirs of medical science. The infant was born dead, literally strangled by internal convulsions. Thus began the illness—temporary conditions had nothing to do with it.—Perhaps you are a medical student?" Godefroid replied with a nod, which might be either negative or affirmative.

"After this disastrous child-bearing," Monsieur Bernard went on—"a scene that made so terrible an impression on my son-in-law that it laid the foundations of the decline of which he died—my daughter, at the end of two or three months, complained of general debility, more particularly affecting her feet, which felt, as she described it, as if they were made of cotton. This weakness became paralysis, but what a strange form of paralysis! You may bend my daughter's feet under her, twist them round, and she feels nothing. The limbs are there, but they seem to have no blood, no flesh, no bones. This condition, which is unlike any recognized disease, has attacked her arms and hands; it was supposed to be connected with her spine. Doctors and remedies have only made her worse; my poor child cannot move without dislocating her hips, shoulders, or wrists. We have had for a long time an excellent surgeon, almost in the house, who makes it his care, with the help of a doctor—or doctors, for several have seen her out of curiosity—to replace the joints—would you believe me, monsieur?—as often as three or four times a day.

"Ah! I was forgetting to tell you—for this illness has so many forms—that during the early weak stage, before paralysis supervened, my daughter was liable to the most extraordinary attacks of catalepsy. You know what catalepsy is. She would lie with her eyes open and staring, sometimes in the attitude in which the fit seized her. She has had the most incredible forms of this affection, even attacks of tetanus.

"This phase of the disease suggested to me the application of mesmerism as a cure when I saw her so strangely paralyzed. Then, monsieur, my daughter became miraculously *clairvoyante,* her mind was subject to every marvel of somnambulism, as her body is to every form of disease."

Godefroid was indeed wondering whether the old man were quite sane.

"For my part," he went on, heedless of the expression of Godefroid's eyes, "I, brought up on Voltaire, Diderot, and Helvétius, am a son of the eighteenth century, of the Revolution; and I laughed to scorn all the records handed down from antiquity and middle ages of persons possessed—yes, and yet *possession* is the only explanation of the state my child is in. Even in her mesmeric sleep she has never been able to reveal the cause of her sufferings; she could not see it; and the methods of treatment suggested by her under those conditions, though carefully followed, have had no good result. For instance, she said she must be wrapped in a freshly-killed pig; then she was to have points of highly magnetized red-hot iron applied to her legs; to have metal sealing-wax on her spine.—And what a wreck she became; her teeth fell out; she became deaf, and then dumb; and suddenly, after six months of perfect deafness and silence, she recovered hearing and speech. She occasionally recovers the use of her hands as unexpectedly as she loses it, but for seven years she has never known the use of her feet.

"She has sometimes had well-defined and characteristic attacks of hydrophobia. Not only may the sight or sound of water, of a glass or a cup, rouse her to frenzy, but she barks like a dog, a melancholy bark, or howls, as dogs do at the sound of an organ.

"She has several times seemed to be dying, and has received the last sacraments, and then come back to life again to suffer with full understanding and clearness of mind, for her faculties of heart and brain remain unimpaired. Though she is alive, she has caused the death of her husband and her mother, who could not stand such repeated trials. Alas!— Nor is this all. Every function of nature is perverted; only a medical man could give you a complete account of the strange condition of every organ.

"In this state did I bring her to Paris from the country in 1829; for the famous physicians to whom I described the case—Desplein, Bianchon, and Haudry—believed I was trying to impose upon them. At that time magnetism was stoutly denied by the schools. Without throwing any doubt on the provincial doctors' good faith or mine, they thought there was some inaccuracy, or, if you like, some exaggeration, such as is common enough in families or in the sufferers themselves. But they have been obliged to change their views; to these phenomena, indeed, it is due that nervous diseases have of late years been made the subject of investigation, for this strange case is now classed as nervous. The last consultation held by these gentlemen led them to give up all medicine; they decided that nature must be studied, but left to itself; and since then I have had but one doctor—the doctor who attends the poor of this district. In fact, all that can be done is done to alleviate her sufferings, since their causes remain unknown."

The old man paused, as if this terrible confession were too much for him.

"For five years now my daughter has lived through alternations of amendment and relapse; but no new symptoms have appeared. She suffers more or less from the various forms of nervous attack which I have briefly described to you; but the paralysis of the legs and organic disturbances are constant. Our narrow means—increasingly narrow—compelled us to move from the rooms I took in 1829 in the Rue du Roule; and as my daughter cannot bear being moved, and I nearly lost her twice, first in coming to Paris, and then in moving her from the Beaujon side, I took the lodging in which we now are, foreseeing the disasters which ere long overtook us; for, after thirty years' service, I was kept waiting for my pension till 1833. I have drawn it only for six months, and the new government has crowned its severities by granting me only the minimum."

Godefroid expressed such surprise as seemed to demand entire confidence, and so the old man understood it, for he went on at once, not without a reproachful glance towards heaven.

"I am one of the thousand victims to political reaction. I carefully hide a name that is obnoxious to revenge; and if the lessons of experience ever avail from one generation to the next, remember, young man, never to lend yourself to the severity of any *side* in politics. Not that I repent of having done my duty, my conscience is at peace; but the powers of to-day have ceased to have that sense of common responsibility which binds governments together, however dissimilar; when zeal meets with a reward, it is the result of transient fear. The instrument, having served its purpose, is, sooner or later, completely forgotten. In me you see one of the staunchest supporters of the throne under the elder branch of the Bourbons, as I was, too, of the Imperial rule, and I am a beggar! As I am too proud to ask charity, no one will ever guess that I am suffering intolerable ills.

"Five days since, monsieur, the district medical officer who attends my daughter, or who watches the case, told me that he had no hope of curing a disease of which the symptoms vary every fortnight. His view is that neurotic patients are the despair of the Faculty because the causes lie in a system that defies investigation. He advises me to call in a certain Jewish doctor, who is spoken of as a quack; but at the same time he remarked that he was a foreigner, a Polish refugee, and that physicians are extremely jealous of certain extraordinary cures that have been much talked of; some people regard him as very learned and skilful.

"But he is exacting and suspicious; he selects his patients, and will not waste time; and then he is—a communist. His name is Halpersohn. My grandson has called on him twice, but in vain; for he has not yet been to the house, and I understand why."

"Why?" asked Godefroid.

"Oh, my grandson, who is sixteen, is worse clothed even than I am; and, will you believe me, monsieur, I dare not show myself to this doctor; my dress is too ill-suited to what is expected in a man of my age, and of some dignity too. If he should see the grandfather so destitute as I am when the grandson has shown himself in the same sorry plight, would he devote due care to my daughter? He would treat her as paupers are always treated.—And you must remember, monsieur, that I love my daughter for the grief she has caused me, as of old I loved her for the care she lavished upon me. She has become a perfect angel. Alas! She is now no more than a soul—a soul that beams on her son and on me; her body is no more, for she has triumphed over pain.

"Imagine what a spectacle for a father! My daughter's world is her bedroom. She must have flowers which she loves; she reads a great deal; and when she has the use of her hands, she works like a fairy. She knows nothing of the misery in which we live. Our life is such a strange one, that we can admit no one to our rooms.—Do you understand me, monsieur? Do you see that a neighbor is intolerable? I should have to ask so much of him that I should be under the greatest obligations—and I could never discharge them. In the first place, I have no time for anything: I am educating my grandson, and I work so hard, monsieur—so hard, that I never sleep for more than three or four hours at night."

"Monsieur," said Godefroid, interrupting the old man, to whom he had listened attentively while watching him with grieved attention, "I will be your neighbor, and I will help you——"

The old gentleman drew himself up with pride, indeed, with impatience, for he did not believe in any good thing in man.

"I will help you," repeated Godefroid, taking the old man's hands and pressing them warmly, "in such ways as I can.—Listen to me. What do you intend to make of your grandson?"

"He is soon to begin studying the law; I mean him to be an advocate."

"Then your grandson will cost you six hundred francs a year, and you——"

The old man said nothing.

"I have nothing," said Godefroid after a pause, "but I have influence; I will get at the Jewish doctor; and if your daughter is curable, she shall be cured. We will find means to repay this Halpersohn."

"Oh, if my daughter were cured, I would make the sacrifice that can be made but once; I would give up what I am saving for a rainy day."

"You may keep that too."

"Ah! what a thing it is to be young!" said the old man, shaking his head. "Good-bye, monsieur, or rather *au revoir*. The library is open, and as I have sold all my books, I have to go there every day for my work.

"I am grateful for the kind feeling you have shown; but we must see whether you can show me such consideration as I am obliged to require of a neighbor. That is all I ask of you——"

"Yes, monsieur, pray accept me as your neighbor; for Barbet, as you know, is not the man to put up long with empty rooms, and you might meet with a worse companion in misery than I.—I do not ask you to believe in me, only to allow me to be of use to you."

"And what interest can you have in serving me?" cried the old man, as he was about to go down the steps of the Cloister of the Carthusians, through which there was at that time a passage from the broad walk of the Luxembourg to the Rue d'Enfer.

"Have you never, in the course of your career, obliged anybody?"

The old man looked at Godefroid with knit brows, his eyes vague with reminiscence, like a man searching through the record of his life for an action for which he might deserve such rare gratitude; then he coldly turned away, after bowing with evident suspicion.

"Come! for a first meeting he was not particularly distant," said the disciple to himself.

Godefroid went at once to the Rue d'Enfer, the address given him by Monsieur Alain, and found Doctor Berton at home—a stern, cold man, who surprised him greatly by assuring him that the details given by Monsieur Bernard of his daughter's illness were absolutely correct; he then went in search of Doctor Halpersohn.

The Polish physician, since so famous, at that time lived at Chaillot in a little house in the Rue Marbeuf, of which he occupied the first floor. General Roman Zarnovicki lived on the ground floor, and the servants of the two refugees occupied the attics of the little hotel, only one story high. Godefroid did not see the doctor; he had been sent for to some distance in the country by a rich patient. But Godefroid was almost glad not to have met him, for in his haste he had neglected to provide himself with money, and was obliged to return to the Hôtel de la Chanterie to fetch some from his room.

These walks, and the time it took to dine in a restaurant in the Rue de l'Odéon, kept him busy till the hour when he was to take possession of his lodgings on the Boulevard Mont-Parnasse.

Nothing could be more wretched than the furniture provided by Madame Vauthier for the two rooms. It seemed as though the woman was in the habit of letting rooms not to be inhabited. The bed, the chairs, the tables, the drawers, the desk, the curtains, had all evidently been purchased at sales under compulsion of the law, where the money-lender had kept them on account, no cash value being obtainable—a not infrequent case.

Madame Vauthier, her arms akimbo, expected thanks, and she took Godefroid's smile for one of surprise.

"Oh yes, I have given you the best of everything, my dear Monsieur Godefroid," said she with an air of triumph. "Look what handsome silk curtains, and a mahogany bedstead that is not at all worm-eaten. It belonged to the Prince de Wissembourg, and was bought out of his mansion. When he left the Rue Louis-le-Grand, in 1809, I was scullery-maid in his kitchen, and from there I went to live with my landlord——"

Godefroid checked this confidential flow by paying his month's lodging in advance, and at the same time gave Madame Vauthier six francs, also in advance, for doing his rooms. At this moment he heard a bark; and if he had not been forewarned, he might have thought that his neighbor kept a dog in his lodgings.

"Does that dog bark at night?" he asked.

"Oh, be easy, sir, and have patience; there will not be above a week of it. Monsieur Bernard will not be able to pay his rent, and he will be turned out.—Still, they are queer folks, I must say! I never saw their dog.—For months that dog— for months, did I say?—for six months at a time you will never hear that dog, and you might think they didn't keep one.

The creature never comes out of madame's room. There is a lady who is very bad; she has never been out of her bed since they carried her in. Old Monsieur Bernard works very hard, and his son too, who is a day pupil at the Collège Louis-le-Grand, where he is in the top class for philosophy, and he is but sixteen. A bright chap that! but that little beggar works like a good 'un.

"You will hear them presently moving the flower pots in the lady's room—for they eat nothing but dry bread, the old man and his grandson, but they buy flowers and nice things for her. She must be very bad, poor thing, never to have stirred out since she came; and if you take Monsieur Berton's word—he is the doctor who comes to see her—she never will go out but feet foremost."

"And what is this Monsieur Bernard?"

"A very learned man, so they say; for he writes and goes to work in the public libraries, and the master lends him money on account of what he writes."

"The master—who?"

"The landlord, Monsieur Barbet, the old bookseller; he has been in business this sixteen years. He is a man from Normandy, who once sold salad in the streets, and who started as a dealer in old books on the quay, in 1818; then he set up a little shop, and now he is very rich.—He is a sort of old Jew who runs six-and-thirty businesses at once, for he was a kind of partner with the Italian who built this great barn to keep silkworms in——"

"And so the house is a place of refuge for authors in trouble?" said Godefroid.

"Are you so unlucky as to be one?" asked the widow Vauthier.

"I am only a beginner," said Godefroid.

"Oh, my good gentleman, for all the ill I wish you, never get any further! A newspaper man, now—I won't say——"

Godefroid could not help laughing, and he bid the woman good-night—a cook unconsciously representing the whole middle class.

As he went to bed in the wretched room, floored with bricks that had not even been colored, and hung with paper at seven sous the piece, Godefroid not only regretted his little lodging in the Rue Chanoinesse, but more especially the society of Madame de la Chanterie. There was a great void in his soul. He had already acquired certain habits of mind, and he could not remember ever having felt such keen regrets for anything in his previous life. This comparison, brief as it was, made a great impression on his mind; he understood that no life he could lead could compare with that he was about to embrace, and his determination to follow in the steps of good Father Alain was thenceforth unchangeable. If he had not the vocation, he had the will.

Next morning, Godefroid, whose new way of life accustomed him to rising very early, saw, out of his window, a youth of about seventeen, wearing a blouse, and coming in evidently from a public fountain, carrying in each hand a pitcher full of water. The lad's face, not knowing that any one could see him, betrayed his thoughts; and never had Godefroid seen one more guileless and more sad. The charm of youth was depressed by misery, study, and great physical fatigue. Monsieur Bernard's grandson was remarkable for an excessively white skin, in strong contrast to very dark-brown hair. He made three expeditions; and the third time he saw a load of wood being delivered which Godefroid had ordered the night before; for the winter, though late, of 1838 was beginning to be felt, and there had been a light fall of snow in the night.

Népomucène, who had just begun his day's work by fetching this wood, on which Madame Vauthier had already levied heavy toll, stood talking to the youth while waiting till the sawyer had cut up the logs for him to take indoors. It was very evident that the sight of this wood, and of the ominous gray sky, had reminded the lad of the desirability of laying in some fuel. And then suddenly, as if reproaching himself for waste of time, he took up the pitchers and hurried into the

house. It was indeed half-past seven; and as he heard the
quarters strike by the clock at the Convent of the Visitation,
he reflected that he had to be at the Collège Louis-le-Grand
by half-past eight.

At the moment when the young man went in, Godefroid
opened his door to Madame Vauthier, who was bringing up
some live charcoal to her new lodger; so it happened that he
witnessed a scene that took place on the landing. A gardener
living in the neighborhood, after ringing several times at Monsieur Bernard's door without arousing anybody, for the bell
was muffled in paper, had a rough dispute with the youth,
insisting on the money due for the hire of plants which
he had supplied. As the creditor raised his voice, Monsieur
Bernard came out.

"Auguste," said he to his grandson, "get dressed. It is
time to be off."

He himself took the pitchers and carried them into the
ante-room of his apartment, where Godefroid could see stands
filled with flowers; then he closed the door and came outside
to talk to the nurseryman. Godefroid's door was ajar, for
Népomucène was passing in and out and piling up the logs in
the second room. The gardener had become silent when Monsieur Bernard appeared, wrapped in a purple silk dressing-
gown, buttoned to the chin, and looking really imposing.

"You might ask for the money we owe you without shouting," said the gentleman.

"Be just, my dear sir," replied the gardener. "You were
to pay me week by week, and now, for three months—ten
weeks—I have had no money, and you owe me a hundred and
twenty francs. We are accustomed to hire out our plants to
rich people, who give us our money as soon as we ask for it,
and I have called here five times. We have our rent to pay
and our workmen, and I am no richer than you are. My wife,
who used to supply you with milk and eggs, will not call this
morning neither; you owe her thirty francs, and she would
rather not come at all than come to nag, for she has a good
heart, has my wife! If I listened to her, trade would never

pay.—And that is why I came, you understand, for that is not my way of looking at things, you see——"

Just then out came Auguste, dressed in a miserable green cloth coat, and trousers of the same, a black cravat, and shabby boots. These clothes, though brushed with care, revealed the very last extremity of poverty, for they were too short and too tight, so that they looked as if the least movement on the lad's part would split them. The whitened seams, the dog's-eared corners, the worn-out button-holes, in spite of mending, betrayed to the least practised eye the stigmata of poverty. This garb contrasted painfully with the youthfulness of the wearer, who went off eating a piece of stale bread, in which his fine strong teeth left their mark. This was his breakfast, eaten as he made his way from the Boulevard du Mont-Parnasse to the Rue Saint-Jacques, with his books and papers under his arm, and on his head a cap far too small for his powerful head and his mass of fine dark hair.

As he passed his grandfather, they exchanged rapid glances of deep dejection; for he saw that the old man was in almost irremediable difficulties, of which the consequences might be terrible. To make way for the student of philosophy, the gardener retreated as far as Godefroid's door; and at the moment when he reached the door, Népomucène, with a load of wood, came up to the landing, driving the creditor quite to the window.

"Monsieur Bernard," exclaimed the widow, "do you suppose that Monsieur Godefroid took these rooms for you to hold meetings in?"

·"I beg pardon, madame," replied the nurseryman, "the landing was crowded——"

"I did not mean it for you, Monsieur Cartier," said the woman.

"Stay here!" cried Godefroid, addressing the nurseryman. —"And you, my dear sir," he added, turning to Monsieur Bernard, whom this insolent remark left unmoved, "if it suits you to settle matters with your gardener in my room, pray come in."

The old gentleman, stupefied with trouble, gave Godefroid a stony look, which conveyed a thousand thanks.

"As for you, my dear Madame Vauthier, do not be so rough to monsieur, who, in the first place, is an old man, and to whom you also owe your thanks for having me as your lodger."

"Indeed!" exclaimed the woman.

"Besides, if poor folks do not help each other, who is to help them?—Leave us, Madame Vauthier; I can blow up my own fire. See to having my wood stowed in your cellar; I have no doubt you will take good care of it."

Madame Vauthier vanished; for Godefroid, by placing his fuel in her charge, had afforded pasture to her greed.

"Come in," said Godefroid, signing to the gardener, and setting two chairs for the debtor and creditor. The old man talked standing; the tradesman took a seat.

"Come, my good man," Godefroid went on, "the rich do not always pay so punctually as you say they do, and you should not dun a worthy gentleman for a few louis. Monsieur draws his pension every six months, and he cannot give you a draft in anticipation for so small a sum; but I will advance the money if you insist on it."

"Monsieur Bernard drew his pension about three weeks since, and he did not pay me. I should be very sorry to annoy him——"

"What, and you have been supplying him with flowers for——"

"Yes, monsieur, for six years, and he has always paid until now."

Monsieur Bernard, who was listening to all that might be going on in his own lodgings, and paying no heed to this discussion, heard screams through the partition, and hurried away in alarm, without saying a word.

"Come, come, my good man, bring some fine flowers, your best flowers, this very morning, to Monsieur Bernard, and let your wife send in some fresh eggs and milk; I will pay you myself this evening."

Cartier looked somewhat askance at Godefroid.

"Well, I suppose you know more about it than Madame Vauthier; she sent me word that I had better look sharp if I meant to be paid," said he. "Neither she nor I, sir, can account for it when people who live on bread, who pick up odds and ends of vegetables, and bits of carrot and potatoes, and turnip outside the eating-house doors—yes, sir, I have seen the boy filling a little basket,—well, when those people spend near on a hundred francs a month on flowers. The old man, they say, has but three thousand francs a year for his pension——"

"At any rate," said Godefroid, "if they ruin themselves in flowers, it is not for you to complain."

"Certainly not, sir, so long as I am paid."

"Bring me your bill."

"Very good, sir," said the gardener, with rather more respect. "You hope to see the lady they hide so carefully, no doubt?"

"Come, come, my good fellow, you forget yourself," said Godefroid stiffly. "Go home and pick out your best flowers to replace those you are taking away. If you can supply me with rich milk and new-laid eggs, you may have my custom. I will go this morning and look at your place."

"It is one of the best in Paris, and I exhibit at the Luxembourg shows. I have three acres of garden on the boulevard, just behind that of the *Grande-Chaumière*."

"Very good, Monsieur Cartier. You are richer than I am, I can see. So have some consideration for us; for who knows but that one day we may need each other."

The nurseryman departed, much puzzled as to what Godefroid could be.

"And time was when I was just like that!" said Godefroid to himself, as he blew the fire. "What a perfect specimen of the commonplace citizen; a gossip, full of curiosity, possessed by the idea of equality, but jealous of other dealers; furious at not knowing why a poor invalid stays in her room and is never seen; secretive as to his profits, but vain enough to let out the secret if he could crow over his neighbor. Such a man ought to be lieutenant at least of his crew. How easily and how often in every age does the scene of Monsieur Dimanche recur! Another minute, and Cartier would have been my sworn ally!"

The old man's return interrupted this soliloquy, which shows how greatly Godefroid's ideas had changed during the past four months.

"I beg your pardon," said Monsieur Bernard, in a husky voice, "I see you have sent off the nurseryman quite satisfied, for he bowed politely. In fact, my young friend, Providence seems to have sent you here for our express benefit at the very moment when all seemed at an end! Alas! The man's chatter must have told you many things.—It is quite true that I drew my half-year's pension a fortnight since; but I had other and more pressing debts, and I was obliged to keep back the money for the rent or be turned out of doors. You, to whom I have confided the secret of my daughter's state—who have heard her——"

He looked anxiously at Godefroid, who nodded affirmation.

"Well, you can judge if that would not be her death-blow. For I should have to place her in a hospital.—My grandson and I have been dreading this day, not that Cartier was our chief fear; it is the cold——"

"My dear Monsieur Bernard, I have plenty of wood; take some!" cried Godefroid.

"But how can I ever repay such kindness?" said the old man.

"By accepting it without ceremony," answered Godefroid cordially, "and by giving me your entire confidence."

"But what claims have I on such generosity?" asked Monsieur Bernard with revived suspicions. "My pride and my grandson's is broken!" he exclaimed. "For we have already fallen so far as to argue with our two or three creditors. The very poor can have no creditors. Only those can owe money who keep up a certain external display which we have utterly lost.—But I have not yet lost my common sense, my reason," he added, as if speaking to himself.

"Monsieur," said Godefroid gravely, "the story you told me yesterday would draw tears from an usurer——"

"No, no! for Barbet the publisher, our landlord, speculates on my poverty, and sets his old servant, the woman Vauthier, to spy it out."

"How can he speculate on it?" asked Godefroid.

"I will tell you at another time," replied the old man. "My daughter may be feeling cold, and since you are so kind, and since I am in a situation to accept charity, even if it were from my worst enemy——"

"I will carry the wood," said Godefroid, who went across the landing with half a score of logs, which he laid down in his neighbor's outer room.

Monsieur Bernard had taken an equal number, and when he beheld this little stock of fuel, he could not conceal the simple, almost idiotic, smile by which men rescued from mortal and apparently inevitable danger express their joy, for there still is fear even in their belief.

"Accept all I can give you, my dear Monsieur Bernard, without hesitation, and when we have saved your daughter, and you are happy once more, I will explain everything. Till then leave everything to me.—I went to call on the Jewish doctor, but unfortunately Halpersohn is absent; he will not be back for two days."

Just then a voice which sounded to Godefroid, and which really was, sweet and youthful, called out, "Papa, papa!" in an expressive tone.

While talking to the old man, Godefroid had already remarked, through the crack of the door opposite to that on the landing, lines of neat white paint, showing that the sick woman's room must be very different from the others that composed the lodging. His curiosity was now raised to the highest pitch; the errand of mercy was to him no more than a means; its end was to see the invalid. He would not believe that any one who spoke in such a voice could be horrible to behold.

"You are taking too mucn trouble, papa," said the voice. "Why do not you have more servants—at your age—Dear me!"

"But you know, dear Vanda, that I will not allow any one to wait on you but myself or your boy."

These two sentences, which Godefroid overheard, though with some difficulty, for a curtain dulled the sound, made him understand the case. The sick woman, surrounded by every luxury, knew nothing of the real state in which her father and son lived. Monsieur Bernard's silk wrapper, the flowers, and his conversation with Cartier had already roused Godefroid's suspicions, and he stood riveted, almost confounded, by this marvel of paternal devotion. The contrast between the invalid's room as he imagined it and what he saw was in fact amazing. The reader may judge:

Through the door of a third room which stood open, Godefroid saw two narrow beds of painted wood like those of the vilest lodging-houses, with a straw mattress and a thin upper mattress; on each there was but one blanket. A small iron stove such as porters use to cook on, with a few lumps of dried fuel by the side of it, was enough to show the destitution of the owner, without other details in keeping with this wretched stove.

Godefroid by one step forward could see the pots and pans of the wretched household—glazed earthenware jars, in which a few potatoes were soaking in dirty water. Two tables of blackened wood, covered with papers and books, stood in front of a window looking out on the Rue Notre-Dame des Champs, and showed how the father and son occupied themselves in the evening. On each table there was a candlestick of wrought iron of the poorest description, and in them candles of the cheapest kind, eight to the pound. On a third table, which served as a dresser, there were two shining sets of silver-gilt forks and spoons, some plates, a basin and cup in Sèvres china, and a knife with a gilt handle lying in a case, all evidently for the invalid's use.

The stove was alight; the water in the kettle was steaming gently. A wardrobe of painted deal contained no doubt the lady's linen and possessions, for he saw on her father's bed the clothes he had worn the day before, spread by way of a covering.

Some other rags laid in the same way on his grandson's bed led him to conclude that this was all their wardrobe; and under the bed he saw their shoes.

The floor, swept but seldom no doubt, was like that of a schoolroom. A large loaf that had been cut was visible on a shelf over the table. In short, it was poverty in the last stage of squalor, poverty reduced to a system, with the decent order of a determination to endure it; driven poverty that has to do everything at home, that insists on doing it, but that finds it impossible, and so puts every poor possession to a wrong use. A strong and sickening smell pervaded the room, which evidently was but rarely cleaned.

The ante-room where Godefroid stood was at any rate decent, and he guessed that it commonly served to hide the horrors of the room inhabited by the old man and the youth. This room, hung with a Scotch plaid paper, had four walnut-wood chairs and a small table, and was graced with portraits—a colored print of Horace Vernet's picture of the Emperor; those of Louis XVIII. and Charles X.; and one of Prince Poniatowski, a friend no doubt of Monsieur Bernard's father-in-law. There were cotton window-curtains bound with red and finished with fringe.

Godefroid, keeping an eye on Népomucène, and hearing him come up with a load of wood, signed to him to stack it noiselessly in Monsieur Bernard's ante-room; and, with a delicate feeling that showed he was making good progress, he shut the bedroom door that Madame Vauthier's boy might not see the old man's squalor.

The ante-room was partly filled up by three flower-stands full of splendid plants, two oval and one round, all three of rosewood, and elegantly finished; and Népomucène, as he placed the logs on the floor, could not help saying:

"Isn't that lovely?—It must cost a pretty penny!"

"Jean, do not make too much noise——" Monsieur Bernard called out.

"There, you hear him?" said Népomucène to Godefroid, "the poor old boy is certainly cracked!"

"And what will you be at his age?"

"Oh, I know sure enough!" said Népomucène; "I shall be in a sugar-basin."

"In a sugar-basin?"

"Yes, my bones will have been made into charcoal. I have seen the sugar-boilers' carts often enough at Mont Souris come to fetch bone-black for their works, and they told me they used it in making sugar." And with this philosophical reply, he went off for another basketful of wood.

Godefroid quietly closed Monsieur Bernard's door, leaving him alone with his daughter.

Madame Vauthier had meanwhile prepared her new lodger's breakfast, and came with Félicité to serve it. Godefroid, lost in meditation, was staring at the fire on the hearth. He was absorbed in reflecting on this poverty that included so many different forms of misery, though he perceived that it had its pleasures too; the ineffable joys and triumphs of fatherly and of filial devotion. They were like pearls sewn on sackcloth.

"What romance—even the most famous—can compare with such reality?" thought he. "How noble is the life that mingles with such lives as these, enabling the soul to discern their cause and effect; to assuage suffering and encourage what is good; to become one with misfortune and learn the secrets of such a home as this; to be an actor in ever-new dramas such as delight us in the works of the most famous authors!—I had no idea that goodness could be more interesting than vice."

"Is everything to your mind, sir?" asked Madame Vauthier, who, helped by Félicité, had placed the table close to Godefroid. He then saw an excellent cup of coffee with milk, a smoking hot omelette, fresh butter, and little red radishes.

"Where did you find those radishes?" asked Godefroid.

"Monsieur Cartier gave them to me," said she. "I thought you might like them, sir.

"And what do you expect me to pay for a breakfast like this every day?" said Godefroid.

"Well, monsieur, to be quite fair—it would be hard to supply it under thirty sous."

"Say thirty sous," said Godefroid. "But how is it that close by this, at Madame Machillot's, they only ask me forty-five francs a month for dinner, which is just thirty sous a day?"

"Oh, but what a difference, sir, between getting a dinner for fifteen people and going to buy everything that is needed for one breakfast: a roll, you see, eggs, butter,—lighting the fire—and then sugar, milk, coffee.—Why, they will ask you sixteen sous for nothing but a cup of coffee with milk in the Place de l'Odéon, and you have to give a sou or two to the waiter!—Here you have no trouble at all; you breakfast at home, in your slippers.

"Well, then it is settled," said Godefroid.

"And even then, but for Madame Cartier, from whom I get the milk and eggs and parsley, I could not do it at all.— You must go and see their place, sir. Oh, it is really a fine sight. They employ five gardeners' apprentices, and Népomucène goes to help with the watering all the summer; they pay me to let him go. And you make a lot of money out of strawberries and melons.—You are very much interested in Monsieur Bernard, it would seem?" asked the widow in her sweetest tones. "For really to answer for their debts in that way!—But perhaps you don't know how much they owe.— There is the lady that keeps the circulating library on the Place Saint-Michel; she calls every three or four days for thirty francs, and she wants it badly too. Heaven above! that poor woman in bed does read and read. And at two sous a volume, thirty francs in two months——"

"Is a hundred volumes a month," said Godefroid.

"There goes the old fellow to fetch madame's cream and roll," the woman went on. "It is for her tea; for she lives on nothing but tea, that lady; she has it twice a day, and then twice a week she wants sweets.—She is dainty, I can tell you! The old boy buys her cakes and tarts at the pastry-cook's in the Rue de Buci. Oh, when it is for her, he sticks at nothing. He says she is his daughter!—Where's the man who would do all he does, and at his age, for his daughter? He is killing himself—himself and his Auguste—and all for her.—If you are like me, sir—I would give twenty francs to see her. Monsieur Berton says she is shocking, an object to make a show of.—They did well to come to this part of the town where nobody ever comes.—And you think of dining at Madame Machillot's, sir?"

"Yes, I thought of making an arrangement with her."

"Well, sir, it is not to interfere with any plan of yours; but, take 'em as you find 'em, you will find a better eating-place in the Rue de Tournon; you need not bind yourself for a month, and you will have a better table——"

"Where in the Rue de Tournon?"

"At the successors of old Madame Girard. That is where the gentlemen upstairs dine, and they are satisfied—they could not be better pleased."

"Very well, Madame Vauthier, I will take your advice and dine there."

"And, my dear sir," the woman went on, emboldened by the easy-going air which Godefroid had intentionally assumed, "do you mean to say, seriously, that you are such a flat as to think of paying Monsieur Bernard's debts?—I should be really very sorry; for you must remember, my good Monsieur Godefroid, that he is very near on seventy, and after him where are you? There's an end to his pension. What will there be to repay you? Young men are so rash. Do you know that he owes above a thousand crowns?"

"But to whom?" asked Godefroid.

"Oh, that is no concern of mine," said Madame Vauthier mysteriously. "He owes the money, and that's enough; and between you and me, he is having a hard time of it; he cannot get credit for a sou in all the neighborhood for that very reason."

"A thousand crowns!" said Godefroid. "Be sure of one thing; if I had a thousand crowns, I should be no lodger of yours. But I, you see, cannot bear to see others suffering; and for a few hundred francs that it may cost me, I will make sure that my neighbor, a man with white hair, has bread and firing. Why, a man often loses as much at cards.—But three thousand francs—why, what do you think? Good Heavens!"

Madame Vauthier, quite taken in by Godefroid's affected candor, allowed a gleam of satisfaction to light up her face, and this confirmed her lodger's suspicions. Godefroid was convinced that the old woman was implicated in some plot against the hapless Monsieur Bernard.

"It is a strange thing, monsieur, what fancies come into one's head. You will say that I am very inquisitive; but yesterday, when I saw you talking to Monsieur Bernard, it struck me that you must be a publisher's clerk—for this is their part of the town. I had a lodger, a foreman printer, whose works are in the Rue de Vaugirard, and he was named the same name as you——"

"And what concern is it of yours what my business is?" said Godefroid.

"Lor'! whether you tell me or whether you don't, I shall know just the same," said the widow. "Look at Monsieur Bernard, for instance; well, for eighteen months I could never find out what he was; but in the nineteenth month I discovered that he had been a judge or a magistrate, or something of the kind, in the law, and that now he is writing a book about it. What does he get by it? That's what I say. And if he had told me, I should have held my tongue; so there!"

"I am not at present a publisher's agent, but I may be, perhaps, before long."

"There, I knew it!" exclaimed the woman eagerly, and turning from the bed she was making as an excuse to stay chattering to her lodger. "You have come to cut the ground from under—— Well, well, 'a nod's as good as a wink'——"

"Hold hard!" cried Godefroid, standing between Madame Vauthier and the door. "Now, tell me, what are you paid to meddle in this?"

"Heyday!" cried the old woman, with a keen look at Godefroid. "You are pretty sharp after all!"

She shut and locked the outer door; then she came back and sat down by the fire.

"On my word and honor, as sure as my name is Vauthier, I took you for a student till I saw you giving your logs to old

Father Bernard. My word, but you're a sharp one! By the Piper! you can play a part well! I thought you were a perfect flat. Now, will you promise me a thousand francs? For as sure as the day above us, old Barbet and Monsieur Métivier have promised me five hundred if I keep my eyes open."

"What? Not they! Two hundred at the very outside, my good woman, and only promised at that—and you cannot summons them for payment!—Look here; if you will put me in a position to get the job they are trying to manage with Monsieur Bernard, I will give you four hundred!—Come, now, what are they up to?"

"Well, they have paid him fifteen hundred francs on account for his work, and made him sign a bill for a thousand crowns. They doled it out to him a hundred francs at a time, contriving to keep him as poor as poor.—They set the duns upon him; they sent Cartier, you may wager."

At this, Godefroid, by a look of cynical perspicacity that he shot at the woman, made it clear to her that he quite understood the game she was playing for her landlord's benefit. Her speech threw a light on two sides of the question, for it also explained the rather strange scene between the gardener and himself.

"Oh yes!" she went on, "they have him fast; for where is he ever to find a thousand crowns! They intend to offer him five hundred francs when the work is in their hands complete, and five hundred francs per volume as they are brought out for sale. The business is all in the name of a bookseller these gentlemen have set up in business on the Quai des Augustins——"

"Oh yes—that little—what's-his-name?"

"Yes, that's your man.—Morand, formerly Monsieur Barbet's agent.—There is a heap of money to be got out of it, it would seem."

"There will be a heap of money to put into it," said Godefroid, with an expressive grimace.

There was a gentle knock at the door, and Godefroid, very glad of the interruption, rose to open it.

"All this is between you and me, Mother Vauthier," said Godefroid, seeing Monsieur Bernard.

"Monsieur Bernard," cried she, "I have a letter for you."

The old man went down a few steps.

"No, no, I have no letter for you, Monsieur Bernard; I only wished to warn you against that young fellow there. He is a publisher."

"Oh, that accounts for everything," said the old man to himself. And he came back to his neighbor's room with a quite altered countenance.

The calmly cold expression on Monsieur Bernard's face when he reappeared was in such marked contrast to the frank and friendly manner his gratitude had lent him, that Godefroid was struck by so sudden a change.

"Monsieur, forgive me for disturbing your solitude, but you have since yesterday loaded me with favors, and a benefactor confers rights on those whom he obliges."

Godefroid bowed.

"I, who for five years have suffered once a fortnight the torments of the Redeemer; I, who for six-and-thirty years was the representative of Society and the Government, who was then the arm of public vengeance, and who, as you may suppose, have no illusions left—nothing, nothing but sufferings,—well, monsieur, your careful attention in closing the door of the dog-kennel in which my grandson and I sleep—that trifling act was to me the cup of water of which Bossuet speaks. I found in my heart, my wornout heart, which is as dry of tears as my withered body is of sweat, the last drop of that elixir which in youth leads us to see the best side of every human action, and I came to offer you my hand, which I never give to any one but my daughter; I came to bring you the heavenly rose of belief, even now, in goodness."

"Monsieur Bernard," said Godefroid, remembering good old Alain's injunctions, "I did nothing with a view to winning your gratitude.—You are under a mistake."

"That is frank and above board," said the old lawyer. "Well, that is what I like. I was about to reproach you. Forgive me; I esteem you.—So you are a publisher, and you want to get my book in preference to Messieurs Barbet, Métivier, and Morand?—That explains all. You are prepared to deal with me as they were; only you do it with a good grace."

"Old Vauthier has just told you, I suppose, that I am a publisher's agent?"

"Yes," said he.

"Well, Monsieur Bernard, before I can say what we are prepared to *pay* more than those gentlemen *offer,* I must understand on what terms you stand with them."

"Very true," said the old man, who seemed delighted to find himself the object of a competition by which he could not fail to benefit. "Do you know what the work is?"

"No; I only know that there is something to be made by it."

"It is only half-past nine; my daughter has had her breakfast, my grandson Auguste will not come in till a quarter to eleven. Cartier will not be here with the flowers for an hour —we have time to talk, monsieur—monsieur who?"

"Godefroid."

"Monsieur Godefroid.—The book in question was planned by me in 1825, at a time when the Ministry, struck by the constant reduction of personal estate, drafted the Law of Entail and Seniority which was thrown out. I had observed many defects in our codes and in the fundamental principle of French law. The codes have been the subject of many important works; but all those treatises are essentially on jurisprudence; no one has been so bold as to study the results of the Revolution—or of Napoleon's rule, if you prefer it—as a whole, analyzing the spirit of these laws and the working of their application. That is, in general terms, the purpose of my book. I have called it the *Spirit of the Modern Laws.* It covers organic law as well as the codes—all the codes, for we have five! My book, too, is in five volumes, and a sixth volume of authorities, quotations, and references. I have still three months' work before me.

"The owner of this house, a retired publisher, scented a speculation. I, in the first instance, thought only of benefiting my country. This Barbet has got the better of me.—You will wonder how a publisher could entrap an old lawyer; but you, monsieur, know my history, and this man is a money-lender. He has the sharp eye and the knowledge of the world that such men must have. His advances have just kept pace with my necessity; he has always come in at the very moment when despair has made me a defenceless prey."

"Not at all, my dear sir," said Godefroid. "He has simply kept Madame Vauthier as a spy.—But the terms, tell me honestly."

"They advanced me fifteen hundred francs, represented at the present rates by three bills for a thousand francs each, and these three thousand francs are secured to them by a lien on the property of my book, which I cannot dispose of elsewhere till I have paid off the bills; the bills have been protested; judgment has been pronounced.—Here, monsieur, you see the complications of poverty.

"At the most moderate estimate, the first edition of this vast work, the result of ten years' labor and thirty-six years' experience, will be well worth ten thousand francs.—Well, just five days since, Morand offered me a thousand crowns and my note of hand paid off for all rights.—As I could never find three thousand two hundred and forty francs, unless you intervene between us, I must yield.

"They would not take my word of honor; for further security they insisted on bills of exchange which have been protested, and I shall be imprisoned for debt. If I pay up, these money-lenders will have doubled their loan; if I deal with them, they will make a fortune, for one of them was a paper-maker, and God only knows how low they can keep the price of materials. And then, with my name on it, they know that they are certain of a sale of ten thousand copies."

"Why, monsieur—you, a retired Judge——!"

"What can I say? I have not a friend, no one remembers me!—And yet I saved many heads even if I sentenced many to fall!—And then there is my daughter, my daughter whose nurse and companion I am, for I work only at night.—Ah!

young man, none but the wretched should be set to judge the wretched. I see now that of yore I was too severe."

"I do not ask you your name, monsieur. I have not a thousand crowns at my disposal, especially if I pay Halper-sohn and your little bills; but I can save you if you will pledge your word not to dispose of your book without due notice to me; it is impossible to embark in so important a matter without consulting professional experts. The persons I work for are powerful, and I can promise you success if you can promise me perfect secrecy, even from your children—and keep your word."

"The only success I care for is my poor Vanda's recovery; for, I assure you, the sight of such sufferings extinguishes every other feeling in a father's heart; the loss of fame is nothing to the man who sees a grave yawning at his feet——"

"I will call on you this evening. Halpersohn may come home at any moment, and I go every day to see if he has returned.—I will spend to-day in your service."

"Oh, if you could bring about my daughter's recovery, mon-sieur——, monsieur, I would make you a present of my book!"

"But," said Godefroid, "I am not a publisher."

The old man started with surprise.

"I could not help letting old Vauthier think so for the sake of ascertaining what snares had been laid for you."

"But who are you, then?"

"Godefroid," was the reply; "and as you have allowed me to supply you with the means of living better," added the young man, smiling, "you may call me Godefroid de Bouil-lon."

The old lawyer was too much touched to laugh at the jest. He held out his hand to Godefroid and grasped the young man's warmly.

"You wish to remain unknown?" said Monsieur Bernard, looking at Godefroid with melancholy, mixed with some un-easiness.

"If you will allow me."

"Well, do as you think proper.—And come in this evening; you will see my daughter, if her state allows."

This was evidently the greatest concession the poor father could make; and seeing Godefroid's grateful look, the old man had the pleasure of feeling that he was understood.

An hour later Cartier came back with some beautiful flowers, replanted the stands with his own hands in fresh moss, and Godefroid paid the bill, as he did the subscription to the lending library, for which the account was sent in soon after. Books and flowers were the staff of life to this poor sick—or rather, tormented woman, who could live on so little food.

As he thought of this family in the toils of disaster, like that of Laocoon—a sublime allegory of many lives!—Godefroid, making his way leisurely on foot to the Rue Marbeuf, felt in his heart that he was curious rather than benevolent. The idea of the sick woman, surrounded with luxuries in the midst of abject squalor, made him forget the horrible details of the strange nervous malady, which is happily an extraordinary exception, though abundantly proved by various historians. One of our gossiping chronicle writers, Tallemant des Réaux, mentions an instance. We like to think of women as elegant even in their worst sufferings, and Godefroid promised himself some pleasure in penetrating into the room which only the physician, the father, and the son had entered for six years past. However, he ended by reproaching himself for his curiosity. The neophyte even understood that his feeling, however natural, would die out by degrees as he carried out his merciful errands, by dint of seeing new homes and new sorrows. Such messengers, in fact, attain to a heavenly benignity which nothing can shock or amaze, just as in love we attain to a sublime quiescence of feeling in the conviction of its strength and duration, by a constant habit of submission and sweetness.

Godefroid was told that Halpersohn had come home during the night, but had been obliged to go out in his carriage the

first thing in the morning to see the patients who were waiting for him. The woman at the gate told Godefroid to come
back next morning before nine.

Remembering Monsieur Alain's advice as to parsimony
in his personal expenses, Godefroid dined for twenty-five sous
in the Rue de Tournon, and was rewarded for his self-denial
by finding himself among compositors and proof-readers. He
heard a discussion about the cost of production, and, joining in, picked up the information that an octavo volume of
forty sheets, of which a thousand copies were printed, would
not cost more than thirty sous per copy under favorable circumstances. He determined on going to inquire the price
commonly asked for such volumes on sale at the law publishers, so as to be in a position to dispute the point with the
publishers who had got a hold on Monsieur Bernard, if he
should happen to meet them.

At about seven in the evening he came back to the Boulevard Mont-Parnasse along the Rue de Vaugirard, the Rue
Madame, and the Rue de l'Ouest, and he saw how deserted
that part of the town is, for he met nobody. It is true that
the cold was severe, snow fell in large flakes, and the carts
made no noise on the stones.

"Ah, here you are, monsieur!" said Madame Vauthier when
she saw him. "If I had known you would come in so early,
I would have lighted your fire."

"It is unnecessary," replied Godefroid, as the woman followed him; "I am going to spend the evening with Monsieur
Bernard."

"Ah! very good. You are cousins, I suppose, that you are
hand and glove with him by the second day. I thought perhaps you would have liked to finish what we were saying——"

"Oh, about the four hundred francs?" said Godefroid in an
undertone. "Look here, Mother Vautier, you would have
had them this evening if you had said nothing to Monsieur
Bernard. You want to hunt with the hounds and run with
the hare, and you will get neither; for, so far as I am concerned, you have spoiled my game—my chances are altogether ruined——"

"Don't you believe that, my good sir. To-morrow, when you are at breakfast——"

"Oh, to-morrow I must be off at daybreak like your authors."

Godefroid's past experience and life as a dandy and journalist had been so far of use to him as to lead him to guess that if he did not take this line, Barbet's spy would warn the publisher that there was something in the wind, and he would then take such steps as would ere long endanger Monsieur Bernard's liberty; whereas, by leaving the three usurious negotiators to believe that their schemes were not in peril, they would keep quiet.

But Godefroid was not yet a match for Parisian humanity when it assumes the guise of a Madame Vauthier. This woman meant to have Godefroid's money and her landlord's too. She flew off to Monsieur Barbet, while Godefroid changed his dress to call on Monsieur Bernard's daughter.

Eight o'clock was striking at the Convent of the Visitation, whose clock regulated the life of the whole neighborhood, when Godefroid, full of curiosity, knocked at his friend's door. Auguste opened it; as it was Saturday, the lad spent his evening at home; Godefroid saw that he wore a jacket of black velvet, black trousers that were quite decent, and a blue silk tie; but his surprise at seeing the youth so unlike his usual self ceased when he entered the invalid's room. He at once understood the necessity for the father and the boy to be presentably dressed.

The walls of the room, hung with yellow silk, paneled with bright green cord, made the room look extremely cheerful; the cold tiled floor was covered by a flowered carpet on a white ground. The two windows, with their handsome curtains lined with white silk, were like bowers, the flower-stands were so full of beauty, and blinds hindered them from being seen from outside in a quarter where such lavishness was rare. The woodwork, painted white, and varnished, was touched up with gold lines. A heavy curtain, embroidered in tent stitch, with grotesque foliage on a yellow ground, hung over

the door and deadened every sound from outside. This splendid curtain had been worked by the invalid, who embroidered
like a fairy when she had the use of her hands.

Opposite the door, at the further end of the room, the
chimney-shelf, covered with green velvet, had a set of very
costly ornaments, the only relic of the wealth of the two families. There was a very curious clock; an elephant supporting
a porcelain tower filled with beautiful flowers; two candelabra
in the same style, and some valuable Oriental pieces. The
fender, the dogs, and fire-irons were all of the finest workmanship.

The largest of the three flower stands stood in the middle
of the room, and above it hung a porcelain chandelier of floral
design.

The bed on which the judge's daughter lay was one of those
fine examples of carved wood, painted white and gold, that
were made in the time of Louis XV. By the invalid's pillow
was a pretty inlaid table, on which were the various objects
necessary for a life spent in bed; a bracket light for two
candles was fixed to the wall, and could be turned backwards
and forwards by a touch. In front of her was a bed-table,
wonderfully contrived for her convenience. The bed was
covered with a magnificent counterpane, and draped with curtains looped back in festoons; it was loaded with books and a
work-basket, and among these various objects Godefroid
would hardly have discovered the sick woman but for the
tapers in the two candle-branches.

There seemed to be nothing of her but a very white face,
darkly marked round the eyes by much suffering; her eyes
shone like fire; and her principal ornament was her splendid
black hair, of which the heavy curls, set out in bunches of
numerous ringlets, showed that the care and arrangement of
her hair occupied part of the invalid's day; a movable mirror
at the foot of the bed confirmed the idea.

No kind of modern elegance was lacking, and a few trifling
toys for poor Vanda's amusement showed that her father's
affection verged on mania.

The old man rose from a very handsome easy-chair of Louis XV. style, white and gold, and covered with needlework, and went forward a few steps to welcome Godefroid, who certainly would not have recognized him; for his cold, stern face had assumed the gay expression peculiar to old men who have preserved their dignity of manner and the superficial frivolity of courtiers. His purple wadded dressing-gown was in harmony with the luxury about him, and he took snuff out of a gold box set with diamonds.

"Here, my dear," said Monsieur Bernard to his daughter, "is our neighbor of whom I spoke to you." And he signed to his grandson to bring forward one of two armchairs, in the same style as his own, which were standing on each side of the fire.

"Monsieur's name is Godefroid, and he is most kind in standing on no ceremony——"

Vanda moved her head in acknowledgment of Godefroid's low bow; and by the movement of her throat as it bent and unbent, he discovered that all this woman's vitality was seated in her head. Her emaciated arms and lifeless hands lay on the fine white sheet like objects quite apart from the body, and that seemed to fill no space in the bed. The things needed for her use were on a set of shelves behind the bed, and screened by a silk curtain.

"You, my dear sir, are the first person, excepting only the doctors—who have ceased to be men to me—whom I have set eyes on for six years; so you can have no idea of the interest I have felt in you ever since my father told me you were coming to call on us. It was passionate, unconquerable curiosity, like that of our mother Eve. My father, who is so good to me; my son, of whom I am so fond, are undoubtedly enough to fill up the vacuum of a soul now almost bereft of body; but that soul is still a woman's after all! I recognized that in the childish joy I felt in the idea of your visit.—You will do us the pleasure of taking a cup of tea with us, I hope?"

"Yes, Monsieur Godefroid has promised us the pleasure of his company for the evening," said the old man, with the air of a millionaire doing the honors of his house.

Auguste, seated in a low, worsted-work chair by a small table of inlaid wood, finished with brass mouldings, was reading by the light of the wax-candles on the chimney-shelf.

"Auguste, my dear, tell Jean to bring tea in an hour's time."

She spoke with some pointed meaning, and Auguste replied by a nod.

"Will you believe, monsieur, that for the past six years no one has waited on me but my father and my boy, and I could not endure anybody else. If I were to lose them, I should die of it.—My father will not even allow Jean, a poor old Normandy peasant who has lived with us for thirty years— will not even let him come into the room."

"I should think not, indeed!" said the old man readily. "Monsieur Godefroid has seen him; he saws and brings in the wood, he cooks and runs errands, and wears a dirty apron; he would have made hay of all these pretty things, which are so necessary to my poor child, to whom this elegance is second nature."

"Indeed, madame, your father is quite right——"

"But why?" she urged. "If Jean had damaged my room, my father would have renewed it."

"Of course, my child; but what would have prevented me is the fact that you cannot leave it; and you have no idea what Paris workmen are. It would take them more than three months to restore your room! Only think of the dust that would come out of your carpet if it were taken up. Let Jean do your room! Do not think of such a thing. By taking the extreme care which only your father and your boy can take, we have spared you sweeping and dust; if Jean came in to help, everything would be done for in a month."

"It is not so much out of economy as for the sake of your health," said Godefroid. "Monsieur your father is quite right."

"Oh, I am not complaining," said Vanda in a saucy tone.

Her voice had the quality of a concert; soul, action, and life were all concentrated in her eyes and her voice; for

Vanda, by careful practice, for which time had certainly
not been lacking, had succeeded in overcoming the difficulties
arising from her loss of teeth.

"I am still happy, monsieur, in spite of the dreadful malady
that tortures me; for wealth is certainly a great help in enduring my sufferings. If we had been in poverty, I should have
died eighteen years ago, and I am still alive. I have many
enjoyments, and they are all the keener because I live on,
triumphing over death.—You will think me a great chatterbox," she added, with a smile.

"Madame," said Godefroid, "I could beg you to talk for
ever, for I never heard a voice to compare with yours
—it is music! Rubini is not more delightful——"

"Do not mention Rubini or the opera," said the old man
sadly. "However rich we may be, it is impossible to give my
daughter, who was a great musician, a pleasure to which she
was devoted."

"I apologize," said Godefroid.

"You will fall into our ways," said the old man.

"This is your training," said the invalid, smiling. "When
we have warned you several times by crying, 'Look out!' you
will know all the blind man's buff of our conversation!"

Godefroid exchanged a swift glance with Monsieur Bernard, who, seeing tears in his new friend's eyes, put his finger
to his lip as a warning not to betray the heroic devotion he
and the boy had shown for the past seven years.

This devoted and unflagging imposture, proved by the
invalid's entire deception, produced on Godefroid at this moment the effect of looking at a precipitous rock whence two
chamois-hunters were on the point of falling.

The splendid gold and diamond snuff-box with which the
old man trifled, leaning over the foot of his daughter's bed,
was like the touch of genius which in a great actor wrings
from us a cry of admiration. Godefroid looked at the snuff-
box, wondering why it had not been sold or pawned, but he
postponed the idea till he could discuss it with the old man.

"This evening, Monsieur Godefroid, my daughter was so

greatly excited by the promise of your visit, that the various strange symptoms of her malady which, for nearly a fortnight past, have driven us to despair, suddenly disappeared. You may imagine my gratitude!"

"And mine!" cried Vanda, in an insinuating voice, with a graceful inclination of her head. "You are a deputation from the outer world.—Since I was twenty I have not known what a drawing-room is like, or a party, or a ball; and I love dancing, I. am crazy about the play, and above all about music. Well, I imagine everything in my mind. I read a great deal, and my father tells me all about the gay world——" As he listened, Godefroid felt prompted to kneel at the feet of this poor old man.

"When he goes to the opera—and he often goes—he describes the dresses to me, and all the singers. Oh! I should like to be well again; in the first place, for my father's sake, for he lives for me alone, as I live for him and through him, and then for my son's—I should like him to know another mother. Oh! monsieur, what perfect men are my dear old father and my admirable son!—Then I could wish for health also, that I might hear Lablache, Rubini, Tamburini, Grisi, the *Puritani* too!—But——"

"Come, my dear, compose yourself. If we talk about music, it is fatal!" said the old father, with a smile.

And that smile, which made him look younger, evidently constantly deceived the sick woman.

"Well, I will be good," said Vanda, with a saucy pout. "But let me have a harmonium."

This instrument had lately been invented; it could, by a little contrivance, be placed by the invalid's bed, and would only need the pressure of the foot to give out an organ-like tone. This instrument, in its most improved form, was as effective as a piano; but at that time it cost three hundred francs. Vanda, who read newspapers and reviews, had heard of such an instrument, and had been longing for one for two months past.

"Yes, madame, and I can procure you one," replied Godefroid at an appealing glance from the old man. "A friend of mine who is setting out for Algiers has a very fine one, which I will borrow of him; for before buying one, you had better try it. It is quite possible that the sound, which is strongly vibrating, may be too much for you."

"Can I have it to-morrow?" she asked, with the eagerness of a Creole.

"To-morrow!" objected Monsieur Bernard. "That is very soon; besides, to-morrow will be Sunday."

"To be sure," said she, looking at Godefroid, who felt as though he saw a soul fluttering, as he admired the ubiquity of Vanda's eyes.

Until now he had never understood what the power of the voice and eyes might be when the entire vitality was concentrated in them. Her glance was more than a glance; it was a flame, or rather a blaze of divine light, a communicative ray of life and intelligence, thought made visible. The voice, with its endless intonations, supplied the place of movement, gesture, and turns of the head. And her changing color, varying like that of the fabled chameleon, made the illusion—or, if you will, the delusion—complete. That weary head, buried in a cambric pillow frilled with lace, was a complete woman.

Never in his life had Godefroid seen so noble a spectacle, and he could hardly endure his emotions. Another grand feature, where everything was strange in a situation so full of romance and of horror, was that the soul alone seemed to be living in the spectators. This atmosphere, where all was sentiment, had a celestial influence. They were as unconscious of their bodies as the woman in bed; everything was pure spirit. By dint of gazing at these frail remains of a pretty woman, Godefroid forgot the elegant luxury of the room, and felt himself in heaven. It was not till half-an-hour after that he noticed a what-not covered with curiosities, over which hung a noble portrait that Vanda desired him to look at, as it was by Géricault.

"Géricault," said she, "was a native of Rouen, and his family being under some obligations to my father, who was

President of the Supreme Court there, he showed his gratitude by painting that masterpiece, in which you see me at the
age of sixteen."

"You have there a very fine picture," said Godefroid, "and
one that is quite unknown to those who have studied the rare
works of that great genius."

"To me it is no longer an object of anything but affectionate regard," said she, "since I live only by my feelings;
and I have a beautiful life," she went on, looking at her father
with her whole soul in her eyes. "Oh, monsieur, if you could
but know what my father is! Who would believe that the austere and dignified Judge to whom the Emperor owed so much
that he gave him that snuff-box, and whom Charles X. rewarded by the gift of that Sèvres tray"—and she looked at
a side-table—"that the staunch upholder of law and authority,
the learned political writer, has in a heart of rock all the tenderness of a mother?—Oh, papa, papa! Come, kiss me—I
insist on it—if you love me."

The old man rose, leaned over the bed, and set a kiss on
his daughter's high poetic brow, for her sickly fancies were
not invariably furies of affection. Then he walked up and
down the room, but without a sound, for he wore slippers—
the work of his daughter's hands.

"And what is your occupation?" she asked Godefroid after
a pause.

"Madame, I am employed by certain pious persons to take
help to the unfortunate."

"A beautiful mission!" said she. "Do you know that the
idea of devoting myself to such work has often occurred to
me? But what ideas have not occurred to me?" said she,
with a little shake of her head. "Pain is a torch that throws
light on life, and if I ever recover my health——"

"You shall enjoy yourself, my child," the old man put in.

"Certainly I long to enjoy life," said she, "but should I be
able for it?—My son, I hope, will be a lawyer, worthy of his
two grandfathers, and he must leave me. What is to be done?
—If God restores me to life, I will dedicate it to Him.—Oh,

not till I have given you both as much of it as you desire!" she exclaimed, looking at her father and her boy. "There are times, my dear father, when Monsieur de Maistre's ideas work in my brain, and I fancy I am expatiating some sin."

"That is what comes of reading so much!" cried the old man, visibly grieved.

"There was that brave Polish General, my great-grandfather; he meddled very innocently in the concerns of Poland——"

"Now we have come back to Poland!" exclaimed Bernard.

"How can I help it, papa? My sufferings are intolerable, they make me hate life, and disgust me with myself. Well, what have I done to deserve them? Such an illness is not mere disordered health; it is a complete wreck of the whole constitution, and——"

"Sing the national air your poor mother used to sing; it will please Monsieur Godefroid, I have spoken to him of your voice," said her father, evidently anxious to divert his daughter's mind from the ideas she was following out.

Vanda began to sing in a low, soft voice a hymn in the Polish tongue, which left Godefroid bewildered with admiration and sadness. This melody, a good deal like the long-drawn melancholy tunes of Brittany, is one of those poetic airs that linger in the mind long after being heard. As he listened to Vanda, Godefroid at first looked at her; but he could not bear the ecstatic eyes of this remnant of a woman now half-crazed, and he gazed at some tassels that hung on each side of the top of the bed.

"Ah, ha!" said Vanda, laughing at Godefroid's evident curiosity, "you are wondering what those are for?"

"Vanda, Vanda, be calm, my child! See, here comes the tea.—This, monsieur, is a very expensive contrivance," he said to Godefroid. "My daughter cannot raise herself, nor can she remain in bed without its being made and the sheets changed. Those cords work over pulleys, and by slipping a sheet of leather under her and attaching it to rings at the corners to those ropes, we can lift her without fatiguing her or ourselves."

"Yes, I am carried up—up!" said Vanda deliriously.

Auguste happily came in with a teapot, which he set on a little table, where he also placed the Sèvres tray, covered with sandwiches and cakes. Then he brought in the cream and butter. This diverted the sick woman's mind; she had been on the verge of an attack.

"Here, Vanda, is Nathan's last novel. If you should lie awake to-night, you will have something to read."

"*La Perle de Dol!* That will be a love-story no doubt.— Auguste, what do you think? I am to have a harmonium!"

Auguste raised his head quickly, and looked strangely at his grandfather.

"You see how fond he is of his mother!" Vanda went on. —"Come and kiss me, dear rogue.—No, it is not your grandfather that you must thank, but Monsieur Godefroid; our kind neighbor promises to borrow one for me to-morrow morning.—What is it like, monsieur?"

Godefroid, at a nod from the old man, gave a long description of the harmonium while enjoying the tea Auguste had made, which was of superior quality and delicious flavor.

At about half-past ten the visitor withdrew, quite overpowered by the frantic struggle maintained by the father and son, while admiring their heroism and the patience that enabled them, day after day, to play two equally exhausting parts.

"Now," said Monsieur Bernard, accompanying him to his own door, "now you know the life I lead! At every hour I have to endure the alarms of a robber, on the alert for everything. One word, one look might kill my daughter. One toy removed from those she is accustomed to see about her would reveal everything to her, for mind sees through walls."

"Monsieur," said Godefroid, "on Monday Halpersohn will pronounce his opinion on your daughter, for he is at home again. I doubt whether science can restore her frame."

"Oh, I do not count upon it," said the old man with a sigh. "If they will only make her life endurable.—I trusted to your tact, monsieur, and I want to thank you, for you understood.

—Ah! the attack has come on!" cried he, hearing a scream. "She has done too much——"

He pressed Godefroid's hand and hurried away.

At eight next morning Godefroid knocked at the famous doctor's door. He was shown up by the servant to a room on the first floor of the house, which he had had time to examine while the porter found the man-servant.

Happily, Godefroid's punctuality had saved him the vexation of waiting, as he had hoped it might. He was evidently the first-comer. He was led through a very plain ante-room into a large study, where he found an old man in a dressing-gown, smoking a long pipe. The dressing-gown, of black moreen, was shiny with wear, and dated from the time of the Polish dispersion.

"What can I do to serve you?" said the Jew, "for you are not ill."

And he fixed Godefroid with a look that had all the sharp inquisitiveness of the Polish Jew, eyes which seem to have ears.

To Godefroid's great surprise, Halpersohn was a man of fifty-six, with short bow-legs and a broad, powerful frame. There was an Oriental stamp about the man, and his face must in youth have been singularly handsome; the remains showed a marked Jewish nose, as long and as curved as a Damascus scimitar. His forehead was truly Polish, broad and lofty, wrinkled all over like crumpled paper, and recalling that of a Saint-Joseph by some old Italian master. His eyes were sea-green, set like a parrot's in puckered gray lids, and expressive of cunning and avarice in the highest degree. His mouth, thin and straight, like a cut in his face, lent this sinister countenance a crowning touch of suspiciousness.

The pale, lean features—for Halpersohn was extraordinarily thin—were crowned by ill-kept gray hair, and graced by a very thick, long beard, black streaked with white, that hid half his face, so that only the forehead and eyes, the cheek-bones, nose, and lips were visible.

This man, a friend of the agitator Lelewel, wore a black velvet cap that came down in a point on his forehead and showed off its mellow hue, worthy of Rembrandt's brush.

The doctor, who subsequently became equally famous for his talents and his avarice, startled Godefroid by his question, and the young man asked himself, "Can he take me for a thief?"

The reply to the question was evident on the doctor's table and chimney-piece. Godefroid had fancied himself the first-comer—he was the last. His patients had laid very handsome sums on the table and shelf, for Godefroid saw piles of twenty and forty-franc pieces and two thousand-franc notes. Was all this the fruit of a single morning? He greatly doubted it, and he suspected an ingenious trick. The infallible but money-loving doctor perhaps tried thus to encourage his patients' liberality, and to make his rich clients believe that he was given banknotes as if they were curl-papers.

Moïse Halpersohn was no doubt largely paid, for he cured his patients, and cured them of those very complaints which the profession gave up in despair. It is very little known in Western Europe that the Slav nations possess a store of medical secrets. They have a number of sovereign remedies derived from their intercourse with the Chinese, the Persians, the Cossacks, the Turks, and the Tartars. Some peasant women, regarded as witches, have been known to cure hydrophobia completely in Poland with the juice of certain plants. There is among those nations a great mass of uncodified information as to the effects of certain plants and the powdered bark of trees, which is handed down from family to family, and miraculous cures are effected there.

Halpersohn, who for five or six years was regarded as a charlatan, with his powders and mixtures, had the innate instinct of a great healer. Not only was he learned, he had observed with great care, and had traveled all over Germany, Russia, Persia, and Turkey, where he had picked up much traditional lore; and as he was learned in chemistry, he became a living encyclopedia of the secrets preserved by "the good women," as they were called, the midwives and "wise women" of every country whither he had followed his father, a wandering trader.

It must not be supposed that the scene in *Richard in Palestine,* in which Saladin cures the King of England, is pure fiction. Halpersohn has a little silk bag, which he soaks in water till it is faintly colored, and certain fevers yield to this infusion taken by the patient. The virtues residing in plants are infinitely various, according to him, and the most terrible maladies admit of cure. He, however, like his brother physicians, pauses sometimes before the incomprehensible. Halpersohn admires the invention of homœopathy, less for its medical system than for its therapeutics; he was at that time in correspondence with Hedenius of Dresden, Chelius of Heidelberg, and the other famous Germans, but keeping his own hand dark though it was full of discoveries. He would have no pupils.

The setting of this figure, which might have stepped out of a picture by Rembrandt, was quite in harmony with it. The study, hung with green flock paper, was poorly furnished with a green divan. The carpet, also of moss green, showed the thread. A large armchair covered with black leather, for the patients, stood near the window, which was hung with green curtains. The doctor's seat was a study-chair with arms, in the Roman style, of mahogany with a green leather seat. Besides the chimney-piece and the long table at which he wrote, there was in the middle of the wall opposite the fireplace a common iron chest supporting a clock of Vienna granite, on which stood a bronze group of Love sporting with Death, the gift of a famous German sculptor whom Halpersohn had, no doubt, cured. A tazza between two candlesticks was all the ornament of the chimney-shelf. Two bracket shelves, one at each end of the divan, served to place trays on, and Godefroid noted that there were silver bowls on them, water-bottles, and table-napkins.

This simplicity, verging on bareness, struck Godefroid, who took everything in at a glance, and he recovered his presence of mind.

"I am perfectly well, monsieur. I have not come to consult you myself, but on behalf of a lady whom you ought long since to have seen—a lady living on the Boulevard du Mont-Parnasse."

"Oh yes, that lady has sent her son to me several times. Well, monsieur, tell her to come to see me?"

"Tell her to come!" cried Godefroid indignantly. "Why, monsieur, she cannot be lifted from her bed to a sofa; she has to be raised by straps."

"You are not a doctor?" asked the Jew, with a singular grimace which made his face look even more wicked.

"If Baron de Nucingen sent to tell you that he was ill and to ask you to visit him, would you reply, 'Tell him to come to me'?"

"I should go to him," said the Jew drily, as he spat into a Dutch spittoon made of mahogany and filled with sand.

"You would go to him," Godefroid said mildly, "because the Baron has two millions a year, and——"

"Nothing else has to do with the matter. I should go."

"Very well, monsieur, you may come and see the lady on the Boulevard du Mont-Parnasse for the same reason. Though I have not such a fortune as the Baron de Nucingen, I am here to tell you that you can name your own price for the cure, or, if you fail, for your care of her. I am prepared to pay you in advance. But how is it, monsieur, that you, a Polish exile, a communist, I believe, will make no sacrifice for the sake of Poland! For this lady is the granddaughter of General Tarlovski, Prince Poniatowski's friend——"

"Monsieur, you came to ask me to prescribe for this lady, and not to give me your advice. In Poland I am a Pole; in Paris a Parisian. Every one does good in his own way, and you may believe me when I tell you that the greed attributed to me has its good reasons. The money I accumulate has its uses; it is sacred. I sell health; rich persons can pay for it, and I make them buy it. The poor have their physicians. —If I had no aim in view, I should not practise medicine. I live soberly, and I spend my time in rushing from one to another; I am by nature lazy, and I used to be a gambler. You may draw your own conclusions, young man!—You are not old enough to judge the aged!"

Godefroid kept silence.

"You live with the granddaughter of the foolhardy soldier who had no courage but for fighting, and who betrayed his country to Catherine II. ?"

"Yes, monsieur."

"Then be at home on Monday at three o'clock," said he, laying down his pipe and taking up his notebook, in which he wrote a few words. "When I call, you will please to pay me two hundred francs; then, if I undertake to cure her, you will give me a thousand crowns.—I have been told," he went on, "that the lady is shrunken as if she had fallen in the fire."

"It is a case, monsieur, if you will believe the first physicians of Paris, of nervous disease, with symptoms so strange that no one can imagine them who has not seen them."

"Ah, yes, now I remember the details given me by that little fellow.—Till to-morrow, monsieur."

Godefroid left with a bow to this singular and extraordinary man. There was nothing about him to show or suggest a medical man, not even in that bare consulting-room, where the only article of furniture that was at all remarkable was the ponderous chest, made by Huret or Fichet.

Godefroid reached the Passage Vivienne in time to purchase a splendid harmonium before the shop was shut, and he despatched it forthwith to Monsieur Bernard, whose address he gave.

Then he went to the Rue Chanoinesse, passing along the Quai des Augustins, where he hoped still to find a bookseller's shop open; he was, in fact, so fortunate, and had a long conversation on the cost of law-books, with the clerk in charge.

He found Madame de la Chanterie and her friend just come in from high mass, and he answered her first inquiring glance with a significant shake.

"And our dear Father Alain is not with you?" said he.

"He will not be here this Sunday," replied Madame de la

Chanterie. "You will not find him here till this day week, unless you go to the place where you know you can meet him."

"Madame," said Godefroid, in an undertone, "you know I am less afraid of him than of these gentlemen, and I intended to confess to him."

"And I?"

"Oh, you—I will tell you everything, for I have many things to say to you. As a beginning, I have come upon the most extraordinary case of destitution, the strangest union of poverty and luxury, and figures of a sublimity which outdoes the inventions of our most admired romancers."

"Nature, and especially moral nature, is always as far above art as God is above His creatures. But come," said Madame de la Chanterie, "and tell me all about your expedition into the unknown lands where you made your first venture."

Monsieur Nicolas and Monsieur Joseph—for the Abbé de Vèze had remained for a few minutes at Notre-Dame—left Madame de la Chanterie alone with Godefroid; and he, fresh from the emotions he had gone through the day before, related every detail with the intensity, the gesticulation, and the eagerness that come of the first impression produced by such a scene and its accessories of men and things. He had a success too; for Madame de la Chanterie, calm and gentle as she was, and accustomed to look into gulfs of suffering, shed tears.

"You did right," said she, "to send the harmonium."

"I wish I could have done much more," replied Godefroid, "since this is the first family through whom I have known the pleasures of charity; I want to secure to the noble old man the chief part of the profits on his great work. I do not know whether you have enough confidence in me to enable me to undertake such a business. From the information I have gained, it would cost about nine thousand francs to bring out an edition of fifteen hundred copies, and their lowest selling value would be twenty-four thousand francs. As we must, in the first instance, pay off the three thousand and odd francs that have been advanced on the manuscript, we should have to risk twelve thousand francs.

"Oh, madame! if you could but imagine how bitterly, as I made my way hither from the Quai des Augustins, I rued having so foolishly wasted my little fortune. The Genius of Charity appeared to me, as it were, and filled me with the ardor of a neophyte; I desire to renounce the world, to live the life of these gentlemen, and to be worthy of you. Many a time during the past two days have I blessed the chance that brought me to your house. I will obey you in every particular till you judge me worthy to join the brotherhood."

"Well," said Madame de la Chanterie very seriously, after a few minutes of reflection, "listen to me, I have important things to say to you. You have been fascinated, my dear boy, by the poetry of misfortune. Yes, misfortune often has a poetry of its own; for, to me, poetry is a certain exaltation of feeling, and suffering is feeling. We live so much through suffering!"

"Yes, madame, I was captured by the demon of curiosity. How could I help it! I have not yet acquired the habit of seeing into the heart of these unfortunate lives, and I cannot set out with the calm resolution of your three pious soldiers of the Lord. But I may tell you, it was not till I had quelled this incitement that I devoted myself to your work."

"Listen, my very dear son," said Madame de la Chanterie, saying the words with a saintly sweetness which deeply touched Godefroid, "we have forbidden ourselves absolutely —and this is no exaggeration, for we do not allow ourselves even to think of what is forbidden—we have forbidden ourselves ever to embark in a speculation. To print a book for sale, and looking for a return, is business, and any transaction of that kind would involve us in the difficulties of trade. To be sure, it looks in this case very feasible, and even necessary. Do you suppose that it is the first instance of the kind that has come before us? Twenty times, a hundred times, we have seen how a family, a concern, could be saved. But, then, what should we have become in undertaking matters of this kind? We should be simply a trading firm. To be a sleeping partner with the unfortunate is not work; it is only

helping misfortune to work. In a few days you may meet
with even harder cases than this; will you do the same thing?
You would be overwhelmed.

"Remember, for one thing, that the house of Mongenod, for
a year past, has ceased to keep our accounts. Quite half of
your time will be taken up by keeping our books. There are,
at this time, nearly two thousand persons in our debt in Paris;
and of those who may repay us, at any rate, it is necessary
that we should check the amounts they owe us. We never sue
—we wait. We calculate that half of the money given out is
lost. The other half sometimes returns doubled.

"Now, suppose this lawyer were to die, the twelve thousand
francs would be badly invested! But if his daughter recovers, if his grandson does well, if he one day gets another
appointment—then, if he has any sense of honor, he will remember the debt, and return the funds of the poor with interest. Do you know that more than one family, raised from
poverty and started by us on the road to fortune by considerable loans without interest, has saved for the poor and returned us sums of double and sometimes treble the amount?

"This is our only form of speculation.

"In the first place, as to this case which interests you, and
ought to interest you, consider that the sale of the lawyer's
book depends on its merits; have you read it? Then, even if
the work is excellent, how many excellent books have remained two or three years without achieving the success they
deserved. How many a wreath is laid on a tomb! And, as
I know, publishers have ways of driving bargains and taking
their charges, which make the business one of the most risky
and the most difficult to disentangle of all in Paris. Monsieur
Nicolas can tell you about these difficulties, inherent in the
nature of book-making. So, you see, we are prudent; we have
ample experience of every kind of misery, as of every branch
of trade, for we have long been studying Paris. The Mongenods give us much help; they are a light to our path, and
through them we know that the Bank of France is always
suspicious of the book-trade, though it is a noble trade—but
it is badly conducted.

"As to the four thousand francs needed to save this noble family from the horrors of indigence, I will give you the money; for the poor boy and his grandfather must be fed and decently dressed.—There are sorrows, miseries, wounds, which we bind up at once without inquiring who it is that we are helping; religion, honor, character, are not inquired into; but as soon as it is a case of lending the money belonging to the poor to assist the unfortunate under the more active form of industry or trade, then we require some guarantee, and are as rigid as the money-lenders. So, for all beyond this immediate relief, be satisfied with finding the most honest publisher for the old man's book. This is a matter for Monsieur Nicolas. He is acquainted with lawyers and professors and authors of works in jurisprudence; next Saturday he will, no doubt, be prepared with some good advice for you.

"Be easy; the difficulty will be got over if possible. At the same time, it might be well if Monsieur Nicolas could read the magistrate's book; if you can persuade him to lend it."

Godefroid was amazed at this woman's sound sense, for he had believed her to be animated solely by the spirit of charity. He knelt on one knee and kissed one of her beautiful hands, saying:

"Then you are Reason too!"

"In our work we have to be everything," said she, with the peculiar cheerfulness of a true saint.

There was a brief silence, broken by Godefroid, who exclaimed:

"Two thousand debtors, did you say, madame? Two thousand accounts! It is tremendous!"

"Two thousand accounts, which may lead, as I have told you, to our being repaid from the delicate honor of the borrowers. But there are three thousand more—families who will never make us any return but in thanks. Thus, as I have told you, we feel that it is necessary to keep books; and if your secrecy is above suspicion, you will be our financial oracle. We ought to keep a day-book, a ledger, a book of current expenses, and a cash-book. Of course, we have receipts, notes of hand, but it takes a great deal of time to look for them—— Here come the gentlemen."

Godefroid, at first serious and thoughtful, took little part in the conversation; he was bewildered by the revelation Madame de la Chanterie had just imparted to him in a way which showed that she meant it to be the reward of his zeal.

"Two thousand families indebted to us!" said he to himself. "Why, if they all cost as much as Monsieur Bernard will cost us, we must have millions sown broadcast in Paris!"

This reflection was one of the last promptings of the worldly spirit which was fast dying out in Godefroid. As he thought the matter over, he understood that the united fortunes of Madame de la Chanterie, of Messieurs Alain, Nicolas, Joseph, and Judge Popinot, with the gifts collected by the Abbé de Vèze, and the loans from the Mongenods, must have produced a considerable capital; also, that in twelve or fifteen years this capital, with the interest paid on it by those who had shown their gratitude, must have increased like a snowball, since the charitable holders took nothing from it. By degrees he began to see clearly how the immense affair was managed, and his wish to co-operate was increased.

At nine o'clock he was about to return on foot to the Boulevard du Mont-Parnasse; but Madame de la Chanterie, distrustful of so lonely a neighborhood, insisted on his taking a cab. As he got out of the vehicle, though the shutters were so closely fastened that not a gleam of light was visible, Godefroid heard the sounds of the instrument; and Auguste, who, no doubt, was watching for Godefroid's return, half opened the door on the landing, and said:

"Mamma would very much like to see you, and my grandfather begs you will take a cup of tea."

Godefroid went in and found the invalid transfigured by the pleasure of the music; her face beamed and her eyes sparkled like diamonds.

"I ought to have waited for you, to let you hear the first chords; but I flew at this little organ as a hungry man rushes on a banquet. But you have a soul to understand me, and I know I am forgiven."

Vanda made a sign to her son, who placed himself where he could press the pedal that supplied the interior of the instrument with wind; and, with her eyes raised to heaven like Saint Cecilia, the invalid, whose hands had for a time recovered their strength and agility, performed some variations on the prayer in *Mosè* which her son had bought for her. She had composed them in a few hours. Godefroid discerned in her a talent identical with that of Chopin. It was a soul manifesting itself by divine sounds in which sweet melancholy predominated.

Monsieur Bernard greeted Godefroid with a look expressing a sentiment long since in abeyance. If the tears had not been for ever dried up in the old man scorched by so many fierce sorrows, his eyes would at this moment have been wet.

The old lawyer was fingering his snuff-box and gazing at his daughter with unutterable rapture.

"To-morrow, madame," said Godefroid, when the music had ceased, "your fate will be sealed, for I have good news for you. The famous Halpersohn will come at three o'clock. —And he has promised," he added in Monsieur Bernard's ear, "to tell me the truth."

The old man rose, and taking Godefroid by the hand, led him into a corner of the room near the fireplace. He was trembling.

"What a night lies before me! It is the final sentence!" said he in a whisper. "My daughter will be cured or condemned!"

"Take courage," said Godefroid, "and after tea come to my rooms."

) "Cease playing, my child," said Monsieur Bernard; "you will bring on an attack. Such an expenditure of strength will be followed by a reaction."

He made Auguste remove the instrument, and brought his daughter her cup of tea with the coaxing ways of a nurse who wants to anticipate the impatience of a baby.

"And what is this doctor like?" asked she, already diverted by the prospect of seeing a stranger.

Vanda, like all prisoners, was consumed by curiosity. When the physical symptoms of her complaint gave her some respite, they seemed to develop in her mind, and then she had the strangest whims and violent caprices. She wanted to see Rossini, and cried because her father, who could, she imagined, do everything, assured her he could not bring him.

Godefroid gave her a minute description of the Jewish physician and his consulting-room, for she knew nothing of the steps taken by her father. Monsieur Bernard had enjoined silence on his grandson as to his visits to Halpersohn; he had so much feared to excite hopes which might not be realized. Vanda seemed to hang on the words that fell from Godefroid's lips; she was spellbound and almost crazy, so ardent did her desire become to see the strange Pole.

"Poland has produced many singular and mysterious figures," said the old lawyer. "Just now, for instance, besides this doctor there is Hoëné Vronski the mathematician and seer, Mickievicz the poet, the inspired Tovianski, and Chopin with his superhuman talent. Great national agitations always produce these crippled giants."

"Oh, my dear papa, what a man you are.! If you were to write down all that we hear you say simply to entertain me, you would make a fortune! For, would you believe me, monsieur, my kind old father invents tales for me when I have no more novels to read, and so sends me to sleep. His voice lulls me, and he often soothes my pain with his cleverness. Who will ever repay him?—Auguste, my dear boy, you ought to kiss your grandfather's footprints for me."

The youth looked at his mother with his fine eyes full of tears; and that look, overflowing with long repressed compassion, was a poem in itself. Godefroid rose, took Auguste's hand, and pressed it warmly.

"God has given you two angels for your companions, madame!" he exclaimed.

"Indeed I know it. And I blame myself for so often pro-

voking them.   Come, dear Auguste, and kiss your mother.
He is a son, monsieur, of whom any mother would be proud.
He is as good as gold, candid—a soul without sin; but a
rather too impassioned creature, like his mamma.   God has
nailed me to my bed to preserve me perhaps from the follies
women commit—when they have too much heart!" she ended
with a smile.

Godefroid smiled in reply and bowed good-night.

"Good-night, monsieur; and be sure to thank your friend,
for he has made a poor cripple very happy."

"Monsieur," said Godefroid when he was in his rooms, alone
with Monsieur Bernard, who had followed him, "I think I
may promise you that you shall not be robbed by those three
sharpers.   I can get the required sum, but you must place the
papers proving the loan in my hands.   If I am to do anything
more, you should allow me to have your book—not to read
myself, for I am not learned enough to judge of it, but to
be read by an old lawyer I know, a man of unimpeachable in-
tegrity, who will undertake, according to the character of the
work, to find a respectable firm with whom you may deal on
equitable terms.—On this, however, I do not insist.

"Meanwhile, here are five hundred francs," he went on,
offering a note to the astonished lawyer, "to supply your more
pressing wants.   I ask for no receipt; you will be indebted
on no evidence but that of your conscience, and your conscience may lie silent till you have to some extent recovered
yourself.—I will settle with Halpersohn."

"But who are you?" asked the old man, sinking on to a
chair.

"I," replied Godefroid, "am nobody; but I serve certain
powerful persons to whom your necessities are now made
known, and who take an interest in you.—Ask no more."

"And what motive can these persons have——?"

"Religion, monsieur," replied Godefroid.

"Is it possible?—Religion!"

"Yes, the Catholic, Apostolic, Roman religion."

"Then you are of the Order of Jesus?"

"No, monsieur," said Godefroid.   "Be perfectly easy.   No

one has any design on you beyond that of helping you and restoring your family to comfort."

"Can philanthropy then wear any guise but that of vanity?"

"Nay, monsieur, do not insult holy Catholic Charity, the virtue described by Saint Paul!" cried Godefroid eagerly.

At this reply Monsieur Bernard began to stride up and down the room.

"I accept!" he suddenly said. "And I have but one way of showing my gratitude—that is, by intrusting you with my work. The notes and quotations are unnecessary to a lawyer; and I have, as I told you, two months' work before me yet in copying them out.—To-morrow then," and he shook hands with Godefroid.

"Can I have effected a conversion?" thought Godefroid, struck by the new expression he saw on the old man's face as he had last spoken.

Next day, at three o'clock, a hackney coach stopped at the door, and out stepped Halpersohn, buried in a vast bearskin coat. The cold had increased in the course of the night, and the thermometer stood at ten degrees below freezing.

The Jewish doctor narrowly though furtively examined the room in which his visitor of yesterday received him, and Godefroid detected a gleam of suspicion sparkling in his eye like the point of a dagger. This swift flash of doubt gave Godefroid an internal chill; he began to think that this man would be merciless in his money dealings; and it is so natural to think of genius as allied to goodness, that this gave him an impulse of disgust.

"Monsieur," said he, "I perceive that the plainness of my lodgings arouses your uneasiness; so you will not be surprised at my manner of proceeding. Here are your two hundred francs, and here, you see, are three notes for a thousand francs each"—and he drew out the notes which Madame de la Chanterie had given him to redeem Monsieur Bernard's manuscript. "If you have any further doubts as to my solvency, I may refer you, as a guarantee for the carrying out of my pledge, to Messrs. Mongenod the bankers, Rue de la Victoire."

"I know them," said Halpersohn, slipping the ten gold pieces into his pocket.

"And he will go there!" thought Godefroid.

"And where does the sick lady live?" asked the doctor, rising, as a man who knows the value of time.

"Come this way, monsieur," said Godefroid, going first to show him the way.

The Jew cast a shrewd and scrutinizing glance on the rooms he went through, for he had the eye of a spy; and he was able to see the misery of poverty through the door into Monsieur Bernard's bedroom, for, unluckily, Monsieur Bernard had just been putting on the dress in which he always showed himself to his daughter, and in his haste to admit his visitors he left the door of his kennel ajar.

He bowed with dignity to Halpersohn, and softly opened his daughter's bedroom door.

"Vanda, my dear, here is the doctor," he said.

He stood aside to let Halpersohn pass, still wrapped in his furs.

The Jew was surprised at the splendor of this room, which in this part of the town seemed anomalous; but his astonishment was of no long duration, for he had often seen in the houses of German and Polish Jews a similar discrepancy between the display of extreme penury and concealed wealth. While walking from the door to the bed he never took his eyes off the sufferer; and when he stood by her side, he said to her in Polish:

"Are you a Pole?"

"I am not; my mother was."

"Whom did your grandfather, General Tarlovski, marry?"

"A Pole."

"Of what province?"

"A Sobolevska of Pinsk."

"Good.—And this gentleman is your father?"

"Yes, monsieur."

"Monsieur," said Halpersohn, "is your wife——"

"She is dead," replied Monsieur Bernard.

"Was she excessively fair?" said Halpersohn, with some impatience at the interruption.

"Here is a portrait of her," replied Monsieur Bernard, taking down a handsome frame containing several good miniatures.

Halpersohn was feeling the invalid's head and hair, while he looked at the portrait of Vanda Tarlovska *née* Comtesse Sobolevska.

"Tell me the symptoms of the patient's illness." And he seated himself in the armchair, gazing steadily at Vanda during twenty minutes, while the father and daughter spoke by turns.

"And how old is the lady?"

"Eight-and-thirty."

"Very good!" he said as he rose. "Well, I undertake to cure her. I cannot promise to give her the use of her legs, but she can be cured. Only, she must be placed in a private hospital in my part of the town."

"But, monsieur, my daughter cannot be moved——"

"I will answer for her life," said Halpersohn sententiously. "But I answer for her only on those conditions.—Do you know she will exchange her present symptoms for another horrible form of disease, which will last for a year perhaps, or six months at the very least?—You can come to see her, as you are her father."

"And it is certain?" asked Monsieur Bernard.

"Certain," repeated the Jew. "Your daughter has a vicious humor, a national disorder, in her blood, and it must be brought out. When you bring her, carry her to the Rue Basse-Saint-Pierre at Chaillot—Dr. Halpersohn's private hospital."

"But how?"

"On a stretcher, as the sick people are always carried to a hospital."

"But it will kill her to be moved."

"No."

And Halpersohn, as he spoke this curt *No,* was at the door, where Godefroid met him on the landing.

The Jew, who was suffocating with heat, said in his ear:

"The charge will be fifteen francs a day, besides the thousand crowns; three months paid in advance."

"Very good, monsieur.—And," asked Godefroid, standing on the step of the cab into which the doctor had hurried, "you answer for the cure?"

"Positively," said the Pole. "Are you in love with the lady?"

"No," said Godefroid.

"You must not repeat what I am about to tell you, for I am saying it only to prove to you that I am sure of the cure; but if you say anything about it, you will be the death of the woman——"

Godefroid replied only by a gesture.

"For seventeen years she has been suffering from the disease known as *Plica Polonica,* which can produce all these torments; I have seen the most dreadful cases. Now I am the only man living who knows how to bring out the *Plica* in such a form as to be curable, for not every one gets over it. You see, monsieur, that I am really very liberal. If this were some great lady—a Baronne de Nucingen or any other wife or daughter of some modern Crœsus—I should get a hundred— two hundred thousand francs for this cure—whatever I might like to ask!—However, that is a minor misfortune."

"And moving her?"

"Oh, she will seem to be dying, but she will not die of it! She may live a hundred years when once she is cured.—Now, Jacques, quick—Rue Monsieur, and make haste!" said he to the driver.

He left Godefroid standing in the street, where he gazed in bewilderment after the retreating cab.

"Who on earth is that queer-looking man dressed in bearskin?" asked Madame Vauthier, whom nothing could escape. "Is it true, as the hackney coachman said, that he is the most famous doctor in Paris?"

"And what can that matter to you, Mother Vauthier?"

"Oh, not at all," said she with a sour face.

"You made a great mistake in not siding with me," said Godefroid, as he slowly went into the house. "You would have done better than by sticking to Monsieur Barbet and Monsieur Métivier; you will get nothing out of them."

"And am I on their side?" retorted she with a shrug. "Monsieur Barbet is my landlord, that is all."

It took two days to persuade Monsieur Bernard to part from his daughter and carry her to Chaillot. Godefroid and the old lawyer walked all the way, one on each side of the stretcher, screened in with striped blue-and-white tickings, on which the precious patient lay, almost tied down to the mattress, so greatly did her father fear the convulsions of a nervous attack. However, having set out at three o'clock, the procession reached the private hospital at five, when it was dusk. Godefroid paid the four hundred and fifty francs demanded for the three months' board, and took a receipt for it; then, when he went down to pay the two porters, Monsieur Bernard joined him and took from under the mattress a very voluminous sealed packet, which he handed to Godefroid.

"One of these men will fetch you a cab," said he, "for you cannot carry those four volumes very far. This is my book; place it in my censor's hands; I will leave it with him for a week. I shall remain at least a week in this neighborhood, for I cannot abandon my daughter to her fate. I know my grandson; he can mind the house, especially with you to help him; and I commend him to your care. If I were myself what once I was, I would ask you my critic's name; for if he was once a magistrate, there were few whom I did not know——"

"It is no mystery," said Godefroid, interrupting Monsieur Bernard. "Since you show such entire confidence in me, I may tell you that the reader is the President Lecamus de Tresnes."

"Oh, of the Supreme Court in Paris. Take it—by all means. He is one of the noblest men of our time. He and the late Judge Popinot, the judge of the Lower Court, were lawyers worthy of the best days of the old Parlements. All my fears, if I had any, must vanish.—And where does he live? I should like to go and thank him when he has taken so much trouble."

"You will find him in the Rue Chanoinesse, under the name of Monsieur Nicolas. I am just going there.—But your agreement with those rascals?"

"Auguste will give it you," said the old man, going back into the hospital.

A cab was found on the Quai de Billy and brought by one of the men; Godefroid got in and stimulated the driver by the promise of drink money if he drove quickly to the Rue Chanoinesse, where he intended to dine.

Half an hour after Vanda's removal, three men, dressed in black, were let in by Madame Vauthier at the door in the Rue Notre-Dame des Champs, where they had been waiting, no doubt, till the coast should be clear. They went upstairs under the guidance of the Judas in petticoats, and gently knocked at Monsieur Bernard's door. As it happened to be a Thursday, the young collegian was at home. He opened the door, and three men slipped like shadows into the outer room.

"What do you want, gentlemen?" asked the youth.

"This is Monsieur Bernard's—that is to say, Monsieur le Baron——?"

"But what do you want here?"

"Oh, you know that pretty well, young man, for your grandfather has just gone off with a closed litter, I am told.—Well, that does not surprise us; he shows his wisdom. I am a bailiff, and I have come to seize everything here. On Monday last you were summoned to pay three thousand francs and the expenses to Monsieur Métivier, under penalty of imprisonment; and as a man who has grown onions knows the smell of chives, the debtor has taken the key of the fields rather than wait for that of the lock-up. However, if we cannot secure him, we can get a wing or a leg of his gorgeous furniture—

for we know all about it, young man, and we are going to make
an official report."

"Here are some stamped papers that your grandpapa would
never take," said the widow Vauthier, shoving three writs
into Auguste's hand.

"Stay here, ma'am; we will put you in possession. The
law gives you forty sous a day; it is not to be sneezed at."

"Ah, ha! Then I shall see what there is in the grand bedroom!" cried Madame Vauthier.

"You shall not go into my mother's room!" cried the lad
in a fury, as he flung himself between the door and the three
men in black.

On a sign from their leader, the two men and a lawyer's
clerk who came in seized Auguste.

"No resistance, young man; you are not master here. We
shall draw up a charge, and you will spend the night in the
lock-up."

At this dreadful threat, Auguste melted into tears.

"Oh, what a mercy," cried he, "that mamma is gone! This
would have killed her!"

The men and the bailiff now held a sort of council with
the widow Vauthier. Auguste understood, though they talked
in a low voice, that what they chiefly wanted was to seize his
grandfather's manuscripts, so he opened the bedroom door.

"Walk in then, gentlemen," said he, "but spoil nothing.
You will be paid to-morrow morning." Then, still in tears, he
went into his own squalid room, snatched up all his grandfather's notes, and stuffed them into the stove, where he knew
that there was not a spark of fire.

The thing was done so promptly, that the bailiff, though
he was keen and cunning, and worthy of his employers Barbet
and Métivier, found the boy in tears on a chair when he rushed
into the room, having concluded that the manuscripts would
not be in the ante-room. Though books and manuscripts may
not legally be seized for debt, the lien signed by the old lawyer
in this case justified the proceeding. Still, it would have been
easy to find means of delaying the distraint, as Monsieur

Bernard would certainly have known.   Hence the necessity for acting with cunning.

The widow Vauthier had been an invaluable ally to her landlord by failing to serve his notices on her lodger; her plan was to throw them on him when entering at the heels of the officers of justice; or, if necessary, to declare to Monsieur Bernard that she had supposed them to be intended for the two writers who had been absent for two days.

The inventory of the goods took above an hour to make out, for the bailiff would omit nothing, and regarded the value as sufficient to pay off the debts.

As soon as the officers were gone, the poor youth took the writs and hurried away to find his grandfather at Halpersohn's hospital; for, as the bailiff assured him that Madame Vauthier was responsible for everything under heavy penalties, he could leave the place without fear.

The idea of his grandfather's being taken to prison for debt drove the poor boy absolutely mad—mad in the way in which the young are mad; that is to say, a victim to the dangerous and fatal excitement in which every energy of youth is in a ferment and may lead to the worst as to the most heroic actions.

When poor Auguste reached the Rue Basse-Saint-Pierre, the doorkeeper told him that he did not know what had become of the father of the patient brought in at five o'clock, but that by Monsieur Halpersohn's orders no one—not even her father—was to be allowed to see the lady for a week, or it might endanger her life.

This reply put a climax to Auguste's desperation. He went back again to the Boulevard du Mont-Parnasse, revolving the most extravagant schemes as he went. He got home by about half-past eight, almost starving, so exhausted by hunger, and grief, that he accepted when Madame Vauthier invited him to share her supper, consisting of a stew of mutton and potatoes. The poor boy dropped half dead into a chair in the dreadful woman's room.

Encouraged by the old woman's coaxing and insinuating

words, he answered a few cunningly arranged questions about Godefroid, and gave her to understand that it was he who would pay off his grandfather's debts on the morrow, and that to him they owed the improvement that had taken place in their prospects during the past week. The widow listened to all this with an affectation of doubt, plying Auguste with a few glasses of wine.

At ten o'clock the wheels of a cab were heard to stop in front of the house, and the woman exclaimed:

"Oh, there is Monsieur Godefroid!"

Auguste took the key of his rooms and went upstairs to see the kind friend of the family; but he found Godefroid so entirely unlike himself, that he hesitated to speak till the thought of his grandfather's danger spurred the generous youth.

This is what had happened in the Rue Chanoinesse, and had caused Godefroid's stern expression of countenance.

The neophyte, arriving in good time, had found Madame de la Chanterie and her adherents in the drawing-room, and he had taken Monsieur Nicolas aside to deliver to him the *Spirit of the Modern Laws.* Monsieur Nicolas at once carried the sealed parcel to his room, and came down to dinner. Then, after chatting during the first part of the evening, he went up again, intending to begin reading the work.

Godefroid was greatly surprised when, a few minutes after, Manon came from the old judge to beg him to go up to speak with him. Following Manon, he was led to Monsieur Nicolas' room; but he could pay no attention to its details, so greatly was he startled by the evident distress of a man usually so placid and firm.

"Did you know," said Monsieur Nicolas, quite the Judge again, "the name of the author of this work?"

"Monsieur Bernard," said Godefroid. "I know him only by that name. I did not open the parcel——"

"True," said Monsieur Nicolas. "I broke the seals myself. —And you made no inquiry as to his previous history?"

"No. I know that he married for love the daughter of General Tarlovski, that his daughter is named Vanda after her mother, and his grandson Auguste. And the portrait I saw of Monsieur Bernard is, I believe, in the dress of a Presiding Judge—a red gown."

"Look here!" said Monsieur Nicolas, and held out the title of the work in Auguste's handwriting, and in the following form:

THE SPIRIT

OF THE MODERN LAWS

BY

M. BERNARD-JEAN-BAPTISTE MACLOUD

BARON BOURLAC

Formerly Attorney-General to the High Court of Justice at Rouen
Commander of the Legion of Honor.

"Oh! The man who condemned Madame, her daughter, and the Chevalier du Vissard!" said Godefroid in a choked voice.

His knees gave way, and the neophyte dropped on to a chair.

"What a beginning!" he murmured.

"This, my dear Godefroid, is a business that comes home to us all. You have done your part; we must deal with it now! I beg you to do nothing further of any kind; go and fetch whatever you left in your rooms; and not a word!—In fact, absolute silence. Tell Baron Bourlac to apply to me. Between this and then, we shall have decided how it will be best to act in such circumstances."

Godefroid went downstairs, called a hackney cab, and hurried back to the Boulevard du Mont-Parnasse, filled with horror as he thought of the examination and trials at Caen, of the hideous drama that ended on the scaffold, and of Madame de la Chanterie's sojourn in Bicêtre. He understood the neg-

13

lect into which this lawyer, almost a second Fouquier-Tinville, had fallen in his old age, and the reasons why he so carefully concealed his name.

"I hope Monsieur Nicolas will take some terrible revenge for poor Madame de la Chanterie!"

He had just thought out this not very Christian wish, when he saw Auguste.

"What do you want of me?" asked Godefroid.

"My dear sir, a misfortune has befallen us which is turning my brain! Some scoundrels have been here to take possession of everything belonging to my mother, and they are hunting for my grandfather to put him into prison. But it is not by reason of these disasters that I turn to you for help," said the lad with Roman pride; "it is to beg you to do me such a service as you would do to a condemned criminal——"

"Speak," said Godefroid.

"They wanted to get hold of my grandfather's manuscripts; and as I believe he placed the work in your hands, I want to beg you to take the notes, for the woman will not allow me to remove a thing.—Put them with the volumes, and then——"

"Very well," said Godefroid, "make haste and fetch them."

While the lad went off, to return immediately, Godefroid reflected that the poor boy was guilty of no crime, that he must not break his heart by telling him about his grandfather, or the desertion which was the punishment in his sad old age of the passions of his political career; he took the packet not unkindly.

"What is your mother's name?" he asked.

"My mother, monsieur, is the Baronne de Mergi. My father was the son of the Presiding Judge of the Supreme Court at Rouen."

"Ah!" said Godefroid, "so your grandfather married his daughter to the son of the famous Judge Mergi?"

"Yes, monsieur."

"Leave me, my little friend," said Godefroid.

He went out on to the landing with the young Baron de Mergi, and called Madame Vauthier.

"Mother Vauthier," said he, "you can relet my rooms; I am never coming back again."

And he went down to the cab.

"Have you intrusted anything to that gentleman?" asked the widow of Auguste.

"Yes," said the lad.

"You're a pretty fool. He is one of your enemies' agents. He has been at the bottom of it all, you may be sure. It is proof enough that the trick has turned out all right that he never means to come back. He told me I could let his rooms."

Auguste flew out, and down the boulevard, running after the cab, and at last succeeded in stopping it by his shouts and cries.

"What is it?" asked Godefroid.

"My grandfather's manuscripts?"

"Tell him to apply for them to Monsieur Nicolas."

The lad took this reply as the cruel jest of a thief who has no shame left; he sat down in the snow as he saw the cab set off again at a brisk trot.

He rose in a fever of fierce energy and went home to bed, worn out with rushing about Paris, and quite heart-broken.

Next morning, Auguste de Mergi awoke to find himself alone in the rooms where yesterday his mother and his grandfather had been with him, and he went through all the miseries of his position, of which he fully understood the extent. The utter desertion of the place, hitherto so amply filled, where every minute had brought with it a duty and an occupation, was so painful to him, that he went down to ask the widow Vauthier whether his grandfather had come in during the night or early morning; for he himself had slept very late, and he supposed that if the Baron Bourlac had come home the woman would have warned him against his pursuers. She replied, with a sneer, that he must know full well where to look for his grandfather; for if he had not come in, it was evident that he had taken up his abode in the "Château de Clichy." This impudent irony from the woman who, the day before, had cajoled him so effectually, again drove the poor boy to frenzy, and he flew to the private hospital in the Rue Basse-Saint-Pierre, in despair, as he thought of his grandfather in prison.

Baron Bourlac had hung about all night in front of the hospital which he was forbidden to enter, or close to the house of Doctor Halpersohn, whom he naturally wished to call to account for this conduct. The doctor did not get home till two in the morning. The old man, who, at half-past one, had been at the doctor's door, had just gone off to walk in the Champs-Élysées, and when he returned at half-past two the gatekeeper told him that Monsieur Halpersohn was now in bed and asleep, and was on no account to be disturbed.

Here, alone, at half-past two in the morning, the unhappy father, in utter despair, paced the quay, and under the trees, loaded with frost, of the sidewalks of the Cours-la-Reine, waiting for the day.

At nine o'clock he presented himself at the doctor's, and asked him why he thus kept his daughter under lock and key.

"Monsieur," said Halpersohn, "I yesterday made myself answerable for your daughter's recovery; and at this moment I am responsible for her life, and you must understand that in such a case I must have sovereign authority. I may tell you that your daughter yesterday took a remedy which will give her the *Plica,* that till the disease is brought out the lady must remain invisible. I will not allow myself to lose my patient or you to lose your daughter by exposing her to any excitement, any error of treatment; if you really insist on seeing her, I shall demand a consultation of three medical men to protect myself against any responsibility, as the patient might die."

The old man, exhausted with fatigue, had dropped on to a chair; he quickly rose, however, saying:

"Forgive me, monsieur; I have spent the night in mortal anguish, for you cannot imagine how much I love my daughter, whom I have nursed for fifteen years between life and death, and this week of waiting is torture to me!"

The Baron left Halpersohn's study, tottering like a drunken man, the doctor giving him his arm to the top of the stairs.

About an hour later, he saw Auguste de Mergi walk into his room. On questioning the lodge-keeper of the private hospital, the poor lad had just heard that the father of the lady admitted the day before had called again in the evening, had asked for her, and had spoken of going early in the day to Doctor Halpersohn, who, no doubt, would know something about him. At the moment when Auguste de Mergi appeared in the doctor's room, Halpersohn was breakfasting off a cup of chocolate and a glass of water, all on a small round table; he did not disturb himself for the youth, but went on soaking his strip of bread in the chocolate; for he ate nothing but a roll, cut into four with an accuracy that argued some skill as an operator. Halpersohn had, in fact, practised surgery in the course of his travels.

"Well, young man," said he as Vanda's son came in, "you too have come to require me to account for your mother?"

"Yes, monsieur," said Auguste.

The young fellow had come forward as far as the large table, and his eye was immediately caught by several bank-notes lying among the little piles of gold pieces. In the position in which the unhappy boy found himself, the temptation was stronger than his principles, well grounded as they were. He saw before him the means of rescuing his grandfather, and saving the fruits of twenty years' labor imperiled by avaricious speculators. He fell. The fascination was as swift as thought, and justified itself by an idea of self-immolation that smiled on the boy. He said to himself:

"I shall be done for, but I shall save my mother and my grandfather."

Under this stress of antagonism between his reason and the impulse to crime, he acquired, as madmen do, a strange and fleeting dexterity, and instead of asking after his grandfather, he listened and agreed to all the doctor was saying.

Halpersohn, like all acute observers, had understood the whole past history of the father, the daughter, and her son.

He had scented or guessed the facts which Madame de Mergi's conversation had confirmed, and he felt in consequence a sort of benevolence towards his new clients;—as to respect or admiration, he was incapable of them.

"Well, my dear boy," said he familiarly, "I am keeping your mother to restore her to you young, handsome, and in good health. Hers is one of those rare diseases which doctors find very interesting; and besides, she is, through her mother, a fellow-countrywoman of mine. You and your grandfather must be brave enough to live without seeing her for a fortnight, and madame——?"

"La Baronne de Mergi."

"If she is a Baroness, you are Baron——?" asked Halpersohn.

At this moment the theft was effected. While the doctor was looking at his bread, heavy with chocolate, Auguste snatched up four folded notes, and had slipped them into his trousers pocket, affecting to keep his hand there out of sheer embarrassment.

"Yes, monsieur, I am a Baron. So too is my grandfather; he was public prosecutor at the time of the Restoration."

"You blush, young man. You need not blush because you are a Baron and poor—it is a very common case."

"And who told you, monsieur, that we are poor?"

"Well, your grandfather told me that he had spent the night in the Champs-Élysées; and though I know no palace where there is so fine a vault overhead as that which was glittering at two o'clock this morning, it was cold, I can tell you, in the palace where your grandfather was taking his airing. A man does not go to the Hôtel *de la belle-Étoile* by preference."

"Has my grandfather been here?" cried Auguste, seizing the opportunity to beat a retreat. "Thank you, monsieur. I will come again, with your permission, for news of my mother."

As soon as he got out, the young Baron went off to the bailiff's office, taking a hackney cab to get there the sooner. The man gave up the agreement, and the bill of costs duly receipted, and then desired the young man to take one of the clerks with him to release the person in charge from her functions.

"And as Messrs. Barbét and Métivier live in your part of the town," added he, "my boy will take them the money and desire them to restore you the deed of lien on the property."

Auguste, who understood nothing of these phrases and formalities, submitted. He received seven hundred francs in silver, the change out of his four thousand-franc notes, and went off in the clerk's company. He got into the cab in a state of indescribable bewilderment, for the end being achieved, remorse was making itself felt; he saw himself disgraced and cursed by his grandfather, whose austerity was well known to him; and he believed that his mother would die of grief if she heard of his guilt. All nature had changed before his eyes. He was lost; he no longer saw the snow, the houses looked like ghosts.

No sooner was he at home than the young Baron decided on his course of action, and it was certainly that of an honest man. He went into his mother's room and took the diamond snuff-box given to his grandfather by the Emperor to send it with the seven hundred francs to Doctor Halpersohn with the following letter, which required several rough copies:

"MONSIEUR,—The fruits of twenty years' labor—my grandfather's work—were about to be absorbed by some moneylenders, who threatened him with imprisonment. Three thousand three hundred francs were enough to save him; and seeing so much gold on your table, I could not resist the idea of seeing my parent free by thus making good to him the earnings of his long toil. I borrowed from you, without your leave, four thousand francs; but as only three thousand three hundred francs were needed, I send you the remaining seven hundred, and with them a snuff-box set with diamonds, given by the Emperor to my grandfather; this will, I hope, indemnify you.

"If you should not after this believe that I, who shall all

my life regard you as my benefactor, am a man of honor, if
you will at any rate preserve silence as to an action so unjusti-
able in any other circumstances, you will have saved my grandfather as you will save my mother, and I shall be for life your
devoted slave.

"AUGUSTE DE MERGI."

At about half-past two, Auguste, who had walked to the
Champs-Élysées, sent a messenger on to deliver at Doctor
Halpersohn's door a sealed box containing ten louis, a five-
hundred-franc note, and the snuff-box; then he slowly went
home across the Pont d'Iéna by the Invalides and the Boulevards, trusting to Doctor Halpersohn's generosity.

The physician, who had at once discovered the theft, had
meanwhile changed his views as to his clients. He supposed
that the old man had come to rob him, and, not having succeeded, had sent this boy. He put no credence in the rank
and titles they had assumed, and went off at once to the public
prosecutor's office to state his case, and desire that immediate
steps should be taken for the prosecution.

The prudence of the law rarely allows of such rapid proceedings as the complaining parties would wish; but, at about
three in the afternoon, a police officer, followed by some detec-
tives, who affected to be lounging on the boulevard, was cate-
chizing Madame Vauthier as to her lodgers, and the widow
quite unconsciously was confirming the constable's suspicions.

Népomucène, scenting the policeman, thought that it was
the old man they wanted; and as he was very fond of Monsieur Auguste, he hurried out to meet Monsieur Bernard,
whom he intercepted in the Avenue de l'Observatoire.

"Make your escape, monsieur," cried he. "They have come
to take you. The bailiffs were in yesterday and laid hands
on everything. Mother Vauthier, who has hidden some
stamped papers of yours, said you would be in Clichy by last
night or this morning. There, do you see those sneaks?"

The old judge recognized the men as bailiffs, and he understood everything.

"And Monsieur Godefroid?" he asked.

"Gone, never to come back. Mother Vauthier says he was a spy for your enemies."

Monsieur Bourlac determined that he would go at once to Barbet, and in a quarter of an hour he was there; the old bookseller lived in the Rue Sainte-Catherine-d'Enfer.

"Oh, you have come yourself to fetch your agreement," said the publisher, bowing to his victim. "Here it is," and, to the Baron's great amazement, he handed him the document, which the old lawyer took, saying:

"I do not understand——"

"Then it was not you who paid up?" said Barbet.

"Are you paid?"

"Your grandson carried the money to the bailiff this morning."

"And is it true that you took possession of my goods yesterday?"

"Have you not been home for two days?" said Barbet. "Still, a retired public prosecutor must know what it is to be threatened with imprisonment for debt!"

On this the Baron bowed coldly to Barbet, and returned home, supposing that the authorities had in fact come in search of the authors living on the first floor. He walked slowly, absorbed in vague apprehensions, for Népomucène's warning seemed to him more and more inexplicable. Could Godefroid have betrayed him? He mechanically turned down the Rue Notre-Dame des Champs, and went in by the back door, which happened to be open, running against Népomucène.

"Oh, monsieur, make haste, come on; they are taking Monsieur Auguste to prison; they caught him on the boulevard; it was him they were hunting—they have been questioning him——"

The old man, with a spring like a tiger's, rushed through the house and garden and out on to the boulevard, as swift as an arrow, and was just in time to see his grandson get into a hackney coach between three men.

"Auguste," he cried, "what is the meaning of this?"

The youth burst into tears, and turned faint.

"Monsieur," said he to the police officer, whose scarf struck his eye, "I am Baron Bourlac, formerly a public prosecutor; for pity's sake, explain the matter."

"Monsieur, if you are Baron Bourlac, you will understand it in two words. I have just questioned this young man, and he has unfortunately confessed——"

"What?"

"A theft of four thousand francs from Doctor Halpersohn."

"Auguste! Is it possible?"

"Grandpapa, I have sent him your diamond snuff-box as a guarantee. I wanted to save you from the disgrace of imprisonment."

"Wretched boy, what have you done?" cried the Baron. "The diamonds are false; I sold the real stones three years ago."

The police officer and his clerk looked at each other with strange meaning. This glance, full of suggestions, was seen by the Baron, and fell like a thunderbolt.

"Monsieur," said he to the officer, "be quite easy; I will go and see the public prosecutor; you can testify to the delusion in which I have kept my daughter and my grandson. You must do your duty, but in the name of humanity, send my grandson to a cell by himself.—I will go to prison.—Where are you taking him?"

"Are you Baron Bourlac?" said the constable.

"Oh! Monsieur——"

"Because the public prosecutor, the examining judge, and I myself could not believe that such men as you and your grandson could be guilty; like the doctor, we concluded that some swindlers had borrowed your names."

He took the Baron aside and said:

"Were you at Doctor Halpersohn's house this morning?"

"Yes, monsieur."

"And your grandson too, about half-an-hour later?"

"I know nothing about that; I have this instant come in, and I have not seen my grandson since yesterday."

"The writs he showed me and the warrant for arrest explain everything," said the police agent. "I know his motive for the crime. I ought indeed to arrest you, monsieur, as abetting your grandson, for your replies confirm the facts alleged by the complainant; but the notices served on you, and which I return to you," he added, holding out a packet of stamped papers which he had in his hand, "certainly prove you to be Baron Bourlac. At the same time, you must be prepared to be called up before Monsieur Marest, the examining judge in this case. I believe I am right in relaxing the usual rule in consideration of your past dignity.

"As to your grandson, I will speak of him to the public prosecutor as soon as I go in, and we will show every possible consideration for the grandson of a retired judge, and the victim of a youthful error. Still, there is the indictment, the accused has confessed; I have sent in my report, and have a warrant for his imprisonment; I cannot help myself. As to the place of detention, your grandson will be taken to the Conciergerie."

"Thank you, monsieur," said the miserable Bourlac. He fell senseless on the snow, and tumbled into one of the rain-water cisterns, which at that time divided the trees on the boulevard.

The police officer called for help, and Népomucène hurried out with Madame Vauthier. The old man was carried indoors, and the woman begged the police constable, as he went by the Rue d'Enfer, to send Doctor Berton as quickly as possible.

"What is the matter with my grandfather?" asked poor Auguste.

"He is crazed, sir. That is what comes of thieving!"

Auguste made a rush as though to crack his skull; but the two men held him back.

"Come, come, young man. Take it quietly," said the officer. "Be calm. You have done wrong, but it is not irremediable."

"But pray, monsieur, tell the woman that my grandfather has probably not touched food for these twenty-four hours."

"Oh, poor creatures!" said the officer to himself.

He stopped the coach, which had started, and said a word in his clerk's ear; the man ran off to speak to old Vauthier, and then returned at once.

Monsieur Berton was of opinion that Monsieur Bernard—for he knew him by no other name—was suffering from an attack of high fever; but when Madame Vauthier had told him of all the events that had led up to it in the way in which a housekeeper tells a story, the doctor thought it necessary to report the whole business next day to Monsieur Alain at the Church of Saint-Jacques du Haut-Pas, and Monsieur Alain sent a pencil note by messenger to Monsieur Nicolas, Rue Chanoinesse.

Godefroid, on reaching home the night before, had given the notes on the book to Monsieur Nicolas, who spent the greater part of the night in reading the first volume of Baron Bourlac's work.

On the following day Madame de la Chanterie told Godefroid that if his determination still held good, he might begin on his work at once.

Godefroid, initiated by her into the financial secrets of the Society, worked for seven or eight hours a day, and for several months, under the supervision of Frédéric Mongenod, who came every Sunday to look through the work, and who praised him for the way in which it was done.

"You are a valuable acquisition for the saints among whom you live," said the banker when all the accounts were clearly set forth and balanced. "Two or three hours a day will now be enough to keep the accounts in order, and during the rest of your time you can help them, if you still feel the vocation as you did six months since."

This was in the month of July 1838. During the time that had elapsed since the affair of the Boulevard du Mont-Parnasse, Godefroid, eager to prove himself worthy of his companions, had never asked a single question as to Baron Bourlac; for, as he had not heard a word, nor found anything in the account-books that bore on the matter, he suspected that the silence that was preserved with regard to the two men who had been so ruthless to Madame de la Chanterie, was intended as a test to which he was being put, or perhaps as proof that the noble lady's friends had avenged her.

But, two months later, in the course of a walk one day, he went as far as the Boulevard du Mont-Parnasse, managed to meet Madame Vauthier, and asked her for some news of the Bernard family.

"Who can tell, my dear Monsieur Godefroid, what has become of those people. Two days after your expedition—for it was you, you cunning dog, who blabbed to my landlord—somebody came who took that old swaggerer off my hands. Then, in four-and-twenty hours, everything was cleared out —not a stick left, nor a word said—perfect strangers to me, and they told me nothing. I believe he packed himself off to Algiers with his precious grandson; for Népomucène, who was very devoted to that young thief—he is no better than he should be himself—did not find him in the Conciergerie, and he alone knows where they are, and the scamp has gone off and left me. You bring up these wretched foundlings, and this is the reward you get; they leave you high and dry. I have not been able to find any one to take his place, and as the neighborhood is very crowded, and the house is full, I am worked to death."

And Godefroid would never have known anything more of Baron Bourlac but for the conclusion of the adventure, which came about through one of the chance meetings which occur in Paris.

In the month of September, Godefroid was walking down the Champs-Élysées, when, as he passed the end of the Rue Marbeuf, he remembered Doctor Halpersohn.

"I ought to call on him," thought he, "and ask if he cured Bourlac's daughter. What a voice, what a gift she had! She wanted to dedicate herself to God!"

As he got to the Rond-Point, Godefroid crossed the road hurriedly to avoid the carriages that came quickly down the grand avenue, and he ran up against a youth who had a young-looking woman on his arm.

"Take care!" cried the young man. "Are you blind?"

"Why, it is you!" cried Godefroid, recognizing Auguste de Mergi.

Auguste was so well dressed, so handsome, so smart, so proud of the lady he was escorting, that, but for the memories that rushed on his mind, Godefroid would hardly have recognized them.

"Why, it is dear Monsieur Godefroid!" exclaimed the lady.

On hearing the delightful tones of Vanda's enchanting voice, and seeing her walking, Godefroid stood riveted to the spot.

"Cured!" he exclaimed.

"Ten days ago he allowed me to walk," she replied.

"Halpersohn?"

"Yes," said she. "And why have you never come to see us? —But, indeed, you were wise. My hair was not cut off till about a week ago. This that you see is but a wig; but the doctor assures me it will grow again!—But we have so much to say to each other. Will you not come to dine with us?—Oh, that harmonium!—Oh, monsieur!" and she put her hand-kerchief to her eyes. "I will treasure it all my life! My son will preserve it as a relic.—My father has sought for you all through Paris, and he is anxiously in search, too, of his un-known benefactors. He will die of grief if you cannot help him to find them. He suffers from the darkest melancholy, and I cannot always succeed in rousing him from it."

Fascinated alike by the voice of this charming woman re-called from the grave, and by that of irresistible curiosity, Godefroid gave his arm to the hand held out by the Baronne de Mergi, who let her son go on in front with an errand, which the lad had understood from his mother's nod.

"I shall not take you far; we are living in the Allée d'Antin in a pretty little house *à l'Anglaise;* we have it all to our-selves, each of us occupies a floor. Oh, we are very comfort-able! And my father believes that you have had a great deal to do with the good fortune that is poured upon us——"

"I?"

"Did you not know that a place has been created for him in consequence of a report from the Minister for Public Instruction, a Chair of Legislature, like one at the Sorbonne? My father will give his first course of lectures in the month of November next. The great work on which he was engaged will be published in a month or so; the house of Cavalier is bringing it out on half-profits with my father, and has paid him thirty thousand francs on account of his share; so he is buying the house we live in. The Minister of Justice allows me a pension of twelve hundred francs as the daughter of a retired magistrate; my father has his pension of a thousand crowns, and he had five thousand francs with his professorship. We are so economical that we shall be almost rich.

"My Auguste will begin studying the law a few months hence; meanwhile, he has employment in the public prosecutor's office, and gets twelve hundred francs.—Oh, Monsieur Godefroid, never mention that miserable business of my poor Auguste's. For my part, I bless him every day for the deed which his grandfather has not yet forgiven. His mother blesses him, Halpersohn is devoted to him, but the old public prosecutor is implacable!"

"What business?" asked Godefroid.

"Ah! that is just like your generosity!" cried Vanda. "You have a noble heart. Your mother must be proud of you!——"

"On my word, I know nothing of the matter you allude to," said Godefroid.

"Really, you did not hear?" And she frankly told the story of Auguste's borrowing from the doctor, admiring her son for the action.

"But if I am to say nothing about this before the Baron," said Godefroid, "tell me how your son got out of the scrape."

"Well," said Vanda, "as I told you, my son is in the public prosecutor's office, and has met with the greatest kindness. He was not kept more than eight-and-forty hours in the Conciergerie, where he was lodged with the governor. The worthy doctor, who did not get Auguste's beautiful, sublime

letter till the evening, withdrew the charge; and by the intervention of a former presiding judge of the Supreme Court—
a man my father had never even seen—the public prosecutor
had the police agent's report and the warrant for arrest both
destroyed. In fact, not a trace of the affair survives but in my
heart, in my son's conscience, and in his grandfather's mind
—who, since that day, speaks to my boy in the coldest terms,
and treats him as a stranger.

"Only yesterday, Halpersohn was interceding for him; but
my father, who will not listen to me, much as he loves me,
replied: 'You are the person robbed, you can and ought to
forgive. But I am answerable for the thief—and when I sat
on the Bench, I never pronounced a pardon!'—'You will kill
your daughter,' said Halpersohn—I heard them. My father
kept silence."

"But who is it that has helped you?"

"A gentleman who is, we believe, employed to distribute
the benefactions of the Queen."

"What is he like?" asked Godefroid.

"He is a grave, thin man, sad-looking—something like my
father. It was he who had my father conveyed to the house
where we now are, when he was in a high fever. And, just
fancy, as soon as my father was well, I was removed from the
private hospital and brought there, where I found my old
bedroom just as though I had never left it.—Halpersohn,
whom the tall gentleman had quite bewitched—how I know
not—then told me all about my father's sufferings, and how he
had sold the diamonds off his snuff-box! My father and my
boy often without bread, and making believe to be rich in my
presence!—Oh, Monsieur Godefroid, those two men are mar-
tyrs! What can I say to my father? I can only repay him
and my son by suffering for them, like them."

"And had the tall gentleman something of a military air?"

"Oh, you know him!" cried Vanda, as they reached the
door of the house.

She seized Godefroid's hand with the grip of a woman in
hysterics, and dragging him into a drawing-room of which

the door stood open, she exclaimed—"Father, Monsieur Godefroid knows your benefactor."

Baron Bourlac, whom Godefroid found dressed in a style
suitable to a retired judge of his high rank, held out his hand
to Godefroid, and said:

"I thought as much."

Godefroid shook his head in negation of any knowledge of
the details of this noble revenge; but the Baron did not give
him time to speak.

"Monsieur," he want on, "only Providence can be more
powerful, only Love can be more thoughtful, only Motherhood can be more clear-sighted, than your friends who are
allied with those great divinities.—I bless the chance that has
led to our meeting again, for Monsieur Joseph has vanished
completely; and as he has succeeded in avoiding every snare I
could lay to ascertain his real name and residence, I should
have died in grief.—But here, read his letter.—And you know
him?"

Godefroid read as follows:

"Monsieur le Baron Bourlac, the money we have laid out
for you by the orders of a charitable lady amounts to a sum
of fifteen thousand francs. Take note of this, that it may be
repaid either by you or by your descendants when your family
is sufficiently prosperous to allow of it, for it belongs to the
poor. When such repayment is possible, deposit the money
you owe with the Brothers Mongenod, bankers. God forgive
you your sins!"

The letter was mysteriously signed with five crosses.

Godefroid returned it.—"The five crosses, sure enough!"
said he to himself.

"Now, since you know all," said the old man, "you who
were this mysterious lady's messenger—tell me her name."

"Her name!" cried Godefroid; "her name! Unhappy man,
never ask it! never try to find it out.—Oh, madame," said he,
taking Madame de Mergi's hand in his own, which shook, "if

you value your father's sanity, keep him in his ignorance; never let him make any attempt——"

The father, the daughter, and Auguste stood frozen with amazement.

"Well, then, the woman who has preserved your daughter for you," said Godefroid, looking at the old lawyer, "who has restored her to you, young, lovely, fresh, and living—who has snatched her from the grave—who has rescued your grandson from disgrace—who has secured to you a happy and respected old age—who has saved you all three——" he paused, "is a woman whom you sent innocent to the hulks for twenty years," he went on, addressing Monsieur Bourlac, "on whom, from your judgment-seat, you poured every insult, whose saintliness you mocked at, and from whom you snatched a lovely daughter to send her to the most horrible death, for she was guillotined!"

Godefroid, seeing Vanda drop senseless on to a chair, rushed out of the room, and from thence into the Allée d'Antin, where he took to his heels.

"If you would earn my forgiveness," said Baron Bourlac to his grandson, "follow that man and find out where he lives."

Auguste was off like a dart.

By half-past eight next morning, Baron Bourlac was knocking at the old yellow gate of the Hôtel de la Chanterie, Rue Chanoinesse. He asked for Madame de la Chanterie, and the porter pointed to the stone steps. Happily they were all going to breakfast, and Godefroid recognized the Baron in the courtyard through one of the loopholes that lighted the stairs. He had but just time to fly down and into the drawing-room where they were all assembled, crying out—"Baron Bourlac."

On hearing this name, Madame de la Chanterie, supported by the Abbé de Vèze, disappeared into her room.

"You shall not come in, you imp of Satan!" cried Manon, who recognized the lawyer, and placed herself in front of the drawing-room door. "Do you want to kill my mistress?"

"Come, Manon, let the gentleman pass," said Monsieur Alain.

Manon dropped on to a chair as if her knees had both given way at once.

"Gentlemen," said the Baron in a voice of deep emotion, as he recognized Godefroid and Monsieur Joseph, and bowed to the two strangers, "Beneficence confers a claim on those benefited by it!"

"You owe nothing to us," said the worthy Alain; "you owe everything to God."

"You are saints, and you have the serenity of saints," replied the old lawyer. "You will hear me, I beg.—I have learned that the superhuman blessings that have been heaped on me for eighteen months past are the work of a person whom I deeply injured in the course of my duty; it was fifteen years before I was assured of her innocence; this, gentlemen, is the single remorse I have known as due to the exercise of my powers.—Listen! I have not much longer to live, but I shall lose that short term of life, necessary still to my children whom Madame de la Chanterie has saved, if I cannot win her forgiveness. Gentlemen, I will remain kneeling on the square of Notre-Dame till she has spoken one word!—I will wait for her there!—I will kiss the print of her feet; I will find tears to soften her heart—I who have been dried up like a straw by seeing my daughter's sufferings——"

The door of Madame de la Chanterie's room was opened, the Abbé de Vèze came through like a shade, and said to Monsieur Joseph:

"That voice is killing Madame."

"What! she is there! She has passed there!" cried Bourlac.

He fell on his knees, kissed the floor, and melted into tears, crying in a heartrending tone:

"In the name of Jesus who died on the Cross, forgive! forgive! For my child has suffered a thousand deaths!"

The old man collapsed so entirely that the spectators believed he was dead.

At this moment Madame de la Chanterie appeared like a spectre in the doorway, leaning, half-fainting, against the side-post.

"In the name of Louis XVI. and Marie Antoinette, whom I see on the scaffold, of Madame Elizabeth, of my daughter, and of yours—in the name of Jesus, I forgive you."

As he heard the words, the old man looked up and said:

"Thus are the angels avenged."

Monsieur Joseph and Monsieur Nicolas helped him to his feet, and led him out to the courtyard; Godefroid went to call a coach; and when they heard the rattle of wheels, Monsieur Nicolas said as he helped the old man into it:

"Come no more, monsieur, or you will kill the mother too. The power of God is infinite, but human nature has its limits."

That day Godefroid joined the Order of the Brethren of Consolation.

VIERZCHOVNIA, UKRAINE, *December* 1847.

A PRINCE OF BOHEMIA

To Henri Heine.

I inscribe this to you, my dear Heine, to you that represent in Paris the ideas and poetry of Germany, in Germany the lively and witty criticism of France; for you better than any other will know whatsoever this Study may contain of criticism and of jest, of love and truth.

DE BALZAC.

"MY dear friend," said Mme. de la Baudraye, drawing a pile of manuscript from beneath her sofa cushion, "will you pardon me in our present straits for making a short story of something which you told me a few weeks ago?"

"Anything is fair in these times. Have you not seen writers serving up their own hearts to the public, or very often their mistress' hearts when invention fails? We are coming to this, dear; we shall go in quest of adventures, not so much for the pleasure of them as for the sake of having the story to tell afterwards."

"After all, you and the Marquise de Rochefide have paid the rent, and I do not think, from the way things are going here, that I ever pay yours."

"Who knows? Perhaps the same good luck that befell Mme. de Rochefide may come to you."

"Do you call it good luck to go back to one's husband?"

"No; only great luck. Come, I am listening."

And Mme. de la Baudraye read as follows:

"Scene—a splendid salon in the Rue de Chartres-du-Roule. One of the most famous writers of the day discovered sitting on a settee beside a very illustrious Marquise, with whom

he is on such terms of intimacy, as a man has a right to claim
when a woman singles him out and keeps him at her side as a
complacent *souffre-douleur* rather than a makeshift."

"Well," says she, "have you found those letters of which
you spoke yesterday? You said that you could not tell me
all about *him* without them?"

"Yes, I have them."

"It is your turn to speak; I am listening like a child when
his mother begins the tale of *Le Grand Serpentin Vert.*"

"I count the young man in question in that group of our
acquaintances which we are wont to style our friends. He
comes of a good family; he is a man of infinite parts and
ill-luck, full of excellent dispositions and most charming
conversation; young as he is, he has seen much, and while
awaiting better things, he dwells in Bohemia. Bohemianism,
which by rights should be called the doctrine of the Boulevard des Italiens, finds its recruits among young men between twenty and thirty, all of them men of genius in their
way, little known, it is true, as yet, but sure of recognition
one day, and when that day comes, of great distinction. They
are distinguished as it is at carnival time, when their ex-
uberant wit, repressed for the rest of the year, finds a vent
in more or less ingenious buffoonery.

"What times we live in! What an irrational central power
which allows such tremendous energies to run to waste!
There are diplomatists in Bohemia quite capable of over-
turning Russia's designs, if they but felt the power of
France at their backs. There are writers, adminis-
trators, soldiers, and artists in Bohemia; every faculty,
every kind of brain is represented there. Bohemia is a
microcosm. If the Czar would buy Bohemia for a score
of millions and set its population down in Odessa—always
supposing that they consented to leave the asphalt of the
boulevards—Odessa would be Paris with the year. In
Bohemia, you find the flower doomed to wither and come
to nothing; the flower of the wonderful young manhood of

France, so sought after by Napoleon and Louis XIV., so neglected for the last thirty years by the modern Gerontocracy that is blighting everything else—that splendid young manhood of whom a witness so little prejudiced as Professor Tissot wrote, 'On all sides the Emperor employed a younger generation in every way worthy of him; in his councils, in the general administration, in negotiations bristling with difficulties or full of danger, in the government of conquered countries; and in all places Youth responded to his demands upon it. Young men were for Napoleon the *missi hominici* of Charlemagne.'

"The word Bohemia tells you everything. Bohemia has nothing and lives upon what it has. Hope is its religion; faith (in oneself) its creed; and charity is supposed to be its budget. All these young men are greater than their misfortune; they are under the feet of Fortune, yet more than equal to Fate. Always ready to mount and ride an *if,* witty as a *feuilleton,* blithe as only those can be that are deep in debt and drink deep to match, and finally—for here I come to my point—hot lovers, and what lovers! Picture to yourself Lovelace, and Henri Quatre, and the Regent, and Werther, and Saint-Preux, and René, and the Maréchal de Richelieu—think of all these in a single man, and you will have some idea of their way of love. What lovers! Eclectic of all things in love, they will serve up a passion to a woman's order; their hearts are like a bill of fare in a restaurant. Perhaps they have never read Stendhal's *De l'Amour,* but unconsciously they put it in practice. They have by heart their chapters —Love-Taste, Love-Passion, Love-Caprice, Love-Crystalized, and more than all, Love-Transient. All is good in their eyes. They invented the burlesque axiom, 'In the sight of man, all women are equal.' The actual text is more vigorously worded, but as in my opinion the spirit is false, I do not stand nice upon the letter.

"My friend, madame, is named Gabriel Jean Anne Victor Benjamin George Ferdinand Charles Edward Rusticoli, Comte de la Palférine. The Rusticolis came to France with

Catherine dei Medici, having been ousted about that time
from their infinitesimal Tuscan sovereignty. They are dis-
tantly related to the house of Este, and connected by marriage with the Guises. On the Day of Saint-Bartholomew
they slew a goodly number of Protestants, and Charles IX.
bestowed the hand of the heiress of the Comte de la Palférine
upon the Rusticoli of that time. The Comté, however, being
a part of the confiscated lands of the Duke of Savoy, was re-
purchased by Henri IV. when that great king so far blundered as to restore the fief; and in exchange, the Rusticoli—
who had borne arms long before the Medici bore them,
to-wit, *argent* a cross flory *azure* (the cross flower-de-luced
by letters patent granted by Charles IX.), and a count's coronet, with two peasants for supporters with the motto IN HOC
SIGNO VINCIMUS—the Rusticoli, I repeat, retained their title,
and received a couple of offices under the crown with the
government of a province.

"From the time of the Valois till the reign of Richelieu, as
it may be called, the Rusticoli played a most illustrious part;
under Louis XIV. their glory waned somewhat, under Louis
XV. it went out altogether. My friend's grandfather wasted
all that was left to the once brilliant house with Mlle. La-
guerre, whom he first discovered, and brought into fashion
before Bouret's time. Charles Edward's own father was an
officer without any fortune in 1789. The Revolution came
to his assistance; he had the sense to drop his title, and became
plain Rusticoli. Among other deeds, M. Rusticoli married a
wife during the war in Italy, a Capponi, a goddaughter of the
Countess of Albany (hence La Palférine's final names). Rusticoli was one of the best colonels in the army. The Emperor
made him a commander of the Legion of Honor and a count.
His spine was slightly curved, and his son was wont to say
of him laughingly that he was *un comte refait* (*contrefait*).

"General Count Rusticoli, for he became a brigadier-gen-
eral at Ratisbon and a general of the division on the field of
Wagram, died at Vienna almost immediately after his promotion, or his name and ability would sooner or later have

brought him the marshal's bâton. Under the Restoration
he would certainly have repaired the fortunes of a great and
noble family so brilliant even as far back as 1100, centuries
before they took the French title—for the Rusticoli had given
a pope to the church and twice revolutionized the kingdom
of Naples—so illustrious again under the Valois; so dexterous
in the days of the Fronde, that obstinate Frondeurs though
they were, they still existed through the reign of Louis XIV.
Mazarin favored them; there was the Tuscan strain in them
still, and he recognized it.

"To-day, when Charles Edward de la Palférine's name is
mentioned, not three persons in a hundred know the history
of his house. But the Bourbons have actually left a Foix-
Grailly to live by his easel.

"Ah! if you but knew how brilliantly Charles Edward accepts his obscure position! how he scoffs at the bourgeois of
1830! What Attic salt in his wit! He would be the king of
Bohemia, if Bohemia would endure a king. His *verve* is inexhaustible. To him we owe a map of the country and the
names of the seven castles which Nodier could not discover."

"The one thing wanting in one of the cleverest skits of
our time," said the Marquise.

"You can form your own opinion of La Palférine from
a few characteristic touches," continued Nathan. "He once
came upon a friend of his, a fellow-Bohemian, involved in a
dispute on the boulevard with a bourgeois who chose to consider himself affronted. To the modern powers that be, Bohemia is insolent in the extreme. There was talk of calling
one another out.

"'One moment,' interposed La Palférine, as much Lauzun
for the occasion as Lauzun himself could have been. 'One
moment. Monsieur was born, I suppose?'

"'What, sir?'

"'Yes, are you born? What is your name?'

"'Godin.'

"'Godin, eh!' exclaimed La Palférine's friend.

"'One moment, my dear fellow,' interrupted La Palférine.
'There are the Trigaudins. Are you one of them?'

"Astonishment.

"'No? Then you are one of the new dukes of Gaëta, I suppose, of imperial creation? No? Oh, well, how can you expect my friend to cross swords with you when he will be secretary of an embassy and ambassador *some day,* and you will owe him respect? *Godin!* the thing is non-existent! You are a nonentity, Godin. My friend cannot be expected to beat the air! When one is somebody, one cannot fight with a nobody! Come, my dear fellow—good-day.'

"'My respects to madame,' added the friend.

"Another day La Palférine was walking with a friend who flung his cigar end in the face of a passer-by. The recipient had the bad taste to resent this.

"'You have stood your antagonist's fire,' said the young Count, 'the witnesses declare that honor is satisfied.'

"La Palférine owed his tailor a thousand francs, and the man instead of going himself sent his assistant to ask for the money. The assistant found the unfortunate debtor up six pairs of stairs at the back of a yard at the further end of the Faubourg du Roule. The room was unfurnished save for a bed (such a bed!), a table, and such a table! La Palférine heard the preposterous demand—'A demand which I should qualify as illegal,' he said when he told us the story, 'made, as it was, at seven o'clock in the morning.'

"'Go,' he answered, with the gesture and attitude of a Mirabeau, 'tell your master in what condition you find me.'

"The assistant apologized and withdrew. La Palférine, seeing the young man on the landing, rose in the attire celebrated in verse in *Britannicus* to add, 'Remark the stairs! Pay particular attention to the stairs; do not forget to tell him about the stairs!'

"In every position into which chance has thrown La Palférine, he has never failed to rise to the occasion. All that he does is witty and never in bad taste; always and in everything he displays the genius of Rivarol, the polished subtlety of the old French noble. It was he who told that delicious anecdote of a friend of Laffitte the banker. A national fund

had been started to give back to Laffitte the mansion in which
the Revolution of 1830 was brewed, and this friend appeared at the offices of the fund with, 'Here are five francs,
give me a hundred sous change!'—A caricature was made of
it.—It was once La Palférine's misfortune, in judicial style,
to make a young girl a mother. The girl, not a very simple innocent, confessed all to her mother, a respectable matron, who
hurried forthwith to La Palférine and asked what he meant
to do.

" 'Why, madame,' said he, 'I am neither a surgeon nor a
midwife.'

"She collapsed, but three or four years later she returned to
the charge, still persisting in her inquiry, 'What did La Palférine mean to do?'

" 'Well, madame,' returned he, 'when the child is seven
years old, an age at which a boy ought to pass out of women's hands'—an indication of entire agreement on the
mother's part—'if the child is really mine'—another gesture
of assent—'if there is a striking likeness, if he bids fair to
be a gentleman, if I can recognize in him my turn of mind,
and more particularly the Rusticoli air; then, oh—ah!'—a
new movement from the matron—'on my word and honor, I
will make him a cornet of—sugar-plums!'

"All this, if you will permit me to make use of the phraseology employed by M. Sainte-Beuve for his biographies of ob-
scurities—all this, I repeat, is the playful and sprightly yet
already somewhat decadent side of a strong race. It smacks
rather of the Parc-aux-Cerfs than of the Hôtel de Rambouillet.
It is a race of the strong rather than of the sweet; I incline
to lay a little debauchery to its charge, and more than I should
wish in brilliant and generous natures; it is gallantry after
the fashion of the Maréchal de Richelieu, high spirits and
frolic carried rather too far; perhaps we may see in it the
outrances of another age, the Eighteenth Century pushed to
extremes; it harks back to the Musketeers; it is an exploit
stolen from Champcenetz; nay, such light-hearted incon-
stancy takes us back to the festooned and ornate period of the

old court of the Valois. In an age as moral as the present, we are bound to regard audacity of this kind sternly; still, at the same time that 'cornet of sugar-plums' may serve to warn young girls of the perils of lingering where fancies, more charming than chastened, come thickly from the first; on the rosy flowery unguarded slopes, where trespasses ripen into errors full of equivocal effervescence, into too palpitating issues. The anecdote puts La Palférine's genius before you in all its vivacity and completeness. He realizes Pascal's *entre-deux,* he comprehends the whole scale between tender-ness and pitilessness, and, like Epaminondas, he is equally great in extremes. And not merely so, his epigram stamps the epoch; the *accoucheur* is a modern innovation. All the refinements of modern civilization are summed up in the phrase. It is monumental."

"Look here, my dear Nathan, what farrago of nonsense is this?" asked the Marquise in bewilderment.

"Madame la Marquise," returned Nathan, "you do not know the value of these 'precious' phrases; I am talking Sainte-Beuve, the new kind of French.—I resume. Walking one day arm in arm with a friend along the boulevard, he was accosted by a ferocious creditor, who inquired:

" 'Are you thinking of me, sir?'

" 'Not the least in the world,' answered the Count.

"Remark the difficulty of the position. Talleyrand, in similar circumstances, had already replied, 'You are very in-quisitive, my dear fellow!' To imitate the inimitable great man was out of the question.—La Palférine, generous as Buckingham, could not bear to be caught empty-handed. One day when he had nothing to give a little Savoyard chimney-sweeper, he dipped a hand into a barrel of grapes in a grocer's doorway and filled the child's cap from it. The little one ate away at his grapes; the grocer began by laughing, and ended by holding out his hand.

" 'Oh, fie! monsieur,' said La Palférine, 'your left hand ought not to know what my right hand doth.'

"With his adventurous courage, he never refuses any odds,

but there is wit in his bravado. In the Passage de l'Opéra he chanced to meet a man who had spoken slightingly of him, elbowed him as he passed, and then turned and jostled him a second time.

"'You are very clumsy!'

"'On the contrary; I did it on purpose.'

"The young man pulled out his card. La Palférine dropped it. 'It has been carried too long in the pocket. Be good enough to give me another.'

"On the ground he received a thrust; blood was drawn; his antagonist wished to stop.

"'You are wounded, monsieur!'

"'I disallow the *botte*,' said La Palférine, as coolly as if he had been in the fencing-saloon; then as he riposted (sending the point home this time), he added, 'There is the right thrust, monsieur!'

"His antagonist kept his bed for six months.

"This, still following on M. Sainte-Beuve's tracks, recalls the *raffinés*, the fine-edged raillery of the best days of the monarchy. In this speech you discern an untrammeled but drifting life; a gaiety of imagination that deserts us when our first youth is past. The prime of the blossom is over, but there remains the dry compact seed with the germs of life in it, ready against the coming winter. Do you not see that these things are symptoms of something unsatisfied, of an unrest impossible to analyze, still less to describe, yet not incomprehensible; a something ready to break out if occasion calls into flying upleaping flame? It is the *accidia* of the cloister; a trace of sourness, of ferment engendered by the enforced stagnation of youthful energies, a vague, obscure melancholy."

"That will do," said the Marquise; "you are giving me a mental shower bath."

"It is the early afternoon languor. If a man has nothing to do, he will sooner get into mischief than do nothing at all; this invariably happens in France. Youth at the present day has two sides to it; the studious or unappreciated, and the ardent or *passionné*."

"That will do!" repeated Mme. de Rochefide, with an authoritative gesture. "You are setting my nerves on edge."

"To finish my portrait of La Palférine, I hasten to make the plunge into the gallant regions of his character, or you will not understand the peculiar genius of an admirable representative of a certain section of mischievous youth—youth strong enough, be it said, to laugh at the position in which it is put by those in power; shrewd enough to do no work, since work profiteth nothing, yet so full of life that it fastens upon pleasure—the one thing that cannot be taken away. And meanwhile a bourgeois, mercantile, and bigoted policy continues to cut off all the sluices through which so much aptitude and ability would find an outlet. Poets and men of science are not wanted.

"To give you an idea of the stupidity of the new court, I will tell you of something which happened to La Palférine. There is a sort of relieving officer on the civil list. This functionary one day discovered that La Palférine was in dire distress, drew up a report, no doubt, and brought the descendant of the Rusticolis fifty francs by way of alms. La Palférine received the visitor with perfect courtesy, and talked of various persons at court.

"'Is it true,' he asked, 'that Mlle. d'Orléans contributes such and such a sum to this benevolent scheme started by her nephew? If so, it is very gracious of her.'

"Now La Palférine had a servant, a little Savoyard, aged ten, who waited on him without wages. La Palférine called him Father Anchises, and used to say, 'I have never seen such a mixture of besotted foolishness with great intelligence; he would go through fire and water for me; he understands everything—and yet he cannot grasp the fact that I can do nothing for him.'

"Anchises was despatched to a livery stable with instructions to hire a handsome brougham with a man in livery behind it. By the time the carriage arrived below, La Palférine had skilfully piloted the conversation to the subject of the functions of his visitor, whom he has since called 'the unmitigated misery man,' and learned the nature of his duties and his stipend.

" 'Do they allow you a carriage to go about the town in this way?'

" 'Oh! no.'

"At that La Palférine and a friend who happened to be with him went downstairs with the poor soul, and insisted on putting him into the carriage. It was raining in torrents. La Palférine had thought of everything. He offered to drive the official to the next house on his list; and when the almoner came down again, he found the carriage waiting for him at the door. The man in livery handed him a note written in pencil:

" 'The carriage has been engaged for three days. Count Rusticoli de la Palférine is too happy to associate himself with Court charities by lending wings to Royal beneficence.'

"La Palférine now calls the civil list the uncivil list.

"He was once passionately loved by a lady of somewhat light conduct. Antonia lived in the Rue du Helder; she had seen and been seen to some extent, but at the time of her acquaintance with La Palférine she had not yet 'an establishment.' Antonia was not wanting in the insolence of old days, now degenerating into rudeness among women of her class. After a fortnight of unmixed bliss, she was compelled, in the interest of her civil list, to return to a less exclusive system; and La Palférine, discovering a certain lack of sincerity in her dealings with him, sent Madame Antonia a note which made her famous.

" 'MADAME,—Your conduct causes me much surprise and no less distress. Not content with rending my heart with your disdain, you have been so little thoughtful as to retain a toothbrush, which my means will not permit me to replace, my estates being mortgaged beyond their value.

" 'Adieu, too fair and too ungrateful friend! May we meet again in a better world.

" 'CHARLES EDWARD.'

"Assuredly (to avail ourselves yet further of Sainte-Béuve's Babylonish dialect), this far outpasses the raillery of Sterne's *Sentimental Journey;* it might be Scarron without his grossness. Nay, I do not know but that Molière in his lighter mood would not have said of it, as of Cyrano de Bergerac's best—'This is mine.' Richelieu himself was not more complete when he wrote to the princess waiting for him in the Palais Royal—'Stay there, my queen, to charm the scullion lads.' At the same time, Charles Edward's humor is less biting. I am not sure that this kind of wit was known among the Greeks and Romans. Plato, possibly, upon a closer inspection approaches it, but from the austere and musical side——"

"No more of that jargon," the Marquise broke in, "in print it may be endurable; but to have it grating upon my ears is a punishment which I do not in the least deserve."

"He first met Claudine on this wise," continued Nathan. "It was one of the unfilled days, when Youth is a burden to itself; days when youth, reduced by the overweening presumption of Age to a condition of potential energy and dejection, emerges therefrom (like Blondet under the Restoration), either to get into mischief or to set about some colossal piece of buffoonery, half excused by the very audacity of its conception. La Palférine was sauntering, cane in hand, up and down the pavement between the Rue de Grammont and the Rue de Richelieu, when in the distance he descried a woman too elegantly dressed, covered, as he phrased it, with a great deal of portable property, too expensive and too carelessly worn for its owner to be other than a princess of the Court or of the stage, it was not easy at first to say which. But after July 1830, in his opinion, there is no mistaking the indications—the princess can only be a princess of the stage.

"The Count came up and walked by her side as if she had given him an assignation. He followed her with a courteous persistence, a persistence in good taste, giving the lady from time to time, and always at the right moment, an authoritative glance, which compelled her to submit to his escort. Any-

body but La Palférine would have been frozen by his reception, and disconcerted by the lady's first efforts to rid herself
of her cavalier, by her chilly air, her curt speeches; but no
gravity, with all the will in the world, could hold out long
against La Palférine's jesting replies. The fair stranger went
into her milliner's shop. Charles Edward followed, took a
seat, and gave his opinions and advice like a man that meant
to pay. This coolness disturbed the lady. She went out.

"On the stairs she spoke to her persecutor.

" 'Monsieur, I am about to call upon one of my husband's relatives, an elderly lady, Mme. de Bonfalot——'

" 'Ah! Mme. de Bonfalot, charmed, I am sure. I am going
there.'

"The pair accordingly went. Charles Edward came in
with the lady, every one believed that she had brought him
with her. He took part in the conversation, was lavish of
his polished and brilliant wit. The visit lengthened out. That
was not what he wanted.

" 'Madame,' he said, addressing the fair stranger, 'do not
forget that your husband is waiting for us, and only allowed
us a quarter of an hour.'

"Taken aback by such boldness (which, as you know, is
never displeasing to you women), led captive by the conqueror's glance, by the astute yet candid air which Charles
Edward can assume when he chooses, the lady rose, took the
arm of her self-constituted escort, and went downstairs, but
on the threshold she stopped to speak to him.

" 'Monsieur, I like a joke——'

" 'And so do I.'

"She laughed.

" 'But this may turn to earnest,' he added; 'it only rests
with you. I am the Comte de la Palférine, and I am delighted
that it is in my power to lay my heart and my fortune at
your feet.'

"La Palférine was at that time twenty-two years old.
(This happened in 1834.) Luckily for him, he was fashion-
ably dressed. I can paint his portrait for you in a few words.

He was the living image of Louis XIII., with the same white forehead and gracious outline of the temples, the same olive skin (that Italian olive tint which turns white where the light falls on it), the brown hair worn rather long, the black 'royale,' the grave and melancholy expression, for La Palférine's character and exterior were amazingly at variance.

"At the sound of the name, and the sight of its owner, something like a quiver thrilled through Claudine. La Palférine saw the vibration, and shot a glance at her out of the dark depths of almond-shaped eyes with purpled lids, and those faint lines about them which tell of pleasures as costly as painful fatigue. With those eyes upon her, she said—'Your address?'

" 'What want of address!'

" 'Oh, pshaw!' she said, smiling. 'A bird on the bough?'

" 'Good-bye, madame, you are such a woman as I seek, but my fortune is far from equaling my desire——'

"He bowed, and there and then left her. Two days later, by one of the strange chances that can only happen in Paris, he had betaken himself to a money-lending wardrobe dealer to sell such of his clothing as he could spare. He was just receiving the price with an uneasy air, after long chaffering, when the stranger lady passed and recognized him.

" 'Once for all,' cried he to the bewildered wardrobe dealer, 'I tell you I am not going to take your trumpet!'

"He pointed to a huge, much-dinted musical instrument, hanging up outside against a background of uniforms, civil and military. Then, proudly and impetuously, he followed the lady.

"From that great day of the trumpet these two understood one another to admiration. Charles Edward's ideas on the subject of love are as sound as possible. According to him, a man cannot love twice, there is but one love in his lifetime, but that love is a deep and shoreless sea. It may break in upon him at any time, as the grace of God found St. Paul; and a man may live sixty years and never know love. Perhaps, to quote Heine's superb phrase, it is 'the secret malady of the heart'—a sense of the Infinite that there is within us, together with the revelation of the ideal Beauty in its visible form. This love, in short, comprehends both the creature and creation. But so long as there is no question of this great poetical conception, the loves that cannot last can only be taken lightly, as if they were in a manner snatches of song compared with Love the epic.

"To Charles Edward the adventure brought neither the thunderbolt signal of love's coming, nor yet that gradual revelation of an inward fairness which draws two natures by degrees more and more strongly each to each. For there are but two ways of love—love at first sight, doubtless akin to the Highland 'second-sight,' and that slow fusion of two natures which realizes Plato's 'man-woman.' But if Charles Edward did not love, he was loved to distraction. Claudine found love made complete, body and soul; in her, in short, La Palférine awakened the one passion of her life; while for him Claudine was only a most charming mistress. The Devil himself, a most potent magician certainly, with all hell at his back, could never have changed the natures of these two unequal fires. I dare affirm that Claudine not unfrequently bored Charles Edward.

" 'Stale fish and the woman you do not love are only fit to fling out of the window after three days,' he used to say.

"In Bohemia there is little secrecy observed over these affairs. La Palférine used to talk a good deal of Claudine; but, at the same time, none of us saw her, nor so much as knew her name. For us Claudine was almost a mythical personage. All of us acted in the same way, reconciling the requirements of our common life with the rules of good taste. Claudine, Hortense, the Baroness, the Bourgeoise, the Empress, the Spaniard, the Lioness,—these were cryptic titles which permitted us to pour out our joys, our cares, vexations, and hopes, and to communicate our discoveries. Further, none of us went. It has been known, in Bohemia, that chance discovered the identity of the fair unknown; and at once, as by tacit convention, not one of us spoke of her again.

This fact may show how far youth possesses a sense of true delicacy. How admirably certain natures of a finer clay know the limit line where jest must end, and all that host of things French covered by the slang word *blague,* a word which will shortly be cast out of the language (let us hope), and yet it is the only one which conveys an idea of the spirit of Bohemia.

"So we often used to joke about Claudine and the Count —'*Toujours Claudine?*' sung to the air of *Toujours Gessler.* —'What are you making of Claudine?'—'How is Claudine?'

" 'I wish you all such a mistress, for all the harm I wish you,' La Palférine began one day. 'No greyhound, no basset-dog, no poodle can match her in gentleness, submissiveness, and complete tenderness. There are times when I reproach myself, when I take myself to task for my hard heart. Claudine obeys with saintly sweetness. She comes to me, I tell her to go, she goes, she does not even cry till she is out in the courtyard. I refuse to see her for a whole week at a time. I tell her to come at such an hour on Tuesday; and be it midnight or six o'clock in the morning, ten o'clock, five o'clock, breakfast time, dinner time, bed time, any particularly inconvenient hour in the day—she will come, punctual to the minute, beautiful, beautifully dressed, and enchanting. And she is a married woman, with all the complications and duties of a household. The fibs that she must invent, the reasons she must find for conforming to my whims would tax the ingenuity of some of us! . . . Claudine never wearies; you can always count upon her. It is not love, I tell her, it is infatuation. She writes to me every day; I do not read her letters; she found that out, but still she writes. See here; there are two hundred letters in this casket. She begs me to wipe my razors on one of her letters every day, and I punctually do so. She thinks, and rightly, that the sight of her handwriting will put me in mind of her.'

"La Palférine was dressing as he told us this. I took up the letter which he was about to put to this use, read it, and kept it, as he did not ask to have it back. Here it is. I looked for it, and found it as I promised.

" 'Well, my dear, are you satisfied with me? I did not
even ask for your hand, yet you might easily have given it
to me, and I longed so much to hold it to my heart, to my
lips. No, I did not ask, I am so afraid of displeasing you.
Do you know one thing? Though I am cruelly sure that anything I do is a matter of perfect indifference to you, I am
none the less extremely timid in my conduct: the woman
that belongs to you, whatever her title to call herself yours,
must not incur so much as the shadow of blame. In so far
as love comes from the angels in heaven, from whom there
are no secrets hid, my love is as pure as the purest; wherever
I am I feel that I am in your presence, and I try to do you
honor.

" 'All that you said about my manner of dress impressed
me very much; I began to understand how far above others
are those that come of a noble race. There was still something of the opera girl in my gowns, in my way of dressing
my hair. In a moment I saw the distance between me and
good taste. Next time you shall receive a duchess, you shall
not know me again! Ah! how good you have been to your
Claudine! How many and many a time I have thanked you
for telling me those things! What interest lay in those few
words! You had taken thought for that thing belonging to
you called Claudine? *This* imbecile would never have opened
my eyes; he thinks that everything I do is right; and besides,
he is much too humdrum, too matter-of-fact to have any feeling for the beautiful.

" 'Tuesday is very slow of coming for my impatient mind!
On Tuesday I shall be with you for several hours. Ah! when
it comes I will try to think that the hours are months, that it
will be so always. I am living in hope of that morning now,
as I shall live upon the memory of it afterwards. Hope is
memory that craves; and recollection, memory sated. What a
beautiful life within life thought makes for us in this way!

" 'Sometimes I dream of inventing new ways of tenderness
all my own, a secret which no other woman shall guess. A

cold sweat breaks out over me at the thought that something may happen to prevent this meeting. Oh, I would break with *him* for good, if need was, but nothing here could possibly interfere; it would be from your side. Perhaps you may decide to go out, perhaps to go to see some other woman. Oh! spare me this Tuesday for pity's sake. If you take it from me, Charles, you do not know what *he* will suffer; I should drive him wild. But even if you do not want me, if you are going out, let me come, all the same, to be with you while you dress; only to see you, I ask no more than that; only to show you that I love you without a thought of self.

"'Since you gave me leave to love you, for you gave me leave, since I am yours; since that day I loved and love you with the whole strength of my soul; and I shall love you for ever, for once having loved *you,* no one could, no one ought to love another. And, you see, when those eyes that ask nothing but to see you are upon you, you will feel that in your Claudine there is a something divine, called into existence by you.

"'Alas! with you I can never play the coquette. I am like a mother with her child; I endure anything from you; I, that was once so imperious and proud. I have made dukes and princes fetch and carry for me; aides-de-camp, worth more than all the court of Charles X. put together, have done my errands, yet I am treating you as my spoilt child. But where is the use of coquetry? It would be pure waste. And yet, monsieur, for want of coquetry I shall never inspire love in you. I know it; I feel it; yet I do as before, feeling a power that I cannot withstand, thinking that this utter self-surrender will win me the sentiment innate in all men (so *he* tells me) for the thing that belongs to them.

"Wednesday.

"'Ah! how darkly sadness entered my heart yesterday when I found that I must give up the joy of seeing you. One single thought held me back from the arms of Death!—It was thy will! To stay away was to do thy will, to obey an order from thee. Oh! Charles, I was so pretty; I looked a lovelier woman for you than that beautiful German princess whom you gave me for an example, whom I have studied at the Opéra. And yet—you might have thought that I had overstepped the limits of my nature. You have left me no confidence in myself; perhaps I am plain after all. Oh! I loathe myself, I dream of my radiant Charles Edward, and my brain turns. I shall go mad, I know I shall. Do not laugh, do not talk to me of the fickleness of women. If we are inconstant, *you* are strangely capricious. You take away the hours of love that made a poor creature's happiness for ten whole days; the hours on which she drew to be charming and kind to all that came to see her! After all, you were the source of my kindness to *him;* you do not know what pain you give him. I wonder what I must do to keep you, or simply to keep the right to be yours sometimes. . . . When I think that you never would come here to me! . . . With what delicious emotion I would wait upon you!—There are other women more favored than I. There are women to whom you say, 'I love you.' To me you have never said more than 'You are a good girl.' Certain speeches of yours, though you do not know it, gnaw at my heart. Clever men sometimes ask me what I am thinking. . . . I am thinking of my self-abasement—the prostration of the poorest outcast in the presence of the Saviour.'

"There are still three more pages, you see. La Palférine allowed me to take the letter, with the traces of tears that still seemed hot upon it! Here was proof of the truth of his story. Marcas, a shy man enough with women, was in ecstacies over a second which he read in his corner before lighting his pipe with it.

" 'Why, any woman in love will write that sort of thing!' cried La Palférine. 'Love gives all women intelligence and style, which proves that here in France style proceeds from the matter and not from the words. See now how well this is thought out, how clear-headed sentiment is'—and with that he reads us another letter, far superior to the artificial and labored productions which we novelists write.

"One day poor Claudine heard that La Palférine was in a critical position; it was a question of meeting a bill of exchange. An unlucky idea occurred to her; she put a tolerably large sum in gold into an exquisitely embroidered purse and went to him.

"'Who has taught you to be so bold as to meddle with my household affairs?' La Palférine cried angrily. 'Mend my socks and work slippers for me, if it amuses you. So!—— you will play the duchess, and you turn the story of Danaë against the aristocracy.'

"He emptied the purse into his hand as he spoke, and made as though he would fling the money in her face. Claudine, in her terror, did not guess that he was joking; she shrank back, stumbled over a chair, and fell with her head against the corner of the marble chimney-piece. She thought she should have died. When she could speak, poor woman, as she lay on the bed, all that she said was, 'I deserved it, Charles!'

"For a moment La Palférine was in despair; his anguish revived Claudine. She rejoiced in the mishap; she took advantage of her suffering to compel La Palférine to take the money and release him from an awkward position. Then followed a variation on La Fontaine's fable, in which a man blesses the thieves that brought him a sudden impulse of tenderness from his wife. And while we are upon this subject, another saying will paint the man for you.

"Claudine went home again, made up some kind of tale as best she could to account for her bruised forehead, and fell dangerously ill. An abscess formed in the head. The doctor —Bianchon, I believe—yes, it was Bianchon—wanted to cut off her hair. The Duchesse de Berri's hair is not more beautiful than Claudine's; she would not hear of it, she told Bianchon in confidence that she could not allow it to be cut without leave from the Comte de Palférine. Bianchon went to

Charles Edward. Charles Edward heard him with much seriousness. The doctor had explained the case at length, and showed that it was absolutely necessary to sacrifice the hair to insure the success of the operation.

"'Cut off Claudine's hair!' cried he in peremptory tones. 'No. I would sooner lose her.'"

"Even now, after a lapse of four years, Bianchon still quotes that speech; we have laughed over it for half an hour together. Claudine, informed of the verdict, saw in it a proof of affection; she felt sure that she was loved. In the face of her weeping family, with her husband on his knees, she was inexorable. She kept her hair. The strength that came with the belief that she was loved came to her aid, the operation succeeded perfectly. There are stirrings of the inner life which throw all the calculations of surgery into disorder and baffle the laws of medical science.

"Claudine wrote a delicious letter to La Palférine, a letter in which the orthography was doubtful and the punctuation all to seek, to tell him of the happy result of the operation, and to add that Love was wiser than all the sciences.

"'Now,' said La Palférine one day, 'what am I to do to get rid of Claudine?'

"'Why, she is not at all troublesome; she leaves you master of your actions,' objected we.

"'That is true,' returned La Palférine, 'but I do not choose that anything shall slip into my life without my consent.'

"From that day he set himself to torment Claudine. It seemed that he held the bourgeoise, the nobody, in utter horror; nothing would satisfy him but a woman with a title. Claudine, it was true, had made progress; she had learned to dress as well as the best-dressed women of the Faubourg Saint-Germain; she had freed her bearing of unhallowed traces; she walked with a chastened, inimitable grace; but this was not enough. This praise of her enabled Claudine to swallow down the rest.

"But one day La Palférine said, 'If you wish to be the mistress of one La Palférine, poor, penniless, and without prospects as he is, you ought at least to represent him worthily. You should have a carriage and liveried servants and a title. Give me all the gratifications of vanity that will never be mine in my own person. The woman whom I honor with my regard ought never to go on foot; if she is bespattered with mud, I suffer. That is how I am made. If she is mine, she must be admired of all Paris. All Paris shall envy me my good fortune. If some little whipper-snapper seeing a brilliant countess pass in her brilliant carriage shall say to himself, "Who can call such a divinity his?" and grow thoughtful—why, it will double my pleasure.'

"La Palférine owned to us that he flung this programme at Claudine's head simply to rid himself of her. As a result he was stupefied with astonishment for the first and probably the only time in his life.

" 'Dear,' she said, and there was a ring in her voice that betrayed the great agitation which shook her whole being, 'it is well. All this shall be done, or I will die.'

"She let fall a few happy tears on his hand as she kissed it.

" 'You have told me what I must do to be your mistress still,' she added; 'I am glad.'

" 'And then' (La Palférine told us) 'she went out with a little coquettish gesture like a woman that has had her way. As she stood in my garret doorway, tall and proud, she seemed to reach the stature of an antique sibyl.'

"All this should sufficiently explain the manners and customs of the Bohemia in which the young *condottiere* is one of the most brilliant figures," Nathan continued after a pause. "Now it so happened that I discovered Claudine's identity, and could understand the appalling truth of one line which you perhaps overlooked in that letter of hers. It was on this wise."

The Marquise, too thoughtful now for laughter, bade Nathan "Go on," in a tone that told him plainly how deeply she had been impressed by these strange things, and even more plainly how much she was interested in La Palférine.

"In 1829, one of the most influential, steady, and clever of dramatic writers was du Bruel. His real name is unknown to the public, on the play-bills he is de Cursy. Under the Restoration he had a place in the Civil Service; and being really attached to the elder branch, he sent in his resignation bravely in 1830, and ever since has written twice as many plays to fill the deficit in his budget made by his noble conduct. At that time du Bruel was forty years old; you know the story of his life. Like many of his brethren, he bore a stage dancer an affection hard to explain, but well known in the whole world of letters. The woman, as you know, was Tullia, one of the *premiers sujets* of the Académie Royale de Musique. Tullia is merely a pseudonym like du Bruel's name of de Cursy.

"For the ten years between 1817 and 1827 Tullia was in her glory on the heights of the stage of the Opéra. With more beauty than education, a mediocre dancer with rather more sense than most of her class, she took no part in the virtuous reforms which ruined the corps de ballet; she continued the Guimard dynasty. She owed her ascendency, moreover, to various well-known protectors, to the Duc de Rhétoré (the Duc de Chaulieu's eldest son), to the influence of a famous Superintendent of Fine Arts, and sundry diplomatists and rich foreigners. During her apogee she had a neat little house in the Rue Chauchat, and lived as Opera nymphs used to live in the old days. Du Bruel was smitten with her about the time when the Duke's fancy came to an end in 1823. Being a mere subordinate in the Civil Service, du Bruel tolerated the Superintendent of Fine Arts, believing that he himself was really preferred. After six years this connection was almost a marriage. Tullia has always been very careful to say nothing of her family; we have a vague idea that she comes from Nanterre. One of her uncles, formerly a simple bricklayer or carpenter, is now, it is said, a very rich contractor, thanks to her influence and generous loans. This fact leaked out through du Bruel. He happened to say that Tullia would inherit a fine fortune sooner or later. The contractor was a bachelor; he had a weakness for the niece to whom he is indebted.

"'He is not clever enough to be ungrateful,' said she.

"In 1829 Tullia retired from the stage of her own accord. At the age of thirty she saw that she was growing somewhat stouter, and she had tried pantomime without success. Her whole art consisted in the trick of raising her skirts, after Noblet's manner, in a pirouette which inflated them balloon-fashion and exhibited the smallest possible quantity of clothing to the pit. The aged Vestris had told her at the very beginning that this *temps,* well executed by a fine woman, is worth all the art imaginable. It is the chest-note C of dancing. For which reason, he said, the very greatest dancers—Camargo, Guimard, and Taglioni, all of them thin, brown, and plain—could only redeem their physical defects by their genius. Tullia, still in the height of her glory, retired before younger and cleverer dancers; she did wisely. She was an aristocrat; she had scarcely stooped below the noblesse in her *liaisons;* she declined to dip her ankles in the troubled waters of July. Insolent and beautiful as she was, Claudine possessed handsome souvenirs, but very little ready money; still, her jewels were magnificent, and she had as fine furniture as any one in Paris.

"On quitting the stage when she, forgotten to-day, was yet in the height of her fame, one thought possessed her—she meant du Bruel to marry her; and at the time of this story, you must understand that the marriage had taken place, but was kept a secret. How do women of her class contrive to make a man marry them after seven or eight years of intimacy? What springs do they touch? What machinery do they set in motion? But, however comical such domestic dramas may be, we are not now concerned with them. Du Bruel was secretly married; the thing was done.

"Cursy before his marriage was supposed to be a jolly companion; now and again he stayed out all night, and to some extent led the life of a Bohemian; he would unbend at a supper-party. He went out to all appearance to a rehearsal at the Opéra-Comique, and found himself in some unaccountable way at Dieppe, or Baden, or Saint-Germain; he gave

dinners, led the Titanic thriftless life of artists, journalists,
and writers; levied his tribute on all the greenrooms of Paris;
and, in short, was one of us. Finot, Lousteau, du Tillet,
Desroches, Bixiou, Blondet, Couture, and des Lupeaulx
tolerated him in spite of his pedantic manner and ponderous
official attitude. But once married, Tullia made a slave of
du Bruel. There was no help for it. He was in love with
Tullia, poor devil.

"'Tullia' (so he said) 'had left the stage to be his alone,
to be a good and charming wife.' And somehow Tullia managed to induce the most Puritanical members of du Bruel's
family to accept her. From the very first, before any one
suspected her motives, she assiduously visited old Mme. de
Bonfalot, who bored her horribly; she made handsome presents to mean old Mme. de Chissé, du Bruel's great-aunt; she
spent a summer with the latter lady, and never missed a
single mass. She even went to confession, received absolution, and took the sacrament; but this, you must remember,
was in the country, and under the aunt's eyes.

"'I shall have real aunts now, do you understand?' she
said to us when she came back in the winter.

"She was so delighted with her respectability, so glad to
renounce her independence, that she found means to compass
her end. She flattered the old people. She went on foot
every day to sit for a couple of hours with Mme. du Bruel
the elder while that lady was ill—a Maintenon's stratagem
which amazed du Bruel. And he admired his wife without
criticism; he was so fast in the toils already that he did not
feel his bonds.

"Claudine succeeded in making him understand that only
under the elastic system of a bourgeois government, only at
the bourgeois court of the Citizen-King, could a Tullia, now
metamorphosed into a Mme. du Bruel, be accepted in the society which her good sense prevented her from attempting
to enter. Mme. de Bonfalot, Mme. de Chissé, and Mme. du
Bruel received her; she was satisfied. She took up the position of a well-conducted, simple, and virtuous woman, and

never acted out of character. In three years' time she was introduced to the friends of these ladies.

" 'And still I cannot persuade myself that young Mme. du Bruel used to display her ankles, and the rest, to all Paris, with the light of a hundred gas-jets pouring upon her,' Mme. Anselme Popinot remarked naïvely.

"From this point of view, July 1830 inaugurated an era not unlike the time of the Empire, when a waiting-woman was received at Court in the person of Mme. Garat, a chief-justice's 'lady.' Tullia had completely broken, as you may guess, with all her old associates; of her former acquaintances, she only recognized those who could not compromise her. At the time of her marriage she had taken a very charming little hôtel between a court and a garden, lavishing money on it with wild extravagance and putting the best part of her furniture and du Bruel's into it. Everything that she thought common or ordinary was sold. To find anything comparable to her sparkling splendor, you could only look back to the days when a Sophie Arnould, a Guimard, or a Duthé, in all her glory, squandered the fortunes of princes.

"How far did this sumptuous existence affect du Bruel? It is a delicate question to ask, and a still more delicate one to answer. A single incident will suffice to give you an idea of Tullia's crotchets. Her bed-spread of Brussels lace was worth ten thousand francs. A famous actress had another like it. As soon as Claudine heard this, she allowed her cat, a splendid Angora, to sleep on the bed. That trait gives you the woman. Du Bruel dared not say a word; he was ordered to spread abroad that challenge in luxury, so that it might reach the other. Tullia was very fond of this gift from the Duc de Rhétoré; but one day, five years after her marriage, she played with her cat to such purpose that the coverlet—fur-belows, flounces, and all—was torn to shreds, and replaced by a sensible quilt, a quilt that was a quilt, and not a symptom of the peculiar form of insanity which drives these women to make up by an insensate luxury for the childish days when they lived on raw apples, to quote the expression of a journalist. The day when the bed-spread was torn to tatters marked a new epoch in her married life.

"Cursy was remarkable for his ferocious industry. Nobody suspects the source to which Paris owes the patch-and-powder eighteenth century vaudevilles that flooded the stage. Those thousand-and-one vaudevilles, which raised such an outcry among the *feuilletonistes,* were written at Mme. du Bruel's express desire. She insisted that her husband should purchase the hôtel on which she had spent so much, where she had housed five hundred thousand francs' worth of furniture. Wherefore Tullia never enters into explanations; she understands the sovereign woman's reason to admiration.

"'People made a good deal of fun of Cursy,' said she; 'but, as a matter of fact, he found this house in the eighteenth century rouge-box, powder, puffs, and spangles. He would never have thought of it but for me,' she added, burying herself in her cushions in her fireside corner.

"She delivered herself thus on her return from a first night. Du Bruel's piece had succeeded, and she foresaw an avalanche of criticisms. Tullia had her At Homes. Every Monday she gave a tea-party; her society was as select as might be, and she neglected nothing that could make her house pleasant. There was bouillotte in one room, conversation in another, and sometimes a concert (always short) in the large drawing-room. None but the most eminent artists performed in her house. Tullia had so much good sense, that she attained to the most exquisite tact, and herein, in all probability, lay the secret of her ascendency over du Bruel; at any rate, he loved her with the love which use and wont at length makes indispensable to life. Every day adds another thread to the strong, irresistible, intangible web, which enmeshes the most delicate fancies, takes captive every most transient mood, and binding them together, holds a man captive hand and foot, heart and head.

"Tullia knew Cursy well; she knew every weak point in his armor, knew also how to heal his wounds.

"A passion of this kind is inscrutable for any observer, even for a man who prides himself, as I do, on a certain expertness. It is everywhere unfathomable; the dark depths in it are darker than in any other mystery; the colors confused even in the highest lights.

"Cursy was an old playwright, jaded by the life of the theatrical world. He liked comfort; he liked a luxurious, affluent, easy existence; he enjoyed being a king in his own house; he liked to be host to a party of men of letters in a hôtel resplendent with royal luxury, with carefully chosen works of art shining in the setting. Tullia allowed du Bruel to enthrone himself amid the tribe; there were plenty of journalists whom it was easy enough to catch and ensnare; and, thanks to her evening parties and a well-timed loan here and there, Cursy was not attacked too seriously—his plays succeeded. For these reasons he would not have separated from Tullia for an empire. If she had been unfaithful, he would probably have passed it over, on condition that none of his accustomed joys should be retrenched; yet, strange to say, Tullia caused him no twinges on this account. No fancy was laid to her charge; if there had been any, she certainly had been very careful of appearances.

"'My dear fellow,' du Bruel would say, laying down the law to us on the boulevard, 'there is nothing like one of these women who have sown their wild oats and got over their passions. Such women as Claudine have lived their bachelor life; they have been over head and ears in pleasure, and make the most adorable wives that could be wished; they have nothing to learn, they are formed, they are not in the least prudish; they are well broken in, and indulgent. So I strongly recommend everybody to take the "remains of a racer." I am the most fortunate man on earth.'

"Du Bruel said this to me himself with Bixiou there to hear it.

"'My dear fellow,' said the caricaturist, 'perhaps he is right to be in the wrong.'

"About a week afterwards, du Bruel asked us to dine with him one Tuesday. That morning I went to see him on a piece of theatrical business, a case submitted to us for arbitration by the commission of dramatic authors. We were obliged to go out again; but before we started he went to Claudine's room, knocked, as he always does, and asked for leave to enter.

"'We live in grand style,' said he, smiling; 'we are free. Each is independent.'

"We were admitted. Du Bruel spoke to Claudine. 'I have asked a few people to dinner to-day——'

"'Just like you!' cried she. 'You ask people without speaking to me; I count for nothing here.—Now' (taking me as arbitrator by a glance) 'I ask you yourself. When a man has been so foolish as to live with a woman of my sort; for, after all, I was an opera dancer—yes, I ought always to remember that, if other people are to forget it—well, under those circumstances, a clever man seeking to raise his wife in public opinion would do his best to impose her upon the world as a remarkable woman, to justify the step he had taken by acknowledging that in some ways she was something more than ordinary women. The best way of compelling respect from others is to pay respect to her at home, and to leave her absolute mistress of the house. Well, and yet it is enough to waken one's vanity to see how frightened he is of seeming to listen to me. I must be in the right ten times over if he concedes a single point.'

"(Emphatic negative gestures from du Bruel at every other word.)

"'Oh, yes, yes,' she continued quickly, in answer to this mute dissent. 'I know all about it, du Bruel, my dear, I that have been like a queen in my house all my life till I married you. My wishes were guessed, fulfilled, and more than fulfilled. After all, I am thirty-five, and at five-and-thirty a woman cannot expect to be loved. Ah, if I were a girl of sixteen, if I had not lost something that is dearly bought at the Opéra, what attention you would pay me, M. du Bruel! I feel the most supreme contempt for men who boast that they can love and grow careless and neglectful in little things as time grows on. You are short and insignificant, you see, du Bruel; you love to torment a woman; it is your only way of showing your strength.

A Napoleon is ready to be swayed by the woman he loves; he loses nothing by it; but as for such as you, you believe that you are nothing apparently, you do not wish to be ruled.——Five-and-thirty, my dear boy,' she continued, turning to me, 'that is the clue to the riddle.——"No," does he say again?——You know quite well that I am thirty-seven. I am very sorry, but just ask your friends to dine at the *Rocher de Cancale*. I *could* have them here, but I will not; they shall not come. And then perhaps my poor little monologue may engrave that salutary maxim, "Each is master at home," upon your memory. That is our charter,' she added, laughing, with a return of the opera girl's giddiness and caprice.

" 'Well, well, my dear little puss; there, there, never mind. We can manage to get on together,' said du Bruel, and he kissed her hands, and we came away. But he was very wroth.

"The whole way from the Rue de la Victoire to the boulevard a perfect torrent of venomous words poured from his mouth like a waterfall in flood; but as the shocking language which he used on the occasion was quite unfit to print, the report is necessarily inadequate.

" 'My dear fellow, I will leave that vile, shameless opera dancer, a worn-out jade that has been set spinning like a top to every operatic air; a foul hussy, an organ-grinder's monkey! Oh, my dear boy, you have taken up with an actress; may the notion of marrying your mistress never get a hold on you. It is a torment omitted from the hell of Dante, you see. Look here! I will beat her; I will give her a thrashing; I will give it to her! Poison of my life, she sent me off like a running footman.'

"By this time we had reached the boulevard, and he had worked himself up to such a pitch of fury that the words stuck in his throat.

" 'I will kick the stuffing out of her!'

" 'And why?'

" 'My dear fellow, you will never know the thousand-and-one fancies that slut takes into her head. When I want to stay at home, she, forsooth, must go out; when I want to go

out, she wants me to stop at home; and she spouts out arguments and accusations and reasoning and talks and talks till
she drives you crazy. Right means any whim that they
happen to take into their heads, and wrong means our notion.
Overwhelm them with something that cuts their arguments
to pieces—they hold their tongues and look at you as if you
were a dead dog. My happiness indeed! I lead the life of a
yard-dog; I am a perfect slave. The little happiness that I
have with her costs me dear. Confound it all. I will leave
her everything and take myself off to a garret. Yes, a garret
and liberty. I have not dared to have my own way once in
these five years.'

"But instead of going to his guests, Cursy strode up and
down the boulevard between the Rue de Richelieu and the
Rue du Mont Blanc, indulging in the most fearful imprecations, his unbounded language was most comical to hear. His
paroxysm of fury in the street contrasted oddly with his
peaceable demeanor in the house. Exercise assisted him to
work off his nervous agitation and inward tempest. About
two o'clock, on a sudden frantic impulse, he exclaimed:

"'These damned females never know what they want. I
will wager my head now that if I go home and tell her that
I have sent to ask my friends to dine with me at the *Rocher
de Cancale,* she will not be satisfied though she made the
arrangement herself.—But she will have gone off somewhere
or other. I wonder whether there is something at the bottom
of all this, an assignation with some goat? No. In the bottom of her heart she loves me!'"

The Marquise could not help smiling.

"Ah, madame," said Nathan, looking keenly at her, "only
women and prophets know how to turn faith to account.—Du
Bruel would have me go home with him," he continued, "and
we went slowly back. It was three o'clock. Before he appeared, he heard a stir in the kitchen, saw preparations
going forward, and glanced at me as he asked the cook the
reason of this.

"'Madame ordered dinner,' said the woman. 'Madame

dressed and ordered a cab, and then she changed her mind
and ordered it again for the theatre this evening.'

" 'Good,' exclaimed du Bruel, 'what did I tell you?'

"We entered the house stealthily. No one was there. We
went from room to room until we reached a little boudoir,
and came upon Tullia in tears. She dried her eyes without
affectation, and spoke to du Bruel.

" 'Send a note to the *Rocher de Cancale*,' she said, 'and ask
your guests to dine here.'

"She was dressed as only women of the theatre can dress,
in a simply-made gown of some dainty material, neither too
costly nor too common, graceful, and harmonious in outline
and coloring; there was nothing conspicuous about her, nothing exaggerated—a word now dropping out of use, to be replaced by the word 'artistic,' used by fools as current coin.
In short, Tullia looked like a gentlewoman. At thirty-seven
she had reached the prime of a Frenchwoman's beauty. At
this moment the celebrated oval of her face was divinely pale;
she had laid her hat aside; I could see a faint down like the
bloom of fruit softening the silken contours of a cheek itself
so delicate. There was a pathetic charm about her face with
its double cluster of fair hair; her brilliant gray eyes were
veiled by a mist of tears; her nose, delicately carved as a
Roman cameo, with its quivering nostrils; her little mouth,
like a child's even now; her long queenly throat, with the
veins standing out upon it; her chin, flushed for the moment
by some secret despair; the pink tips of her ears, the hands
that trembled under her gloves, everything about her told
of violent feeling. The feverish twitching of her eyebrows
betrayed her pain. She looked sublime.

"Her first words had crushed du Bruel. She looked at us
both, with that penetrating, impenetrable cat-like glance
which only actresses and great ladies can use. Then she held
out her hand to her husband.

" 'Poor dear, you had scarcely gone before I blamed myself
a thousand times over. It seemed to me that I had been
horribly ungrateful. I told myself that I had been unkind.

—Was I very unkind?' she asked, turning to me.—'Why not receive your friends? Is it not your house? Do you want to know the reason of it all? Well, I was afraid that I was not loved; and indeed I was half-way between repentance and the shame of going back. I read the newspapers, and saw that there was a first night at the Variétés, and I thought you had meant to give the dinner to a collaborator. Left to myself, I gave way, I dressed to hurry out after you—poor pet.'

Du Bruel looked at me triumphantly, not a vestige of a recollection of his orations *contra Tullia* in his mind.

" 'Well, dearest, I have not spoken to any one of them,' he said.

" 'How well we understand each other!' quoth she.

"Even as she uttered those bewildering sweet words, I caught sight of something in her belt, the corner of a little note thrust sidewise into it; but I did not need that indication to tell me that Tullia's fantastic conduct was referable to occult causes. Woman, in my opinion, is the most logical of created beings, the child alone excepted. In both we behold a sublime phenomenon, the unvarying triumph of one dominant, all-excluding thought. The child's thought changes every moment; but while it possesses him, he acts upon it with such ardor that others give way before him, fascinated by the ingenuity, the persistence of a strong desire. Woman is less changeable, but to call her capricious is a stupid insult. Whenever she acts, she is always swayed by one dominant passion; and wonderful it is to see how she makes that passion the very centre of her world.

"Tullia was irresistible; she twisted du Bruel round her fingers, the sky grew blue again, the evening was glorious. And ingenious writer of plays as he is, he never so much as saw that his wife had buried a trouble out of sight.

" 'Such is life, my dear fellow,' he said to me, 'ups and downs and contrasts.'

" 'Especially life off the stage,' I put in.

" 'That is just what I mean,' he continued. 'Why, but for these violent emotions, one would be bored to death! Ah! that woman has the gift of rousing me.'

"We went to the Variétés after dinner; but before we left the house I slipped into du Bruel's room, and on a shelf among a pile of waste papers found the copy of the *Petites-Affiches,* in which, agreeably to the reformed law, notice of the purchase of the house was inserted. The words stared me in the face—'At the request of Jean François du Bruel and Claudine Chaffaroux, his wife——' *Here* was the explanation of the whole matter. I offered my arm to Claudine, and allowed the guests to descend the stairs in front of us. When we were alone—'If I were La Palférine,' I said, 'I would not break an appointment.'

"Gravely she laid her finger on her lips. She leant on my arm as we went downstairs, and looked at me with almost something like happiness in her eyes because I knew La Palférine. Can you see the first idea that occurred to her? She thought of making a spy of me, but I turned her off with the light jesting talk of Bohemia.

"A month later, after a first performance of one of du Bruel's plays, we met in the vestibule of the theatre. It was raining; I went to call a cab. We had been delayed for a few minutes, so that there were no cabs in sight. Claudine scolded du Bruel soundly; and as we rolled through the streets (for she set me down at Florine's), she continued the quarrel with a series of most mortifying remarks.

" 'What is this about?' I inquired.

" 'Oh, my dear fellow, she blames me for allowing you to run out for a cab, and thereupon proceeds to wish for a carriage.'

" 'As a dancer,' said she, 'I have never been accustomed to use my feet except on the boards. If you have any spirit, you will turn out four more plays or so in a year; you will make up your mind that succeed they must, when you think of the end in view, and that your wife will not walk in the mud. It is a shame that I should have to ask for it. You ought to have guessed my continual discomfort during the five years since I married you.'

" 'I am quite willing,' returned du Bruel. 'But we shall ruin ourselves.'

" 'If you run into debt,' she said, 'my uncle's money will clear it off some day.'

" 'You are quite capable of leaving me the debts and taking the property.'

" 'Oh! is that the way you take it?' retorted she. 'I have nothing more to say to you; such a speech stops my mouth.'

"Whereupon du Bruel poured out his soul in excuses and protestations of love. Not a word did she say. He took her hands, she allowed him to take them; they were like ice, like a dead woman's hands. Tullia, you can understand, was playing to admiration the part of corpse that women can play to show you that they refuse their consent to anything and everything; that for you they are suppressing soul, spirit, and life, and regard themselves as beasts of burden. Nothing so provokes a man with a heart as this strategy. Women can only use it with those who worship them.

"She turned to me. 'Do you suppose,' she said scornfully, 'that a Count would have uttered such an insult even if the thought had entered his mind? For my misfortune I have lived with dukes, ambassadors, and great lords, and I know their ways. How intolerable it makes bourgeois life! After all, a playwright is not a Rastignac nor a Rhétoré——'

"Du Bruel looked ghastly at this. Two days afterwards we met in the *foyer* at the Opéra, and took a few turns together. The conversation fell on Tullia.

" 'Do not take my ravings on the boulevard too seriously,' said he; 'I have a violent temper.'

"For two winters I was a tolerably frequent visitor at du Bruel's house, and I followed Claudine's tactics closely. She had a splendid carriage. Du Bruel entered public life; she made him abjure his Royalist opinions. He rallied himself; he took his place again in the administration; the National Guard was discreetly canvassed, du Bruel was elected major, and behaved so valorously in a street riot, that he was decorated with the rosette of an officer of the Legion of Honor. He was appointed Master of Requests and head of a department. Uncle Chaffaroux died and left his niece forty thou-

sand francs per annum, three-fourths of his fortune. Du
Bruel became a deputy; but beforehand, to save the necessity
of re-election, he secured his nomination to the Council of
State. He reprinted divers archæological treatises, a couple
of political pamphlets, and a statistical work, by way of pretext for his appointment to one of the obliging academies of
the Institut. At this moment he is a Commander of the Legion, and (after fishing in the troubled waters of political
intrigue) has quite recently been made a peer of France and
a count. As yet our friend does not venture to bear his
honors; his wife merely puts 'La Comtesse du Bruel' on her
cards. The sometime playwright has the Order of Leopold,
the Order of Isabella, the Cross of Saint-Vladimir, second
class, the Order of Civil Merit of Bavaria, the Papal Order of
the Golden Spur,—all the lesser orders, in short, besides the
Grand Cross.

"Three months ago Claudine drove to La Palférine's door
in her splendid carriage with its armorial bearings. Du
Bruel's grandfather was a farmer of taxes ennobled towards
the end of Louis Quatorze's reign. Chérin composed his coat-
of-arms for him, so the Count's coronet looks not amiss above
a scutcheon innocent of Imperial absurdities. In this way,
in the short space of three years, Claudine had carried out
the programme laid down for her by the charming, light-
hearted La Palférine.

"One day, just a month ago, she climbed the miserable
staircase to her lover's lodging; climbed in her glory, dressed
like a real countess of the Faubourg Saint-Germain, to our
friend's garret. La Palférine, seeing her, said, 'You have
made a peeress of yourself I know. But it is too late, Claudine; every one is talking just now about the Southern Cross,
I should like to see it!'

"'I will get it for you.'

"La Palférine burst into a peal of Homeric laughter.

"'Most distinctly,' he returned, 'I do *not* wish to have a
woman as ignorant as a carp for my mistress, a woman that
springs like a flying fish from the green-room of the Opéra

to Court, for I should like to see you at the Court of the Citizen King.'

"She turned to me.

" 'What is the Southern Cross?' she asked, in a sad, downcast voice.

"I was struck with admiration for this indomitable love, outdoing the most ingenious marvels of fairy tales in real life—a love that would spring over a precipice to find a roc's egg, or to gather the singing flower. I explained that the Southern Cross was a nebulous constellation even brighter than the Milky Way, arranged in the form of a cross, and that it could only be seen in southern latitudes.

" 'Very well, Charles, let us go,' said she.

"La Palférine, ferocious though he was, had tears in his eyes; but what a look there was in Claudine's face, what a note in her voice! I have seen nothing like the thing that followed, not even in the supreme touch of a great actor's art; nothing to compare with her movement when she saw the hard eyes softened in tears; Claudine sank upon her knees and kissed La Palférine's pitiless hand. He raised her with his grand manner, his 'Rusticoli air,' as he calls it—'There, child!' he said, 'I will do something for you; I will put you— in my will.'

"Well," concluded Nathan, "I ask myself sometimes whether du Bruel is really deceived. Truly there is nothing more comic, nothing stranger than the sight of a careless young fellow ruling a married couple, his slightest whims received as law, the weightiest decisions revoked at a word from him. That dinner incident, as you can see, is repeated times without number, it interferes with important matters. Still, but for Claudine's caprices, du Bruel would be de Cursy still, one vaudevillist among five hundred; whereas he is in the House of Peers."

"You will change the names, I hope!" said Nathan, addressing Mme. de la Baudraye.

"I should think so! I have only set names to the masks for

you. My dear Nathan," she added in the poet's ear, "I know another case in which the wife takes du Bruel's place."

"And the catastrophe?" queried Lousteau, returning just at the end of Mme. de la Baudraye's story.

"I do not believe in catastrophes. One has to invent such good ones to show that art is quite a match for chance; and nobody reads a book twice, my friend, except for the details."

"But there is a catastrophe," persisted Nathan.

"What is it?"

"The Marquise de Rochefide is infatuated with Charles Edward. My story excited her curiosity."

"Oh, unhappy woman!" cried Mme. de la Baudraye.

"Not so unhappy," said Nathan, "for Maxime de Trailles and La Palférine have brought about a rupture between the Marquis and Mme. Schontz, and they mean to make it up between Arthur and Béatrix."

1839–1845.

A MAN OF BUSINESS

*To Monsieur le Baron James de Rothschild, Banker and
Austrian Consul-General at Paris.*

THE word *lorette* is a euphemism invented to describe the
status of a personage, or a personage of a status, of which it
is awkward to speak; the French Académie, in its modesty,
having omitted to supply a definition out of regard for the
age of its forty members. Whenever a new word comes to
supply the place of an unwieldy circumlocution, its fortune
is assured; the word *lorette* has passed into the language of
every class of society, even where the lorette herself will never
gain an entrance. It was only invented in 1840, and derived
beyond a doubt from the agglomeration of such swallows'
nests about the Church of Our Lady of Loretto. This information is for etymologists only. Those gentlemen would not
be so often in a quandary if mediæval writers had only taken
such pains with details of contemporary manners as we take
in these days of analysis and description.

Mlle. Turquet, or Malaga, for she is better known by her
pseudonym,* was one of the earliest parishioners of that
charming church. At the time to which this story belongs,
that lighthearted and lively damsel gladdened the existence
of a notary with a wife somewhat too bigoted, rigid, and frigid
for domestic happiness.

Now, it so fell out that one Carnival evening Maître Cardot
was entertaining guests at Mlle. Turquet's house—Desroches
the attorney, Bixiou of the caricatures, Lousteau the journalist, Nathan, and others; it is quite unnecessary to give any
further description of these personages, all bearers of illustrious names in the *Comédie Humaine.* Young La Palférine,

*See *La fausse Maîtresse.*

(251)

in spite of his title of Count and his great descent, which, alas! means a great descent in fortune likewise, had honored the notary's little establishment with his presence.

At dinner, in such a house, one does not expect to meet the patriarchal beef, the skinny fowl and salad of domestic and family life, nor is there any attempt at the hypocritical conversation of drawing-rooms furnished with highly respectable matrons. When, alas! will respectability be charming? When will the women in good society vouchsafe to show rather less of their shoulders and rather more wit or geniality? Marguerite Turquet, the Aspasia of the Cirque-Olympique, is one of those frank, very living personalities to whom all is forgiven, such unconscious sinners are they, such intelligent penitents; of such as Malaga one might ask, like Cardot—a witty man enough, albeit a notary—to be well "deceived." And yet you must not think that any enormities were committed. Desroches and Cardot were good fellows grown too gray in the profession not to feel at ease with Bixiou, Lousteau, Nathan, and young La Palférine. And they on their side had too often had recourse to their legal advisers, and knew them too well to try to "draw them out," in lorette language.

Conversation, perfumed with seven cigars, at first was as fantastic as a kid let loose, but finally it settled down upon the strategy of the constant war waged in Paris between creditors and debtors.

Now, if you will be so good as to recall the history and antecedents of the guests, you will know that in all Paris you could scarcely find a group of men with more experience in this matter; the professional men on one hand, and the artists on the other, were something in the position of magistrates and criminals hobnobbing together. A set of Bixiou's drawings to illustrate life in the debtors' prison, led the conversation to take this particular turn; and from debtors' prisons they went to debts.

It was midnight. They had broken up into little knots round the table and before the fire, and gave themselves up

to the burlesque fun which is only possible or comprehensible
in Paris and in that particular region which is bounded
by the Faubourg Montmartre, the Rue Chaussée d'Antin, the
upper end of the Rue de Navarin and the line of the boulevards.

In ten minutes' time they had come to an end of all the
deep reflections, all the moralizings, small and great, all the
bad puns made on a subject already exhausted by Rabelais
three hundred and fifty years ago. It is not a little to their
credit that the pyrotechnic display was cut short with a final
squib from Malaga.

"It all goes to the shoemakers," she said. "I left a milliner
because she failed twice with my hats. The vixen has been
here twenty-seven times to ask for twenty francs. She did
not know that we never have twenty francs. One has a thousand francs, or one sends to one's notary for five hundred;
but twenty francs I have never had in my life. My cook and
my maid may, perhaps, have so much between them; but for
my own part, I have nothing but credit, and I should lose that
if I took to borrowing small sums. If I were to ask for twenty
francs, I should have nothing to distinguish me from my colleagues that walk the boulevard."

"Is the milliner paid?" asked La Palférine.

"Oh, come now, are you turning stupid?" said she, with a
wink. "She came this morning for the twenty-seventh time,
that is how I came to mention it."

"What did you do?" asked Desroches.

"I took pity upon her, and—ordered a little hat that I
have just invented, a quite new shape. If Mlle. Amanda
succeeds with it, she will say no more about the money, her
fortune is made."

"In my opinion," put in Desroches, "the finest things that
I have seen in a duel of this kind give those who know Paris
a far better picture of the city than all the fancy portraits
that they paint. Some of you think that you know a thing
or two," he continued, glancing round at Nathan, Bixiou, La
Palférine, and Lousteau, "but the king of the ground is a

certain Count, now busy ranging himself. In his time, he was supposed to be the cleverest, adroitest, canniest, boldest, stoutest, most subtle and experienced of all the pirates, who, equipped with fine manners, yellow kid gloves, and cabs, have ever sailed or ever will sail upon the stormy sea of Paris. He fears neither God nor man. He applies in private life the principles that guide the English Cabinet. Up to the time of his marriage, his life was one continual war, like—Lousteau's, for instance. I was, and am still his solicitor."

"And the first letter of his name is Maxime de Trailles," said La Palférine.

"For that matter, he has paid every one, and injured no one," continued Desroches. "But as our friend Bixiou was saying just now, it is a violation of the liberty of the subject to be made to pay in March when you have no mind to pay till October. By virtue of this article of his particular code, Maxime regarded a creditor's scheme for making him pay at once as a swindler's trick. It was long since he had grasped the significance of the bill of exchange in all its bearings, direct and remote. A young man once, in my place, called a bill of exchange the 'asses' bridge' in his hearing. 'No,' said he, 'it is the Bridge of Sighs; it is the shortest way to an execution.' Indeed, his knowledge of commercial law was so complete, that a professional could not have taught him anything. At that time he had nothing, as you know. His carriage and horses were jobbed; he lived in his valet's house; and, by the way, he will be a hero to his valet to the end of the chapter, even after the marriage that he proposes to make. He belonged to three clubs, and dined at one of them whenever he did not dine out. As a rule, he was to be found very seldom at his own address——"

"He once said to me," interrupted La Palférine, " 'My one affectation is the pretence that I make of living in the Rue Pigalle.' "

"Well," resumed Desroches, "he was one of the combatants; and now for the other. You have heard more or less talk of one Claparon?"

"Had hair like this!" cried Bixiou, ruffling his locks till they stood on end. Gifted with the same talent for mimicking absurdities which Chopin the pianist possesses to so high a degree, he proceeded forthwith to represent the character with startling truth.

"He rolls his head like this when he speaks; he was once a commercial traveler; he has been all sorts of things——"

"Well, he was born to travel, for at this minute, as I speak, he is on the sea on his way to America," said Desroches. "It is his only chance, for in all probability he will be condemned by default as a fraudulent bankrupt next session."

"Very much at sea!" exclaimed Malaga.

"For six or seven years this Claparon acted as man of straw, cat's-paw, and scapegoat to two friends of ours, du Tillet and Nucingen; but in 1829 his part was so well known that——"

"Our friends dropped him," put in Bixiou.

"They left him to his fate at last, and he wallowed in the mire," continued Desroches. "In 1833 he went into partnership with one Cérizet——"

"What! he that promoted a joint-stock company so nicely that the Sixth Chamber cut short his career with a couple of years in jail?" asked the lorette.

"The same. Under the Restoration, between 1823 and 1827, Cérizet's occupation consisted in first putting his name intrepidly to various paragraphs, on which the public prosecutor fastened with avidity, and subsequently marching off to prison. A man could make a name for himself with small expense in those days. The Liberal party called their provincial champion 'the courageous Cérizet,' and towards 1828 so much zeal received its reward in 'general interest.'

" 'General interest' is a kind of civic crown bestowed on the deserving by the daily press. Cérizet tried to discount the 'general interest' taken in him. He came to Paris, and, with some help from capitalists in the Opposition, started as a broker, and conducted financial operations to some extent, the capital being found by a man in hiding, a skilful gambler who overreached himself, and in consequence, in July 1830, his capital foundered in the shipwreck of the Government."

"Oh! it was he whom we used to call the System," cried Bixiou.

"Say no harm of him, poor fellow," protested Malaga. "D'Estourny was a good sort."

"You can imagine the part that a ruined man was sure to play in 1830 when his name in politics was 'the courageous Cérizet.' He was sent off into a very snug little sub-prefecture. Unluckily for him, it is one thing to be in opposition—any missile is good enough to throw, so long as the fight lasts; but quite another to be in office. Three months later, he was obliged to send in his resignation. Had he not taken it into his head to attempt to win popularity? Still, as he had done nothing as yet to imperil his title of 'courageous Cérizet,' the Government proposed by way of compensation that he should manage a newspaper; nominally an Opposition paper, but Ministerialist *in petto*. So the fall of this noble nature was really due to the Government. To Cérizet, as manager of the paper, it was rather too evident that he was as a bird perched on a rotten bough; and then it was that he promoted that nice little joint-stock company, and thereby secured a couple of years in prison; he was caught, while more ingenious swindlers succeeded in catching the public."

"We are acquainted with the more ingenious," said Bixiou; "let us say no ill of the poor fellow; he was nabbed; Couture allowed them to squeeze his cash-box; who would ever have thought it of him?"

"At all events, Cérizet was a low sort of fellow, a good deal damaged by low debauchery. Now for the duel I spoke about. Never did two tradesmen of the worst type, with the worst manners, the lowest pair of villains imaginable, go into partnership in a dirtier business. Their stock-in-trade consisted of the peculiar idiom of the man about town, the audacity of poverty, the cunning that comes of experience, and a special knowledge of Parisian capitalists, their origin, connections, acquaintances, and intrinsic value. This partnership of two 'dabblers' (let the Stock Exchange term pass, for it is the only word which describes them), this partnership of dabblers did not last very long. They fought like famished curs over every bit of garbage.

"The earlier speculations of the firm of Cérizet and Claparon were, however, well planned. The two scamps joined forces with Barbet, Chaboisseau, Samanon, and usurers of that stamp, and bought up hopelessly bad debts.

"Claparon's place of business at that time was a cramped entresol in the Rue Chabannais—five rooms at a rent of seven hundred francs at most. Each partner slept in a little closet, so carefully closed from prudence, that my head-clerk could never get inside. The furniture of the other three rooms—an ante-chamber, a waiting-room, and a private office—would not have fetched three hundred francs altogether at a distress-warrant sale. You know enough of Paris to know the look of it; the stuffed horsehair-covered chairs, a table covered with a green cloth, a trumpery clock between a couple of candle sconces, growing tarnished under glass shades, the small gilt-framed mirror over the chimney-piece, and in the grate a charred stick or two of firewood which had lasted them for two winters, as my head-clerk put it. As for the office, you can guess what it was like—more letter-files than business letters, a set of common pigeon-holes for either partner, a cylinder desk, empty as the cash-box, in the middle of the room, and a couple of armchairs on either side of a coal fire. The carpet on the floor was bought cheap at second-hand (like the bills and bad debts). In short, it was the mahogany furniture of furnished apartments which usually descends from one occupant of chambers to another during fifty years of service. Now you know the pair of antagonists.

"During the first three months of a partnership dissolved four months later in a bout of fisticuffs, Cérizet and Claparon bought up two thousand francs' worth of bills bearing Maxime's signature (since Maxime is his name), and filled a couple of letter files to bursting with judgments, appeals, orders of the court, distress-warrant, application for stay of proceedings, and all the rest of it; to put it briefly, they had bills for three thousand two hundred francs odd centimes, for which they had given five hundred francs; the transfer being made under private seal, with special power of attorney, to save the expense of registration. Now it so happened at this juncture, Maxime, being of ripe age, was seized with one of the fancies peculiar to the man of fifty——"

"Antonia!" exclaimed La Palférine. "That Antonia whose fortune I made by writing to ask for a toothbrush!"

"Her real name is Chocardelle," said Malaga, not over well pleased by the fine-sounding pseudonym.

"The same," continued Desroches.

"It was the only mistake Maxime ever made in his life. But what would you have, no vice is absolutely perfect?" put in Bixiou.

"Maxime had still to learn what sort of a life a man may be led into by a girl of eighteen when she is minded to take a header from her honest garret into a sumptuous carriage; it is a lesson that all statesmen should take to heart. At this time, de Marsay had just been employing his friend, our friend de Trailles, in the high comedy of politics. Maxime had looked high for his conquests; he had no experience of untitled women; and at fifty years he felt that he had a right to take a bite of a little so-called wild fruit, much as a sportsman will halt under a peasant's apple-tree. So the Count found a reading-room for Mlle. Chocardelle, a rather smart little place to be had cheap, as usual——"

"Pooh!" said Nathan. "She did not stay in it six months. She was too handsome to keep a reading-room."

"Perhaps you are the father of her child?" suggested the lorette.

Desroches resumed.

"Since the firm bought up Maxime's debts, Cérizet's likeness to a bailiff's officer grew more and more striking, and one morning after seven fruitless attempts he succeeded in penetrating into the Count's presence. Suzon, the old man-servant, albeit he was by no means in his novitiate, at last mistook the visitor for a petitioner, come to propose a thousand crowns if Maxime would obtain a license to sell postage stamps for a young lady. Suzon, without the slightest suspicion of the little scamp, a thoroughbred Paris street-boy into whom prudence had been rubbed by repeated personal experience of the police-courts, induced his master to receive him. Can you see the man of business, with an uneasy eye, a bald forehead, and scarcely any hair on his head, standing in his threadbare jacket and muddy boots——"

"What a picture of a Dun!" cried Lousteau.

"——standing before the Count, that image of flaunting Debt, in his blue flannel dressing-gown, slippers worked by some Marquise or other, trousers of white woolen stuff, and a dazzling shirt? There he stood, with a gorgeous cap on his black dyed hair, playing with the tassels at his waist——"

" 'Tis a bit of genre for anybody who knows the pretty little morning room, hung with silk and full of valuable paintings, where Maxime breakfasts," said Nathan. "You tread on a Smyrna carpet, you admire the sideboards filled with curiosities and rarities fit to make a King of Saxony envious——"

"Now for the scene itself," said Desroches, and the deepest silence followed.

" 'Monsieur le Comte,' began Cérizet; 'I have come from a M. Charles Claparon, who used to be a banker——'

" 'Ah! poor devil, and what does he want with me?' .

" 'Well, he is at present your creditor for a matter of three thousand two hundred francs, seventy-five centimes, principal, interest, and costs——"

" 'Coutelier's business?' put in Maxime, who knew his affairs as a pilot knows his coast.

" 'Yes, Monsieur le Comte,' said Cérizet with a bow. 'I have come to ask your intentions.'

" 'I shall only pay when the fancy takes me,' returned Maxime, and he rang for Suzon. 'It was very rash of Claparon to buy up bills of mine without speaking to me beforehand. I am sorry for him, for he did so very well for such a long time as a man of straw for friends of mine. I always said that a man must really be weak in his intellect to work for men that stuff themselves with millions, and to serve them so faithfully for such low wages. And now here he gives me another proof of his stupidity! Yes, men deserve what they get. It is your own doing whether you get a crown on your forehead or a bullet through your head; whether you are a millionaire or a porter, justice is always done you. I cannot help it, my dear fellow; I myself am not a king, I stick to my principles. I have no pity for those that put me to expense or do not know their business as creditors.—Suzon! my tea! Do you see this gentleman?' he continued when the man came in. 'Well, you have allowed yourself to be taken in, poor old boy. This gentleman is a creditor; you ought to have known him by his boots. No friend nor foe of mine, nor those that are neither and want something of me, come to see me on foot. —My dear M. Cérizet, do you understand? You will not wipe your boots on my carpet again' (looking as he spoke at the mud that whitened the enemy's soles). 'Convey my compliments and sympathy to Claparon, poor buffer, for I shall file this business under the letter Z.'

"All this with an easy good-humor fit to give a virtuous citizen the colic.

" 'You are wrong, Monsieur le Comte,' retorted Cérizet, in a slightly peremptory tone. 'We will be paid in full, and that in a way which you may not like. That was why I came to you first in a friendly spirit, as is right and fit between gentlemen——'

" 'Oh! so that is how you understand it?' began Maxime, enraged by this last piece of presumption. There was something of Talleyrand's wit in the insolent retort, if you have quite grasped the contrast between the two men and their costumes. Maxime scowled and looked full at the intruder; Cérizet not merely endured the glare of cold fury, but even returned it, with an icy, cat-like malignance and fixity of gaze.

" 'Very good, sir, go out——'

" 'Very well, good-day, Monsieur le Comte. We shall be quits before six months are out.'

" 'If you can steal the amount of your bill, which is legally due I own, I shall be indebted to you, sir,' replied Maxime.

'You will have taught me a new precaution to take. I am very much your servant.'

" 'Monsieur le Comte,' said Cérizet, 'it is I, on the contrary, who am yours.'

"Here was an explicit, forcible, confident declaration on either side. A couple of tigers confabulating, with the prey before them, and a fight impending, would have been no finer and no shrewder than this pair; the insolent fine gentleman as great a blackguard as the other in his soiled and mud-stained clothes.

"Which will you lay your money on?" asked Desroches, looking round at an audience, surprised to find how deeply it was interested.

"A pretty story!" cried Malaga. "My dear boy, go on, I beg of you. This goes to one's heart."

"Nothing commonplace could happen between two fighting-cocks of that calibre," added La Palférine.

"Pooh!" cried Malaga, "I will wager my cabinet-maker's invoice (the fellow is dunning me) that the little toad was too many for Maxime."

"I bet on Maxime," said Cardot. "Nobody ever caught him napping."

Desroches drank off a glass that Malaga handed to him.

"Mlle. Chocardelle's reading-room," he continued, after a pause, "was in the Rue Coquenard, just a step or two from the Rue Pigalle where Maxime was living. The said Mlle. Chocardelle lived at the back on the garden side of the house, beyond a big, dark place where the books were kept. Antonia left her aunt to look after the business——"

"Had she an aunt even then?" exclaimed Malaga. "Hang it all, Maxime did things handsomely."

"Alas! it was a real aunt," said Desroches; "her name was —let me see——"

"Ida Bonamy," said Bixiou.

"So as Antonia's aunt took a good deal of the work off her hands, she went to bed late and lay late of a morning, never showing her face at the desk until the afternoon, some time

between two and four. From the very first her appearance
was enough to draw custom. Several elderly men in the quarter used to come, among them a retired coach-builder, one
Croizeau. Beholding this miracle of female loveliness
through the window-panes, he took it into his head to read
the newspapers in the beauty's reading-room; and a sometime
custom-house officer, named Denisart, with a ribbon in his
button-hole, followed the example. Croizeau chose to look
upon Denisart as a rival. *'Môsieur,'* he said afterwards, 'I
did not know what to buy for you!'

"That speech should give you an idea of the man. The
Sieur Croizeau happens to belong to a particular class of old
man which should be known as 'Coquerels' since Henri Monnier's time; so well did Monnier render the piping voice, the
little mannerisms, little queue, little sprinkling of powder,
little movements of the head, prim little manner, and tripping
gait in the part of Coquerel in *La Famille Improvisée.* This
Croizeau used to hand over his halfpence with a flourish and a
'There, fair lady!'

"Mme. Ida Bonamy the aunt was not long in finding out
through the servant that Croizeau, by popular report of the
neighborhood of the Rue de Buffault, where he lived, was a
man of exceeding stinginess, possessed of forty thousand
francs per annum. A week after the instalment of the charming librarian he was delivered of a pun:

"'You lend me books (*livres*), but I give you plenty of
francs in return,' said he.

"A few days later he put on a knowing little air, as much
as to say, 'I know you are engaged, but my turn will come one
day; I am a widower.'

"He always came arrayed in fine linen, a cornflower blue
coat, a paduasoy waistcoat, black trousers, and black ribbon
bows on the double soled shoes that creaked like an abbé's; he
always held a fourteen franc silk hat in his hand.

"'I am old and I have no children,' he took occasion to
confide to the young lady some few days after Cérizet's visit to
Maxime. 'I hold my relations in horror. They are peasants

born to work in the fields. Just imagine it, I came up from
the country with six francs in my pocket, and made my fortune here. I am not proud. A pretty woman is my equal.
Now would it not be nicer to be Mme. Croizeau for some years
to come than to do a Count's pleasure for a twelvemonth? He
will go off and leave you some time or other; and when that
day comes, you will think of me . . . your servant, my
pretty lady!'

"All this was simmering below the surface. The slightest
approach at love-making was made quite on the sly. Not a
soul suspected that the trim little old fogy was smitten with
Antonia; and so prudent was the elderly lover, that no rival
could have guessed anything from his behavior in the reading-
room. For a couple of months Croizeau watched the retired
custom-house official; but before the third month was out he
had good reason to believe that his suspicions were groundless.
He exerted his ingenuity to scrape an acquaintance with Denisart, came up with him in the street, and at length seized his
opportunity to remark, 'It is a fine day, sir!'

"Whereupon the retired official responded with, 'Austerlitz
weather, sir. I was there myself—I was wounded indeed, I
won my Cross on that glorious day.'

"And so from one thing to another the two drifted wrecks
of the Empire struck up an acquaintance. Little Croizeau
was attached to the Empire through his connection with Napoleon's sisters. He had been their coach-builder, and had
frequently dunned them for money; so he gave out that he
'had had relations with the Imperial family.' Maxime, duly
informed by Antonia of the 'nice old man's' proposals (for so
the aunt called Croizeau), wished to see him. Cérizet's declaration of war had so far taken effect that he of the yellow
kid gloves was studying the position of every piece, however
insignificant, upon the board; and it so happened that at
the mention of that 'nice old man,' an ominous tinkling
sounded in his ears. One evening, therefore, Maxime seated
himself among the book-shelves in the dimly lighted back
room, reconnoitred the seven or eight customers through the

chink between the green curtains, and took the little coach-
builder's measure. He gauged the man's infatuation, and
was very well satisfied to find that the varnished doors of a
tolerably sumptuous future were ready to turn at a word
from Antonia so soon as his own fancy had passed off.

"'And that other one yonder?' asked he, pointing out the
stout fine-looking elderly man with the Cross of the Legion
of Honor. 'Who is he?'

"'A retired custom-house officer.'

"'The cut of his countenance is not reassuring,' said Maxime, beholding the Sieur Denisart.

"And indeed the old soldier held himself upright as a
steeple. His head was remarkable for the amount of powder
and pomatum bestowed upon it; he looked almost like a postilion at a fancy ball. Underneath that felted covering,
moulded to the top of the wearer's cranium, appeared an elderly profile, half-official, half-soldierly, with a comical admixture of arrogance,—altogether something like caricatures
of the *Constitutionnel*. The sometime official finding that
age, and hair-powder, and the conformation of his spine made
it impossible to read a word without spectacles, sat displaying a very creditable expanse of chest with all the pride
of an old man with a mistress. Like old General Montcornet,
that pillar of the Vaudeville, he wore earrings. Denisart was
partial to blue; his roomy trousers and well-worn greatcoat
were both of blue cloth.

"'How long is it since that old fogy came here?' inquired
Maxime, thinking that he saw danger in the spectacles.

"'Oh, from the beginning,' returned Antonia, 'pretty
nearly two months ago now.'

"'Good,' said Maxime to himself, 'Cérizet only came to me
a month ago.—Just get him to talk,' he added in Antonia's
ear; 'I want to hear his voice.'

"'Pshaw,' said she, 'that is not so easy. He never says a
word to me.'

"'Then why does he come here?' demanded Maxime.

"'For a queer reason,' returned the fair Antonia. 'In the
first place, although he is sixty-nine, he has a fancy; and be-

cause he is sixty-nine, he is as methodical as a clock face.
Every day at five o'clock the old gentleman goes to dine with
her in the Rue de la Victoire. (I am sorry for her.) Then
at six o'clock, he comes here, reads steadily at the papers for
four hours, and goes back at ten o'clock. Daddy Croizeau says
that he knows M. Denisart's motives, and approves his conduct; and in his place, he would do the same. So I know
exactly what to expect. If ever I am Mme. Croizeau, I shall
have four hours to myself between six and ten o'clock.'

"Maxime looked through the directory, and found the following reassuring item:

" DENISART,* retired custom-house officer, Rue de la Victoire.

"His uneasiness vanished.

"Gradually the Sieur Denisart and the Sieur Croizeau began to exchange confidences. Nothing so binds two men together as a similarity of views in the matter of womankind.
Daddy Croizeau went to dine with 'M. Denisart's fair lady,'
as he called her. And here I must make a somewhat important observation.

"The reading-room had been paid for half in cash, half in
bills signed by the said Mlle. Chocardelle. The *quart d'heure
de Rabelais* arrived; the Count had no money. So the first
bill of three thousand-franc bills was met by the amiable
coach-builder; that old scoundrel Denisart having recommended him to secure himself with a mortgage on the reading-
room.

" 'For my own part,' said Denisart, 'I have seen pretty
doings from pretty women. So, in all cases, even when I
have lost my head, I am always on my guard with a woman.
There is this creature, for instance; I am madly in love with
her; but this is not her furniture; no, it belongs to me. The
lease is taken out in my name.'

"You know Maxime! He thought the coach-builder uncommonly green. Croizeau might pay all three bills, and get
nothing for a long while; for Maxime felt more infatuated
with Antonia than ever."

"I can well believe it," said La Palférine. "She is the *bella Imperia* of our day."

"With her rough skin!" exclaimed Malaga; "so rough, that she ruins herself in bran baths!"

"Croizeau spoke with a coach-builder's admiration of the sumptuous furniture provided by the amorous Denisart as a setting for his fair one, describing it all in detail with diabolical complacency for Antonia's benefit," continued Desroches. "The ebony chests inlaid with mother-of-pearl and gold wire, the Brussels carpets, a mediæval bedstead worth three thousand francs, a Boule clock, candelabra in the four corners of the dining-room, silk curtains, on which Chinese patience had wrought pictures of birds, and hangings over the doors, worth more than the portress that opened them.

" 'And that is what *you* ought to have, my pretty lady.— And that is what I should like to offer you,' he would conclude. 'I am quite aware that you scarcely care a bit about me; but, at my age, we cannot expect too much. Judge how much I love you; I have lent you a thousand francs. I must confess that, in all my born days, I have not lent anybody *that* much——'

"He held out his penny as he spoke, with the important air of a man that gives a learned demonstration.

"That evening at the Variétés, Antonia spoke to the Count.

" 'A reading-room is very dull, all the same,' said she; 'I feel that I have no sort of taste for that kind of life, and I see no future in it. It is only fit for a widow that wishes to keep body and soul together, or for some hideously ugly thing that fancies she can catch a husband with a little finery.'

" 'It was your own choice,' returned the Count. Just at that moment, in came Nucingen, of whom Maxime, king of lions (the 'yellow kid gloves' were the lions of that day) had won three thousand francs the evening before. Nucingen had come to pay his gaming debt.

" 'Ein writ of attachment haf shoost peen served on me by der order of dot teufel Glabaron,' he said, seeing Maxime's astonishment.

" 'Oh, so that is how they are going to work, is it?' cried Maxime. 'They are not up to much, that pair——'

" 'It makes not,' said the banker, 'bay dem, for dey may apply demselfs to oders pesides, und do you harm. I dake dees bretty voman to vitness dot I haf baid you dees morning, long pefore dat writ vas serfed.' "

"Queen of the boards," smiled La Palférine, looking at Malaga, "thou art about to lose thy bet."

"Once, a long time ago, in a similar case," resumed Desroches, "a too honest debtor took fright at the idea of a solemn declaration in a court of law, and declined to pay Maxime after notice was given. That time we made it hot for the creditor by piling on writs of attachment, so as to absorb the whole amount in costs——"

"Oh, what is that?" cried Malaga; "it all sounds like gibberish to me. As you thought the sturgeon so excellent at dinner, let me take out the value of the sauce in lessons in chicanery."

"Very well," said Desroches. "Suppose that a man owes you money, and your creditors serve a writ of attachment upon him; there is nothing to prevent all your other creditors from doing the same thing. And now what does the court do when all the creditors make application for orders to pay? *The court divides the whole sum attached, proportionately among them all.* That division, made under the eye of a magistrate, is what we call a *contribution.* If you owe ten thousand francs, and your creditors issue writs of attachment on a debt due to you of a thousand francs, each one of them gets so much per cent, 'so much in the pound,' in legal phrase; so much (that means) in proportion to the amounts severally claimed by the creditors. But—the creditors cannot touch the money without a special order from the clerk of the court. Do you guess what all this work drawn up by a judge and prepared by attorneys must mean? It means a quantity of stamped paper full of diffuse lines and blanks, the figures almost lost in vast spaces of completely empty ruled columns. The first proceeding is to deduct the costs. Now, as the costs are precisely the same whether the amount attached is one thousand or one million francs, it is not difficult to eat up three thousand francs (for instance) in costs, especially if you can manage to raise counter applications."

"And an attorney always manages to do it," said Cardot. "How many a time one of you has come to me with, 'What is there to be got out of the case?'"

"It is particularly easy to manage it if the debtor eggs you on to run up costs till they eat up the amount. And, as a rule, the Count's creditors took nothing by that move, and were out of pocket in law and personal expenses. To get money out of so experienced a debtor as the Count, a creditor should really be in a position uncommonly difficult to reach; it is a question of being creditor and debtor both, for then you are legally entitled to work the confusion of rights, in law language——"

"To the confusion of the debtor?" asked Malaga, lending an attentive ear to this discourse.

"No, the confusion of rights of debtor and creditor, and pay yourself through your own hands. So Claparon's innocence in merely issuing writs of attachment eased the Count's mind. As he came back from the Variétés with Antonia, he was so much the more taken with the idea of selling the reading-room to pay off the last two thousand francs of the purchase-money, because he did not care to have his name made public as a partner in such a concern. So he adopted Antonia's plan. Antonia wished to reach the higher ranks of her calling, with splendid rooms, a maid, and a carriage; in short, she wanted to rival our charming hostess, for instance——"

"She was not woman enough for that," cried the famous beauty of the Circus; "still, she ruined young d'Esgrignon very neatly."

"Ten days afterwards, little Croizeau, perched on his dignity, said almost exactly the same thing, for the fair Antonia's benefit," continued Desroches.

" 'Child,' said he, 'your reading-room is a hole of a place. You will lose your complexion; the gas will ruin your eyesight. You ought to come out of it; and, look here, let us take advantage of an opportunity. I have found a young lady for you that asks no better than to buy your reading-room. She is a ruined woman with nothing before her but a plunge into the river; but she has four thousand francs in cash, and the best thing to do is to turn them to account, so as to feed and educate a couple of children.'

"'Very well. It is kind of you, Daddy Croizeau,' said Antonia.

"'Oh, I shall be much kinder before I have done. Just imagine it, poor M. Denisart has been worried into the jaundice! Yes, it has gone to the liver, as it usually does with susceptible old men. It is a pity he feels things so. I told him so myself; I said, "Be passionate, there is no harm in that, but as for taking things to heart—draw the line at that! It is the way to kill yourself."—Really, I would not have expected him to take on so about it; a man that has sense enough and experience enough to keep away as he does while he digests his dinner——'

"'But what is the matter?' inquired Mlle. Chocardelle.

"'That little baggage with whom I dined has cleared out and left him! . . . Yes. Gave him the slip without any warning but a letter, in which the spelling was all to seek.'

"'There, Daddy Croizeau, you see what comes of boring a woman——'

"'It is indeed a lesson, my pretty lady,' said the guileful Croizeau. 'Meanwhile, I have never seen a man in such a state. Our friend Denisart cannot tell his left hand from his right; he will not go back to look at the "scene of his happiness," as he calls it. He has so thoroughly lost his wits, that he proposes that I should buy all Hortense's furniture (Hortense was her name) for four thousand francs.'

"'A pretty name,' said Antonia.

"'Yes. Napoleon's stepdaughter was called Hortense. I built carriages for her, as you know.'

"'Very well, I will see,' said cunning Antonia; 'begin by sending this young woman to me.'

"Antonia hurried off to see the furniture, and came back fascinated. She brought Maxime under the spell of antiquarian enthusiasm. That very evening the Count agreed to the sale of the reading-room. The establishment, you see, nominally belonged to Mlle. Chocardelle. Maxime burst out laughing at the idea of little Croizeau's finding him a buyer. The firm of Maxime and Chocardelle was losing two thousand francs, it is true, but what was the loss compared with four glorious thousand-franc notes in hand? 'Four thousand francs of live coin!—there are moments in one's life when one would sign bills for eight thousand to get them,' as the Count said to me.

"Two days later the Count must see the furniture himself, and took the four thousand francs upon him. The sale had been arranged; thanks to little Croizeau's diligence, he pushed matters on; he had 'come round' the widow, as he expressed it. It was Maxime's intention to have all the furniture removed at once to a lodging in a new house in the Rue Tronchet, taken in the name of Mme. Ida Bonamy; he did not trouble himself much about the nice old man that was about to lose his thousand francs. But he had sent beforehand for several big furniture vans.

"Once again he was fascinated by the beautiful furniture which a wholesale dealer would have valued at six thousand francs. By the fireside sat the wretched owner, yellow with jaundice, his head tied up in a couple of printed handkerchiefs, and a cotton night-cap on the top of them; he was huddled up in wrappings like a chandelier, exhausted, unable to speak, and altogether so knocked to pieces that the Count was obliged to transact his business with the man-servant. When he had paid down the four thousand francs, and the servant had taken the money to his master for a receipt, Maxime turned to tell the man to call up the vans to the door; but even as he spoke, a voice like a rattle sounded in his ears.

"'It is not worth while, Monsieur le Comte. You and I are quits; I have six hundred and thirty francs fifteen centimes to give you!'

"To his utter consternation, he saw Cérizet, emerged from his wrappings like a butterfly from the chrysalis, holding out the accursed bundle of documents.

"'When I was down on my luck, I learned to act on the stage,' added Cérizet. 'I am as good as Bouffé at old men.'

"'I have fallen among thieves!' shouted Maxime.

"'No, Monsieur le Comte, you are in Mlle. Hortense's house. She is a friend of old Lord Dudley's; he keeps her hidden away here; but she has the bad taste to like your humble servant.'

"'If ever I longed to kill a man,' so the Count told me afterwards, 'it was at that moment; but what could one do? Hortense showed her pretty face, one had to laugh. To keep my dignity, I flung her the six hundred francs. "There's for the girl," said I.'"

"That is Maxime all over!" cried La Palférine.

"More especially as it was little Croizeau's money," added Cardot the profound.

"Maxime scored a triumph," continued Desroches, "for Hortense exclaimed, 'Oh! if I had only known that it was you!'"

"A pretty 'confusion' indeed!" put in Malaga. "You have lost, milord," she added, turning to the notary.

And in this way the cabinetmaker, to whom Malaga owed a hundred crowns, was paid.

PARIS, 1845.

GAUDISSART II.

*To Madame la Princesse Cristina de Belgiojoso, née
Trivulzio.*

To know how to sell, to be able to sell, and to sell. People
generally do not suspect how much of the stateliness of Paris
is due to these three aspects of the same problem. The brilliant display of shops as rich as the salons of the noblesse
before 1789; the splendors of cafés which eclipse, and easily
eclipse, the Versailles of our day; the shop-window illusions,
new every morning, nightly destroyed; the grace and elegance
of the young men that come in contact with fair customers;
the piquant faces and costumes of young damsels, who cannot
fail to attract the masculine customer; and (and this especially of late) the length, the vast spaces, the Babylonish
luxury of galleries where shopkeepers acquire a monopoly of
the trade in various articles by bringing them all together,—
all this is as nothing. Everything, so far, has been done to
appeal to a single sense, and that the most exacting and jaded
human faculty, a faculty developed ever since the days of the
Roman Empire, until, in our own times, thanks to the efforts
of the most fastidious civilization the world has yet seen, its
demands are grown limitless. That faculty resides in the
"eyes of Paris."

Those eyes require illuminations costing a hundred thousand francs, and many-colored glass palaces a couple of miles
long and sixty feet high; they must have a fairyland at some
fourteen theatres every night, and a succession of panoramas
and exhibitions of the triumphs of art; for them a whole
world of suffering and pain, and a universe of joy, must re-
volve through the boulevards or stray through the streets of
Paris; for them encyclopædias of carnival frippery and a

score of illustrated books are brought out every year, to say nothing of caricatures by the hundred, and vignettes, lithographs, and prints by the thousand. To please those eyes, fifteen thousand francs' worth of gas must blaze every night; and, to conclude, for their delectation the great city yearly spends several millions of francs in opening up views and planting trees. And even yet this is as nothing—it is only the material side of the question; in truth, a mere trifle compared with the expenditure of brain power on the shifts, worthy of Molière, invented by some sixty thousand assistants and forty thousand damsels of the counter, who fasten upon the customer's purse, much as myriads of Seine whitebait fall upon a chance crust floating down the river.

Gaudissart in the mart is at least the equal of his illustrious namesake, now become the typical commercial traveler. Take him away from his shop and his line of business, he is like a collapsed balloon; only among his bales of merchandise do his faculties return, much as an actor is sublime only upon the boards. A French shopman is better educated than his fellows in other European countries; he can at need talk asphalt, Bal Mabille, polkas, literature, illustrated books, railways, politics, parliament, and revolution; transplant him take away his stage, his yardstick, his artificial graces; he is foolish beyond belief; but on his own boards, on the tight-rope of the counter, as he displays a shawl with a speech at his tongue's end, and his eye on his customer, he puts the great Talleyrand into the shade; he has more wit than a Désaugiers, more wiles than Cleopatra; he is a match for a Monrose and a Molière to boot. Talleyrand in his own house would have outwitted Gaudissart, but in the shop the parts would have been reversed.

An incident will illustrate the paradox.

Two charming duchesses were chatting with the above-mentioned great diplomatist. The ladies wished for a bracelet; they were waiting for the arrival of a man from a great Parisian jeweler. A Gaudissart accordingly appeared with three bracelets of marvelous workmanship. The great ladies hesi-

tated. Choice is a mental lightning flash; hesitate—there
is no more to be said, you are at fault. Inspiration in matters
of taste will not come twice. At last, after about ten minutes,
the Prince was called in. He saw the two duchesses confronting doubt with its thousand facets, unable to decide between
the transcendent merits of two of the trinkets, for the third
had been set aside at once. Without leaving his book, without
a glance at the bracelets, the Prince looked at the jeweler's
assistant.

"Which would you choose for your sweetheart?" asked he.

The young man indicated one of the pair.

"In that case, take the other, you will make two women
happy," said the subtlest of modern diplomatists, "and make
your sweetheart happy too, in my name."

The two fair ladies smiled, and the young shopman took
his departure, delighted with the Prince's present and the
implied compliment to his taste.

A woman alights from her splendid carriage before one of
the expensive shops where shawls are sold in the Rue Vivienne. She is not alone; women almost always go in pairs on
these expeditions; always make the round of half a score of
shops before they make up their minds, and laugh together in
the intervals over the little comedies played for their benefit.
Let us see which of the two acts most in character—the fair
customer or the seller, and which has the best of it in such
miniature vaudevilles?

If you attempt to describe a sale, the central fact of Parisian trade, you are in duty bound, if you attempt to give the
gist of the matter, to produce a type, and for this purpose a
shawl or a châtelaine costing some three thousand francs is a
more exciting purchase than a length of lawn or dress that
costs three hundred. But know, oh foreign visitors from the
Old World and the New (if ever this study of the physiology
of the Invoice should be by you perused), that this selfsame
comedy is played in haberdashers' shops over a barège at two
francs or a printed muslin at four francs the yard.

And you, princess, or simple citizen's wife, whichever you

may be, how should you distrust that good-looking, very young
man, with those frank, innocent eyes, and a cheek like a peach
covered with down? He is dressed almost as well as your—
cousin, let us say. His tones are as soft as the woolen stuffs
which he spreads before you. There are three or four more of
his like. One has dark eyes, a decided expression, and an
imperial manner of saying, "This is what you wish"; another,
that blue-eyed youth, diffident of manner and meek of speech,
prompts the remark, "Poor boy! he was not born for business"; a third, with light auburn hair, and laughing tawny
eyes, has all the lively humor, and activity, and gaiety of the
South; while the fourth, he of the tawny red hair and fan-
shaped beard, is rough as a communist, with his portentous
cravat, his sternness, his dignity, and curt speech.

These varieties of shopmen, corresponding to the principal
types of feminine customers, are arms, as it were, directed
by the head, a stout personage with a full-blown countenance,
a partially bald forehead, and a chest measure befitting a
Ministerialist deputy. Occasionally this person wears the ribbon of the Legion of Honor in recognition of the manner
in which he supports the dignity of the French draper's wand.
From the comfortable curves of his figure you can see that he
has a wife and family, a country house, and an account with
the Bank of France. He descends like a *deus ex machinâ,*
whenever a tangled problem demands a swift solution. The
feminine purchasers are surrounded on all sides with urban-
ity, youth, pleasant manners, smiles, and jests; the most
seeming-simple human products of civilization are here. all
sorted in shades to suit all tastes.

Just one word as to the natural effects of architecture, op-
tical science, and house decoration; one short, decisive, terrible word, of history made on the spot. The work which
contains this instructive page is sold at number 76 Rue de
Richelieu, where above an elegant shop, all white and gold
and crimson velvet, there is an entresol into which the light
pours straight from the Rue de Ménars, as into a painter's
studio—clean, clear, even daylight. What idler in the streets

has not beheld the Persian, that Asiatic potentate, ruffling
it above the door at the corner of the Rue de la Bourse and
the Rue de Richelieu, with a message to deliver *urbi et orbi,*
"Here I reign more tranquilly than at Lahore"?   Perhaps
but for this immortal analytical study, archæologists might
begin to puzzle their heads about him five hundred years
hence, and set about writing quartos with plates (like M.
Quatremère's work on Olympian Jove) to prove that Napoleon
was something of a Sofi in the East before he became "Emperor of the French."   Well, the wealthy shop laid siege to
the poor little entresol; and after a bombardment with banknotes, entered and took possession.   The Human Comedy gave
way before the comedy of cashmeres.   The Persian sacrificed
a diamond or two from his crown to buy that so necessary
daylight; for a ray of sunlight shows the play of the colors,
brings out the charms of a shawl, and doubles its value; 'tis
an irresistible light; literally, a golden ray.   From this fact
you may judge how far Paris shops are arranged with a view
to effect.

But to return to the young assistants, to the beribboned
man of forty whom the King of the French receives at his
table, to the red-bearded head of the department with his
autocrat's air.   Week by week these emeritus Gaudissarts are
brought in contact with whims past counting; they know
every vibration of the cashmere chord in the heart of woman.
No one, be she lady or lorette, a young mother of a family,
a respectable tradesman's wife, a woman of easy virtue, a
duchess or a brazen-fronted ballet-dancer, an innocent young
girl or a too innocent foreigner, can appear in the shop, but
she is watched from the moment when she first lays her fingers upon the door-handle.   Her measure is taken at a glance
by seven or eight men that stand, in the windows, at the counter, by the door, in a corner, in the middle of the shop, meditating, to all appearance, on the joys of a bacchanalian Sunday holiday.   As you look at them, you ask yourself involuntarily, "What can they be thinking about?"   Well, in the
space of one second, a woman's purse, wishes, intentions, and

whims are ransacked more thoroughly than a traveling carriage at a frontier in an hour and three-quarters. Nothing is
lost on these intelligent rogues. As they stand, solemn as
noble fathers on the stage, they take in all the details of a
fair customer's dress; an invisible speck of mud on a little
shoe, an antiquated hat-brim, soiled or ill-judged bonnet-
strings, the fashion of the dress, the age of a pair of gloves.
They can tell whether the gown was cut by the intelligent
scissors of a Victorine IV.; they know a modish gewgaw or a
trinket from Froment-Meurice. Nothing, in short, which can
reveal a woman's quality, fortune, or character passes unre-
marked.

Tremble before them. Never was the Sanhedrim of Gaudissarts, with their chief at their head, known to make a mistake. And, moreover, they communicate their conclusions to
one another with telegraphic speed, in a glance, a smile, the
movement of a muscle, a twitch of the lip. If you watch
them, you are reminded of the sudden outbreak of light along
the Champs-Élysées at dusk; one gas-jet does not succeed another more swiftly than an idea flashes from one shopman's
eyes to the next.

At once, if the lady is English, the dark, mysterious, portentous Gaudissart advances like a romantic character out of
one of Byron's poems.

If she is a city madam, the oldest is put forward. He
brings out a hundred shawls in fifteen minutes; he turns
her head with colors and patterns; every shawl that he shows
her is like a circle described by a kite wheeling round a hapless rabbit, till at the end of half an hour, when her head is
swimming and she is utterly incapable of making a decision
for herself, the good lady, meeting with a flattering response
to all her ideas, refers the question to the assistant, who
promptly leaves her on the horns of a dilemma between two
equally irresistible shawls.

"This, madame, is very becoming—apple-green, the color
of the season; still, fashions change; while as for this other
black-and-white shawl (an opportunity not to be missed),

you will never see the end of it, and it will go with any dress."

This is the A B C of the trade.

"You would not believe how much eloquence is wanted in that beastly line," the head Gaudissart of this particular establishment remarked quite lately to two acquaintances (Duronceret and Bixiou) who had come trusting in his judgment to buy a shawl. "Look here; you are artists and discreet, I can tell you about the governor's tricks, and of all the men I ever saw, he is the cleverest. I do not mean as a manufacturer, there M. Fritot is first; but as a salesman. He discovered the 'Selim shawl,' *an absolutely unsalable* article, yet we never bring it out but we sell it. We keep always a shawl worth five or six hundred francs in a cedar-wood box, perfectly plain outside, but lined with satin. It is one of the shawls that Selim sent to the Emperor Napoleon. It is our Imperial Guard; it is brought to the front whenever the day is almost lost; *il se vend et ne meurt pas*—it sells its life dearly time after time."

As he spoke, an Englishwoman stepped from her jobbed carriage and appeared in all the glory of that phlegmatic humor peculiar to Britain and to all its products which make believe they are alive. The apparition put you in mind of the Commandant's statue in *Don Juan,* it walked along, jerkily by fits and starts, in an awkward fashion invented in London, and cultivated in every family with patriotic care.

"An Englishwoman!" he continued for Bixiou's ear. "An Englishwoman is our Waterloo. There are women who slip through our fingers like eels; we catch them on the staircase. There are lorettes who chaff us, we join in the laugh, we have a hold on them because we give credit. There are sphinx-like foreign ladies; we take a quantity of shawls to their houses, and arrive at an understanding by flattery; but an Englishwoman!—you might as well attack the bronze statue of Louis Quatorze! That sort of woman turns shopping into an occupation, an amusement. She quizzes us, forsooth!"

The romantic assistant came to the front.

"Does madame wish for real Indian shawls or French, something expensive or——"

"I will see." (*Je véraie.*)

"How much would madame propose——"

"I will see."

The shopman went in quest of shawls to spread upon the mantle-stand, giving his colleagues a significant glance. "What a bore!" he said plainly, with an almost imperceptible shrug of the shoulders.

"These are our best quality in Indian red, blue, and pale orange—all at ten thousand francs. Here are shawls at five thousand francs, and others at three."

The Englishwoman took up her eyeglass and looked round the room with gloomy indifference; then she submitted the three stands to the same scrutiny, and made no sign.

"Have you any more?" (*Havaivod'hôte?*) demanded she.

"Yes, madame. But perhaps madame has not quite decided to take a shawl?"

"Oh, quite decided" (*trei-deycidai*).

The young man went in search of cheaper wares. These he spread out solemnly as if they were things of price, saying by his manner, "Pay attention to all this magnificence!"

"These are much more expensive," said he. "They have never been worn; they have come by courier direct from the manufacturers at Lahore."

"Oh! I see," said she; "they are much more like the thing I want."

The shopman kept his countenance in spite of inward irritation, which communicated itself to Duronceret and Bixiou. The Englishwoman, cool as a cucumber, appeared to rejoice in her phlegmatic humor.

"What price?" she asked, indicating a sky-blue shawl covered with a pattern of birds nestling in pagodas.

"Seven thousand francs."

She took it up, wrapped it about her shoulders, looked in the glass, and handed it back again.

"No, I do not like it at all." (*Je n'ame pouinte.*)

A long quarter of an hour went by in trying on other shawls; to no purpose.

"This is all we have, madame," said the assistant, glancing at the master as he spoke.

"Madame is fastidious, like all persons of taste," said the head of the establishment, coming forward with that tradesman's suavity in which pomposity is agreeably blended with subservience. The Englishwoman took up her eyeglass and scanned the manufacturer from head to foot, unwilling to understand that the man before her was eligible for Parliament and dined at the Tuileries.

"I have only one shawl left," he continued, "but I never show it. It is not to everybody's taste; it is quite out of the common. I was thinking this morning of giving it to my wife. We have had it in stock since 1805; it belonged to the Empress Josephine."

"Let me see it, monsieur."

"Go for it," said the master, turning to a shopman. "It is at my house."

"I should be very much pleased to see it," said the English lady.

This was a triumph. The splenetic dame was apparently on the point of going. She made as though she saw nothing but the shawls; but all the while she furtively watched the shopmen and the two customers, sheltering her eyes behind the rims of her eyeglasses.

"It cost sixty thousand francs in Turkey, madame."

"Oh!" (*hâu!*)

"It is one of seven shawls which Selim sent, before his fall, to the Emperor Napoleon. The Empress Josephine, a Creole, as you know, my lady, and very capricious in her tastes, exchanged this one for another brought by the Turkish ambassador, and purchased by my predecessor; but I have never seen the money back. Our ladies in France are not rich enough; it is not as it is in England. The shawl is worth seven thousand francs; and taking interest and compound interest altogether, it makes up fourteen or fifteen thousand by now—"

"How does it make up?" asked the Englishwoman.

"Here it is, madame."

With precautions, which a custodian of the Dresden *Grüne Gewölbe* might have admired, he took out an infinitesimal key and opened a square cedar-wood box. The Englishwoman was much impressed with its shape and plainness. From that box, lined with black satin, he drew a shawl worth about fifteen hundred francs, a black pattern on a golden-yellow ground, of which the startling color was only surpassed by the surprising efforts of the Indian imagination.

"Splendid," said the lady, in a mixture of French and English, "it is really handsome. Just my ideal" (*idéol*) "of a shawl; it is very magnificent." The rest was lost in a madonna's pose assumed for the purpose of displaying a pair of frigid eyes which she believed to be very fine.

"It was a great favorite with the Emperor Napoleon; he took——"

"A great favorite," repeated she with her English accent. Then she arranged the shawl about her shoulders and looked at herself in the glass. The proprietor took it to the light, gathered it up in his hands, smoothed it out, showed the gloss on it, played on it as Liszt plays on the pianoforte keys.

"It is very fine; beautiful, sweet!" said the lady, as composedly as possible.

Duronceret, Bixiou, and the shopmen exchanged amused glances. "The shawl is sold," they thought.

"Well, madame?" inquired the proprietor, as the Englishwoman appeared to be absorbed in meditations infinitely prolonged.

"Decidedly," said she; "I would rather have a carriage" (*une vôteure*).

All the assistants, listening with silent rapt attention, started as one man, as if an electric shock had gone through them.

"I have a very handsome one, madame," said the proprietor with unshaken composure; "it belonged to a Russian princess, the Princess Narzicof; she left it with me in payment for goods received. If madame would like to see it, she would be astonished. It is new; it has not been in use altogether for ten days; there is not its like in Paris."

The shopmen's amazement was suppressed by profound admiration.

"I am quite willing."

"If madame will keep the shawl," suggested the proprietor, "she can try the effect in the carriage." And he went for his hat and gloves.

"How will this end?" asked the head assistant, as he watched his employer offer an arm to the English lady and go down with her to the jobbed brougham.

By this time the thing had come to be as exciting as the last chapter of a novel for Duronceret and Bixiou, even without the additional interest attached to all contests, however trifling, between England and France.

Twenty minutes later the proprietor returned.

"Go to the Hôtel Lawson (here is the card, 'Mrs. Noswell'), and take an invoice that I will give you. There are six thousand francs to take."

"How did you do it?" asked Duronceret, bowing before the king of invoices.

"Oh, I saw what she was, an eccentric woman that loves to be conspicuous. As soon as she saw that every one stared at her, she said, 'Keep your carriage, monsieur, my mind is made up; I will take the shawl.' While M. Bigorneau (indicating the romantic-looking assistant) was serving, I watched her carefully; she kept one eye on you all the time to see what you thought of her; she was thinking more about you than of the shawls. Englishwomen are peculiar in their *distaste* (for one cannot call it taste); they do not know what they want; they make up their minds to be guided by circumstances at the time, and not by their own choice. I saw the kind of woman at once, tired of her husband, tired of her brats, regretfully virtuous, craving excitement, always posing as a weeping willow. . . ."

These were his very words.

Which proves that in all other countries of the world a shopkeeper is a shopkeeper; while in France, and in Paris more particularly, he is a student from a Collège Royal, a well-read man with a taste for art, or angling, or the theatre, and consumed, it may be, with a desire to be M. Cunin-Gridaine's successor, or a colonel of the National Guard, or a member of the General Council of the Seine, or a referee in the Commercial Court.

"M. Adolphe," said the mistress of the establishment, addressing the slight fair-haired assistant, "go to the joiner and order another cedar-wood box."

"And now," remarked the shopman who had assisted Duronceret and Bixiou to choose a shawl for Mme. Schontz, *"now* we will go through our old stock to find another Selim shawl."

PARIS, *November* 1844.

SARRASINE

SARRASINE

To Monsieur Charles Bernard du Grail.

I was buried in one of those profound reveries to which everybody, even a frivolous man, is subject in the midst of the most uproarious festivities. The clock on the Élysée-Bourbon had just struck midnight. Seated in a window recess and concealed behind the undulating folds of a curtain of watered silk, I was able to contemplate at my leisure the garden of the mansion at which I was passing the evening. The trees, being partly covered with snow, were outlined indistinctly against the grayish background formed by a cloudy sky, barely whitened by the moon. Seen through the medium of that strange atmosphere, they bore a vague resemblance to spectres carelessly enveloped in their shrouds, a gigantic image of the famous *Dance of Death.* Then, turning in the other direction, I could gaze admiringly upon the dance of the living! a magnificent salon, with walls of silver and gold, with gleaming chandeliers, and bright with the light of many candles. There the loveliest, the wealthiest women in Paris, bearers of the proudest titles, moved hither and thither, fluttered from room to room in swarms, stately and gorgeous, dazzling with diamonds; flowers on their heads and breasts, in their hair, scattered over their dresses or lying in garlands at their feet. Light quiverings of the body, voluptuous movements, made the laces and gauzes and silks swirl about their graceful figures. Sparkling glances here and there eclipsed the lights, and the blaze of the diamonds, and fanned the flame of hearts already burning too brightly. I detected also significant nods of the head for lovers and repellent attitudes for husbands. The exclamations of the card-players at every unexpected *coup,* the jingle of gold, mingled with the music and the mur-

mur of conversation; and to put the finishing touch to the
vertigo of that multitude, intoxicated by all the seductions the
world can offer, a perfume-laden atmosphere and general exaltation acted upon their over-wrought imaginations.   Thus,
at my right was the depressing, silent image of death; at my
left the decorous bacchanalia of life; on the one side nature,
cold and gloomy, and in mourning garb; on the other side,
man on pleasure bent.   And, standing on the borderland of
those two incongruous pictures, which, repeated thousands
of times in diverse ways, make Paris the most entertaining
and most philosophical city in the world, I played a mental
*macédoine,** half jesting, half funereal.   With my left foot I
kept time to the music, and the other felt as if it were in a
tomb.   My leg was, in fact, frozen by one of those draughts
which congeal one half of the body while the other suffers
from the intense heat of the salons—a state of things not unusual at balls.

"Monsieur de Lanty has not owned this house very long,
has he?"

"Oh, yes! It is nearly ten years since the Maréchal de Carigliano sold it to him."

"Ah!"

"These people must have an enormous fortune."

"They surely must."

"What a magnificent party! It is almost insolent in its
splendor."

"Do you imagine they are as rich as Monsieur de Nucingen or Monsieur de Gondreville?"

"Why, don't you know?"

I leaned forward and recognized the two persons who were
talking as members of that inquisitive genus which, in Paris,
busies itself exclusively with the *Whys* and *Hows*.   *Where
does he come from? Who are they? What's the matter with
him? What has she done?*   They lowered their voices and

Macédoine, in the sense in which it is here used, is a game, or rather a series of
games, of cards, each player, when it is his turn to deal, selecting the game to
be played.

walked away in order to talk more at their ease on some retired couch. Never was a more promising mine laid open to
seekers after mysteries. No one knew from what country
the Lanty family came, nor to what source—commerce, extortion, piracy, or inheritance—they owed a fortune estimated
at several millions. All the members of the family spoke
Italian, French, Spanish, English, and German, with sufficient fluency to lead one to suppose that they had lived long
among those different peoples. Were they gypsies? were they
buccaneers?

"Suppose they're the devil himself," said divers young politicians, "they entertain mighty well."

"The Comte de Lanty may have plundered some *Casbah* for
all I care; I would like to marry his daughter!" cried a philosopher.

Who would not have married Marianina, a girl of sixteen,
whose beauty realized the fabulous conceptions of Oriental
poets! Like the Sultan's daughter in the tale of the *Wonderful Lamp,* she should have remained always veiled. Her
singing obscured the imperfect talents of the Malibrans, the
Sontags, and the Fodors, in whom some one dominant quality
always mars the perfection of the whole; whereas Marianina
combined in equal degree purity of tone, exquisite feeling,
accuracy of time and intonation, science, soul, and delicacy.
She was the type of that hidden poesy, the link which con-
nects all the arts and which always eludes those who seek it.
Modest, sweet, well-informed, and clever, none could eclipse
Marianina unless it were her mother.

Have you ever met one of those women whose startling
beauty defies the assaults of time, and who seem at thirty-
six more desirable than they could have been fifteen years
earlier? Their faces are impassioned souls; they fairly
sparkle; each feature gleams with intelligence; each possesses
a brilliancy of its own, especially in the light. Their capti-
vating eyes attract or repel, speak or are silent; their gait is
artlessly seductive; their voices unfold the melodious treasures
of the most coquettishly sweet and tender tones. Praise of

their beauty, based upon comparisons, flatters the most sensitive self-esteem. A movement of their eyebrows, the slightest play of the eye, the curling of the lip, instils a sort of terror in those whose lives and happiness depend upon their favor. A maiden inexperienced in love and easily moved by words may allow herself to be seduced; but in dealing with women of this sort, a man must be able, like M. de Jaucourt, to refrain from crying out when, in hiding him in a closet, the lady's maid crushes two of his fingers in the crack of a door. To love one of these omnipotent sirens is to stake one's life, is it not? And that, perhaps, is why we love them so passionately! Such was the Comtesse de Lanty.

Filippo, Marianina's brother, inherited, as did his sister, the Countess' marvelous beauty. To tell the whole story in a word, that young man was a living image of Antinoüs, with somewhat slighter proportions. But how well such a slender and delicate figure accords with youth, when an olive complexion, heavy eyebrows, and the gleam of a velvety eye promise virile passions, noble ideas for the future! If Filippo remained in the hearts of young women as a type of manly beauty, he likewise remained in the memory of all mothers as the best match in France.

The beauty, the great wealth, the intellectual qualities, of these two children came entirely from their mother. The Comte de Lanty was a short, thin, ugly little man, as dismal as a Spaniard, as great a bore as a banker. He was looked upon, however, as a profound politician, perhaps because he rarely laughed, and was always quoting M. de Metternich or Wellington.

This mysterious family had all the attractiveness of a poem by Lord Byron, whose difficult passages were translated differently by each person in fashionable society; a poem that grew more obscure and more sublime from strophe to strophe. The reserve which Monsieur and Madame de Lanty maintained concerning their origin, their past lives, and their relations with the four quarters of the globe would not, of itself, have been for long a subject of wonderment in Paris. In no other country, perhaps, is Vespasian's maxim more thoroughly understood. Here gold pieces, even when stained with blood or mud, betray nothing, and represent everything. Provided that good society knows the amount of your fortune, you are classed among those figures which equal yours, and no one asks to see your credentials, because everybody knows how little they cost. In a city where social problems are solved by algebraic equations, adventurers have many chances in their favor. Even if this family were of gypsy extraction, it was so wealthy, so attractive, that fashionable society could well afford to overlook its little mysteries. But, unfortunately, the enigmatical history of the Lanty family offered a perpetual subject of curiosity, not unlike that aroused by the novels of Anne Radcliffe.

People of an observing turn, of the sort who are bent upon finding out where you buy your candelabra, or who ask you what rent you pay when they are pleased with your apartments, had noticed, from time to time, the appearance of an extraordinary personage at the fêtes, concerts, balls, and routs given by the countess. It was a man. The first time that he was seen in the house was at a concert, when he seemed to have been drawn to the salon by Marianina's enchanting voice.

"I have been cold for the last minute or two," said a lady near the door to her neighbor.

The stranger, who was standing near the speaker, moved away.

"This is very strange! now I am warm," she said, after his departure. "Perhaps you will call me mad, but I cannot help thinking that my neighbor, the gentleman in black who just walked away, was the cause of my feeling cold."

Ere long the exaggeration to which people in society are naturally inclined, produced a large and growing crop of the most amusing ideas, the most curious expressions, the most absurd fables concerning this mysterious individual. Without being precisely a vampire, a ghoul, a fictitious man, a sort of Faust or Robin des Bois, he partook of the nature of all these anthropomorphic conceptions, according to those persons who were addicted to the fantastic. Occasionally some German would take for realities these ingenious jests of Parisian evil-speaking. The stranger was simply *an old man.* Some young men, who were accustomed to decide the future of Europe every morning in a few fashionable phrases, chose to see in the stranger some great criminal, the possessor of enormous wealth. Novelists described the old man's life and gave some really interesting details of the atrocities committed by him while he was in the service of the Prince of Mysore. Bankers, men of a more positive nature, devised a specious fable.

"Bah!" they would say, shrugging their broad shoulders pityingly, "that little old fellow's a *Genoese head!*"

"If it is not an impertinent question, monsieur, would you have the kindness to tell me what you mean by a Genoese head?"

"I mean, monsieur, that he is a man upon whose life enormous sums depend, and whose good health is undoubtedly essential to the continuance of this family's income. I remember that I once heard a mesmerist, at Madame d'Espard's, undertake to prove by very specious historical deductions, that this old man, if put under the magnifying glass, would turn out to be the famous Balsamo, otherwise called Cagliostro. According to this modern alchemist, the Sicilian had escaped death, and amused himself making gold for his grandchildren. And the Bailli of Ferette declared that he recognized in this extraordinary personage the Comte de Saint-Germain."

Such nonsense as this, put forth with the assumption of superior cleverness, with the air of raillery, which in our day characterize a society devoid of faith, kept alive vague suspicions concerning the Lanty family. At last, by a strange combination of circumstances, the members of that family justified the conjectures of society by adopting a decidedly mysterious course of conduct with this old man, whose life was, in a certain sense, kept hidden from all investigations.

If he crossed the threshold of the apartment he was sup-

posed to occupy in the Lanty mansion, his appearance always
caused a great sensation in the family. One would have supposed that it was an event of the greatest importance. Only
Filippo, Marianina, Madame de Lanty, and an old servant
enjoyed the privilege of assisting the unknown to walk, to rise,
to sit down. Each one of them kept a close watch on his
slightest movements. It seemed as if he were some enchanted
person upon whom the happiness, the life, or the fortune of all
depended. Was it fear or affection? Society could discover
no indication which enabled them to solve this problem. Concealed for months at a time in the depths of an unknown
sanctuary, this familiar spirit suddenly emerged, furtively as
it were, unexpectedly, and appeared in the salons like the fair-
ies of old, who alighted from their winged dragons to disturb
festivities to which they had not been invited. Only the most
experienced observers could divine the anxiety, at such times,
of the masters of the house, who were peculiarly skilful in
concealing their feelings. But sometimes, while dancing a
quadrille, the too ingenuous Marianina would cast a terrified
glance at the old man, whom she watched closely from the
circle of dancers. Or perhaps Filippo would leave his place
and glide through the crowd to where he stood, and remain beside him, affectionate and watchful, as if the touch of man,
or the faintest breath, would shatter that extraordinary creature. The countess would try to draw nearer to him without
apparently intending to join him; then, assuming a manner
and an expression in which servility and affection, submissiveness and tyranny, were equally noticeable, she would say two
or three words, to which the old man almost always deferred;
and he would disappear, led, or I might better say carried
away, by her. If Madame de Lanty were not present, the
Count would employ a thousand ruses to reach his side; but
it always seemed as if he found difficulty in inducing him to
listen, and he treated him like a spoiled child, whose mother
gratifies his whims and at the same time suspects mutiny.
Some prying persons having ventured to question the Comte
de Lanty indiscreetly, that cold and reserved individual

seemed not to understand their questions. And so, after many attempts, which the circumspection of all the members of the family rendered fruitless, no one sought to discover a secret so well guarded. Society spies, triflers, and politicians, weary of the strife, ended by ceasing to concern themselves about the mystery.

But at that moment, it may be, there were in those gorgeous salons philosophers who said to themselves, as they discussed an ice or a sherbet, or placed their empty punch glasses on a tray:

"I should not be surprised to learn that these people are knaves. That old fellow who keeps out of sight and appears only at the equinoxes or solstices, looks to me exactly like an assassin."

"Or a bankrupt."

"There's very little difference. To destroy a man's fortune is worse sometimes than to kill the man himself."

"I bet twenty louis, monsieur; there are forty due me."

"Faith, monsieur; there are only thirty left on the cloth."

"Just see what a mixed company there is here! One can't play cards in peace."

"Very true. But it's almost six months since we saw the Spirit. Do you think he's a living being?"

"Well, barely."

These last remarks were made in my neighborhood by persons whom I did not know, and who passed out of hearing just as I was summarizing in one last thought my reflections, in which black and white, life and death, were inextricably mingled. My wandering imagination, like my eyes, contemplated alternately the festivities, which had now reached the climax of their splendor, and the gloomy picture presented by the gardens. I have no idea how long I meditated upon those two faces of the human medal; but I was suddenly aroused by the stifled laughter of a young woman. I was stupefied at the picture presented to my eyes. By virtue of one of the strangest of nature's freaks, the thought half draped in black, which was tossing about in my brain, emerged from it and stood before me personified, living; it had come forth like Minerva from Jupiter's brain, tall and strong; it was at once a hundred years old and twenty-two; it was alive and dead. Escaped from his chamber, like a madman from his cell, the little old man had evidently crept behind a long line of people who were listening attentively to Marianina's voice as she finished the cavatina from *Tancred*. He seemed to have come up through the floor, impelled by some stage mechanism. He stood for a moment motionless and sombre, watching the festivities, a murmur of which had perhaps reached his ears. His almost somnambulistic preoccupation was so concentrated upon things that, although he was in the midst of many people, he saw nobody. He had taken his place unceremoniously beside one of the most fascinating women in Paris, a young and graceful dancer, with slender figure, a face as fresh as a child's, all pink and white, and so fragile, so transparent, that it seemed that a man's glance must pass through her as the sun's rays pass through flawless glass. They stood there before me, side by side, so close together, that the stranger rubbed against the gauze dress, and the wreaths of flowers, and the hair, slightly crimped, and the floating ends of the sash.

I had brought that young woman to Madame de Lanty's ball. As it was her first visit to that house, I forgave her her stifled laugh; but I hastily made an imperious sign which abashed her and inspired respect for her neighbor. She sat down beside me. The old man did not choose to leave the charming creature, to whom he clung capriciously with the silent and apparently causeless obstinacy to which very old persons are subject, and which makes them resemble children. In order to sit down beside the young lady he needed a folding-chair. His slightest movements were marked by the inert heaviness, the stupid hesitancy, which characterize the movements of a paralytic. He sat slowly down upon his chair with great caution, mumbling some unintelligible words. His cracked voice resembled the noise made by a stone falling into a well. The young woman nervously pressed my hand, as if she were trying to avoid a precipice, and shivered when that man, at whom she happened to be looking, turned upon her two lifeless, sea-green eyes, which could be compared to nothing save tarnished mother-of-pearl.

"I am afraid," she said, putting her lips to my ear.

"You can speak," I replied; "he hears with great difficulty."

"You know him, then?"

"Yes."

Thereupon she summoned courage to scrutinize for a moment that creature for which no human language has a name, form without substance, a being without life, or life without action. She was under the spell of that timid curiosity which impels women to seek perilous excitement, to gaze at chained tigers and boa-constrictors, shuddering all the while because the barriers between them are so weak. Although the little old man's back was bent like a day-laborer's, it was easy to see that he must formerly have been of medium height. His excessive thinness, the slenderness of his limbs, proved that he had always been of slight build. He wore black silk breeches which hung about his fleshless thighs in folds, like a lowered veil. An anatomist would instinctively have recognized the symptoms of consumption in its advanced stages, at sight of the tiny legs which served to support that strange frame. You would have said that they were a pair of cross-bones on a gravestone. A feeling of profound horror seized the heart when a close scrutiny revealed the marks made by decrepitude upon that frail machine.

He wore a white waistcoat embroidered with gold, in the old style, and his linen was of dazzling whiteness. A shirt-frill of English lace, yellow with age, the magnificence of which a queen might have envied, formed a series of yellow ruffles on his breast; but upon him the lace seemed rather a worthless rag than an ornament. In the centre of the frill a diamond of inestimable value gleamed like a sun. That superannuated splendor, that display of treasure, of great intrinsic worth, but utterly without taste, served to bring out in still bolder relief the strange creature's face. The frame was worthy of the portrait. That dark face was full of angles

and furrowed deep in every direction; the chin was furrowed;
there were great hollows at the temples; the eyes were sunken
in yellow orbits. The maxillary bones, which his indescribable
gauntness caused to protrude, formed deep cavities in the
centre of both cheeks. These protuberances, as the light fell
upon them, caused curious effects of light and shadow which
deprived that face of the last vestige of resemblance to the
human countenance. And then, too, the lapse of years had
drawn the fine, yellow skin so close to the bones that it described a multitude of wrinkles everywhere, either circular like
the ripples in the water caused by a stone which a child throws
in, or star-shaped like a pane of glass cracked by a blow; but
everywhere very deep, and as close together as the leaves of a
closed book. We often see more hideous old men; but what
contributed more than aught else to give to the spectre that
rose before us the aspect of an artificial creation was the red
and white paint with which he glistened. The eyebrows shone
in the light with a lustre which disclosed a very well executed
bit of painting. Luckily for the eye, saddened by such a mass
of ruins, his corpse-like skull was concealed beneath a light
wig, with innumerable curls which indicated extraordinary
pretensions to elegance. Indeed, the feminine coquettishness
of this fantastic apparition was emphatically asserted by the
gold ear-rings which hung at his ears, by the rings containing stones of marvelous beauty which sparkled on his fingers,
like the brilliants in a river of gems around a woman's neck.
Lastly, this species of Japanese idol had constantly upon his
blue lips, a fixed, unchanging smile, the shadow of an implacable and sneering laugh, like that of a death's head. As silent
and motionless as a statue, he exhaled the musk-like odor of
the old dresses which a duchess' heirs exhume from her wardrobe during the inventory. If the old man turned his eyes
toward the company, it seemed that the movements of those
globes, no longer capable of reflecting a gleam, were accomplished by an almost imperceptible effort; and, when the eyes
stopped, he who was watching them was not certain finally
that they had moved at all. As I saw, beside that human ruin,

a young woman whose bare neck and arms and breast were
white as snow; whose figure was well-rounded and beautiful
in its youthful grace; whose hair, charmingly arranged above
an alabaster forehead, inspired love; whose eyes did not receive but gave forth light, who was sweet and fresh, and whose
fluffy curls, whose fragrant breath, seemed too heavy, too
harsh, too overpowering for that shadow, for that man of dust
—ah! the thought that came into my mind was of death and
life, an imaginary arabesque, a half-hideous chimera, divinely
feminine from the waist up.

"And yet such marriages are often made in society!" I said
to myself.

"He smells of the cemetery!" cried the terrified young woman, grasping my arm as if to make sure of my protection,
and moving about in a restless, excited way, which convinced
me that she was very much frightened. "It's a horrible
vision," she continued; "I cannot stay here any longer. If I
look at him again I shall believe that Death himself has come
in search of me. But is he alive?"

She placed her hand on the phenomenon, with the boldness
which women derive from the violence of their wishes, but a
cold sweat burst from her pores, for, the instant she touched
the old man, she heard a cry like the noise made by a rattle.
That shrill voice, if indeed it were a voice, escaped from a
throat almost entirely dry. It was at once succeeded by a
convulsive little cough like a child's, of a peculiar resonance.
At that sound, Marianina, Filippo, and Madame de Lanty
looked toward us, and their glances were like lightning
flashes. The young woman wished that she were at the bottom of the Seine. She took my arm and pulled me away toward a boudoir. Everybody, men and women, made room for
us to pass. Having reached the farther end of the suite of
reception-rooms, we entered a small semi-circular cabinet.
My companion threw herself on a divan, breathing fast with
terror, not knowing where she was.

"You are mad, madame," I said to her.

"But," she rejoined, after a moment's silence, during which

I gazed at her in admiration, "is it my fault? Why does Madame de Lanty allow ghosts to wander round her house?"

"Nonsense," I replied; "you are doing just what fools do. You mistake a little old man for a spectre."

"Hush," she retorted, with the imposing, yet mocking, air which all women are so well able to assume when they are determined to put themselves in the right. "Oh! what a sweet boudoir!" she cried, looking about her. "Blue satin hangings always produce an admirable effect. How cool it is! Ah! the lovely picture!" she added, rising and standing in front of a magnificently framed painting.

We stood for a moment gazing at that marvel of art, which seemed the work of some supernatural brush. The picture represented Adonis stretched out on a lion's skin. The lamp, in an alabaster vase, hanging in the centre of the boudoir, cast upon the canvas a soft light which enabled us to grasp all the beauties of the picture.

"Does such a perfect creature exist?" she asked me, after examining attentively, and not without a sweet smile of satisfaction, the exquisite grace of the outlines, the attitude, the color, the hair, in fact everything.

"He is too beautiful for a man," she added, after such a scrutiny as she would have bestowed upon a rival.

Ah! how sharply I felt at that moment those pangs of jealousy in which a poet had tried in vain to make me believe! the jealousy of engravings, of pictures, of statues, wherein artists exaggerate human beauty, as a result of the doctrine which leads them to idealize everything.

"It is a portrait," I replied. "It is a product of Vien's genius. But that great painter never saw the original, and your admiration will be modified somewhat perhaps, when I tell you that this study was made from a statue of a woman."

"But who is it?"

I hesitated.

"I insist upon knowing," she added earnestly.

"I believe," I said, "that this *Adonis* represents a—a relative of Madame de Lanty."

I had the chagrin of seeing that she was lost in contemplation of that figure. She sat down in silence, and I seated myself beside her and took her hand without her noticing it. Forgotten for a portrait! At that moment we heard in the silence a woman's footstep and the faint rustling of a dress. We saw the youthful Marianina enter the boudoir, even more resplendent by reason of her expression of innocence than by reason of her grace and her fresh costume; she was walking slowly and leading with motherly care, with a daughter's solicitude, the spectre in human attire, who had driven us from the music-room; as she led him, she watched with some anxiety the slow movement of his feeble feet. They walked painfully across the boudoir to a door hidden in the hangings. Marianina knocked softly. Instantly a tall, thin man, a sort of familiar spirit, appeared as if by magic. Before entrusting the old man to this mysterious guardian, the lovely child, with deep veneration, kissed the ambulatory corpse, and her chaste caress was not without a touch of that graceful playfulness, the secret of which only a few privileged women possess.

"Addio, addio!" she said, with the sweetest inflection of her young voice.

She added to the last syllable a wonderfully executed trill, in a very low tone, as if to depict the overflowing affection of her heart by a poetic expression. The old man, suddenly arrested by some memory, remained on the threshold of that secret retreat. In the profound silence we heard the sigh that came forth from his breast; he removed the most beautiful of the rings with which his skeleton fingers were laden, and placed it in Marianina's bosom. The young madcap laughed, plucked out the ring, slipped it on one of her fingers over her glove, and ran hastily back toward the salon, where the orchestra were, at that moment, beginning the prelude of a contra-dance.

She spied us.

"Ah! were you here?" she said, blushing.

After a searching glance at us as if to question us, she ran away to her partner with the careless petulance of her years.

"What does this mean?" queried my young partner. "Is he her husband? I believe I am dreaming. Where am I?"

"You!" I retorted, "you, madame, who are easily excited, and who, understanding so well the most imperceptible emotions, are able to cultivate in a man's heart the most delicate of sentiments, without crushing it, without shattering it at the very outset, you who have compassion for the tortures of the heart, and who, with the wit of the Parisian, combine a passionate temperament worthy of Spain or Italy——"

She realized that my words were heavily charged with bitter irony; and, thereupon, without seeming to notice it, she interrupted me to say:

"Oh! you describe me to suit your own taste. A strange kind of tyranny! You wish me not to be *myself!*"

"Oh! I wish nothing," I cried, alarmed by the severity of her manner. "At all events, it is true, is it not, that you like to hear stories of the fierce passions kindled in our hearts by the enchanting women of the South?"

"Yes. And then?"

"Why, I will come to your house about nine o'clock to-morrow evening, and elucidate this mystery for you."

"No," she replied, with a pout; "I wish it done now."

"You have not yet given me the right to obey you when you say, 'I wish it.'"

"At this moment," she said, with an exhibition of coquetry of the sort that drives men to despair, "I have a most violent desire to know this secret. To-morrow it may be that I will not listen to you."

She smiled and we parted, she still as proud and as cruel, I as ridiculous, as ever. She had the audacity to waltz with a young aide-de-camp, and I was by turns angry, sulky, admiring, loving, and jealous.

"Until to-morrow," she said to me, as she left the ball about two o'clock in the morning.

"I won't go," I thought. "I give you up. You are a thousand times more capricious, more fanciful, than—my imagination."

The next evening we were seated in front of a bright fire
in a dainty little salon, she on a couch, I on cushions almost
at her feet, looking up into her face. The street was silent.
The lamp shed a soft light. It was one of those evenings
which delight the soul, one of those moments which are never
forgotten, one of those hours passed in peace and longing,
whose charm is always in later years a source of regret, even
when we are happier. What can efface the deep imprint of
the first solicitations of love?

"Go on," she said. "I am listening."

"But I dare not begin. There are passages in the story
which are dangerous to the narrator. If I become excited,
you will make me hold my peace."

"Speak."

"I obey.

"Ernest-Jean Sarrasine was the only son of a prosecuting
attorney of Franche-Comté," I began, after a pause. "His
father had, by faithful work, amassed a fortune which yielded
an income of six to eight thousand francs, then considered a
colossal fortune for an attorney in the provinces. Old Maître
Sarrasine, having but one child, determined to give him a
thorough education; he hoped to make a magistrate of him,
and to live long enough to see, in his old age, the grandson
of Mathieu Sarrasine, a ploughman in the Saint-Dié country,
seated on the lilies, and dozing through the sessions for the
greater glory of the Parliament; but Heaven had not that joy
in store for the attorney. Young Sarrasine, entrusted to the
care of the Jesuits at an early age, gave indications of an extraordinarily unruly disposition. His was the childhood of a
man of talent. He would not study except as his inclination
led him, often rebelled, and sometimes remained for whole
hours at a time buried in tangled meditations, engaged now
in watching his comrades at play, now in forming mental
pictures of Homer's heroes. And, when he did choose to
amuse himself, he displayed extraordinary ardor in his games.
Whenever there was a contest of any sort between a comrade
and himself, it rarely ended without bloodshed. If he were

the weaker, he would use his teeth. Active and passive by
turns, either lacking in aptitude, or too intelligent, his ab-
normal temperament caused him to distrust his masters as
much as his schoolmates. Instead of learning the elements of
the Greek language, he drew a picture of the reverend father
who was interpreting a passage of Thucydides, sketched the
teacher of mathematics, the prefect, the assistants, the man
who administered punishment, and smeared all the walls with
shapeless figures. Instead of singing the praises of the Lord
in the chapel, he amused himself, during the services, by
notching a bench; or, when he had stolen a piece of wood, he
would carve the figure of some saint. If he had no wood or
stone or pencil, he worked out his ideas with bread. Whether
he copied the figures in the pictures which adorned the choir,
or improvised, he always left at his seat rough sketches whose
obscene character drove the young fathers to despair; and the
evil-tongued alleged that the Jesuits smiled at them. At last,
if we are to believe college traditions, he was expelled because,
while awaiting his turn to go to the confessional one Good
Friday, he carved a figure of the Christ from a stick of wood.
The impiety evidenced by that figure was too flagrant not to
draw down chastisement on the artist. He had actually had
the hardihood to place that decidedly cynical image on the top
of the tabernacle!

"Sarrasine came to Paris to seek a refuge against the
threats of a father's malediction. Having one of those strong
wills which know no obstacles, he obeyed the behests of his
genius and entered Bouchardon's studio. He worked all day
and went about at night begging for subsistence. Bouchardon,
marveling at the young artist's intelligence and rapid progress, soon divined his pupil's destitute condition; he assisted
him, became attached to him, and treated him like his own
child. Then, when Sarrasine's genius stood revealed in one
of those works wherein future talent contends with the effervescence of youth, the generous Bouchardon tried to restore
him to the old attorney's good graces. The paternal wrath
subsided in face of the famous sculptor's authority. All Be-

sançon congratulated itself on having brought forth a future
great man. In the first outburst of delight due to his flattered vanity, the miserly attorney supplied his son with the
means to appear to advantage in society. The long and laborious study demanded by the sculptor's profession subdued
for a long time Sarrasine's impetuous temperament and unruly genius. Bouchardon, foreseeing how violently the passions would some day rage in that youthful heart, as highly
tempered perhaps as Michelangelo's, smothered its vehemence
with constant toil. He succeeded in restraining within reasonable bounds Sarrasine's extraordinary impetuosity, by forbidding him to work, by proposing diversions when he saw
that he was carried away by the violence of some idea, or by
placing important work in his hands when he saw that he was
on the point of plunging into dissipation. But with that
passionate nature, gentleness was always the most powerful of
all weapons, and the master did not acquire great influence
over his pupil until he had aroused his gratitude by fatherly
kindness.

"At the age of twenty-two Sarrasine was forcibly removed
from the salutary influence which Bouchardon exercised over
his morals and his habits. He paid the penalty of his genius
by winning the prize for sculpture founded by the Marquis de
Marigny, Madame de Pompadour's brother, who did so much
for art. Diderot praised Bouchardon's pupil's statue as a
masterpiece. Not without profound sorrow did the king's
sculptor witness the departure for Italy of a young man whose
profound ignorance of the things of life he had, as a matter
of principle, refrained from enlightening. Sarrasine was
Bouchardon's guest for six years. Fanatically devoted to his
art, as Canova was at a later day, he rose at dawn and went
to the studio, there to remain until night, and lived with his
muse alone. If he went to the Comédie-Française, he was
dragged thither by his master. He was so bored at Madame
Geoffrin's, and in the fashionable society to which Bouchardon
tried to introduce him, that he preferred to remain alone, and
held aloof from the pleasures of that licentious age. He had

no other mistresses than sculpture and Clotilde, one of the celebrities of the Opéra. Even that intrigue was of brief duration. Sarrasine was decidedly ugly, always badly dressed, and naturally so independent, so irregular in his private life, that the illustrious nymph, dreading some catastrophe, soon remitted the sculptor to love of the arts. Sophie Arnould made some witty remark on the subject. She was surprised, I think, that her colleague was able to triumph over statues.

"Sarrasine started for Italy in 1758. On the journey his ardent imagination took fire beneath a sky of copper and at sight of the marvelous monuments with which the fatherland of the arts is strewn. He admired the statues, the frescoes, the pictures; and, fired with a spirit of emulation, he went on to Rome, burning to inscribe his name between the names of Michelangelo and Bouchardon. At first, therefore, he divided his time between his studio work and examination of the works of art which abound in Rome. He had already passed a fortnight in the ecstatic state into which all youthful imaginations fall at sight of the queen of ruins, when he happened one evening to enter the Argentina theatre, in front of which there was an enormous crowd. He inquired the reasons for the presence of so great a throng, and every one answered by two names:

" 'Zambinella! Jomelli!'

"He entered and took a seat in the pit, crowded between two unconscionably stout *abbati;* but luckily he was quite near the stage. The curtain rose. For the first time in his life he heard the music whose charms Monsieur Jean-Jacques Rousseau had extolled so eloquently at one of Baron d'Holbach's evening parties. The young sculptor's senses were lubricated, so to speak, by Jomelli's harmonious strains. The languorous peculiarities of those skilfully blended Italian voices plunged him in an ecstasy of delight. He sat there, mute and motionless, not even conscious of the crowding of the two priests. His soul poured out through his ears and his eyes. He seemed to be listening with every one of his pores. Suddenly a whirlwind of applause greeted the appear-

ance of the prima donna. She came forward coquettishly to
the footlights and courtesied to the audience with infinite
grace. The brilliant light, the enthusiasm of a vast multitude,
the illusion of the stage, the glamour of a costume which was
most attractive for the time, all conspired in that woman's
favor. Sarrasine cried aloud with pleasure. He saw before
him at that moment the ideal beauty whose perfections he had
hitherto sought here and there in nature, taking from one
model, often of humble rank, the rounded outline of a shapely
leg; from another the contour of the breast; from another
her white shoulders; stealing the neck of that young girl, the
hands of this woman, and the polished knees of yonder child,
but never able to find beneath the cold skies of Paris the rich
and satisfying creations of ancient Greece. La Zambinella
displayed in her single person, intensely alive and delicate
beyond words, all those exquisite proportions of the female
form which he had so ardently longed to behold, and of which
a sculptor is the most severe and at the same time the most
passionate judge. She had an expressive mouth, eyes instinct
with love, flesh of dazzling whiteness. And add to these details, which would have filled a painter's soul with rapture, all
the marvelous charms of the Venuses worshiped and copied
by the chisel of the Greeks. The artist did not tire of admiring the inimitable grace with which the arms were attached
to the body, the wonderful roundness of the throat, the graceful curves described by the eyebrows and the nose, and the
perfect oval of the face, the purity of its clean-cut lines, and
the effect of the thick, drooping lashes which bordered the
large and voluptuous eyelids. She was more than a woman;
she was a masterpiece! In that unhoped-for creation there
was love enough to enrapture all mankind, and beauties calculated to satisfy the most exacting critic.

"Sarrasine devoured with his eyes what seemed to him Pygmalion's statue descended from its pedestal. When La Zambinella sang, he was beside himself. He was cold; then suddenly he felt a fire burning in the secret depths of his being,
in what, for lack of a better word, we call the heart. He did

not applaud, he said nothing; he felt a mad impulse, a sort
of frenzy of the sort that seizes us only at the age when there
is a something indefinably terrible and infernal in our desires.
Sarrasine longed to rush upon the stage and seize that woman.
His strength, increased a hundredfold by a moral depression
impossible to describe,—for such phenomena take place in a
sphere inaccessible to human observation,—insisted upon manifesting itself with deplorable violence. Looking at him, you
would have said that he was a cold, dull man. Renown, science, future, life, prizes, all vanished.

" 'To win her love or die!' Such was the sentence Sarrasine
pronounced upon himself.

"He was so completely intoxicated that he no longer saw
theatre, audience, or actors, no longer heard the music. Nay,
more, there was no space between him and La Zambinella;
he possessed her; his eyes, fixed steadfastly upon her, took
possession of her. An almost diabolical power enabled him
to feel the breath of that voice, to inhale the fragrant powder
with which her hair was covered, to see the slightest inequalities of her face, to count the blue veins which threaded their
way beneath the satiny skin. And that fresh, brisk voice of
silvery *timbre*, flexible as a thread to which the faintest breath
of air gives form, which it rolls and unrolls, tangles and blows
away, that voice attacked his heart so fiercely that he more
than once uttered an involuntary exclamation, extorted by
the convulsive ecstasy too rarely evoked by human passions.
He was soon obliged to leave the theatre. His trembling legs
almost refused to bear him. He was prostrated, weak, like a
nervous man who has given way to a terrible burst of anger.
He had had such exquisite pleasure, or perhaps had suffered
so, that his life had flowed away like water from an overturned
vessel. He felt a void within him, a sense of goneness like
the utter lack of strength which discourages a convalescent
just recovering from a serious sickness. Overwhelmed by inexplicable melancholy, he sat down on the steps of a church.
There, with his back resting against a pillar, he lost himself
in a fit of meditation as confused as a dream. Passion had

dealt him a crushing blow. On his return to his apartments
he was seized by one of those paroxysms of activity which reveal to us the presence of new principles in our existence. A
prey to that first fever of love which resembles pain as much
as pleasure, he sought to defeat his impatience and his frenzy
by sketching La Zambinella from memory. It was a sort of
material meditation. Upon one leaf La Zambinella appeared
in that pose, apparently calm and cold, affected by Raphael,
Georgione, and all the great painters. On another, she was
coyly turning her head as she finished a roulade, and seemed
to be listening to herself. Sarrasine drew his mistress in all
poses: he drew her unveiled, seated, standing, reclining,
chaste, and amorous—interpreting, thanks to the delirious activity of his pencil, all the fanciful ideas which beset our
imagination when our thoughts are completely engrossed by
a mistress. But his frantic thoughts outran his pencil. He
met La Zambinella, spoke to her, entreated her, exhausted a
thousand years of life and happiness with her, placing her
in all imaginable situations, trying the future with her, so
to speak. The next day he sent his servant to hire a box near
the stage for the whole season. Then, like all young men of
powerful feelings, he exaggerated the difficulties of his undertaking, and gave his passion, for its first pasturage, the joy
of being able to admire his mistress without obstacle. The
golden age of love, during which we enjoy our own sentiments,
and in which we are almost as happy by ourselves, was not
likely to last long with Sarrasine. However, events surprised
him when he was still under the spell of that springtime hal-
lucination, as naïve as it was voluptuous. In a week he lived
a whole lifetime, occupied through the day in molding the
clay with which he succeeded in copying La Zambinella, notwithstanding the veils, the skirts, the waists, and the bows of
ribbon which concealed her from him. In the evening, in-
stalled at an early hour in his box, alone, reclining on a sofa,
he made for himself, like a Turk drunk with opium, a happiness as fruitful, as lavish, as he wished. First of all, he fa-
miliarized himself gradually with the too intense emotions

which his mistress' singing caused him; then he taught his eyes to look at her, and was finally able to contemplate her at his leisure without fearing an explosion of concealed frenzy, like that which had seized him the first day. His passion became more profound as it became more tranquil. But the unsociable sculptor would not allow his solitude, peopled as it was with images, adorned with the fanciful creations of hope, and full of happiness, to be disturbed by his comrades. His love was so intense and so ingenuous, that he had to undergo the innocent scruples with which we are assailed when we love for the first time. As he began to realize that he would soon be required to bestir himself, to intrigue, to ask where La Zambinella lived, to ascertain whether she had a mother, an uncle, a guardian, a family,—in a word, as he reflected upon the methods of seeing her, of speaking to her, he felt that his heart was so swollen with such ambitious ideas, that he postponed those cares until the following day, as happy in his physical sufferings as in his intellectual pleasures."

"But," said Madame de Rochefide, interrupting me, "I see nothing of Marianina or her little old man in all this."

"You see nothing but him!" I cried, as vexed as an author for whom some one has spoiled the effect of a *coup de théâtre*.

"For some days," I resumed after a pause, "Sarrasine had been so faithful in attendance in his box, and his glances expressed such passionate love, that his passion for La Zambinella's voice would have been town-talk in Paris, if the episode had happened here; but in Italy, madame, every one goes to the theatre for his own enjoyment, with all his own passions, with a heartfelt interest which precludes all thought of espionage with opera-glasses. However, the sculptor's frantic admiration could not long escape the notice of the performers, male and female. One evening the Frenchman noticed that they were laughing at him in the wings. It is hard to say what violent measures he might have resorted to, had not La Zambinella come on the stage. She cast at Sarrasine one of those eloquent glances which often say more than women intend. That glance was a complete revelation in itself. Sarrasine was beloved!

" 'If it is a mere caprice,' he thought, already accusing his mistress of too great ardor, 'she does not know the sort of domination to which she is about to become subject. Her caprice will last, I trust, as long as my life.'

"At that moment, three light taps on the door of his box attracted the artist's attention. He opened the door. An old woman entered with an air of mystery.

" 'Young man,' she said, 'if you wish to be happy, be prudent. Wrap yourself in a cloak, pull a broad-brimmed hat over your eyes, and be on the Rue du Corso, in front of the Hôtel d'Espagne, about ten o'clock to-night.' "

" 'I will be there,' he replied, putting two louis in the duenna's wrinkled hand.

"He rushed from his box, after a sign of intelligence to La Zambinella, who lowered her voluptuous eyelids modestly, like a woman overjoyed to be understood at last. Then he hurried home, in order to borrow from his wardrobe all the charms it could loan him. As he left the theatre, a stranger grasped his arm.

" 'Beware, Signor Frenchman,' he said in his ear. 'This is a matter of life and death. Cardinal Cicognara is her protector, and he is no trifler.'

"If a demon had placed the deep pit of hell between Sarrasine and La Zambinella, he would have crossed it with one stride at that moment. Like the horses of the immortal gods described by Homer, the sculptor's love had traversed vast spaces in a twinkling.

" 'If death awaited me on leaving the house, I would go the more quickly,' he replied.

" 'Poverino!' cried the stranger, as he disappeared.

"To talk of danger to a man in love is to sell him pleasure. Sarrasine's valet had never seen his master so painstaking in the matter of dress. His finest sword, a gift from Bouchardon, the bow-knot Clotilde gave him, his coat with gold braid, his waistcoat of cloth of silver, his gold snuff-box, his valuable watch, everything was taken from its place, and he arrayed himself like a maiden about to appear before her first lover.

At the appointed hour, drunk with love and boiling over with
hope, Sarrasine, his nose buried in his cloak, hurried to the
rendezvous appointed by the old woman. She was waiting.

" 'You are very late,' she said. 'Come.'

"She led the Frenchman through several narrow streets and
stopped in front of a palace of attractive appearance. She
knocked; the door opened. She led Sarrasine through a laby-
rinth of stairways, galleries, and apartments which were
lighted only by uncertain gleams of moonlight, and soon
reached a door through the cracks of which stole a bright light,
and from which came the joyous sound of several voices. Sarrasine was suddenly blinded when, at a word from the old
woman, he was admitted to that mysterious apartment and
found himself in a salon as brilliantly lighted as it was sump-
tuously furnished; in the centre stood a bountifully supplied
table, laden with inviolable bottles, with laughing decanters
whose red facets sparkled merrily. He recognized the singers
from the theatre, male and female, mingled with charming
women, all ready to begin an artists' spree and waiting only
for him. Sarrasine restrained a feeling of displeasure and
put a good face on the matter. He had hoped for a dimly
lighted chamber, his mistress leaning over a brazier, a jealous
rival within two steps, death and love, confidences exchanged
in low tones, heart to heart, hazardous kisses, and faces so
near together that La Zambinella's hair would have touched
caressingly his desire-laden brow, burning with happiness.

" *'Vive la folie!'* he cried. *'Signori e belle donne,* you will
allow me to postpone my revenge and bear witness to my gratitude for the welcome you offer a poor sculptor."

"After receiving congratulations not lacking in warmth
from most of those present, whom he knew by sight, he tried
to approach the couch on which La Zambinella was noncha-
lantly reclining. Ah! how his heart beat when he spied a tiny
foot in one of those slippers which—if you will allow me to
say so, madame—formerly imparted to a woman's feet such a
coquettish, voluptuous look that I cannot conceive how men
could resist them. Tightly fitting white stockings with green

clocks, short skirts, and the pointed, high-heeled slippers of
Louis XV.'s time contributed somewhat, I fancy, to the de-
moralization of Europe and the clergy."

"Somewhat!" exclaimed the marchioness. "Have you read
nothing, pray?"

"La Zambinella," I continued, smiling, "had boldly crossed
her legs, and as she prattled swung the upper one, a duchess'
attitude very well suited to her capricious type of beauty, overflowing with a certain attractive suppleness. She had laid
aside her stage costume, and wore a waist which outlined a
slender figure, displayed to the best advantage by a *panier*
and a satin dress embroidered with blue flowers. Her breast,
whose treasures were concealed by a coquettish arrangement
of lace, was of a gleaming white. Her hair was dressed almost like Madame du Barry's; her face, although overshad-
owed by a large cap, seemed only the daintier therefor, and
the powder was very becoming to her. To see her thus was
to adore her. She smiled graciously at the sculptor. Sarrasine, disgusted beyond measure at finding himself unable to
speak to her without witnesses, courteously seated himself
beside her, and discoursed of music, extolling her prodigious
talent; but his voice trembled with love and fear and hope.

" 'What do you fear?' queried Vitagliani, the most celebrated singer in the troupe. 'Go on, you have no rival here
to fear.'

"After he had said this the tenor smiled silently. The lips
of all the guests repeated that smile, in which there was a
lurking expression of malice likely to escape a lover. The
publicity of his love was like a sudden dagger-thrust in Sarrasine's heart. Although possessed of a certain strength of
character, and although nothing that might happen could
subdue the violence of his passion, it had not before occurred
to him that La Zambinella was almost a courtesan, and that
he could not hope to enjoy at one and the same time the pure
delights which make a maiden's love so sweet, and the passionate transports with which one must purchase the perilous
favors of an actress. He reflected and resigned himself to his

fate. The supper was served. Sarrasine and La Zambinella seated themselves side by side without ceremony. During the first half of the feast the artists exercised some restraint, and the sculptor was able to converse with the singer. He found that she was very bright and quick-witted; but she was amazingly ignorant and seemed weak and superstitious. The delicacy of her organs was reproduced in her understanding. When Vitagliani opened the first bottle of champagne, Sarrasine read in his neighbor's eyes a shrinking dread of the report caused by the release of the gas. The involuntary shudder of that thoroughly feminine temperament was interpreted by the amorous artist as indicating extreme delicacy of feeling. This weakness delighted the Frenchman. There is so much of the element of protection in a man's love!

" 'You may make use of my power as a shield!'

"Is not that sentence written at the root of all declarations of love? Sarrasine, who was too passionately in love to make fine speeches to the fair Italian, was, like all lovers, grave, jovial, meditative, by turns. Although he seemed to listen to the guests, he did not hear a word that they said, he was so wrapped up in the pleasure of sitting by her side, of touching her hand, of waiting on her. He was swimming in a sea of concealed joy. Despite the eloquence of divers glances they exchanged, he was amazed at La Zambinella's continued reserve toward him. She had begun, it is true, by touching his foot with hers and stimulating his passion with the mischievous pleasure of a woman who is free and in love; but she had suddenly enveloped herself in maidenly modesty, after she had heard Sarrasine relate an incident which illustrated the extreme violence of his temper. When the supper became a debauch, the guests began to sing, inspired by the Peralta and the Pedro-Ximenes. There were fascinating duets, Calabrian ballads, Spanish *sequidillas,* and Neapolitan *canzonettes*. Drunkenness was in all eyes, in the music, in the hearts and voices of the guests. There was a sudden overflow of bewitching vivacity, of cordial unconstraint, of Italian good nature, of which no words can convey an idea to those who know only the evening parties of Paris, the routs of London, or the clubs of Vienna. Jests and words of love flew from side to side like bullets in a battle, amid laughter, impieties, invocations to the Blessed Virgin or the *Bambino*. One man lay on a sofa and fell asleep. A young woman listened to a declaration, unconscious that she was spilling Xeres wine on the table-cloth. Amid all this confusion La Zambinella, as if terror-stricken, seemed lost in thought. She refused to drink, but ate perhaps a little too much; but gluttony is attractive in women, it is said. Sarrasine, admiring his mistress' modesty, indulged in serious reflections concerning the future.

" 'She desires to be married, I presume,' he said to himself.

"Thereupon he abandoned himself to blissful anticipations of marriage with her. It seemed to him that his whole life would be too short to exhaust the living spring of happiness which he found in the depths of his heart. Vitagliani, who sat on his other side, filled his glass so often that, about three in the morning, Sarrasine, while not absolutely drunk, was powerless to resist his delirious passion. In a moment of frenzy he seized the woman and carried her to a sort of boudoir which opened from the salon, and toward which he had more than once turned his eyes. The Italian was armed with a dagger.

" 'If you come near me,' she said, 'I shall be compelled to plunge this blade into your heart. Go! you would despise me. I have conceived too great a respect for your character to abandon myself to you thus. I do not choose to destroy the sentiment with which you honor me.'

" 'Ah!' said Sarrasine, 'to stimulate a passion is a poor way to extinguish it! Are you already so corrupt that, being old in heart, you act like a young prostitute who inflames the emotions in which she trades?"

" 'Why, this is Friday,' she replied, alarmed by the French-man's violence.

"Sarrasine, who was not piously inclined, began to laugh. La Zambinella gave a bound like a young deer, and darted into the salon. When Sarrasine appeared, running after her,

he was welcomed by a roar of infernal laughter. He saw La
Zambinella swooning on a sofa. She was very pale, as if exhausted by the extraordinary effort she had made. Although
Sarrasine knew but little Italian, he understood his mistress
when she said to Vitagliani in a low voice:

" 'But he will kill me!'

"This strange scene abashed the sculptor. His reason returned. He stood still for a moment; then he recovered his
speech, sat down beside his mistress, and assured her of his
profound respect. He found strength to hold his passion in
check while talking to her in the most exalted strain; and, to
describe his love, he displayed all the treasures of eloquence
—that sorcerer, that friendly interpreter, whom women rarely
refuse to believe. When the first rays of dawn surprised the
boon companions, some woman suggested that they go to Frascati. One and all welcomed with loud applause the idea of
passing the day at Villa Ludovisi. Vitagliani went down to
hire carriages. Sarrasine had the good fortune to drive La
Zambinella in a phaeton. When they had left Rome behind,
the merriment of the party, repressed for a moment by the
battle they had all been fighting against drowsiness, suddenly
awoke. All, men and women alike, seemed accustomed to that
strange life, that constant round of pleasures, that artistic
energy, which makes of life one never ending *fête*, where
laughter reigns, unchecked by fear of the future. The sculptor's companion was the only one who seemed out of spirits.

" 'Are you ill?' Sarrasine asked her. 'Would you prefer to
go home?'

" 'I am not strong enough to stand all this dissipation,'
she replied. 'I have to be very careful; but I feel so happy
with you! Except for you, I should not have remained to
this supper; a night like this takes away all my freshness.'

" 'You are so delicate!' rejoined Sarrasine, gazing in rapture at the charming creature's dainty features.

" 'Dissipation ruins my voice.'

" 'Now that we are alone,' cried the artist, 'and that you
no longer have reason to fear the effervescence of my passion,
tell me that you love me.'

" 'Why?' said she; 'for what good purpose? You think me pretty. But you are a Frenchman, and your fancy will pass away. Ah! you would not love me as I should like to be loved.'

" 'How?'

" 'Purely, with no mingling of vulgar passion. I abhor men even more, perhaps, than I hate women. I need to take refuge in friendship. The world is a desert to me. I am an accursed creature, doomed to understand happiness, to feel it, to desire it, and like many, many others, compelled to see it always fly from me. Remember, signor, that I have not deceived you. I forbid you to love me. I can be a devoted friend to you, for I admire your strength of will and your character. I need a brother, a protector. Be both of these to me, but nothing more.'

" 'And not love you!' cried Sarrasine; 'but you are my life, my happiness, dear angel!'

" 'If I should say a word, you would spurn me with horror.'

" 'Coquette! nothing can frighten me. Tell me that you will cost me my whole future, that I shall die two months hence, that I shall be damned for having kissed you but once——'

"And he kissed her, despite La Zambinella's efforts to avoid that passionate caress.

" 'Tell me that you are a demon, that I must give you my fortune, my name, all my renown! Would you have me cease to be a sculptor? Speak.'

" 'Suppose I were not a woman?' queried La Zambinella, timidly, in a sweet, silvery voice.

" 'A merry jest!' cried Sarrasine. 'Think you that you can deceive an artist's eye? Have I not, for ten days past, admired, examined, devoured, thy perfections? None but a woman can have this soft and beautifully rounded arm, these graceful outlines. Ah! you seek compliments!'

"She smiled sadly, and murmured:

" 'Fatal beauty!'

"She raised her eyes to the sky. At that moment, there

was in her eyes an indefinable expression of horror, so startling, so intense, that Sarrasine shuddered.

"'Signor Frenchman,' she continued, 'forget forever a
moment's madness. I esteem you, but as for love, do not ask
me for that; that sentiment is suffocated in my heart. I have
no heart!' she cried, weeping bitterly. 'The stage on which
you saw me, the applause, the music, the renown to which I
am condemned—those are my life; I have no other. A few
hours hence you will no longer look upon me with the same
eyes, the woman you love will be dead.'

"The sculptor did not reply. He was seized with a dull
rage which contracted his heart. He could do nothing but
gaze at that extraordinary woman, with inflamed, burning
eyes. That feeble voice, La Zambinella's attitude, manners,
and gestures, instinct with dejection, melancholy, and discouragement, reawakened in his soul all the treasures of passion. Each word was a spur. At that moment, they arrived
at Frascati. When the artist held out his arms to help his
mistress to alight, he felt that she trembled from head to foot.

"'What is the matter? You would kill me,' he cried, seeing
that she turned pale, 'if you should suffer the slightest pain
of which I am, even innocently, the cause.'

"'A snake!' she said, pointing to a reptile which was glid-
ing along the edge of a ditch. 'I am afraid of the disgusting
creatures.'

"Sarrasine crushed the snake's head with a blow of his foot.

"'How could you dare to do it?' said La Zambinella, gazing at the dead reptile with visible terror.

"'Aha!' said the artist, with a smile, 'would you venture
to say now that you are not a woman?'

"They joined their companions and walked through the
woods of Villa Ludovisi, which at that time belonged to Cardinal Cicognara. The morning passed all too swiftly for the
amorous sculptor, but it was crowded with incidents which
laid bare to him the coquetry, the weakness, the daintiness, of
that pliant, inert soul. She was a true woman with her sudden terrors, her unreasoning caprices, her instinctive worries,

her causeless audacity, her bravado, and her fascinating delicacy of feeling. At one time, as the merry little party of singers ventured out into the open country, they saw at some distance a number of men armed to the teeth, whose costume was
by no means reassuring. At the words, 'Those are brigands!'
they all quickened their pace in order to reach the shelter of
the wall enclosing the cardinal's villa. At that critical moment Sarrasine saw from La Zambinella's manner that she no
longer had strength to walk; he took her in his arms and carried her for some distance, running. When he was within
call of a vineyard near by, he set his mistress down.

"'Tell me,' he said, 'why it is that this extreme weakness,
which in another woman would be hideous, would disgust me,
so that the slightest indication of it would be enough to destroy my love,—why is it that in you it pleases me, fascinates
me? Oh, how I love you!' he continued. 'All your faults,
your frights, your petty foibles, add an indescribable charm
to your character. I feel that I should detest a Sappho, a
strong, courageous woman, overflowing with energy and passion. O sweet and fragile creature! how couldst thou be
otherwise? That angel's voice, that refined voice, would have
been an anachronism coming from any other breast than
thine.'

"'I can give you no hope,' she said. 'Cease to speak thus
to me, for people would make sport of you. It is impossible
for me to shut the door of the theatre to you; but if you love
me, or if you are wise, you will come there no more. Listen to
me, monsieur,' she continued in a grave voice.

"'Oh, hush!' said the excited artist. 'Obstacles inflame the
love in my heart.'

"La Zambinella maintained a graceful and modest attitude;
but she held her peace, as if a terrible thought had suddenly
revealed some catastrophe. When it was time to return to
Rome she entered a berlin with four seats, bidding the sculptor, with a cruelly imperious air, to return alone in the phaeton. On the road, Sarrasine determined to carry off La Zambinella. He passed the whole day forming plans, each more

extravagant than the last. At nightfall, as he was going out to inquire of somebody where his mistress lived, he met one of his fellow-artists at the door.

" 'My dear fellow,' he said, 'I am sent by our ambassador to invite you to come to the embassy this evening. He gives a magnificent concert, and when I tell you that La Zambinella will be there——'

" 'Zambinella!' cried Sarrasine, thrown into delirium by that name; 'I am mad with love of her.'

" 'You are like everybody else,' replied his comrade.

" 'But if you are friends of mine, you and Vien and Lauterbourg and Allegrain, you will lend me your assistance for a *coup de main,* after the entertainment, will you not?' asked Sarrasine.

" 'There's no cardinal to be killed? no——?'

" 'No, no!' said Sarrasine, 'I ask nothing of you that men of honor may not do.'

"In a few moments the sculptor laid all his plans to assure the success of his enterprise. He was one of the last to arrive at the ambassador's, but he went thither in a traveling carriage drawn by four stout horses and driven by one of the most skilful *vetturini* in Rome. The ambassador's palace was full of people; not without difficulty did the sculptor, whom nobody knew, make his way to the salon where La Zambinella was singing at that moment.

" 'It must be in deference to all the cardinals, bishops, and *abbés* who are here,' said Sarrasine, 'that *she* is dressed as a man, that *she* has curly hair which *she* wears in a bag, and that *she* has a sword at her side?'

" 'She! what she?' rejoined the old nobleman whom Sarrasine addressed.

" 'La Zambinella.'

" 'La Zambinella!' echoed the Roman prince. 'Are you jesting? Whence have you come? Did a woman ever appear in a Roman theatre? And do you not know what sort of creatures play female parts within the domains of the Pope? It was I, monsieur, who endowed Zambinella with his voice. I

paid all the knave's expenses, even his teacher in singing. And
he has so little gratitude for the service I have done him that
he has never been willing to step inside my house. And yet,
if he makes his fortune, he will owe it all to me.'

"Prince Chigi might have talked on forever, Sarrasine did
not listen to him. A ghastly truth had found its way into his
mind. He was stricken as if by a thunderbolt. He stood like
a statue, his eyes fastened on the singer. His flaming glance
exerted a sort of magnetic influence on Zambinella, for he
turned his eyes at last in Sarrasine's direction, and his divine
voice faltered. He trembled! An involuntary murmur escaped the audience, which he held fast as if fastened to his
lips; and that completely disconcerted him; he stopped in
the middle of the aria he was singing and sat down. Cardinal
Cicognara, who had watched from the corner of his eye the
direction of his *protégé's* glance, saw the Frenchman; he
leaned toward one of his ecclesiastical aides-de-camp, and apparently asked the sculptor's name. When he had obtained
the reply he desired he scrutinized the artist with great attention and gave orders to an *abbé,* who instantly disappeared.
Meanwhile Zambinella, having recovered his self-possession,
resumed the aria he had so capriciously broken off; but he
sang badly, and refused, despite all the persistent appeals
showered upon him, to sing anything else. It was the first
time he had exhibited that humorsome tyranny, which, at a
later date, contributed no less to his celebrity than his talent
and his vast fortune, which was said to be due to his beauty
as much as to his voice.

" 'It's a woman,' said Sarrasine, thinking that no one could
overhear him. 'There's some secret intrigue beneath all this.
Cardinal Cicognara is hoodwinking the Pope and the whole
city of Rome !'

"The sculptor at once left the salon, assembled his friends,
and lay in wait in the courtyard of the palace. When Zambinella was assured of Sarrasine's departure he seemed to
recover his tranquillity in some measure. About midnight,
after wandering through the salons like a man looking for an

enemy, the *musico* left the party. As he passed through the
palace gate he was seized by men who deftly gagged him with
a handkerchief and placed him in the carriage hired by Sarrasine. Frozen with terror, Zambinella lay back in a corner,
not daring to move a muscle. He saw before him the terrible
face of the artist, who maintained a deathlike silence. The
journey was a short one. Zambinella, kidnapped by Sarrasine, soon found himself in a dark, bare studio. He sat, half
dead, upon a chair, hardly daring to glance at a statue of a
woman, in which he recognized his own features. He did not
utter a word, but his teeth were chattering; he was paralyzed
with fear. Sarrasine was striding up and down the studio.
Suddenly he halted in front of Zambinella.

" 'Tell me the truth,' he said, in a changed and hollow voice.
'Are you not a woman? Cardinal Cicognara——'

"Zambinella fell on his knees, and replied only by hanging
his head.

" 'Ah! you are a woman!' cried the artist in a frenzy; 'for
even a——'

"He did not finish the sentence.

" 'No,' he continued, 'even *he* could not be so utterly base.'

" 'Oh, do not kill me!' cried Zambinella, bursting into tears.
'I consented to deceive you only to gratify my comrades, who
wanted an opportunity to laugh.'

" 'Laugh!' echoed the sculptor, in a voice in which there was
a ring of infernal ferocity. 'Laugh! laugh! You dared to
make sport of a man's passion—you?'

" 'Oh, mercy!' cried Zambinella.

" 'I ought to kill you!' shouted Sarrasine, drawing his sword
in an outburst of rage. 'But,' he continued, with cold disdain, 'if I searched your whole being with this blade, should I
find there any sentiment to blot out, anything with which to
satisfy my thirst for vengeance? You are nothing! If you
were a man or a woman, I would kill you, but——'

"Sarrasine made a gesture of disgust, and turned his face
away; thereupon he noticed the statue.

" 'And that is a delusion!' he cried.

"Then, turning to Zambinella once more, he continued:

" 'A woman's heart was to me a place of refuge, a fatherland. Have you sisters who resemble you? No. Then die! But no, you shall live. To leave you your life is to doom you to a fate worse than death. I regret neither my blood nor my life, but my future and the fortune of my heart. Your weak hand has overturned my happiness. What hope can I extort from you in place of all those you have destroyed? You have brought me down to your level. *To love, to be loved!* are henceforth meaningless words to me, as to you. I shall never cease to think of that imaginary woman when I see a real woman.'

"He pointed to the statue with a gesture of despair.

" 'I shall always have in my memory a divine harpy who will bury her talons in all my manly sentiments, and who will stamp all other women with a seal of imperfection. Monster! you, who can give life to nothing, have swept all women off the face of the earth.'

"Sarrasine seated himself in front of the terrified singer. Two great tears came from his dry eyes, rolled down his swarthy cheeks, and fell to the floor—two tears of rage, two scalding, burning tears.

" 'An end of love! I am dead to all pleasure, to all human emotions!'

"As he spoke, he seized a hammer and hurled it at the statue with such excessive force that he missed it. He thought that he had destroyed that monument of his madness, and thereupon he drew his sword again, and raised it to kill the singer. Zambinella uttered shriek after shriek. Three men burst into the studio at that moment, and the sculptor fell, pierced by three daggers.

" 'From Cardinal Cicognara,' said one of the men.

" 'A benefaction worthy of a Christian,' retorted the Frenchman, as he breathed his last.

"These ominous emissaries told Zambinella of the anxiety of his patron, who was waiting at the door in a closed carriage in order to take him away as soon as he was set at liberty."

"But," said Madame de Rochefide, "what connection is there between this story and the little old man we saw at the Lantys'?"

"Madame, Cardinal Cicognara took possession of Zambinella's statue and had it reproduced in marble; it is in the Albani Museum to-day. In 1794 the Lanty family discovered it there, and asked Vien to copy it. The portrait which showed you Zambinella at twenty, a moment after you had seen him as a centenarian, afterward figured in Girodet's *Endymion;* you yourself recognized the type in *Adonis.*"

"But this Zambinella, male or female——"

"Must be, madame, Marianina's maternal great uncle. You can conceive now Madame de Lanty's interest in concealing the source of a fortune which comes——"

"Enough!" said she, with an imperious gesture.

We remained for a moment in the most profound silence.

"Well?" I said at last.

"Ah!" she cried, rising and pacing the floor.

She came and looked me in the face, and said in an altered voice:

"You have disgusted me with life and passion for a long time to come. Leaving monstrosities aside, are not all human sentiments dissolved thus, by ghastly disillusionment? Children torture mothers by their bad conduct, or their lack of affection. Wives are betrayed. Mistresses are cast aside, abandoned. Talk of friendship! Is there such a thing! I would turn pious to-morrow if I did not know that I can remain like the inaccessible summit of a cliff amid the tempests of life. If the future of the Christian is an illusion too, at all events it is not destroyed until after death. Leave me to myself."

"Ah!" said I, "you know how to punish."

"Am I in the wrong?"

"Yes," I replied, with a sort of desperate courage. "By finishing this story, which is well known in Italy, I can give you an excellent idea of the progress made by the civilization of the present day. There are none of those wretched creatures now."

"Paris," said she, "is an exceedingly hospitable place; it welcomes one and all, fortunes stained with shame, and fortunes stained with blood. Crime and infamy have a right of asylum here; virtue alone is without altars. But pure hearts have a fatherland in heaven! No one will have known me! I am proud of it."

And the marchioness was lost in thought.

FACINO CANE

I once used to 1 ve in a little street which probably is not known to you—the Rue de Lesdiguières. It is a turning out of the Rue Saint-Antoine, beginning just opposite a fountain near the Place de la Bastille, and ending in the Rue de la Cerisaie. Love of knowledge stranded me in a garret; my nights I spent in work, my days in reading at the Bibliothèque d'Orléans, close by. I lived frugally, I had accepted the conditions of the monastic life, necessary conditions for every worker, scarcely permitting myself a walk along the Boulevard Bourdon when the weather was fine. One passion only had power to draw me from my studies; and yet, what was that passion but a study of another kind? I used to watch the manners and customs of the Faubourg, its inhabitants, and their characteristics. As I dressed no better than a working man, and cared nothing for appearances, I did not put them on their guard; I could join a group and look on while they drove bargains or wrangled among themselves on their way home from work. Even then observation had come to be an instinct with me; a faculty of penetrating to the soul without neglecting the body; or rather, a power of grasping external details so thoroughly that they never detained me for a moment, and at once I passed beyond and through them. I could enter into the life of the human creatures whom I watched, just as the dervish in the *Arabian Nights* could pass into any soul or body after pronouncing a certain formula.

If I met a working man and his wife in the streets between eleven o'clock and midnight on their way home from the Ambigu Comique, I used to amuse myself by following them from the Boulevard du Pont aux Choux to the Boulevard Beaumarchais. The good folk would begin by talking about the play; then from one thing to another they would come to their own affairs, and the mother would walk on and on, heedless of complaints or question from the little one that dragged at her hand, while she and her husband reckoned up the wages to be paid on the morrow, and spent the money in a score of different ways. Then came domestic details, lamentations over the excessive dearness of potatoes, or the length of the winter and the high price of block fuel, together with forcible representations of amounts owing to the baker, ending in an acrimonious dispute, in the course of which such couples reveal their characters in picturesque language. As I listened, I could make their lives mine, I felt their rags on my back, I walked with their gaping shoes on my feet; their cravings, their needs, had all passed into my soul, or my soul had passed into theirs. It was the dream of a waking man. I waxed hot with them over the foreman's tyranny, or the bad customers that made them call again and again for payment.

To come out of my own ways of life, to be another than myself through a kind of intoxication of the intellectual faculties, and to play this game at will, such was my recreation. Whence comes the gift? Is it a kind of second sight? Is it one of those powers which when abused end in madness? I have never tried to discover its source; I possess it, I use it, that is all. But this it behoves you to know, that in those days I began to resolve the heterogeneous mass known as the People into its elements, and to evaluate its good and bad qualities. Even then I realized the possibilities of my suburb, that hotbed of revolution in which heroes, inventors, and practical men of science, rogues and scoundrels, virtues and vices, were all packed together by poverty, stifled by necessity, drowned in drink, and consumed by ardent spirits.

You would not imagine how many adventures, how many tragedies, lie buried away out of sight in that Dolorous City; how much horror and beauty lurks there. No imagination can reach the Truth, no one can go down into that city to make discoveries; for one must needs descend too low into its depths to see the wonderful scenes of tragedy or comedy enacted there, the masterpieces brought forth by chance.

I do not know how it is that I have kept the following story so long untold. It is one of the curious things that stop in the bag from which Memory draws out stories at haphazard, like numbers in a lottery. There are plenty of tales just as strange and just as well hidden still left; but some day, you may be sure, their turn will come.

One day my charwoman, a working man's wife, came to beg me to honor her sister's wedding with my presence. If you are to realize what this wedding was like, you must know that I paid my charwoman, poor creature, four francs a month; for which sum she came every morning to make my bed, clean my shoes, brush my clothes, sweep the room, and make ready my breakfast, before going to her day's work of turning the handle of a machine, at which hard drudgery she earned five-pence. Her husband, a cabinetmaker, made four francs a day at his trade; but as they had three children, it was all that they could do to gain an honest living. Yet I have never met with more sterling honesty than in this man and wife. For five years after I left the quarter, Mère Vaillant used to come on my birthday with a bunch of flowers and some oranges for me—she that had never a sixpence to put by! Want had drawn us together. I never could give her more than a ten-franc piece, and often I had to borrow the money for the occasion. This will perhaps explain my promise to go to the wedding; I hoped to efface myself in these poor people's merry-making.

The banquet and the ball were given on a first floor above a wineshop in the Rue de Charenton. It was a large room, lighted by oil lamps with tin reflectors. A row of wooden benches ran round the walls, which were black with grime to the height of the tables. Here some eighty persons, all in their Sunday best, tricked out with ribbons and bunches of flowers, all of them on pleasure bent, were dancing away with heated visages as if the world were about to come to an end. Bride and bridegroom exchanged salutes to the general satisfaction, amid a chorus of facetious "Oh, ohs!" and "Ah, ahs!"

less really indecent than the furtive glances of young girls that have been well brought up. There was something inde-scribably infectious about the rough, homely enjoyment in all countenances.

But neither the faces, nor the wedding, nor the wedding-guests have anything to do with my story. Simply bear them in mind as the odd setting to it. Try to realize the scene, the shabby red-painted wineshop, the smell of wine, the yells of merriment; try to feel that you are really in the faubourg, among old people, working men and poor women giving them-selves up to a night's enjoyment.

The band consisted of a fiddle, a clarionet, and a flageolet from the Blind Asylum. The three were paid seven francs in a lump sum for the night. For the money, they gave us, not Beethoven certainly, nor yet Rossini; they played as they had the will and the skill; and every one in the room (with charming delicacy of feeling) refrained from finding fault. The music made such a brutal assault on the drum of my ear, that after a first glance round the room my eyes fell at once upon the blind trio, and the sight of their uniform in-clined me from the first to indulgence. As the artists stood in a window recess, it was difficult to distinguish their faces except at close quarters, and I kept away at first; but when I came nearer (I hardly know why) I thought of nothing else; the wedding party and the music ceased to exist, my curiosity was roused to the highest pitch, for my soul passed into the body of the clarionet player.

The fiddle and the flageolet were neither of them interest-ing; their faces were of the ordinary type among the blind—earnest, attentive, and grave. Not so the clarionet player; any artist or philosopher must have come to a stop at the sight of him.

Picture to yourself a plaster mask of Dante in the red lamp-light, with a forest of silver-white hair above the brows. Blind-ness intensified the expression of bitterness and sorrow in that grand face of his; the dead eyes were lighted up, as it were, by a thought within that broke forth like a burning flame, lit

by one sole insatiable desire, written large in vigorous characters upon an arching brow scored across with as many lines
as an old stone wall.

The old man was playing at random, without the slightest
regard for time or tune. His fingers traveled mechanically
over the worn keys of his instrument; he did not trouble himself over a false note now and again (a *canard,* in the language of the orchestra), neither did the dancers, nor, for that
matter, did my old Italian's acolytes; for I had made up my
mind that he must be an Italian, and an Italian he was. There
was something great, something too of the despot about this
old Homer bearing within him an *Odyssey* doomed to oblivion.
The greatness was so real that it triumphed over his abject position; the despotism so much a part of him, that it rose above
his poverty.

There are violent passions which drive a man to good or
evil, making of him a hero or a convict; of these there was
not one that had failed to leave its traces on the grandly-hewn,
lividly Italian face. You trembled lest a flash of thought
should suddenly light up the deep sightless hollows under the
grizzled brows, as you might fear to see brigands with torches
and poniards in the mouth of a cavern. You felt that there
was a lion in that cage of flesh, a lion spent with useless raging against iron bars. The fires of despair had burned themselves out into ashes, the lava had cooled; but the tracks of
the flames, the wreckage, and a little smoke remained to bear
witness to the violence of the eruption, the ravages of the fire.
These images crowded up at the sight of the clarionet player,
till the thoughts now grown cold in his face burned hot within
my soul.

The fiddle and the flageolet took a deep interest in bottles
and glasses; at the end of a country-dance, they hung their
instruments from a button on their reddish-colored coats, and
stretched out their hands to a little table set in the window
recess to hold their liquor supply. Each time they did so they
held out a full glass to the Italian, who could not reach it for
himself because he sat in front of the table, and each time

the Italian thanked them with a friendly nod. All their movements were made with the precision which always amazes you so much at the Blind Asylum. You could almost think that they can see. I came nearer to listen; but when I stood beside them, they evidently guessed I was not a working man, and kept themselves to themselves.

"What part of the world do you come from, you that are playing the clarionet?"

"From Venice," he said, with a trace of Italian accent.

"Have you always been blind, or did it come on afterwards——?"

"Afterwards," he answered quickly. "A cursed gutta serena."

"Venice is a fine city; I have always had a fancy to go there."

The old man's face lighted up, the wrinkles began to work, he was violently excited.

"If I went with you, you would not lose your time," he said.

"Don't talk about Venice to our Doge," put in the fiddle, "or you will start him off, and he has stowed away a couple of bottles as it is—has the prince!"

"Come, strike up, Daddy Canard!" added the flageolet, and the three began to play. But while they executed the four figures of a square dance, the Venetian was scenting my thoughts; he guessed the great interest I felt in him. The dreary, dispirited look died out of his face, some mysterious hope brightened his features and slid like a blue flame over his wrinkles. He smiled and wiped his brow, that fearless, terrible brow of his, and at length grew gay like a man mounted on his hobby.

"How old are you?" I asked.

"Eighty-two."

"How long have you been blind?"

"For very nearly fifty years," he said, and there was that in his tone which told me that his regret was for something more than his lost sight, for great power of which he had been robbed.

"Then why do they call you 'the Doge' ?" I asked.

"Oh, it is a joke. I am a Venetian noble, and I might have been a doge like any one else."

"What is your name?"

"Here, in Paris, I am Père Canet," he said. "It was the only way of spelling my name on the register. But in Italy I am Marco Facino Cane, Prince of Varese."

"What, are you descended from the great *condottiere* Facino Cane, whose lands won by the sword were taken by the Dukes of Milan?"

"*E vero,*" returned he. "His son's life was not safe under the Visconti; he fled to Venice, and his name was inscribed on the Golden Book. And now neither Cane nor Golden Book are in existence." His gesture startled me; it told of patriotism extinguished and weariness of life.

"But if you were once a Venetian senator, you must have been a wealthy man. How did you lose your fortune?"

"In evil days."

He waved away the glass of wine handed to him by the flageolet, and bowed his head. He had no heart to drink. These details were not calculated to extinguish my curiosity.

As the three ground out the music of the square dance, I gazed at the old Venetian noble, thinking thoughts that set a young man's mind afire at the age of twenty. I saw Venice and the Adriatic; I saw her ruin in the ruin of the face before me. I walked to and fro in that city, so beloved of her citizens; I went from the Rialto Bridge, along the Grand Canal, and from the Riva degli Schiavoni to the Lido, returning to St. Mark's, that cathedral so unlike all others in its sublimity. I looked up at the windows of the Casa Doro, each with its different sculptured ornaments; I saw old palaces rich in marbles, saw all the wonders which a student beholds with the more sympathetic eyes because visible things take their color of his fancy, and the sight of realities cannot rob him of the glory of his dreams. Then I traced back a course of life for this latest scion of a race of condottieri, tracking down his misfortunes, looking for the reasons of the deep moral and

physical degradation out of which the lately revived sparks
of greatness and nobility shone so much the more brightly.
My ideas, no doubt, were passing through his mind, for all
processes of thought-communications are far more swift, I
think, in blind people, because their blindness compels them
to concentrate their attention. I had not long to wait for
proof that we were in sympathy in this way. Facino Cane
left off playing, and came up to me. "Let us go out!" he said;
his tones thrilled through me like an electric shock. I gave
him my arm, and we went.

Outside in the street he said, "Will you take me back to
Venice? will you be my guide? Will you put faith in me?
You shall be richer than ten of the richest houses in Amsterdam or London, richer than Rothschild; in short, you shall
have the fabulous wealth of the *Arabian Nights.*"

The man was mad, I thought; but in his voice there was a
potent something which I obeyed. I allowed him to lead, and
he went in the direction of the Fossés de la Bastille, as if he
could see; walking till he reached a lonely spot down by the
river, just where the bridge has since been built at the
junction of the Canal Saint-Martin and the Seine. Here he
sat down on a stone, and I, sitting opposite to him, saw the
old man's hair gleaming like threads of silver in the moonlight. The stillness was scarcely troubled by the sound of the
far-off thunder of traffic along the boulevards; the clear
night air and everything about us combined to make a
strangely unreal scene.

"You talk of millions to a young man," I began, "and do
you think that he will shrink from enduring any number of
hardships to gain them? Are you not laughing at me?"

"May I die unshriven," he cried vehemently, "if all that
I am about to tell you is not true. I was one-and-twenty
years old, like you at this moment. I was rich, I was handsome, and a noble by birth. I began with the first madness
of all—with Love. I loved as no one can love nowadays. I
I have hidden myself in a chest, at the risk of a dagger thrust,
for nothing more than the promise of a kiss. To die for Her

Here he sat down on a stone

·—it seemed to me to be a whole life in itself. In 1760 I fell in love with a lady of the Vendramin family; she was eighteen years old, and married to a Sagredo, one of the richest senators, a man of thirty, madly in love with his wife. My mistress and I were guiltless as cherubs when the *sposo* caught us together talking of love. He was armed, I was not, but he missed me; I sprang upon him and killed him with my two hands, wringing his neck as if he had been a chicken. I wanted Bianca to fly with me; but she would not. That is the way with women! So I went alone. I was condemned to death, and my property was confiscated and made over to my next-of-kin; but I had carried off my diamonds, five of Titian's pictures taken down from their frames and rolled up, and all my gold.

"I went to Milan, no one molested me, my affair in nowise interested the State.—One small observation before I go further," he continued, after a pause, "whether it is true or no that the mother's fancies at the time of conception or in the months before birth can influence her child, this much is certain, my mother during her pregnancy had a passion for gold, and I am the victim of a monomania, of a craving for gold which must be gratified. Gold is so much of a necessity of life for me, that I have never been without it; I must have gold to toy with and finger. As a young man I always wore jewelry, and carried two or three hundred ducats about with me wherever I went."

He drew a couple of gold coins from his pocket and showed them to me as he spoke.

"I can tell by instinct when gold is near. Blind as I am, I stop before the jeweler's shop windows. That passion was the ruin of me; I took to gambling to play with gold. I was not a cheat, I was cheated, I ruined myself. I lost all my fortune. Then the longing to see Bianca once more possessed me like a frenzy. I stole back to Venice and found her again. For six months I was happy; she hid me in her house and fed me. I thought thus deliciously to finish my days. But the Provveditore courted her, and guessed that he had a rival;

we in Italy can feel that. He played the spy upon us, and surprised us together in bed, base wretch. You may judge what a fight for life it was; I did not kill him outright, but I wounded him dangerously.

"That adventure broke my luck. I have never found another Bianca; I have known great pleasures; but among the most celebrated women at the court of Louis XV. I never found my beloved Venetian's charm, her love, her great qualities.

"The Provveditore called his servants, the palace was surrounded and entered; I fought for my life that I might die beneath Bianca's eyes; Bianca helped me to kill the Provveditore. Once before she had refused flight with me; but after six months of happiness she wished only to die with me, and received several thrusts. I was entangled in a great cloak that they flung over me, carried down to a gondola, and hurried to the Pozzi dungeons. I was twenty-two years old. I gripped the hilt of my broken sword so hard, that they could only have taken it from me by cutting off my hand at the wrist. A curious chance, or rather the instinct of self-preservation, led me to hide the fragment of the blade in a corner of my cell, as if it might still be of use. They tended me; none of my wounds were serious. At two-and-twenty one can recover from anything. I was to lose my head on the scaffold. I shammed illness to gain time. It seemed to me that the canal lay just outside my cell. I thought to make my escape by boring a hole through the wall and swimming for my life. I based my hopes on the following reasons.

"Every time that the jailer came with my food, there was light enough to read directions written on the walls— 'Side of the Palace,' 'Side of the Canal,' 'Side of the Vaults.' At last I saw a design in this, but I did not trouble myself much about the meaning of it; the actual incomplete condition of the Ducal Palace accounted for it. The longing to regain my freedom gave me something like genius. Groping about with my fingers, I spelled out an Arabic inscription on the wall. The author of the work informed those to come after him that he had loosed two stones in the lowest course of masonry and hollowed out eleven feet beyond underground. As he went on with his excavations, it became necessary to spread the fragments of stone and mortar over the floor of his cell. But even if jailers and inquisitors had not felt sure that the structure of the buildings was such that no watch was needed below, the level of the Pozzi dungeons being several steps below the threshold, it was possible gradually to raise the earthen floor without exciting the warder's suspicions.

"The tremendous labor had profited nothing—nothing at least to him that began it. The very fact that it was left unfinished told of the unknown worker's death. Unless his devoted toil was to be wasted for ever, his successor must have some knowledge of Arabic, but I had studied Oriental languages at the Armenian Convent. A few words written on the back of the stone recorded the unhappy man's fate; he had fallen a victim to his great possessions; Venice had coveted his wealth and seized upon it. A whole month went by before I obtained any result; but whenever I felt my strength failing as I worked, I heard the chink of gold, I saw gold spread before me, I was dazzled by diamonds.—Ah! wait.

"One night my blunted steel struck on wood. I whetted the fragment of my blade and cut a hole; I crept on my belly like a serpent; I worked naked and mole-fashion, my hands in front of me, using the stone itself to gain a purchase. I was to appear before my judges in two days' time, I made a final effort, and that night I bored through the wood and felt that there was space beyond.

"Judge of my surprise when I applied my eye to the hole. I was in the ceiling of a vault, heaps of gold were dimly visible in the faint light. The Doge himself and one of the Ten stood below; I could hear their voices and sufficient of their talk to know that this was the Secret Treasury of the Republic, full of the gifts of Doges and reserves of booty called the Tithe of Venice from the spoils of military expeditions. I was saved!

"When the jailer came I proposed that he should help me to escape and fly with me, and that we should take with us as much as we could carry. There was no reason for hesitation; he agreed. Vessels were about to sail for the Levant. All possible precautions were taken. Bianca furthered the schemes which I suggested to my accomplice. It was arranged that Bianca should only rejoin us in Smyrna for fear of exciting suspicion. In a single night the hole was enlarged, and we dropped down into the Secret Treasury of Venice.

"What a night that was! Four great casks full of gold stood there. In the outer room silver pieces were piled in heaps, leaving a gangway between by which to cross the chamber. Banks of silver coins surrounded the walls to the height of five feet.

"I thought the jailer would go mad. He sang and laughed and danced and capered among the gold, till I threatened to strangle him if he made a sound or wasted time. In his joy he did not notice at first the table where the diamonds lay. I flung myself upon these, and deftly filled the pockets of my sailor jacket and trousers with the stones. Ah! Heaven, I did not take the third of them. Gold ignots lay underneath the table. I persuaded my companion to fill as many bags as we could carry with the gold, and made him understand that this was our only chance of escaping detection abroad.

"'Pearls, rubies, and diamonds might be recognized,' I told him.

"Covetous though we were, we could not possibly take more than two thousand livres weight of gold, which meant six journeys across the prison to the gondola. The sentinel at the water gate was bribed with a bag containing ten livres weight of gold; and as for the two gondoliers, they believed they were serving the Republic. At daybreak we set out.

"Once upon the open sea, when I thought of that night, when I recollected all that I had felt, when the vision of that great hoard rose before my eyes, and I computed that I had left behind thirty millions in silver, twenty in gold, and many more in diamonds, pearls, and rubies—then a sort of madness began to work in me. I had the gold fever.

"We landed at Smyrna and took ship at once for France. As we went on board the French vessel, Heaven favored me by ridding me of my accomplice. I did not think at the time of all the possible consequences of this mishap, and rejoiced not a little. We were so completely unnerved by all that had happened, that we were stupid, we said not a word to each other, we waited till it should be safe to enjoy ourselves at our ease. It was not wonderful that the rogue's head was dizzy. You shall see how heavily God has punished me.

"I never knew a quiet moment until I had sold two-thirds of my diamonds in London or Amsterdam, and held the value of my gold dust in a negotiable shape. For five years I hid myself in Madrid, then in 1770 I came to Paris with a Spanish name, and led as brilliant a life as may be. Then in the midst of my pleasures, as I enjoyed a fortune of six millions, I was smitten with blindness. I do not doubt but that my infirmity was brought on by my sojourn in the cell and my work in the stone, if, indeed, my peculiar faculty for 'seeing' gold was not an abuse of the power of sight which predestined me to lose it. Bianca was dead.

"At this time I had fallen in love with a woman to whom I thought to link my fate. I had told her the secret of my name; she belonged to a powerful family; she was a friend of Mme. du Barry; I hoped everything from the favor shown me by Louis XV.; I trusted in her. Acting on her advice, I went to England to consult a famous oculist, and after a stay of several months in London she deserted me in Hyde Park. She had stripped me of all that I had, and left me without resource. Nor could I make complaint, for to disclose my name was to lay myself open to the vengeance of my native city; I could appeal to no one for aid, I feared Venice. The woman put spies about me to exploit my infirmity. I spare you a tale of adventures worthy of Gil Blas.—Your Revolution followed. For two whole years that creature kept me at the Bicêtre as a lunatic, then she gained admit-

tance for me at the Blind Asylum; there was no help for it,
I went. I could not kill her; I could not see; and I was so
poor that I could not pay another arm.

"If only I had taken counsel with my jailer, Benedetto
Carpi, before I lost him, I might have known the exact position of my cell, I might have found my way back to the Treasury and returned to Venice when Napoleon crushed the Republic——

"Still, blind as I am, let us go back to Venice! I shall find
the door of my prison, I shall see the gold through the prison
walls, I shall hear it where it lies under the water; for the
events which brought about the fall of Venice befell in such
a way that the secret of the hoard must have perished with
Bianca's brother, Vendramin, a doge to whom I looked to
make my peace with the Ten. I sent memorials to the First
Consul; I proposed an agreement with the Emperor of Austria; every one sent me about my business for a lunatic. Come!
we will go to Venice; let us set out as beggars, we shall come
back millionaires. We will buy back my estates, and you shall
be my heir! You shall be Prince of Varese!"

My head was swimming. For me his confidences reached
the proportions of tragedy; at the sight of that white head
of his and beyond it the black water in the trenches of the
Bastille lying still as a canal in Venice, I had no words to
answer him. Facino Cane thought, no doubt, that I judged
him, as the rest had done, with a disdainful pity; his gesture
expressed the whole philosophy of despair.

Perhaps his story had taken him back to happy days and to
Venice. He caught up his clarionet and made plaintive music,
playing a Venetian boat-song with something of his lost
skill, the skill of the young patrician lover. It was a sort of
Super flumina Babylonis. Tears filled my eyes. Any belated
persons walking along the Boulevard Bourdon must have stood
still to listen to an exile's last prayer, a last cry of regret for a
lost name, mingled with memories of Bianca. But gold soon
gained the upper hand, the fatal passion quenched the light
of youth.

"I see it always," he said; "dreaming or waking, I see it; and as I pace to and fro, I pace in the Treasury, and the diamonds sparkle. I am not as blind as you think; gold and diamonds light up my night, the night of the last Facino Cane, for my title passes to the Memmi. My God! the murderer's punishment was not long delayed! *Ave Maria,*" and he repeated several prayers that I did not heed.

"We will go to Venice!" I said, when he rose.

"Then I have found a man!" he cried, with his face on fire.

I gave him my arm and went home with him. We reached the gates of the Blind Asylum just as some of the wedding guests were returning along the street, shouting at the top of their voices. He squeezed my hand.

"Shall we start to-morrow?" he asked.

"As soon as we can get some money."

"But we can go on foot. I will beg. I am strong, and you feel young when you see gold before you."

Facino Cane died before the winter was out after a two months' illness. The poor man had taken a chill.

PARIS, *March* 1896.

Z. MARCAS

To His Highness Count William of Wurtemberg, as a token
of the Author's respectful gratitude.

De Balzac.

I NEVER saw anybody, not even among the most remarkable
men of the day, whose appearance was so striking as this
man's; the study of his countenance at first gave me a feeling of great melancholy, and at last produced an almost painful impression.

There was a certain harmony between the man and his
name. The Z. preceding Marcas, which was seen on the addresses of his letters, and which he never omitted from his
signature, as the last letter of the alphabet, suggested some
mysterious fatality.

MARCAS! say this two-syllabled name again and again; do
you not feel as if it had some sinister meaning? Does it not
seem to you that its owner must be doomed to martyrdom?
Though foreign, savage, the name has a right to be handed
down to posterity; it is well constructed, easily pronounced,
and has the brevity that beseems a famous name. Is it not
pleasant as well as odd? But does it not sound unfinished?

I will not take it upon myself to assert that names have
no influence on the destiny of men. There is a certain secret
and inexplicable concord or a visible discord between the
events of a man's life and his name which is truly surprising;
often some remote but very real correlation is revealed. Our
globe is round; everything is linked to everything else. Some
day perhaps we shall revert to the occult sciences.

Do you not discern in that letter Z an adverse influence?
Does it not prefigure the wayward and fantastic progress of a

storm-tossed life? What wind blew on that letter, which,
whatever language we find it in, begins scarcely fifty words?
Marcas' name was Zephirin; Saint Zephirin is highly
venerated in Brittany, and Marcas was a Breton.

Study the name once more: Z. Marcas! The man's whole
life lies in this fantastic juxtaposition of seven letters; seven!
the most significant of all the cabalistic numbers. And he
died at five-and-thirty, so his life extended over seven lustres.

Marcas! Does it not hint of some precious object that is
broken with a fall, with or without a crash?

I had finished studying the law in Paris in 1836. I lived
at that time in the Rue Corneille in a house where none but
students came to lodge, one of those large houses where there
is a winding staircase quite at the back, lighted below from
the street, higher up by borrowed lights, and at the top by a
skylight. There were forty furnished rooms—furnished as
students' rooms are! What does youth demand more than was
here supplied? A bed, a few chairs, a chest of drawers, a
looking-glass, and a table. As soon as the sky is blue the student opens his window.

But in this street there are no fair neighbors to flirt with.
In front is the Odéon, long since closed, presenting a wall
that is beginning to go black, its tiny gallery windows and its
vast expanse of slate roof. I was not rich enough to have a
good room; I was not even rich enough to have a room to myself. Juste and I shared a double-bedded room on the fifth
floor.

On our side of the landing there were but two rooms—
ours and a smaller one, occupied by Z. Marcas, our neighbor.
For six months Juste and I remained in perfect ignorance
of the fact. The old woman who managed the house had
indeed told us that the room was inhabited, but she had added
that we should not be disturbed, that the occupant was exceedingly quiet. In fact, for those six months, we never
met our fellow-lodger, and we never heard a sound in his room,
in spite of the thinness of the partition that divided us—one

of those walls of lath and plaster which are common in Paris houses.

Our room, a little over seven feet high, was hung with a vile cheap paper sprigged with blue. The floor was painted, and knew nothing of the polish given by the *frotteur's* brush. By our beds there was only a scrap of thin carpet. The chimney opened immediately to the roof, and smoked so abominably that we were obliged to provide a stove at our own expense. Our beds were mere painted wooden cribs like those in schools; on the chimney shelf there were but two brass candlesticks, with or without tallow candles in them, and our two pipes with some tobacco in a pouch or strewn abroad, also the little piles of cigar-ash left there by our visitors or ourselves.

A pair of calico curtains hung from the brass window rods, and on each side of the window was a small bookcase in cherry-wood, such as every one knows who has stared into the shop windows of the Quartier Latin, and in which we kept the few books necessary for our studies.

The ink in the inkstand was always in the state of lava congealed in the crater of a volcano. May not any inkstand nowadays become a Vesuvius? The pens, all twisted, served to clean the stems of our pipes; and, in opposition to all the laws of credit, paper was even scarcer than coin.

How can young·men be expected to stay at home in such furnished lodgings? The students studied in the cafés, the theatre, the Luxembourg gardens, in *grisettes'* rooms, even in the law schools—anywhere rather than in their horrible rooms —horrible for purposes of study, delightful as soon as they are used for gossiping and smoking in. Put a cloth on the table, and the impromptu dinner sent in from the best eating-house in the neighborhood—places for four—two of them in petticoats—show a lithograph of this "Interior" to the veriest bigot, and she will be bound to smile.

We thought only of amusing ourselves. The reason for our dissipation lay in the most serious facts of the politics of the time. Juste and I could not see any room for us in the two professions our parents wished us to take up. There are a hundred doctors, a hundred lawyers, for one that is wanted. The crowd is choking these two paths which are supposed to lead to fortune, but which are merely two arenas; men kill each other there, fighting, not indeed with swords or fire-arms, but with intrigue and calumny, with tremendous toil, campaigns in the sphere of the intellect as murderous as those in Italy were to the soldiers of the Republic. In these days, when everything is an intellectual competition, a man must be able to sit forty-eight hours on end in his chair before a table, as a General could remain for two days on horseback and in his saddle.

The throng of aspirants has necessitated a division of the Faculty of Medicine into categories. There is the physician who writes and the physician who practises, the political physi-cian, and the physician militant—four different ways of being a physician, four classes already filled up. As to the fifth class, that of physicians who sell remedies, there is such a competition that they fight each other with disgusting ad-vertisements on the walls of Paris.

In all the law courts there are almost as many lawyers as there are cases. The pleader is thrown back on journalism, on politics, on literature. In fact, the State, besieged for the smallest appointments under the law, has ended by requiring that the applicants should have some little fortune. The pear-shaped head of the grocer's son is selected in preference to the square skull of a man of talent who has not a sou. Work as he will, with all his energy, a young man, starting from zero, may at the end of ten years find himself below the point he set out from. In these days, talent must have the good luck which secures success to the most incapable; nay, more, if it scorns the base compromises which insure advancement to crawling mediocrity, it will never get on.

If we thoroughly knew our time, we also knew ourselves, and we preferred the indolence of dreamers to aimless stir, easy-going pleasure to the useless toil which would have ex-hausted our courage and worn out the edge of our intelligence.

We had analyzed social life while smoking, laughing, and loafing. But, though elaborated by such means as these, our reflections were none the less judicious and profound.

While we were fully conscious of the slavery to which youth is condemned, we were amazed at the brutal indifference of the authorities to everything connected with intellect, thought, and poetry. How often have Juste and I exchanged glances when reading the papers as we studied political events, or the debates in the Chamber, and discussed the proceedings of a Court whose wilful ignorance could find no parallel but in the platitude of the courtiers, the mediocrity of the men forming the hedge round the newly-restored throne, all alike devoid of talent or breadth of view, of distinction or learning, of influence or dignity!

Could there be a higher tribute to the Court of Charles X. than the present Court, if Court it may be called? What a hatred of the country may be seen in the naturalization of vulgar foreigners, devoid of talent, who are enthroned in the Chamber of Peers! What a perversion of justice! What an insult to the distinguished youth, the ambitions native to the soil of France! We looked upon these things as upon a spectacle, and groaned over them, without taking upon ourselves to act.

Juste, whom no one ever sought, and who never sought any one, was, at five-and-twenty, a great politician, a man with a wonderful aptitude for apprehending the correlation between remote history and the facts of the present and of the future. In 1831, he told me exactly what would and did happen—the murders, the conspiracies, the ascendency of the Jews, the difficulty of doing anything in France, the scarcity of talent in the higher circles, and the abundance of intellect in the lowest ranks, where the finest courage is smothered under cigar ashes.

What was to become of him? His parents wished him to be a doctor. But if he were a doctor, must he not wait twenty years for a practice? You know what he did? No? Well, he is a doctor; but he left France, he is in Asia. At this mo-

ment he is perhaps sinking under fatigue in a desert, or dying
of the lashes of a barbarous horde—or perhaps he is some Indian prince's prime minister.

Action is my vocation. Leaving a civil college at the age
of twenty, the only way for me to enter the army was by enlisting as a common soldier; so, weary of the dismal outlook
that lay before a lawyer, I acquired the knowledge needed
for a sailor. I imitate Juste, and keep out of France, where
men waste, in the struggle to make way, the energy needed
for the noblest works. Follow my example, friends; I am
going where a man steers his destiny as he pleases.

These great resolutions were formed in the little room in
the lodging-house in the Rue Corneille, in spite of our haunt-
ing the Bal Musard, flirting with girls of the town, and leading a careless and apparently reckless life. Our plans and
arguments long floated in the air.

Marcas, our neighbor, was in some degree the guide who
led us to the margin of the precipice or the torrent, who made
us sound it, and showed us beforehand what our fate would
be if we let ourselves fall into it. It was he who put us on
our guard against the time-bargains a man makes with
poverty under the sanction of hope, by accepting precarious
situations whence he fights the battle, carried along by the
devious tide of Paris—that great harlot who takes you up or
leaves you stranded, smiles or turns her back on you with
equal readiness, wears out the strongest will in vexatious waiting, and makes misfortune wait on chance.

At our first meeting, Marcas, as it were, dazzled us. On our
return from the schools, a little before the dinner-hour, we
were accustomed to go up to our room and remain there a
while, either waiting for the other, to learn whether there were
any change in our plans for the evening. One day, at four
o'clock, Juste met Marcas on the stairs, and I saw him in the
street. It was in the month of November, and Marcas had no
cloak; he wore shoes with heavy soles, corduroy trousers, and
a blue double-breasted coat buttoned to the throat, which gave

a military air to his broad chest, all the more so because he wore a black stock. The costume was not in itself extraordinary, but it agreed well with the man's mien and countenance.

My first impression on seeing him was neither surprise, nor distress, nor interest, nor pity, but curiosity mingled with all these feelings. He walked slowly, with a step that betrayed deep melancholy, his head forward with a stoop, but not bent like that of a conscience-stricken man. That head, large and powerful, which might contain the treasures necessary for a man of the highest ambition, looked as if it were loaded with thought; it was weighted with grief of mind, but there was no touch of remorse in his expression. As to his face, it may be summed up in a word. A common superstition has it that every human countenance resembles some animal. The animal for Marcas was the lion. His hair was like a mane, his nose was short and flat; broad and dented at the tip like a lion's; his brow, like a lion's, was strongly marked with a deep median furrow, dividing two powerful bosses. His high, hairy cheek-bones, all the more prominent because his cheeks were so thin, his enormous mouth and hollow jaws, were accentuated by lines of haughty significance, and marked by a complexion full of tawny shadows. This almost terrible countenance seemed illuminated by two lamps—two eyes, black indeed, but infinitely sweet, calm and deep, full of thought. If I may say so, those eyes had a humiliated expression.

Marcas was afraid of looking directly at others, not for himself, but for those on whom his fascinating gaze might rest; he had a power, and he shunned using it; he would spare those he met, and he feared notice. This was not from modesty, but from resignation—not Christian resignation, which implies charity, but resignation founded on reason, which had demonstrated the immediate inutility of his gifts, the impossibility of entering and living in the sphere for which he was fitted. Those eyes could at times flash lightnings. From those lips a voice of thunder must surely proceed; it was a mouth like Mirabeau's.

"I have seen such a grand fellow in the street," said I to Juste on coming in.

"It must be our neighbor," replied Juste, who described, in fact, the man I had just met. "A man who lives like a wood-louse would be sure to look like that," he added.

"What dejection and what dignity!"

"One is the consequence of the other."

"What ruined hopes! What schemes and failures!"

"Seven leagues of ruins! Obelisks—palaces—towers!— The ruins of Palmyra in the desert!" said Juste, laughing. So we called him the Ruins of Palmyra.

As we went out to dine at the wretched eating-house in the Rue de la Harpe to which we subscribed, we asked the name of Number 37, and then heard the weird name Z. Marcas. Like boys, as we were, we repeated it more than a hundred times with all sorts of comments, absurd or melancholy, and the name lent itself to the jest. Juste would fire off the Z like a rocket rising, *z-z-z-z-zed;* and after pronouncing the first syllable of the name with great importance, depicted a fall by the dull brevity of the second.

"Now, how and where does the man live?"

From this query, to the innocent espionage of curiosity there was no pause but that required for carrying out our plan. Instead of loitering about the streets, we both came in, each armed with a novel. We read with our ears open. And in the perfect silence of our attic rooms, we heard the even, dull sound of a sleeping man breathing.

"He is asleep," said I to Juste, noticing this fact.

"At seven o'clock!" replied the Doctor.

This was the name by which I called Juste, and he called me the Keeper of the Seals.

"A man must be wretched indeed to sleep as much as our neighbor!" cried I, jumping on to the chest of drawers with a knife in my hand, to which a corkscrew was attached.

I made a round hole at the top of the partition, about as big as a five-sou piece. I had forgotten that there would be no light in the room, and on putting my eye to the hole, I saw only darkness. At about one in the morning, when we had finished our books and were about to undress, we heard a noise in our neighbor's room. He got up, struck a match, and lighted his dip. I got on to the drawers again, and I then saw Marcas seated at his table and copying law-papers.

His room was about half the size of ours; the bed stood in a recess by the door, for the passage ended there, and its breadth was added to his garret; but the ground on which the house was built was evidently irregular, for the party-wall formed an obtuse angle, and the room was not square. There was no fireplace, only a small earthenware stove, white blotched with green, of which the pipe went up through the roof. The window, in the skew side of the room, had shabby red curtains. The furniture consisted of an armchair, a table, a chair, and a wretched bed-table. A cupboard in the wall held his clothes. The wall-paper was horrible; evidently only a servant had ever lodged there before Marcas.

"What is to be seen?" asked the Doctor as I got down.

"Look for yourself," said I.

At nine next morning, Marcas was in bed. He had breakfasted off a saveloy; we saw on a plate, with some crumbs of bread, the remains of that too familiar delicacy. He was asleep; he did not wake till eleven. He then set to work again on the copy he had begun the night before, which was lying on the table.

On going downstairs we asked the price of that room, and were told fifteen francs a month.

In the course of a few days, we were fully informed as to the mode of life of Z. Marcas. He did copying, at so much a sheet no doubt, for a law-writer who lived in the courtyard of the Sainte-Chapelle. He worked half the night; after sleeping from six till ten, he began again and wrote till three. Then he went out to take the copy home before dinner, which he ate at Mizerai's in the Rue Michel-le-Comte, at a cost of nine sous, and came in to bed at six o'clock. It became known to us that Marcas did not utter fifteen sentences in a month; he never talked to anybody, nor said a word to himself in his dreadful garret.

"The Ruins of Palmyra are terribly silent!" said Juste.

This taciturnity in a man whose appearance was so imposing was strangely significant. Sometimes when we met him, we exchanged glances full of meaning on both sides, but they never led to any advances. Insensibly this man became the object of our secret admiration, though we knew no reason for it. Did it lie in his secretly simple habits, his monastic regularity, his hermit-like frugality, his idiotically mechanical labor, allowing his mind to remain neuter or to work on its own lines, seeming to us to hint at an expectation of some stroke of good luck, or at some foregone conclusion as to his life?

After wandering for a long time among the Ruins of Palmyra, we forget them—we were young! Then came the Carnival, the Paris Carnival, which, henceforth, will eclipse the old Carnival of Venice, unless some ill-advised Prefect of Police is antagonistic.

Gambling ought to be allowed during the Carnival; but the stupid moralists who have had gambling suppressed are inert financiers, and this indispensable evil will be re-established among us when it is proved that France leaves millions at the German tables.

This splendid Carnival brought us to utter penury, as it does every student. We got rid of every object of luxury; we sold our second coats, our second boots, our second waistcoats—everything of which we had a duplicate, except our friend. We ate bread and cold sausages; we looked where we walked; we had set to work in earnest. We owed two months' rent, and were sure of having a bill from the porter for sixty or eighty items each, and amounting to forty or fifty francs. We made no noise, and did not laugh as we crossed the little hall at the bottom of the stairs; we commonly took it at a flying leap from the lowest step into the street. On the day when we first found ourselves bereft of tobacco for our pipes, it struck us that for some days we had been eating bread without any kind of butter.

Great was our distress.

"No tobacco!" said the Doctor.

"No cloak!" said the Keeper of the Seals.

"Ah, you rascals, you would dress as the postillon de Longjumeau, you would appear as Débardeurs, sup in the morning, and breakfast at night at Véry's—sometimes even at the *Rocher de Cancale.*—Dry bread for you, my boys! Why," said I, in a big bass voice, "you deserve to sleep under the bed, you are not worthy to lie in it——"

"Yes, yes; but, Keeper of Seals, there is no more tobacco!" said Juste.

"It is high time to write home, to our aunts, our mothers, and our sisters, to tell them we have no underlinen left, that the wear and tear of Paris would ruin garments of wire. Then we will solve an elegant chemical problem by transmuting linen into silver."

"But we must live till we get the answer."

"Well, I will go and bring out a loan among such of our friends as may still have some capital to invest."

"And how much will you find?"

"Say ten francs!" replied I with pride.

It was midnight. Marcas had heard everything. He knocked at our door.

"Messieurs," said he, "here is some tobacco; you can repay me on the first opportunity."

We were struck, not by the offer, which we accepted, but by the rich, deep, full voice in which it was made; a tone only comparable to the lowest string of Paganini's violin. Marcas vanished without waiting for our thanks.

Juste and I looked at each other without a word. To be rescued by a man evidently poorer than ourselves! Juste sat down to write to every member of his family, and I went off to effect a loan. I brought in twenty francs lent me by a fellow-provincial. In that evil but happy day gambling was still tolerated, and in its lodes, as hard as the rocky ore of Brazil, young men, by risking a small sum, had a chance of winning a few gold pieces. My friend, too, had some Turkish tobacco brought home from Constantinople by a sailor, and

he gave me quite as much as we had taken from Z. Marcas.
I conveyed the splendid cargo into port, and we went in triumph to repay our neighbor with a tawny wig of Turkish
tobacco for his dark *Caporal*.

"You are determined not to be my debtors," said he.
"You are giving me gold for copper.—You are boys—good
boys——"

The sentences, spoken in varying tones, were variously emphasized. The words were nothing, but the expression !—
That made us friends of ten years' standing at once.

Marcas, on hearing us coming, had covered up his papers;
we understood that it would be taking a liberty to allude to his
means of subsistence, and felt ashamed of having watched
him. His cupboard stood open; in it there were two shirts,
a white necktie, and a razor. The razor made me shudder.
A looking-glass, worth five francs perhaps, hung near the
window.

The man's few and simple movements had a sort of savage
grandeur. The Doctor and I looked at each other, wondering what we could say in reply. Juste, seeing that I was
speechless, asked Marcas jestingly :

"You cultivate literature, monsieur?"

"Far from it !" replied Marcas. "I should not be so
wealthy."

"I fancied," said I, "that poetry alone, in these days, was
amply sufficient to provide a man with lodgings as bad as
ours."

My remark made Marcas smile, and the smile gave a charm
to his yellow face.

"Ambition is not a less severe taskmaster to those who fail,"
said he. "You, who are beginning life, walk in the beaten
paths. Never dream of rising superior, you will be ruined !"

"You advise us to stay just as we are?" said the Doctor,
smiling.

There is something so infectious and childlike in the pleasantries of youth, that Marcas smiled again in reply.

"What incidents can have given you this detestable philosophy?" asked I.

"I forgot once more that chance is the result of an immense equation of which we know not all the factors. When we start from zero to work up to the unit, the chances are incalculable. To ambitious men Paris is an immense roulette table, and every young man fancies he can hit on a successful progression of numbers."

He offered us the tobacco I had brought that we might smoke with him; the Doctor went to fetch our pipes; Marcas filled his, and then he came to sit in our room, bringing the tobacco with him, since there were but two chairs in his. Juste, as brisk as a squirrel, ran out, and returned with a boy carrying three bottles of Bordeaux, some Brie cheese, and a loaf.

"Hah!" said I to myself, "fifteen francs," and I was right to a sou.

Juste gravely laid five francs on the chimney-shelf.

There are immeasurable differences between the gregarious man and the man who lives closest to nature. Toussaint Louverture, after he was caught, died without speaking a word. Napoleon, transplanted to a rock, talked like a magpie —he wanted to account for himself. Z. Marcas erred in the same way, but for our benefit only. Silence in all its majesty is to be found only in the savage. There never is a criminal who, though he might let his secrets fall with his head into the basket of sawdust, does not feel the purely social impulse to tell them to somebody.

Nay, I am wrong. We have seen one Iroquois of the Faubourg Saint-Marceau who raised the Parisian to the level of the natural savage—a republican, a conspirator, a Frenchman, an old man, who outdid all we have heard of Negro determination, and all that Cooper tells us of the tenacity and coolness of the Redskins under defeat. Morey, the Guatimozin of the "Mountain," preserved an attitude unparalleled in the annals of European justice.

This is what Marcas told us during the small hours, sandwiching his discourse with slices of bread spread with cheese and washed down with wine. All the tobacco was burned out.

Now and then the hackney coaches clattering across the Place de l'Odéon, or the omnibuses toiling past, sent up their dull rumbling, as if to remind us that Paris was still close to us.

His family lived at Vitré; his father and mother had fifteen hundred francs a year in the funds. He had received an education gratis in a Seminary, but had refused to enter the priesthood. He felt in himself the fires of immense ambition, and had come to Paris on foot at the age of twenty, the possessor of two hundred francs. He had studied the law, working in an attorney's office, where he had risen to be superior clerk. He had taken his doctor's degree in law, had mastered the old and modern codes, and could hold his own with the most famous pleaders. He had studied the law of nations, and was familiar with European treaties and international practice. He had studied men and things in five capitals—London, Berlin, Vienna, Petersburg, and Constantinople.

No man was better informed than he as to the rules of the Chamber. For five years he had been reporter of the debates for a daily paper. He spoke extempore and admirably, and could go on for a long time in that deep, appealing voice which had struck us to the soul. Indeed, he proved by the narrative of his life that he was a great orator, a concise orator, serious and yet full of piercing eloquence; he resembled Berryer in his fervor and in the impetus which commands the sympathy of the masses, and was like Thiers in refinement and skill; but he would have been less diffuse, less in difficulties for a conclusion. He had intended to rise rapidly to power without burdening himself first with the doctrines necessary to begin with, for a man in opposition, but an incubus later to the statesman.

Marcas had learned everything that a real statesman should know; indeed, his amazement was considerable when he had occasion to discern the utter ignorance of men who have risen to the administration of public affairs in France. Though in him it was vocation that had led to study, nature had been generous and bestowed all that cannot be acquired—keen perceptions, self-command, a nimble wit, rapid judgment, decisiveness, and, what is the genius of these men, fertility in resource.

By the time when Marcas thought himself duly equipped, France was torn by intestine divisions arising from the triumph of the House of Orleans over the elder branch of the Bourbons.

The field of political warfare is evidently changed. Civil war henceforth cannot last for long, and will not be fought out in the provinces. In France such struggles will be of brief duration and at the seat of government; and the battle will be the close of the moral contest which will have been brought to an issue by superior minds. This state of things will continue so long as France has her present singular form of government, which has no analogy with that of any other country; for there is no more resemblance between the English and the French constitutions than between the two lands.

Thus Marcas' place was in the political press. Being poor and unable to secure his election, he hoped to make a sudden appearance. He resolved on making the greatest possible sacrifice for a man of superior intellect, to work as subordinate to some rich and ambitious deputy. Like a second Bonaparte, he sought his Barras; the new Colbert hoped to find a Mazarin. He did immense services, and he did them then and there; he assumed no importance, he made no boast, he did not complain of ingratitude. He did them in the hope that his patron would put him in a position to be elected deputy; Marcas wished for nothing but a loan that might enable him to purchase a house in Paris, the qualification required by law. Richard III. asked for nothing but his horse.

In three years Marcas had made his man—one of the fifty supposed great statesmen who are the battledores with which two cunning players toss the ministerial portfolios exactly as the man behind the puppet-show hits Punch against the constable in his street theatre, and counts on always getting paid. This man existed only by Marcas, but he had just brains enough to appreciate the value of his "ghost" and to know that Marcas, if he ever came to the front, would remain there, would be indispensable, while he himself would be translated to the polar zone of the Luxembourg. So he determined to put insurmountable obstacles in the way of his Mentor's advancement, and hid his purpose under the semblance of the utmost sincerity. Like all mean men, he could dissimulate to perfection, and he soon made progress in the ways of ingratitude, for he felt that he must kill Marcas, not to be killed by him. These two men, apparently so united, hated each other as soon as one had once deceived the other.

The politician was made one of a ministry; Marcas remained in the opposition to hinder his man from being attacked; nay, by skilful tactics he won him the applause of the opposition. To excuse himself for not rewarding his subaltern, the chief pointed out the impossibility of finding a place suddenly for a man on the other side, without a great deal of manœuvring. Marcas had hoped confidently for a place to enable him to marry, and thus acquire the qualification he so ardently desired. He was two-and-thirty, and the Chamber ere long must be dissolved. Having detected his man in this flagrant act of bad faith, he overthrew him, or at any rate contributed largely to his overthrow, and covered him with mud.

A fallen minister, if he is to rise again to power, must show that he is to be feared; this man, intoxicated by Royal glibness, had fancied that his position would be permanent; he acknowledged his delinquencies; besides confessing them, he did Marcas a small money service, for Marcas had got into debt. He subsidized the newspaper on which Marcas worked, and made him the manager of it.

Though he despised the man, Marcas, who, practically, was being subsidized too, consented to take the part of the fallen minister. Without unmasking at once all the batteries of his superior intellect, Marcas came a little further than before; he showed half his shrewdness. The Ministry lasted only a hundred and eighty days; it was swallowed up. Marcas had put himself into communication with certain deputies, had moulded them like dough, leaving each impressed with a high

opinion of his talent; his puppet again became a member of
the Ministry, and then the paper was ministerial. The Ministry united the paper with another, solely to squeeze out
Marcas, who in this fusion had to make way for a rich and
insolent rival, whose name was well known, and who already
had his foot in the stirrup.

Marcas relapsed into utter destitution; his haughty patron
well knew the depths into which he had cast him.

Where was he to go? The ministerial papers, privily
warned, would have nothing to say to him. The opposition
papers did not care to admit him to their offices. Marcas
could side neither with the Republicans nor with the Legitimists, two parties whose triumph would mean the overthrow of everything that now is.

"Ambitious men like a fast hold on things," said he with a
smile.

He lived by writing a few articles on commercial affairs,
and contributed to one of those encyclopedias brought out by
speculation and not by learning. Finally a paper was
founded, which was destined to live but two years, but which
secured his services. From that moment he renewed his connection with the minister's enemies; he joined the party who
were working for the fall of the Government; and as soon as
his pickaxe had free play, it fell.

This paper had now for six months ceased to exist; he had
failed to find employment of any kind; he was spoken of as a
dangerous man, calumny attacked him; he had unmasked a
huge financial and mercantile job by a few articles and a pamphlet. He was known to be the mouthpiece of a banker who
was said to have paid him largely, and from whom he was supposed to expect some patronage in return for his champion-
ship. Marcas, disgusted by men and things, worn out by five
years of fighting, regarded as a free lance rather than as a
great leader, crushed by the necessity for earning his daily
bread, which hindered him from gaining ground, in despair
at the influence exerted by money over mind, and given over
to dire poverty, buried himself in a garret, to make thirty

sous a day, the sum strictly answering to his needs. Meditation had leveled a desert all round him. He read the papers to be informed of what was going on. Pozzo di Borgo
had once lived like this for some time.

Marcas, no doubt, was planning a serious attack, accustom-
ing himself to dissimulation, and punishing himself for his
blunders by Pythagorean muteness. But he did not tell us
the reasons for his conduct.

It is impossible to give you an idea of the scenes of the
highest comedy that lay behind this algebraic statement of
his career; his useless patience dogging the footsteps of fortune, which presently took wings, his long tramps over the
thorny brakes of Paris, his breathless chases as a petitioner,
his attempts to win over fools; the schemes laid only to fail
through the influence of some frivolous woman; the meetings
with men of business who expected their capital to bring
them places and a peerage, as well as large interest. Then the
hopes rising in a towering wave only to break in foam on the
shoal; the wonders wrought in reconciling adverse interests
which, after working together for a week, fell asunder; the
annoyance, a thousand times repeated, of seeing a dunce decorated with the Legion of Honor, and preferred, though as
ignorant as a shop-boy, to a man of talent. Then, what Marcas called the stratagems of stupidity—you strike a man, and
he seems convinced, he nods his head—everything is settled;
next day, this india-rubber ball, flattened for a moment, has
recovered itself in the course of the night; it is as full of wind
as ever; you must begin all over again; and you go on till you
understand that you are not dealing with a man, but with a
lump of gum that loses shape in the sunshine.

These thousand annoyances, this vast waste of human
energy on barren spots, the difficulty of achieving any good,
the incredible facility of doing mischief; two strong games
played out, twice won, and then twice lost; the hatred of a
statesman—a blockhead with a painted face and a wig,
but in whom the world believed—all these things, great

and small, had not crushed, but for the moment had dashed, Marcas. In the days when money had come into his hands, his fingers had not clutched it; he had allowed himself the exquisite pleasure of sending it all to his family—to his sisters, his brothers, his old father. Like Napoleon in his fall, he asked for no more than thirty sous a day, and any man of energy can earn thirty sous for a day's work in Paris.

When Marcas had finished the story of his life, intermingled with reflections, maxims, and observations, revealing him as a great politician, a few questions and answers on both sides as to the progress of affairs in France and in Europe were enough to prove to us that he was a real statesman; for a man may be quickly and easily judged when he can be brought on to the ground of immediate difficulties: there is a certain Shibboleth for men of superior talents, and we were of the tribe of modern Levites without belonging as yet to the Temple. As I have said, our frivolity covered certain purposes which Juste has carried out, and which I am about to execute.

When we had done talking, we all three went out, cold as it was, to walk in the Luxembourg gardens till the dinner hour. In the course of that walk our conversation, grave throughout, turned on the painful aspects of the political situation. Each of us contributed his remarks, his comment, or his jest, a pleasantry or a proverb. This was no longer exclusively a discussion of life on the colossal scale just described by Marcas, the soldier of political warfare. Nor was it the distressful monologue of the wrecked navigator, stranded in a garret in the Hôtel Corneille; it was a dialogue in which two well-informed young men, having gauged the times they lived in, were endeavoring, under the guidance of a man of talent, to gain some light on their own future prospects.

"Why," asked Juste, "did you not wait patiently for an opportunity, and imitate the only man who has been able to keep the lead since the Revolution of July by holding his head above water?"

"Have I not said that we never know where the roots of

chance lie? Carrel was in identically the same position as the orator you speak of. That gloomy young man, of a bitter spirit, had a whole government in his head; the man of whom you speak had no idea beyond mounting on the crupper of every event. Of the two, Carrel was the better man. Well, one became a minister, Carrel remained a journalist; the incomplete but craftier man is living; Carrel is dead.

"I may point out that your man has for fifteen years been making his way, and is but making it still. He may yet be caught and crushed between two cars full of intrigues on the highroad to power. He has no house; he has not the favor of the palace like Metternich; nor, like Villèle, the protection of a compact majority.

"I do not believe that the present state of things will last ten years longer. Hence, supposing I should have such poor good luck, I am already too late to avoid being swept away by the commotion I foresee. I should need to be established in a superior position."

"What commotion?" asked Juste.

"August, 1830," said Marcas in solemn tones, holding out his hand towards Paris; "August, the offspring of Youth which bound the sheaves, and of Intellect which had ripened the harvest, forgot to provide for Youth and Intellect.

"Youth will explode like the boiler of a steam-engine. Youth has no outlet in France; it is gathering an avalanche of underrated capabilities, of legitimate and restless ambitions; young men are not marrying now; families cannot tell what to do with their children. What will the thunderclap be that will shake down these masses? I know not, but they will crash down into the midst of things, and overthrow everything. These are laws of hydrostatics which act on the human race; the Roman Empire had failed to understand them, and the Barbaric hordes came down.

"The Barbaric hordes now are the intelligent class. The laws of overpressure are at this moment acting slowly and silently in our midst. The Government is the great criminal; it does not appreciate the two powers to which it owes everything; it has allowed its hands to be tied by the absurdities of the Contract; it is bound, ready to be the victim.

"Louis XIV., Napoleon, England, all were or are eager for intelligent youth. In France the young are condemned by the new legislation, by the blundering principles of elective rights, by the unsoundness of the ministerial constitution.

"Look at the elective Chamber; you will find no deputies of thirty; the youth of Richelieu and of Mazarin, of Turenne and of Colbert, of Pitt and of Saint-Just, of Napoleon and of Prince Metternich, would find no admission there; Burke, Sheridan, or Fox could not win seats. Even if political majority had been fixed at one-and-twenty, and eligibility had been relieved of evey disabling qualification, the Departments would have returned the very same members, men devoid of political talent, unable to speak without murdering French grammar, and among whom, in ten years, scarcely one statesman has been found.

"The causes of an impending event may be seen, but the event itself cannot be foretold. At this moment the youth of France is being driven into Republicanism, because it believes that the Republic would bring it emancipation. It will always remember the young representatives of the people and the young army leaders! The imprudence of the Government is only comparable to its avarice."

That day left its echoes in our lives. Marcas confirmed us in our resolution to leave France, where young men of talent and energy are crushed under the weight of successful commonplace, envious, and insatiable middle age.

We dined together in the Rue de la Harpe. We thenceforth felt for Marcas the most respectful affection; he gave us the most practical aid in the sphere of the mind. That man knew everything; he had studied everything. For us he cast his eye over the whole civilized world, seeking the country where openings would be at once the most abundant and the most favorable to the success of our plans. He indicated what should be the goal of our studies; he bid us make haste, explaining to us that time was precious, that emigration would presently begin, and that its effect would be to deprive France of the cream of its powers and of its youthful talent; that their intelligence, necessarily sharpened, would select the best places, and that the great thing was to be first in the field.

Thenceforward, we often sat late at work under the lamp. Our generous instructor wrote some notes for our guidance— two pages for Juste and three for me—full of invaluable advice—the sort of information which experience alone can supply, such landmarks as only genius can place. In those papers, smelling of tobacco, and covered with writing so vile as to be almost hieroglyphic, there are suggestions for a fortune, and forecasts of unerring acumen. There are hints as to certain parts of America and Asia which have been fully justified, both before and since Juste and I could set out.

Marcas, like us, was in the most abject poverty. He earned, indeed, his daily bread, but he had neither linen, clothes, nor shoes. He did not make himself out any better than he was; his dreams had been of luxury as well as of power. He did not admit that this was the real Marcas; he abandoned his person, indeed, to the caprices of life. What he lived by was the breath of ambition; he dreamed of revenge while blaming himself for yielding to so shallow a feeling. The true states- man ought, above all things, to be superior to vulgar passions; like the man of science, he should have no passion but for his science. It was in these days of dire necessity that Marcas seemed to us so great—nay, so terrible; there was something awful in the gaze which saw another world than that which strikes the eye of ordinary men. To us he was a subject of contemplation and astonishment; for the young—which of us has not known it?—the young have a keen craving to ad- mire; they love to attach themselves, and are naturally in- clined to submit to the men they feel to be superior, as they are to devote themselves to a great cause.

Our surprise was chiefly aroused by his indifference in mat- ters of sentiment; woman had no place in his life. When we spoke of this matter, a perennial theme of conversation among Frenchmen, he simply remarked:

"Gowns cost too much."

He saw the look that passed between Juste and me, and went on:

"Yes, far too much. The woman you buy—and she is the least expensive—takes a great deal of money. The woman who gives herself takes all your time! Woman extinguishes every energy, every ambition. Napoleon reduced her to what she should be. From that point of view, he really was great. He did not indulge such ruinous fancies of Louis XIV. and Louis XV.; at the same time, he could love in secret."

We discovered that, like Pitt, who made England his wife, Marcas bore France in his heart; he idolized his country; he had not a thought that was not for his native land. His fury at feeling that he had in his hands the remedy for the evils which so deeply saddened him, and could not apply it, ate into his soul, and this rage was increased by the inferiority of France at that time, as compared with Russia and England. France a third-rate power! This cry came up again and again in his conversation. The intestinal disorders of his country had entered into his soul. All the contests between the Court and the Chamber, showing, as they did, incessant change and constant vacillation, which must injure the prosperity of the country, he scoffed at as backstairs squabbles.

"This is peace at the cost of the future," said he.

One evening Juste and I were at work, sitting in perfect silence. Marcas had just risen to toil at his copying, for he had refused our assistance in spite of our most earnest entreaties. We had offered to take it in turns to copy a batch of manuscript, so that he should do but a third of his distasteful task; he had been quite angry, and we had ceased to insist.

We heard the sound of gentlemanly boots in the passage, and raised our heads, looking at each other. There was a tap at Marcas' door—he never took the key out of the lock—and we heard the hero answer:

"Come in." Then—"What! you here, monsieur?"

"I myself," replied the retired minister.

It was the Diocletian of this unknown martyr.

For some time he and our neighbor conversed in an under tone. Suddenly Marcas, whose voice had been heard but rarely, as is natural in a dialogue in which the applicant begins by setting forth the situation, broke out loudly in reply to some offer we had not overheard.

"You would laugh at me for a fool," cried he, "if I took you at your word. Jesuits are a thing of the past, but Jesuitism is eternal. Your Machiavelism and your generosity are equally hollow and untrustworthy. You can make your own calculations, but who can calculate on you? Your Court is made up of owls who fear the light, of old men who quake in the presence of the young, or who simply disregard them. The Government is formed on the same pattern as the Court. You have hunted up the remains of the Empire, as the Restoration enlisted the Voltigeurs of Louis XIV.

"Hitherto the evasions of cowardice have been taken for тne manœuvring of ability; but dangers will come, and the younger generation will rise as they did in 1790. They did grand things then.—Just now you change ministries as a sick man turns in his bed; these oscillations betray the weakness of the Government. You work on an underhand system of policy which will be turned against you, for France will be tired of your shuffling. France will not tell you that she is tired of you; a man never knows whence his ruin comes; it is the historian's task to find out; but you will undoubtedly perish as the reward of not having the youth of France to lend you its strength and energy; for having hated really capable men; for not having lovingly chosen them from this noble generation; for having in all cases preferred mediocrity.

"You have come to ask my support, but you are an atom in that decrepit heap which is made hideous by self-interest, which trembles and squirms, and, because it is so mean, tries to make France mean too. My strong nature, my ideas, would work like poison in you; twice you have tricked me, twice have I overthrown you. If we unite a third time, it must be a very serious matter. I should kill myself if I allowed myself to be duped; for I should be to blame, not you."

Then we heard the humblest entreaties, the most fervent adjurations, not to deprive the country of such superior talents. The man spoke of patriotism, and Marcas uttered a significant *"Ouh! ouh!"* He laughed at his would-be patron. Then the statesman was more explicit; he bowed to the superiority of his erewhile counselor; he pledged himself to enable Marcas to remain in office, to be elected deputy; then he offered him a high appointment, promising him that he, the speaker, would thenceforth be the subordinate of a man whose subaltern he was only worthy to be. He was in the newly-formed ministry, and he would not return to power unless Marcas had a post in proportion to his merit; he had already made it a condition, Marcas had been regarded as indispensable.

Marcas refused.

"I have never before been in a position to keep my promises; here is an opportunity of proving myself faithful to my word, and you fail me."

To this Marcas made no reply. The boots were again audible in the passage on the way to the stairs.

"Marcas! Marcas!" we both cried, rushing into his room. "Why refuse? He really meant it. His offers are very handsome; at any rate, go to see the ministers."

In a twinkling, we had given Marcas a hundred reasons. The minister's voice was sincere; without seeing him, we had felt sure that he was honest.

"I have no clothes," replied Marcas.

"Rely on us," said Juste, with a glance at me.

Marcas had the courage to trust us; a light flashed in his eye, he pushed his fingers through his hair, lifting it from his forehead with a gesture that showed some confidence in his luck; and when he had thus unveiled his face, so to speak, we saw in him a man absolutely unknown to us—Marcas sublime, Marcas in his power! His mind in its element—the bird

restored to the free air, the fish to the water, the horse gal-
loping across the plain.

It was transient. His brow clouded again; he had, it
would seem, a vision of his fate. Halting doubt had followed
close on the heels of white-winged hope.

We left him to himself.

"Now, then," said I to the Doctor, "we have given our
word; how are we to keep it?"

"We will sleep upon it," said Juste, "and to-morrow morning we will talk it over."

Next morning we went for a walk in the Luxembourg.

We had had time to think over the incident of the past
night, and were both equally surprised at the lack of address
shown by Marcas in the minor difficulties of life—he, a man
who never saw any difficulties in the solution of the hardest
problems of abstract or practical politics. But these elevated
characters can all be tripped up on a grain of sand, and will,
like the grandest enterprise, miss fire for want of a thousand
francs. It is the old story of Napoleon, who, for lack of a
pair of boots, did not set out for India.

"Well, what have you hit upon?" asked Juste.

"I have thought of a way to get him a complete outfit."

"Where?"

"From Humann."

"How?"

"Humann, my boy, never goes to his customers—his customers go to him; so that he does not know whether I am
rich or poor. He only knows that I dress well and look
decent in the clothes he makes for me. I shall tell him that
an uncle of mine has dropped in from the country, and that
his indifference in matters of dress is quite a discredit to me
in the upper circles where I am trying to find a wife.—It will
not be Humann if he sends in his bill before three months."

The Doctor thought this a capital idea for a vaudeville,
but poor enough in real life, and doubted my success. But
I give you my word of honor, Humann dressed Marcas, and,
being an artist, turned him out as a political personage ought
to be dressed.

Juste lent Marcas two hundred francs in gold, the product of two watches bought on credit, and pawned at the Mont-de-Piété. For my part, I had said nothing of six shirts and all necessary linen, which cost me no more than the pleasure of asking for them from a forewoman in a shop whom I had treated to Musard's during the carnival.

Marcas accepted everything, thanking us no more than he ought. He only inquired as to the means by which we had got possession of such riches, and we made him laugh for the last time. We looked on our Marcas as shipowners, when they have exhausted their credit and every resource at their command to fit out a vessel, must look on it as it puts to sea.

Here Charles was silent; he seemed crushed by his memories.

"Well," cried the audience, "and what happened?"

"I will tell you in a few words—for this is not romance—it is history."

We saw no more of Marcas. The administration lasted for three months; it fell at the end of the session. Then Marcas came back to us, worked to death. He had sounded the crater of power; he came away from it with the beginnings of brain fever. The disease made rapid progress; we nursed him. Juste at once called in the chief physician of the hospital where he was working as house-surgeon. I was then living alone in our room, and I was the most attentive attendant; but care and science alike were in vain. By the month of January, 1838, Marcas himself felt that he had but a few days to live.

The man whose soul and brain he had been for six months never even sent to inquire after him. Marcas expressed the greatest contempt for the Government; he seemed to doubt what the fate of France might be, and it was this doubt that had made him ill. He had, he thought, detected treason in the heart of power, not tangible, seizable treason, the result of facts, but the treason of a system, the subordination of national interests to selfish ends. His belief in the degradation of the country was enough to aggravate his complaint.

I myself was witness to the proposals made to him by one of the leaders of the antagonistic party which he had fought against. His hatred of the men he had tried to serve was so virulent, that he would gladly have joined the coalition that was about to be formed among certain ambitious spirits who, at least, had one idea in common—that of shaking off the yoke of the Court. But Marcas could only reply to the envoy in the words of the Hôtel de Ville:

"It is too late!".

Marcas did not leave money enough to pay for his funeral. Juste and I had great difficulty in saving him from the ignominy of a pauper's bier, and we alone followed the coffin of Z. Marcas, which was dropped into the common grave of the cemetery of Mont-Parnasse.

We looked sadly at each other as we listened to this tale, the last we heard from the lips of Charles Rabourdin the day before he embarked at le Havre on a brig that was to convey him to the islands of Malay. We all knew more than one Marcas, more than one victim of his devotion to a party, repaid by betrayal or neglect.

LES JARDIES, *May* 1840.

AN EPISODE UNDER THE TERROR

AN EPISODE UNDER THE TERROR

To Monsieur Guyonnet-Merville.

Is it not a necessity to explain to a public curious to know everything, how I came to be sufficiently learned in the law to carry on
the business of my little world? And in so doing, am I not bound
to put on record the memory of the amiable and intelligent man
who, meeting Scribe (another clerk-amateur) at a ball, said, "Just
give the office a turn; there is work for you there, I assure you"?
But do you need this public testimony to feel assured of the affection of the writer?

DE BALZAC.

ON the 22d of January, 1793, towards eight o'clock in the
evening, an old lady came down the steep street that comes
to an end opposite the Church of Saint Laurent in the
Faubourg Saint Martin. It had snowed so heavily all day
long that the lady's footsteps were scarcely audible; the
streets were deserted, and a feeling of dread, not unnatural
amid the silence, was further increased by the whole extent
of the Terror beneath which France was groaning in those
days; what was more, the old lady so far had met no one by
the way. Her sight had long been failing, so that the few
foot passengers dispersed like shadows in the distance over
the wide thoroughfare through the faubourg, were quite
invisible to her by the light of the lanterns.

She had passed the end of the Rue des Morts, when she
fancied that she could hear the firm, heavy tread of a man
walking behind her. Then it seemed to her that she had
heard that sound before, and dismayed by the idea of being
followed, she tried to walk faster toward a brightly lit shop
window, in the hope of verifying the suspicions which had
taken hold of her mind.

So soon as she stood in the shaft of light that streamed out across the road, she turned her head suddenly, and caught sight of a human figure looming through the fog. The dim vision was enough for her. For one moment she reeled beneath an overpowering weight of dread, for she could not doubt any longer that the man had followed her the whole way from her own door; then the desire to escape from the spy gave her strength. Unable to think clearly, she walked twice as fast as before, as if it were possible to escape from a man who of course could move much faster; and for some minutes she fled on, till, reaching a pastry-cook's shop, she entered and sank rather than sat down upon a chair by the counter.

A young woman busy with embroidery looked up from her work at the rattling of the door-latch, and looked out through the square window-panes. She seemed to recognize the old-fashioned violet silk mantle, for she went at once to a drawer as if in search of something put aside for the newcomer. Not only did this movement and the expression of the woman's face show a very evident desire to be rid as soon as possible of an unwelcome visitor, but she even permitted herself an impatient exclamation when the drawer proved to be empty. Without looking at the lady, she hurried from her desk into the back shop and called to her husband, who appeared at once.

"Wherever have you put?——" she began mysteriously, glancing at the customer by way of finishing her question.

The pastry-cook could only see the old lady's head-dress, a huge black silk bonnet with knots of violet ribbon round it, but he looked at his wife as who should say, "Did you think I should leave such a thing as that lying about in your drawer?" and then vanished.

The old lady kept so still and silent that the shopkeeper's wife was surprised. She went back to her, and on a nearer view a sudden impulse of pity, blended perhaps with curiosity, got the better of her. The old lady's face was naturally pale; she looked as though she secretly practised austerities;

but it was easy to see that she was paler than usual from recent agitation of some kind. Her head-dress was so arranged as almost to hide hair that was white, no doubt with age, for there was not a trace of powder on the collar of her dress. The extreme plainness of her dress lent an air of austerity to her face, and her features were proud and grave. The manners and habits of people of condition were so different from those of other classes in former times that a noble was easily known, and the shopkeeper's wife felt persuaded that her customer was a *ci-devant,* and that she had been about the Court.

"Madame," she began with involuntary respect, forgetting that the title was proscribed.

But the old lady made no answer. She was staring fixedly at the shop window as though some dreadful thing had taken shape against the panes. The pastry-cook came back at that moment, and drew the lady from her musings, by holding out a little cardboard box wrapped in blue paper.

"What is the matter, citoyenne?" he asked.

"Nothing, nothing, my friends," she answered, in a gentle voice. She looked up at the man as she spoke, as if to thank him by a glance; but she saw the red cap on his head, and a cry broke from her. "Ah! *You* have betrayed me!"

The man and his young wife replied by an indignant gesture, that brought the color to the old lady's face; perhaps she felt relief, perhaps she blushed for her suspicions.

"Forgive me!" she said, with a childlike sweetness in her tones. Then, drawing a gold louis from her pocket, she held it out to the pastry-cook. "That is the price agreed upon," she added.

There is a kind of want that is felt instinctively by those who know want. The man and his wife looked at one another, then at the elderly woman before them, and read the same thoughts in each other's eyes. That bit of gold was so plainly the last. Her hands shook a little as she held it out, looking at it sadly but ungrudgingly, as one who knows the full extent of the sacrifice. Hunger and penury had carved lines as easy to read in her face as the traces of asceticism and fear. There were vestiges of bygone splendor in her clothes. She was dressed in threadbare silk, a neat but well-worn mantle, and daintily mended lace,—in the rags of former grandeur, in short. The shopkeeper and his wife, drawn two ways by pity and self-interest, began by lulling their consciences with words.

"You seem very poorly, citoyenne——"

"Perhaps madame might like to take something," the wife broke in.

"We have some very nice broth," added the pastry-cook.

"And it is so cold," continued his wife; "perhaps you have caught a chill, madame, on your way here. But you can rest and warm yourself a bit."

"We are not so black as the devil!" cried the man.

The kindly intention in the words and tones of the charitable couple won the old lady's confidence. She said that a strange man had been following her, and she was afraid to go home alone.

"Is that all!' returned he of the red bonnet; "wait for me, citoyenne."

He handed the gold coin to his wife, and then went out to put on his National Guard's uniform, impelled thereto by the idea of making some adequate return for the money; an idea that sometimes slips into a tradesman's head when he has been prodigiously overpaid for goods of no great value. He took up his cap, buckled on his sabre, and came out in full dress. But his wife had had time to reflect, and reflection, as not unfrequently happens, closed the hand that kindly intentions had opened. Feeling frightened and uneasy lest her husband might be drawn into something unpleasant, she tried to catch at the skirt of his coat, to hold him back, but he, good soul, obeying his charitable first thought, brought out his offer to see the lady home, before his wife could stop him.

"The man of whom the citoyenne is afraid is still prowling about the shop, it seems," she said sharply.

"I am afraid so," said the lady innocently.

"How if it is a spy?   .   .   .   a plot?   .   .   .   Don't go. And take the box away from her——"

The words whispered in the pastry-cook's ear cooled his hot fit of courage down to zero.

"Oh! I will just go out and say a word or two. I will rid you of him soon enough," he exclaimed, as he bounced out of the shop.

The old lady meanwhile, passive as a child and almost dazed, sat down on her chair again. But the honest pastry-cook came back directly. A countenance red enough to begin with, and further flushed by the bake-house fire, was suddenly blanched; such terror perturbed him that he reeled as he walked, and stared about him like a drunken man.

"Miserable aristocrat! Do you want to have our heads cut off?" he shouted furiously. "You just take to your heels and never show yourself here again. Don't come to me for materials for your plots."

He tried, as he spoke, to take away the little box which she had slipped into one of her pockets. But at the touch of a profane hand on her clothes, the stranger recovered youth and activity for a moment, preferring to face the dangers of the street with no protector save God, to the loss of the thing that she had just paid for. She sprang to the door, flung it open, and disappeared, leaving the husband and wife dumfounded and quaking with fright.

Once outside in the street, she started away at a quick walk; but her strength soon failed her. She heard the sound of the snow crunching under a heavy step, and knew that the pitiless spy was on her track. She was obliged to stop. He stopped likewise. From sheer terror, or lack of intelligence, she did not dare to speak or to look at him. She went slowly on; the man slackened his pace and fell behind so that he could still keep her in sight. He might have been her very shadow.

Nine o'clock struck as the silent man and woman passed again by the Church of Saint Laurent. It is in the nature of things that calm must succeed to violent agitation, even in the weakest soul; for if feeling is infinite, our capacity to feel is limited. So, as the stranger lady met with no harm from her supposed persecutor, she tried to look upon him as an unknown friend anxious to protect her. She thought of all the circumstances in which the stranger had appeared, and put them together, as if to find some ground for this comforting theory, and felt inclined to credit him with good intentions rather than bad.

Forgetting the fright that he had given the pastry-cook, she walked on with a firmer step through the upper end of the Faubourg Saint Martin; and another half-hour's walk brought her to a house at the corner where the road to the Barrière de Pantin turns off from the main thorough-fare. Even at this day, the place is one of the least fre-quented parts of Paris. The north wind sweeps over the Buttes-Chaumont and Belleville, and whistles through the houses (the hovels rather), scattered over an almost unin-habited low-lying waste, where the fences are heaps of earth and bones. It was a desolate-looking place, a fitting refuge for despair and misery.

The sight of it appeared to make an impression upon the relentless pursuer of a poor creature so daring as to walk alone at night through the silent streets. He stood in thought, and seemed by his attitude to hesitate. She could see him dimly now, under the street lamp that sent a faint, flickering light through the fog. Fear gave her eyes. She saw, or thought she saw, something sinister about the stranger's features. Her old terrors awoke; she took advantage of a kind of hesitation on his part, slipped through the shadows to the door of the solitary house, pressed a spring, and van-ished swiftly as a phantom.

For awhile the stranger stood motionless, gazing up at the house. It was in some sort a type of the wretched dwellings in the suburb; a tumble-down hovel, built of rough stones, daubed over with a coat of yellowish stucco, and so riven with great cracks that there seemed to be danger lest the slightest puff of wind might blow it down. The roof, covered with brown moss-grown tiles, had given way in several places, and looked as though it might break down altogether under the weight of the snow. The frames of the three windows on each story were rotten with damp and warped by the sun; evidently the cold must find its way inside. The house standing thus quite by itself looked like some old tower that Time had forgotten to destroy. A faint light shone from the attic windows pierced at irregular distances in the roof; otherwise the whole building was in total darkness.

Meanwhile the old lady climbed not without difficulty up the rough, clumsily built staircase, with a rope by way of a hand-rail. At the door of the lodging in the attic she stopped and tapped mysteriously; an old man brought forward a chair for her. She dropped into it at once.

"Hide! hide!" she exclaimed, looking up at him. "Seldom as we leave the house, everything that we do is known, and every step is watched——"

"What is it now?" asked another elderly woman, sitting by the fire.

"The man that has been prowling about the house yesterday and to-day, followed me to-night——"

At those words all three dwellers in the wretched den looked in each other's faces and did not try to dissimulate the profound dread that they felt. The old priest was the least overcome, probably because he ran the greatest danger. If a brave man is weighed down by great calamities or the yoke of persecution, he begins, as it were, by making the sacrifice of himself; and thereafter every day of his life becomes one more victory snatched from fate. But from the way in which the women looked at him it was easy to see that their intense anxiety was on his account.

"Why should our faith in God fail us, my sisters?" he said, in low but fervent tones. "We sang His praises through the shrieks of murderers and their victims at the Carmelites. If it was His will that I should come alive out of that butchery, it was, no doubt, because I was reserved for some fate which I am bound to endure without murmuring. God will protect His own; He can do with them according to His will. It is for you, not for me that we must think."

"No," answered one of the women. "What is our life compared with a priest's life?"

"Once outside the Abbaye de Chelles, I look upon myself as dead," added the nun who had not left the house, while the Sister that had just returned held out the little box to the priest.

"Here are the wafers . . . but I can hear some one coming up the stairs."

At this, the three began to listen. The sound ceased.

"Do not be alarmed if somebody tries to come in," said the priest. "Somebody on whom we could depend was to make all necessary arrangements for crossing the frontier. He is to come for the letters that I have written to the Duc de Langeais and the Marquis de Beauséant, asking them to find some way of taking you out of this dreadful country, and away from the death or the misery that waits for you here."

"But are you not going to follow us?" the nuns cried under their breath, almost despairingly.

"My post is here where the sufferers are," the priest said simply, and the women said no more, but looked at their guest in reverent admiration. He turned to the nun with the wafers.

"Sister Marthe," he said, "the messenger will say *Fiat Voluntas* in answer to the word *Hosanna.*"

"There is some one on the stairs!" cried the other nun, opening a hiding-place contrived in the roof.

This time it was easy to hear, amid the deepest silence, a sound echoing up the staircase; it was a man's tread on the steps covered with dried lumps of mud. With some difficulty the priest slipped into a kind of cupboard, and the nun flung some clothes over him.

"You can shut the door, Sister Agathe," he said in a muffled voice.

He was scarcely hidden before three raps sounded on the door. The holy women looked into each other's eyes for counsel, and dared not say a single word.

They seemed both to be about sixty years of age. They had lived out of the world for forty years, and had grown so accustomed to the life of the convent that they could scarcely imagine any other. To them, as to plants kept in a hot-house, a change of air meant death. And so, when the grating was broken down one morning, they knew with a shudder that they were free. The effect produced by the Revolution upon their simple souls is easy to imagine; it produced a temporary imbecility not natural to them. They could not bring the ideas learned in the convent into harmony with life and its difficulties; they could not even understand their own position. They were like children whom mothers have always cared for, deserted by their maternal providence. And as a child cries, they betook themselves to prayer. Now, in the presence of imminent danger, they were mute and passive, knowing no defence save Christian resignation.

The man at the door, taking silence for consent, presented himself, and the women shuddered. This was the prowler that had been making inquiries about them for some time past. But they looked at him with frightened curiosity, much as shy children stare silently at a stranger; and neither of them moved.

The newcomer was a tall, burly man. Nothing in his behavior, bearing, or expression suggested malignity as, following the example set by the nuns, he stood motionless, while his eyes traveled round the room.

Two straw mats laid upon planks did duty as beds. On the one table, placed in the middle of the room, stood a brass candlestick, several plates, three knives, and a round loaf. A small fire burned in the grate. A few bits of wood in a heap in a corner bore further witness to the poverty of the recluses. You had only to look at the coating of paint on the walls to discover the bad condition of the roof, and the ceiling was a perfect network of brown stains made by rain-water.

A relic, saved no doubt from the wreck of the Abbaye de Chelles, stood like an ornament on the chimney-piece. Three chairs, two boxes, and a rickety chest of drawers completed the list of the furniture, but a door beside the fireplace suggested an inner room beyond.

The brief inventory was soon made by the personage introduced into their midst under such terrible auspices. It was with a compassionate expression that he turned to the two women; he looked benevolently at them, and seemed, at least, as much embarrassed as they. But the strange silence did not last long, for presently the stranger began to understand. He saw how inexperienced, how helpless (mentally speaking), the two poor creatures were, and he tried to speak gently.

"I am far from coming as an enemy, citoyennes——" he began. Then he suddenly broke off and went on, "Sisters, if anything should happen to you, believe me, I shall have no share in it. I have come to ask a favor of you."

Still the women were silent.

"If I am annoying you—if—if I am intruding, speak freely, and I will go; but you must understand that I am entirely at your service; that if I can do anything for you, you need not fear to make use of me. I, and I only, perhaps, am above the law, since there is no King now."

There was such a ring of sincerity in the words that Sister Agathe hastily pointed to a chair as if to bid their guest be seated. Sister Agathe came of the house of Langeais; her manner seemed to indicate that once she had been familiar with brilliant scenes, and had breathed the air of courts. The stranger seemed half pleased, half distressed when he understood her invitation; he waited to sit down until the women were seated.

"You are giving shelter to a reverend father who refused to take the oath, and escaped the massacres at the Carmelites by a miracle——"

"*Hosanna!*" Sister Agathe exclaimed eagerly, interrupting the stranger, while she watched him with curious eyes.

"That is not the name, I think," he said.

"But, monsieur," Sister Marthe broke in quickly, "we have no priest here, and——"

"In that case you should be more careful and on your guard," he answered gently, stretching out his hand for a breviary that lay on the table. "I do not think that you know Latin, and——"

He stopped; for, at the sight of the great emotion in the faces of the two poor nuns, he was afraid that he had gone too far. They were trembling, and the tears stood in their eyes.

"Do not fear," he said frankly. "I know your names and the name of your guest. Three days ago I heard of your distress and devotion to the venerable Abbé de——"

"Hush!" Sister Agathe cried, in the simplicity of her heart, as she laid her finger on her lips.

"You see, Sisters, that if I had conceived the horrible idea of betraying you, I could have given you up already, more than once——"

At the words the priest came out of his hiding-place and stood in their midst.

"I cannot believe, monsieur, that you can be one of our persecutors," he said, addressing the stranger, "and I trust you. What do you want with me?"

The priest's holy confidence, the nobleness expressed in every line in his face, would have disarmed a murderer. For a moment the mysterious stranger, who had brought an element of excitement into lives of misery and resignation, gazed at the little group; then he turned to the priest and said, as if making a confidence, "Father, I came to beg you to celebrate a mass for the repose of the soul of—of—of an august personage whose body will never rest in consecrated earth——"

Involuntarily the abbé shivered. As yet, neither of the Sisters understood of whom the stranger was speaking; they sat with their heads stretched out and faces turned towards the speaker, curiosity in their whole attitude. The priest.

meanwhile, was scrutinizing the stranger; there was no mistaking the anxiety in the man's face, the ardent entreaty in his eyes.

"Very well," returned the abbé. "Come back at midnight. I shall be ready to celebrate the only funeral service that it is in our power to offer in expiation of the crime of which you speak."

A quiver ran through the stranger, but a sweet yet sober satisfaction seemed to prevail over a hidden anguish. He took his leave respectfully, and the three generous souls felt his unspoken gratitude.

Two hours later, he came back and tapped at the garret door. Mademoiselle de Beauséant showed the way into the second room of their humble lodging. Everything had been made ready. The Sisters had moved the old chest of drawers between the two chimneys, and covered its quaint outlines over with a splendid altar cloth of green watered silk.

The bare walls looked all the barer, because the one thing that hung there was the great ivory and ebony crucifix, which of necessity attracted the eyes. Four slender little altar candles, which the Sisters had contrived to fasten into their places with sealing-wax, gave a faint, pale light, almost absorbed by the walls; the rest of the room lay well-nigh in the dark. But the dim brightness, concentrated upon the holy things, looked like a ray from Heaven shining down upon the unadorned shrine. The floor was reeking with damp. An icy wind swept in through the chinks here and there, in a roof that rose sharply on either side, after the fashion of attic roofs. Nothing could be less imposing; yet perhaps, too, nothing could be more solemn than this mournful ceremony. A silence so deep that they could have heard the faintest sound of a voice on the Route d'Allemagne, invested the night-piece with a kind of sombre majesty; while the grandeur of the service—all the grander for the strong contrast with the poor surroundings—produced a feeling of reverent awe.

The Sisters kneeling on each side the altar, regardless of the deadly chill from the wet brick floor, were engaged in prayer, while the priest, arrayed in pontifical vestments, brought out a golden chalice set with gems; doubtless one of the sacred vessels saved from the pillage of the Abbaye de Chelles. Beside a ciborium, the gift of royal munificence, the wine and water for the holy sacrifice of the mass stood ready in two glasses such as could scarcely be found in the meanest tavern. For want of a missal, the priest had laid his breviary on the altar, and a common earthenware plate was set for the washing of hands that were pure and undefiled with blood. It was all so infinitely great, yet so little, poverty-stricken yet noble, a mingling of sacred and profane.

The stranger came forward reverently to kneel between the two nuns. But the priest had tied crape round the chalice of the crucifix, having no other way of marking the mass as a funeral service; it was as if God himself had been in mourning. The man suddenly noticed this, and the sight appeared to call up some overwhelming memory, for great drops of sweat stood out on his broad forehead.

Then the four silent actors in the scene looked mysteriously at one another; and their souls in emulation seemed to stir and communicate the thoughts within them until all were melted into one feeling of awe and pity. It seemed to them that the royal martyr whose remains had been consumed with quicklime, had been called up by their yearning and now stood, a shadow in their midst, in all the majesty of a king. They were celebrating an anniversary service for the dead whose body lay elsewhere. Under the disjointed laths and tiles, four Christians were holding a funeral service without a coffin, and putting up prayers to God for the soul of a King of France. No devotion could be purer than this. It was a wonderful act of faith achieved without an afterthought. Surely in the sight of God it was like the cup of cold water which counterbalances the loftiest virtues. The prayers put up by two feeble nuns and a priest represented the whole Monarchy, and possibly at the same time, the Revolution found expression in the stranger, for the remorse in his face was so great that it was impossible not to think that he was fulfilling the vows of a boundless repentance.

When the priest came to the Latin words, *Introïbo ad altare Dei,* a sudden divine inspiration flashed upon him; he looked at the three kneeling figures, the representatives of Christian France, and said instead, as though to blot out the poverty of the garret, "We are about to enter the Sanctuary of God!"

These words, uttered with thrilling earnestness, struck reverent awe into the nuns and the stranger. Under the vaulted roof of St. Peter's at Rome, God would not have revealed Himself in greater majesty than here for the eyes of, the Christians in that poor refuge; so true is it that all intermediaries between God and the soul of man are super- fluous, and all the grandeur of God proceeds from Himself alone.

The stranger's fervor was sincere. One emotion blended the prayers of the four servants of God and the King in a single supplication. The holy words rang like the music of heaven through the silence. At one moment, tears gath- ered in the stranger's eyes. This was during the *Pater Noster;* for the priest added a petition in Latin, and his audience doubtless understood him when he said: *"Et remitte scelus regicidis sicut Ludovicus eis remisit semetipse"*—for- give the regicides as Louis himself forgave them.

The Sisters saw two great tears trace a channel down the stranger's manly cheeks and fall to the floor. Then the office for the dead was recited; the *Domine salvum fac regem* chanted in an undertone that went to the hearts of the faith- ful Royalists, for they thought how the child-King for whom they were praying was even then a captive in the hands of his enemies; and a shudder ran through the stranger, as he thought that a new crime might be committed, and that he could not choose but take his part in it.

The service came to an end. The priest made a sign to the Sisters, and they withdrew. As soon as he was left alone with the stranger, he went toward him with a grave, gentle face, and said in fatherly tones:

"My son, if your hands are stained with the blood of the royal martyr, confide in me. There is no sin that may not be blotted out in the sight of God by penitence as sincere and touching as yours appears to be."

At the first words, the man started with terror, in spite of himself. Then he recovered composure, and looked quietly at the astonished priest.

"Father," he said, and the other could not miss the tremor in his voice, "no one is more guiltless than I of the blood shed——"

"I am bound to believe you," said the priest. He paused a moment, and again he scrutinized his penitent. But, persisting in the idea that the man before him was one of the members of the Convention, one of the timorous voters who betrayed an inviolable and anointed head to save their own, he began again gravely:

"Remember, my son, that it is not enough to have taken no active part in the great crime; that fact does not absolve you. The men who might have defended the King and left their swords in their scabbards, will have a very heavy account to render to the King of Heaven—Ah! yes," he added, with an eloquent shake of the head, "heavy indeed!—for by doing nothing they became accomplices in the awful wickedness——"

"But do you think that an indirect participation will be punished?" the stranger asked with a bewildered look. "There is the private soldier commanded to fall into line—is he actually responsible?"

The priest hesitated. The stranger was glad; he had put the Royalist precisian in a dilemma, between the dogma of passive obedience on the one hand (for the upholders of the Monarchy maintained that obedience was the first principle of military law), and the equally important dogma which turns respect for the person of a King into a matter of religion. In the priest's indecision he was eager to see a favorable solution of the doubts which seemed to torment him. To prevent too prolonged reflection on the part of the reverend Jansenist, he added:

"I should blush to offer remuneration of any kind for the

funeral service which you have just performed for the repose of the King's soul and the relief of my conscience.
The only possible return for something of inestimable value
is an offering likewise beyond price. Will you deign, monsieur, to take my gift of a holy relic? A day will perhaps
come when you will understand its value."

As he spoke the stranger held out a box; it was very small
and exceedingly light. The priest took it mechanically, as
it were, so astonished was he by the man's solemn words, the
tones of his voice, and the reverence with which he held out
the gift.

The two men went back together into the first room. The
Sisters were waiting for them.

"This house that you are living in belongs to Mucius
Scævola, the plasterer on the first floor," he said. "He is
well known in the Section for his patriotism, but in reality
he is an adherent of the Bourbons. He used to be a huntsman in the service of his Highness the Prince de Conti, and
he owes everything to him. So long as you stay in the house,
you are safer here than anywhere else in France. Do not go
out. Pious souls will minister to your necessities, and you
can wait in safety for better times. Next year, on the 21st
of January,"—he could not hide an involuntary shudder as
he spoke,—"next year, if you are still in this dreary refuge,
I will come back again to celebrate the expiatory mass with
you——"

He broke off, bowed to the three, who answered not a word,
gave a last look at the garret with its signs of poverty, and
vanished.

Such an adventure possessed all the interest of a romance
in the lives of the innocent nuns. So, as soon as the venerable
abbé told them the story of the mysterious gift, it was placed
upon the table, and by the feeble light of the tallow dip an
indescribable curiosity appeared in the three anxious faces.
Mademoiselle de Langeais opened the box, and found a very
fine lawn handkerchief, soiled with sweat; darker stains appeared as they unfolded it.

"That is blood!" exclaimed the priest.

"It is marked with a royal crown!" cried Sister Agathe.

The women, aghast, allowed the precious relic to fall. For their simple souls the mystery that hung about the stranger grew inexplicable; as for the priest, from that day forth he did not even try to understand it.

Before very long the prisoners knew that, in spite of the Terror, some powerful hand was extended over them. It began when they received firewood and provisions; and next the Sisters knew that a woman had lent counsel to their protector, for linen was sent to them, and clothes in which they could leave the house without causing remark upon the aristocrat's dress that they had been forced to wear. After awhile Mucius Scævola gave them two civic cards; and often and often tidings necessary for the priest's safety came to them in roundabout ways. Warnings and advice reached them so opportunely that they could only have been sent by some person in the possession of state secrets. And, at a time when famine threatened Paris, invisible hands brought rations of "white bread" for the proscribed women in the wretched garret. Still they fancied that Citizen Mucius Scævola was only the mysterious instrument of a kindness always ingenious, and no less intelligent.

The noble ladies in the garret could no longer doubt that their protector was the stranger of the expiatory mass on the night of the 22d of January, 1793; and a kind of cult of him sprung up among them. Their one hope was in him; they lived through him. They added special petitions for him to their prayers; night and morning the pious souls prayed for his happiness, his prosperity, his safety; entreating God to remove all snares far from his path, to deliver him from his enemies, to grant him a long and peaceful life. And with this daily renewed gratitude, as it may be called, there blended a feeling of curiosity which grew more lively day by day. They talked over the circumstances of his first sudden appearance, their conjectures were endless; 'the

stranger had conferred one more benefit upon them by divert-
ing their minds. Again, and again, they said, when he next
came to see them as he promised, to celebrate the sad anniversary of the death of Louis XVI., he should not escape their
friendship.

The night so impatiently awaited came at last. At midnight the old wooden staircase echoed with the stranger's
heavy footsteps. They had made the best of their room for
his coming; the altar was ready, and this time the door stood
open, and the two Sisters were out at the stairhead, eager to
light the way. Mademoiselle de Langeais even came down a
few steps, to meet their benefactor the sooner.

"Come," she said, with a quaver in the affectionate tones,
"come in; we are expecting you."

He raised his face, gave her a dark look, and made no
answer. The Sister felt as if an icy mantle had fallen over
her, and said no more. At the sight of him, the glow of
gratitude and curiosity died away in their hearts. Perhaps
he was not so cold, not so taciturn, not so stern as he seemed
to them, for in their highly wrought mood they were ready
to pour out their feeling of friendship. But the three poor
prisoners understood that he wished to be a stranger to them;
and submitted. The priest fancied that he saw a smile on
the man's lips as he saw their preparations for his visit, but
it was at once repressed. He heard mass, said his prayer,
and then disappeared, declining, with a few polite words,
Mademoiselle de Langeais' invitation to partake of the little
collation made ready for him.

After the 9th Thermidor, the Sisters and the Abbé de
Marolles could go about Paris without the least danger.
The first time that the abbé went out he walked to a perfumer's shop at the sign of *The Queen of Roses,* kept by the
Citizen Ragon and his wife, court perfumers. The Ragons
had been faithful adherents of the Royalist cause; it was
through their means that the Vendéan leaders kept up a
correspondence with the Princes and the Royalist Committee
in Paris. The abbé, in the ordinary dress of the time, was

standing on the threshold of the shop—which stood between Saint Roch and the Rue des Frondeurs—when he saw that the Rue Saint Honoré was filled with a crowd and he could not go out.

"What is the matter?" he asked Madame Ragon.

"Nothing," she said; "it is only the tumbril cart and the executioner going to the Place Louis XV. Ah! we used to see it often enough last year; but to-day, four days after the anniversary of the twenty-first of January, one does not feel sorry to see the ghastly procession."

"Why not?" asked the abbé. "That is not said like a Christian."

"Eh! but it is the execution of Robespierre's accomplices. They defended themselves as long as they could, but now it is their turn to go where they sent so many innocent people."

The crowd poured by like a flood. The abbé, yielding to an impulse of curiosity, looked up above the heads, and there in the tumbril stood the man who had heard mass in the garret three days ago.

"Who is it?" he asked; "who is the man with——"

"That is the headsman," answered M. Ragon, calling the executioner—the *exécuteur des hautes œuvres*—by the name he had borne under the Monarchy.

"Oh! my dear, my dear! M. l'Abbé is dying!" cried out old Madame Ragon. She caught up a flask of vinegar, and tried to restore the old priest to consciousness.

"He must have given me the handkerchief that the King used to wipe his brow on the way to his martyrdom," murmured he. " . . . Poor man! . . . There was a heart in the steel blade, when none was found in all France. . . ."

The perfumers thought that the poor abbé was raving.

PARIS, *January* 1831.

THE COMÉDIE HUMAINE

INDEX

THE COMÉDIE HUMAINE as arranged by Balzac is a curious example of subdivision and inter-subdivision. It is composed of some eighty-eight separate stories which, however, are connected —nearly all of them—with the general scheme of the Comédie. This scheme embraces six Scenes and two Studies, as follows:

Scenes from Private Life.

Scenes from Provincial Life.

Scenes from Parisian Life.

Scenes from Political Life.

Scenes from Military Life.

Scenes from Country Life.

Philosophical Studies.

Analytical Studies.

The above Scenes or Studies, in turn, are divided into groups including stories which the author desired to connect as intimately as possible. The stories themselves are liable to subdivision, being made up possibly of two or more narratives strung together on the slightest thread under some general title. As an example of this may be cited The Thirteen, a book composed of three distinct tales—Ferragus, The Duchesse de Langeais, and The Girl with the Golden Eyes.

Granted that a story were entirely coherent in plot, it was not always or often suffered to lie undisturbed by its restless author. It was wrought upon, both internally and externally. Internally it met with the frequent decapitation or addition of chapter heads. Perchance all the chapters might be merged in one. Perchance some incident lightly dwelt upon might reveal another sit-

uation for the same actors; a budding process would begin, and
thus a new story of the Comédie would be born. Externally a
story might be changed in title, in grouping, or even in its position in the Comédie; it might lose its identity entirely (in a reverse process to one described above) by being incorporated into
another story, in the form of a chapter. All these operations
might and did happen in the evolution of the Comédie, which fact
explains the difficulty oftentimes experienced in locating tales by
the titles given in the earlier French editions; also for the varying number of stories accredited to the Comédie.

The present edition does not give the original grouping in absolute order; this was not possible in a given number of volumes of
uniform size. The original grouping has never been considered
vital—the author himself was constantly changing it, up to the
very day of his death. Nevertheless, the arrangement as finally
left by him has been maintained in so far as mechanical convenience would permit. And for those who desire to follow the
Balzacian scheme, or to consider a story in relation to its group-
mates and the general plan, these Indices have been prepared,
showing: (1) Alphabetical Index of stories and their position
in the accompanying edition; (2) Titles of Volumes; (3) Original Balzac Scheme.—J. WALKER McSPADDEN, Publisher's Editor.

ALPHABETICAL INDEX

THE STORIES CONSTITUTING THE COMÉDIE HUMAINE AND THEIR POSITION IN THE ACCOMPANYING EDITION

TITLES OF VOLUMES

(401)

Another Study of Woman,	*Autre Étude de Femme.*
La Grande Bretêche,	*La Grande Bretêche.*
Albert Savarus,	*Albert Savarus.*

BOOK 3.

LETTERS OF TWO BRIDES,	*Mémoires de Deaux Jeunes.*
	Mariées.
A Daughter of Eve,	*Une Fille d'Eve.*

BOOK 4.

A WOMAN OF THIRTY,	*La Femme de Trente Ans.*
The Deserted Woman,	*La Femme Abandonée.*
La Grenadière,	*La Grenadière.*
The Message,	*Le Message.*
Gobseck,	*Gobseck.*

BOOK 5.

| A MARRIAGE SETTLEMENT, | *Le Contrat de Mariage.* |
| A Start in Life, | *Un Début dans la Vie.* |

BOOK 6.

| MODESTE MIGNON, | *Modeste Mignon.* |

BOOK 7.

| BÉATRIX. | *Béatrix.* |

BOOK 8.

HONORINE,	*Honorine.*
Colonel Chabert,	*Le Colonel Chabert.*
The Atheist's Mass,	*La Messe de l'Athée.*
The Commission in Lunacy,	*L'Interdiction.*
Pierre Grassou,	*Pierre Grassou.*

TITLES OF VOLUMES

1.   I.   THE MAGIC SKIN.
     II.   THE QUEST OF THE ABSOLUTE.

2.   I.   ABOUT CATHERINE DE' MEDICI.
     II.   SERAPHITA.

3.   I.   EUGÉNIE GRANDET.
     II.   URSULE MIROUËT.

4.   I.   AT THE SIGN OF THE CAT AND RACKET.
     II.   A BACHELOR'S ESTABLISHMENT.

5.   I.   A DAUGHTER OF EVE.
     II.   A WOMAN OF THIRTY.

6.   I.   A MARRIAGE SETTLEMENT.
     II.   MODESTE MIGNON.

7.   I.   BEATRIX.
     II.   THE JEALOUSIES OF A COUNTRY TOWN.

8.   I.   LOST ILLUSIONS.
     II.   A DISTINGUISHED PROVINCIAL AT PARIS.

9.   I.   THE LILY OF THE VALLEY.
     II.   THE COUNTRY DOCTOR.

10.   I.   THE COUNTRY PARSON.
     II.   THE PEASANTRY.

11.   I.   COUSIN BETTY.
     II.   COUSIN PONS.

THE BALZAC PLAN

OF THE COMÉDIE HUMAINE

The form in which the Comédie Humaine was left by its author, with the exceptions of *Le Député d'Arcis* (incomplete) and *Les Petits Bourgeois*, both of which were added, some years later, by the Edition Définitive.

[On the right hand side is given the original French titles; on the left, their English equivalents. Literal translations have been followed, excepting a few instances where preference is shown for a clearer or more comprehensive English title.]

COMÉDIE HUMAINE

SCENES FROM PRIVATE LIFE

(*Scènes de la Vie Privée*)

BOOK 1.

AT THE SIGN OF THE CAT AND RACKET,	*La Maison du Chat-qui-Pelote.*
The Ball at Sçeaux,	*Le Bal de Sçeaux.*
The Purse,	*La Bourse.*
The Vendetta,	*La Vendetta.*
Madame Firmiani,	*Mme. Firmiani.*
A Second Home,	*Une Double Famille.*

BOOK 2.

DOMESTIC PEACE,	*La Paix du Ménage.*
The Imaginary Mistress,	*La Fausse Maitresse.*
A Study of Woman,	*Etude de Femme.*

Another Study of Woman,   *Autre Étude de Femme.*
La Grande Bretêche,   *La Grande Bretêche.*
Albert Savarus,   *Albert Savarus.*

Book 3.

LETTERS OF TWO BRIDES,   *Mémoires de Deaux Jeunes.*
                               Mariées.
A Daughter of Eve,   *Une Fille d'Eve.*

Book 4.

A WOMAN OF THIRTY,   *La Femme de Trente Ans.*
The Deserted Woman,   *La Femme Abandonée.*
La Grenadière,   *La Grenadière.*
The Message,   *Le Message.*
Gobseck,   *Gobseck.*

Book 5.

A MARRIAGE SETTLEMENT,   *Le Contrat de Mariage.*
A Start in Life,   *Un Début dans la Vie.*

Book 6.

MODESTE MIGNON,   *Modeste Mignon.*

Book 7.

BÉATRIX.   *Béatrix.*

Book 8.

HONORINE,   *Honorine.*
Colonel Chabert,   *Le Colonel Chabert.*
The Atheist's Mass,   *La Messe de l'Athée.*
The Commission in Lunacy,   *L'Interdiction.*
Pierre Grassou,   *Pierre Grassou.*

SCENES FROM PROVINCIAL LIFE

(Scènes de la Vie Province)

SCENES FROM PARISIAN LIFE

(*Scènes de la Vie Parisienne*)

* The fourth and final part of Scenes from a Courtesan's Life.

* This book is not numbered, inasmuch as it was included after Balzac's death.

SCENES FROM POLITICAL LIFE

(*Scènes de la Vie Politique*)

BOOK 26.

THE GONDREVILLE MYSTERY,	*Une Ténébreuse Affaire.*
An Episode Under the Terror,	*Un Episode sous la Terreur.*

BOOK 27.

THE SEAMY SIDE OF HISTORY,	*L'Envers de l'Histoire Contemporaine:*
Madame de la Chanterie,	*Mme. de la Chanterie,*
Initiated,	*L'Initié.*
Z. Marcas,	*Z. Marcas.*

BOOK 28.

THE MEMBER FOR ARCIS,*	*Le Député d'Arcis.*

SCENES FROM MILITARY LIFE

(*Scènes de la Vie Militaire*)

BOOK 29.

THE CHOUANS,	*Les Chouans.*
A Passion in the Desert,	*Une Passion dans le Désert.*

SCENES FROM COUNTRY LIFE

(*Scènes de la Vie de Champagne*)

BOOK 30.

THE COUNTRY DOCTOR,	*Le Médecin de Campagne.*

BOOK 31.

THE COUNTRY PARSON.	*Le Curé de Village.*

* Though not included until after the author's death, its exact position had been previously indicated.

The Ruggieri's Secret,   *La Confidence des Ruggieri.*
The Two Dreams,   *Les Deux Rêves.*

Book 38.

LOUIS LAMBERT,   *Louis Lambert.*
The Exiles,   *Les Proscrits.*
Seraphita,   *Séraphita.*

ANALYTICAL STUDIES.

Book 39.

THE PHYSIOLOGY OF MARRIAGE,   *Physiologie du Mariage.*

Book 40.

PETTY TROUBLES OF MARRIED   *Petite Misères de la Vie*
    LIFE,   *Conjugale.*

The above list comprises the entire *Human Comedy*, but in addition to the same there are included in this New Saintsbury Balzac:

I. THE DRAMAS (2 volumes).

VAUTRIN,   *Vautrin.*
QUINOLA'S RESOURCES,   *Les Ressources de Quinola.*
THE STEP-MOTHER,   *La Maratre.*
MERCADET,   *Mercadet.*
PAMELA GIRAUD,   *Pamela Giraud.*

II. A REPERTORY OF THE HUMAN COMEDY (1 volume).

In which the various appearances of the personages in the novels are reduced to a biographical dictionary.